REVOLUTIONARY MOVEMENTS
IN LATIN AMERICA

REVOLUTIONARY MOVEMENTS IN LATIN AMERICA

El Salvador's FMLN & Peru's Shining Path

C y n t h i a   M c C l i n t o c k

United States Institute of Peace Press
Washington, D.C.

United States Institute of Peace
1550 M Street NW
Washington, DC 20005

First published 1998

Printed in the United States of America

The paper used in this publication meets the minimum requirements of American National Standards for Information Sciences—Permanence of Paper for Printed Library Materials, ANSI Z39.48-1984.

Library of Congress Cataloging-in-Publication Data
McClintock, Cynthia.
    Revolutionary movements in Latin America : El Salvador's FMLN and Peru's Shining Path / Cynthia McClintock.
      p. cm.
    Includes bibliographical references (p. –) and index.
    ISBN 1-878379-77-1 (hardcover). — ISBN 1-878379-76-3 (pbk.)
    1. El Salvador—Politics and government—1979–1992. 2. Peru—Politics and government—1980– 3. Frente Farabundo Martí para la Liberación Nacional. 4. Sendero Luminoso (Guerrilla group) 5. El Salvador—Economic conditions— 1945– 6. Peru—Economic conditions—1968– 7. United States—Foreign relations—El Salvador. 8. El Salvador—Foreign relations—United States. 9. United States—Foreign relations—Peru. 10. Peru—Foreign relations—United States. I. Title.
F1488.3.M375 1998
303.6'4'09728409048—dc21   98-13334
                                                             CIP

To my daughter,
Jeannette Alicia McClintock,

in the hope that one day her native land
will be peaceful and prosperous

CONTENTS

FIGURES AND TABLES

FOREWORD

*C*ynthia McClintock's remarkably well-written book, *Revolutionary Movements in Latin America,* has much to say to a variety of readers, and says it with precision and an engaging candor and clarity.

At first glance, one sees that the author concentrates primarily on the formidable revolutionary movements in Peru and El Salvador between the late 1970s and early 1990s, and one might conclude that the book is meant mostly for students of the politics of those two countries. At second glance, however, one finds that McClintock also discusses the politics, revolutions, and regimes of Ecuador, Cuba, Nicaragua, and Bolivia. This comparative perspective broadens the book's audience to include scholars of Latin America generally and anyone with an interest in revolutionary movements and regime stability.

Indeed, Professor McClintock's book makes a significant contribution to the literature on theories of revolution. Displaying great breadth and depth of reading, and the ability to marshal armies of facts and arguments into clear and purposeful order, McClintock tests the well-known theory that revolution occurs when a certain type of authoritarian regime denies its political opponents the space to compete for power. She finds this theory persuasive in the case of El Salvador, but not in the case of Peru. It was not regime type that precipitated the emergence of Peru's brutally effective Shining Path, but rather an economic structure that devastated the peasants of the rural highlands and dashed the middle-class expectations of new university graduates who became revolutionary leaders. The case she makes is a strong one, and the book is sure to find many readers among students and scholars of theories of revolution.

The book also seems certain to appeal to those interested in examining the details of the practice, as distinguished from the theory, of revolution. Not only has McClintock sifted through an enormous amount of data to arrive at what are probably the most reliable figures available on such controversial topics as the death tolls inflicted by rebels and government forces, but also she has undertaken significant new research on the opinions of a wide variety of groups within Peru and El Salvador, including the revolutionaries themselves. The aims, strategies, and ideologies of the two guerrilla movements differed significantly: the fundamentalist Shining Path was a highly authoritarian and rigidly Maoist organization that extolled the use of violence and sought to sweep away Peru's existing political and social system; the FMLN was a fractious, relatively democratic grouping of five movements that adhered to a variety of Marxist and social democratic views, did not regard political terror as a primary tactic, and looked to overthrow El Salvador's regime but wanted primarily to reform its political and economic system.

This solid empirical base makes the book pertinent to policymakers in Latin America but also—indeed, especially—to U.S. policymakers. The readiness of the United States to support beleaguered Latin American regimes has been critical to their survival. The FMLN posed probably the most severe military challenge faced by any Latin American regime in recent decades, yet because of massive U.S. economic and military support, conditioned on opening of the political process, the El Salvadoran regime survived. This fact, underscored by McClintock's analysis, is widely known. What is less well known, however, is how serious was the challenge posed to the more-or-less democratic regime in Peru by the Maoist Shining Path, and how (according to the author) U.S. policy, which stressed free market reforms and anti-drug efforts, failed to bolster the Peruvian government's counterinsurgency efforts. Only fairly late in the day, with the Shining Path poised to topple Peruvian democracy, did the United States apparently play a key but covert role by dint of CIA support for the police unit that ultimately captured the Shining Path's leader, Abimael Guzmán.

Perhaps McClintock's most interesting conclusion is that "revolutionary conflict of the kind that emerged during the Cold War is over; revolutionary conflict is not." Post–Cold War revolutionary movements, of the kind we have seen in Chiapas in Mexico and in Colombia, are not mere throwbacks to the Cold War era, but rather attest to other long-standing problems. Those problems include regimes that are judged "democratic" by the often loose standards of foreign observers but that enjoy only limited legitimacy in the eyes of their people; and economies that have been opened to free market forces but that have spawned greater dissatisfaction among frustrated aspirants to the middle class, as well as greater abject poverty. New revolutionary movements, says McClintock, "are likely to reject elections . . . and rather base their claims to legitimacy on quasi-religious and ideological grounds. The Shining Path sought to present itself as a group of virtually 'born-again' Peruvians: honest, dedicated, and effective, fighting against a hopelessly corrupt state." The author suggests that the kind of U.S. support traditionally provided to endangered regimes may no longer be appropriate, and she offers U.S. policymakers a variety of practical recommendations for helping to combat both these new-style movements and the conditions that foster them. McClintock urges that priority be given to alleviating hunger and poverty, to promoting economic and democratic development, and to reducing levels of government cronyism and corruption.

Finally, we can add yet another category of reader for McClintock's book: the informed lay reader. *Revolutionary Movements in Latin America* is a challenging book to be sure, but it is also a distinctly intelligible, engaging, and illuminating one. For the reader who would like to learn something about the recent history of Latin America, about the motives, strategies, and actions of two quite different kinds of revolutionaries, and about the prospects for peace and stability in the Western Hemisphere, there is no more reliable and readable a guide than Professor McClintock's.

We are pleased to have given Cynthia McClintock the opportunity to begin drafting her study during her year as a Jennings Randolph fellow at the United States Institute of Peace in 1990–91. As might be expected of a book that speaks to so many different audiences, *Revolutionary Movements in Latin America* complements a range of Institute-sponsored work on Latin America, including the analysis of the negotiation and implementation of the peace treaty in El Salvador in Fen Hampson's book *Nurturing Peace;* Francisco Villagrán de León's two reports on the OAS and democratization and the OAS and regional security; and Raymond Cohen's assessment of U.S.-Mexican negotiating encounters in

Negotiating across Cultures. In addition, Institute grants have supported work on such topics as indigenous protest and democratization, the role of NGOs in El Salvador, transitions to democracy, and a comparison of peace processes in the region.

Revolutionary Movements in Latin America is a prime example of the efforts by the Institute of Peace to overcome the intellectual tunnel vision that often clouds our understanding and obscures the lessons of experience. This book is a much-needed remedy for the ailment of overspecialization.

Richard H. Solomon, President
United States Institute of Peace

ACKNOWLEDGMENTS

This book has been almost a decade in the making, and throughout this time I have benefited greatly in many ways from numerous institutions and individuals. Friends and colleagues in the United States, El Salvador, and Peru generously contributed their time, knowledge, and moral support to help bring this book to fruition.

The individual whose assistance was most critical to the research for this book was Rodolfo Osores Ocampo, a Peruvian sociologist who worked with me on my dissertation research in 1973 and continued to provide research assistance until his death from cancer in January 1997. Rodolfo was the key to the successful implementation of numerous surveys—most notably, thirty-three interviews with Shining Path members—the results of which are presented in this book. Undertaking such surveys in the Peruvian central highlands in the early 1990s was a brave endeavor. Rodolfo was not only a capable and wise researcher but also a trusted friend whose thoughts about his country's politics have been essential to the development of my own perspectives. My greatest regret in the writing of this book is that he did not live to see its publication.

I am also very grateful to the United States Institute of Peace; without the Jennings Randolph Peace Fellowship I was awarded for 1990–91, this book would not have been undertaken. The Institute was an excellent scholarly home that enabled frequent travel to both El Salvador and Peru during my fellowship year. At the Institute, I benefited greatly from the able research assistance of Jocelyn Nieva and from the thoughtful insights of Vice President Charles Nelson. Last but far from least, the Institute's editor, Nigel Quinney, offered both the encouragement and the prodding that were essential to the completion of the book.

When I began this research, my knowledge about El Salvador was relatively limited. I am very grateful that Hugh Byrne spent many hours making comments, asking questions, and sharing information that greatly sharpened my analysis of the Salvadoran revolutionary movement and its trajectory. Salvador Cortes, William Stanley, and George Vickers also played critical roles in advancing my understanding of Salvadoran politics. While I was in El Salvador, I was fortunate to be welcomed and helped by Roberto Codas, Alberto Enríquez, Tom Gibb, Leonel Gómez, Marta Guevara, David Holiday, Ian McNabb, Margaret Popkin, and especially Antonio Orellana, who coordinated most of my survey work in El Salvador.

Over the years that I have been carrying out research in Peru, I have been gratified and warmed by the willingness of so many people—peasants, political leaders, military officers, scholars, and others from different walks of life—to offer their insights and friendship to a North American researcher. Among the many whose help has been invaluable are Rolando Ames, José Bailetti, Enrique Bernales, Alberto Bolívar, Mercedes Calderon, Miguel Candiotti, Juan Carlos Capuñay, Carlos Iván Degregori, Luis Deustua, Eduardo Ferrero, José Gonzales, Raúl Gonzales, Gustavo Gorriti, Admiral (r) Jorge Hesse, Carlos Indacochea, General (r) Sinesio Jarama, General (r) Edgardo Mercado Jarrín, Enrique Obando, Felipe Ortiz de Zevallos, Piedad Pareja Pflucker, Henry Pease, Alberto Quevedo, Francisco Sagasti, Leoncio Ramón Veliz, Fernando Rospigliosi, Marcial Rubio, Diego García-Sayan, Carlos Tapia, Manuel Torrado, Fernando Tuesta, Fabian Vallas, Mónica Villalobos, and Lorenzo Villareal. I also especially value the affection shared with my *comadres* Justina Bedón and Carmen Osores and their families.

Various friends and colleagues took the time to provide thoughtful critiques of parts or all of manuscript drafts: Jeremy Bigwood, Charles Brockett, Hugh Byrne, Ernest Evans, Mark Katz, Abraham F. Lowenthal, Kevin Middlebrook, David Scott Palmer, Jim Rudolph, Richard Webb, and Robert White. At panels of professional meetings or other seminars, helpful comments were made by numerous colleagues, including Julio Cotler, Larry Diamond, Henry Dietz, Jonathan Hartlyn, David Little, Michael Lund, Tommie Sue Montgomery, Charles Nelson, Michael Shifter, and Alexander Wilde. I am especially grateful to two of the United States Institute of Peace reviewers for the book, Michael Foley and Timothy Wickham-Crowley, for their excellent suggestions. All these scholars were essential in prompting me to clarify and even rethink important questions in the study, in particular questions about the impact of economic variables on the revolutionary movements' expansion in the two nations.

After the completion of my fellowship at the United States Institute of Peace, the George Washington University's Elliott School of International Affairs and Department of Political Science provided funds for research assistance. Diane Bartz, David Collis, Luis Deustua, Jacqueline Kellachan, Katherine Landauer, Victoria Layne, Chad Metzler, Estelle McKemie, Usha Pitts, Brandon Scheid, Max Skolnik, and John R. Wagley helped to review materials, code and tabulate data, carry out bibliographical searches, and perform other important tasks. Helen Atkinson-Barnes tracked down material for me while she was in Ecuador in 1992.

I have dedicated this book to my daughter, Jeannette Alicia McClintock, who was born in Peru. For most of my research trips to El Salvador and Peru, she accompanied me. Of course, there was agony in these countries at the time. Thousands of Salvadorans and Peruvians, including numerous friends and acquaintances of mine, lost their lives or feared losing their lives. For me, to look at Alicia's resplendent smile and see her optimism was to know that a different future was possible.

REVOLUTIONARY MOVEMENTS
IN LATIN AMERICA

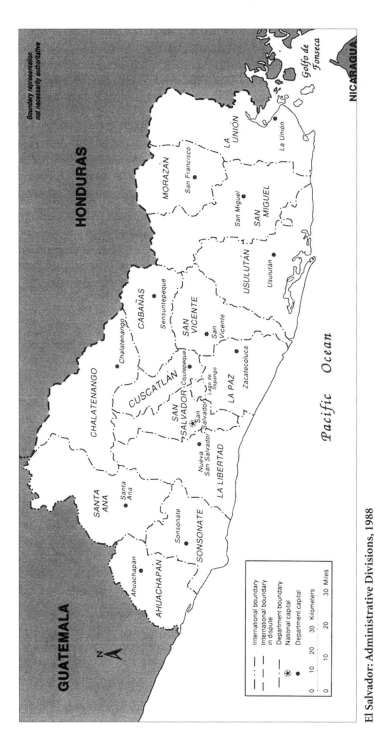

El Salvador: Administrative Divisions, 1988

From Richard A. Haggerty, ed., *El Salvador: A Country Study* (Washington, D.C.: Federal Research Division, Library of Congress, 1990).

Peru: Administrative Divisions (Departments), 1992
From Rex A. Hudson, ed., *Peru: A Country Study* (Washington, D.C.: Federal Research Division, Library of Congress, 1993).

INTRODUCTION

The study of revolutions remains much like the study of earthquakes. When one occurs, scholars try to make sense of the data they have collected and to build theories to account for the next one. Gradually, we gain a fuller understanding of revolutions and the conditions behind them. And yet the next one still surprises us.

Jack A. Goldstone, *Revolutions:*
Theoretical, Comparative, and Historical Studies

As the twenty-first century approaches, has liberal democracy triumphed in the world?[1] And, amid democratization, is social revolution doomed?[2] Are democracies immune to insurgencies?

Logically, in a democracy, opponents of an elected regime should compete at the ballot box rather than risk their lives fighting the regime. As Samuel P. Huntington pointed out, "Perhaps the most important and obvious but also most neglected fact about successful great revolutions is that they do not occur against democratic political systems. . . . Revolution requires political institutions which resist the expansion of participation."[3] The same point is made by Jeff Goodwin and Theda Skocpol: "The ballot box . . . has proven to be the coffin of revolutionary movements."[4] The principle was also endorsed by Ché Guevara:

> One should never try to start a revolution against an elected government, for the populace will not turn in a revolutionary direction while electoral alternatives remain an option and retain an appeal.[5]

The historical record suggests validity for the argument that democracy stymies social revolution. Not one established, elected regime has been overthrown by a Marxist guerrilla movement—at any time, in any place in the world.[6] During the 1960s and 1970s, various elected Latin American governments—namely the Venezuelan, the Uruguayan, the Argentine, and the Colombian—confronted guerrilla movements, and none of these governments even came close to defeat by the revolutionaries.[7] All four governments received considerable support from the United States.[8]

In the first three nations, the challenges endured only a few years, ending amid greater democratization in Venezuela and intense repression in Uruguay and Argentina. In Venezuela after 1959, the new government of Rómulo Betancourt confronted between one and two thousand guerrillas, most of them university students influenced by the recent victory of Fidel Castro in Cuba and disturbed that Betancourt had shifted rightward after their joint ousting of a dictator. Popular support for the guerrillas was, however, minimal and dissolved almost entirely after a successful election in 1963.[9] In Uruguay, between roughly 1967 and 1972, elected governments faced about fifteen hundred Tupamaros; at first, these youthful urban guerrillas' spectacular, selective attacks were supported by many disaffected Uruguayans, but then the guerrillas' violence became more random, and the movement "totally estranged itself from public opinion."[10] In Argentina between 1973 and 1976, Presidents Juan Perón and then his widow Isabel Perón were challenged by perhaps five thousand urban guerrillas, among whom the Montoneros were the most salient; most of the guerrillas had worked for the return of Perón to Argentina in the hope that his government would initiate socialist policies and were angry when it did not.[11]

Only in Colombia has an elected, civilian regime confronted enduring guerrilla violence. Indeed, in comparison with the revolutionaries in Venezuela, Uruguay, and Argentina, the number of Colombian guerrillas was greater; they were also able to dominate parts of the national territory.[12] However, various caveats are necessary. Although the Colombian government was elected and civilian, during the 1960s and 1970s it was in various respects less deserving of the democratic label than were the Venezuelan, Uruguayan, and Argentine governments during the periods mentioned above.[13] Also, despite the guerrillas' strength in particular regions of the country, at no time did they pose a challenge to the

Colombian state.[14] Originating to a greater degree than elsewhere amid long-standing patterns of local political violence, Colombia's guerrilla groups were divided among themselves and failed to develop a coherent strategy for taking power.[15] Indeed, revolutionary victory was not necessarily their goal, especially as more of the guerrillas mingled with drug traffickers and bandits.[16]

The four governments that did fall to social revolution in Latin America during this century were all authoritarian; three were personalist dictatorships.[17] In Mexico in 1910, Porfirio Díaz had ruled for more than forty years. In Bolivia in 1952, a military junta had nullified an election won the previous year. In Cuba in 1959, Fulgencio Batista had canceled elections and ruled repressively for more than six years. And, in Nicaragua in 1979, Anastasio Somoza had been the third member of a dynasty ruling Nicaragua since the 1930s. All three revolutionary movements that came to power in the world in 1979 toppled despots: Somoza in Nicaragua, Eric Gairy in Grenada, and Shah Mohammed Reza Pahlavi in Iran.

According to the current conventional wisdom, social revolution in Latin America should be doomed not only because the democratic wave is flowing in the region but also because East bloc support for leftist revolution has ended.[18] As the Berlin Wall crumbled in November 1989, Mikhail Gorbachev's government discarded conventional Marxist principles and Deng Xiaoping's regime introduced free market reforms in the People's Republic of China. In Cuba, Fidel Castro's regime struggled. Major external support for Marxist movements in Latin America became a virtual impossibility.

In contradiction to the conventional wisdom and the historical record, however, the thrust of this book is to suggest that revolution is not a Cold War relic in Latin America. Although liberal democracy is the historical current and a major factor deterring revolution in Latin America, significant attempts to struggle against the current will continue. Although Latin America has not seen a successful revolution since the initiation of the third democratic wave and the collapse of the East bloc, it has seen two very strong revolutionary movements, even after 1989.

This book examines the two revolutionary movements in Latin America that seriously challenged incumbent governments at the end of the 1980s and into the 1990s: the Farabundo Martí National Liberation

Front (Frente Farabundo Martí de Liberación Nacional, FMLN) in El Salvador and the Shining Path (Sendero Luminoso) in Peru. Given my interest in revolutionary movements that posed actual threats to the state, I did not compare the Salvadoran and Peruvian experiences with those in Colombia or Guatemala, two other nations where revolutionary movements have endured. The Colombian guerrillas did not seriously endanger the government at any time during the 1980s. In Guatemala, the guerrilla coalition did threaten the regime in the early 1980s but only briefly, for about a year.[19] By contrast, in both El Salvador and Peru, the possibilities were real that the revolutionary movements would take power.

There is widespread awareness in the United States that the Salvadoran government was imperiled by the FMLN. Said a U.S. diplomat in December 1979: "If confronted with a Nicaragua-type situation the El Salvadoran military establishment could easily collapse in four to six weeks."[20] Commented a U.S. scholar: "By 1983 the rebels were actually winning the war."[21] Looking in hindsight at the Salvadoran conflict, a U.S. Green Beret concluded, "El Salvador has survived what appeared to be its probable demise in the early 1980s."[22]

Although the period of greatest threat to the Salvadoran government was probably between 1979 and 1982, the FMLN's challenge continued until the signing of peace agreements in January 1992 (see chapter 2). The year 1989—the year that the Berlin Wall fell—was one of intense guerrilla action in El Salvador. When the FMLN's proposals for modifications of the March presidential elections were rejected, the guerrillas coordinated more serious sabotage of the elections than ever before: "They [the FMLN] succeeded in severely disrupting the vote. . . . Their transport ban left almost all roads deserted except for military convoys. Petrol stations were bombed, about 90% of the country's electricity supplies were sabotaged, and water was cut."[23] Later in the year, on 11 November, the FMLN launched its largest offensive: thirty-five hundred insurgents occupied San Salvador, and other units attacked military positions in most major cities. Having surprised the Salvadoran military by the scale of their attack, the rebels defended their positions for some two weeks, even after the Salvadoran military resorted to aerial bombing. The offensive was deemed the "military high point of the war" by FMLN commander Joaquín Villalobos.[24]

Scholars and political leaders agree virtually unanimously that U.S. aid to the Salvadoran government prevented a takeover by the FMLN.[25] Proclaimed European scholar Harald Jung in 1984: "Since the January offensive in 1981, the guerrilla force in El Salvador has gained such a military strength that only massive support from the United States could save the Salvadoran army from defeat."[26] Manus Midlarsky and Kenneth Roberts echoed this sentiment: "There would appear to be little doubt that only extensive U.S. military assistance . . . has prevented the military defeat of the Salvadoran government since 1981."[27] Political leaders made similar assessments. Villalobos commented that "the level of intervention developed by the North American government constituted an external factor that began to alter the correlation and, as a result, the war changed its character. This was the most decisive factor of them all."[28] Said another FMLN commander in 1981: "Only one thing still holds up this government, and it is the same thing that props up all puppet regimes: imperialism's dollars and the political alliance of the most retrogressive sectors."[29] A different tone was struck by Alvaro Magaña, provisional president of El Salvador between 1982 and 1984: "The attitude of the U.S. government, during my tenure as interim president, was what definitely saved this country."[30]

By contrast, there is no widespread awareness in the United States that the Peruvian government was endangered by Sendero Luminoso. Many Americans do not believe that a movement as savage and brutal as Sendero could threaten an elected government. But it did. Only when Sendero leader Abimael Guzmán was captured in September 1992 did the threat posed to the Peruvian state end. Because there is limited knowledge of the threat posed by the Shining Path, I will cite numerous statements to that effect, most of them made between 1990 and the capture of Guzmán in 1992, first by Peruvian and then by non-Peruvian analysts.[31]

Peruvian expert Enrique Obando worried that "the state is on the verge of defeat. The armed forces could tumble down at any moment."[32] Reflecting after the capture of Guzmán on the fears of 1991 and 1992, Obando described the period as "extremely black . . . when people thought Sendero was about to take Lima, the government would fall. There was real fear, in the population and in the armed forces."[33] Warned Gustavo Gorriti: "If they [the Shining Path] continue this way, they will be able to beat the Peruvian state."[34] In another assessment,

Gorriti explained his pessimistic view: "If this is a war of apparatuses, Shining Path will win because it is more efficient, better organized and has better intelligence."[35] Agreed Carlos Iván Degregori: "In the early 1990s, the Shining Path was the most important guerrilla movement in Latin America, and it posed a real threat to the state."[36] The scholar Luis Pásara referred to the problem of "a Sendero Luminoso that threatens to take over the entire country."[37] Among the Peruvian public, 32 percent of respondents in one Lima poll in 1991 thought that Sendero would win.[38] By August 1992, even government officials acknowledged that Peru was "at war" and that Lima had become "the Beirut of the Andes."[39]

By the early 1990s, non-Peruvian analysts were also very worried about the possibility of a Shining Path victory. Simon Strong, a British journalist and author of a book in English devoted exclusively to the Shining Path, was a pessimist: "[In my book] I say that [the triumph of Sendero Luminoso] is probable."[40] A U.S.-based specialist concluded that "the Shining Path has become a direct threat to the government of Peru."[41] Warned two other analysts: "The potential of Guzmán's followers to bring down the elected government in Lima should not be underestimated."[42] Newspaper headlines for articles on events in Peru threatened a fall: "Plagued by a Host of Ills, Peru May be Beyond Help";[43] "Peru Risks Slide into Terrorist State beyond Rescue;"[44] and "Terrorist Noose Tightens in Peru."[45] At a hearing on Peru, both Bernard W. Aronson, assistant secretary of state for Inter-American Affairs, and Representative Robert G. Torricelli, head of the House Western Hemisphere subcommittee, speculated about what a Sendero victory would mean for the world.[46] Pleaded one expert to the U.S. public and policymakers: "Save Peru from Sendero."[47] Reflecting on Sendero after the capture of Guzmán, the respected Inter-American Dialogue reported that "many knowledgeable observers believed by the early 1990s that the Shining Path might overwhelm the Peruvian state."[48]

This book asks one primary question and several corollaries: Why were the FMLN and the Shining Path able to mount such serious revolutionary challenges between 1980 and 1992? Why were they able to recruit thousands of militants and gain the support of at least 10 percent of their respective populations? Why were they able to do this despite the fact that the Peruvian government had been elected since the onset of the movement, and the Salvadoran since 1984? And why, despite the fact that in the Peruvian case external support was almost nonexistent?

In social science terms, I seek to identify the cause of the expansion of the revolutionary movements—the trigger, the catalyst, the sine qua non, or the independent variable. For social scientists, the demonstration of cause is difficult.[49] The cause of a revolutionary movement cannot be something that was always present or that has not changed in some way; if something had always been present or had not changed, then it cannot explain the timing of the emergence of the movement. In other words, the cause of the revolutionary movement beginning in El Salvador in the late 1970s and the movement expanding in Peru in the 1980s must be something that was different from previous years or different from other nations—or else, in the logic of social science, a similar revolutionary movement should have occurred earlier or elsewhere as well. For social scientists, causation requires evidence that something different happened, and it is logical to assume a link between the changes in the independent variable and the dependent variable (in this case, the revolutionary movement).

During the course of my research, it became clear that the reasons for the emergence, expansion, and ultimate fate of the two revolutionary movements were different.[50] I argue that the pattern of variables that made up the revolutionary trajectory in El Salvador was essentially similar to those in other countries during the Cold War and, accordingly, does not sharply contradict recent scholarly theories of revolution, developed primarily on the basis of cases from the Cold War era. By contrast, the interplay of variables in the Peruvian case may be a harbinger of new revolutionary patterns during the post–Cold War era—and does contradict recent scholarly theories of revolution, which we now perceive to have been theories appropriate only for their historical moment.

The most prominent theorists of revolution writing during the Cold War identified an authoritarian regime type as the key variable in the emergence of revolutionary movements; they distinguished regime-type variables from economic variables and argued that regime-type variables are the most important (see chapter 1). It is agreed in this book that, despite the holding of elections in El Salvador during the 1980s, political exclusion was the sine qua non in the Salvadoran revolutionary equation. During the period of the formation of the groups that composed the FMLN, the authoritarian Salvadoran regime committed human rights violations on a massive scale unprecedented since the 1930s. Political opening—as the U.S. role in El Salvador increased and a civilian, Christian Democratic president was elected in 1984—reduced support for the FMLN, among the middle classes in particular. Still, for most Salvadorans, "democracy" meant more than elections—especially elections that were not especially free or fair (see chapter 3).

By contrast, during the period of the formation of the FMLN in the 1970s, the Salvadoran macroeconomy performed relatively well; economic concerns were not salient for the Salvadoran middle classes or recent university graduates aspiring to enter the middle classes. Nor, despite increasing land scarcity, was there a clear pattern of deepening poverty that threatened peasants' food security in El Salvador.

Accordingly, the Salvadoran case conforms to the dominant scholarly theories of revolution during the 1970s and 1980s. But it is also important to ask about the outcome stage of the revolutionary trajectory: why did the FMLN not win power, given that by most criteria the FMLN's revolutionary organization was stronger than, say, Fidel Castro's in Cuba prior to 1959?[51] The answer lies in the large-scale U.S. support for the Salvadoran government. This support was an important boon, enhancing living standards for the Salvadoran middle classes and enabling the U.S. government to pressure the regime for political reforms. The continuing human rights violations in El Salvador, however, made U.S. support for the regime controversial within the United States; U.S. support would probably have been less massive if the Salvadoran government had not responded at least somewhat to U.S. demands for political opening. In previous cases, when Latin American dictatorships had refused U.S. requests for a political opening, the U.S. government had decided not to rescue the threatened despot—and in those cases the revolutionary movement had succeeded.

Accordingly, in Latin American countries during the Cold War, there was a particular interplay among the variables in the revolutionary trajectory. The strength of the revolutionary organization was not key to whether it actually achieved power. The "successful" revolutionary movements in Cuba and Nicaragua did not defeat the regime's security forces on the battlefields of the capital city; rather, the Cuban and Nicaraguan dictators left their countries. One of the primary reasons why both dictators left was their realization that, since they were unwill-

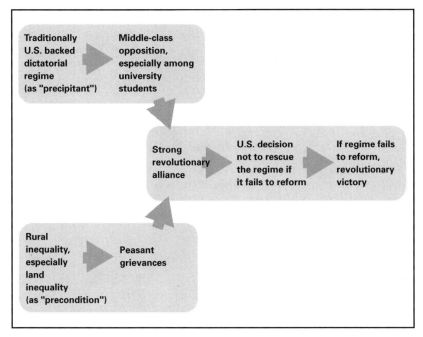

Figure I.1. Revolution in Latin America during the Cold War
Source: A composite of Huntington (1968), Blasier (1972), Booth (1991), Brockett (1991), and Wickham-Crowley (1992), based especially upon the cases of Cuba and Nicaragua. Among these scholars, only Wickham-Crowley incorporates the variable of U.S. policy.

ing to democratize their regimes, they would not be rescued by the U.S. government—and in both cases U.S. support had been critical to their maintenance of power. Lobbied by prodemocratic groups within the United States and from each country, the U.S. administration assessed (according to its ideological orientation and intelligence capability at the time) the character of the incumbent regime relative to the character of the revolutionary organization challenging it and decided not to rescue the regime from the revolutionaries' challenge. (See figure I.1.)

In Peru, by contrast, the interplay of variables contradicts scholarly theories of revolution developed during the Cold War. Political exclusion was not a key impetus to revolution. Rather, between 1980 and 1991, elections in Peru were fair and the electoral process was inclusive. Marxist parties participated in the political process, electorally and otherwise. Whereas FMLN militants in El Salvador frequently cited political exclusion as the main reason for their decision to join the movement, Shining Path guerrillas did not (see chapter 6).

Rather, the sine qua non in Peru's revolutionary experience was the nation's economic debacle. During the 1970s, not only were rural inequality and land scarcity increasing in the highlands of Peru—despite an ambitious agrarian reform effort—but also a threat to peasants' subsistence emerged. In addition, despite brief macroeconomic upturns between 1980 and 1982 and again between 1985 and 1987, Peru's overall economic performance during the 1980s was disastrous (see chapter 4). The economic decline exacerbated the already serious plight of Peru's rural highlands poor; it also dashed the middle-class expectations of the vast numbers of new university graduates. Peru's teachers, many of whom were the first in their families to gain an education and had aspired to professional lifestyles, found themselves unable to provide for their families' basic human needs; they were especially angry. The economic devastation was so severe that it was perceived as causing death and thereby, for some Peruvians, justifying Sendero's killings; salaries were "inhuman" and "[government officials through their policies] are killing the people."[52]

Of course, economic catastrophe alone is insufficient to create revolutionary equations; rather, it must interact with organizational, political, and international variables. As an organization, Sendero was extremely adept at taking advantage of the new kind of revolutionary space that had become available in Peru: Sendero targeted teachers and students, whose numbers were much larger than in the past and whose expectations had been severely dashed; its ideology was fundamentalist, repudiating elections—an ideology that would have been anomalous in previous years; and, although its exaltation of violence alienated most Peruvians, at some places and in some times violence facilitated an image of an organization that punished wrongdoers and that achieved its objectives. Confronted by economic crisis and a shrewd, savage revolutionary movement, the traditionally weak capabilities of Peru's state eroded further. Neither the Belaúnde nor the García government effectively countered either the guerrilla movement or the security forces' human rights abuses. And, in the late 1980s and early 1990s, when Sendero became a very real threat to the survival of the Peruvian state, the movement was underestimated in most sectors of the U.S. government, which continued to prioritize antidrug and economic liberalization policies; in some respects U.S. antidrug policy actually abetted Sendero.[53] The Peruvian

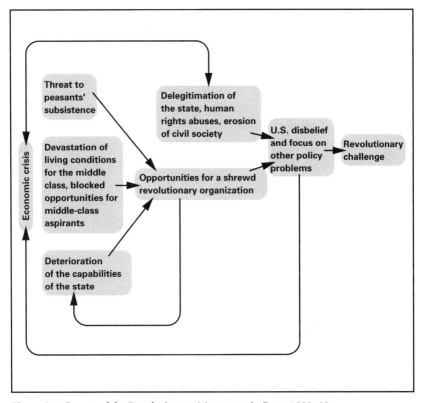

Figure I.2. Causes of the Revolutionary Movement in Peru, 1980–92

revolutionary equation—economic crisis that weakens a formally democratic but not particularly legitimate state, multiplied by a revolutionary organization that shrewdly takes advantage of these adverse conditions amidst minimal U.S. support—may be a harbinger of a post–Cold War revolutionary pattern. (See figure I.2.)

Chapter 1 of this book presents its scholarly framework. The first section summarizes the theories of revolution that are to be tested and ultimately modified in this study. Then I discuss my research design and in particular my choice of Ecuador as a negative or control case for comparison and contrast with Peru. The final section defines the key terms "revolution" and "democracy."

Chapter 2 describes the FMLN and the Shining Path as revolutionary organizations. The chapter highlights the major differences between the two, indicating that, if these very different organizations were both relatively successful, there is no set of criteria for an "effective" revolutionary organization that can be determined by social scientists. Rather, the effective organization is one that is appropriate to its context; both the FMLN and Sendero presented an alternative for those citizens who were angry about the most salient problems in their countries. The chapter undermines voluntarist interpretations of revolution by emphasizing that what matters is not the organization, but the fit between the organization and its context. Revolutionary organization is a necessary but never sufficient variable in a revolutionary equation.

Subsequent chapters describe three key variables in revolutionary equations: politics, economics, and the international context. As chapter 1 highlights, these are the key variables whose significance to revolutionary outcomes has been most intensely debated by theorists of revolution.

Chapter 3 examines the degree to which Peru and El Salvador meet democratic standards. The chapter analyzes the extent to which electoral processes in the two nations have been "free and fair." The thrust of the chapter is that, by and large, between 1980 and 1991 Peru was characterized by a free and fair electoral process including participants of Marxist inclinations. By contrast, although political space for the opposition increased in El Salvador and elections became more competitive, in my judgment they fell short of classification as free and fair. Accordingly, it is not surprising that the Peruvian militants rarely mention political exclusion as an explanation for their adherence to the revolutionary organization, whereas their Salvadoran counterparts do (see chapter 6).

I also suggest in this chapter that, even though conventional international standards for democracy were met in Peru during this period and perhaps even met in El Salvador by the early 1990s, many citizens were dissatisfied with their governments and were not as ready as were international analysts to label them democratic. Citizens in both countries were concerned about the performance of their governments: they worried that the governments were not resolving the problems of economic crisis and insurgency. Citizens believed that the governments should have been able to combat corruption and human rights violations more effectively; they wondered why both the governing parties and the opposition parties seemed unable to present cogent alternative policies.

Chapter 4 compares the Peruvian and Salvadoran economies during the 1970s and 1980s. In El Salvador, most national economic trends were positive during the 1970s, when the guerrilla groups were forming. The expectations of high-school and university graduates for entry into the Salvadoran middle classes were being met. Living standards among the peasantry improved in numerous respects; there was no widespread threat to subsistence. For many peasants, land scarcity was a serious grievance —but for the most part these were not the peasants who composed the FMLN's key social bases. By the 1980s, most Salvadoran economic trends were negative; but in Peru after 1976, the trends were much worse. The economic debacle both endangered peasants' food security and blocked educated young persons' access to the middle class. Economic reversal eroded state institutions—perhaps provoking greater corruption, perhaps not, but certainly sparking greater popular anger about corruption.

Chapter 5 analyzes the international context, specifically U.S. policy toward Latin American revolutions. First, it demonstrates a key theoretical point: during the Cold War, revolutionary movements in Latin America succeeded not when they met the government head on and won, but when they confronted a regime that had become illegitimate—not only to middle-class and popular groups within the country but also to the U.S. government—and that the U.S. government did not seek to rescue.

The chapter then examines the U.S. responses to the crises in El Salvador and Peru. In El Salvador, the U.S. response to the growth of the FMLN drew upon past responses to similar Latin American revolutionary organizations supported by East bloc countries during the Cold War. The U.S. government was able to bolster the Salvadoran regime financially and militarily at the same time that it prodded the regime toward greater political openness. By contrast, in Peru, Sendero was expanding as the Cold War ebbed. The movement was Maoist, unaligned with any superpower rival to the United States and unlikely to become so aligned in the future. Accordingly, the extent to which Sendero threatened U.S. strategic interests in Latin America was not clear. The appropriate U.S. response was also not clear, given that Sendero arose in response to a very different set of problems than had traditionally triggered Latin American revolutionary movements. The set of policies that served U.S. interests in previous revolutionary contexts would not succeed in Peru. Amid U.S. officials' uncertainties and competing policy priorities for the Peruvian government, neither the Reagan nor the Bush administration significantly bolstered the Peruvian regime.[54] Until 1992, the U.S. priorities in Peru appeared to be the implementation of free market reforms and the prosecution of the antidrug campaign, despite the fact that both efforts created difficulties for counterinsurgency, at least in the short run.

Drawing upon the information about the political and economic conditions in El Salvador and Peru presented in chapters 3 and 4 and upon the description of the U.S. role in chapter 5, chapter 6 offers integral explanations of why the two revolutionary movements expanded. The chapter first describes the revolutionary militants' backgrounds and experiences, and provides their own explanations for their actions. Then, based on the premise that citizens' attitudes about their nation's politics matter, the chapter compares Salvadorans' and Peruvians' interpretations of their circumstances. Finally, integrating various scholarly emphases about the differences in political regimes, economic conditions, revolutionary organizations, and U.S. policy, the chapter assesses the two countries' revolutionary equations.

Revolutionary movements will recur in the post–Cold War era in Latin America. Indeed, the embers of Cold War revolutionary movements continued to flicker in Guatemala until a peace agreement in December 1996, and sharply reignited in Colombia in 1996–97.[55] Moreover, since the initiation of the research for this book, a revolutionary challenge has been raised by two different groups in Mexico: first, the Zapatista National Liberation Army (Ejército Zapatista de Liberación Nacional, EZLN) in Chiapas, and then the Revolutionary Popular Army (Ejército Popular Revolucionario, EPR) in Guerrero and Oaxaca. The EZLN, although sparked in part by the authoritarianism of the Mexican regime in Chiapas, resembles the Shining Path in its roots in an increasingly destitute part of the country and in its militant protest against the prevailing economic order; for neither the Senderistas nor the Zapatistas were reasonably fair elections a sufficient response to their concerns.[56] Although information about the EPR is limited, it appears to be more similar to the Shining Path: the EPR is predominantly Maoist, it is not cautious about the use of violence, and its leaders appear to be well organized but not particularly articulate.[57] Together, the emergence of the Sendero Luminoso and the Mexican revolutionary movements as well as the expansion of the movements in Colombia suggest that revolutionary movements will endure in the post–Cold War era, but that the factors that make up a successful revolutionary equation will be different.

1

ANALYTICAL FRAMEWORK

*I*n the first section of this chapter, contending perspectives on revolution are reviewed and criticized. The second section outlines the research design and methodology of this study. In the third section, key concepts—namely, "democracy" and "revolution"—are defined.

Theories of Revolution

Scholarly arguments about revolution tend to pit political variables—in particular, the state and regime type—against economic variables, advancing either one or the other as the most important, virtually regardless of time or place. During the 1970s and 1980s, the predominant school of thought asserted the primacy of the state and regime type. This book, however, presents revolutionary equations that include not only both economic and political variables but also the variables of international context and revolutionary organization. Furthermore, this book suggests that the interplay of these variables is different in different times and places. As noted in the introduction, it is here argued that political variables may be the triggering variables (the variables that changed most dramatically in the areas of the country where the revolutionary movement expanded) in some equations, such as the Salvadoran, whereas economic variables may be the triggering variables in other revolutionary equations, such as the Peruvian.

The Predominant Scholarly Emphasis on the State and Regime Type
By far the most influential work on revolution in recent years has been *States and Social Revolutions* by Theda Skocpol, published in 1979.[1]

Skocpol's study has provided a conceptual framework for numerous subsequent books, including Farideh Farhi's *States and Urban-Based Revolutions* and Timothy P. Wickham-Crowley's *Guerrillas and Revolution in Latin America*; it has been a primary subject of numerous review essays; and it has been the target of scores of critiques.[2] Among the scholars who emphasize the primacy of political variables and regime type in the emergence of an intense revolutionary challenge, however, Skocpol is one of the most adamant in her dismissal of the importance of economic variables.

Skocpol's key argument is that "the realm of the state is likely to be central [to the causes and outcomes of revolution]."[3] The state is defined as "a set of administrative, policing, and military organizations headed, and more or less well coordinated by, an executive authority."[4] Comparing the successful revolutions in France, Russia, and China with failed revolutions in Japan and Germany, Skocpol contends that social revolutions occurred as a result of "crises centered in the structures and situations of the states of the Old Regimes."[5] The crises are catalyzed by military pressures from economically more developed nations, and they persist in part because of landlords' resistance to efforts at crisis resolution by the state.[6] In turn, the breakdown of the state's repressive capacity "finally created conditions directly or ultimately favorable to widespread and irreversible peasant revolts against landlords."[7]

Skocpol identifies a certain agrarian structure as most susceptible to peasant revolt: peasant smallholders who are autonomous from landlords and reside in communities with considerable peasant solidarity.[8] For Skocpol, "agrarian structure" refers to the relations of the peasant community to local, regional, and national power—not to patterns of grievances within the community. Although Skocpol uses the term "social classes" and occasionally mentions the phrase "economic conditions," she does not identify socioeconomic deprivation as a factor in peasant revolt. She contends that socioeconomic deprivation is a constant for peasants and in any case cannot be empirically assessed.[9] Indeed, she characterizes the agrarian economies in prerevolutionary Russia and France as "growing" and that in China not as declining but as "near limits to growth."[10]

In short, for Skocpol, the key variables in the revolutionary equation are international pressures, the state and its autonomy or lack thereof from the landed upper class, and agrarian landowning structures.[11] Skocpol explicitly rejects previous theories that emphasize, in the terms of political science, "society" rather than "the state." Considering in particular the work of Ted Robert Gurr, Chalmers Johnson, and Charles Tilly, Skocpol argues that these theorists present revolution as a three-step process: first, "grievances, social disorientation, or new class or group interests and potentials for collective mobilization" emerge; second, "there develops a purposive, mass-based movement"; and third, the revolutionary movement fights the authorities, either winning or losing.[12] Skocpol points out that this interpretation incorrectly implies that the survival of a regime depends directly upon its popular support (when in fact most regimes are not widely supported), and that it neglects the essential coercive function of the state.[13]

During the 1980s, Skocpol's interest in the state as the key variable in revolutionary equations led her to analyze regime typologies and their relative vulnerability to revolutionary challenges. Collaborating with Jeff Goodwin, Skocpol contends that "closed authoritarian regimes" are most vulnerable to the growth of revolutionary movements.[14] The reasons are several: under such regimes, the economic grievances of excluded sectors are quickly politicized; a visible, common enemy is available to groups whose grievances and goals are different; and opponents tend to be radicalized, as they cannot compete in honest elections.[15]

Among exclusionary authoritarian regimes of the current era, moreover, a specific type is most vulnerable to actual overthrow: "neopatrimonial or Sultanistic dictatorships identified with a foreign power."[16] These personal dictatorships are especially vulnerable because they often provoke elite and middle-class opposition, in which case foreign support may be withdrawn, and because the dictator organizes the military toward the goal of his personal political survival rather than professional competence.[17]

In her article with Goodwin, Skocpol derides socioeconomic explanations of revolution more vehemently than in her earlier work. Goodwin and Skocpol oversimplify socioeconomic explanations. They claim, for example, that

> the "misery breeds revolt" hypothesis does not explain very much. Leon Trotsky once wrote that "the mere existence of privations is not enough to cause an insurrection; if it were, the masses would be always in revolt."[18]

Perhaps the best-known recent work that seeks to exalt regime type as not only a necessary but also a sufficient condition of revolutionary success is that by Robert Dix. In his 1984 work "Why Revolutions Succeed and Fail," Dix identifies two successful revolutions in Latin America (the 1959 Cuban and the 1979 Nicaraguan revolutions) and eight failed ones. He argues that there are no significant differences between the cases of success and failure on such key socioeconomic variables as GNP per capita, percentages of the population literate or urban, rates of growth in per capita income, income distribution, or dependency. Again contrasting the two cases of revolutionary success to the eight of revolutionary failure, Dix claims that the key variables are exclusively political. As for Goodwin and Skocpol, for Dix the crucial catalyst is a narrowly based dictatorship that provokes a broad-based opposition coalition against it.[19]

For most other scholars, economic variables are not irrelevant; rather, economic grievances are essential to the establishment of favorable preconditions for revolutionary movements, but they do not determine the ultimate fate of a movement. This group of scholars includes Wickham-Crowley (1992), Booth (1991), Brockett (1991), Booth and Walker (1993), and, in a much earlier but influential work, Blasier (1967).

In *Guerrillas and Revolution in Latin America*, Wickham-Crowley assesses the validity of Skocpol's theory for twenty-four cases of winning, losing, and "also-ran" revolutionary movements in Latin America between 1956 and the mid-1980s. In his thoughtful and empirically rich study, Wickham-Crowley finds considerable support for Skocpol's theory from recent Latin American experience. Post-1956 winning revolutionary movements occurred in the two cases (again, Cuba and Nicaragua) where a "patrimonial, praetorian" state was challenged by a peasant-supported guerrilla movement. In nations where a peasant-supported guerrilla movement emerged but the state was not a personalistic dictatorship, the revolutionary movement either lost or merely achieved the status of contender for national political power.

In contrast to Skocpol, Wickham-Crowley is concerned about the economic grievances of the peasantry;[20] however, his focus is not on poverty or overall changes in living standards but on peasants' ownership of land, or lack thereof. He finds that physical dislocation of the peasants from their land (grabbing of the land by elites) is a common catalyst to revolt, whereas agrarian reform is usually a bulwark against revolt. He finds also that certain types of peasants who do not own land—specifically squatters, sharecroppers, and migratory estate laborers —are prone to revolt.

Although the empirical focus of the studies by Brockett (1991), Booth (1991), and Booth and Walker (1993) is upon Central America, the thrust of their analysis is similar to Wickham-Crowley's. These scholars examine the trajectory of revolutionary movements in Central America during the 1970s and 1980s, distinguishing the nations where strong revolutionary movements occurred—namely, El Salvador, Nicaragua, and Guatemala—from those where strong revolutionary movements did not emerge—namely, Costa Rica and Honduras. They agree that the expansion of commercial agriculture displaced significant numbers of peasants from the land and lowered peasants' living standards through-out Central America. As a result, peasants mobilized in all five nations. Whether the flames of peasant mobilization were fanned into national revolt, as in El Salvador, Nicaragua, and Guatemala, or were dampened, as in Costa Rica and Honduras, depended upon regime type. National revolt occurred against the three governments that were exclusively repressive in their response to peasant mobilization. By contrast, revolt did not occur against the two governments that were not highly repres-sive but rather open to the discussion of grievances and willing to offer modest concessions.

In various key respects, these analyses by Wickham-Crowley, Booth, Brockett, and Walker resemble the theory proposed some twenty-five years earlier by Blasier (1967). Studying the winning revolutions in Mexico, Bolivia, and Cuba, he distinguishes between the "preconditions" of revolution and the "precipitants." He notes that land concentration was a serious problem in Mexico and Bolivia prior to the revolutions, and that inefficiency and insufficient employment on Cuba's commer-cial plantations were widely criticized in Cuba before 1959. Accordingly, "economic conditions were a source of popular discontent."[21] But, he cautions, "similar economic conditions have plagued most countries in Latin America which have never experienced social revolution."[22] Again, as for Wickham-Crowley, Booth, and Brockett, the key variable determining the relative success of the revolutionary movement is regime type. The Mexican, Bolivian, and Cuban regimes were "despotic dictatorships."[23] Blasier emphasizes that "in each case, a dictatorial figure or group openly and cynically denied the electorate the opportunity to select its own leadership. . . . [providing] moral and political justification for revolution."[24]

There are also important similarities between the recent theories and the much earlier but influential analysis by Huntington (1968). Huntington was one of the first scholars to highlight the fact that democratic regimes are not vulnerable to revolution. For Huntington, as for the other scholars discussed here, regime type is the variable most critical to the trajectory of revolution:

> The great revolutions of history have taken place either in highly centralized traditional monarchies (France, China, Russia), or in narrowly based military dictatorships (Mexico, Bolivia, Guatemala, Cuba), or in colonial regimes (Vietnam, Algeria). All these political systems demonstrated little if any capacity to expand their power and to provide channels for the participation of new groups in politics.[25]

But Huntington is also very interested in the emergence of a revolutionary challenge, for which he believes an alliance between the peasants and "the first middle-class elements to appear on the scene"—"intellectuals with traditional roots but modern values"—is necessary.[26] In his view, the revolutionary potential of the peasantry in a country depends considerably on their "social and economic conditions," which may have deteriorated as patterns of land inequality become more extreme with the advance of "modernization."[27] Huntington also highlights the impact of foreign intervention on the revolutionary movement; rather than perceiving the capacity of an external power to rescue threatened regimes, however, he emphasizes that foreign intervention may provoke the nationalism that becomes "the cement of the revolutionary alliance" between the intellectuals and the peasants.[28]

Although regime type is crucial for these scholars, Huntington is one of the few who actually uses the term "democracy." The primary reason is simply that, in the eras that these scholars are discussing, few Latin American regimes even approached the criteria for democracy. In other words, authoritarianism was just as common as poverty. Accordingly, scholars focus on whether the authoritarian government is personal or institutional and on the intensity of repression and degree of corruption —in Goodwin and Skocpol's terminology, on neopatrimonialism and sultanism. At the same time, it is clear that, for these scholars, democratic regimes should not be vulnerable to revolution.

Criticisms of Scholars Emphasizing the Primacy of the State and Regime Type

Recent scholarship highlighting the state does not put it into the context of other important variables. In particular, in their discussions of revolution in Latin America during the Cold War, these scholars underestimate the importance of the international context and of U.S. policy.[29] Both Goodwin and Skocpol and Wickham-Crowley recognize that the loss of U.S. support was an important factor in the downfalls of Fulgencio Batista in Cuba and Anastasio Somoza in Nicaragua.[30] Both would acknowledge too that one of the reasons for the vulnerability of the sultanistic dictatorship relative to other authoritarian regimes was the greater threat represented to it by the loss of U.S. support. But, in their works to date, international context is neither described cogently nor linked analytically to domestic revolutionary variables. For example, the Batista and Somoza regimes are "personalistic" and "mafiacracies"; they are not client governments of the United States.

If international context is analyzed in relation to domestic revolutionary variables, it becomes easier to understand why the triumphant revolutionary movements during the Cold War were not necessarily the strongest. (Among scholarly criteria for the strength of a revolutionary movement are the number of peasants and other citizens willing to commit resources to the guerrillas' cause, the range of resources committed, and the capacity to establish "dual power.")[31] The Cuban revolutionary movement was much weaker by these criteria than the Colombian or the Salvadoran, but it won in part because Batista left the country when he could no longer count on U.S. support.[32] By contrast, although the Salvadoran FMLN was comparatively strong, it could not defeat a strong regime—strong in part because of U.S. support.

Indeed, the strength of the revolutionary movement in El Salvador posed numerous analytical problems for the mainstream theorists of the 1980s. These theorists could explain without difficulty why the revolutionary movement did not win: the Salvadoran state was not a personalistic dictatorship, and it enjoyed substantial support from El Salvador's own socioeconomic and political elites as well as from the

United States. But why was the FMLN as strong as it was? In numerous works, scholars hedged their bets about the prospects for an FMLN victory—despite the fact that such a victory would have roundly contradicted the key arguments of their studies.[33]

Accordingly, the Salvadoran case raised a key question: Are the factors that are important to the development of a strong revolutionary movement similar to those that are important to revolutionary triumph, or not? Do we study revolutionary movements only out of interest in which ones win, and consider cases of revolutionary activity only because they might win? Or are we interested in what John Walton calls "national revolts" regardless of their potential for seizing state power?[34] Are distinct theories necessary for the analyses of "national revolts" and revolutionary movements that win power?

These questions are important not only for analytical reasons but also for methodological ones. Methodologists would point out that a very small number of cases of revolutions that have won state power are available for scholarly analysis. In other words, the *N* is tiny.[35] Theda Skocpol's 1979 work is built around a mere three successful cases—France, Russia, and China. Dix's analysis focuses upon two successful cases, Cuba and Nicaragua, relegating all other cases except El Salvador to the category of failure. Wickham-Crowley (1992) also emphasizes Cuba and Nicaragua as "winning" revolutions, although his more nuanced study distinguishes "also-ran" or contending movements from failed efforts.

Criticisms have also been voiced of some of the key concepts used by these scholars. In particular, critics have suggested that it is tautological to argue that a revolution succeeds because the state "breaks down" "amid political crisis." For Skocpol, notes Davidheiser, "revolution is the collapse of the old state; it occurs where the state is weak and collapses."[36] Further, Snyder (1992) points out that during the 1980s, numerous neopatrimonial regimes—such as those in the Philippines, Haiti, Paraguay, and Zaire—were not overthrown by revolutionary movements and asks why not. Everingham (1995) poses the question: If it is the dictatorial regime type alone that provokes negative coalitions and multiclass revolution, why did the revolutionary movement in Nicaragua not win a decade or more earlier?

Critics have also targeted the terms "precondition" and "precipitant." Asks Colburn: How can we determine the precise impact of "preconditions" when they were evident in most poor nations during the same time period?[37] Further, those scholars who assert that the type of regime determines revolutionary outcomes do not rigorously assess exactly how or why the nature of the state changed, or how or why the nature of repression by the state changed, so that this change became the precipitant or the trigger to the revolutionary movement.

Alternative Arguments: Misery Matters Most

The leading scholars of the late 1970s and 1980s scorned economic grievances as an explanation for revolution, pointing out that poverty is common but revolution is rare. However, scholars whose work sought to explain not only successful revolutions but also major revolts, as well as many scholars whose work was not restricted to the Cold War era, have argued for the primacy of economic problems.

Several of the leading advocates of the "misery matters" approach were writing in the 1960s or early 1970s, and theirs were the studies against which Skocpol and other proponents of the primacy of the state reacted. The first widely noted work was "Toward a Theory of Revolution" (1962) by James C. Davies. Analyzing revolutionary movements in the United States in 1842, Russia in 1917, and Egypt in 1952, Davies found that these movements emerged when a prolonged era of prosperity ended and was followed by a sharp decline in living standards. Under these conditions, Davies posited, the rising expectations that had developed while living standards improved were left unfulfilled, frustrations mounted, and rebellion became likely.

A second leading advocate of the "misery matters" approach—and Skocpol's theoretical nemesis—is Ted Robert Gurr. At first glance, Gurr's work does not appear to be about economics. In Gurr's *Why Men Rebel* (1970), most of the key concepts are drawn from the psychological realm: "perceptions" of "deprivation" spark "frustration" and "aggression." However, Gurr is much more precise in his formulations about "deprivation" and much more emphatic about the importance of economic factors to deprivation than his critics admit.

Gurr's thesis is that the likelihood of "internal war" (defined as "large-scale, organized violence aimed at overthrowing a regime or dissolving a state and accompanied by extensive violence") "varies directly with the intensity and scope of elite and mass relative deprivation."[38]

Gurr defines relative deprivation as "actors' perception of discrepancy between their value expectations and their value capabilities."[39] Although these are terms from the psychological literature, Gurr underscores economic factors as the most important dimension of these values:

> Another general point is that economic factors are more salient for most people than other values . . . a cross-national study shows that for 114 nations in the early 1960s a composite measure of short-term economic deprivation correlates .44 with magnitude of civil strife.[40]

Gurr also highlights economic decline as key to political violence. In cases of "decremental deprivation," he notes, men "are angered over the loss of what they once had or thought they could have. . . . decremental deprivation has probably been a more common source of collective violence than any other pattern of RD."[41] The types of decremental deprivation identified by Gurr include inc reases in taxation; declines in the number or appropriateness of job opportunities, especially for university students in developing nations; natural disasters; and wartime material sacrifices.

A second major, but much more recent, study that emphasizes the importance of economic grievances is Jack A. Goldstone's *Revolution and Rebellion in the Early Modern World* (1991). For Goldstone, the deus ex machina of revolt is demographic: population increase. Especially in the traditional agrarian economies of 1500 to 1850, economic output in general and food supply in particular often did not increase at the same pace as the population. Amid more intense competition for land and flooded labor markets, real wages decline, unemployment increases, and consumer prices rise—and, concomitantly, popular unrest grows.

Although both Gurr and Goldstone highlight economic grievances in their analyses, and both perceive these grievances as much more important than a "precondition," they do not ignore political variables in general or the state in particular. Gurr distinguishes the "potential for collective violence" from the "potential for political violence" and the "magnitude of political violence"—or, in other words, distinguishes discontent from the politicization and expression of discontent—and emphasizes the importance of ideological justifications and the balance of coercion to these latter phenomena.

One of Goldstone's main arguments is that economic and political factors should not be considered as competing explanations for rebellions; rather, there is a crucial interplay between the economic and political dimensions. Goldstone (1991) demonstrates that population growth, urban migration, and increasing poverty and unemployment can lead to a fiscal crisis for the state. Often, the state under-taxes, in part because elites are more financially hard-pressed and even more likely than previously to evade taxes. Amid the demographic and economic changes, greater turnover, displacement, and factionalization are probable among elites; in turn, elite factionalization intensifies conflict for state office and patronage and thereby also debilitates the state.

Among scholars whose primary focus is the phenomenon of revolt among peasants, economics is widely considered to be the leading explanatory factor. There are two primary competing interpretations of how economic factors have shaped peasant revolt, those of James C. Scott and Jeffery M. Paige. (Although the work of Samuel Popkin is often discussed alongside Scott's and Paige's within the "political economy" set, Popkin's emphasis is not upon economic grievance, but upon economic rationality and organizational capacity, and accordingly is summarized in the next section.)

In *The Moral Economy of the Peasant* (1976), James Scott focuses on peasant rebellions in Southeast Asia. Scott argues that the peasants' guiding moral principle, the standard by which they assess the actions of landlords and government officials, is their own subsistence. Especially in cohesive villages with strong communal traditions, peasants become morally outraged and consider revolt when they judge their right to subsistence to be seriously threatened. Analyzing rebellions in Burma and Vietnam during the twentieth century, Scott argues that population growth, the expansion of capitalism, and increasing fiscal claims on the peasantry by the state all exposed peasants to greater risks of subsistence crises.

Scott's argument is supported for the Mexican case by Tutino (1986). Tutino argues that successive crop failures caused by drought and frost in 1907–10, population growth, and the advance of large-scale export agriculture in Mexico under Díaz threatened subsistence in many rural regions of Mexico. He concludes: "Facing social changes that denied them autonomy and forced them into deepening poverty, dependence, and insecurity, agrarian Mexicans became outraged at the injustice of their lives."[42] Tutino indicates that similar socioeconomic grievances were important to the 1810 Hidalgo revolt in Mexico but did not result in revolution because of elite unity at that time; however, socioeconomic grievances were not a backdrop or precondition to the revolution in 1910 but an integral factor in the division among Mexican elites at that time.

A rival explanation of peasant rebellion is provided by Jeffery Paige (1975 and 1983). In his classic study *Agrarian Revolution: Social Movements and Export Agriculture in the Underdeveloped World* (1975), as well as in his more recent article "Social Theory and Peasant Revolution in Vietnam and Guatemala" (1983), Paige advances what he calls a class conflict model. In his view, the key to revolt in the countryside is not the intensity of peasants' deprivation but the intensity of class conflict between landowners and the rural or semirural proletariat. For Peru in the 1960s, as for Angola, Vietnam, and Guatemala, Paige argues against Scott's contention that smallholders dependent on their own plots for their subsistence are the most rebellion-prone group. Paige believes that smallholders were divided by conflicts over land and water rights and could not unite. Moreover, they were averse to property risks, and many depended on large landowners for marketing or other services. Rather, Paige believes that the classes most disposed to insurrection were migrant laborers or sharecroppers who, working on estates under more or less uniform contracts, were able to make common cause against landlords and had less to lose in the effort.

Much more recently, Paige (1996) and Mitchell Seligson (1996) have offered competing interpretations of the nature of peasant revolt, with a particular focus on El Salvador. In accord with the emphases in his earlier work, Paige argues that, within the context of the social organization of Salvadoran agrarian production, the large numbers of landless and land-poor peasants in El Salvador were a key factor in the FMLN's expansion (and could be a key factor in similar revolutionary movements in the future). By contrast, Seligson contends that landlessness was perhaps a "necessary condition for rebellion," but not "a central causal factor."[43] Seligson's argument in this article reflects in part his previous work with Edward N. Muller, in which these scholars have advanced income inequality rather than land inequality or landlessness as the variable critical to insurrection.[44]

Scholars who emphasize economic variables have focused on the peasantry for the obvious reason that this group is usually the most impoverished. At the same time, however, misery of course affects other groups as well. As chapters 4 and 6 in this book argue, in Peru teachers were particularly frustrated and particularly drawn to Sendero. As noted above, Huntington highlighted the possible revolutionary inclinations of the first generation of intellectuals in a country in his 1968 study of the topic. Alvin Gouldner (1979) makes essentially the same point but develops it much more rigorously. Analyzing teachers as a newly important social class in many nations, he argues that they are often separated from their community roots, are confident that they are right, and are angry at their relative lack of prestige and income, and accordingly may become politically radical.

Recent Additional Emphases

The theoretical direction of this book—the emphasis on economic grievances, regime type, revolutionary organization, and international context as a set of variables in an equation that fit together in particular patterns during particular eras—is, to my knowledge, new. However, I am joining other scholars who in recent years have been arguing that international context and revolutionary organization are variables that were neglected in the 1970s and 1980s.

The almost simultaneous triumph in 1979 of three distinct revolutionary movements—in Nicaragua, Iran, and Grenada—signaled to many scholars that international context should be incorporated as an important factor in revolutionary outcomes. Especially when the reduced opposition toward revolutionary movements of the Carter administration was followed by the aggressive antagonism of the Reagan administration, and two Latin American movements triumphed under Carter and none under Reagan, it was hard to argue that U.S. policy was insignificant.

Accordingly, numerous scholars writing during the 1980s and early 1990s have bowed to international context as important, although none to my knowledge has elaborated a sustained argument about the ways in which international context might affect the kind of revolutionary organization that might come to power. Analyzing the 1979 revolutions in Nicaragua and Iran, Farhi (1988 and 1990) reintroduced the term "permissive world context," a concept originally coined by Walter Goldfrank (1979) to explain the triumph of the Mexican revolutionaries.

Examining peasant revolution in the Philippines, Hawes (1990) calls for more attention to international context, as does Foran (1992) in a sophisticated treatment of the Mexican, Cuban, and Nicaraguan experiences.

While Wickham-Crowley (1992) emphasizes that massive U.S. aid did not rescue the South Vietnamese government, nor U.S. indifference doom the Guatemalan regime of late 1970s and early 1980s, he yet includes "loss of U.S. support" as one among five favorable conditions for revolution. Wickham-Crowley, Dix, and Midlarsky and Roberts, among other authors, concur that U.S. foreign aid bolstered the Salvadoran government at a time of structural crisis and guerrilla threat.[45]

From the 1960s to the 1980s, scholars downplayed the role of revolutionary organization. Skocpol was vehement in her criticism of "voluntarist" explanations of revolutions as events made by purposive organizations.[46] During this period, some scholars may have hesitated to discuss the roles of revolutionary organizations because they feared that their interpretations would be grist for the mills of intelligence agencies. Other scholars may have considered revolutionary movements unamenable to rigorous empirical analysis and more appropriate to study by journalists than by political scientists.

Although Skocpol's argument was perhaps valid for the French, Mexican, and Russian cases, purposive organization is evident in most post–World War II cases of revolution (revolutions occurring after the worldwide emergence of Marxism as an ideology), and its importance to revolutionary expansion in Bolivia, Cuba, Nicaragua, Iran, and El Salvador is rarely denied. Indeed, confronting the case of the victory of mass-mobilizing revolutionaries in Iran, Skocpol herself (1982) concedes the point.

Although the concept of revolutionary organization is rarely defined, for many scholars the term includes the organization's ideology, strategy, structure, and leadership. In one model, Desai and Eckstein (1990) emphasize the importance of visionary and innovative ideas that are advanced with zeal, as well as of a "combat party" that can "make fervor efficient" —that is, identify where it is likely to gain adherents, mobilize and retain members, identify friends and enemies, and plot a plausible path to power.[47] In a recent study of Latin American revolutions, Selbin (1993) seeks to "bring people back in" to the analysis. Both he and Colburn (1994) emphasize that social scientists "should evaluate the power and promise of ideas and ideals by studying the manner in which social revolutionary leaders invoke, manipulate, and build on timeless conceptions to arouse and mobilize the population."[48]

Organizational capacity has been highlighted by various scholars. Wickham-Crowley deems one of his five favorable conditions for revolution to be the "military strength of guerrilla movements," which he believes is strongly related to the numbers of peasant combatants that the guerrilla group mobilizes.[49] Samuel Popkin (1979) also stresses organizational capacity. In his classic work *The Rational Peasant: The Political Economy of Rural Society in Vietnam*, Popkin argues that the key factor is the capacity of the revolutionary organization to provide attractive benefits to peasants, because peasants are rational utility-maximizers who respond to individual incentives offered by political organizers. As chapter 6 discusses, scholarly analysts of Peru's Shining Path have also emphasized this movement's organizational capacity in their explanations of its expansion.

Other scholars emphasize ideology and strategy. Farideh Farhi highlights the importance of Christian liberation theology to the success of the Nicaraguan revolt and the significance of Muslim fundamentalism to the success of the Iranian revolt.[50] In an extremely thoughtful analysis of the Salvadoran experience, Byrne (1996) points to the important role of FMLN strategy in the evolution of the conflict during the 1980s.

Research Design and Methodology

In the terminology of political science, the goal of this book is to test the prevailing theories of revolution against the empirical evidence of the 1980s and early 1990s. I seek to identify which, if any, independent variables—or, more colloquially put, which causes of social revolution—explain the dependent variable—national revolt during this period.

Perhaps to an even greater degree than the discipline of comparative politics generally, the study of revolution is impeded by the "small *N*" problem—the small number of cases of revolutionary triumph. As noted above, there have been at most four cases of revolutionary victory in Latin America in the twentieth century, and two cases (the Cuban and the Nicaraguan) are the focus of most scholarly work. Of course, social science theory should be constructed on a much larger number of cases. In part because of the absolute paucity of cases, it seems appropriate that scholars examine cases of "national revolt." As defined by Walton, national revolts are "protracted, intermittently violent, nonlocal struggles [with extensive] mobilization of classes and status groups that become recognized claimants of rival sovereignty and engage the state."[51] For the reasons indicated directly below, among the four cases of national revolt in Latin America that endured into the 1980s, I selected the Peruvian and Salvadoran.

In the terminology of comparative politics, my research design is neither the method of agreement nor the method of difference. The method of agreement would attempt to identify similarities in independent variables that are associated with a common outcome—in other words, similar reasons for national revolt in both El Salvador and Peru. The method of difference would attempt to identify independent variables associated with differing outcomes.

Rather, my approach is closer to research strategies proposed by Alexander George (1979), George and McKeown (1985), and Collier and Collier (1991). As George and George and McKeown recommend, my two-case comparison is "focused": I am analyzing selectively those aspects of the Salvadoran and Peruvian experiences that are relevant to my research objectives and my data requirements. I am posing uniform questions in each case. In contrast, however, to a method of agreement design, I am not assuming that the answers to these questions will be the same for El Salvador and Peru. As Collier and Collier emphasize, comparativists have been prone to either lumping cases together or splitting them apart—exaggerating either the similarities or the differences among cases.[52] In line with Collier and Collier's approach, to achieve my research goals I examine similarities *and* contrasts between my two cases.[53]

There is at least one unfortunate consequence of my approach, however: to a rigorous comparativist, El Salvador and Peru become individual case studies rather than two cases exemplifying one theory. Given that, overall, my analysis of the Salvadoran case does not dramatically contradict the predominant school's theories of revolution, my interpretation could be considered as an additional case and does not pose questions of scientific rigor. However, my analysis of the Peruvian case does contradict the most recent conventional wisdom; without other cases to bolster my argument, do I have any grounds on which to assert that my interpretation is valid more generally—that Peru is not just an idiosyncratic, sui generis case? Not really; my argument about Peru is more akin to hypothesis forming than to hypothesis testing.[54]

However, I try to maximize rigor for my analysis of Peru by the introduction of a negative case. Just as Skocpol contrasts the experiences of successful revolution in France, Russia, and China to the nonrevolutionary experiences of England, Prussia/Germany, and Japan, and Wickham-Crowley contrasts the successful revolutionary movements in Nicaragua and Cuba to numerous "also-ran" and failed movements in the region, I contrast the national revolt in Peru to the relative political calm of Ecuador.[55]

The purpose of the introduction of the Ecuadorean case is to test my argument about why Peru's revolutionary movement expanded. Among all the Latin American countries, Ecuador is most similar to Peru in a wide range of areas usually considered relevant to a revolutionary outcome; thus, one might expect that the independent variables I identify as the most important to Peru's revolt would also be present in the Ecuadorean case. If these independent variables were indeed present in the Ecuadorean case, however, my analysis would be invalidated. In other words, the pattern of variables that I identify as key to the expansion of Sendero Luminoso in Peru must not be evident in Ecuador, given the absence of a revolutionary threat there.

Table 1.1 shows the similarities in the two countries' geography, preindependence heritage, socioeconomic inequalities, economies, and recent political trajectories. Although differences between Peru and Ecuador in terms of variables relevant to revolutionary outcomes do become evident upon in-depth analysis, overall these differences are secondary. The only other nation that shares (almost) as many similarities with Peru is Bolivia. Bolivia, however, is more traditional on most socioeconomic indicators than Peru or Ecuador, and it had already experienced what most analysts called a revolution in 1952.[56]

As mentioned in the introduction to this book, the demonstration of causality is difficult for social scientists; evidence of correlation is easier to advance than evidence of cause. We social scientists imply cause much more frequently than we try to prove cause empirically. For example, as noted above, it is not always clear why scholars have identified

Table 1.1. Peru and Ecuador: Two Countries That Are Similar (except for the intensity of revolutionary threat)

Geography
The steep Andean mountain range divides coast and jungle in both countries.

Preindependence Heritage
Prior to the Spanish conquest, most parts of both countries were controlled by the Incas. After the conquest, both were governed as the Vice Royalty of Peru.

Socioeconomic Inequality
Sharp in both nations. Class cleavage is reinforced by geography and ethnicity: i.e., the poorest people are indigenous highlands peasants. In 1976, the annual per capita incomes of 30 percent of Peruvians and 33 percent of Ecuadoreans were estimated at under $200, higher percentages than for other nations at similar overall income levels.[a]

Economy
Per capita GNP at $1,120 in Ecuador and $1,300 in Peru in 1988. Between 1945 and 1988, primary commodities accounted for more than 80 percent of exports in both countries. In the late 1980s, the percentage of GDP in manufacturing was about 20 percent in both countries.[b]

Politics, 1930–79
Unstable civilian and military regimes. Leftist militaries governed in both countries toward the end of this period.

Politics during the 1980s
Inclusive elections were held in Ecuador in 1979 and in Peru in 1980. Between 1979 and 1992, four presidents were fairly elected in Ecuador and three in Peru.

---

[a]Luzuriaga C. and Zuvekas (1983, 17). Honduras was the exception to this pattern.
[b]World Bank (1990, 178, 208–209, 182–183).

some problems as "precipitants" of revolutionary movements while characterizing others as "preconditions." How much more severe must a problem become to graduate from the level of precondition to that of precipitant? Are precise indicators of the problem available? Is the severity of the problem determined by objective data on the extent of change, by the subjective assessment of the citizens who are suffering the problem, or by both objective and subjective criteria?

This study draws on both objective and subjective data about trends in political regimes, economic conditions, and U.S. policy toward El Salvador and Peru. To gather such data, I traveled to El Salvador and Peru for extended periods during 1990–91, and returned to both nations more briefly thereafter. Having lived in Peru for more than twelve months in 1973–74 and for four months during 1987, as well as having visited for briefer periods almost annually, I already had a wealth of information about Peru on which I could build. This was not the case for El Salvador, although I had visited the country with a Center for Development Policy delegation in 1983.

In my research, I sought out objective data of various types. Data about military/paramilitary violence and electoral processes are critical to chapter 3; chapter 4 relies on data about economic and social trends, especially in the agrarian sector; and chapter 5 draws on data about U.S. aid. Although all the data in this book are in my view helpful indicators of the phenomenon in question, many are also rough indicators; specific problems are mentioned in the relevant sections. Perhaps the most controversial data are those on political violence. I have reported data from the institutions that emerged as the most respected sources for data on political violence in their respective countries: the Bernales Commission in Peru and Tutela Legal in El Salvador.[57] Appendix II discusses the controversies surrounding these two institutions and the collection and accuracy of political violence data in Peru and El Salvador generally.

To gain citizens' own evaluations, I worked with respected Peruvian and Salvadoran research teams to carry out sample surveys, as well as informal surveys, of particular groups in the two countries. In Peru, I worked primarily with the polling agency Datum and with my own long-standing research assistant, Rodolfo Osores Ocampo, and his team, based in Huancayo. In El Salvador, I collaborated with Antonio Orellana, the director of the Salvadoran Institute of Education and Technical Assistance for Cooperatives (Instituto Salvadoreño de Educación y Asesoría Cooperativa, ISEAC), who had worked on public opinion research at the Catholic University in El Salvador (the UCA—the university's formal name is Universidad Centroamericana José Simeón Cañas) and who came highly recommended by several Salvadoran social scientists. To the extent possible on key items in the sample surveys, my goal was to ask identical questions to identically selected samples of people in the two countries. Surveys were carried out in areas of both Peru and El Salvador where the guerrillas were especially strong—the department of Junín in Peru and what are called the "eastern departments" in El Salvador. Further information about the survey teams and the conduct of the various surveys in the two countries is provided in appendix I.

One of the scholarly contributions this book makes is what I believe to be the most rigorous and most numerous set of interviews with Shining Path militants ever conducted. In 1993, my Osores research team carried out thirty-three interviews with Senderistas in the Huancayo area of Peru. Although the interviews were carried out through a process of informal contacts rather than a rigorous sample and although a larger number of interviews would have been desirable (see appendix I), the interviews add greatly to our knowledge about the kinds of Peruvians who became Shining Path members and about their reasons for joining the movement (see chapter 6). We also conducted informative informal surveys with security force personnel in Huancayo and with various sets of government officials in both countries.

Definitions

Two concepts are key throughout this study and must be defined at the outset: revolution and democracy. "Revolution" is generally defined as a violent change in government, social structure, and culture. Among scholars in recent years, the term is almost exclusively restricted to social revolutions, usually of Marxist or Islamist orientation and mobilized from below at the grassroots, rather than from above by a military institution or other elite sector. The following definitions are representative:

> A revolution is a rapid, fundamental, and violent domestic change in the dominant values and myths of a society, in its political institutions, social structure, leadership, and government activities and policies.[58]

> Social revolutions are rapid, basic transformations of a society's state and class structures; and they are accompanied and in part carried through by class-based revolts from below.[59]

Although scholarly disagreement about the definition of revolution is slight, analysts do not concur about the elaboration of specific criteria in the definition and, accordingly, the application of the revolutionary label to various cases. For example, although most scholars perceive revolution to have occurred four times in Latin America—in Mexico in 1910, Bolivia in 1952, Cuba in 1959, and Nicaragua in 1979—some scholars doubt the applicability of the term to each of these cases. Some analysts believe that in both the Mexican and Bolivian cases the revolution was "uncompleted": the most popularly based, leftist sector of the revolutionary movement did not achieve power. With respect to the Cuban case, Marxist analysts in particular often perceived the revolution as an accident, winning because of good luck and fortuitous political circumstances rather than strong, popularly based organization. Prior to 1990, scholars would have been unanimous that the Nicaraguan case met the criteria for revolution—but then the revolutionary movement accepted electoral defeat and its revolutionary president left office. It is not yet clear how analysts of revolution will interpret such a transition only eleven years after apparent revolutionary triumph.

As indicated in the first section of this chapter, scholars also disagree about the classification of cases of "national revolt." Whereas many scholars focus on revolutionary movements that win power, others are also interested in movements that, in Walton's phrase, "become recognized claimants of rival sovereignty and engage the state." Clearly, in this book we are interested in national revolts—in the reasons why they became strong, and also to a lesser degree in the reasons why they did not actually win. At least one scholar defines "revolution" to include movements that seek the overthrow of a political regime, even if they fail to attain this goal:

> Political revolution refers to abrupt, illegal mass violence aimed at the overthrow of the political regime as a step toward over-all social change.[60]

Historically more controversial than the definition of revolution has been the definition of democracy. In the 1960s and 1970s, many definitions of democracy were "maximalist"; scholars suggested that "true democracy" or "full democracy" signified more active citizens' participation and greater economic and political equality than was the case in "formal democracy" or "bourgeois democracy."[61] For example, in the classic work *Polyarchy,* Dahl reserved the term "democracy" for "a political system one of the characteristics of which is the quality of being completely or almost completely responsive to all its citizens" and used the term "polyarchy" for real-world regimes that were "highly inclusive and extensively open to public contestation."[62] Some scholars today continue to advocate a definition of democracy that includes criteria of government responsiveness or accountability, but they are in a minority.[63]

In recent years, most scholars in the United States have adopted a definition of democracy based on the procedure for the selection of the regime.[64] The key criterion for the classification of a regime as democratic has been free and fair elections. Democracy so defined has been called not only "procedural," but also "formal," "representative," "liberal," "bourgeois," and "constitutional," as well as of course the classic "polyarchy." One representative definition is by Huntington:

> [The] most powerful collective decision makers are selected through fair, honest, and periodic elections in which candidates freely compete for votes and in which virtually all the adult population is eligible to vote. . . . It also implies the existence of civil and political freedoms to speak, publish, assemble and organize that are necessary to political debate and the conduct of electoral campaigns.[65]

However, as with respect to the term "revolution," scholars have not specified and agreed upon the criteria for the evaluation of the freedom and fairness of an election.[66] Usually, if the political opposition in a country does not protest the quality of an election and continues to participate in subsequent elections, scholars assume that the election was free and fair. But what if the political opposition does protest the quality of the election or does not participate? How are its charges to be judged? How many deaths of politically salient individuals attributed to paramilitary or military groups indicate that an election is not free? What kinds of data tell us that registration procedures are so exclusive, or voting tables so inaccessible, or ballot tabulation so irregular that an election is not fair? Even Freedom House, which has established seven-point scales for political rights and civil liberties, has not specified the precise indicators in its scales, let alone the thresholds for the seven points in its scales (see chapter 3).

As is the case with the term "revolution," the lack of precise criteria for the freedom and fairness of elections leads to disagreement about the qualification of a nation as democratic or not. Currently, scholars who specialize in a country whose qualification as democratic is dubious tend to be cautious about the application of the democratic label to the country—although they rarely explicitly check the country into the "not democratic" column. In more general analyses by comparative politics scholars, however, the country is usually allowed into the ranks of democratic nations without serious comment (see chapter 3).

In Latin America, the formal authority of civilian governments has often been undermined by powerful military institutions; the civilian winners of an election have not invariably been the actual key decision-makers in the country. Accordingly, scholars have added stipulations about the role of the military to their definition of democracy. Terry Karl's definition of democracy has been widely cited by Latin Americanists because of its inclusion of the subordination of the military to civilian authority as a criterion:

> a set of institutions that permits the entire adult population to act as citizens by choosing their leading decision-makers in competitive, fair, and regularly scheduled elections which are held in the context of the rule of law, guarantees for political freedom, *and limited military prerogatives.*[67]

The effort to establish precise indicators for military subordination to civilian authority has been undertaken by David Pion-Berlin and Samuel Fitch, among other Latin Americanists.[68]

Some scholars, in particular Carothers, have suggested that assessments of democracy in Latin American nations should more rigorously include the functioning of democratic institutions, such as the judiciary, the legislature, and political parties.[69] As chapter 3 indicates, I agree with Carothers's argument; to date, however, it has not been incorporated into most official or scholarly assessments of Latin American democracies—much less given precise thresholds for rankings.

2

TWO REVOLUTIONARY ORGANIZATIONS
THE FMLN AND THE SHINING PATH

*T*he FMLN and the Shining Path were very different guerrilla organizations. Whereas the FMLN resembled previous Latin American guerrilla movements in important respects, in its ideology and strategy the Shining Path resembled not the FMLN but Cambodia's Khmer Rouge. The only significant similarity between the FMLN and the Shining Path is the intensity of the challenge each made to the respective governments.

This chapter describes the FMLN and Sendero Luminoso and the threats that they mounted against the Salvadoran and Peruvian states. As noted in chapter 1, an issue current among today's scholars of revolutions is the role of the guerrilla organization as a variable in the revolutionary equation. Here the question is, To what extent did the FMLN and Sendero Luminoso themselves autonomously "make" the revolution? Should revolutionary organization and leadership be considered a "cause" of guerrilla expansion, independent of popular discontent?

On the one hand, I believe that revolutionary organization and leadership matter (see chapter 1). A revolutionary organization must be able to channel social discontent; it must be able to identify the kind of political space available to it and advance itself within that space; it must be able to identify likely allies and likely enemies and plot a credible strategy for power.

On the other hand, rigorous analysis of the advantages and disadvantages, the strengths and the weaknesses, of a specific revolutionary organization is difficult, if not impossible. Many characteristics of an organization have ambiguous implications for its success or failure. This ambiguity is evident in comparing the FMLN and Sendero as organizations: they were very different, but both were relatively successful. The FMLN could be assessed as pragmatic and open to debate—or as opportunistic and irresolute. The Shining Path could be assessed as dedicated and steadfast—or as fundamentalist and uncompromising. Analysts of the FMLN have tended to perceive this coalition's divisions and conflicts as a weakness and perhaps would be tempted to perceive the coherence and discipline of Sendero under one leader as a strength. But, by the same token, many analysts of Sendero have perceived the organization not as "coherent" and "disciplined" so much as inflexible, dogmatic, and authoritarian—and, accordingly, repugnant to large sectors of Peruvian society. Clearly, if only one kind of organization can "make" a revolution, then both the FMLN and Sendero would not have done so well.

The intensity of the challenge to the state posed by a guerrilla movement is also difficult to measure objectively. On the basis of quantifiable indicators of military strength, the FMLN was the strongest guerrilla movement ever to emerge in Latin America; yet the FMLN probably was closest to a successful revolutionary takeover several years before it achieved its greatest military strength. Especially in Latin America, revolutionary movements have triumphed in part because of their capacity to challenge the regime militarily, and in part because of the demoralization of the regime's army and leadership. No matter how strong an organization may be, citizens will not stand up for it at critical moments if they believe that the government, with its international allies, is stronger. Accordingly, an element of tautology impairs the analyst's assessment of the intensity of a revolutionary challenge: citizens' beliefs that an organization is powerful make it in fact powerful, which in turn further affects citizens' beliefs.

Rigorous assessment of the strengths and weaknesses of a guerrilla organization is thus very difficult. To a considerable degree, arguments are tautological: revolutionary victory is the independent variable to be explained by a strong and effective revolutionary organization, but the strength and effectiveness of the revolutionary organization are measured by its victory. We assess a leader as "effective" if the leader's decisions produce results. In other words, in the terminology of political science, the dependent and independent variables are the same. We usually do not take into account the range of options, or lack thereof, that were available at the time; nor can we replay events under the conditions of an alternative strategic decision. "Control" leaders and organizations are absent.

It is in good part due to the virtual impossibility of objective analysis that traditional scholarly theories of revolution ignored organization and leadership as factors in revolutionary outcomes (see chapter 1). And it is also due to this impossibility that I do not perceive either the FMLN or Sendero to have autonomously "made" the revolution, apart from the political and economic contexts in which they arose. My view is that, as "successful" guerrilla organizations, both the FMLN and Sendero recognized the degree and nature of people's anger and channeled that anger effectively. As revolutionary organizations, the FMLN and Sendero were important variables but only within the context of an entire revolutionary equation.

A salient example of a revolutionary organization that was inappropriate to the revolutionary space available in Peru in the 1980s and early 1990s was the Túpac Amaru Revolutionary Movement (Movimiento Revolucionario Túpac Amaru, MRTA). Despite what might appear to be the contrary evidence from the MRTA's dramatic seizure of the Japanese ambassador's residence on 17 December 1996, the MRTA never posed a threat to the Peruvian state.[1] Numbering approximately 1,000 militants at its apex and based primarily in Lima, Huancayo, and the coca-producing San Martín department, in the late 1980s the MRTA was responsible for about 10 percent of all political attacks and roughly 5 percent of all deaths from political violence (in comparison to Sendero's approximately 75 percent and 50 percent).[2] As a revolutionary movement, the MRTA was relatively similar to the movements in Nicaragua, El Salvador, and Colombia. Influenced by the Cuban model, its strategy was *foquista*: the emphasis on the popular attack that commands great publicity and accordingly, without any need for a coherent revolutionary organization, gains popular support. Whereas this strategy proved successful in Cuba and Nicaragua where a widely despised dictator was ruling and a spectacular attack showing his vulnerability was significant, it was inappropriate in the Peru of the 1980s and early 1990s. In this context, where successive democratically elected governments were deemed not despotic but ineffectual and undisciplined, citizens were unlikely to be engaged by a revolutionary opposition that also appeared undisciplined.

Accordingly, although the MRTA might have successfully channeled popular discontent in Cuba or Nicaragua, it did not in Peru. Both the FMLN and Sendero fit the revolutionary space in their respective nations much better than the MRTA did. On the other hand, as will be evident below, both the FMLN and Sendero were far from perfect fits; both were deficient in significant respects. Other organizations might have emerged in both countries that fit the available revolutionary space better.

The FMLN

The discipline and hierarchy that were hallmarks of the Shining Path did not characterize the FMLN. To the contrary, the FMLN was fractious. Established in 1980, the FMLN was a coalition of five guerrilla groups that had been active previously; each group maintained its own leaders, internal practices, and ideological perspectives.[3] There was no single leader of the organization; for key decisions, agreement was supposed to be reached among the commanders of the five groups. Although the leftist orientations within the FMLN were diverse, none of the groups extolled political violence for its own sake; terrorism was reserved primarily for military targets. Also, in contrast to Sendero Luminoso, the FMLN maintained numerous important alliances: domestically, with the civilian opposition the Democratic Revolutionary Front (Frente Democrático Revolucionario, FDR) and internationally, with the Cuban and Nicaraguan governments and with social democratic movements in the United States and Europe.

The Formation of the FMLN

The identities of the five groups composing the FMLN were forged during the 1970s, amid intense ideological debate in the capital city, San Salvador—primarily at its main university, the National University of El Salvador. Most of the leaders of the groups were dissidents from both the traditional pro-Soviet Communist Party in El Salvador and the then center-left Christian Democratic Party.

Until 1970, the Communist Party of El Salvador (Partido Comunista de El Salvador, PCS) was the only significant Marxist group in the country.

Founded by Farabundo Martí in 1930, the party spearheaded the planning for the insurrection of 1932. After the capture of Martí, the failure of the insurrection, and the brutal killing of more than thirty thousand Salvadorans, the party was essentially destroyed. More than a decade later, the party regrouped in a new organization that included some survivors of the 1932 massacre. The party was one of the many communist parties at that time in Latin America closely linked to the Soviet Communist Party. The party's stronghold was at the National University. Although the party was illegal, many of its members were activists in another organization linked to the party by the late 1960s, the Democratic Nationalist Union (Unión Democrática Nacionalista, UDN), which ran candidates in Salvadoran elections.

In 1970, the leader of the PCS, Salvador Cayetano Carpio, argued to the party's central committee that the PCS should abandon the traditional Soviet approach to revolution—the development of popular consciousness through peaceful participation in the electoral process. He believed that the PCS, in trying to restrain popular action within legal limits, was a "fireman," "pouring cold water on the combativity of the masses until it lost them the capacity to be the vanguard"; he advocated "military struggle" as well as "mass struggle."[4] When he did not prevail, he withdrew from the party; Shafik Handal, who was about a decade younger than Carpio, became head of the PCS. Under Handal, in both 1972 and 1977 the PCS joined the Christian Democratic Party and the National Revolutionary Movement (Movimiento Revolucionario Nacional, MNR) in an electoral coalition. The party was never large, numbering only about one hundred fifty members in 1972.[5] However, Handal's long-standing connections with officials in the Soviet Union and other communist countries were a benefit that the PCS was to bring to the FMLN.

After Carpio left the PCS in 1970, he and six other dissidents formed the Popular Forces for Liberation (Fuerzas Populares de Liberación, FPL).[6] Carpio, originally a bakery worker, was one of the few leftist leaders from the popular classes, and his background apparently influenced the greater emphasis on orthodox Marxist issues in the FPL. Rejecting participation in the Salvadoran electoral process, as well as the *foco* theory advocated by Ché Guevara, the FPL advocated a prolonged popular war strategy *(guerra popular prolongada)* that was modeled in part after the Vietnamese experience. Aspiring to achieve a true Marxist-Leninist party, the FPL worked more intensely than any of the other Salvadoran groups to incorporate large numbers of workers and peasants into the organization. In 1975, the FPL established an alliance with the Revolutionary Popular Bloc (Bloque Popular Revolucionario, BPR), a popular organization that included many unionized teachers, students, and peasants among its members.[7] By the late 1970s the BPR was the largest leftist organization in El Salvador, numbering approximately sixty thousand, and it regularly coordinated mass demonstrations and strikes.[8] When the FPL used violence, often in an effort to free its jailed members, it most commonly attacked policemen and other security force personnel. The FPL was especially active in the northeastern department of Chalatenango.

In 1970, the same year that Carpio withdrew from the PCS, other dissidents from the PCS, as well as from Christian Youth and New Left groups, were also despairing of an electoral approach to social change. Some of these leftists formed "El Grupo," which in 1972 evolved into the Revolutionary Army of the People (Ejército Revolucionario del Pueblo, ERP). Relative to the leaders of the FPL, the founders of the ERP were younger, more middle class, and usually formerly affiliated with the Christian Democratic Party rather than with the PCS.[9] Unlike the FPL's founders, the ERP's leaders had not developed among themselves a clear ideological position at the time of the ERP's establishment; for the most part, in the words of a high-ranking defector from the FPL, "the ERP was a day-to-day movement that thought little about ideological things. . . . Ideologically, they weren't Marxist-Leninists."[10]

In general, however, the ERP adopted a *foquista* strategy influenced by the Cuban and Nicaraguan revolutionary models, emphasizing spectacular military action as a prelude to insurrection in the short term—rather than long-term political mobilization—as the key to the revolutionary triumph. As Villalobos put it, many years later: "Who would have thought that, with a few attacks on some barracks, Somoza would have fallen? And the same was true in Cuba. You have to seize the moment."[11] The ERP's preferred violent tactic was bombing. As early as 1974, the ERP chose the eastern department of Morazán as its regional stronghold. Relative to the other leftist organizations, the ERP was slow to build an allied popular organization, working only as of

1978 with the Popular Leagues—28th of February (Ligas Populares—28 de Febrero, LP-28).

After the death of the original leader of the ERP, Sebastián Urquilla, Joaquín Villalobos emerged as the group's leader despite his youth. To the extent that the youthful Villalobos had established a formal political affiliation prior to joining the ERP, it was with the Christian Student movement.[12] Villalobos was more a pragmatist than an ideologue.[13] During the early years his image was that of a particularly ruthless leader. Along with heads of the ERP, he approved the 1975 assassination of Roque Dalton, El Salvador's leading contemporary poet and an internationally renowned Marxist intellectual. Dalton was arguing that the ERP's strategy should not be exclusively military and that greater attention to political mobilization was necessary. Dalton was charged with treason by the ERP leadership and executed.

Protesting the murder, a sizable number of members withdrew from the ERP to form the Resistencia Nacional (RN).[14] Agreeing with Dalton's criticism of the ERP, the RN put a major emphasis on political action; its allied political organization was considered second only to the BPR in size. The RN's guerrilla organization was named the Armed Forces of National Resistance (Fuerzas Armadas de Resistencia Nacional, FARN), and at times it is referred to by this acronym. The FARN carried out many of the kidnappings of the late 1970s and early 1980s in El Salvador.

The fifth party within the FMLN was the Workers' Revolutionary Party (Partido Revolucionario de los Trabajadores, PRTC). It was the last to be founded, and the smallest. Like the majority of the other parties' leaders, however, the PRTC's founders were students from the University of El Salvador who had become militants in the early 1970s. The primary difference between the PRTC and the other parties was the greater ideological emphasis placed by the PRTC on the Central American region, rather than just on El Salvador, as the appropriate context for a revolution.[15] The party had actually been founded in Costa Rica, but gradually the party developed a group of Salvadoran supporters, primarily in the department of San Vicente. Given its small size, however, the PRTC had few options other than flexibility and mediation among the other groups.

Several attempts at unification of the revolutionary groups failed. The ideological differences that had given rise to the formation of the five groups had been serious, and to a considerable degree endured even after unification. As late as May 1979, long after the military coup in Chile against Salvador Allende and just before the Sandinista National Liberation Front (Frente Sandinista de Liberación Nacional, FSLN) in Nicaragua was preparing its final offensive against the dictatorial regime, the PCS continued to extol the electoral process as the exclusive revolutionary path in El Salvador.[16] For their parts, the FPL and the ERP were intense rivals. As the largest group during the 1970s and the most ideologically sophisticated, led by the man with the longest experience in revolutionary movements (Carpio), the FPL believed that it was the superior organization. For the ERP, however, the FPL's emphasis on pro-longed political mobilization raised the risk of missing the revolutionary moment; the ERP believed that El Salvador was ready for insurrection. The FPL's "prolonged popular war" strategy was also rejected by the RN; for the RN, the FPL was encouraging popular combat without sufficient analysis of possible outcomes—without sufficient consideration of tac-tics and strategic ends.[17] Believing that there were no reformist elements in the Salvadoran armed forces or bourgeoisie, the FPL rejected any alliances with sectors of these groups, whereas the ERP and the RN did not.[18]

Ultimately, however, the five movements formed the FMLN in Octo-ber 1980. Both the Salvadoran insurgents and the Cuban leadership were persuaded by the example of the Sandinista victory in Nicaragua that revolutionary unity was necessary. Possibly, in December 1979, Fidel Castro conditioned his support for the Salvadoran guerrillas upon their unification.[19] Still, although in the mid-1980s the ERP argued strongly that the FMLN should become one united party, each move-ment retained its own leadership, ideology, and organizational structure.

In 1980 and for most of the rest of the decade, the FMLN was allied with the FDR.[20] The FDR was established in April 1980, at the height of the death squad activity that had included the assassination of Arch-bishop Romero. The FDR's formation signified the rupture between the Salvadoran government and its social democratic sector. Virtually immediately after its establishment, the FDR joined with the precursor organization to the FMLN; the FDR's essential objective was to unite left and center-left groups, both political parties and social organizations. The three political parties in the FDR were the MNR, the UDN, and the

Popular Christian Social Movement (Movimiento Popular Social Cristiano, MPSC). After the original leaders of the FDR were assassinated in November 1980, the MNR's Guillermo Ungo became the group's president. One of the group's leaders best known in the United States, and a member of its Political-Diplomatic Commission, was the MPSC's Rubén Zamora.

Gradually, the relationship between the FMLN and the FDR became more distant. The FDR was at times critical of human rights abuses by the FMLN, and the FDR was also quicker than the FMLN to believe that political space was opening again in El Salvador.[21] Although the FDR was not formally dissolved, it had little practical significance after 1987, when Ungo, Zamora, and other FDR members returned to El Salvador, assessed the possibility of their participation in the country's elections, and ultimately founded the Democratic Convergence (Convergencia Democrática, CD). Still, the relationship among these groups was sufficiently cordial that, in 1994, Zamora was the presidential candidate of a coalition integrating the FMLN, the CD, and the MNR.

Internal Divisions within the FMLN and the Failed "Final Offensive"

A serious dispute emerged in 1980 about the leadership of the coalition. Carpio, the FPL's leader, fervently believed that he should be number one in the FMLN hierarchy; he was senior to the others in years and experience, he was the leader of the largest organization, and (as he apparently argued ad nauseam) he was the only leader of working-class background and was accordingly the "vanguard of the vanguard."[22] For a brief period in 1980, Carpio did formally become the FMLN's number one. Gradually, however, Carpio was perceived as arrogant, dogmatic, and sectarian by other groups within the FMLN as well as by many members of the FPL, and he lost his number-one rank. He also apparently became a carping critic, rejecting others' proposals but not offering alternatives of his own.

The differences among the groups seriously weakened the "final offensive" of January 1981.[23] The FMLN's plan was that its armed offensive against all the country's main garrisons would coincide with a nationwide strike, and that these events would spark defection and rebellion within the armed forces. In the event, although there were more than eighty FMLN attacks on military posts in two-thirds of El Salvador, no garrison was actually taken; having suffered massive repression and fearing more, a smaller number of citizens heeded the strike than in previous months; and only in one military garrison did troops mutiny. One of the reasons for the failure of the offensive was division among the FMLN commanders. Neither the FPL nor the RN favored the offensive, and the RN apparently failed to attack.[24] The ERP declined to share arms with the other groups.[25]

Overall, the differences among the insurgent groups may have cost them victory during 1979–81. This critical period, just before and after General Carlos Humberto Romero was ousted by a military coup led by a young, reformist faction of the military, was the most unstable in El Salvador (see chapter 3). U.S. and upper-class Salvadoran support for the regime was fragile—at different moments and for different reasons—and popular mobilization was at its apex. In December 1979, the entire cabinet of the first civilian-military junta had resigned; on 22 January 1980, between one and two hundred thousand persons marched against the government.[26] The number of guerrillas was approximately similar to that in Nicaragua in the spring of 1979, and their level of training was similar to that of Nicaragua's core guerrillas in late 1978.[27] Together, the insurgent groups might have been able to forge a successful challenge to the Romero dictatorship or the subsequent civilian-military juntas. As Handal commented years later:

> The delay in the unity of the revolutionary organizations did not allow us to take advantage of the revolutionary insurrection situation of 1980. Unity should have been consummated a year earlier, but analysis is slower than objective reality. The people were hoping that we would unite and launch the struggle. . . . Tens of thousands of persons went defiantly to demonstrations knowing that they would be massacred. . . . They were ready to give their lives for the revolution. But we were only in the conditions to launch a great offensive by January 1981. . . . When the offensive was produced on January 10, 1981, the insurrectional situation had declined.[28]

A virtually identical analysis was provided by Villalobos:

> In the first stage, during the years 1979, 1980, and 1981, the military development of the revolutionary movement was scanty and we can say that different factors made impossible the maturation of the historical conditions that would have permitted progress towards the taking of power. . . . In the

first place, the lack of unification upon a strategic line within the revolutionary movement. This lack prevented our taking advantage to the maximum of our accumulated political and military power.[29]

Another FMLN leader made a similar comment:

That [1980] was a difficult time. . . . We didn't have arms. And we had setbacks in the unity process. There was a great popular surge. If we had been able to rise on that wave, things would have been more successful. But we weren't ready. And we were ready when the wave had already passed.[30]

As this leader indicates, however, even if the groups had been closely united during 1979–81, they would still have been trying to defeat, with few weapons, a relatively well-equipped and well-trained military.[31] As the leftist movements gained a military capability, the Salvadoran regime too was becoming stronger.

Gradually, the FMLN became more cohesive. FMLN unity was advanced by the death of Carpio, the long-time leader of the FPL.[32] As it became clear that Carpio would not be number one in the FMLN hierarchy, he became skeptical that the FPL should participate in the FMLN at all. The FPL's second-in-command "Comandante Ana María" (Melida Anaya Montes), was an advocate of FMLN unity. In February 1983 in Managua, Carpio ordered the assassination of Ana María, hoping that his deed would remain a secret. When Carpio was questioned by Sandinista leaders about the assassination, he apparently realized that his order would be revealed, and he committed suicide.

The bloodshed shook the FPL and its supporters outside of El Salvador. Although the Cuban leadership had at first been close to the FPL, and presumably viewed the ERP as other leftists did during the 1970s—as a group of ideologically ignorant, immature upstarts whose former friends' blood was on their hands—Fidel Castro gradually came to favor Villalobos.[33] Villalobos's pragmatic, can-do approach was, after all, much more similar to the way that Fidel Castro had come to power than Carpio's doctrinaire, go-slow style. Despite Villalobos's part in the history of violent infighting within the Salvadoran left, by the 1980s he appeared to be the only charismatic leader among the various FMLN commanders. For leftist Salvadorans, he was congenial and articulate. ERP members who worked with him perceived him as accessible, diligent, and thoughtful.[34]

In any case, the FMLN gradually resolved contentious issues more effectively. There was a great deal of discussion and debate, but ultimately more-or-less common positions were established on such policies as the November 1989 offensive and the subsequent negotiations. Reported a sympathetic U.S. doctor:

> The high price of this unity was everlasting meetings, since no one was about to grant uninformed consent on strategic or tactical issues. My impression, however, was that he [Raúl Hercules] fully endorsed this time-consuming process. I chuckle to think what a U.S. general would say if his every command decision were put to a vote of five political blocs within his ranks![35]

Although fractiousness was still perceived as a problem by many analysts, a certain level of comfort seemed to have been achieved among the leaders—a recognition that they might not like one another or agree politically, but that their fates were inextricably bound together:

> There's a real danger of each group going its own way, but it's also difficult to decree unity. We have genuine differences of approach, and the answer is not for every organization to renounce its beliefs in the name of unity. That smells of Stalinism to me.[36]

The FMLN as an Organization: Ideology, Structure, International Alliances, and Resources

The FMLN and the Shining Path were vastly different in their ideology, structure, international alliances, and resources. The FMLN's ideology was much more pragmatic and moderate, its structure more democratic, its international alliances vastly more elaborate; although the FMLN received considerable amounts of weapons from the East bloc during the early 1980s, its total income was less than Sendero's.

The thrust of the stated principles of the FMLN were social democratic rather than Marxist, even during the organization's initial period. Most militants indicated that the authoritarian political regime was the primary reason behind their decision to join the guerrilla movement (see chapter 6); consequently, the revolutionaries' appeals emphasized political vices. In an April 1980 FPL radio announcement, for example, the guerrillas' calls are "Let us defeat the genocidal armed forces! Let us put an end to this regime of persecution and massacre! A river of blood separates the junta from the people! The peace offered by the junta is the peace of the grave! Not one more year of tyranny in El Salvador!"[37] In May 1980, the ERP began a radio message condemning the Salvadoran political regime: "The murderous military-Christian Democratic dictatorship, loyal to the orders of imperialism and the oligarchs who exploit the country, have tried to cover up their repression with a ridiculous curtain of demagogic reforms."[38]

Consider also the more formal FMLN statements, such as its "six-point platform of principles" presented in December 1980:

1. The revolutionary democratic government will guarantee national sovereignty and independence. It will secure and defend the right to self-determination of the Salvadoran people.
2. It will guarantee peace, liberty, well-being and progress to the Salvadoran people. For this purpose, it will carry out political, economic, and social reforms that will assure a just distribution of wealth, the enjoyment of culture and health and an effective exercise of the democratic rights of the majorities.
3. It will follow a foreign policy of peace and nonalignment.
4. It will guarantee democratic representation of all popular, democratic and revolutionary sectors that actively contribute to the overthrow of the military dictatorship.
5. It will create a new-type army composed of the People's Revolutionary Army, honest individuals among the troops and officers of the present army, who will be incorporated into it, and the FMLN.
6. It will support all private businessmen who cooperate and promote the economic development of the country and the revolutionary government's program.[39]

FMLN leaders repeatedly sought to assure middle-class businessmen that the FMLN would not implement wholesale nationalizations. Even the FPL's Carpio, widely considered the most committed Marxist among the FMLN commanders at the time, declared:

The revolutionary government . . . will not be socialist. . . . the revolutionary democratic government will support all private businessmen, the small industrialists and merchants, and all of those who promote the development of the country and the application of a revolutionary democratic program.[40]

Villalobos was even more emphatic on this point:

The government claims that the FMLN is against any form of private property and that its plans include the expropriation and destruction of all the coffee and cotton bosses, industrial managers, and businessmen of the country. All of this is absolutely false. The plans of the FMLN rest on an objective and realistic basis, not on pipe-dreams and non-doable goals. It is not reasonable or logical, for reasons of stability and economic development, to expropriate all the private sector. . . . Any plan of economic development . . . must . . . take advantage of the potential of the private sector.[41]

Even in the early 1980s, FMLN leaders were also explicit that they did not seek a communist-style government. Said the PRTC's commander, "Roberto Roca":

> We want democracy and stability and we'll want help from abroad. We're an expression of . . . pluralism [the broad spectrum of Marxist and democratic views represented in the opposition]. Our new society cannot be built under the domination of one political force.[42]

Echoed Villalobos:

> The FMLN is struggling for a government of full participation, with representation from all the democratic political forces, including of course the FMLN-FDR. . . . The FMLN maintains that a government of full participation should guarantee freedom of expression and organization, respect for Human Rights, and truly free elections with participation by all parties and forces.[43]

Did these declarations reflect the actual views and aspirations of the FMLN leaders? Probably, the answer is "yes" for some of the FMLN commanders, and "no" for others. As mentioned above, Villalobos, the commander who became "first among equals," was very much a pragmatist; he had not been affiliated with a Marxist movement prior to becoming an ERP leader.[44] Villalobos dedicated one of his publications to a fallen friend, an ERP founder, remembering that "he insisted that political theory should never be converted into political-religious doctrine."[45] Although Villalobos at times advocated Marxism in his discussions with other leftists, in his published writings and interviews, Marxist terminology is rare; Villalobos's focus is usually on current political conditions in El Salvador, and on the way in which the FMLN will achieve power.[46] He often declares that Marxism is an important influence within the FMLN, but never says this about himself. Although during the 1980s Villalobos's moderation—especially when expressed in a mainstream U.S. journal such as *Foreign Policy*—was frequently dismissed as a public relations gambit, during the 1990s Villalobos did shift dramatically toward El Salvador's political center.[47]

Nor was Marxism evident in statements by other ERP leaders. For example, *New York Times* journalist Raymond Bonner reported an ERP commander's explanation for the guerrilla movement as given to several hundred peasants at a funeral for a slain boy:

> The electoral process has never worked in El Salvador. . . . in 1972, when José Napoleon Duarte won the presidential election, the army threw him into exile. After that, . . . peasants, students, workers and professionals began to organize and engage in marches and demonstrations to protest the absence of democracy and to demand better living conditions for the poor. . . . We were met with the bullets from tanks and machine guns. Now we must fight with those same bullets.[48]

Bonner did report that some Marxist concepts were defined in political courses taught by the ERP, and among a list of possible themes for students' writings was "What is Marxism?"[49] Still, the use of Marxist terms by ERP militants was rare (see chapter 6).

For the FPL, however, the largest group within the FMLN for most of the 1970s and 1980s, Marxism was important.[50] As indicated above, FPL founders had been members of the Salvadoran Communist Party who came to reject the PCS's electoralism. Marxist concepts of social class and terms such as "capitalism" and "imperialism" appear frequently in FPL members' literature and discussions.[51] FPL leaders acknowledge their Marxist views:

> [We are] clear that Marxism is an instrument for the interpretation of reality . . . a scientific instrument for the analysis and interpretation of reality that permits us to find the most correct solutions and proposals for each situation.[52]

They also acknowledge that they encouraged the discussion of basic Marxist concepts among their recruits:

> [For popular education] we used materials of Mao . . . and also materials about dialectical materialism, historical materialism.[53]

In contrast to Sendero, for no FMLN group was political terror a primary tactic. During the 1970s, the emphasis by the guerrilla groups was on popular organization; although wealthy businessmen were kidnapped for ransom and some government officials were assassinated, for the most part violent attacks were infrequent.[54] Throughout the 1980s, the overwhelming majority of victims of the FMLN were security force personnel. The FMLN assassinated an average of forty civilians each year between 1983 and 1990; the number was never as large as

10 percent of the number of civilians killed at the hands of the security forces.[55] (By contrast, approximately 1,250 civilians, representing more than 80 percent of all deaths attributed to the Shining Path, were killed annually by this group during 1989 and 1990.) [56] When civilians were killed (and forty civilian deaths a year is a considerable number), the FMLN tried to justify the assassinations by claiming that, for one reason or another, the individuals were legitimate military targets.[57]

Also in contrast to the Shining Path, the organizational structure of the FMLN was relatively democratic. As discussed above, the five commanders and their immediate colleagues met frequently to debate FMLN strategy and policy. Although the FMLN commanders were often outside of El Salvador, and they were not elected by their followers, Villalobos and other top leaders did mingle at least occasionally with other guerrillas.[58] In most zones, commanders met frequently with peasant sympathizers, who criticized some decisions and influenced demotions and promotions among local commanders.[59] In Chalatenango during the early 1980s, in a system of local government called Local Popular Power (Poder Popular Local, PPL), officials representing about five hundred people were elected at popular assemblies.[60] In Guazapa, judicial authorities were elected by the population.[61] In general, in the guerrilla strongholds there were numerous collective initiatives, including collective agricultural production, and a strong sense of community among the FMLN militants.[62] Whereas the emphasis of FMLN militants about life in the guerrilla-controlled zones was on cooperation, the emphasis of Shining Path sympathizers about life in these zones was on discipline and order (see below).

In contrast to the Shining Path, the FMLN maintained a network of international alliances, receiving resources as well as advice (perhaps wanted and unwanted). There were ties to the East bloc but also to other Latin American nations and to solidarity groups in the United States and Europe.

Probably the FMLN's most important alliances were with the Cuban and Nicaraguan leaderships.[63] Indeed, most FMLN and FDR leaders lived in Nicaragua for periods during the 1980s.[64] Meetings among the FMLN commanders, Nicaraguan president Daniel Ortega, and Fidel Castro were common. At least at times, the Cubans advised the FMLN commanders on strategy for the war.[65]

Although these relationships were close, they were also tense.[66] The Cubans and the Nicaraguans often acted as if they knew what was best for the FMLN and pressured the Salvadoran commanders on various issues. The Cubans and the Sandinistas may often have allocated weapons among the FMLN groups according to their own preferences—a practice that could only have alienated those groups receiving smaller quantities of weapons. Furthermore, not only the Sandinista government but also Fidel Castro gave a higher priority to the Sandinistas' survival than to the FMLN's victory and, accordingly, took various decisions that angered the FMLN commanders. For their part, FMLN members may at times have resented their dependence on the Sandinistas and the Cubans and these foreigners' ability to influence the Salvadoran revolutionary movement.

How much material support the FMLN received from East bloc governments during different periods is an extremely controversial question, to which a precise answer is not yet available. Probably, during the course of the 1980s, more than one thousand Salvadoran revolutionaries received political and military training in Cuba, Nicaragua, Eastern Europe, Vietnam, or the Soviet Union.[67] The FMLN also received weapons, but specific indications of the amounts and their significance are available only in reports by defectors and by the U.S. government. Apparently, in preparation for the 1981 "final offensive" and over the next few years, a kind of "triangular trade" was established, whereby the FMLN would be sent arms by the Sandinistas, the Sandinistas would be sent weapons by the Cubans, and the Cubans would be sent weapons by the Soviets.[68] Some weapons were also received from Vietnam.[69] According to a defector from the FMLN, as of 1983 there were about seven thousand East bloc arms in El Salvador, constituting approximately 60 percent of the FMLN's total arsenal; roughly 30 percent were bought on the black market or captured from the Salvadoran army.[70] During the later 1980s, the Defense Intelligence Agency estimated that 70 percent of FMLN ammunition came from outside El Salvador, primarily routed through Nicaragua.[71]

Other analysts believe that the amount of East bloc arms sent to the FMLN was a smaller percentage of their total arsenal.[72] During the 1970s, primarily as a result of kidnappings of wealthy businessmen, the rebels had collected some $50 to $65 million, and considerable amounts apparently remained for arms purchases.[73] Later, the insurgents levied war taxes upon land holdings.[74] The guerrillas captured substantial quantities of weapons from the Salvadoran army itself. Also, especially in later years, the FMLN became adept at the manufacture of land mines.

There is general agreement that, after approximately 1983, East bloc nations continued to support the FMLN, but to a lesser degree than in previous years.[75] Concerned about U.S. retaliation against Nicaragua and pessimistic about the FMLN's chances for victory, the Sandinista leadership became more cautious—to the dismay of the FMLN.[76] Arms shipments became irregular and smaller; ammunition became a primary part of the shipments. Also, the Sandinista leadership denied the FMLN's repeated requests for surface-to-air antiaircraft missiles.[77] In late 1990, after the FSLN had been ousted from the presidency in Nicaragua, Sandinista army officers did turn more than twenty surface-to-air missiles over to the FMLN, and subsequently the Cuban government also may have sent some missiles; they were apparently very helpful to the FMLN, but presumably would have been more helpful if supplied earlier.[78]

The FMLN's international ties were not exclusively to East bloc leaders. The FMLN sought advice and resources from political groups around the world. In the late 1970s and early 1980s, the guerrilla organizations enjoyed considerable support from the governments of Mexico and Panama, as well as from social democratic parties in Costa Rica, Venezuela, and the Dominican Republic.[79] In the fall of 1988, Joaquín Villalobos and Leonel González traveled to nine Latin American countries, exchanging views about the course of the Salvadoran war and hearing the opinion of these nations' leaders that the FMLN should move toward negotiations.[80] The FMLN also maintained contact and gained resources from the governments of France, West Germany, Sweden, Austria, and Canada, as well as from solidarity groups in other First World countries.[81] For example, in 1981 alone an "Arms for El Salvador" campaign in West Germany provided $1 million; the U.S.-based "Medical Aid for El Salvador" gave more than $5 million during the 1980s.[82]

Overall, the FMLN gained more weapons but less cash from its external alliances than the Shining Path, as the following section discusses.

The weapons facilitated the FMLN's direct military confrontations with the Salvadoran armed forces, confrontations that were especially large scale during 1981–84. However, the FMLN's annual budget was probably less than $5 million; the insurgents' communications equipment appears to have been limited, and the organization was not providing its rebels with amounts of cash that qualified as salaries.[83] By contrast, Sendero did not mount sophisticated military attacks, but it did have substantial amounts of money—probably at least ten times as much as the FMLN—for logistical communication and general maintenance of its guerrilla force.

The Shining Path

Sendero resembled not the FMLN but the Khmer Rouge. Although Guzmán dominated the Shining Path to a greater degree than Pol Pot dominated the Khmer Rouge, in ideology, strategy, and social base there were strong similarities between the two organizations.[84] It is possible that Guzmán and Pol Pot met; Pol Pot visited China several times between 1975 and 1979, and Guzmán was also there for a time in 1975.[85] Both the Shining Path and the Khmer Rouge strictly adhered to the tenets of Maoism during the period of the Cultural Revolution, scorning all other Marxist models.[86] Both attributed a fundamental role in the revolutionary process to political violence, and systematically terrorized and murdered not only military but also civilian opponents.[87] Both recruited extensively among schoolteachers, and both enjoyed their most secure social base in this group.[88] Both employed similar tactics: training children to enjoy tormenting others, for example.[89] Descriptions of both organizations highlight an unusual amalgam: emotional rage and total conviction of their own rectitude against a pervasively corrupt society—joined with a tightly disciplined, well-controlled military organization.[90]

Sendero was created and led by one man: Abimael Guzmán Reynoso.[91] Dubbing himself the "Fourth Sword of Marxism" (the first three being Marx, Lenin, and Mao), Guzmán was regarded like a deity by his followers, who themselves behaved like disciples. His organizational role has been described as that of "philosopher-king." Among Quechua-speaking peoples, who traditionally revered the sun, he was called Doctor "Puka Inti"—the Red Sun. In one Shining Path hymn, a stanza is dedicated to Guzmán, who used the alias "Gonzalo": "The masses roar Gonzalo! and the Andes tremble."[92] After Guzmán's capture, he was extolled in the Shining Path newspaper as

> our dear, heroic, eminent chief, President Gonzalo, the greatest existing Marxist-Leninist-Maoist, the greatest political and military strategist, philosopher, master of Communists, center of unification of the motherland, who, by creatively applying the Marxist-Leninist-Maoist principles to the concrete conditions of the Peruvian revolution has generated Gonzalo Thought, which guarantees the triumph of the revolution. . . . we reassert our unmovable decision of giving our life for President Gonzalo, the Party, and the Revolution.[93]

Actually, there were assets but also deficiencies to Guzmán's leadership. In small groups, he had an extraordinary capacity to win people to his views; but, having gone underground when the armed struggle began in 1980 and not strikingly handsome in any case, he was not charismatic in the style of a Fidel Castro or a Maurice Bishop. Presumably in good part due to Guzmán's iron rule, the organization's goals were clear throughout the twelve years of war, and strategic plans were well coordinated. But when the sun god was captured and revealed to be an ordinary mortal, not only was Sendero's strategic capacity crippled but also its mystique was almost destroyed.

Whereas the FMLN was a coalition bringing together the various Marxist groups active in El Salvador in the 1970s, Guzmán's Shining Path was a faction that had repeatedly split from other Peruvian Marxist movements.[94] In the early 1960s, Guzmán became an important communist leader in Ayacucho; in part due to an intransigent Guzmán demand, the original pro-Soviet communist party fragmented into pro-Moscow and pro-Peking factions in 1964. The pro-Peking group was called the Red Flag (Bandera Roja). At almost the same time, Cuban-inspired guerrilla groups became active in Peru, and there was pressure on the Red Flag to support these groups and their Guevarist *foco* ideology; Guzmán and the pro-Chinese party resisted this pressure and the Guevarist group left. However, Guzmán was impatient with what he saw as Red Flag's insufficiently militaristic leader, and in Ayacucho in 1970 he formed a new party. The new party called itself the "Partido Comunista del Perú," implying that it was the only legitimate communist party in the country. The name Sendero Luminoso was taken from a statement by Peru's first prominent Marxist, José Carlos Mariátegui, that "Marxism-Leninism will open the shining path to revolution."

Guzmán claimed that his ideology was the "fourth sword of Marxism," a doctrine that was heir to Marxism, Leninism, and Maoism but distinct from them. In practice, however, Guzmán's ideology was overwhelmingly Maoist.[95] In the phrase of Harding (1988: 65), Guzmán's devotion to the tenets of Maoism was "slavish." Guzmán's adherence to Maoism developed during his experiences in China in 1964, 1967, and 1975, for a total period of about two years, including extended study at a cadre school in Peking.[96] Several key Guzmán lieutenants—including his wife Augusta and the intellectual Antonio Díaz Martínez—also traveled to China during the era of the Cultural Revolution (commonly dated as from 1966 until Mao's death in 1976).[97]

Mao described China as "semifeudal" and "semicolonial," and the Chinese political economy as a dysfunctional "bureaucratic capitalism."[98] Guzmán adopts an identical vocabulary in his description of Peru and its political economy:

> Contemporary Peru is a semifeudal and semicolonial society in which bureaucratic capitalism is unfolding: a delayed capitalism subjected completely to imperialism, in our case Yankee imperialism, and accordingly does not develop the great productive forces of our country, but rather damages it.... [Bureaucratic capitalism] is totally opposed to our national interests, to the most essential and most urgent needs of the masses of our people.[99]

Given Peru's "semifeudal" social structure, "democracy" was deemed impossible in the country. The Shining Path judged all Peruvian governments—despite the wide range in character attributed to them by most analysts—as "fascist, corporatist, and reactionary."[100]

Guzmán's original strategy for winning power was also Maoist.[101] Like Mao, Guzmán identified three key phases of guerrilla war: first, "defensive"; then, "equilibrium"; and finally, "offensive."[102] The leading revolutionary role was attributed to the peasantry. The peasant guerrilla war would be prolonged; gradually, from a firm rural base, the cities would be encircled. Ultimately, the nation's capital would be besieged: its supplies of food, water, and electricity from the interior of the country would be blocked. After Sendero's first congress in 1988, however, the Maoist prioritization of the countryside was modified; Guzmán said that sufficient progress had been made in the countryside, and that the main theater of insurrection should now be the cities, in particular Lima.[103] The decision was controversial; a faction led by Guzmán's own wife, and including top lieutenant Osmán Morote, argued that Guzmán's strategy contradicted Maoism and that urban action was premature and would excessively expose the organization's leadership.[104]

By the time of Guzmán's capture in September 1992, it is not entirely clear how the leader precisely envisioned taking power. As of September 1992, Sendero was beginning "the first campaign" of the "Sixth Great Plan," entitled the "Plan to Establish the Conquest of Peru," including "Operation Conquer Lima."[105] While these terms sound military, Sendero's previous, predominantly nonmilitary tactics were apparently to continue: bombing attacks that would terrorize elites and constitute a kind of psychological war, and political work that would incorporate "the masses" into the movement to an even greater extent, leading to gigantic "waves" of "popular struggle."[106] Predictions by some Shining Path leaders of a coup by the Peruvian military and intervention by the United States seemed to imply a larger military dimension in the future, but no specifics on this score were provided.[107] Rather, in the view of several top Senderólogos, Guzmán's belief was that terror and economic sabotage would provoke panic among both Peru's economic elites, who would flee the country, and its security forces, who would disperse in the face of only a minimal military threat.[108]

Sectarian and uncompromising in its Maoism, the Shining Path denounced all other communist parties as "rotten revisionists."[109] Brezhnev was "the boss of Russian revisionism and grand puppet-master of revisionism at the world level."[110] After Mao's death and the ascendance of Deng Xiaoping in China, the new Chinese leaders were repudiated as "the dogs who betrayed the Cultural Revolution."[111] The Cuban revolutionary approach "was a petit bourgeois 'militaristic' deviation, doomed to sure defeat, against which President Mao had written long ago"; Fidel Castro was "a puppet of social imperialism."[112] The Shining Path hostility toward the Soviet Union and China was not merely verbal; violent attacks against their embassies and representatives were common.[113]

Sendero's most vitriolic insults were reserved for its Marxist rivals within Peru. In particular, Guzmán denounced the other Marxist parties' decision to participate in Peru's elections during the 1980s. He claimed that every social advance in Peru was a result exclusively of "popular struggle," not "parliamentary activity."[114] For Guzmán, the United Left (Izquierda Unida) coalition was

> the old opportunistic electoral coalition-making that we have seen many times in Peru; this electoral front is the negation of a Party that leads, and if there is no party of the proletariat that leads, then there is no transformation, no revolution; the revolution has never been made via Parliament, nor will it ever be. . . . The Izquierda Unida is a sewer of contradictions. What unites them? Collusion, ambition . . .[115]

Just as Sendero's authoritarian leadership was a double-edged sword, so its rigid Maoist political creed attracted some citizens who yearned for a political religion, but alienated others. For example, insisting that rural Peru was semifeudal, Sendero's leaders did not recognize that most of Peru's rural communities were in fact economically linked to markets; they did not anticipate that their prohibition against sales of peasants' products in local markets would spark as much resentment as it did, and they failed to modify their thinking upon the outbreak of this resentment.[116]

Perhaps even more important, many of Peru's indigenous peoples eagerly sought a political movement that would incorporate their long-standing millenarianist beliefs, as well as their concerns about ethnic identity and discrimination.[117] For the most part, however, the "hyper-classist" Sendero not only rejected ethnicity as an issue but did not respect traditional indigenous culture.[118] Even so, Sendero was at times perceived through an ethnic lens; we noted above, for example, that Guzmán was at times called Doctor Puka Inti. But many more indigenous persons presumably would have seen Sendero as an expression of ethnic concerns if Sendero had not made such an interpretation so difficult.

In Shining Path ideology, just as in Maoism, violence is extolled, both as revolutionary strategy and as socialization. Recall the Maoist proverb: "From the barrel of a gun grows political power."[119] As Mauceri notes, "Violence takes on an almost mystical quality, not only destroying the old but creating the new. For Mao, revolutionary violence is an immense force which can transform many things, or open the way for their transformation."[120] Similarly, for Sendero, "popular war is the principal form of struggle" and "the war itself forges the militant."[121]

Adulation of bravery in revolutionary war is prominent throughout Shining Path tracts. Several publications begin with the citation, apparently from Mao, that "he who is not afraid of being cut into a thousand pieces is bold enough to bring down the Emperor."[122] A poem commemorating Shining Path militants who died in a massacre in Lima's prisons in June 1986 reads: "Glory to the fallen heroes, long live the revolution! Blood does not drown the revolution, but irrigates it!"[123]

For Sendero Luminoso, those who stood in its way were the enemy, and—even if they were unarmed civilians—should be assassinated. Said one Senderista: "This is a revolution, and anyone who opposes it will be crushed like an insect."[124] Whereas the military and police were the principal targets of the FMLN and most previous Latin American guerrilla movements, only 17 percent of Shining Path's victims were members of the military or police; most victims were unarmed civilians.[125] For perhaps the first time in the history of Latin America, nuns, priests, journalists, agronomists, food aid workers, and even human rights activists were directly targeted and killed—not by the government, but by the guerrillas. Between 1980 and 1992, Sendero murdered at least 8 ecclesiastics, 9 foreign development workers, 44 grassroots leaders, 203 businessmen, 244 teachers, 303 students, 424 workers, 502 political officials (primarily local officials such as mayors), 1,100 urban residents, and 2,196 peasants.[126]

Sendero killed not only routinely, but savagely. Perhaps the most notorious example is the murder of María Elena Moyano, a grassroots leader in a Lima shanty town; after her assassination, her body was blown to bits in front of her children. One of the most common tactics was the beheading of victims. Also, eyes were gouged out; men were castrated; children were disemboweled; and human bonfires were set.[127] Sendero socialized its young recruits to violence; children of five and six were taught to kill chickens so that they would be accustomed to blood, and by the age of nine were smashing skulls with stones.[128]

As with other characteristics of the Sendero guerrilla organization, the key role of political violence was both an asset and a liability. On the one hand, for many Senderistas, the capacity to intimidate was one of the attractions of the organization. Said Carlos Iván Degregori, for example, "For the first time in their lives, they can command respect. They are the ones who instill fear."[129] Added a leading Peruvian psychoanalyst,

"Sendero is a compensation for impotence."[130] Also, the consistency and severity of Sendero's "execution of justice" and "discipline" brought results. Where schoolteachers had worked from Tuesday through Thursday, they began to work Monday through Friday.[131] In many communities, abusive people who had been hated for years by most of the residents were shot, and the action was popular.[132] Ironically, many citizens welcomed the "law and order" that Sendero was able to impose:

> Now, there are very few abuses because the people complain to the compañeros. . . . Now, Shining Path is the law. If you leave your camera or your car with keys in the ignition . . . , nobody will touch them. . . . Perhaps Shining Path is a necessary evil here. The government has never been able to impose order.[133]

On the other hand, the Shining Path's terror was repugnant to a larger number of Peruvian citizens. Critics of Sendero likened the movement to a death cult; given Sendero's indoctrination that the militant should expect to give his or her life for the party, how many Peruvians could find membership appealing? Although some Peruvians joined Sendero because of the opportunity to instill fear, many of these same people left the organization charging that it was excessively brutal.[134] Frequently, for example, a person punished by Sendero was innocent— or the punishment appeared very severe relative to the crime. In one notorious case, the mayor of a town in Puno was assassinated by Sendero, and the assassination was so repudiated by the people in the area that Sendero's expansion in the entire department was checked.[135] In various areas where Sendero was unable to make inroads or where it gradually lost support, the explanation given was excessive violence: "The Senderistas have killed too many innocent people, too many elected officials."[136] One former Senderista's comment imputed irrationality to Sendero's violence: "When the Sendero leaders were in a bad mood, you knew for sure that there'd be killing."[137]

Relative to the FMLN leadership, Guzmán put greater emphasis on building the Shining Path as a strong party organization. Of course, Guzmán did not share the voluntarist or *foquista* beliefs of some Latin American Marxists. Rather, Guzmán repeated the Maoist dictum, "the party commands the gun and not the gun the party" and proclaimed his goal "to create organizations that are superior to those of the reactionaries."[138] Accordingly, the organization of the Shining Path was disciplined and cohesive.[139] There was a great deal of ritual bonding: singing, chanting, and marching, for example.[140] In at least one community, no more than two people were allowed to gather on a street except when Sendero called a meeting.[141] Even marriage and family were regulated; members were allowed to marry only other members at the same level in the organization, the vows were to "better serve the revolution," and the wedding date was set by the party.[142] The couples' priority was expected to be the revolution, not children; leaders Osmán Morote and Teresa Durand were held up as an exemplary revolutionary couple because they left both their infant children to be raised by others.[143]

As with other characteristics of the Shining Path organization, such cohesion and discipline were attractive to some but repugnant to others. On the one hand, the organization provided identity, belonging, and purpose for its members. Commented one Peruvian writer: "For certain people, Sendero is like an addictive drug. It's something that helps you get through life without the complications of having to act on your own."[144] On the other hand, Sendero was perceived as rigid and totalitarian by most Peruvians.

The organizational structure of Sendero was also extremely hierarchical. Of course, the permanent number one leader was Guzmán; there was no publicly acknowledged number two. Of the various possible second-in-commands, two were no longer with Guzmán at the time of his capture and one was in custody. Guzmán's wife Augusta La Torre was probably informally the most influential person with her husband until 1988. At that time, however, she disagreed with Guzmán about the decision to prioritize the war in Lima and openly opposed it at the 1988 congress; apparently, her political conflict with her husband was an important factor in her suicide shortly thereafter.[145] A key Guzmán colleague in the 1960s and early 1970s was Luis Kawata Makabe; he was purged from the movement after he was caught in bed by Guzmán with one of Guzmán's lovers.[146] If there were an internally designated number two during the 1970s and 1980s, it was most likely to have been Osmán Morote, a student and then a professor at the university in Ayacucho whose family was closely linked to the Shining Path movement (see chapter 6); Morote was captured in 1988.[147] A possible sometime rival for this position, who may have left the movement in the late 1980s, was Julio César Mezzich.[148]

By 1989, Guzmán's inner circle—all members of the elite "Political Bureau"—was quite different. The new apparent number two, and his new lover, was Elena Iparaguirre ("Comrade Miriam"), a reputed "iron lady" who kept Guzmán's personal schedule.[149] Number three after Iparaguirre was the head of Sendero's military apparatus, Oscar Alberto Ramírez Durand ("Feliciano"), who emerged as the leader of the at-large sector of the organization after Guzmán's capture.[150] Possibly, the relationship between Guzmán and "Feliciano" was tense; Guzmán's preferred choice as his successor may have been another member of the Political Bureau, Deodato Hugo Juárez Cruzzat ("Germán"), but he was captured in 1990 and subsequently killed.[151] A final member of the elite Political Bureau was Elizabeth Gonzáles Otoya Santisteban ("Aurora").[152]

At the formal apex of Sendero's organizational chart was the Central Committee. As of approximately 1989, it was composed of nineteen regular members, three alternates, and three candidates.[153] At that time, about half of the members were male and half were female.[154] Beyond Central Committee members who were also on the Political Bureau, one of the most important Central Committee members was Laura Zambrano Padilla ("Comrade Meche"), head of the Lima Metropolitan Committee and at Guzmán's hideout at the time of his arrest.[155]

Directly below the Central Committee were six regional committees: the "primary" (Ayacucho, Huancavelica, and Apurímac), the "metropolitan" (Lima and Callao), and the southern, eastern, central, and northern, each made up of several departments. Below the regional committees were, in turn, zones, sectors, and cells. Most cells included five to nine members, only one of whom was in communication with the next higher level of leadership. Among the thirty-three former and current Sendero members interviewed by my research team in 1993, none had actually seen Guzmán; twenty-seven of the thirty-three (81 percent) said that they did not know the "Sendero leaders" well.[156]

Guzmán's authority over the decisions made by the regional committees was considerable. Guzmán received frequent reports from the regional committees.[157] Captured minutes from the Shining Path's 1988 congress and other meetings indicate that Guzmán met frequently with regional leaders and, with the Central Committee, issued orders such as the following: "The Huancavelica Zonal Committee was told that the group of roving Senderistas who have been carrying out actions in that department had to become the main one and that another secondary group had to operate in the 'half moon' to 'stir up the land problem.'"[158] Apparently, Guzmán supervised the allocation of virtually all the organization's financial resources.[159] Overall strategy and decisions about nationwide attacks, such as those for Guzmán's birthday and Peru's independence day, were coordinated by Guzmán. Presumably, however, most decisions about local attacks were made by the leaders in the particular area. Said one Senderista, "In the party they teach us that we are not loose pearls, but rather a pearl necklace."[160]

The Shining Path also classified individuals according to the degree of their commitment and the character of their contribution to the movement.[161] At the top of the hierarchy was the Central Committee; the next rank were the "commanders," who were responsible for the political and military activity in their geographic areas; then the military personnel in the "Popular Guerrilla Army"; and finally, two nonmilitary ranks, "activists" and "sympathizers." These "activists" and "sympathizers" were organized in a vast array of groups.[162] The most important of these groups was the People's Aid of Peru (Socorro Popular del Perú), which provided legal, medical, financial, and other professional services to the movement.

After its expansion into the drug-producing Upper Huallaga Valley, Sendero enjoyed ample financial resources from its activities there— primarily charges levied against drug traffickers for use of Sendero-controlled airstrips. Estimates of the amount of money gained by Sendero from its activities in the Upper Huallaga Valley range from a "mere" $20 million per year to a huge $550 million per year.[163] Additional sums were obtained from *cupos*—taxes levied on businesses and citizens; smaller amounts were probably received from various support groups in Great Britain, France, Sweden, Germany, Belgium, and Spain.[164]

How was this war chest used by Sendero? The answer is not entirely clear. A considerable amount—possibly as much as $200 million—may have been deposited in foreign bank accounts; Guzmán may have believed that the organization should save in order to have ample reserves for the difficult days after it assumed power.[165] But the organization also used its funds for its own maintenance. Especially by the 1990s, activists received not only salaries, but very good salaries by

Peruvian standards—approximately \$250 to \$500 per month.[166] The guerrilla organization also bought weapons and equipment. Although Senderistas probably used dynamite stolen from mines more often than any other weapon, they also used machine guns, G-3 and FAL automatic rifles, U.S.-made hand grenades, and mortars.[167] Finally, too, Guzmán and his inner circle lived well: in the ten-bedroom safe house in Lima where he was captured were found not only computers, radios, fax machines, and police interception equipment but also French wines, imported vitamins, and first-class food.[168]

The Challenges Mounted by the FMLN and the Shining Path

Although the FMLN and the Shining Path were very different organizations, they both posed extremely serious challenges to their countries' governments. In both El Salvador and Peru, triumph by the revolutionaries was a real possibility—not only, of course, in the eyes of the revolutionaries themselves but also in the estimates of political analysts.

As noted in the introduction to this chapter, objective assessment of the exact intensity of the challenge to a government mounted by a revolutionary movement is difficult. This section first assesses the intensity of the challenge by the FMLN and the Shining Path on the basis of four quantifiable indicators of revolutionary strength: the number of full-time combatants; the amount of popular support; the number of deaths inflicted by the guerrillas; and the extent of territorial control (see table 2.1). The year for the comparison is 1989, when the challenge posed by

Table 2.1. Intensity of the Challenge to the State Mounted by the FMLN and Sendero Luminoso, circa 1989

	Combatants (full-time)	Deaths Inflicted (per year)	Popular Support (% of citizens)	Territorial Control (% of municipalities)
El Salvador	8,000[a]	684[b]	25[a]	15[a]
Peru	10,000	1,526[c]	15[a]	28

[a]See discussion and sources in text.

[b]Source: Tutela Legal for 1989, including only deaths. In the early 1980s, the toll was higher—at about 2,000 annually. See discussion and sources in text.

[c]Comisión Especial de Estudio e Investigación y Estudio sobre Terrorismo y Otras Manifestaciones de la Violencia (1990, 45).

Sendero Luminoso was increasing and when the FMLN's military threat was at its apex (although its political support had eroded relative to the early 1980s). If the year for the comparison had been in the early 1980s, the figures for Peru would have been lower and some of those for El Salvador higher. Next, the section examines the revolutionary strategies of the FMLN and Sendero, and assesses how close each insurgency was to actually accomplishing a takeover.

Strength of the FMLN and the Shining Path

The number of combatants in the FMLN and the Shining Path is the first quantifiable indicator of revolutionary strength in table 2.1. The figures are estimates. The exact number of guerrillas is rarely known, as there are reasons why both governments and insurgents may want to inflate or deflate their figures. Moreover, although the term "combatants" suggests members with a capacity to participate in military operations of some sort, the usefulness of this distinction was not entirely clear in the Peruvian case, where a "committed supporter" could presumably help with the detonation of a bomb or the destruction of an electricity pylon, although not with actual fighting.

In general, however, it can be said that the number of FMLN and Shining Path combatants was roughly similar. For the FMLN, the figure of eight thousand full-time combatants as of 1989 is common to a variety of sources.[169] This figure is slightly lower than the ten thousand or so that was a typical estimate in the early 1980s.[170] The number of committed supporters was perhaps fifty thousand during most of the 1980s.[171] For Sendero Luminoso, the figure of ten thousand militants was the conventional estimate in the early 1990s, and it remains a sensible figure in light of documents that have been revealed more recently.[172] Estimates of the number of "committed people" in Sendero ranged from fifty thousand to one hundred thousand.[173]

For the Shining Path, estimates of the number of combatants varied more widely than for the FMLN.[174] It has gradually become clear that the Peruvian authorities intentionally deflated their figures.[175] On the basis of information recovered from Guzmán's own computer, however, one of the most respected Senderólogos reported that Guzmán numbered his "People's Guerrilla Army" at 23,430, including 816 members of the "principal force," 4,674 members of the "local force," and

17,940 members of the "base force."[176] Tapia believes that only the members of the "principal force" and the "local force" had "some capacity to participate in diverse kinds of military operations"; but how he makes this conclusion is unclear, given that he also states that members of the "base force" were sometimes "rudimentarily armed."[177] Peruvian intelligence officers considered Guzmán's figures for his "People's Guerrilla Army" to be "armed guerrillas."[178] Newmont Mining apparently did as well; for its gold mine in Cajamarca—a department where the guerrillas were weak—they hired enough armed guards to repel an attack by as many as four hundred Senderistas.[179] The problem in the distinction between "armed and trained combatant" and "committed supporter" is suggested in the comment by a U.S. analyst about the strength of Sendero in the Upper Huallaga Valley: the Shining Path could *"mobilize thousands* of sympathizers with little notice."[180]

As just mentioned, the number of "committed people" (predominantly unarmed) was estimated at fifty thousand to one hundred thousand. Said a French priest about Shining Path militants, "They are everywhere."[181] The number of Shining Path militants was apparently sufficient by 1992 to affect the instruction given to about 60 percent of Peruvian schoolchildren.[182] As early as May 1988, Sendero was estimated to have infiltrated twenty-five companies.[183]

The figures for Sendero membership should also be considered in the context of other relevant numbers. Between 1980 and 1991, more than eleven thousand "assumed terrorists" were reportedly killed. Also, by mid-1994 approximately forty-eight hundred prisoners were in jail on terrorist charges; another four thousand or more had "repented" of terrorism; and large numbers had left the Sendero organization surreptitiously.[184]

In the second column of table 2.1, the number of deaths inflicted in 1989 by the FMLN (684) and the Shining Path (1,526) is estimated. The figures for El Salvador are especially uncertain. The number in the table is from Tutela Legal (see appendix II for a discussion of this organization). The figure does not include those wounded by the FMLN, which had become a major toll by the late 1980s—approximately 2,000 annually—as the FMLN was deploying land mines extensively. Tutela Legal's estimate was not shared by either of the belligerent parties, however. The FMLN was reporting higher death tolls—at 4,910 in 1990, for example[185]—while Salvadoran officials reported lower tolls.[186] During the early 1980s, the toll was higher—about 2,000 annually according to Tutela Legal. For this period, the figures do not vary greatly by source.[187]

The figure on the number of deaths for Peru is not controversial. Similar figures are reported in a variety of sources; virtually all are based on data provided by the Peruvian government. (Figures for the number of attacks by the guerrillas varied considerably, however, because figures were provided by both government officials and journalists.)

Popular support for the FMLN and for Sendero Luminoso is, of course, also difficult to measure precisely. This is especially the case for El Salvador, where expressions of support for the FMLN were dangerous and no public opinion agencies directly asked respondents whether they supported the movement.[188] Also, in El Salvador to a greater degree than in Peru, support for the guerrillas was concentrated in areas where pollsters did not venture. In the Orellana survey for this research, we approached the issue of the respondent's attitude indirectly, not inquiring whether the respondent supported the FMLN but asking for the respondent's estimate of how much support the guerrillas had. The item did not work very well, for reasons that were not entirely clear.[189] To the extent that a conclusion could be drawn from the answers, it seemed to be that there was a great deal of uncertainty about the amount of support that the FMLN might have. Among the respondents to the Orellana team's question about the amount of support among Salvadorans for the FMLN, roughly similar percentages (20 percent to 35 percent of the respondents) estimated support at 2 percent, at 10 percent, and at 20 percent. Raymond Bonner, the *New York Times* journalist in El Salvador in the early 1980s, found a similar confusion; one resident of lower-middle-class Mejicanos told him in 1982 that "no one supports the guerrillas," and his next interviewee in the neighborhood said, "I think most people support the guerrillas."[190]

One estimate for popular support for the FMLN is an inference from the data in UCA publications.[191] Before 1989, when neither the CD nor the FMLN was a participant in national elections, more than 20 percent of respondents would report that they had "no" political party preference or "no" presidential candidate preference; another 20 percent or so said they did not know; and another 10 percent to 15 percent responded that "the vote is secret." From these negative and cautious response patterns, it can be estimated that some 20 percent to 25 percent of Salvadoran citizens supported the FMLN. Another important indicator is the 24.9 percent of the vote that the FMLN, CD, and MNR coalition won in the 1994 presidential election (see chapter 3). The 24.9 percent figure might be lower than actual support for these parties because of their leaders' errors during the campaign or electoral irregularities, or it might be higher than support would have been during the period of intense fighting. In any case, it now appears clear that the 10 percent figure previously cited by some analysts was low.[192]

The 25 percent figure is probably below the support that the revolutionary movements would have enjoyed during the late 1970s and early 1980s.[193] Between 1979 and 1982, a considerable number of Salvadorans believed that revolution was a positive and viable alternative. On 22 January 1980, between 150,000 and 200,000 people demonstrated against the government and celebrated the formation of a unified front among the mass organizations in El Salvador, on the anniversary of the 1932 Farabundo Martí uprising.[194] At least among analysts sympathetic to the political opposition, the perception was that the unified front enjoyed majority support among those who paid attention to politics.[195] But, as the war and its violence dragged on, support eroded. After the death or flight of thousands of militants, and the withdrawal of the FMLN and FDR leaders from the capital, the FMLN was not able to communicate effectively with most Salvadorans; the government's viewpoints dominated the country's media.[196] The 1982 and 1984 elections provided a degree of democratic legitimacy to the Salvadoran government, especially among the middle classes.[197] In certain areas during some periods, the FMLN resorted to forced recruitment, alienating families in these areas. Those FMLN attacks that caused innocent deaths and those acts of economic sabotage that cut off electricity and exacerbated the problems of everyday life alienated even more Salvadorans.[198] Most Salvadorans came to blame the guerrillas rather than the government for the war.[199]

In Peru, because of the nature of the Shining Path, many analysts did not like to acknowledge the evidence of popular support for the movement. But the evidence is incontrovertible. Unlike in El Salvador, pollsters in Peru openly asked respondents questions about their support for revolutionary movements. The most widely cited poll was carried out by the prestigious Apoyo agency in Lima in July and August 1991. In this poll, 7 percent of the respondents said that they had a "favorable" opinion of the Shining Path; in the view of the director of Apoyo's survey, a conservative estimate is that half of the 10 percent of respondents who did not answer the question should also be considered to hold "favorable" opinions.[200] Accordingly, a total of 12 percent of the Lima population assessed Sendero favorably.[201] In the survey, respondents were also asked a vaguer question: "Do you believe subversion is justifiable [*justificable*] in today's Peru?" Seventeen percent of the sample said "Yes."[202] Among the poorest group in the Apoyo sample—which tends to be underrepresented in Peruvian surveys—11 percent of the respondents had a "favorable" view of Sendero and 31 percent did not answer, implying (according to the formula of the survey's director) that 26 percent actually held a "favorable" view.[203] Thirty-eight percent of the poorest stratum said either that they "did not care about a terrorist act" or that they "condoned it."[204]

Other surveys suggested similar or higher levels of support for Sendero. Manuel Torrado, the director of the Datum public opinion agency, assessed support for Sendero at 10 to 12 percent in cities nationwide.[205] In a 1991 Imasen poll in Lima, 47 percent of the respondents said that the Shining Path "punishes the corrupt"; incredibly, 20 percent claimed that it did not "kill and torture innocent people."[206] In an Imasen poll taken in Lima a few weeks after the capture of Guzmán, 20 percent of the respondents expressed "compassion" for the imprisoned leader.[207] Given that (1) the poor tend to be underrepresented in Peruvian surveys (see appendix II); (2) the rest of Peru is poorer than Lima; and (3) support was greater among predominantly rural areas where pollsters did not venture, I estimate the figure of 15 percent for popular support (see table 2.1).

The greater support for the Shining Path in numerous predominantly rural, agriculture-based departments is evident from scholars' and journalists' reports. Especially in the early 1980s, support was found to be substantial among southern highlands peasants.[208] Support in the town of Ayacucho and in the department generally was also strong at this time; an Ayacucho police chief estimated that "eighty percent of the townspeople of Ayacucho sympathize with Sendero."[209]

Similar reports of popular support for Sendero were provided by journalists for the Huánuco and San Martín coca-growing departments. As described by Strong, "Basic justice, administered under the threat of the death penalty for severe offenses or regular offenders, won Shining Path considerable popular goodwill. . . . The party is liked everywhere; people feel protected by it and believe in its justice rather than the police."[210] Reported a Peruvian journalist: "The people of Tingo María and Tocache never talk about 'terrorists' but about the 'movement,' 'compañeros' and 'the party.' The Shining Path has a high level of support from the population."[211]

Popular support was also evident in Junín by the late 1980s. Journalists reported that "twenty-five percent of those interviewed in regular informal polls in the market zones of Junín categorically declare their support for Sendero Luminoso."[212] Manrique also indicated substantial support among peasant community members in the department.[213]

Further, electoral data suggest considerable support for Sendero in these departments. Given that the Shining Path sought electoral absenteeism and frequently retaliated against voters, however, absenteeism may reflect either support for Sendero or fear of it. Perhaps the best indicator of support is the "null" ballot—which at times was marked by pro-Sendero signs.[214] A second kind of invalid vote, the blank vote, could also reflect support for Sendero. Some "null" and some "blank" ballots are, however, merely errors. In any case, the rates of absenteeism and invalid ballots in the departments where Sendero was considered to be strong were much higher than elsewhere. For example, in the 1989 municipal elections, absenteeism nationwide was 36 percent and invalid ballots were 22 percent of the total; by contrast, in Ayacucho absenteeism was 85 percent and invalid ballots 70 percent; in Huánuco, absenteeism was 59 percent and invalid ballots 45 percent; in Junín, absenteeism was 68 percent and invalid ballots 35 percent.[215] The data for Junín represent an especially marked change, corresponding to Sendero's large increase in power.[216]

Table 2.1 indicates that approximately 15 percent of Salvadoran municipalities were estimated to be controlled by the FMLN in the late 1980s, and about 28 percent of Peruvian municipalities by the Shining Path. The term "guerrilla control" indicates the displacement of the Salvadoran or Peruvian state and the establishment of a proguerrilla governing structure. The best (although imperfect) indicator for the two countries is the ability of the guerrillas to prevent official elections from being held in the area.

But the term implies more: the ability of the guerrillas to determine who could reside in the area, to decide the curricula of the schools, and to restrict speech. Guerrillas may control an area even when they do not enjoy popular support in it, through terror or other strategies. The greater resort to terror by Sendero is suggested in table 2.1; the figure for "popular support" for Sendero is lower than that for the FMLN, but the figure for "territorial control" is higher. The Shining Path systematically targeted not only political leaders but also church people and all kinds of foreigners—development technicians, researchers, archeologists, and tourists—to frighten them into leaving the area.[217] Sendero killed teachers who resisted instructing its line.[218] Even aid workers in soup kitchens obediently read Shining Path tracts aloud.[219] Sendero also frequently called "armed strikes" to demonstrate its control, and it enforced the work stoppage by the threat of death against any violator.

The 15 percent figure for territorial control in El Salvador in the late 1980s was down from between 25 and 33 percent in the early 1980s.[220] The estimates are based primarily on the number of municipalities where elections were not held, and/or where the elected authorities could not reside.[221] The two departments where the FMLN's influence was strongest were Chalatenango and Morazán, dominated by the FPL and the ERP, respectively. The support achieved by each guerrilla group in the department was solid in rural communities; when the guerrillas shifted their primary focus from San Salvador to these departments in the early 1980s, their opponents (primarily larger landowners) left their estates to reside in the departmental capitals.[222] The FMLN also controlled the Guazapa volcano in Cuscatlán (just to the north of San Salvador), southeastern sections of Usulután and La Unión (affording access to the Pacific shore and the Gulf of Fonseca, respectively), and a few small areas in other departments.

As of 1989, according to official tallies, Sendero was able to stop the renewal of state authorities in 28 percent of Peru's electoral districts—a larger percentage than in El Salvador by that date but about the same as in El Salvador in the earlier part of the decade.[223] In the Peruvian case, these official figures underestimate the extent of Sendero control; to a greater degree than in El Salvador, the areas controlled by Sendero were remote and inaccessible, and some local authorities abandoned their positions without the knowledge of the central authorities in Lima. Another possible estimate of intense Sendero threat is the declaration of a province as an "emergency zone," where the government suspends civil rights and establishes de facto military command; while this measure probably overestimates the extent of Sendero control, it is yet noteworthy that 47 percent of Peru's provinces were declared "in a state of emergency" by December 1991.[224] Perhaps a better estimate of actual Sendero control is that of leading Senderólogos: 40 percent by Gustavo Gorriti and Simon Strong in 1991–92.[225]

The departments where Sendero was generally considered to have gained control over a significant swathe of territory were its original social base, Ayacucho and its neighboring departments Huancavelica and Apurímac (sometimes referred to as "the southern highlands"); by the mid-1980s, Huánuco and, to a lesser degree, San Martín (which include the lucrative coca-producing Upper Huallaga Valley); by the late 1980s, the strategically crucial central highlands (in particular Junín), where a key road connects Lima to most of highlands and jungle Peru;[226] and finally, in the early 1990s, most of the Lima shanty towns located on key routes between the capital and other areas.[227] Overall, these departments showed the largest percentages of districts that had no government authorities. Relative to the figure of 28 percent of electoral districts nationwide that were not renewed in 1989 according to official data, 60 percent were not renewed in Ayacucho, 48 percent in Huancavelica, and 24 percent in Apurímac, the southern highlands departments.[228] In another count using official data, 62 percent of the district offices in the provinces making up the "Andrés Avelino Cáceres" region (Huánuco, Junín, Pasco, and one Huancavelica province) were officially vacant between 1989 and 1991.[229] In a third count, 50 percent of the district offices in Junín were vacant, and 24 percent of those in Lima.[230] In an unofficial report by a "senior police official," however, 90 percent of Junín's district authorities had left their posts.[231]

Strategies for Taking Power and Their Effectiveness

We noted above that the intensity of the challenge posed to the state by a guerrilla group should not be assessed solely on the basis of quantifiable indicators. An essential unquantifiable indicator is the insurgency's strategy for victory, and the appropriateness of the strategy to the particular political and international context. Is the strategy working? And, perhaps even more important, has the revolutionary movement persuaded citizens that its strategy is working, so that they believe it will win and, accordingly, will stand up for it at critical moments?

It is evident that the military strength of the FMLN during the mid- and late 1980s—probably greater than that of any other Latin American guerrilla organization and certainly greater than the Shining Path's— was not a sufficient condition for victory.[232] Given the commitment of the United States to the Salvadoran regime, and the concomitant combativeness of the Salvadoran army, there was scant popular expectation of a revolutionary victory and scant popular willingness to participate in risky uprisings. Rather, the FMLN was closer to victory when it was militarily weaker, during the late 1970s and early 1980s, because the Salvadoran regime was less legitimate and U.S. support for it less certain. Similarly, even though the Shining Path could not possibly have defeated a combative Peruvian army in the late 1980s or early 1990s, its strategy was to assure that, in a context of pervasive terror and demoralization, neither Peru's soldiers nor any one else would fight effectively. Variations of this strategy have been successful in Latin America's history (see chapter 5).

During the 1981 "final offensive," the FMLN expected that a spectacular military offensive would provoke a popular uprising as well as the collapse of the Salvadoran military, and soon thereafter the revolutionary movement would be able to take power. Their strategy might have succeeded; as one U.S. analyst commented, "The guerrillas launched a 'final offensive' in early 1981, and they almost pulled it off."[233] As discussed at the beginning of this chapter, if the revolutionary organizations had been militarily ready for an offensive slightly earlier, or if the guerrilla organizations had been more united during 1979–81, the FMLN's chances would have been good.

After the failure of the 1981 offensive in El Salvador, there was ambiguity among the FMLN leaders and their allies about whether the FMLN's objective should be to prod the Salvadoran government to the negotiating table or to continue to seek victory outright.[234] But most FMLN leaders continued to hope that victory was possible.

Between 1981 and 1984, influenced by what the Cuban, Nicaraguan, and ERP leaders perceived as an insurrectionist opportunity in El Salvador similar to that in Nicaragua in 1979, the FMLN's hopes were pinned primarily on conventional military combat and its political implications.[235] In early 1981, amid relentless repression and the failed "final offensive," the FMLN withdrew from El Salvador's cities. The first goal was to develop a revolutionary army that could secure a strategic rearguard in its own "zones of control." Gaining much more equipment and training than in previous years, the FMLN was able to develop battalions of some five hundred guerrillas that successfully forced the Salvadoran military to withdraw from approximately 25 percent of the country's territory.[236] In September 1983, an ERP brigade held San Miguel, El Salvador's third largest city, for the better part of a day.[237] The FMLN hoped that guerrilla-controlled territories would receive formal recognition by some international entities, enabling the FMLN to receive weapons openly under international law; this hope was not fulfilled.[238]

In 1984, however, the FMLN decided that this conventional military approach was not viable and adopted a Salvadoran version of the Vietnamese "prolonged popular war" strategy, the strategy originally advocated by the FPL. A key reason for this change was that, in the wake of the election of Napoleon Duarte to the presidency (see chapter 3), the U.S. government provided even more substantial support to the Salvadoran military, in particular enhancing the Salvadoran military's air attack capability. In this context, the FMLN decided that battalion-size units were too vulnerable and shifted to smaller, more mobile units that harassed urban garrisons and ambushed army units in the countryside. The strategy was no longer conventional military confrontation, but a war of attrition, in which gradually the Salvadoran military—like the South Vietnamese military—would be exhausted and would suffer the withdrawal of U.S. support.

The election of Duarte signified important changes not only on the battlefield but also in the political arena. The opening of political space enabled the FMLN to carry out political work in Salvadoran cities again. Although Duarte's election reduced the appeal of the FMLN's claims to be the exclusive democratic voice in El Salvador, Duarte's government was seriously flawed (see chapter 3). Between 1984 and 1989, the FMLN successfully renewed its political networks in San Salvador and other cities. Although more and more FMLN leaders were suggesting that negotiations should be the ultimate objective, they also believed that greater pressure was necessary to get the Salvadoran government to the negotiating table.[239] Some top commanders and most of the FMLN's rank and file continued to hope for outright victory, arguing that El Salvador's political reforms were a sham, economic conditions were worse, the Salvadoran military was being worn down, and the hearts of the Salvadoran people were really with the FMLN.[240] Consider U.S. journalist Janet Shenk's report on her discussion with Villalobos on New Year's Eve, 1987:

> "Anyone with his eyes closed and blindfolded can see that this war is won!" says Villalobos. He insists that the rebels have the sympathy of the urban and rural poor, but he also admits that's not enough. The FMLN has to channel those sympathies into concrete action, to "integrate" political support and military readiness. In 1981, insurrection in the cities was easily crushed because the rebels were militarily weak. In 1983, they were militarily strong, driving the army to the brink of defeat, but the urban movement was only beginning to recuperate from the terror of previous years. Soon, says Villalobos, both elements will be in place.
>
> Even if he is right, I can't imagine the United States standing by and watching its most costly ally in the region go up in smoke. . . . "But [says Villalobos] . . . I think there are limitations on how much they [the North Americans] can escalate this war. . . ." Villalobos says there is little more the United States can do—short of direct intervention. U.S. ground forces, unfamiliar with the terrain, wouldn't necessarily be an improvement over Salvadoran troops. . . . escalation of the air war would imply . . . tens of thousands of civilian deaths. He believes the American public doesn't have the stomach for that, and that even U.S. policymakers know the cost in international terms would be too high.[241]

Accordingly, FMLN attacks continued. In early 1989, after the FMLN's proposals for its participation in the presidential election conditioned upon electoral reform were rejected by the government, the FMLN sabotaged the election more seriously than ever before (see chapter 3 and the introduction). These attacks culminated in the November 1989 offensive—similar in many respects to the 1968 Vietcong Tet Offensive. On 11 November, the FMLN besieged San Salvador and much of the rest of the country. The offensive was the biggest of the Salvadoran war and also, in all probability, the biggest guerrilla offensive ever mounted against a Latin American government.[242] The unity of the previously fractious FMLN factions behind the offensive was impressive.[243]

In preparation for the offensive, the FMLN successfully concealed the movement of more than fifteen hundred combatants and tons of arms into the capital, primarily though sewer pipes, and accordingly was able to catch the Salvadoran government and the U.S. Embassy by surprise. Roughly thirty-five hundred FMLN insurgents occupied San Salvador, and other guerrilla units attacked in seven major cities of the country. Small units entered the poor neighborhoods at the outskirts of the cities, trying to spark an uprising among the residents. In San Salvador, the FMLN mounted barricades, dug trenches, and seized tall apartment buildings from which they could fire at government soldiers and aircraft. The FMLN occupied the capital's wealthiest neighborhoods: for example, the exclusive Sheraton Hotel, where twelve U.S. Green Berets were trapped on one floor. The rebels defended their positions for some two weeks, even after the Salvadoran military resorted to aerial bombardment. The bombs were the primary cause of the estimated one thousand deaths during the offensive.[244]

However, the offensive did not bring the FMLN to power. Probably in part because popular support for the revolutionary movement was not as great as in the 1979–81 period and in part because popular fears of government repression continued, popular insurrection did not materialize.[245] For those FMLN leaders who had continued to hope for outright victory, this hope was definitively dashed.

For those FMLN leaders whose primary goal in the offensive was to prod the government toward negotiations, however, the offensive was a success. The offensive shattered the belief of the political right in El Salvador and in the United States that the Salvadoran military could achieve a military victory. Rather, it was apparent that the FMLN might continue to torment the Salvadoran military indefinitely. Also, during the offensive, members of the U.S.-trained Atlacatl Battalion committed an egregious atrocity: the murder of six Jesuit priests, their housekeeper, and her daughter at their home in the UCA. It was obvious that, despite years of rhetoric to the contrary, Salvadoran military officers were continuing to flout basic human rights. Raising obstacles to the U.S. Congress's approval of the Bush administration's aid requests for El Salvador, the atrocity distanced the U.S. government somewhat from the Salvadoran regime; negotiations became a more attractive alternative.

To a greater degree than the FMLN, the Shining Path worked to achieve the perception that it was a "winner"—that it invariably met its strategic goals, and that accordingly it was the Shining Path rather than the government that should be supported or feared. To this end, the Shining Path touted its successful expansion in key parts of the Peruvian countryside and provincial cities as evidence that it was fulfilling its Maoist strategic plan.[246] At the time of Guzmán's capture, in September 1992, the Shining Path was elaborating its penultimate plan (just prior to the anticipated actual takeover): "the great plan for the construction of the conquest of power."[247]

The Shining Path expanded in different areas at different times during the 1980s.[248] The expansion surprised most analysts, who had doubted the capacity of such an ideologically rigid group to recruit in diverse regions of the country. First, of course, Sendero began in the destitute, remote, and predominantly rural southern highlands department of Ayacucho and its two neighboring departments, Apurímac and Huancavelica.[249] In the mid-1980s, it expanded in the coca-producing Upper Huallaga Valley, located in the departments of Huánuco and San Martín—departments for the most part newly settled by peasants who cultivated coca for sale to the drug lords.[250] As noted above, Sendero's activities in Peru's drug-producing area netted the organization substantial sums. Then, in the late 1980s, Sendero advanced in central highlands departments, especially Junín—departments much more accessible, commercial, and sophisticated than those in the southern highlands.[251] Junín is of great strategic significance because it supplies most of Lima's water and electricity, as well as considerable amounts of food. Despite considerable popular resistance in the mid- to late 1980s, at the end of the decade and the beginning of the 1990s Sendero made headway in Puno, a department that could provide the guerrilla movement with a corridor between its primary Peruvian highlands bases and Bolivia.[252] At the same time, guerrilla attacks were also extending into Cuzco, Arequipa, and Ica.[253]

Still, most analysts believed that Sendero would not succeed in Lima. The capital was not only relatively prosperous, politically well organized, and culturally sophisticated, but it was also the base of much of

Peru's security personnel. Where would fleeing Senderistas take refuge? As noted above, these concerns were shared even by a faction of the guerrilla leadership.

But Sendero did penetrate Lima. Sendero sought to dominate first the towns on the key strategic artery between Lima and the interior (the "central highway") and then the large slums on the outskirts of the city. In 1990, Sendero spearheaded the establishment of a town that came to be called "Raucana" at Lima's edge on the main highway between the capital and the central highlands.[254] Asked a journalist: "Red Raucana: Is there a 'liberated zone' only eight kilometers from the presidential palace?"[255] From sites such as Raucana, Sendero recruited in the poor shanty towns to the east, north, and south of the capital, such as Ate-Vitarte, Huaycán, and San Juan de Lurigancho.[256] Sendero even recruited effectively in Villa El Salvador, which had been well organized by Peru's democratic political left during the 1970s and had been considered its political stronghold for much of the 1980s.[257] Senderistas took cover from the security forces in huge caves that overlook Lima.[258] In the eyes of many analysts, Sendero had successfully built an "iron belt" around central Lima.[259] In May 1991, the guerrilla leadership proclaimed that it had achieved "strategic equilibrium" (strategic parity).[260]

Given that Sendero's goal was as much to demoralize and neutralize its opposition as to gain actual support, it frequently employed terror. Terrorist attacks were rampant in Lima in 1992. On 9 February, during a blackout of the capital, two powerful bombs exploded, killing at least four Peruvians and wounding thirty-nine; a few days later, a car bomb attack on the residence of the U.S. ambassador killed three Peruvian guards at the residence and wounded twelve bystanders.[261] On 15 February 1992, María Elena Moyano—the Villa El Salvador vice mayor, head of its Glass of Milk program, and "person of the year" for the newspaper *La República*, who had spoken out firmly against Sendero Luminoso and just the day before her death had led a march repudiating an "armed strike" called by the guerrillas—was savagely murdered during a barbecue.[262]

After President Fujimori's *autogolpe* on 5 April 1992, Shining Path attacks escalated.[263] By mid-1992, Sendero was preparing for full-scale insurrection. The car bombs became truck bombs. On 22 May, 660 pounds of dynamite exploded in the center of Peru's banking district—killing one, wounding three, and causing damages estimated at more than $2 million.[264] On 5 June, an attack was launched against one of Peru's major television stations, killing its news program director as well as two guards, and heavily damaging installations.[265] On 16 July, in the worst terrorist incident of the war, Sendero detonated a truck bomb on the small street of Tarata in Miraflores, a neighborhood that is the center of middle-class Lima life. The truck bomb was as destructive as many an aerial bomb: 22 people were killed, their bodies scattered across the street; about 250 people were injured; 400 homes, 20 shops, 10 banks, and 6 hotels were damaged; windows were shattered in buildings within a fifteen-block radius.[266] The Tarata bomb was the start of a weeklong wave of terror—daily attacks against police stations, factories, schools, commercial enterprises, and even a think tank.[267]

Sendero's key objective was to sow sufficient terror to assure the success of its first two-day Lima "armed strike" (a total cessation of activity imposed under the threat of reprisals, a common Sendero tactic), and once again their objective was achieved. On 22 and 23 July, the insurgents' two-day armed strike paralyzed Lima.[268] Road and rail links to the highland interior were cut by bombs. The major avenues from shanty towns into Lima were blocked by stones and burning tires. Public transport halted. Most offices, shops, and schools closed. As the Shining Path enforced the strike by bombs and assaults, some forty people were killed and roughly one hundred were wounded. One taxi driver who did not heed the strike call was burned alive inside his car. Although Lima was the primary focus of the armed strike, a simultaneous offensive was carried out nationwide. Meanwhile, Fujimori huddled in private with his advisers. Commented Simon Strong: "[These attacks] show that Fujimori is getting absolutely nowhere against Sendero."[269]

Although in the past the insurgents had directly confronted members of the Peruvian security forces only rarely, they began to work in larger groups—platoons of fifty to a hundred—and increasingly to target police stations.[270] When confrontations occurred, the record did not inspire much confidence in the fighting spirit of the Peruvian security forces.

Consider: (1) In March 1989, about three hundred Senderistas attacked the police post at Uchiza in the Upper Huallaga Valley; the police commander called for help to nearby military bases as well as to Lima, but none came. The guerrillas seized the post, captured the three police officers in charge, subjected them to a "popular trial," and executed them. The failure of the security forces to mount a rescue mission was widely attributed to deficient military coordination, equipment, and lack of will.[271] (2) On 1 December 1990, Sendero occupied a Mobil Oil camp in the Upper Huallaga Valley—seizing helicopters, destroying trucks, and setting fire to almost all the buildings. Although Sendero controlled the camp for seventeen days (in part as a celebration of Guzmán's birthday), the security forces did nothing.[272] (3) On 21 January 1992, the guerrillas overran a police post in Puquio in the southern highlands and then freed about twenty-five of their Sendero comrades from the Puquio jail. The soldiers at the army base down the road stayed in their barracks.[273]

By the end of July 1992, Sendero had achieved almost the degree of panic that was necessary to preclude effective resistance by the Peruvian state. Said a retired Peruvian colonel: "A growing feeling of impotence and defeatism took over the people."[274] Agreed one Shining Path analyst: "In the opinion of the majority of people, there was the idea that it was impossible to control the Sendero movement."[275] Businessmen, doctors, and many other members of Peru's middle class were trying to leave the country.[276] A *Washington Post* reporter concluded that Lima was "on the edge of nervous breakdown."[277]

Among the panic-stricken were the Peruvian armed forces. Rates of desertion, among both the rank and file and the officers, were very high by the late 1980s. For example, between mid-1989 and mid-1992, about half the naval officers between the ranks of second lieutenant and commander asked to leave the service.[278] Observed Senderólogo Gustavo Gorriti, "The war [against Sendero] might be lost without the army losing even one battle."[279] Shining Path analyst Enrique Obando summarized the situation in July 1992 as

really alarming. The risk was that, facing an average of eight car-bomb attacks monthly, businessmen, industrialists, merchants, and bankers would decide to evacuate the city [Lima], withdrawing their money from the banks, which in turn would have bankrupted the banking system and paralyzed industry and most commerce. The result would be hunger, provoking looting by a badly paid, badly trained, badly equipped and demoralized armed forces. The risk was being run of a disintegration of military units that had a high rate of desertion. This is how close we were to defeat.[280]

An Assessment

Both the FMLN and Sendero Luminoso were poised to take power at certain junctures. There was a real possibility in both El Salvador and Peru that the revolutionary organization would win. While the two organizations were similar in the intensity of the challenges they posed to the respective governments, they were very different in most other important respects.

The FMLN was an unwieldy coalition of quarrelsome groups. The acrimony among these groups may have cost the FMLN victory during the period 1979–81, when both international and popular alienation from the Salvadoran regime was deepest. In particular, the insistence by the erstwhile leader of the FPL, Salvador Cayetano Carpio, that the FPL be the dominant group in the coalition and that he be the dominant leader alienated the others.

After Carpio's death, the FMLN achieved some cohesion. Decisions were made through the forging of a consensus among the leaders of all five organizations within the FMLN. In both the Salvadoran and the international arenas, however, the best-known leader was Villalobos. Was Villalobos a plus or a minus for the FMLN? Assessment is difficult. To Villalobos's admirers, he was not only congenial, intelligent, and an outstanding military strategist, but also articulate and handsome— qualities that approximated charisma. However, Villalobos was rarely mentioned by rank-and-file FMLN members as the catalyst for their decision to join the organization (see chapter 6). To Villalobos's critics—who are many, including most of the other guerrilla leaders—Villalobos was a ruthless opportunist. At a minimum, Villalobos's actions were a factor in the development in some quarters of the image of the FMLN as a group of "enemy colleagues" who killed one another.[281]

By many indicators the FMLN was the strongest guerrilla group ever to emerge in Latin America. Commented, for example, a U.S. colonel, "I think what we're seeing in El Salvador today are some of the best guerrillas, probably the best guerrillas, we've seen in this hemisphere to date. They are certainly better than anything we saw in Nicaragua or in Cuba."[282] Ultimately, the FMLN lost because the United States, the Salvadoran upper classes, and the Salvadoran military all remained relatively supportive of the regime—certainly more supportive than in neighboring Nicaragua (see chapter 5). Under these conditions, no guerrilla movement could have defeated the government; the FMLN did well to continue to mount a serious challenge. Overall, the constant deliberation and negotiation that went on within the FMLN during the 1980s appeared to give the movement resilience and helped it adapt to the changing conditions of the decade. Remarkable unity was achieved for the November 1989 offensive. When peace negotiations finally began, the FMLN's long-standing experience with consultation and argument stood the movement in good stead.

By contrast, the Shining Path was an authoritarian organization dominated by one man, Abimael Guzmán. From 1980 until 12 September 1992, authoritarianism appeared to abet the organization's advance. Virtually deified in Shining Path ideology, Guzmán inspired total commitment from his disciples, who did not hesitate to surrender their lives for the movement. Also, of course, having one man decide what was right and what was wrong enabled the organization to be cohesive, purposeful, and efficient—at a time when no other organization in Peru seemed to be "working."

But on 12 September 1992, when Guzmán was captured, all the assets of authoritarianism suddenly appeared as deficiencies.[283] The image of Guzmán as an invincible god may have seduced many desperate Peruvians, but it also ultimately deceived the leader himself. Guzmán apparently thought that he was invulnerable and the security forces were hopelessly incompetent. He became careless. For example, the funeral of Guzmán's wife Augusta La Torre was videotaped, presumably for the museum of the revolution that would be established after Sendero's victory; but the video was seized at a safe house in January 1991 and for the first time Peru's security forces knew that Guzmán was alive and could identify many of the members of his inner circle.[284] Especially given that various hideouts had been captured, Guzmán was reckless to set up a safe house in another well-to-do Lima neighborhood, and he took minimal safety procedures there.[285]

Of course, too, given that the image of Guzmán as an invincible philosopher-king was such a key factor in Sendero's appeal, the destruction of that image was devastating to the organization.[286] Guzmán's image was probably damaged somewhat by the video of his wife's funeral, in which he appeared inebriated, dancing to Greek music.[287]

In the event of the actual capture, however, Guzmán's heroic, mythical image was virtually destroyed. Not only was the "invincible" leader captured, but in a tape played repeatedly on Peruvian television, he revealed himself to be not only mortal but also an apparently ordinary mortal—a paunchy, middle-aged man with a ragged beard and thick glasses, who meekly followed the orders of Peru's antiterrorist police to take off his pants, revealing his psoriasis.[288]

Probably the most controversial decision made by Guzmán was the decision to prioritize the war in the cities, in particular in Lima, which was of course essentially the decision that led to his capture. The decision sparked the only major known internal conflict within the organization. The opponents of the decision, including both Guzmán's wife and his top lieutenant Osmán Morote,[289] argued that support in the countryside was insufficient and that the risks of exposure were too great in Lima. Of course, ultimately their fears were proven well founded. But was the decision really incorrect? Perhaps, as some analysts believed, Guzmán had become impatient.[290] But, in my own view, Guzmán's decision was the correct bet, albeit a lost bet; if the organization had been more patient, the historical moment would have been lost and the organization would have lost its momentum.[291]

Just as the chances for an FMLN victory would have been greater if its revolutionary components had been more united in the 1979–81 period, however, the possibility of a Sendero victory might have been greater if the organization had been less dogmatic and more attuned to peasants' concerns. I have suggested in this chapter that many of Sendero's "strengths" were double-edged swords, that its authoritarian leadership, rigid Maoist creed, and intemperate use of violence against civilians were strengths and deficiencies at the same time.

It is not, however, certain that a "kinder, gentler" Sendero would have done better than Sendero itself. As mentioned above, the MRTA was much more cautious in its use of violence than Sendero, but it was perceived as incoherent and undisciplined and never threatened the Peruvian state. In Peru's relatively democratic 1980–92 context, Sendero's fundamentalism and discipline probably were appropriate to the revolutionary space available in Peru at the time. However, a less savage movement that was more receptive to the millenarian beliefs and ethnic concerns of many Peruvians might have proven most appropriate of all.

3

POLITICAL TRENDS
MILITARY REPRESSION? ELECTORAL FRAUD? OR DEMOCRACY?

*I*n accord with virtually all previous assessments of Salvadoran governments between 1931 and 1982, the analysis in this chapter is that those governments were not democratic.[1] Governing between 1931 and 1979 in El Salvador, military elites increasingly resorted to repression and electoral fraud to exclude the political "left" from power.[2] The data in the first and second sections of the chapter show that, between 1979 and 1982 when unconstitutional civilian-military juntas presided, human rights violations reached egregious levels, afflicting a greater variety of social groups than ever before in El Salvador.[3] The timing of the fraud and repression—which became evident at about the same time as the revolutionary movement emerged, and much more severe as the movement expanded—strongly suggests that this political variable was the key catalyst to the Salvadoran movement. Political exclusion as the sine qua non variable is confirmed by the militants' own statements (see chapter 6). This, of course, is just what Skocpol, Goodwin, Dix, Blasier, and other influential scholars of revolution who emphasize the primacy of the state and regime type would have assumed.

By contrast, this chapter shows the Peruvian experience to have been very different, contradicting "the state matters most" school. Indeed, between 1980 and 1992, scholars agreed that Peru met the standard criteria for the democratic label.[4] The various sections of this chapter make clear why the Peruvian regime during this period was characterized as democratic. In the first section of the chapter, the Peruvian military tradition is shown to have been very different from the Salvadoran. The

Peruvian military did not systematically seek to repress the Marxist left as it became an important political actor during the 1970s. The second section shows that, not only when Sendero Luminoso initiated its actions in 1980 but also during its growth throughout the decade, Peruvian elections were fair and open to all who chose to participate. Finally, the third section of the chapter indicates that there was considerable civilian authority over the military in Peru during the 1980s. In sum, political exclusion was not a factor in the expansion of the Shining Path; militants' references to political exclusion as a factor in their decisions to join the movement are scant (see chapter 6).

Accordingly, the Peruvian experience contradicts the prevailing scholarly wisdom that the ballot box is the coffin of guerrilla movements. This key point is elaborated primarily in the second section of this chapter, which documents the fairness and relative freedom from political violence of Peruvian elections during the 1980s.

However, the chapter also suggests that, in the common adage, "the baby should not be thrown out with the bath water." To argue that the ballot box is not necessarily the coffin of revolutionary movements is not to argue that politics is irrelevant. Rather, as this book's introduction discusses, my argument is that, although political variables did not trigger the Shining Path, they became important as the movement expanded. In part because of Sendero's actions and in part because of successive elected governments' own vices, Peru's democratic regime as it was fashioned during this period became less legitimate. In particular, as the fourth section of this chapter shows, despite the considerable subordination of the military to civilian authority in Peru, the Peruvian regime was unable to develop a counterinsurgency strategy that was both effective and respectful of human rights. Although the 1980–92 Peruvian regime met standard U.S.-based scholarly criteria for the democratic label, increasingly it did not meet most Peruvians' criteria.

Furthermore, even judgments made according to standard U.S.-based scholarly criteria about the democratic or nondemocratic character of a state can be much more complex than some scholars suggest.[5] As mentioned in chapter 1, to warrant the democratic label, scholars mandate that the electoral context be free (that is, there is no official intimidation or repression of any group trying to participate), that electoral processes be fair (that is, balloting procedures are accessible to all citizens and votes are accurately tabulated), and that the military be subordinate to civilian authority. There are numerous indicators that may be relevant; cross-national thresholds for the awarding of the label "free and fair" to elections and for deeming the military to be subordinate to civilian authority are yet to be established.

It is well known that the assessment of the Salvadoran regime as democratic or not democratic after 1982 is controversial. When elections were held in El Salvador during the 1980s, the U.S. government and some scholars judged them free and fair and awarded El Salvador the democratic label.[6] Indeed, the second section of this chapter shows that after 1982 Salvadoran civilian and military elites did begin to open the country's electoral processes to center and center-left groups; after 1989, they began to do so to groups of Marxist inclination as well. (And, in further support of the "state matters most" argument, at the same time middle-class support for the FMLN gradually eroded.) But were the levels of freedom from political violence, of electoral fairness, and of military subordination to civilian authority sufficient to warrant a democratic label for El Salvador between 1982 and 1991? Based in part on my comparisons with Peruvian levels, I suggest not.

The chapter begins by showing the major differences in the origins and trajectories of the Peruvian and Salvadoran militaries, which culminated in El Salvador in the electoral frauds and political repression of the 1970s that triggered the revolutionary movement. The next two sections assess two of the key conditions for the democratic label in the two nations. First, patterns of political violence and electoral fraud between 1980 and 1991 are compared; it is concluded that, especially during the early 1980s, political exclusion in El Salvador remained severe and continued to propel many Salvadorans toward the FMLN. By contrast, at least until the final years of the decade, Peruvian electoral outcomes were not distorted by problems of political violence or fraud. Then, the third section of the chapter assesses the relationship between military and civilian elites in the two countries during the 1980s, finding that the traditional powers of the Salvadoran military endured, whereas the Peruvian military was relatively subordinate to civilian authority. The final section turns to the key problem that was not resolved in either nation and that gradually eroded the legitimacy of the Peruvian government despite its otherwise democratic character: the failure to implement a counterinsurgency strategy that was both effective and respectful of human rights and democratic principles.

The Militaries prior to the Elections of the 1980s

During the 1970s, when the political groups that were to be known as the Shining Path and the FMLN were forming, military governments were in power in both Peru and El Salvador. Neither the Peruvian nor the Salvadoran political process approximated "democracy," according to almost any definition; however, the militaries in the two nations were very different. In Peru, the military did not systematically seek to repress the political left, whereas in El Salvador it did. Accordingly, political exclusion and repression were not important factors in the emergence of Peru's revolutionary movement but were important in the rise of the Salvadoran movement.

The Peruvian and Salvadoran Militaries prior to 1930

At its inception, the major focus of the Peruvian military was on the nation's security in the event of external war. The Peruvian military was not closely allied to landowning elites and was not preoccupied with these elites' domestic political concerns. In contrast, the Salvadoran military institution grew primarily for the function of internal war; the military institution was closely allied with landowning elites and was highly absorbed in these elites' domestic political concerns.

During the nineteenth century, the Peruvian military fought numerous battles against external enemies. Even during colonial rule, as one of Spain's two vice royalties in Spanish America, Peru hosted a large and powerful military, and the battle for the country's independence was fierce.[7] After independence in 1824, Peru fought first with Chile, then briefly with Bolivia, and even with Spain.

The war that most affected the Peruvian military was the War of the Pacific (1879–83), which Peru and its ally Bolivia lost to Chile.[8] After the Chileans advanced up Peru's coast and even occupied Lima, the peace treaty gave Chile its desired prize: Tarapacá, Peru's southernmost maritime department, which held vast nitrate deposits. The Peruvian military still ponders and regrets what it perceives as Peru's humiliation at the hands of the Chileans.[9] For the military, the key question raised by

Peru's loss was whether or not Peru's economic elites impeded a greater incorporation of Indian peasants into the struggle, out of fear that if the Indian peasants were mobilized against the Chileans, the peasants would subsequently turn against their own nation's elites.[10] In Peru's central highlands, General Andrés A. Cáceres had effectively mobilized Indian peasants against the Chileans—but also against landowners who collaborated with the Chileans.

These Peruvian anxieties endured in part because the 1883 peace treaty between Peru and Chile did not decide the fate of two border departments; the two nations verged upon war on several occasions until a definitive settlement in 1929. Moreover, Peru was also engaged in an intense dispute over its border with Colombia. Debates about a 1922 treaty between Peru and Colombia, which ceded the Amazonian district of Leticia to Colombia, were intense. Major sectors of the Peruvian population, including the military, perceived the treaty as unduly favorable to Colombia and another humiliation for Peru; these perceptions were important to the 1930 fall of the civilian dictator Leguía (who had negotiated the treaty) and to a short-lived attempt to regain the district in 1932–33.[11]

By contrast, the external defense role of the Salvadoran military was slight.[12] The Spanish colonial presence in Central America was centered on the captaincy-general of Guatemala City. Central America gained its independence not through successful military battles between patriot and royalist armies but indirectly as a result of Mexican independence. Although boundary conflicts emerged in Central America after independence, the "armies" were generally ragtag militia of about one hundred men, financed by local landowners. Until the one-hundred-hour 1969 frontier war with Honduras, the Salvadoran military did not fight any war of long-standing import for the nation.

The development of the Salvadoran military was greatly affected by the decision made by the Salvadoran elites during the late nineteenth century that, in the context of a weakening market for indigo, coffee should become the nation's primary resource.[13] The elites' decision implied repression of the peasantry: the land where the coffee could be grown was held in communal *ejidos* by peasants who could not afford to wait the three-year minimum period between the planting of coffee and the first harvest. In 1882, the government abolished the *ejido* system, giving a private property title to anyone planting coffee on the former communal land. Tens of thousands of peasants were evicted by force or the threat of force.[14] To this end, the Salvadoran army was expanded and private armies were established by the coffee planters themselves; remnants of these private armies would be institutionalized in 1912 as the National Guard, and later in 1966 as the official paramilitary organization the Nationalist Democratic Organization (Organización Democrática Nacionalista, ORDEN).

As the relatively labor-intensive coffee industry expanded, planters also wanted a large, cheap rural proletariat. García (1982) contrasts the political implications of the expansion of coffee in El Salvador to those of the expansion of the banana industry in Honduras: the more labor-intensive, domestically owned Salvadoran coffee industry resisted labor demands for higher wages and benefits more militantly than the relatively capital-intensive, foreign-owned Honduran banana industry. One upshot: a military budget in El Salvador during the first decades of the twentieth century that used more than 20 percent of the national budget, versus a much smaller military budget in Honduras.[15]

At approximately the same time that El Salvador's export economy was shifting from indigo to coffee, Peru's guano deposits were nearing exhaustion and Peruvian elites were also required to identify a new export base. In Peru's case, however, exports became diverse; the most important new exports were sugar and cotton.[16] Sugar and cotton hacendados were to become the core constituency of Peru's oligarchical families.[17] The cultivation of sugar and cotton products, which were grown on Peru's coast, did not require a large displacement of Peru's indigenous peoples, whose communities lay primarily in the Andean highlands.[18] Until 1875 on the coastal cotton and sugar haciendas, landowners imported Chinese coolie labor rather than recruit indigenous workers from the highlands.[19] Accordingly, there was no major role for the military or for private armies in the establishment of these haciendas (although subsequently hacendados did call upon the military to repress political organization and strikes).[20]

In the highlands, the dynamics of agroexport expansion were more varied and complex.[21] In most of the highlands, the norm prior to 1930 was the purchase by more entrepreneurial, export-minded persons of traditional haciendas established during colonial rule.[22] However, especially in the southern highlands department of Puno where the wool industry was concentrated, haciendas did expand at the expense of peasant communities.[23] Military force was one strategy that landowners used to displace indigenous peasants; legal chicanery, "purchase" of lands from peasant community leaders who had been bribed, and surreptitious relocation of boundary fences during the night were other common tactics.

Still, at no time did the military as an institution become engaged in a nationally sanctioned policy of evicting peasants from their lands on behalf of would-be agroexporters.[24] Highlands hacendados were not a strong political lobby; their only agroexport, wool from the sheep and alpaca that can graze at high altitudes, represented about 15 percent of the value of total exports in 1895 and declined to a mere 3 percent after 1930.[25] Also, in part because landowners needed labor nearby, and in part because they feared a revolt that they could not control, their goal was not to force indigenous peoples entirely from their lands.

The Peruvian Military (1930–80) and the Salvadoran Military (1931–82)

Between 1930 and 1980, the Peruvian military intermittently ceded the reins of power to civilians, whereas with only the briefest of interruptions the Salvadoran military ruled the country directly. Although for many years the Peruvian military and landowning elites allied to bar the main reformist political party from executive power, sectors of the Peruvian military gradually became critical of the country's traditional elites. In 1968, a reformist military government led by General Juan Velasco Alvarado came to power, and it endured for twelve years. By contrast, although several reformist movements erupted in the Salvadoran military, none consolidated power. The collaboration between landed oligarchs and military officers was tense by the 1970s, but it endured.

In both Peru and El Salvador, as in most of the Latin American region, the post-1929 global depression provoked political crisis.[26] In the Peruvian case, a dark-skinned lieutenant colonel, Luis M. Sánchez Cerro, overthrew an eleven-year-old authoritarian regime led by the civilian Augusto Leguía, and in 1931 Sánchez Cerro won a relatively open and fair election. Sánchez Cerro defeated the political party APRA (the American Popular Revolutionary Alliance, Alianza Popular Revolucionaria Americana), Peru's first mass political party, which at this time perceived itself and was perceived as a militantly leftist party. Without substantiation, APRA leaders (Apristas) denounced the 1931 electoral outcome as fraudulent. Sánchez Cerro arrested APRA's leaders. In turn, Aprista activists rebelled in Trujillo, capturing the local army garrison and executing about sixty soldiers and officers. In retaliation, when the army regained control of the city, they rounded up and shot more than one thousand suspected Apristas. Then, in 1933, Sánchez Cerro was assassinated by an Aprista. The conflict between the Peruvian military and APRA established a strong mutual interest between the military and Peru's traditional elites: the exclusion of APRA from power.[27]

However, a collaboration based primarily on one common enemy, as in Peru, is unlikely to be as strong or as stable as one based on common financial and ideological interests (as in the case of the military-elite collaboration in El Salvador). Unlike the Salvadoran upper class, the Peruvian upper class did not forsake indefinitely its right to govern; nor did it welcome military officers into its clubs or onto its boards of directors.[28] Nor did the Peruvian military restrict its perception of Peru's "national security" to the elites' perceptions of internal security needs. Rather, as the border tensions between Peru and its neighbors continued, the development of a professional military institution and an effective external defense capability were major concerns of Peruvian officers.[29] In 1941, Peru won its first military victory against a neighbor: in the first-ever use of airborne troops in a Latin American conflict, the Peruvians advanced far into Ecuadorean territory in a five-week war and then secured a favorable peace treaty.[30] Accordingly, as the APRA party shifted toward the political center and eschewed violence after 1948, the raison d'être of the collaboration between the military and the oligarchy was gone.

During the late 1950s and the 1960s, the Peruvian military distanced itself further and further from Peru's traditional order. Perhaps because of its self-perceived inglorious record, the Peruvian military became unusually concerned about strategic analysis and, concomitantly, its officers' education.[31] Affirmed two analysts: "The Peruvian military officer is, on average, one of the most highly schooled in the world."[32] At the pinnacle of the educational system was the Center for High Military Studies (Centro de Altos Estudios Militares, CAEM), which by the late 1950s became a prized assignment for officers and an important step toward the rank of general.[33] A full year was devoted to the analysis of Peru's social and political problems; instruction tended to be critical of civilian political leaders for their apparent failure to promote national development.[34]

During the 1960s, military criticism of the perceived failures of civilian elites mounted.[35] In the early 1960s, in the wake of the Cuban revolution, guerrilla groups emerged in the Peruvian highlands, and the civilian government, led by President Fernando Belaúnde, sent the military to counter them. Although the counterinsurgency effort was successful, the military became concerned about the plight of Peru's highlands peasants; many officers decided that, without agrarian reform, guerrilla movements would inevitably reemerge. Officers were distressed that President Belaúnde, who had been elected on a platform of agrarian reform and other progressive measures, was not advancing toward these goals. Many officers found Belaúnde ineffectual, and his opposition (an opportunistic alliance between APRA and its former arch-rival, the party of Odría) worse.

The Peruvian military also became critical of the United States during the 1960s. The Peruvian air force wanted to buy Northrop F-5 jets from the United States; however, the U.S. Congress held up the sale, and finally the Peruvian air force bought Mirage fighters from France.[36] Peruvian officers were also disturbed that the Johnson administration adamantly supported the International Petroleum Company in its dispute with the Belaúnde administration.[37]

The military's tendency toward a critical interpretation of civilian elites and the U.S. government was in part a result of the socioeconomic background of officers relative to these elites. To an unusual degree among Latin American nations, Peru's officers were drawn from lower-middle-class, provincial backgrounds; whereas during 1900–19, 38 percent of army officers were born in the highlands or the jungle, by 1940–59, 52 percent were.[38] Also, during 1955–65, 56 percent of officers attaining the rank of general were born in the highlands or the jungle; the birthplace of the generals may be contrasted to those of the directors of Peru's largest corporations during this period—94 percent of whom were born on Peru's coast.[39]

The reformist concerns of the Peruvian military were evident in the 1968 coup against Belaúnde led by General Juan Velasco Alvarado.[40]

The junta did not deem the previous political order "democratic" but rather a "sellout of the national interest" by "bad politicians," who "acted only to defend the interests of the powerful" and who kowtowed to the United States.[41] President Velasco vowed that his government would ultimately make "real" democracy viable in Peru; he promised a "fully participatory social democracy." The Velasco government nationalized a subsidiary of the U.S.-based Standard Oil Company and many other major foreign-owned firms; it also carried out one of the region's most ambitious agrarian reforms.

Although the Velasco government had a relatively coherent program of socioeconomic reform, its political agenda was unclear. Officers were undecided about the length of time they should govern. While their claim was to build a "fully participatory social democracy," their own decisionmaking style was hierarchical and closed to input from most civilian groups. The government was not repressive by Latin American standards; there was no pattern of torture or disappearances. Indeed, the Velasco government opened a large space for leftist political organizers, and worker and peasant organization under leftist banners expanded dramatically.[42] However, numerous opposition political leaders were deported, and political party activity was severely restricted.

For various reasons, in particular Velasco's ill health and mounting economic problems, General Francisco Morales Bermúdez ousted Velasco in 1975. Considered a moderate and an "institutionalist," Morales Bermúdez implemented a severe austerity program. Propelled in part—ironically—by the political organizations that had been established under Velasco, popular protest mounted. Calling for economic change and for democratic freedoms, the protesters organized a general strike on 19 July 1977 that virtually shut the entire nation down; the general strike was Peru's first since 1919 and the most massive in the country's history. Again, the military government's immediate response was not violent (although approximately 700 union militants were detained and about 3,500 workers were fired).[43] And, less than two weeks later in his annual 28 July address to the nation, President Morales Bermúdez announced a transition to democracy—a decision in sharp contrast to that of his Salvadoran counterparts, as will be evident below.

In June 1978, elections were held for the Constituent Assembly that would write a new constitution for the country. The political context was similar to that of the year before: intense unrest and numerous strikes led by leftist political activists, including another massive general strike on 22 and 23 May. Once again, the military government's response was to detain militants, but not for long periods of time and not to resort to torture. Most remarkably, the electoral process was relatively fair and inclusive of the Marxist left. Indeed, together the leftist parties that were later to join the United Left (Izquierda Unida, IU) coalition won a larger percentage of the national vote than they ever had before or would later: 29 percent.[44]

The post-1929 global depression provoked political crisis in El Salvador also. The depression undermined El Salvador's coffee-growing elite, which had dominated the government since 1870. In 1931, amid increasing political unrest, a reformist civilian president was overthrown in a coup led by General Maximiliano Hernández Martínez. In January 1932, an uprising planned by the Marxist political leader Agustín Farabundo Martí was crushed by the military. Despite the ease of this triumph, General Martínez's soldiers joined with local oligarchs' vigilante bands to massacre about thirty thousand peasants in the coffee lands in western departments of the country; perhaps a mere 10 percent of these peasants had participated in the rebellion.[45] *La matanza*, as the massacre is called, is one of El Salvador's most notorious events.

While in part a result of the established tradition of repression by the Salvadoran military, *la matanza* also initiated a more formal military-oligarchy pact in El Salvador: the oligarchy would cede the benefits of executive office to the military in return for the military's protection of oligarchical interests. As Stanley writes:

> The military's capacity and will to carry out extreme and completely unconstrained violence against civilians became the fundamental legitimating basis for military control of the state. . . . the military was allowed to control most of the state apparatus in exchange for periodically deploying force to protect the oligarchy's interest.[46]

Accordingly, after 1948, military rule was not by a personalistic dictator, but by the military as an institution, whose leaders formed part of a political party competing in elections (the National Conciliation Party—Partido de Conciliación Nacional, PCN). The regular elections gave an appearance of democracy, but the reality was fraud and, by the 1970s, intimidation.[47]

Political crises did occur; at several intervals, entrenched hard-line military presidents were ousted by reformist officers appealing to the causes of democracy and social justice. But these intervals were brief: a five-month period under General Andrés Ignacio Menéndez in 1944, a fourteen-month Revolutionary Council in 1948, and a three-month military-civilian junta in 1960. After each successful coup, the reformists were overthrown by officers concerned about the maintenance and coherence of the military institution, or their reformist impulses were muted amid co-optation.[48] The only one of these governments that had any long-standing impact was the 1948 Revolutionary Council, which advanced the political star of Major Oscar Osorio; elected to the presidency in 1950, Osorio encouraged industrialization, the diversification of agriculture, public works, and human needs projects. (This historical pattern was ultimately to be repeated, with some variations, in the coup of 1979.)

By the 1970s, the Salvadoran political model was in trouble.[49] The key problem was that the model "encouraged an active opposition but, by definition, forbade that opposition to come to power."[50] As a larger percentage of the Salvadoran people became politically mobilized and the political opposition became better institutionalized, the military resorted not only to fraud but also to violence to retain its monopoly of executive power. In 1966, for example, the paramilitary organization ORDEN was established; most of ORDEN's leaders were retired security officers and army reservists, and its ranks ultimately included between fifty thousand and one hundred thousand armed peasants.[51] During the 1970s, ORDEN was increasingly aggressive in stuffing ballot boxes and in attacking popular organizations and political opponents.[52]

For the first time in El Salvador, in 1972 the political opposition believed that it would win the presidential election. The Christian Democratic Party, the social democratic MNR, and the communist UD allied under the banner of the National Opposition Union (Unión Nacional Opositora, UNO). The popular, thrice-elected Christian Democratic mayor of San Salvador, José Napoleon Duarte, was the coalition's presidential candidate and the MNR's Guillermo Ungo was its vice presidential candidate. The governing PCN had been hurt politically by the outbreak of the war with Honduras and its aftermath. For the political opposition, the 1972 elections were a long-awaited moment—and a key test of the viability of the electoral path toward political and economic change.[53]

The Salvadoran government failed this test. When it became clear that the UNO coalition was leading the early returns in the 1972 election, the military government stopped media coverage of the results. The next announcement was that the official party's candidate, Colonel Arturo Molina, had won by 1.3 percent.[54] The coalition's militants urged Duarte to call a general strike, but, to their consternation, Duarte demurred, seemingly at a loss for what to do.[55] Outraged young army officers did stage a two-day rebellion in San Salvador, which was defeated by units from outside the capital.[56] Duarte had given his support to this rebellion; after its defeat, he was captured, badly beaten, and put on a plane to political exile.[57]

Most importantly for this study, in the aftermath of the fraudulent 1972 election, Marxist groups espousing violent alternatives grew dramatically, especially among students at the National University of El Salvador (see chapter 2). The FPL began to operate as a guerrilla organization immediately after the fraud, and the ERP was also formed soon afterward.[58] In an effort to quell the unrest at the university, it was attacked in July 1972 by military tanks and airplanes. Approximately eight hundred people were arrested in one day; perhaps as many as fifteen university leaders, including the president and the dean of the medical school, were flown into forced exile.[59] The university was closed down for two years by the Molina government.

Five years later, the obstruction of the electoral path to power for the Salvadoran political opposition was confirmed once again. With Duarte still in exile, the UNO coalition's standard-bearers were more mainstream than in 1972: Colonel Ernesto Claramont, a respected retired military officer, was the presidential candidate and Antonio Morales Erlich, a conservative Christian Democrat, was the vice presidential candidate.[60] These mainstream credentials did not sway the Salvadoran government to accept a UNO electoral victory, however. The government was more careful than in 1972 that the electoral "result" would be the desired one: 150,000 nonexistent voters were created, all of San Salvador's four hundred voting booths were situated on the outskirts of the city far from poor neighborhoods, opposition poll watchers were arrested or removed from numerous polling places, and ballot boxes were stuffed.[61]

The opposition's standard-bearer Claramont denounced the rigged elections and led a protest against them. For three consecutive days after the announcement of the electoral results, Claramont and his UNO supporters demonstrated in a main square in downtown San Salvador; by the end of the third day, their numbers had grown to as many as fifty thousand.[62] The option of a general strike was discussed. On the final night, however, security force personnel blocked the routes out of the square and then hosed, tear-gassed, and assaulted the demonstrators. In numerous other protests and strikes, crowds attacked official buildings and burned cars.[63] Some two hundred persons were killed by the military, and Claramont angrily followed Duarte into exile.[64]

The 1977 "elections" brought to power General Carlos Humberto Romero, who was more hard-line than his predecessor Molina.[65] Romero spurned all reformist measures and sought only to repress the nation's increasingly militant popular organizations. Political violence surged. Although precise counts of the victims of political violence were not being attempted at this time, by Dunkerley's estimate the average number of victims of political violence rose from dozens per month in 1977 to scores in 1978 and hundreds by mid-1979.[66] By another estimate, about 450 persons were assassinated by the military and paramilitary under Romero's government.[67] At the same time, leftist guerrillas increased their attacks; roughly 130 security force personnel were killed by guerrillas and more than a dozen businessmen kidnapped during Romero's tenure.[68]

Romero faced challenges both from his own military and from the international arena. Generational conflict erupted within the Salvadoran military; Romero was governing primarily with his colleagues from the military academy class of 1955 and was blocking the professional rise of a powerful group of officers from the class of 1957.[69] In the international arena, the general was criticized for his human rights record by U.S. president Jimmy Carter. Also, especially after July 1979, the Salvadoran security forces feared that the revolutionary movement would triumph in El Salvador as it had in Nicaragua. On 15 October 1979, General Romero was ousted, and El Salvador's post-1948 political regime ended.

Between 1979 and 1982, various civilian-military juntas governed El Salvador. Although a young, reformist military faction led the planning and execution of the coup against Romero, this faction proved as unable as its counterparts in similar previous political upheavals to consolidate its power.[70] Although the preparations for the coup had been directed by a colonel who was considered very astute, René Guerra, he was gradually sidelined; the apparently naive Colonel Adolfo Majano became the reformist faction's representative at the head of the Coordinating Committee. Through a variety of machinations, Colonel Jaime Abdul Gutiérrez, a bureaucrat allied with the military faction most concerned about the maintenance and coherence of the military institution (the "institutionalist" faction), became this group's representative at the head of the Coordinating Committee.[71] Immediately after the October coup, Gutiérrez appointed Colonel José Guillermo García, who was also a member of the institutionalist faction, as minister of defense; the reformist faction did not protest effectively.[72] García held effective control of the military apparatus.

Gradually, the reformist faction dissipated. In May 1980 Majano was demoted from his position as commander of the armed forces; in September, his reformist allies were removed from important troop commands; in November, an attempt was made upon his life; and, finally, in December, he was removed from the junta. The reasons were various. First, Majano was an inept and indecisive leader, failing to take advantage of political opportunities against opponents.[73] Second, among many officers there were perceptions that the U.S. embassy supported the institutionalist orientation.[74] Probably most important, however, was the fact that there was a third military faction—known as "the hard-liners." It was never entirely ousted from the post-1979 Salvadoran military, and it reasserted its power adeptly.

The hard-liner faction was headed by ex-Major Roberto D'Aubuisson, who had resigned from the intelligence unit of the National Guard in 1979 to protest the new junta's reformist program, and cooperated closely with the junta's deputy minister of defense, Colonel Nicolás Carranza.[75] Among the key resources of the hard-liner faction in its political reascendance were the military's fear of political division, given the severity of the guerrilla challenge; greater pressure on army officers to operate alongside the security forces, increasing the likelihood that these officers would commit human rights violations and then abandon reformist ideals; and the clarity and simplicity of the hard-liners' message relative to that of the reformists.[76] Important, too, were both economic rewards and physical intimidation.[77]

The years 1979–82 were the period of most intense repression by the military and paramilitary in El Salvador (see table 3.4, page 114). Although the Christian Democratic Party was a nominal governing partner in most of the civilian-military juntas during this period, it appeared unable to moderate the behavior of the Salvadoran military. Judicial Assistance (Socorro Jurídico, the legal support group of the Roman Catholic Archdiocese of San Salvador) estimated total civilian deaths at 1,000 in 1979, 9,000 to 10,000 in 1980, and 12,500 in 1981.[78] The military and paramilitary were responsible for approximately 85 percent of these deaths.[79] The victims included political party leaders, members of the popular organizations, and peacefully demonstrating groups, against whose ranks security force personnel frequently fired shots.[80]

Not only was the military and paramilitary violence intense, but its savage spiral extended to important civilian groups that at most critical moments in other Latin American nations had not been attacked (see also table 3.4). Approximately five hundred Christian Democratic political activists were killed.[81] A serious target was the Catholic Church: among the murdered were Archbishop Oscar Romero and four U.S. churchwomen. There was even an attack upon the tens of thousands of mourners who gathered for Archbishop Romero's funeral. In fear and anger, in 1980 many prominent leftist civilian political leaders (including Guillermo Ungo, the 1972 vice presidential candidate and a civilian member of the first 1979 junta) forged the FDR, expressing their support for the revolutionary path but not themselves taking up arms; five of its most important leaders were killed.[82]

Elections, 1980–91: Free from Political Violence and Fair?

In 1980 in Peru and 1982 in El Salvador, the electoral process was restored as the means by which the nation's government was to be decided. Table 3.1 provides the results for the presidential contests in the two countries during the 1980s. Presidential and legislative elections

Table 3.1. Results of Presidential Contests in Peru and El Salvador, 1980–90

Peru

	1980	1985	1990
Winning party	Acción Popular	APRA	Cambio 90
President-elect	Fernando Belaúnde	Alan García	Alberto Fujimori
Winning party's tally	45%	53%	29%
Party in second place	APRA (27%)	Izquierda Unida (25%)	FREDEMO[a] (33%)

El Salvador

	1982 (Constituent Assembly)	1984	1989
Winning party	Christian Democratic	Christian Democratic	ARENA
Ensuing president	Alvaro Magaña[b]	Napoleon Duarte	Alfredo Cristiani
Winning party's tally	40%	43%	54%
Party in second place	ARENA (30%)	ARENA (30%)	Christian Democratic (35%)

Sources: For Peru, Webb and Fernández Baca (1991, 1028–1030). For El Salvador, Montgomery (1995, 161).

Note: All percentages are percentages of valid votes in the first round. In Peru, both Izquierda Unida and FREDEMO were coalitions of parties.

[a]Coalition of parties led by Mario Vargas Llosa, which won the first round but lost the second.

[b]See discussion in text. Although the Christian Democratic Party won a plurality, its tally was exceeded by the combined votes of ARENA and PCN, which (after discussions with the U.S. ambassador) chose Magaña as president.

were held concurrently in Peru in 1980, 1985, and 1990; the winners of the respective presidential contests were Acción Popular's Fernando Belaúnde Terry, APRA's Alan García, and Cambio 90's Alberto Fujimori. Municipal elections were also held in 1980, 1983, 1986, and 1989. In El Salvador, Constituent Assembly elections were held in 1982; presidential elections followed in 1984 and 1989, bringing first the Christian Democrats' Napoleon Duarte to the executive office and then Alfredo Cristiani of ARENA (National Republican Alliance, Alianza Républicana Nacionalista). Midterm legislative and municipal elections were held concurrently in 1985, 1988, and 1991.

The assessment of elections is a complex task.[83] Unfortunately, this section does not establish threshold numbers for political violence above which an election is not "free," nor threshold percentages of disputed ballot counts or voters excluded from balloting above which an election is not "fair." However, the comparison between Salvadoran and Peruvian elections here holds each country up to the standard of the other—and consistently shows Salvadoran elections to fall far short.[84] In particular, comparison of tables 3.3, 3.4, and 3.5 indicates that military and paramilitary violence against politically salient civilians in El Salvador was many times more intense than in Peru, especially during the critical early 1980s period as the FMLN was attaining its strategic apex and the Shining Path was expanding in Peru's southern highlands. Also, comparison of tables 3.2, 3.7, 3.8, and 3.9 suggests that "irregularities" were much more prevalent in the Salvadoran elections than in the Peruvian, and that, after 1984, the Salvadoran government was not trying to implement procedures that would make the vote accessible to all citizens, whereas the Peruvian government was. Accordingly, the data in this section also support my argument that political exclusion was the catalyst of the revolutionary movement in El Salvador, but not in Peru.

Judgments of Freedom and Fairness by Opposing Political Parties and by the Country's Citizens

Without empirical thresholds for the classification of an election as "free and fair," scholars should consider the classifications of the opposing political parties themselves, as well as those of the country's citizens. It is indeed astounding, given the paucity of objective summary indicators, how rarely scholars include evaluations by a country's citizens as at least a guidepost. Although it is true that both opposing political actors' and citizens' judgments may be colored by the electoral practices of the past, these judgments are one of the few summary indicators available. And, of course, elections are believed to matter because it is hoped they will be perceived as the legitimate arbiter of political power by the country's citizens.

In Peru, the freedom and fairness of elections were rarely questioned by the opposing political parties during the 1980s. The Marxist left participated in elections throughout the period without systematic harassment from government authorities. Especially by the late 1980s and in rural areas, the quality of elections was damaged by fears of political violence, but most electorally related violence was perpetrated by the guerrillas themselves.

Table 3.2. Citizens' Evaluations of Electoral Freedom and Fairness
(percentages)

	Lima 1990 (N = 400)	El Salvador 1991 (N = 415)	Ecuador 1991 (N = 500)
1. There is liberty rather than fear in the expression of opinions here.[a]	37	17	34
2. Elections here have been correct and accessible to all.[b]	60	33	20

Sources: Datum 1990 Lima survey; Orellana 1991 El Salvador survey; CEDATOS 1991 Ecuador survey. See appendix 1 for more information about the surveys.

[a]Item: "In (Peru/El Salvador/Ecuador) is there fear in the expression of opinions or is there liberty?"

[b]Item: "During the last ten years or so, there have been various elections in (Peru/El Salvador/Ecuador). In general, do you think that these elections have been fraudulent and/or inaccessible to all, or have they been correct and accessible to all?"

By contrast, throughout this period the FMLN maintained that its members would not be accepted as legitimate participants in the electoral process by traditional civilian and military elites. Gradually, however, during the course of the decade, the center, center-left, and left did perceive a political opening by Salvadoran elites and did accede to electoral competition: in the mid-1980s, the centrist or center-leftist Christian Democratic Party was accepted as a legitimate contender for presidential power by most traditional civilian and military elites; and, in the late 1980s, social democratic and Marxist leaders who had formed the CD and not actually fought as guerrillas seemed to be on the path toward acceptance as legitimate contenders for power by traditional elites. Only after the 1992 peace accord, however, was the FMLN sufficiently confident of the quality of the Salvadoran electoral process that it decided to participate.

Citizens' evaluations of electoral processes in Peru, El Salvador, and Ecuador circa 1990–91 are reported in table 3.2. The table shows that, in all three countries, fear of expressing opinions was marked—but that it was most widespread in El Salvador. Only 17 percent of Salvadorans believed that there was freedom of expression in their country. The figure for the Peruvian sample was 37 percent—low, but more than double the percentage for El Salvador and (surprisingly) more than the figure for Ecuador. In another survey in the same year, the number of

Salvadorans who said that there was liberty rather than fear in the expression of opinions was similarly low: 20 percent.[85] When the Salvadoran and Peruvian figures are compared, it should be noted also that the security forces in El Salvador were the perpetrators of a larger percentage of the total deaths than in Peru (see table 3.5, page 117)—suggesting greater government complicity in the climate of fear in El Salvador than in Peru. Still, the fact that most Peruvians did not believe that there was liberty of expression raises questions about the quality of Peruvian democracy at the time.

Table 3.2 also shows dramatically more positive attitudes in Peru than in El Salvador about the correctness and openness of elections. Sixty percent of the Peruvian sample believed that their country's elections were procedurally correct and accessible to all citizens—almost double the 33 percent figure in El Salvador and (surprisingly) almost triple the 20 percent figure in Ecuador. Other datasets demonstrate similar differences in the assessments of fairness of elections in Peru and El Salvador. In one nationwide 1990 survey, only 20 percent of Peruvian respondents did not have "confidence that the National Elections Council would act independently and impartially in the upcoming elections."[86] The percentages were reversed in El Salvador: a scant 19 percent of Salvadorans were confident that "there would not be electoral fraud"; 41 percent thought that there would be fraud and another 40 percent were not sure.[87] Slightly later, in 1993, when the quality of Peruvian elections had declined and the quality of Salvadoran elections had improved, a cross-national survey indicated that 62 percent of Peruvian respondents "trusted" the elections in Peru, versus 42 percent in El Salvador and a mere 35 percent in Ecuador.[88]

Peruvian and Salvadoran Elections: How Free from Fear?

The assessments by Peruvians and Salvadorans in table 3.2 indicating fear in the expression of opinions are borne out by the empirical data on political violence in the two countries. The data in this section show that, in Peru, paramilitary and military violence against civilian groups was minimal during the initial years of the decade, as the conflict began. By the end of the decade, however, human rights violations in Peru had risen to harrowing levels; still, even during the years of the most extreme numbers of violations (roughly, 1989–91), the toll was much

Table 3.3. Military/Paramilitary Violence against Politically Salient Civilian Groups: Peru, 1982–91

	1982–85	1986–90	1991
		(total number of deaths during the period)	
Political Activists[a]	2	10	6
Union Activists[b]	2	11	0
Journalists	2[c]	3	3
Human Rights Monitors	0	4	0
Church People	7	0	0

Sources: U.S. Department of State *Country Reports on Human Rights Practices*, 1982–90; all Americas Watch publications on Peru 1984–92; Instituto de Defensa Legal (1990, 1991, and 1992); Amnesty International (1989 and 1992); Lawyers' Committee for Human Rights (1990). Data compiled primarily by Kathy Landauer, research assistant.

[a]Includes government officials, former government officials, and members of political parties.

[b]Includes leaders of peasant communities.

[c]Peruvian journalists killed at Uchuraccay are not included. The journalists were killed by peasants, but the peasants may have received signals that the military would approve the killings.

less heavy than in El Salvador in the early 1980s. In El Salvador, the early 1980s were a period of egregious military and paramilitary violence; after 1984, the level of violence was still considerable in absolute terms—roughly similar to Peru on some indicators—but was much less than in the early 1980s. The contrasting trends in the two countries suggest that military/paramilitary violence was primarily a result of the guerrilla conflict in Peru, but a cause of it in El Salvador.

These points are documented in the subsequent tables in this section. The tables represent various kinds of efforts at comparison of the levels of political violence in the two countries. The first two tables—tables 3.3 and 3.4—report the numbers of civilian deaths in politically salient groups in Peru and El Salvador, respectively. The two tables are based on precisely the same research strategy: the reading of all relevant available documents, in English and Spanish, by my research assistant, and her tally of all deaths for which precise identifications were given in the texts—usually the actual names of the dead individuals, or at least dates and professional backgrounds. Given that it is certain that the methodology for the tallying of the figures in the two tables is the same, these figures are the most rigorously comparable in the section. Of course, the numbers in the two tables are very different from total numbers of

Table 3.4. Military/Paramilitary Violence against Politically Salient Civilian Groups: El Salvador, 1979–90

	October 1979–March 1982[a] (calculated on annual basis)	1982	1983	1984	1985	1986	1987	1988	1989	1990
Political Activists[b]	*200*[c]	26	7					1	3	2
Union Activists[d]	*1,500*[e]	22	27		21	1	8	7	28	2
Journalists	10	4							3	
Human Rights Monitors	2	2					1		2	
Church People	24		10						5	

Sources (unless otherwise indicated): All Americas Watch and American Civil Liberties Union publications; 1982–90 figures reflect only confirmed deaths and disappearances (when the latter are identified by name). Data compiled primarily by Jocelyn Nieva, research assistant, United States Institute of Peace. Numbers in *italics* are rough estimates.

[a]Although approximately 50 percent of all deaths occurred during 1980 and 1981 (United Nations Commission on the Truth for El Salvador, 1993, 44), formal human rights monitoring was impossible, primarily because of attacks against monitors. Annual calculations were made for many figures by dividing by 2.5.

[b]Includes civilian authorities, political candidates, party members, and people formerly in these positions. Figure for 1989 includes three leaders from the Popular Social Christian Movement. See Leogrande (1990, 341).

[c]Well-documented assasinations include one PDC and six FDR leaders in 1980. However, President Duarte reported that 600 Christian Democratic Party members, including 20 mayors, were killed during this period (U.S. Senate, 1982, 8). Given the determination by the United Nations Commission on the Truth for El Salvador that 85 percent of acts of political violence were attributed to military or paramilitary groups, I calculated 510 Christian Democrat victims (and divided by 2.5 for an annual figure).

[d]Figures include agricultural cooperative members, teachers' union members, and others.

[e]FENASTRAS reported 8,329 members murdered, abducted, disappeared, or wounded during this period (Americas Watch and American Civil Liberties Union, 1982b, 122). My estimate is made by assuming that half of these were killed and that 85 percent of deaths were the responsibility of the military or paramilitary, and then dividing by 2.5 for an annual figure.

civilian deaths. Rather, the figures report the deaths that were most salient to human rights groups in the United States and in the two countries; the deaths were also likely to have been those most politically intimidating to the nations' citizens.

Table 3.3 provides the figures for assassinations of politically salient civilians in Peru between 1982 and 1991. (There were virtually no assassinations of politically salient civilians in Peru between 1980 and 1982.)[89] The years in the columns in the table correspond as closely as possible to presidential terms: the 1982–85 column for the Belaúnde administration, the 1986–90 column for García, and 1991 for Fujimori. The figures in the table are totals for these periods; of course, they must be divided by the relevant number of years to yield the figure that may be compared with the data in the table for El Salvador.

When the data in Table 3.3 are calculated on an annual basis, it is clear that military and paramilitary violence was increasing in Peru during the decade. In particular, in 1987 a death squad appeared in Peru. Taking its name from a prominent Aprista killed by the Shining Path, the Comando Rodrigo Franco claimed as its first victim a lawyer who defended Shining Path suspects. Its later assassinations included various prominent political leaders: two members of the Chamber of Deputies and the president of the miners' union.[90] Between 1989 and the end of García's term in mid-1990, about thirteen civilian deaths were attributed to the death squad.[91] The political and intellectual auspices of the Comando Rodrigo Franco have not yet been clearly identified.[92]

Table 3.4 shows the comparable figures for El Salvador. Between October 1979 and the March 1982 Constituent Assembly elections, military/paramilitary violence against politically salient civilian groups in El Salvador was extraordinarily savage—much more so than at any time in Peru. During this period, the Salvadoran military and civilian elites were reluctant to open the electoral process not only to Marxist-left participants but also to the Christian Democrats. Death squads killed approximately 500 Christian Democratic Party members, including about seventeen mayors (see table 3.4, footnote c). Severe repression also hit union activists, church people, and journalists. The repression blatantly restricted free speech; in 1980, there were two newspapers critical of the government in El Salvador, but both were closed during the months prior to the Constituent Assembly election.[93]

After the Constituent Assembly elections and the return to a formal constitutional order, military/paramilitary violence declined in El Salvador. Still, as of 1983, the number of politically salient civilian deaths attributed to the military or paramilitary was much higher than for any year in Peru. Only during the presidential term of the Christian Democrat Duarte did the number of politically salient civilian deaths decline to the approximate level in Peru during the same period. The figures in the table may, however, be overly positive, reflecting perhaps a slight decline in international human rights groups' monitoring of El Salvador.[94] Carothers reports that in 1987 and 1988 "hundreds of human rights activists, labor leaders, community organizers, student leaders, and other civilian actors were tortured and murdered."[95] Political violence again surged way beyond Peruvian levels in 1989, as ARENA led the field for the presidential election and the FMLN set the stage for the November offensive.[96]

The data in tables 3.5 and 3.6 represent a different approach to comparison of the levels of political violence in Peru and El Salvador. In contrast to tables 3.3 and 3.4, tables 3.5 and 3.6 report data compiled by human rights institutions in the two countries, using their own methodologies. Also, whereas tables 3.3 and 3.4 report the deaths of civilians for whom precise references are given in human rights reports, the figures in tables 3.5 and 3.6 approximate as closely as possible the total numbers of deaths—sometimes exclusively civilian deaths and sometimes not—in the two countries. Given differences in the research strategies and research conditions in the two countries, the validity of cross-national comparison of the data is uncertain.

Table 3.5 first reports the total death toll from political violence (including not only civilians but also security force personnel and guerrilla combatants) in the two countries between 1982 and 1992. Given that the source for the Salvadoran data is Tutela Legal and that it only initiated its reports in May 1982, the data for El Salvador for 1982 omit one-third of the year; the figure for El Salvador for the entire year would almost certainly exceed five thousand.[97] The table again shows extremely high levels of political violence in El Salvador in 1982 and 1983, declining slightly in 1984 and 1985 and then dropping considerably thereafter, with the exception of 1989. In Peru, the death toll in 1982 is tiny relative to the toll in the country after that year or at any time in

Table 3.5. Political Violence in Peru and El Salvador, 1982–92

	1982[a]	1983	1984	1985	1986	1987	1988	1989	1990	1991	1992
Peru											
Total Deaths	193	1,979	3,588	1,437	1,376	1,136	1,511	2,877	3,745	3,044	2,683
Deaths Attributed to Military/ Paramilitary in Military Clashes[b]	109	1,226	1,721	630	781	341	404	1,175	1,879	1,375	934
Assassinations[c]	N.A.	N.A.	N.A.	N.A.	N.A.	N.A.	N.A.	39	82	99	114
El Salvador											
Total Deaths	3,371	6,639	4,274	3,036	1,709	1,434	1,387	2,875	1,525	N.A.	N.A.
Deaths Attributed to Military/ Paramilitary in Military Clashes[d]	1,839	3,856	3,027	1,999	1,120	851	829	2,074	863	N.A.	N.A.
Assassinations[e]	1,231	1,286	225	146	59	34	66	43	46	N.A.	N.A.

Sources: For first two rows for Peru, DESCO, *Reporte Especial*, no. 32 (December 1993): 6. For "assassinations": for 1989 and 1990, Chipoco (1992, 220); and for 1990–92, Coordinadora Nacional de Derechos Humanos data (including deaths by *ronderos*) reported in *Ideele*, no. 48 (March 1993): 28. For El Salvador, Tutela Legal annual reports.

Note: The figures are estimates; some are my own tabulations of data that do not otherwise precisely fit my categories. N.A. = not available.

[a] 1982 figures for El Salvador are May–December only and do not include deaths of guerillas.

[b] Generally, civilians could not be distinguished from combatants; in Peru, all victims were listed as "presumed subversives."

[c] Killings believed by human rights groups to be of civilians. Drug traffickers' deaths are excluded.

[d] Includes civilians and combatants, who could not be distinguished from one another.

[e] The figure is for deaths attributed to death squads (and, when indicated, other security forces) in Tutela Legal's annual report. Tutela Legal staff indicated to me that these were targeted killings (presumably primarily of civilians). Figures are low, as other progovernment armed groups committed targeted assassinations.

Table 3.6. Forced Disappearances in Peru and El Salvador, 1982–92

	Peru	El Salvador
1982[a]	2	363
1983	433	535
1984	416	53
1985	208	60
1986	257	96
1987	133	118
1988	230	123
1989	440	218
1990	246	91
1991	304	N.A.
1992	287	N.A.

Note: As these data were compiled by different institutions using different methodologies, the validity of cross-national comparison is uncertain. However, all figures are for new complaints of disappearances made during the year against progovernment forces and exclude "reappearances." The Peruvian and Salvadoran governments denied the validity of many complaints.

Sources: For Peru data: *PerúPaz,* 13, no. 18 (January 1994): 20. The compilation of these data was directed by Enrique Bernales, first when he was a member of a special committee on political violence in the Peruvian senate and later as president of the institute publishing *PerúPaz.* The special committee in the Peruvian senate worked with local human rights groups to present documented cases of disappearances to the United Nations Human Rights Commission Working Group on Forced or Involuntary Disappearances. Local human rights groups' figures varied widely; for example, preliminary estimates for 1991 included 43, 62, 199, 208, and 207, according to Comision Especial de Investigacion y Estudio sobre la Violencia y Alternativas de Pacificacion (1992, chapter 4, table 18). In part due to the severe geographic obstacles, investigations into disappearances and clarification of the character of the human rights violation were especially difficult in Peru.

For El Salvador data: Annual reports by Tutela Legal. The figures for 1982 and 1983 are for the precise number of "disappeared" reported by Tutela Legal; for 1984–90, the figures include both "disappeared" and "captured-disappeared" (captured and subsquently disappeared). The figures exclude those "captured," although those captured were often tortured prior to submission to a military trial; they also exclude those captured who were subsequently released.

[a]1982 data for El Salvador are for May–December only.

El Salvador. Deaths skyrocket in Peru in 1983 and 1984—primarily as a result of indiscriminate attacks by the armed forces in the southern highlands during the final years of the Belaúnde government. During the initial years of the García administration, the death toll declines, only to jump again after 1988 (see table 3.5).

The second row of data for Peru and El Salvador in table 3.5 reports the annual figures for "deaths attributed to military/paramilitary in military clashes." For obvious reasons, in neither country was it possible for any organization to distinguish between guerrillas and civilians among those killed in a military confrontation; the ratios would have varied by year and area within the country.[98] The figures for Peru correspond to the tallies for "presumed subversives" in most reports on the death toll in the country.[99] In general, the figures for deaths in military clashes are considerably lower in Peru than in El Salvador, and a considerably lower percentage of the overall death toll, indicating that conventional military clashes were a less significant component of the war in Peru than in El Salvador.

The data in table 3.5 most relevant to the theme of this section are the figures for "assassinations." Unfortunately, in Peru these figures were compiled only for a few years toward the end of the conflict.[100] The lack of compilation reflects the relative paucity of such assassinations in the early 1980s, as well as the difficulties of confirmation of such assassinations, most of which occurred in remote, war-torn areas where mass grave sites were hard to find. Given that the bodies of many victims of assassinations were never identified, these deaths were recorded as forced disappearances. It is for this reason that there were fewer assassinations but more forced disappearances in Peru than in El Salvador.[101] In any case, for the purposes of this section, the most significant figures in table 3.5 are those for assassinations by the military or paramilitary in El Salvador in 1982 and 1983—figures that are much higher than for the sum of assassinations and forced disappearances in Peru in any year.

Table 3.6 reports the number of forced disappearances in Peru and El Salvador. For the reasons just mentioned, whereas on most indicators of human rights violations the record of the Peruvian security forces was not as poor as that of the Salvadoran security forces, with respect to forced disappearances the record of the Peruvian security forces was worse for most of the decade. However, when the figures for forced disappearances are added to those for assassinations to provide a sum of civilian victims of security forces, the sum for Peru is considerably lower than for El Salvador during the early 1980s.

Did the political violence intimidate potential candidates, poll-watchers, and voters? As table 3.2 suggests, the overall effect was chilling in both countries. In Peru, however, given that it was the Shining Path that was opposed to elections and that the military accepted universal participation in electoral processes, citizens' fears were almost exclusively of violence from the guerrillas.[102] In El Salvador, by contrast, there was widespread fear that becoming a candidate for the "left" (however "left" was defined at the time), serving as a poll-watcher for the "left," or even voting for a "left" candidate would spark retaliation by the political right.[103]

Consider, for example, the intensity of attacks against the CD party in 1991—even as peace negotiations were under way and FDR leaders had opted to form the CD and participate in the midterm legislative elections. The CD's headquarters in Usulután was damaged by a grenade; one party member was captured, beaten, and burned with cigarettes on his chest by members of the Salvadoran Artillery Brigade; another party member in Santa Ana was detained and threatened; death threats were made against grassroots activists in diverse parts of the country; and many party rallies were harassed by soldiers or civil defense members.[104] The gravest attack was the assassination of a municipal candidate for the small communist party, the UDN, after he had ignored telephone threats on his life.[105] Also, the Salvadoran newspaper that was most critical of the government, *El Diario Latino,* was badly damaged in a fire; although the cause of the fire was not determined, the incident was interpreted by many Salvadorans as harassment against the political left.[106]

As a result, in many villages where support for the political left was known to be strong, no leftist candidates dared to come forward in 1991.[107] The CD fielded candidates for less than 30 percent of the country's municipalities.[108] Whereas on election day ARENA enjoyed phalanxes of voting-table officials and poll monitors wearing large smocks with the party's colors and emblem, and the PCN and the Christian Democrats were also relatively well represented, the CD was frequently absent.[109] It should be noted too that, between 1982 and 1988 in El Salvador, ballots were numbered and urns were transparent, reinforcing many Salvadorans' fears that the government "has ways of knowing how you voted."[110]

Peruvian and Salvadoran Elections: How Fair?

As with respect to freedom of expression, citizens' views about the fairness of elections are borne out by the available empirical evidence. In Peru, there was widespread commitment to the principle of universal access to the electoral process, and "transparent," clean electoral procedures; in El Salvador, there was no such commitment.[111] During the

Table 3.7. Electoral Turnout in Peru, 1980–90
(all figures except percentages in millions)

	Estimated Potentially Eligible Population	Registered Voters	Actual Voters	Turnout (% of eligible voters)	Turnout (% of registered voters)
Presidential Elections					
1980	9.2	6.5	5.3	58	82
1985	10.3	8.3	7.6	74	92
1990[a]	11.4	10.0	7.7	67	77
Midterm Elections					
1980	9.2	6.5	4.6	50	71
1983	9.8	7.5	4.8	49	64
1986	10.4	8.3	6.5	63	78
1989	11.2	9.9	6.3	56	64

Sources: Estimated annual population from Webb and Fernández Baca (1991, 115). United Nations demographic yearbooks during the 1980s indicate that the percentage of the population aged 18 and over was 53 percent. All electoral data from 1980 through 1986 from Fernando Tuesta Soldevilla (1987, 191, 199, 207, 215, and 223). For the 1989 election and 1990 elections, data from Webb and Fernández Baca (1991, 1021 and 1030).
[a]First round. Turnout was slightly up in the second round.

decade, improvement on these scores in El Salvador was scant—less evident than with respect to the human rights violations and the opening to center-left and left parties indicated in the previous section.

The commitment in Peru to universal access to the electoral process was reflected in the high rate of voter turnout in the country between 1980 and 1990 (see table 3.7). Turnout averaged 66 percent of the eligible population during the three presidential elections of the decade, a percentage higher than that in many industrialized countries and much higher than in El Salvador (see table 3.8).[112] Turnout was at an apex during the 1985 presidential election, when the charismatic Alan García was riding into power on a tremendous wave of political popularity. As would be expected, turnout was greater for presidential elections than for the midterm municipal elections. The table also shows that, during the decade, a gradually increasing percentage of the potentially eligible population registered to vote, until by 1990 more than 87 percent of the eligible population was registered.

Table 3.8. Estimated Electoral Turnout in El Salvador, 1980–94
(all figures except percentages in millions)

	Eligible Population[a]	Registered Voters	Actual Voters	Turnout (% of eligible voters)	Turnout (% of registered voters)
Presidential Elections					
1984[b]	2.3	N.A.	1.5*	65*	N.A.
1989[c]	2.5	1.8	1.0	40	55
1994[d]	2.7	2.3	1.4	52	61
Midterm Elections					
1985[e]	2.3	N.A.	1.1*	48*	N.A.
1988[f]	2.4	1.65	1.15	48	69
1991[g]	2.6	2.18	1.15	44	53

Note: N.A. = not applicable. There was no voter registration in El Salvador until 1988.

*Figures are overestimates because of double-voting, etc., without a registration system.

[a]Calculation is imprecise because there was no recent census until 1993. At briefings on 10 September 1993, Tommie Sue Montgomery and on 9 March 1994, Ken Ellis, director of the Central America Office of U.S. AID, provided the figure of 2.7 million "voting age population." Calculations for earlier years are based on this figure, reduced for estimates of rate of adult population growth in United Nations Demographic Yearbook, and estimates in data from Ministerio de Planificación, *Indicadores ecónomicos y sociales, años 1987–1989* (San Salvador, 1990), 112. Both these sources indicate 58 percent of the Salvadoran population to be age 18 and over. For similar estimates for 1984, see *New York Times*, 24 March 1984, 4, and 25 March 1984, 12; for 1988, *Economist*, 26 March 1988; for 1989, USCEOM (1994, 7) and *Economist*, 25 March 1989, 44; and for 1991, the United Nations (1990, 4).

[b]Second round. Source: Ricardo Cordova M., "Periodización del proceso de crisis (1979–1988)," in CINAS (1988, 98).

[c]Montes (1989, 205–207).

[d]First Round. USCEOM (1994, 3); Ken Ellis, director of Central America Office, U.S. AID; *Washington Post*, 20 March 1994, A33, and 22 March 1994, A11.

[e]CINAS (1988, 100).

[f]Montes (1989, 205–207).

[g]Acevedo (1991, 10–15).

These high figures reflected in part the mandatory character of registration and voting in Peru. On reaching eighteen years of age, individuals were required to register; the voting card *(libreta electoral)* was functionally akin to a driver's license in many industrialized countries, necessary for all kinds of transactions. Obtaining the card was relatively easy, normally requiring only one visit to the relevant authorities. At no time during the decade were there charges either that the electoral authorities were issuing more than one card per voter, or that they were denying cards to political opponents. On election day, the card was stamped, and this stamp was also necessary for transactions; nonvoters had to pay a fine to secure the stamp. While the principle of mandatory voting is not universally endorsed, it does suggest a national commitment to popular participation. However, compulsory voting was not the only factor in Peru's high turnout rates during this period; turnout rates fell after Fujimori's *autogolpe* and were not very high in El Salvador in the 1984 and 1985 elections, when voting was mandatory there.[113]

No political party alleged widespread fraud in any of Peru's three presidential elections.[114] In most cases, electoral results were similar to public opinion forecasts as well as to exit polls.[115] Certain relatively minor questions did emerge: In 1980, registration efforts were less intensive than they were to become, and several parties complained about the lack of voting tables for transients.[116] In 1985, the primary issue was the withdrawal from the expected runoff of the United Left's Alfonso Barrantes (who had finished second, but way behind Alan García, in the first round); some parties charged that his withdrawal was unconstitutional but, especially in the wake of an assassination attempt against the president of the National Elections Tribunal, the view that the runoff was unnecessary prevailed.[117] Despite Fujimori's surprising showing in the first round of the 1990 elections, the result was not questioned.[118]

Nor were there any significant complaints about the municipal process in 1980 or 1983.[119] However, the 1986 and 1989 municipal elections were both deficient in various respects. The 1986 contest was the only election of the decade in which the governing party (in this case, APRA) was perceived to be taking advantage of official resources and several important results were seriously questioned.[120] In particular, the triumph of APRA's Jorge del Castillo in the Lima mayoralty contest was challenged by both the United Left and the Popular Christian Party (Partido Popular Cristiano, PPC).[121]

The 1989 municipal contest was also marred. There were no significant irregularities in Lima or departmental capitals; the competing parties endorsed the electoral tallies.[122] Preliminary results (which were generally unfavorable for the governing party) were announced for Lima on election night and for departmental capitals within a day or two.[123] But, amid the increasing political violence and Shining Path control of many rural areas, elections were not viable in many parts of Peru. In approximately 28 percent of Peru's electoral districts, state authorities were not renewed, largely because, fearing Sendero, no candidates would run.[124] Frightened electoral authorities delivered voting materials incorrectly and tardily.[125] Also, many electoral authorities apparently lacked the resources or the courage to contact remote municipalities and finalize electoral tallies for these areas; official results for the 1989 election were delayed for more than a year, and the validity of the ultimate tallies is dubious.[126]

By contrast, in El Salvador, incumbent governments were not committed to the principles of universal access to the electoral process or transparency of electoral counts. Before the introduction of registration procedures in 1988, double-voting, ballot stuffing, and other partisan efforts to manipulate electoral outcomes were blatant. After 1988, incumbent governments seemed most intent on suppressing the country's potential vote for the political left. Throughout the period, suspicions that ballots were not honestly counted were rampant. Also, as chapter 5 discusses, U.S. pressures skewed electoral results on several occasions; although U.S. intervention may have secured outcomes that were ultimately more favorable for political peace in El Salvador than would otherwise have been the case, the U.S. role may also have persuaded some Salvadorans that the winners of elections were determined in the proverbial smoke-filled rooms, rather than at the ballot boxes. All these factors seem to be reflected in the low voter turnout rates in El Salvador after 1984 (see table 3.8).

For the 1982 constituent assembly elections, the 1984 presidential elections, and the 1985 midterm elections, no comprehensive registration system was in place; an identity card was all that was necessary to vote. Accordingly, municipal electoral authorities would issue many identity cards to their political allies. Commented Arriaza Meléndez: "It was known that the mayoralties would issue identity cards in great quantities to persons who did not meet the age requirements, and issue various cards to the same person, just changing the name, or even with the same name but assigned to a different voting district."[127]

The 1982 Constituent Assembly election was probably the least fair of all Salvadoran elections during this period. Voter turnout was inflated not only by double-voting but also by ballot stuffing and even manipulating tallies forwarded from municipalities by the military-controlled communications company.[128] All these practices led to inflation of the official turnout figures (see table 3.8). No less an authority than the next Central Elections Council (Consejo Central de Elecionnes, CCE) president asserted that more than 25 percent of the votes in the 1982 election were false; other CCE members estimated 15 percent to 25 percent.[129] The estimate by scholars on the political left was as high as 87 percent, based on their calculation of the total amount of voting time available at polling sites and the amount of time necessary to cast a ballot.[130]

Given the blatant character of the inflation of the 1982 vote, corrective measures were taken. For the 1984 election, a master list of potential voters was compiled by the CCE, based on birth, identity card, and death records, and for the 1988 election an actual registration procedure was introduced. Although the new procedure reduced the incidence of double-voting and ballot stuffing, other strategies that skewed electoral outcomes were initiated. In particular, obtaining the voting card and identifying the correct voting table became onerous for many Salvadorans; the new burdens fell disproportionately upon the poor and the illiterate, who were assumed to be more likely to vote for the political left.

Whereas in earlier years the Salvadoran electoral procedures falsely inflated the number of voters, the later procedures reduced turnout. In contrast to Peru, voting was not mandatory, and a voting card was not akin to a driver's license in the United States. Accordingly, when it became apparent that securing a voting card was a demanding process —requiring a minimum of two visits to the electoral authorities—many Salvadorans opted out. In 1989, 17 percent of Salvadorans who applied for their voting cards could not return to pick them up.[131]

The onerousness of the new procedures was an important factor in the declining turnout in El Salvador's 1989 and 1991 elections (see table 3.8). Consider, in particular, the small number of voters in El Salvador in 1988, 1989, and 1991 relative to 1994 (see table 3.8). Turnout as a percentage of eligible voters in El Salvador's 1989 election was 34 percentage points below that in Peru in 1985 and 27 percentage points below that in Peru in 1990 (see tables 3.7 and 3.8). (Of course, other factors were at work too, in particular disillusionment among Christian Democratic voters.)

It also became much more difficult for unsophisticated Salvadorans to locate and reach their voting table. Salvadoran and Peruvian voters cast their ballots at the table corresponding to the number on their identity card or voting card; at the table, their names were checked against the authorities' master list. In contrast to Peruvian (and U.S.) practice, however, voting tables in El Salvador were not assigned on the basis of the citizen's neighborhood within a municipality but exclusively on an alphabetical basis for the entire municipality; citizens in one neighborhood of San Salvador, for example, often had to travel to the other side of the city to vote—only to discover that there was a mistake and their actual voting site was miles away in another neighborhood of the city. One journalist's comment about the 1984 presidential election has applied virtually ever since: "Anti-fraud rules . . . may have disenfranchised a quarter of the electorate. People were shuttled from voting table to voting table, unable to find the proper place to cast their ballots; many never found it and left frustrated and discouraged."[132] One Salvadoran poll-watcher in the eastern city of San Miguel reported that 50 percent of the people approaching her voting table were turned away.[133] Also, whereas in Peru traditionally two hundred voters were assigned to a table, in El Salvador the number was four hundred. This arrangement only exacerbated delays and confusion.

Although it has not been possible to prove that electoral authorities discriminated against leftist political opponents in the distribution of voting cards or in access to the ballot box on election day, there have been strong suspicions of such discrimination. Some municipal councils were perceived to reject or delay applications for electoral cards from political enemies or to purposely omit their names from the registry.[134] Many analysts believed also that areas of strong leftist support were more affected by election-day irregularities (late arrival of ballots, errors in the printing of the ballots, marked ballots thrown out, last-minute shifting of the polling place, and so forth).[135]

Other problems were common as well. Voters were pressured by security force personnel in favor of ARENA; votes were bought by parties; indelible ink, to be applied so that voters could not cast their ballots twice, was not used.[136] (The ink was applied regularly in Peru.)

Also of great importance was that ballots may not have been tabulated honestly in Salvadoran elections between 1982 and 1991. In contrast to

Table 3.9. Citizens' Explanations of Low Turnout in El Salvador in 1991
(percentages)

Obstacles raised by electoral authorities[a]	26
There is mistrust and lack of credibility	16
There is fear and insecurity	18
They don't have *carnets*[b]	14
There is lack of motivation and civic spirit	8
They don't like the parties/candidates	4
Obstacles raised by the guerillas	7
Other, don't know	10

Source: Orellana survey. For information about the survey, see appendix I. $N = 415$. Survey item: "Why did many people not vote in the March 10 (municipal and legislative) elections?"

[a]Includes: "*carnet* was not given out"; "they didn't find themselves on the electoral list"; "problems caused by the Consejo Central de Elecciones"; "no transportation."

[b]In contrast to the response "*carnet* was not given out," implying blame on the electoral authorities, this answer could assign blame to authorities or to individuals.

Peruvian elections and to the 1994 Salvadoran election, independent exit polls or "quick count" samples from voting tables were not conducted, and there were long delays in the reporting of the official results. As late as the 1988 and 1991 elections, after the introduction of modern communications and computer systems by the United States, almost two weeks elapsed between election day and the announcement of any real results.[137] The only available explanation for the long delay in El Salvador seemed to be political negotiation among the higher-level councils in the "scrutiny" of votes (about invalid votes, for example) or—worse yet, but frequently rumored—manipulation of the results by computer.[138]

Overall, was there an improvement in the fairness of Salvadoran elections between 1982 and 1991? In my view, improvement is difficult to demonstrate. In 1991, the FMLN declared a truce for the elections and the political left was competing in earnest for a significant share of political power. But the problems noted above continued. The election was called "a shambles"[139] and "a rigged vote for peace."[140] Table 3.8 shows that, despite the cease-fire, turnout was down relative to the 1988 municipal race. Salvadorans' own explanations for the low turnout are provided in table 3.9. Considerable blame is placed on the electoral authorities, primarily for not duly providing the electoral card or for losing names of voters from the electoral register. Election-day violence remained an important concern also; in contrast to previous elections, the FMLN provoked no attacks, but the military was aggressive in various contested areas.[141]

At the root of the problem of the skewed Salvadoran electoral playing field may have been the partisan structure of Salvadoran electoral institutions. Whereas in Peru electoral authorities were chosen on the assumption that they would serve the nation as a whole, in El Salvador they were chosen on the assumption that service to the nation as a whole was unrealistic, and that the only route to electoral fairness was the representation of the various political parties. Until after the May 1991 reforms, the Salvadoran Central Elections Council was composed of three members, each of whom represented one of the three political parties with the most votes in the preceding presidential election; its president was from the winning party in the most recent presidential election.[142] The departmental and municipal elections councils, as well as voting-table officials, were also composed of members chosen by the political parties.[143] Obviously, it is in the interest of incumbent political parties to raise obstacles for newcomers. Also, when there are three members of a group, two may ally and discriminate against the third, whatever the actual right or wrong of the situation. The partisanship of the electoral bodies was criticized by none other than the 1991 head of the Salvadoran Electoral Registry: "The problem here is that, as soon as you get a new electoral code, each party sets about trying to manipulate it in its interest."[144] In Ecuador, where table 3.2 showed intense skepticism about the electoral process, electoral councils are similarly composed of political party representatives.[145]

By contrast, in Peru, electoral councils were composed of well-educated citizens; political party leaders were not to serve.[146] The National Elections Tribunal (Jurado Nacional de Elecciones, JNE) was composed of seven members: one representative each of the Supreme Court, the National Federations of Peruvian Law Schools, the Lima Law School, and the deans of the law faculties at the national universities; and three members chosen by lot among citizens proposed by regional tribunals. The Departmental Electoral Commission was composed of a representative of the relevant Superior Court and four citizens chosen by lot from a list of names drawn up by the Superior Court and then reviewed by the public. The three voting-table officials were selected by lot from among the twenty-five citizens with the most years of education registered to vote at the particular table. One shortcoming of the Peruvian institutional structure, however, was that if well-educated citizens' interest in the elections decreased and they did not materialize on election day, there were opportunities for leaders from incumbent parties to monopolize voting-table positions.

The Power of the Militaries in the Elected Regimes

This section examines civilian authority over the military in the two nations. It explores the overall political power of the Peruvian versus Salvadoran militaries and also military authority on key issues, including the military budget and personnel decisions.[147]

The argument is that, during the 1980s, civilian authority was much greater in Peru than in El Salvador (even though international pressure for the assertion of civilian authority at this time was virtually nil in Peru, but considerable in El Salvador). Whereas the outcomes of key controversies facing the military were significantly influenced by changes in presidential administrations in Peru, outcomes of such controversies in El Salvador were affected primarily by changes within the military itself as well as among U.S. political actors, and at most secondarily by changes in presidential administrations.

As the next section indicates, however, the subordination of the military to civilian authority is not in itself an adequate response to a guerrilla challenge. First, the civilian leadership may not necessarily endorse the principle of respect for human rights amid a guerrilla challenge (as in the cases of Presidents Belaúnde and Fujimori). Second (as in the case of President García) an attempt to subordinate military to civilian authority may create conflicts that are disadvantageous to the antiguerrilla effort. Third and perhaps most basically, while military leaders by themselves are unlikely to have all the answers to the problems of insurgency, civilian leaders may not either.

Overall Political Power of the Peruvian and Salvadoran Militaries

After the inauguration of civilian presidents in Peru in 1980 and El Salvador in 1982, the political power of the Peruvian military was much less than that of its Salvadoran counterpart. Not until at least the late

1980s and perhaps at no time during the decade could the Peruvian military seriously threaten a coup against the civilian leadership, whereas such a threat by the Salvadoran military appeared to weigh heavily upon Salvadoran civilian leaders.[148]

One of Peru's public opinion agencies annually ranks the top ten most powerful people in Peru, as judged by several hundred Peruvian elites from numerous sectors. In no year between 1981 and 1992 was more than one military officer ranked among the ten most powerful people in Peru; in no year was a military officer among the top three most powerful, and only in two years (all during the Belaúnde administration) was one among the top five.[149] While no comparable survey is available for El Salvador, it seems likely that during this period the defense minister would have been ranked among the top three and the chief of staff of the armed forces would have been a second military officer among the top ten.[150]

Why was the Peruvian military much less influential than its Salvadoran counterpart? First, the Peruvian military did not enjoy powerful civilian political allies as the Salvadoran did. Traditional Peruvian civilian elites loathed the military as a result of Velasco's reforms, especially his agrarian reform. The Peruvian military did not enjoy its own political party; nor was it a major actor in any other political party. By contrast, as discussed in the first section of this chapter, the Salvadoran military institution governed the country without interruption between 1931 and 1979; it enjoyed various strong alliances, in particular with landowning elites and with sectors of the Salvadoran peasantry through paramilitary networks such as ORDEN.

Nor did most Peruvian citizens perceive the military as an effective institution. Many Peruvians blamed the military government for Peru's severe economic crisis of the late 1970s and considered military officers abusive. In Peru's three presidential elections, a party affiliated with the military ran only in 1985—and it received less than 1 percent of the vote.[151] By contrast, of course, parties affiliated with the military in El Salvador (first the PCN and then ARENA) finished in either first or second place in Salvadoran elections throughout this period. In opinion polls, support for democratic principles was prevalent in both countries, but in El Salvador this support did not translate into rejection of military-affiliated political parties at the ballot box.[152]

The political power of the Peruvian military was also limited by officers' factionalism. The Peruvian military, numbering about 125,000 troops, included not only an army but also a substantial navy and air force.[153] The Peruvian army was widely considered the most concerned about the welfare of Peru's poor, and the most eager to diversify Peru's international ties away from the United States, while the navy was perceived as conservative.[154] There were also at least ten times as many officers in the Peruvian military than in the Salvadoran, and the larger number of officers implied greater diversity.[155]

By contrast, the Salvadoran military numbered approximately 43,250 in the late 1980s—about one-third the size of the Peruvian—and its army was the overwhelmingly predominant service.[156] Salvadoran officers were a smaller and more cohesive group than Peruvian officers, in good part also due to what is referred to as the *tanda* system. Each graduating class at the Gerardo Barrios Military School is a *tanda*; traditionally, each class had only about twenty to twenty-five officers, and all the officers of one *tanda* were promoted together, until they reached the rank of colonel.[157] Although the size of the graduating class grew during the 1980s to about one hundred officers, this number was still small enough to allow close bonds of loyalty and reciprocity.[158]

As indicated in the first section of this chapter, however, the 1979 coup by reformist Salvadoran military officers did signal important divisions within the military. The reformist faction that led the 1979 coup gave way to an institutionalist faction that retained some independence from traditional Salvadoran elites and supported at least in part the reforms launched by the 1979 civilian-military juntas. This faction favored policies that it perceived to advance the military institution, policies that for much of this period were synonymous with policies promoted by the United States. Politically, this military group accepted the election of Duarte in 1984 and the subsequent relative restraint upon human rights violations. These political positions were rewarded by large amounts of U.S. aid and were probably conditioned upon this aid (see chapter 5).

Another military sector known as the hard-liners rejected the reforms initiated in 1979, demonstrated scant acceptance of democratic norms, and supported a hard-line strategy against the FMLN. This military sector was politically affiliated with ex-Major Roberto D'Aubuisson; in

1981, he founded ARENA. The traditional alliance between the Salvadoran oligarchy and most military officers was revived in ARENA, although gradually a "moderate" sector emerged in the party.[159] In September 1985, D'Aubuisson resigned as president; he was replaced by Alfredo Cristiani, a Georgetown University–educated coffee magnate without ties to the Salvadoran death squads. Although Cristiani's political mentor was D'Aubuisson himself, and D'Aubuisson remained active in the party, Cristiani's leadership of ARENA greatly enhanced support for the party among Salvadoran elites and reduced opposition to it in the United States. As indicated above, ARENA won first the legislative and municipal elections of 1988 and then the presidential elections of March 1989.

The Military Budget

Table 3.10 presents the best available comparable data on military expenditure in Peru and El Salvador between the 1970s and the early 1990s.[160] The table indicates that military expenditure varied by presidential administration as well as by year to a much greater degree in Peru than in El Salvador, implying a much greater role for the Peru's civilian leadership in the determination of the size of the budget.[161]

The table shows that military expenditure rose dramatically in Peru under Belaúnde, dropped sharply during the first years of the García administration, and then increased in the final years of his administration; the trend under Fujimori is not clear from the data available. By contrast, expenditure in El Salvador increased gradually during most of the 1980s, without major shifts under Duarte or Cristiani, until the decline at the turn of the decade as peace negotiations began.

In different respects, the shifts in military expenditure under Belaúnde and García were startling. Why, between 1982 and 1984, would a civilian president preside over such a sharp increase in the military budget? One interpretation has been that Belaúnde perceived the budget as the most sensitive issue in civil-military relations and believed that, if the military's budget were accepted by the civilian leaders, the civilians could freely exert their own priorities on all other issues.[162] A more cynical view was that civilian as well as military leaders viewed arms acquisitions as excellent opportunities to obtain "commissions" from the arms vendors for their own pockets.[163]

Table 3.10. Military Expenditures in Peru and El Salvador

	Peru		El Salvador	
	Millions of Current Dollars	Percentage of Government Expenditure	Millions of Current Dollars	Percentage of Government Expenditure
1993	699	N.A.	102	N.A.
1992	783	N.A.	175	16.0
1991	750	16.4	142	20.6
1990	642	11.2	N.A.	24.5
1989	544	20.0	224	27.9
1988	702	20.0	N.A.	25.7
1987	217	N.A.	208	26.8
1986	703	N.A.	60	28.7
1985	641	N.A.	252	20.3
1984	1,327	N.A.	192	N.A.
1983	1,412	27.6	168	15.8
1982	1,626	N.A.	139	11.9
1981	398[a]	13.8	101[a]	16.8
1980	665	21.0	96	8.8
1979	533[a]	12.3	89[a]	9.3
1978	850[a]	N.A.	81[a]	N.A.
1977	406	N.A.	N.A.	N.A.
1972	N.A.	14.8	N.A.	6.6

Sources: See discussion on sources in the note in the text. Source for expenditures in millions of current dollars is *The Military Balance* (London: International Institute for Strategic Studies). Often, figures vary from one edition to the next; in cases of discrepancy, I have used the figure reported in the later edition. At times, figures are not for actual expenditure, but for the budgeted amount. Source for expenditure as a percentage of central government expenditure is *World Development Report* (Washington, D.C.: World Bank), annual editions. Neither source indicates the reasons for data not available.

Note: N.A. = not available in the source.

[a]Figures in 1980 dollars.

The cutback in expenditure under García in 1985 was also extraordinary in the context of Peru's guerrilla war.[164] It should be kept in mind, however, that most of the Peruvian government's expenditure was allocated not for the purposes of internal war but rather for external activities. Even in the late 1980s, less than 20 percent of Peru's military forces were pitted against the country's guerrillas; the jobs of the vast majority were to protect Peru's borders against Ecuador and Chile.[165] García's most publicized cutback was halving the number of sophisticated Mirage 2000 jet fighters to be purchased from France, down from a planned twenty-six (under Belaúnde) to twelve, presumably saving about $400 million.[166] Another significant cutback was in repairs and upgrades for a navy flagship.[167]

Still, some cutbacks in military expenditure under García were likely to have eroded the military's effectiveness against Peru's guerrillas. Military salaries declined drastically: whereas a second lieutenant earned roughly $450 per month during the Belaúnde administration and the first two years of García's term, a second lieutenant's salary was a mere $76 per month at its nadir in 1989.[168] At virtually all ranks, salaries in September 1990 were less than one-third of their January 1988 levels.[169]

Although the Fujimori government was much more sympathetic to the military's concerns than was the García government, Fujimori's capacity to respond to these concerns was constrained by his commitment to reducing the budget deficit in order to return Peru to the good graces of the international financial community.[170] Military salaries remained at very low levels relative to their pre-1987 levels and to levels in other Latin American nations. In 1991, the monthly salary for a Peruvian army division general was about $350, versus an average of $1,272 in neighboring nations.[171] The conscripted soldier earned a mere $10 per month in Peru, versus about $70–$85 per month in El Salvador.[172] Between 1991 and 1993, Peruvian officers' salaries continued to decline.[173]

Not surprisingly, the drastic salary cutbacks fostered demoralization and unrest at all ranks. In my research team's interviews with sixty middle-ranking members of the army and police in June and July 1990, predominantly in Huancayo, 77 percent of the respondents said that salaries should be raised to enhance morale and limit abuses.[174] During 1991, senior officers were requesting early retirement at the rate of at least one every day; between 1989 and 1992, about half the naval officers between the ranks of second lieutenant and commander asked to leave the service.[175] Approximately 20 percent of National Police personnel requested retirement in 1992 and roughly 3 percent deserted.[176] Ultimately, the requests for retirement were so numerous that the government suspended consideration of them.[177] Midlevel officers formed a clandestine group known as COMACA (Commanders, Majors, and Captains), demanding salary and budget increases.[178] Lower-ranking police and army personnel also formed a clandestine union and even threatened strikes.[179] At a 1991 press conference, masked representatives of the union denounced abuses by their superiors, and "the chains that bind us to a humiliating and increasingly degrading life."[180] Officers' demoralization exacerbated the traditional problem of corruption; for example, it was estimated that only one-third of the monthly gasoline ration distributed to the police was used, while two-thirds was sold to service stations.[181]

By contrast, in part because of U.S. military aid, the trend in El Salvador appeared to be toward higher morale among officers and soldiers. Military salaries in El Salvador were not declining, requests for retirement were not increasing, and neither soldiers' nor officers' unions were forming.[182] Especially after 1984, analysts' concerns about the Salvadoran military were focused upon what they considered the relative ease of military life, particularly for officers; by one estimate, Salvadoran generals were earning at least $1,600 per month in the late 1980s—more than quadruple the income of their Peruvian counterparts.[183]

Personnel Decisions

Peruvian civilian leaders also enjoyed greater power over military appointments than did their Salvadoran counterparts. In Peru, the president was influential in the appointment of the top military position in his cabinet, the minister of defense (the minister of war, prior to 1987), and in the appointment of the minister of the interior (whose primary responsibility was supervision of the police forces) and at times other key officers as well.[184] Retired as well as active-duty officers were eligible for cabinet positions. Also, according to the 1979 constitution, promotions within the ranks of general and admiral required approval by the Peruvian senate, and candidates to these ranks lobbied senators on their own behalf.[185] By contrast, in El Salvador, the minister of defense was an active-duty officer appointed primarily as a result of his standing within his graduating class from the military school (his *tanda*). Promotions to the ranks of general or admiral did not require approval by the legislature.

In the making of top military appointments, Belaúnde played a role. Political or family considerations were important to the appointment of three of his four ministers of war.[186] Belaúnde's first and third appointments, retired General Jorge Muñiz Luna in 1980 and General Oscar Brush Noel, were officers who were known as critics of the military government. Only Belaúnde's second war minister—General Luis Cisneros Vizquerra—had held a leadership position within the former military government; but Cisneros was Prime Minister Manuel Ulloa's relative and was appointed in good part for this reason.[187] Of the four war ministers, Cisneros was judged the most powerful; he was ranked the fourth most powerful Peruvian in 1982, the highest ranking for an active or retired military officer in Peru between 1981 and 1992.[188] Only Belaúnde's final appointment, General Julián Juliá Freyre, was made almost exclusively due to his military rank and support within the military institution.[189]

García sought to influence top military appointments to a much greater degree than Belaúnde. As his first war minister, García named General Jorge Flores Torres, an Aprista and godfather to one of García's children; he was serving in only the eighth-ranking command in the army hierarchy prior to his appointment.[190] After the New Year promotions beginning in 1987, the chief of staff and the commander of the navy became Vice Admiral Juan Soría, an APRA sympathizer. All of García's interior ministers were Apristas; one interior minister, Agustín Mantilla, had never served in the military or police and was one of García's closest friends. None of these leaders enjoyed great power; from 1987 through 1989, no active or retired military officer was ranked among the nine most powerful Peruvians.[191]

In 1987, García established a new defense ministry in a professed attempt to coordinate the activities of the army, navy, and air force more effectively; however, the ministry would subordinate the navy and air force to the army and was perceived, especially within these two services, as another initiative to increase presidential power over the military.[192] Whereas the military at first feared that García would appoint an Aprista civilian as the first minister of defense, ultimately García bowed to military pressure and the first defense minister was a highly respected officer with political ties to both Acción Popular and APRA. Overall, however, many officers complained that García was trying to *apristizar* (make entirely Aprista) the security forces and was co-opting dissident officers with promises of promotions and appointments.[193]

Under Fujimori, the president's influence over military appointments increased much more. The nature of Fujimori's influence was not that of a civilian president over a military institution; rather, the pattern of influence was personalistic. Fujimori sought not to coopt officers who had risen to reasonably high ranks according to the military's own criteria (as García did), but rather to establish a network of personalist alliances that overrode the professional criteria of the military institution. Working with his national security adviser, the lawyer and cashiered army captain Vladimiro Montesinos,[194] Fujimori sought not only that the members of his cabinet responsible for the security forces be politically congenial, but also that they be among his most loyal allies; moreover, he sought to place political allies at the top ranks of each armed service.[195] Even more contrary to military norms, Fujimori wanted, and ultimately achieved, an end to annual turnover at the top ranks, allowing his military allies to consolidate their power over promotions and retirements.[196] A prime example of these trends was the rise of General Nicolás de Bari Hermoza, who was not considered a particularly able commander but, working well with Montesinos and Fujimori, became commander of the army in 1992 and commander of the armed forces in 1994—despite the fact that by that date he had been in active service for more than thirty-five years.[197]

Gradually, the Fujimori government approximated a three-person civilian-military triumvirate. Although in 1990 and 1991 the only military officer judged among the ten most powerful Peruvians was army commander General Jorge Zegarra, and although during these two years Vladimiro Montesinos was not ranked among the top ten, by 1992 Montesinos reached the number four position, and Hermoza number seven.[198] By 1993, Fujimori was at number one, Montesinos at number two, and Hermoza at number three—rankings that they retained through 1995.[199]

By contrast, there is much greater continuity throughout different presidential administrations in the names of powerful Salvadoran military officers. Neither Duarte nor Cristiani decided the appointment of defense minister, even though this was an appointment to their own cabinets. Indeed, on the eve of his inauguration, Duarte apparently made a secret agreement with the minister of defense, General Carlos Eugenio Vides Casanova, that assured the institutional autonomy of the armed forces.[200] Vides Casanova, who had been commander of the National Guard during the years of intense death squad activity after the October 1979 coup, had become minister of defense upon the exit of General García in April 1983; he was the top military officers' choice for the position, and his candidacy was supported by U.S. military officers in

El Salvador as well.[201] Vides Casanova remained in this post after Duarte's election. General Adolfo Blandón remained the armed forces' chief of staff. Hard-liner General Juan Rafael Bustillo remained commander of the air force.

Under Vides Casanova, the *tanda* system endured. In general, the first member of a class to be promoted sought the promotions of his classmates as soon as possible—whatever their merits or demerits. Changes in top ministerial positions reflected the passage of power to a new *tanda* rather than to a new president. Commented one expert critic of the Salvadoran military in 1991, "To reach power in the army, you have to reassure those waiting for power that you aren't ruining the system. You have to link up with the *tandas* leaving power and cover their killings and gross corruption."[202]

In late 1988 (during Duarte's final year as president), Defense Minister Vides Casanova appointed numerous members of the *tandona* (an exceptionally large, cohesive, and hard-line class of forty-six graduates of 1966) to top positions within the armed forces.[203] *Tandona* member General René Emilio Ponce became chief of staff. The *tandona* remained the dominant military class in El Salvador through 1991. Despite disgruntlement among *tandas* before and after the *tandona*, and despite perceptions that *tandona* members were not particularly distinguished officers, its members soon occupied the vast majority of top military positions in the Cristiani government.[204] When *tandona* member Ponce became minister of defense in 1990, the promotion was apparently supported by Cristiani; but the primary force behind Ponce's appointment was the *tandona*.[205]

Although presidential influence over top military appointments was much greater in Peru than in El Salvador, gradually a modicum of influence was realized in El Salvador. Some important reassignments were made by Duarte—in particular, the transfer of Colonel Nicolás Carranza, former commander of the treasury police and vice minister of defense, to a foreign post.[206] Duarte disbanded the S-2 intelligence unit, which had been notorious for human rights abuses. He also established a new vice ministry of public security under Colonel Reynaldo López Nuila, who favored curbing the country's death squads.

It may be that Cristiani reassigned a larger number of officers, and higher-ranking officers, than did Duarte.[207] General Juan Rafael Bustillo, a hard-liner who had commanded the air force since 1979 and who had almost become defense minister in 1989, was dispatched to Israel as military attaché. Also, in November 1989, the commander of the National Police was transferred to Costa Rica.

Democracy and Counterinsurgency

The development of an effective counterinsurgency strategy that respects democratic norms is often difficult. First, of course, amidst a guerrilla challenge, the role of the nation's security forces becomes more important, and the civilian leadership may be more inclined to tolerate abuses by the security forces. But human rights abuses alienate citizens and increase the likelihood that they will support the guerrillas. In Latin American nations where revolutionary movements became strong during the Cold War, the critical challenge for the government was usually to recognize that these abuses were fueling the insurgency and to assert civilian control over the military, despite the military's resistance. Certainly, this was the critical challenge in El Salvador.

In Peru, the development of an effective counterinsurgency policy respecting democratic norms was even more difficult in various respects. Not only did the Peruvian government have to deal with the problem indicated above—the necessity for both a real counterinsurgency effort by the security forces and for respect for human rights by these same forces—but it also had to cope with the fact that the root cause of the guerrilla challenge was not perceived as political, as in the case of El Salvador and other Cold War revolutionary movements in Latin America, but economic. The path toward the amelioration of Peru's economic crisis was far from clear, and for various reasons the U.S. government was much less inclined to try to help Peru with this economic crisis than it was to help El Salvador with its political crisis (see chapter 5).

The Peruvian Experience

In contrast to El Salvador, the decimation of the revolutionary movements in Peru did not address what was widely believed to be the root causes of the guerrilla challenge. Table 3.11 shows that the vast majority of Peruvians emphasized economic and social routes toward political peace; a similar pattern of responses was evident in other surveys.[208]

Table 3.11. Citizens' Opinions about the Way to Achieve Political Peace
(percentages)

	Peru		El Salvador		
	Junín, 1990 (N = 200)	Junín, 1991 (N = 130)	Nationwide, 1988[a]	San Salvador, 1991 (N = 175)	Eastern Depts., 1991 (N = 231)
More employment, end to economic crisis	34	42	5	17	14
Reduce social injustice	18	20	0	6	5
Dialogue, political space for guerrillas	12	21	43	56	52
Destroy the guerrillas	7	4	5	11	10
Divine solution	0	0	9	6	5
Other	15	10	17	3	5
Don't know, no answer	14	3	19	1	1

Source: Author's commissioned surveys; see appendix I. Exception is data for El Salvador in 1988. In all surveys, item read, "In your view, what would be the best way to resolve the war, ending the political violence?"

[a]Martín Baró (1989, 76). Sample size is not given.

Both Presidents García and Fujimori were elected on platforms that specified Peru's socioeconomic problems as the root causes of the insurgency; according to democratic norms, they had thus committed themselves to efforts on this score. But, as of 1992 and the decimation of Sendero and the MRTA, economic conditions had not improved in Peru.

Ultimately, Sendero and the MRTA were decimated due to improved performance by the security forces and the military, as well as by various new antiterrorist laws and these revolutionary groups' own errors. Although President Fujimori has tried to take sole credit for these changes, his comments have more to do with justification of his *autogolpe* than with the historical record.[209] Actually, the improvement was gradual; it began under García and to a considerable degree reflected trial and error by various governments (as seems appropriate in a democratic polity).

President Belaúnde's Effort.[210] President Belaúnde, in the unfortunate position of being the first president who had to try to counter Sendero, had to do so during a period when the movement enjoyed greater support in its southern highlands base than at any other time. Ultimately, the government's counterinsurgency was considered the most seriously flawed of all its policies.[211]

In the first few years of his administration, Belaúnde doubted that Sendero represented a serious challenge and did not respond in any significant way, either by trying to improve the desperate socioeconomic problems in the southern highlands or by establishing an appropriate role for the security forces in the area. Until late December 1982, Belaúnde authorized action only by the antiterrorist police, not by the military, in Ayacucho. Also, fearing that the National Intelligence Service (Servicio de Inteligencia Nacional, SIN) would be used against civilian political leaders as it had been in the 1960s, Belaúnde dismantled it—and lost what would probably have been an important intelligence capability against Sendero.[212]

After December 1982, Belaúnde attempted an exclusively repressive strategy that was totally at odds with democratic norms. Belaúnde believed that the counterinsurgency effort of the 1960s—an overwhelmingly military effort in which human rights were not respected and in which socioeconomic reforms were not made—would be effective again in the 1980s. Belaúnde perceived the Senderistas as mere delinquents whose primary support was among foreigners, and accordingly believed attention to the concerns of southern highlands citizens was unnecessary. Although of course a civilian president, Belaúnde shared the views of two of his key "hard-liner" war ministers—Cisneros and Noel—that human rights violations were inevitable and should not be a preoccupation.[213]

In December 1982, most provinces in Ayacucho became an "emergency zone" under the control of the armed forces; most civil rights were suspended.[214] Soldiers or antiterrorist police occupied communities; they usually could not speak the language of the indigenous peasants, and they could not distinguish Senderistas from civilians. Security force personnel attempted to establish civil defense patrols (or, as they were called in later years, *rondas*) and at times may have encouraged peasants to attack strangers; one apparent tragic upshot was the massacre of eight journalists in the peasant community of Uchuraccay in January 1983. Human rights violations escalated dramatically (see tables 3.5 and 3.6). In one community alone, security force personnel may have "disappeared" as many as fifty young people.[215]

The Belaúnde government's strategy was increasingly questioned not only by its civilian political opponents but also by military officers. The tensions culminated in 1984 when the head of the political-military command in Ayacucho, General Adrián Huamán, severely criticized the government's counterinsurgency policy on Peru's most-watched news program, saying it ignored the social and economic roots of the guerrilla problem.[216] As Huamán's criticisms echoed among Peruvians, Belaúnde and the top military officers agreed to dismiss Huamán.[217]

President García's Effort. During the first half of his term, President Alan García attempted a counterinsurgency policy that respected human rights and that sought to ameliorate the destitution of Peru's southern highlands. Unfortunately, however, given the degree to which Sendero was entrenched in these areas and Sendero's savage character, this strategy could not succeed without a military component, and García's approach so alienated the military that it refused to work with the civilian leadership.

Like Huamán and most Peruvians at this time (recall table 3.11), García perceived Sendero as a serious problem that was the result of the destitution and marginalization of Peru's southern highlands. Accordingly, García greatly increased economic aid to Peru's southern highlands. The interest rate on Agrarian Bank loans in the southern highlands was reduced to zero, and the number and real value of agrarian bank loans more than doubled.[218] Public investment in Ayacucho approximately quadrupled between 1985 and 1986, to about $30 million.[219] In 1987, about one hundred thousand southern highland residents were provided jobs through a short-term public employment program.[220]

Ultimately, however, the economic aid effort failed to stop Sendero's expansion. Already entrenched in many of these provinces, Sendero attacked development workers; without military protection, these civilian workers were unable to implement many of the projects.[221] Also, especially in later years, resources for development programs were scant and embezzlement common.[222]

The García government also worked to address peasants' concerns through reorganization of some of the previously established agrarian cooperatives so that larger numbers of peasants would be included in the cooperatives. In 1986 and 1987, large meetings with peasants were held to this end, and expectations rose. However, the initiative stalled amid resistance from the peasants and managers in the established cooperatives and conflicts among the various interested political groups. In some areas, including Junín and Puno, peasants' frustrations at the failure of the reorganization effort were exploited by Sendero.[223]

García also sought to raise human rights standards. In September 1985, mass graves were found in Accomarca and Pucayacu (two Ayacucho villages), suggesting that two massacres had been committed by army officers in these sites. When the joint command's investigative report was evasive, García dismissed three of the military's highest-ranking officers: the head of the joint command, the commander of the Lima-based Second Military Zone, and the commander of the Ayacucho emergency zone.[224] Never before in the history of Peru—and never yet in El Salvador—had a civilian president fired three of the nation's most powerful generals simultaneously. Also, within the next year, legal charges were brought against numerous other higher- and lower-ranking security force personnel.[225] In good part as a result of García's policy, human rights violations in 1985–87 were less than half the numbers in 1983–84 (see tables 3.5 and 3.6).

However, García's human rights initiative infuriated the military. Many officers were so angry that they did not send their soldiers out of the barracks—in effect, calling a strike against García.[226] Military officers refused to share their information on human rights cases with civilian leaders.[227] The majority of officers believed that—at least in the Peruvian context of ill-paid, ill-equipped, and ill-trained soldiers without an effective intelligence capability against a clandestine, savage, disciplined foe—the war against the Shining Path could not be won without serious human rights violations.[228] Officers were especially angry because they considered García hypocritical: it gradually became clear that García himself bore some of the responsibility for the massacre of at least 250 suspected and convicted Shining Path guerrillas in June 1986, but the president never acknowledged his complicity, merely blaming security force personnel.[229]

By early 1988, as the García government became engulfed in economic crisis and Sendero expanded, popular support for García plummeted and the military began to scorn the civilian leadership. A military coup loomed as a possibility.[230] Worried, García made various cabinet appointments more accommodating of military concerns, and he also appeared resigned to human rights abuses.[231] For example, after the massacre of some thirty peasants by military troops in the Ayacucho village of Cayara in May 1988, no officer was dismissed or charged.[232] For the first time human rights groups recorded military assassinations of civilians, and in 1989 the number of forced disappearances returned to 1983–84 levels.[233] Other abuses, such as theft and rape, were rampant as well.[234] The number of provinces declared in emergency—under military control—increased sharply.

By the end of García's term, his counterinsurgency policy appeared to have failed. Most obviously, the Shining Path continued its expansion.[235] The president had abandoned his original emphasis upon economic aid and allowed human rights violations to escalate. However, the last half of García's term saw important counterinsurgency initiatives that reflected the administration's willingness to try new tactics—including tactics that were not warmly endorsed by the Peruvian military. In other words, seeds for a more effective counterinsurgency policy were planted in the final years of the García government, seeds that did not sprout and become visible until the Fujimori period.

Probably of greatest importance at this point was an effort to enhance the government's intelligence capability—an effort that culminated in the capture of Abimael Guzmán, which most analysts perceive as the critical turning point in the anti-Sendero effort.[236] At the time, however, the enhancement of intelligence was perceived as a significant initiative by only small minorities of Peruvians—either civilian or military.[237]

In any case, working with his close friend Agustín Mantilla at the Interior Ministry, García established a cooperative relationship with the police (in contrast to his acrimonious relationship with the military). The antiterrorist police unit's resources and staff were augmented.[238] The first salient achievement was the June 1988 capture of Osmán Morote, the number-two Senderista leader at the time. In February 1989, primarily in a stroke of good luck, police also arrested Víctor Polay Campos, then head of the MRTA, at the Hotel de Turistas in Huancayo.

In March 1990, the Special Intelligence Group (Grupo Especial de Inteligencia, GEIN), the group that was ultimately the primary architect of the capture of Guzmán, was formed within the antiterrorist police unit National Agency Against Terrorism (Dirección Nacional Contra el

Terrorismo, DINCOTE).[239] It is very likely that, soon after its inception, the GEIN enjoyed support from the U.S. government.[240] The GEIN was a small, specialized unit authorized by and responsible to Interior Minister Mantilla and charged with the capture of Guzmán and other top Senderista leaders. The premise of the GEIN's formation was that DINCOTE had become too large and unwieldy, and that a smaller unit that would concentrate its efforts against the apex of the Senderista hierarchy was necessary. Whereas conventionally DINCOTE seized Senderista suspects as quickly as possible and interrogated them, hoping to gain information from them about the Senderista leadership's whereabouts, the GEIN opted to track them, believing that eventually their trails would lead to Guzmán.

In the last two months of García's administration, the GEIN apparently came close to capturing the Senderista leader.[241] On 1 June 1990, a Sendero safe house in the wealthy Monterrico suburb of Lima was seized, and many valuable documents gained. Guzmán left the safe house only about one week prior to the seizure.[242] But the bottom line remained that Guzmán had not been captured, and the GEIN was disparaged by many DINCOTE officials as "Mantilla's guys."[243]

A second important initiative during García's final two years was the establishment of peasant self-defense patrols *(rondas)*. García promoted this strategy over considerable military and civilian opposition.[244] For the most part, the opposition's concerns were understandable, especially in the context of the failed *rondas* strategy only about five years earlier under Belaúnde. Many military officers feared that most peasants did not oppose Sendero, and might use their weapons for rather than against revolutionary groups.[245] There were other worries as well. Many analysts feared that peasants might use their weapons against rival communities, and that the *rondas* would immediately be targeted by Sendero, reducing the *ronderos* to cannon fodder.[246] Also, for leftist political leaders in particular, the precedents in Guatemala and El Salvador were not encouraging; they feared what was called "militarization"—in particular, peasant communities' subordination to military authority.[247] Against these concerns, García argued that peasants had a right to defend themselves in what was a war first and foremost against the peasants themselves, and the president prevailed.[248] García's first major public demonstration of his support for the *rondas* was his gift of his pistol to "Comandante Huayhuaco," who had organized *rondas*, in Ayacucho in December 1989.

A third effort at change in counterinsurgency strategy under García was in the judicial realm, although unfortunately here the effort produced no results. It was blatantly obvious by the late 1980s that Peru's judicial process was woefully inadequate to the country's guerrilla challenge.[249] The Senderista organization was very adept at threatening, and sometimes also bribing, judges. The vast majority of terrorist cases did not even come to trial because judges ruled that there was "insufficient evidence to proceed." For the most part, conviction required evidence that the suspect had actually committed a terrorist crime—but Senderista leaders usually only planned attacks, and did not personally carry them out. For all these reasons, during the late 1980s only 5 percent to 12 percent of terrorist suspects were convicted.[250] The low conviction rate was an important factor provoking human rights violations:

> Human rights violations often stem from a combination of frustration and fear. Say I'm an officer and I have a battle with Shining Path and I arrest 15 guerrillas. . . . I know that if I take them to the judge, they're going to go in one door and out the other, because the justice system doesn't work. Then, I know that while they're in custody they're going to start claiming "human rights" and they might say something that would screw up my career. And finally, I know that Shining Path believes in revenge, and if I send these people to jail they might come after my children, my wife, or me. So I kill everybody. No witnesses.[251]

García recognized that many judges were intimidated or bribed by Sendero, and that conviction of terrorist suspects was too difficult.[252] The president backed various legal reforms.[253] In June 1987, in Law 24,700, García authorized the establishment of special civilian tribunals for cases of terrorism, in which greater protection would be provided for judges. Both this law and its 1989 successor, Law 25,103, included provision for repentance, under which a repentant terrorist could receive clemency in return for information that led to the arrest of other terrorists.

But these new legal provisions were not implemented. Apparently, they were opposed for various reasons by the judges themselves, by opposition political parties, and by military officers (many of whom doggedly sought military jurisdiction for cases of terrorism as well as the death penalty and did not want compromise measures).[254] For his part, President García did not push hard enough to see his reforms through. The problem of judicial reform received minimal public attention; it was not cited at all in responses to our survey item about counterinsurgency performance, either by civilians or by security force personnel.

President Fujimori's Effort. Almost universally, presidents take credit for successes on their watch, whether or not that credit is truly deserved, and Fujimori is no exception. The innovations that were key to the decimation of Sendero and the MRTA had either already been made or had at least been attempted under García. With the exception of the capture of Guzmán, Fujimori's own changes in counterinsurgency strategy were double-edged swords—helping the anti-Sendero effort but increasing the power of the military and violating democratic norms.

Soon after his inauguration, Fujimori established a much more cooperative relationship with the military than had García. For example, Fujimori backed the promotion of various generals whose respect for human rights when they had been directing counterinsurgency efforts was at best questionable. Although the number of forced disappearances decreased, the number of extrajudicial assassinations rose considerably (see tables 3.5 and 3.6). Among the most salient of these assassinations was the killing of sixteen people in the Barrios Altos neighborhood of Lima in November 1991, and the abduction of nine students and a professor from the La Cantuta teacher's college and their subsequent execution in July 1992. As of March 1993, 32 percent in an Apoyo poll believed that the violation of human rights was a policy of the government, another 7 percent that it was a policy of the armed forces—while 63 percent also believed that human rights violations were not necessary to achieve the defeat of terrorism.[255] As will be noted below, the successful implementation of *rondas* in many parts of the Peruvian countryside appeared to depend on respect for the military—not on fear—among Peruvian peasants.

As indicated above, the key counterinsurgency breakthrough was the capture of Guzmán by the GEIN on 12 September 1992. The GEIN's leadership and strategy did not change under Fujimori.[256] Although there were several leadership changes at DINCOTE in Fujimori's first two years, including the appointment of General Ketín Vidal as its head in November 1991, there were no significant policy changes; DINCOTE was not considered especially important.[257] Rather, Fujimori was focusing on the development of the intelligence capability of the SIN, the military intelligence service that had been dismantled under Belaúnde. The GEIN's progress toward the capture of Guzmán was slow but steady.[258]

On 31 January 1991, a second major safe house was seized in Lima, this time in the prosperous suburb of Chacarilla del Estanque, which held videotapes of the funeral of Guzmán's wife and also images of a drunken Guzmán—important to the beginning of the tarnishing of Guzmán's image. Then, in June 1992, after many months of surveillance, the GEIN decided to arrest a Senderista chief of logistics, Luis Alberto Arana Franco, who pointed the GEIN to the neighborhood of Los Sauces as the general area of Guzmán's current safe house. The GEIN undertook careful detective work in this neighborhood; especially critical, for example, was apparently the discovery of Winston Light cigarettes—the same brand as at the Chacarilla del Estanque house—in the rubbish bin of what was to prove to be Guzmán's safe house.

At the time, credit for the capture was taken almost exclusively by Ketín Vidal and DINCOTE. President Fujimori was not informed that the capture was likely to be imminent, and he was fishing out of Lima on September 12. Fujimori was furious that he was not informed and could not be present to stake his claim to be directing the counterinsurgency struggle and emphasizing the role of the SIN and other institutions that his government had augmented. The SIN had played a role in the capture by securing more U.S. support for DINCOTE and the GEIN and by planting reports in the media that the government believed Guzmán was in Bolivia (persuading Guzmán that the government was poorly informed of his whereabouts, so that he would let down his guard), but Vidal did not acknowledge this role.[259]

As noted above, García reinitiated the *rondas* policy in December 1989; in the first six months of 1990, the results of the policy appeared positive, and Fujimori promoted the *rondas* vigorously. Established first in southern highlands departments, the *rondas* were extended to most highlands areas and provided with better weapons. Also very important, in many areas the military was encouraged to develop a more collaborative and trusting relationship with the peasants, and to this end was provided funds for civic action programs.[260] By mid-1993, there were more than four thousand *rondas* in Peru, involving approximately three hundred thousand peasants.[261] Important as the *rondas* appeared to be in the defeat of Sendero, it is also the case that the *rondas* were supervised by soldiers and that military supervision by definition undermines civilian authority in peasant communities.

Under Fujimori, the long-overdue judicial reform was finally achieved —but the reform was a double-edged sword, shifting policies against the rights of the accused and in favor of the state, and in particular the military, to such a degree that democratic principles were violated.[262] It is also anomalous, given the consensus on the need for judicial reform among the FREDEMO, PPC, and Cambio 90 parties that composed a large majority of the Peruvian congress, that Fujimori waited until November 1991 to advance judicial reform.

The most draconian new law was the decree that crimes of "treason against the mother country" be tried in "faceless" military courts. There was more consensus with respect to the new law that crimes of "terrorism" would continue to be tried in civilian courts, but that the judges would also be "faceless." DINCOTE was granted extraordinarily broad investigative powers, trial procedures became summary in the extreme, and the rights of defense counsel were drastically reduced. Finally, a new repentance law encouraged disillusioned guerrillas to surrender, offering reductions in penalties in exchange for relevant information. Together, these legal changes dramatically increased the number of Senderista suspects who were captured, and they also dramatically increased the rate of conviction.[263] However, the pendulum had swung very far; of an estimated five thousand persons jailed for crimes of terrorism since 1992, it was estimated that more than 30 percent were innocent.[264] The percentage of suspects tried in military courts who were convicted was 97 percent.[265]

The Salvadoran Experience

As indicated in the previous sections of this chapter and in chapter 6, the critical challenge throughout the 1980s in El Salvador was to establish democratic norms, in particular respect for human rights in a military institution that traditionally considered itself above the law and traditionally perceived even Christian Democrats as enemies of the nation. Table 3.11 indicates that the vast majority of Salvadorans who would express an opinion on the question of the path toward peace in the country perceived that path as dialogue and political space for the guerrillas. Indeed, even when answering a question about the improvement of military performance, most Salvadorans cited respect for human rights and political dialogue as key.[266]

It appears that, from the beginning of their terms, Presidents Duarte and Cristiani also believed that the military's respect for human rights and negotiations were key to the resolution of the conflict. However, both apparently perceived their power relative to the military institution as limited and sought to affect the military's behavior primarily to the extent that they could gain support for their initiatives from the U.S. government or other key international actors (see chapter 5). Whereas the U.S. government supported both civilian presidents in their efforts to reduce human rights violations (although to a much lesser degree in any efforts that were made to achieve accountability for past human rights violations), only the Bush administration backed negotiations.

President Duarte's Effort. As indicated in tables 3.4, 3.5, and 3.6, when Duarte assumed the presidency in 1984, the Salvadoran military's human rights record improved dramatically. Military/paramilitary violence against politically salient civilian groups as recorded by international human rights organizations declined sharply; the number of military/paramilitary assassinations recorded by Tutela Legal in 1984 was less than 20 percent of the number recorded in 1983; and the number of forced disappearances in 1984 was less than 10 percent of the figure recorded in 1983. Although by 1984 most leftist political activists had already been killed, had fled the country, or had joined the FMLN, the record still indicates a better human rights performance.

As indicated in the discussion of military appointments, Duarte sought this improvement and initiated various reassignments and structural changes to this end. However, Duarte's success also appears to have depended on a clearer message by Reagan administration officials to the Salvadoran military that, if its human rights performance did not improve, U.S. aid to El Salvador would be reduced (see also chapter 5). The progress in the military's human rights record began not with the inauguration of Duarte but with the arrival in San Salvador of Ambassador Thomas Pickering in the fall of 1983.[267] Under Pickering, U.S. pressure against human rights violations increased. On 11 December

1983, Vice President George Bush visited San Salvador, met with the country's thirty-odd top military commanders, and apparently gave President Magaña a list of nine men identified by U.S. intelligence as death squad leaders and told Magaña they had to be sidelined; in one way or another, most were.[268]

The new resoluteness of Reagan administration officials was to bolster not only Duarte but also the institutionalist sector within the Salvadoran military that argued for improved human rights performance on the basis of the military's institutional interest.[269] Commented, for example, Defense Minister Vides Casanova himself, who was generally considered an institutionalist: "We know that improving our image is worth millions of dollars of aid for the country."[270] A similar interpretation was made by chief of staff General Adolfo Blandón: "We knew that public opinion in the United States and the view of many senators and congressmen opposed to military aid for El Salvador were largely due to our bad image because of the death squads. . . . Knowing that the aid was absolutely vital for us, we concluded we had to take a strong decision to get rid of them."[271]

The major role of U.S. pressure in improving the Salvadoran military's human rights record raised doubts that the advance was either a triumph of civilian over military authority or a change in the core values of the Salvadoran military (doubts that for most analysts were confirmed by the murder of the Jesuit priests at the UCA in November 1989).[272] An improvement in human rights performance made from a desire to secure external aid rather than from a conviction that such improvement is the best policy means that the improvement is likely to be reversed as soon as the external aid is withdrawn. This fear was expressed in 1984 by Central Intelligence Agency officials themselves:

> We believe efforts by the civilian government and the military high command to crackdown on right-wing violence have made little progress and have been aimed almost exclusively at placating Washington. Salvadoran officials understandably feel uneasy about openly confronting right-wing extremists; death threats and other forms of intimidation against national leaders are commonplace and often are carried out. Defense Minister Vides—whose room to maneuver is limited—appears both personally disinclined and professionally unable to effect a major cleanup within the armed forces any time soon.[273]

With respect to Duarte's other positions advancing human rights, however, the president did not enjoy support from the Reagan administration and his policy preferences did not prevail. In particular, Duarte could not achieve accountability for past human rights violations.[274] Although Duarte formed a presidential commission to investigate five of the most notorious death squad assassination cases, in only one of the five cases (the killing at the Sheraton Hotel of two American land reform advisers and the director of the Salvadoran government's land reform program) were security force personnel convicted. Even in this case, the officers believed to have ordered the murders were not tried, and the killers were released from prison in the wake of an amnesty law in December 1987. In the other four cases, there were no convictions, despite considerable evidence implicating officers—in particular in the murder of Archbishop Romero, widely considered to have been the responsibility of D'Aubuisson.

Nor was Duarte able to advance other new counterinsurgency strategies during his administration. Rather, it was U.S. officials who took these initiatives. They were vigorous—but not very successful—in promoting such policies as the end of the *tanda* system and the implementation of small unit tactics and civil defense programs (see chapter 5). The most dramatic shifts in counterinsurgency policy in El Salvador were occasioned not by Duarte's presidency but in April 1983, when Defense Minister General José Guillermo García, after a rebellion by Colonel Sigifredo Ochoa in Cabañas, was replaced by Vides Casanova.[275] As mentioned above, Vides Casanova was more partial to the policies advanced by U.S. officials than his predecessor.

Duarte apparently favored a negotiated end to the war in El Salvador. However, his preference did not prevail over the expectation of an outright military victory, held by many Salvadoran officers and by the Reagan administration.[276] It was expected that negotiations would involve major reform of the military institution, and such reform by definition threatened military prerogatives, in particular the long-standing principle of impunity. Also, especially in the context of the large-scale U.S. support, war was lucrative for the military.[277]

Why did Duarte simply not advance toward his human rights and peace goals, warning the Salvadoran military that a coup would reduce American aid? Perhaps Duarte believed that he was indispensable to the political opening that was going on in El Salvador, and that, if a rightist coup did succeed, it would be devastating for the country—with or without U.S. aid in the wake of such a coup.[278] Also, Duarte himself became personally indebted to the Salvadoran military. First, in 1984 and then to an even greater degree in 1985, the apparent electoral victories of the Christian Democrats were upheld against the right's charges of fraud only by a clear endorsement of the elections by El Salvador's military leaders, obligating Duarte to these officers.[279] Second, in October 1985, Duarte's daughter Inés was kidnapped by the guerrillas, and the traumatic event embittered the president against the FMLN and further indebted him to the military.[280] By the mid-1980s, Duarte was a much more cautious, conservative man than he had been in the 1970s.[281]

President Cristiani's Effort. Cristiani's personal political perspectives are less clear than Duarte's. As not only an ARENA leader but also D'Aubuisson's protegé, Cristiani was not outspoken about human rights or about political dialogue in El Salvador.

At first, buoyed by ARENA's victories in the March 1988 legislative elections and then in the March 1989 presidential elections, the Salvadoran death squads appeared to be reviving.[282] Cristiani did not take a vigorous stand on human rights either during the campaign (in which he appeared frequently with D'Aubuisson) or in his first months as president. The expectation that Cristiani would relax human rights standards was a factor in the increase in military and paramilitary violence against politically salient civilians in 1989 (see table 3.4) and in the increase in the number of forced disappearances (see table 3.6). Indeed, the bombing of the National Trade Union Federation of Salvadoran Workers (Federación Nacional Salvadoreña de Trabajadores, FENESTRAS) office in late October 1989, killing eight and wounding thirty-five, was apparently the catalyst for the FMLN's decision to launch the November offensive.[283] Whatever Cristiani's views on the issue, however, as negotiations began and the United Nations became a key actor in El Salvador, the human rights record improved (see tables 3.4, 3.5, and 3.6).

In Cristiani's inaugural address, he proposed a process of negotiations. Apparently, as a member of the Salvadoran business elite, Cristiani was especially concerned that the war was continuing to exact a heavy economic toll.[284] But, like Duarte, Cristiani was apparently unable to convince the Salvadoran military of the need for concessions; talks between government and FMLN representatives began in September 1989 but produced scant results.[285] Although the Bush administration was from its inception much more inclined toward negotiations than the Reagan administration had been, it did not take decisive action at this time.[286]

Then, in November 1989, two crucial events (both discussed at greater length in chapter 2) focused the key actors on the need for negotiations.[287] First, the November 1989 FMLN offensive destroyed the belief of the civilian political right, both in El Salvador and in the United States, that the military was gradually becoming more professional and would soon win the war. Second, during the offensive, U.S.-trained soldiers murdered six Jesuit priests, their housekeeper, and her daughter at the UCA. Although not only the Salvadoran military but also Cristiani tried for years to protect the intellectual authors of the crime, it gradually became clear that they were top Salvadoran officers, including chief of staff Ponce and air force commander Bustillo.[288]

Dismayed, the U.S. government began to push much more vigorously for negotiations. In October 1990, the U.S. Congress voted to withhold 50 percent of the U.S. military assistance requested for El Salvador for fiscal year 1991, conditioning its release of the funds on progress in the investigation of the murders of the Jesuit priests and in peace negotiations. President Bush signed the bill into law soon thereafter.[289] The law was a clear signal to the Salvadoran military that the U.S. funds that had been available for the war in the 1980s were diminishing.

Between April 1990 and 31 December 1991, negotiations advanced under the auspices of the United Nations and culminated in the signing of peace accords in Mexico City on 16 January 1992. Although President Cristiani supported the process, he did not by any means lead it.[290] The key factors in the path toward peace were the realizations by both Salvadoran officers and FMLN leaders that they could not win the war outright and that they had lost external support.[291]

An Assessment

This chapter has indicated that for the most part between 1980 and 1992 Peru deserved the democratic label as democracy is conventionally defined by U.S. scholars, but El Salvador did not. One recent description of Latin American politics was, "the vote, but not always much more."[292] This characterization was apt for Peru during this period. But rigorously examining "the vote" in El Salvador, we found that Salvadoran citizens did not really have even that much. It is thus not surprising that, as chapter 6 elaborates, fraudulent elections, political exclusiveness, and repression triggered the emergence of the FMLN, but played no role in the rise of Sendero Luminoso.

Over the course of the 1980s, however, Salvadoran electoral processes did gradually become more open to center-leftist and even leftist political parties. As mainstream scholars would suggest, the opening of the Salvadoran polity eroded popular support for the revolutionary movement. The opening also was critical to the ultimate decision by the FMLN to seek a negotiated solution to the war. However, it was doubtful that this opening would have occurred without intense pressures by the U.S. government (see chapter 5).

By contrast, although Peruvian electoral processes remained open and correct during the decade, and although civilian authority over the military was considerable—qualifying the government as democratic for U.S.-based social scientists—these achievements were insufficient to qualify the government as democratic for most Peruvian citizens. In particular, despite civilian control over the military in many respects, human rights violations became egregious. As chapters 4 and 6 discuss, the Shining Path guerrillas also shrewdly highlighted the problem of corruption in the democratic regime; amid the ongoing economic debacle, the legitimacy of the regime eroded. For example, in our 1990 Lima survey, only 38 percent of the respondents considered Peru "a lot" or a "good deal" "democratic."[293] This 38 percent figure was higher than the 23 percent in our nationwide 1991 Salvadoran sample, but not by very much.[294]

Accordingly, U.S. scholars' definitions of democracy do not currently incorporate all the political concerns of most Latin American citizens. For many Latin American citizens, an election per se is an insufficient component of democracy; even an election judged free and fair, as well as a military subordinate by conventional criteria to civilian authority, are insufficient components. Citizens may judge a regime democratic or not on the basis of its performance in key policy areas. Only if Latin American citizens' own criteria for a democratic regime are met will "democracy" constitute a bulwark against revolutionary movements in the twenty-first century.

4

ECONOMIC TRENDS
INTENSIFIED POVERTY? DASHED MIDDLE-CLASS EXPECTATIONS?

*F*or Theda Skocpol, misery is a constant in much of the Third World. Given that poverty is pervasive and permanent, in Skocpol's view it does not distinguish one nation or one era from another, and is not a variable triggering revolutionary movements. Most other mainstream political scientists analyzing revolutionary experiences during the Cold War consider economic deprivation—in particular, peasants' economic deprivation—in much greater depth than Skocpol, but ultimately relegate peasants' grievances to a more or less similar status: poverty is an enduring problem that makes peasants available for revolutionary movements but does not explain why one movement becomes strong and another does not. For these scholars as for Skocpol, the variable that best explains the expansion of the movement is the state and its actions or inactions.

As we saw in chapter 1, however, there is an alternative "misery matters most" perspective. For these scholars, the lot of the peasantry has been especially important. James Scott emphasizes that a threat to peasants' subsistence is crucial to their decision to support a revolutionary movement. Jeffery Paige discerns landlessness and land inequality, within the context of particular class conflicts, as key factors in the expansion of rebellion. Timothy Wickham-Crowley perceives the most important factor in peasants' support for guerrilla movements to be not landlessness but the process of physical displacement from land. Other scholars focus not primarily on the peasantry but on middle-class groups, or would-be middle-class groups. Ted Gurr (1970, 46) highlights citizens' "anger over the loss of what they once had, or thought they could have" as key to social revolt, and assesses in particular expectations for entry into the middle class. For Gurr and for Alvin Gouldner, a group especially inclined toward rebellion are recent university graduates and teachers whose expectations for entry into the middle class are frustrated.

This chapter explores economic trends and patterns in El Salvador and Peru during the 1970s and 1980s both at the national level and among relevant social groups to determine how the revolutionary movements' trajectory corresponds, or does not correspond, to these trends and patterns. The eras and areas of the expansion of the revolutionary movements in the two nations were described in detail in chapter 2. Briefly, the movements that were to compose the FMLN grew during the 1970s, and their challenge to the Salvadoran state was at its apex between 1979 and the early 1980s, but continued through the decade. The movements were vigorous in San Salvador until the severe repression of the late 1970s and early 1980s; then, they withdrew to their rural social bases, primarily in the departments of Morazán and Chalatenango, where they had been building substantial peasant support since the mid-1970s. In Peru, the Shining Path originated in the late 1970s and early 1980s in Ayacucho and other predominantly rural departments of the southern highlands. In the mid-1980s, the movement expanded in coca-growing areas. By the late 1980s and early 1990s, Sendero was vigorous not only virtually throughout Peru's highlands but also in major cities, including Lima.

For El Salvador, this chapter shows that, for the most part, national living standards were not declining during the period that the FMLN was emerging, and accordingly there was no change in the national economy that could be considered a trigger to a revolutionary movement with a significant base in the capital city in its early years. The expectations of most recent university graduates and teachers for middle-class status were being met. During the 1980s, most national economic trends in El Salvador became negative; however, the trends were not as negative as in Peru and absolute living standards were not as low, and at the same time popular support for the FMLN was not increasing.

Analysis of trends among Salvadoran peasants is more complex. Various trends in Salvadoran peasants' living standards were positive, while others were negative. Which economic variable was most important? How much change is necessary in the variable if it is to be assessed not as a constant precondition, but rather a changing precipitant? Is inequality or deprivation relative to others most important, or is absolute deprivation? How does the analyst determine a link between the negative economic trend and the emergence of the revolutionary movement? Is it necessary that there be a correlation between the areas of the country where the trend is most severe and the areas where the movement emerged? Is it necessary that militants cite the factor in their explanations for their adherence to the movement? As chapter 1 indicated, scholars do not agree on the answers to these questions.

The most serious negative trend among Salvadoran peasants during the 1970s was landlessness. If the scholar focuses only on this variable, and disregards the facts that landlessness was not more severe in Chalatenango and Morazán than in other rural areas and that landlessness was not frequently cited by FMLN militants as one of the key factors in their decision to join the movement (see chapter 6), the scholar could conclude that economic variables were not just a constant or precondition of the Salvadoran revolutionary movement, but were also a changing precipitant.

This view is rejected in this chapter. Here, although I acknowledge that evidence on some indicators is not ideal, I emphasize that other socioeconomic trends in the countryside were positive, that peasants' subsistence was rarely threatened, that the correlation between areas of more severe poverty and FMLN membership was scant, and that economic variables were not emphasized by militants in their explanations of their decisions to join the FMLN. Accordingly, I contend that poverty among Salvadoran peasants during the 1970s was more of a constant than a catalyst: Peasants were not happy about their living standards; if they had been, they would have been less likely to rebel. But economic variables cannot explain when, where, or ultimately why the revolutionary movement expanded in El Salvador.[1]

By contrast, in Peru poverty was far from a constant either at the national level or among peasants. From the late 1970s through the early 1990s, national economic trends in Peru were among the most negative in the region. In the late 1970s and early 1980s, living standards declined most precipitously among southern highlands peasants, many of whom were frustrated that the government's agrarian reform program had not brought them significant benefits. Especially during

1982–83, when the exceptionally warm Pacific Ocean currents of what is commonly called "El Niño" brought severe drought to the southern highlands, peasants' subsistence was threatened. The correlation between the predominantly rural departments of most severe misery and the emergence of Sendero is clear. When the problem of rural poverty began to be seriously addressed in 1985 and 1986 by the new García government, the effort was too little, too late; Sendero was already ensconced in the southern highlands and attacked agronomists, engineers, and others who were trying to implement development programs.

Outside the southern highlands, living standards declined between the late 1970s and 1985, but for the most part during these years subsistence was not threatened in Peru's cities. Also, despite the long-term negative trend, a modicum of economic recovery occurred between 1980 and 1982 and again between 1985 and 1987.[2] It was not until 1988 and the second half of García's term that a deep, prolonged plunge in living standards occurred in most Peruvian cities. The plunge deepened further in August 1990, when President Fujimori administered the "Fujishock" that ultimately enabled Peru to return to the good graces of the international financial community but also sent hundreds of thousands of previously middle-class persons to soup kitchens. Again, there is a clear correlation between the timing of the economic decline in Peru's cities and the revolutionary movement's expansion in them.

Importantly for my argument, the data in this chapter show that the economic performance of the control case, Ecuador, was considerably better than Peru's. Indeed, among the variables considered in this book as factors in the origins of revolutionary movements, it is in economic performance during the 1970s and 1980s that Peru stands out as faring worse than Ecuador. (See chapter 1 for a discussion of Ecuador as a "control case.")

As was evident in chapter 1, the "misery matters most" school focuses on the peasantry and other social sectors; in this chapter, however, I also examine the interplay between economic reversal and the capabilities of the state. Whereas Skocpol perceives the capabilities of the state to be undermined primarily by international pressures rather than by internal economic problems, I suggest here that the capabilities of Peru's state were undermined considerably by the country's internal economic problems. In the fourth section of this chapter, I examine the capabilities of the state agencies in Peru's health sector relative to those of the state agencies in Ecuador's and El Salvador's health sectors. (Some of the data in this section also document the inferior health standards in Peru relative to Ecuador and El Salvador.) The section argues that the erosion of the Peruvian state's capabilities was primarily a result of scant economic resources. I assess an alternative explanation for the inferior capabilities of the Peruvian state—corruption—and find this explanation wanting.

A question that cannot be fully addressed in this book is why Peru experienced a more severe economic decline in the 1980s and early 1990s than most Latin American nations. In other words, to what extent did economic decline reflect other noneconomic problems?

One noneconomic problem can be addressed, however. It was noted in chapter 1 that Jack Goldstone posits that demographic growth is the underlying variable that weakens economies and burdens states. In the cases of Peru and El Salvador, demographic growth was indeed marked. Between 1961 and 1970, the average annual population growth rate was 2.6 percent in Peru and 3 percent in El Salvador; between 1971 and 1980, the rate was 2.7 percent in Peru and 2.3 percent in El Salvador; and, between 1981 and 1990, 2.2 percent in Peru and 1.5 percent in El Salvador; however, the rate of population growth was similar throughout the region during these three decades and indeed was greater in Ecuador.[3] Accordingly, the problem was not demographic growth per se but how demographic growth intensified popular pressures for land and employment, and how these pressures were met or not met.

I do not argue that economic decline was the only factor in the expansion of the Shining Path. Peru's economic plunge was a spark igniting dry political timbers; it provided an unprecedented opportunity to a shrewd revolutionary organization and provoked new problems for a state whose legitimacy was limited in any case. Nor do I argue that economic grievances were unimportant to the expansion of the FMLN. Rather, the argument here is that, relative to El Salvador, the economic plunge in Peru was extraordinarily deep and severely afflicted not only peasants but also university-educated aspirants to the middle class; especially given that the correlations between the onset of misery and the emergence of Sendero are strong and that economic conditions are frequently cited by Sendero militants as a key reason for their joining the movement (see chapter 6), it is appropriate to conclude that the plunge was the triggering variable in Peru's revolutionary equation. In sum, the Peruvian but not the Salvadoran case supports the scholarly school that "misery matters most."

National Economic Trends

Tables 4.1, 4.2, and 4.3 provide official data about trends in per capita economic product, unemployment, and the real minimum wage in Peru, El Salvador, and Ecuador. These official statistics are subject to many reservations. In particular, in all three countries many economic activities are within what Hernando de Soto first dubbed the "informal sector"—the unofficial sector of underground economic activity beyond government regulation and taxation, which includes street vendors in urban areas as well as coca growers in rural areas.[4] Outside the formal framework of the economy, this sector is very difficult to measure. In Peru in particular, the informal sector is very large, but by definition its precise size is unknown.[5] Accordingly, official figures on per capita product and other economic phenomena are estimates, but they are the only data available for over-time and cross-national analysis.[6]

Table 4.1 documents trends in per capita product in Peru, El Salvador, and Ecuador, as well as in Latin America as a whole.[7] The data indicate Peru's exceptionally poor performance during the 1970s and 1980s. The first three columns of the table demonstrate that, whereas in the early 1970s GNP per capita in Peru was at $1,000, roughly double GNP per capita in El Salvador or Ecuador, by 1989 GNP per capita in El Salvador and Ecuador had edged higher than in Peru. In 1989, Peru's GNP per capita was still the same in current dollars as in the early 1970s; using real 1989 dollars, economists calculate that the $1,000 per capita income in Peru in 1989 is about 25 percent less than that recorded fifteen to twenty years earlier (in the early 1970s), and similar to the level recorded in 1961.[8]

The data in the second set of columns in the table demonstrate that, whereas the rate of growth in GDP per capita was almost at the regional average in Peru in the 1960s, it was way below regional standards in the 1970s and 1980s. Indeed, considering both decades, Peru's decline in GDP per capita was among the most severe in the region: decline was more marked only in Guyana and Nicaragua.[9]

Table 4.1. Trends in Per Capita Product, 1961–90

	GNP Per Capita (in current U.S. $)			GDP Per Capita (average annual growth rate)		
	circa 1959–64	circa 1971–75	1989	1961–70	1971–80 (percentages)	1981–90
Peru	390	1,000	1,010	2.5	0.9	−3.2
El Salvador	270	430	1,070	2.3	0.2	−1.9
Ecuador	250[a]	540	1,020	1.9	5.7	−0.9
Regional Average	431	931	1,519	2.6	3.4	−1.1

Sources: GNP per capita: Data from World Bank, *Social Indicators of Development 1990* (Baltimore: Johns Hopkins University Press, 1991), 89, 93, and 125.

GDP per capita: For 1961–70, Inter-American Development Bank (1990, 263); for 1971–80 and 1981–90, Inter-American Development Bank, (1992, 286).

[a]World Bank, *Social Indicators of Development 1993* (Baltimore: Johns Hopkins University Press, 1993), 96.

The contrast between Peru and Ecuador in table 4.1 is the sharpest between the two countries in this book. The IDB's per capita growth-rate figures suggest a better economic performance in Ecuador than the World Bank's absolute GNP per capita figures, but the data of both agencies indicate an Ecuadorean performance superior to Peru's. In part because of a boom in export revenues from petroleum, Ecuador's GDP per capita growth rate was exceptionally high during the 1970s and not as negative as the regional average during the 1980s.

Table 4.1 also indicates that overall economic performance in El Salvador was below regional averages, although not as far below as in Peru. Moreover, average annual GDP growth in El Salvador was moderate not only between 1961 and 1970 but also until 1979.[10] Salvadoran per capita income attained an apex in 1978.[11] The 0.2 percent figure for average annual GDP growth between 1971 and 1980 would have been much higher but for a plummet by 10 percent in 1980—a plummet that was to a significant degree a result of the armed conflict.[12] In other words, given that per capita income was rising until the onset of severe political violence in 1979 and that popular support for the revolutionary movement peaked in approximately 1980–81, macroeconomic decline could not have been a major cause of guerrilla expansion in El Salvador.

Table 4.2 demonstrates trends in unemployment and underemployment in Peru and El Salvador as well as in the region as a whole.

Table 4.2. Trends in Unemployment and Underemployment, Mid-1980s–1990
(percentages of economically active population)

	1984–88			1990		
	Inadequately employed	Under-employed	Unemployed	Inadequately employed	Under-employed	Unemployed
Lima, Peru[a]	47	40	7	94	86	8
San Salvador[b]	52	44	8	41	31	10
El Salvador[c]	55	34	11	Slight positive change likely[d]		
Ecuador[e]	N.A.	N.A.	11	65	50	15
Regional Average[f]	N.A.	N.A.	N.A.	42	37	5

Note: "Open urban enemployment" is the figure conventionally reported by multilateral institutions, but it is not a good indicator of poverty in Latin America; see discussion in the text. N.A. = not available.

[a]Data from the Ministry of Labor in Cuánto (1991, 30). My 1984–88 numbers average the figures for 1984 and 1986, which are similar.

[b]Grupo Asesor Económico y Social, Ministerio de Planificación (1990, 110).

[c]Data for El Salvador from the 1985 national household survey by the Salvadoran Planning Ministry, reported in Francisco Sorto Rivas, "El estado actual de la economía: Fragilidad y retrocesos en la establización," *Política Económica* 1, no. 8 (August–September 1991): 17.

[d]Unemployment and underemployment declined according to official figures, but analysts were skeptical of the data and precise figures were not given. See *Proceso* 11, no. 457 (December 1990): 25–26, and 13, no. 531 (23 September 1992): 8–9; and Zuvekas (1993, 14).

[e]Consejo Nacional de Modernicación del Estado, "Estrategia de modernización," *La estrategia de modernización* (Quito: ANESSE and CEQUIPUS), 79.

[f]Data for 1989, probably for urban areas, from CEPAL, reported by Salvador Arias Peñate and Mariá Concepción Orozco, "Pobreza e inseguridad alimentaria en América Latina," *Estudios Centroamericanos*, no. 525–526 (July–August 1992): 626.

Unfortunately, the data in most international reports are usually only for unemployment; the variation in rates of unemployment per se in Latin America is small, only between about 5 percent and 15 percent, and the variation that is observed does not correspond to widely observed patterns of poverty in the region.[13] Rates of "inadequate employment," summing unemployment and underemployment, appear to be a better indicator, with greater variation across the region and closer correspondence to analysts' perceptions of unemployment problems.[14]

The most striking statistic in table 4.2 is the extremely high rate of inadequate employment in Lima in 1990: 94 percent. This is double the figure for the mid-1980s, and more than double the rate in San Salvador and in Latin America as a whole in 1990.[15] While rates of inadequate employment in El Salvador were probably higher than the regional

Table 4.3. Trends in the Real Minimum Wage, 1969–91

	1979–80[a] (1969–70 = 100)	1988–89[a] (1969–70 = 100)	1989[b] (1980 = 100)	1989[c] Dollar value
Peru	81	38	23	$35
El Salvador	109	47	36	$90
Ecuador	N.A.	N.A.	44	$47
Regional Average	N.A.	N.A.	75	N.A.

[a]For Peru, calculated from Webb and Fernández Baca (1991, 811). Data for Lima only. For El Salvador, calculated from Carlos Mauricio Funes, "El Salvador: Déficit fiscal y gestión macroeconómica, 1970/89," *Cuadernos de Investigación* 3, no. 11 (January 1992): 51. Data for the country as a whole. Authors' sources are official data from the Labor Ministry and the Economics Ministry, respectively. These data are consistent with other sources.

[b]Inter-American Development Bank (1990, 28). Use of 1980 as the base year exaggerates the depth of the plummet in El Salvador, as the minimum wage peaked in 1980 at a level 4 percent higher than in any year between 1969 and 1989; in Peru, wages were higher in 1980 than in the late 1970s but lower than in the early and mid-1970s.

[c]*Perú Económico* 13, no. 8 (August 1990): 43–44.

average during most of this period, at no time did they approach Peru's 94 percent figure.

Table 4.3 shows trends in the real minimum wage in Peru, El Salvador, Ecuador, and the region as a whole.[16] The first column of the table demonstrates that, during the 1970s, the real minimum wage fell almost 20 percentage points in Peru but increased slightly in El Salvador.[17] The next two columns in the table indicate that, during the 1980s, the real minimum wage plunged further in Peru, and also declined in El Salvador. By 1989 in Peru, the real minimum wage had deteriorated to 23 percent of its 1980 value, and in El Salvador to 36 percent of its 1980 value. The decline in Peru was the worst by 13 percentage points among the nineteen Latin American nations for which figures were reported by the Inter-American Development Bank, and the decline in El Salvador was the second worst.[18]

How much were people earning? In contrast to wage trends, dollar wage values are rarely if ever reported in international economic databases, in part because the calculation of dollar values can be difficult.[19] However, providing the figures from a highly respected Peruvian journal, table 4.3 indicates that the dollar value of the minimum wage in Peru in 1989 was roughly 80 percent of the dollar value of the minimum wage in Ecuador, and less than half the dollar value of the minimum wage in El Salvador. Of the fourteen nations included in *Perú Económico*'s table, only in Bolivia was the dollar value of the minimum wage lower than in Peru.[20]

In addition, by 1991 wages had plummeted even further in Peru. Whereas in 1989, the real minimum wage was 23 percent of the 1980 figure, in 1991 it was an even scantier 16 percent.[21] By contrast, the real minimum wage did not appear to decline further in El Salvador.[22] In August 1990, at the moment of the "Fujishock," the monthly minimum wage in Peru was about $20—less than $1 a day.[23] Only after mid-1991 did the minimum wage "rebound"—to about $50 per month.[24]

What do these wages buy? Complained a Venezuelan woman living in a shanty town on about $100–$150 a month: "We used to be able to eat meat. Now we eat noodles."[25] If the Venezuelans could eat only noodles on a wage roughly quadruple the Peruvian level, what were the Peruvians eating? The answer, of course, is not much. During the late 1970s and early 1980s, when the Shining Path was expanding in the highlands, hunger was critical primarily among the peasantry, and for this reason the data on calorie supply and malnutrition are discussed in the next section. (As of 1984, chronic malnutrition was estimated to be more than twice as prevalent in rural areas as in urban.)[26] By the end of the 1980s, however, hunger was pronounced in cities, including Lima. In one rigorous study of a poor community on Lima's outskirts, family income fell by 56 percent between March 1988 and June 1989, and half the people in these communities were unable to buy enough food to meet basic calorie requirements.[27] By the early 1990s, roughly 20 percent to 50 percent of Limeños were eating regularly at soup kitchens, where meals cost less than 25 cents—a trend that did not occur in El Salvador.[28]

The Peasantry

During the 1960s and 1970s, peasants did not fare well in either El Salvador or Peru. Land scarcity was a serious problem in both countries— more serious than in most of the region, and becoming more serious every year. In some areas of El Salvador, land displacement was severe.

However, the availability of land is only one among numerous factors that affect peasants' living standards; these factors include diverse agricultural policies, opportunities for reasonably paid seasonal work, and public health programs (described later in this chapter). Accordingly, despite increasing landlessness, there is no evidence of a sharp overall decline in Salvadoran peasants' living standards or of a threat to peasants' subsistence. There is such evidence, however, for Peru's peasants. Also, given that many peasants consider not only their absolute living standards and changes over time in these standards but also their living standards relative to others, it is important to note that inequality was more severe in Peru than in El Salvador.[29] Further, in Peru there is a clear correlation between the departments of most severe poverty and the rise of the guerrilla movement, but in El Salvador there is not.

Landlessness, Poverty, and Inequality in the 1960s and 1970s

Traditionally, both Peru and El Salvador were among the Latin American nations where land was most scarce and land distribution severely skewed. As of 1979, only one-fifth of an arable hectare of land was available per capita in Peru, and an even more meager one-sixth of an arable hectare in El Salvador. Land per capita was scarcer in Peru and El Salvador than in any of the twelve Latin American nations for which data were reported.[30] By comparison, Ecuador enjoyed 70 percent more land per capita than Peru.[31] Too little land for the rural population in Peru and El Salvador was a problem that could not be ameliorated even in the medium term, and a problem that limited the positive effects that even an ideal agrarian reform could yield.

In both Peru and El Salvador, landholding was grossly unequal. As discussed in chapter 3, during the agroexport boom between 1890 and 1930, indigenous peoples throughout Latin America were driven from their lands by elite families. In popular lore, the "forty families" owning Peru's largest haciendas made up that country's oligarchy, whereas the "fourteen families" owning El Salvador's largest estates made up its oligarchy. By empirical estimates, as of the 1950s and early 1960s, a mere 280 families—or 0.1 percent of all farm families—owned approximately 30 percent of the land in Peru, or well over half of Peru's best arable soil.[32] In El Salvador in the 1970s, the disparity was almost as extreme: about 0.3 percent of all farm families owned 28 percent of the land.[33]

In 1961, the Gini index of land distribution in Peru was the most unequal among fifty-four nations for which data were reported. Ecuador tied for sixth most unequal, and El Salvador was tenth.[34] In this 1961 study, land distribution was not quite as skewed in El Salvador as in Guatemala but was more skewed than in Nicaragua, Honduras, or Costa Rica—a rank order of inequality among the five Central American countries that is also apparent in most datasets on landholding in the region.[35]

Although rigorously comparable data over time are not available for either Peru or El Salvador, it is clear that landlessness was increasing in both countries. For Peru, an approximate estimate of landlessness among farm families prior to the agrarian reform is 30 percent.[36] For El Salvador, estimates that landlessness increased from 12 percent of families in 1961, to 29 percent in 1971, and even further to 41 percent in 1975 were common;[37] but, in a thorough review of this data, Mitchell Seligson has indicated serious flaws, some of which led to underestimation of landlessness and some to overestimation.[38] Still, Seligson indicates that landless and land-poor populations increased from 51 percent of the economically active population in agriculture in 1961 to 60 percent in 1971.[39] Among families with land, an overwhelming 83 percent of the Peruvian families and 87 percent of the Salvadoran held fewer than five hectares.[40]

In Peru, landlessness was increasing primarily as a result of population growth. Haciendas were not expanding and encroaching upon peasant community lands in the 1960s as they had in the first decades of the twentieth century; nor were they reducing their work forces significantly. Indeed, for most hacienda workers, economic conditions were improving during the 1960s.[41]

In El Salvador, landlessness was increasing not only as a result of demographic pressure but also as a result of landowners' actions. Whereas in previous decades Salvadoran elites had encroached upon indigenous communities' lands primarily in the western part of the country to cultivate coffee, in the 1950s and 1960s elites encroached upon lands primarily in the eastern lowlands to grow cotton. Facilitated in the 1950s by the control of tropical diseases and the construction of a paved highway, cotton estates proliferated in the eastern lowlands along the Pacific coast, in the departments of La Paz, San Vicente, Usulután, San Miguel, and La Unión.[42] But these areas did not become key areas of FMLN support. Comments Douglas Kincaid:

> The most thorough and disruptive process of rural proletarianization was undoubtedly that of cotton development in the Pacific lowlands. Yet the wellsprings [of the revolutionary movement] were found [elsewhere]. . . . In the cotton belt the dispersed and fragmented hamlets of landless laborers presented much more difficult terrain for creating local organizations.[43]

Also, especially in the wake of a minimum wage law covering agricultural workers in 1965, landowners were terminating traditional agreements with the sharecroppers *(colonos)* who had resided permanently on the haciendas. Instead of exchanging the *colono* family's labor for its right to work a plot on the hacienda, the landowner would mechanize the hacienda, hire temporary workers, and rent the parcels.[44] Many *colono* families were displaced.

What kinds of land tensions were evident in Chalatenango and Morazán, the two departments where the FMLN became strongest? In both departments, relatively large numbers of peasants owned or rented small plots. Not only was landlessness not severe by Salvadoran standards in these two departments, but the ratio of landholders to landless laborers in El Salvador's fourteen departments was the second greatest in Chalatenango and the fifth greatest in Morazán in 1961.[45] The relatively large percentages of landed peasants in the two departments did not mean that these departments were especially prosperous, however. Rather, much of the land there is stony and mountainous—useful only for the cultivation of basic grains and the grazing of livestock. Indeed, it was due to the unadaptability of this land for export crops such as coffee, cotton, and sugar that there was not the degree of hacienda penetration in these areas as occurred elsewhere in El Salvador.[46] Also, despite the relatively large numbers of landed peasants in these departments, there were high rates of expulsion of sharecroppers as well as demographic pressure in the wake of the return of thousands of Salvadoran peasants from Honduras to this border area in the wake of the 1969 Soccer War.[47] There is no doubt that peasants in Chalatenango and Morazán were poor, and that despite relatively high rates of landedness, they were increasingly obliged to seek seasonal labor on haciendas to subsist.[48] But it was not these economic factors that drew the revolutionary movement to these departments. Explained the ERP's leader Villalobos:

> There was food in Morazán, and people could eat enough to live. There was not extreme poverty. Poverty was worse in Usulután, where there were many

landless peasants and high rates of delinquency. We saw that it was possible to organize. There was not a great deal of migration outside of the department for temporary work. Rather, families were cohesive. The Catholic Church had a strong education effort there, and the Jesuits had organized a peasant confederation.[49]

Further, despite the increasing landlessness in El Salvador, the overall living standards for disadvantaged peasants were considerably higher in El Salvador than in Peru. Commented a former FPL member who was familiar with both Peru and El Salvador:

> The entire eastern fringe of El Salvador was poor, the poorest part of El Salvador. But it was not as poor as Peru, where the poverty shocked me.[50]

The data available on this issue are not ideal; they are neither from the same source nor in the Salvadoran case commonly broken down by department. But data do exist. For example, as of 1970–71, annual family peasant incomes in the Peruvian highlands averaged about $188.[51] By comparison, as of 1975, annual family incomes for the rural Salvadoran landless averaged roughly $315, and incomes for those with less than one hectare of land averaged approximately $400.[52] In the late 1970s, annual per capita income among peasants in eight communities of the central and southern highlands was approximately $75 in Peru versus somewhat below $225 for landless farmworker families in El Salvador.[53]

Data on trends in rural incomes in the two countries are incomplete, in particular for El Salvador. It appears that the incomes of the rural poor declined by roughly similar percentages in the two countries during the 1970s—about 15 percent to 20 percent in both.[54] In Peru, however, this decline was on top of another drop in the 1960s; accordingly, highlands farm income was estimated to be about 30 percent less in the early 1980s than in 1950.[55]

Table 4.4 compares poverty indicators for Ayacucho, other southern highlands departments, and more advantaged departments in Peru, relative to those for Chalatenango and more advantaged departments in El Salvador. Unfortunately, comparative data for other indicators and at later periods were not available for El Salvador.[56] The table indicates exceptionally high levels of infant mortality and lack of safe water in Ayacucho—worse on most indicators than for Chalatenango ten to fifteen years earlier. In 1968, the infant mortality rate in Ayacucho was 197 per 1,000 live births, and in the southern highlands as a whole 208—

Table 4.4. Poverty in Regions of Core Support for Sendero Luminoso and the FMLN

	Infant Mortality Rates (per 1,000 live births)	Number of Inhabitants per Doctor	Without Safe Water (% of population)
Peru, Late 1970s–Early 1980s			
Lima Department	56	525	26
Nationwide	92	1,255	56
Ayacucho	128	16,779	85
Southern Highlands[a]	131	25,028	86
El Salvador, 1967–71			
San Salvador Department	104	1,106	N.A.
Nationwide	118	3,779	45
Chalatenango	124	34,164	70
Morazán	121	N.A.	N.A.

Sources: Peru: Infant mortality data for 1979 from Zschock (1988, 50–51); number of inhabitants per doctor for 1981 from Consejo Nacional de Población, "Perú: Guía demográfica y socioeconomica"; data on percentage of population without safe water from Banco Central de Reserva del Perú, "Perú: Indicadores sociales" (Lima, June 1986), 22.

El Salvador: Infant mortality data for 1967, from CELADE (1988, 18); data on number of inhabitants per doctor apparently for 1971 from Fiedler (1986, appendix E); percentage without potable water for 1971 from Pearce (1986, 51).

[a]Average for Ayacucho, Huancavelica, and Apurímac (the three departments most affected by the Shining Path rebellion in the early 1980s).

more than 50 percent worse than in Chalatenango in almost the same year.[57] The percentage of the population in Ayacucho and the southern highlands lacking safe water in the mid-1980s was also larger than in Chalatenango about fifteen years earlier. Only with respect to the number of inhabitants per doctor did Peru in 1981 fare as well as El Salvador in 1971.

The available cross-regional data for Ecuador also suggest that the lot of Ecuadoreans in the poorest areas of Ecuador was somewhat better than the lot of Peruvians in the poorest areas of Peru. In 1979, the Ecuadorean department with the highest infant mortality rate was Cotopaxi, at 119 deaths per 1,000; Peru's highest rate the same year was 142, almost 20 percent worse, in the southern highlands department of Huancavelica.[58]

Table 4.4 shows too that inequality between disadvantaged and advantaged departments was much more severe in Peru than in El Salvador or Ecuador. The infant mortality rate was 36 percentage points higher in Ayacucho than in Peru nationwide in 1979—versus 6 percentage points higher in Chalatenango than in El Salvador nationwide. Also, in Ayacucho there were thirteen times as many people for each doctor as nationwide and thirty-two times as many people for each doctor as in the department of Lima; the difference between Chalatenango and other Salvadoran departments is not quite as severe. The only indicator in the table in which inequality is not more severe in Peru than in El Salvador is access to safe water.

Considering other poverty indicators, we see that Ayacucho and the other southern highlands departments almost invariably clustered at the nadir. Compared with residents of northern and central highlands departments and with residents of coastal departments in the late 1970s and early 1980s, southern highlands residents earned much less, died much younger, and were much less likely to be literate or enjoy basic services such as potable water and an available doctor.[59] For example, in 1961, agricultural incomes in the southern highlands were less than half of those in the northern and central highlands, and less than one seventh of incomes in Lima.[60] Moreover, agricultural incomes in three Ayacucho provinces of early core support for Sendero—Huanta, Huamanga, and Cangallo—were lower than for all but 9 of Peru's 155 provinces.[61]

In El Salvador and in Ecuador, the map of poverty was more blurred. There is a broad consensus among Salvadorans that, in general, Chalatenango and Morazán are disadvantaged departments; however, these departments do not almost invariably cluster at the nadir on indicators of poverty. For example, as table 4.4 shows, with respect to infant mortality, the rates in Chalatenango and Morazán were not much worse than nationwide; the department where the rate was the worst was La Libertad.[62] On stunted growth, the indicators were the worst in three departments, Morazán, Ahuachapán, and Cabañas; La Libertad fared relatively well.[63] On number of people per doctor, the department of Cabañas fared the worst, while Chalatenango and Morazán fared poorly, but about the same as Cuscatlán and La Unión.[64] On percentages of the urban population in extreme poverty in 1990, Chalatenango and Morazán scored worse, but the difference between these two departments and several others was small.[65]

Also significant, because of the similarities in topography between Peru and Ecuador, is that the map of poverty in Ecuador was more blurred than in Peru. To an even greater degree than in El Salvador, departments that score high or low on one indicator do not necessarily score high or low on other indicators. For example, the department with the highest infant mortality rate in 1979 was Cotopaxi; the department with the least number of hospital beds per person was Bolívar; and the department with the lowest per capita rural income was Loja.[66] Also, Ecuador's largest coastal city and its department, Guayaquil and Guayas, do not stand out at the apex of socioeconomic indicators in Ecuador as Lima does in Peru.[67]

For many key indicators in Ecuador, the degree of inequality was less severe than in Peru. For example, whereas in 1961 per capita farm income in Lima was more than nine times per capita farm income in Ayacucho, the figure for the Ecuadorean department with the highest per capita rural income (Guayas) was less than triple the figure for the Ecuadorean department with the lowest per capita rural income.[68]

Why was inequality less severe in Ecuador than in Peru, despite their similar topography? Perhaps in part because Lima is on the country's coast and Quito is in the highlands. Accordingly, the social and physical infrastructure in Quito and its department of Pichincha are better than in any Peruvian highlands city or department.

Agrarian Reform

The severe problems of landlessness, rural poverty, and inequality were to be addressed in both Peru and El Salvador by agrarian reform programs. The material results of the reforms were not greatly different in the two countries: in both, a small group of peasants—for the most part, peasants who were not among the most disadvantaged—benefited, while most did not. The political implications of the reforms were, however, very different.

In El Salvador, the reform was implemented after the emergence of the FMLN; the reform did not appear to dramatically affect political attitudes toward the FMLN or toward the government. In Peru, by contrast, the reform was implemented prior to the emergence of the Shining Path, and its political implications were considerable, although not at all uniform. On the one hand, the peasants who gained the most from the Peruvian reform (predominantly, the members of coastal cooperatives) were among those Peruvian groups that the Shining Path was least able to attract. On the other hand, the peasants who gained virtually nothing from the reform (predominantly, southern highlands peasants) were more frustrated politically after the reform than before it. They had been promised a reform, and their expectations had been raised; but no benefits were forthcoming.

The key reason for the failure of the Peruvian agrarian reform in the southern highlands was geography; in the remote, arid, precipitous, and windswept departments of Peru's southern highlands, there were few prosperous haciendas to be transferred to peasants.[69] By the late 1970s, there was not a great deal more that agrarian reform per se could really do for large numbers of Peruvian peasants; the Velasco government had expropriated virtually all the country's major profitable haciendas and swept landowning elites from the countryside.[70] In El Salvador, by contrast, the government could have extended major agrarian reform benefits to more peasants; the overwhelming majority of enterprises in the key export sector, coffee, remained unaffected by the reform.[71]

Both the Peruvian and Salvadoran reforms benefited a sector of the peasantry, but in both cases this sector constituted a minority of the total agricultural population (see table 4.5). In Peru, according to the official data reported in the table, 39 percent of the country's agricultural families benefited from the reform, but for various reasons this figure is an exaggeration; 25 percent is more likely, and this figure includes many families whose gains were meager, as we will discuss below.[72]

Only about 10 percent of all agricultural families were clearly "winners" from the reform. These were the 140,000-odd permanent workers on haciendas, who became members of cooperative enterprises, especially those on Peru's coast.[73] Given that the haciendas had been established on Peru's best land, and that the reform was implemented rapidly against the largest, best-capitalized estates (reducing the owners' opportunity to sell livestock or machinery), most ex-hacienda workers gained substantially. The average value of the property transferred to each cooperative member was about $1,900.[74]

In the first decade after the reform, the standard of living among Peruvian cooperative members improved considerably. In the three cooperatives that I studied during this period, real wages approximately doubled between 1973 and 1980.[75] Members gained rights to larger private plots; as the number of nonmanual positions (for instance, accountant,

Table 4.5. Agrarian Reform in Peru and El Salvador

	Were Large Estates Still Owned by Elites?	Hectares in Reform Sector (number)	Hectares in Reform Sector (% of total)	Agricultural Families Benefited (number)	Agricultural Families Benefited[a] (% of total)	Agricultural Families Landless Post-reform[b] (% of total)
Peru	No	10,298,453	55	399,576	39	19
El Salvador	Yes	308,363	21	98,905	23	41

Sources (except for landless): For Peru: Figures as of October 1980 from Martínez and Tealdo (1982, 20). Figures for absolute numbers in reform sector are considerably higher than a year earlier, probably reflecting the military government's taking its last opportunity to report an ambitious reform program. See also Deere (1990, 223); Caballero and Alvarez (1980, 20); and McClintock (1981, 61). For El Salvador: Figures as of June 1991 on the advance of the reform from reports by U.S. AID in San Salvador; they are slightly higher than those reported in Seligson (1995) and most Salvadoran domestic sources. The figures for total hectares (1,451,000) and total agricultural families (420,000) are more consensual than in Peru; see Diskin (1989, 443); Prosterman, Riedinger, and Temple (1981, 60); and Barraclough and Scott (1987, 100), among others.
[a]These figures are controversial and hard to calculate. Calculations of the number of peasants per "agricultural family" vary according to the analyst's goals, as Seligson (1995, 46); Matos Mar and Mejía (1980, 68); and Diskin (1989, 443) discuss.
[b]Figure for 1988 from Jazairy, Alamgir, and Panuccio (1992, 406–407).

truck driver, construction supervisor) increased, many members secured promotions to these positions for themselves or their children. During the 1970s, major improvements were evident in the housing, school, transportation, and other facilities at the cooperatives. In my 1974 sample survey in the two coastal cooperatives, 80 percent of respondents believed that, overall, the cooperatives were either "a lot" or "somewhat" helpful, and 51 percent perceived themselves as better off than before the reform.[76]

In El Salvador, about 23 percent of agricultural families benefited from the reform—a lower number than the official Peruvian figure reported in table 4.5 but similar to the more realistic estimate of 25 percent suggested above.[77] In El Salvador, there were two major sets of beneficiaries: the permanent hacienda workers who became members of large cooperative enterprises by the decrees of "Phase 1" and accounted for perhaps as many as 10 percent of all agricultural families, and the tenants who gained individual ownership rights by the decrees of "Phase 3" and accounted for about 13 percent of all agricultural families.[78]

It appears that about as many Phase 1 and Phase 3 Salvadoran benefi-ciaries as Peruvian cooperative members viewed their country's agrarian reform positively. In a nationwide 1987 survey encompassing 411 agricul-tural households and 69 beneficiaries, 61 percent said that the reform had been "good," 22 percent "bad," and 17 percent "mixed."[79] While only about 30 percent of the beneficiaries in this survey believed that their quality of life was better in 1987 than it had been in 1978, this percent-age was 26 percent higher than for nonbeneficiaries.[80] Among a set of relatively privileged reform sites at a later date (when there had been a reduction in political violence), perceptions of improved living con-ditions in the wake of the reform were much more common; about 90 percent of the respondents in an Orellana survey said that their liv-ing conditions were better than before the reform, and almost all said that the cooperatives had helped at least a little.[81]

The Salvadoran Phase 1 beneficiaries gave reasons similar to those of their Peruvian counterparts for their positive evaluations of the reform. Job security, better housing with private plots, improved education, and medical services were cited.[82] Incomes also apparently increased.[83] Among Phase 3 beneficiaries, who had gained individual property rights, the most common positive comment was about land ownership.[84] Making capital improvements on their land and also increasing their off-farm remunerative pursuits, Phase 3 beneficiaries nearly doubled their annual family income between 1982 and 1984.[85]

Still, many beneficiaries were unenthusiastic. Some of the problems for Peruvian and Salvadoran cooperative members were similar.[86] In both nations, serious problems included corruption; disincentives to hard work, given that usually all members received the same wages; and conflicts between cooperative members and technical managers, who were often appointed at least in part by the government. In the early years especially, members' fears that they would not be able to pay their debts to the state for the adjudication of the cooperative were pronounced, but ultimately the financial burden was not severe in either country.[87]

In El Salvador, however, the benefits of the reform were seriously compromised by various additional problems. In particular, violence against the reform process was intense. In 1980–81, more than five hun-dred peasant leaders and dozens of land reform officials (including the head of the Salvadoran Institute of Agrarian Transformation) were assassinated by right-wing death squads.[88] The FMLN also opposed the agrarian reform. Although assassinations of peasants by the FMLN were rare, the guerrillas exacted war taxes from many cooperatives and carried out economic sabotage against some.[89]

Also, between 1982 and 1984, ARENA controlled the Salvadoran agrarian reform agency, and top officials facilitated sabotage of the reform by landowners.[90] Landowners were able to remove an estimated 25 percent of their farm machinery and slaughter 30 percent of the cattle.[91] They overvalued their land and the capital on the hacienda (for the purposes of their compensation by the state).[92] They also credibly threatened eviction against beneficiaries who had not yet received land titles.[93]

Accordingly, many potential beneficiaries of the Salvadoran reform opted out. About two-thirds of the peasants expected to request land under Phase 3 did not make a claim.[94] Also, about 15 percent of original Phase 1 beneficiaries had deserted their cooperatives by 1985.[95]

To what extent were the beneficiaries of the Peruvian and Salvadoran reforms the most disadvantaged peasants? In Peru, almost not at all. As noted above, the majority of the significant beneficiaries of Peru's reform were the ex-hacienda workers who became members of coastal cooperatives. However, enjoying stable employment on lucrative estates, ex-hacienda workers had earned prereform incomes approximately quadruple those of average families in the poorest areas of the rural highlands.[96] After the reform, the differential was to become much greater.

In El Salvador, data distinguishing among the agricultural poor are relatively scant; however, the Salvadoran beneficiaries appear closer to median peasant strata than their Peruvian counterparts. Data on the prereform incomes of Phase 1 beneficiaries are especially meager; although they were presumably somewhat better off than average, they were not on the country's most lucrative estates, and they were probably less well paid and more vulnerable to expulsion than residents on the coffee haciendas. For Phase 3 beneficiaries, data are available, and their socioeconomic position was similar to that of Salvadoran peasants overall; roughly 40 percent of Phase 3 families were among the "rural poor."[97]

Both the Peruvian and the Salvadoran reforms were least effective in precisely the departments where guerrilla movements either were to become strong, as in Peru, or already were strong, as in El Salvador. In El

Salvador, the reason was straightforward: these departments were already dominated by the FMLN when the reform began, and the FMLN effectively blocked the reform.[98] Peasants applying for benefits from Phase 3 of the reform were less than 25 percent of the estimated number of eligible beneficiaries in Chalatenango and Morazán, versus more than 80 percent in three coffee-producing, relatively prosperous northwestern departments: Sonsonate, Ahuachapán, and La Libertad.[99] Although the amount of land in Chalatenango and Morazán is similar to that in Ahuachapán and La Libertad,[100] the land adjudicated under Phase 1 was much less.[101] About eight thousand hectares were adjudicated as Phase 1 cooperatives in the two departments along the Salvadoran border, versus approximately sixty-two thousand in the two southwestern departments.[102]

In Peru, however, the reasons for the ineffectiveness of the reform in the country's highlands, and in its southern highlands in particular, were complex, rooted in the marginality of the area and its history of tensions between peasant groups. In Peru, as in other Andean nations where indigenous communities endured despite the encroachment of haciendas on their land, community members were usually at odds with hacienda workers. For their part, peasant community members believed that "agrarian reform" was the return of the land taken from them by the haciendas. But the hacienda workers, who generally enjoyed higher living standards than the peasant community members, did not want the dissolution of the enterprises or the end of their jobs.

What to do? Some highlands peasants—about one-sixth of all beneficiaries in Peru—became members of "Peasant Groups."[103] These groups were established on ex-haciendas that had not been well capitalized and that had not rigorously organized their labor force, and peasants generally opted to work the land individually.[104] The average value of property received by a Peasant Group beneficiary was about $325—only approximately one-sixth the valued received by an average cooperative member.[105]

Also, some highlands peasant community members—about one-third of all beneficiaries in Peru—received additional pasture lands and the like from contiguous ex-haciendas.[106] Again, however, these ex-haciendas had usually not been very prosperous, and most of the land was poor. The average value of the property transferred to a peasant community member was only about $50 nationwide, and it was even less in the southern highlands.[107]

By far the most controversial strategy, however, was the establishment of the Agrarian Social Interest Societies (Sociedades agrícolas de interes social, SAIS), which joined ex-haciendas and peasant communities.[108] The goal of the enterprise was to maintain the capitalist advances that had been made in Peru's more prosperous haciendas and to provide some benefits to nearby disadvantaged peasant communities. Approximately one-sixth of official Peruvian reform beneficiaries were members of the SAIS.[109] However, as chapter 6 discusses in detail, the SAIS did not satisfy either its ex-hacienda members or its peasant-community members. Although the ex-hacienda members generally remained better off than their peasant-community counterparts, they complained that they should not be required to share the fruits of their labor with others. For their part, although peasant-community members often did receive at least some benefits from the SAIS, they continued to want the ex-hacienda land.

Overall, the reform benefits that were received by disadvantaged southern highlands peasants were even scantier than those received elsewhere in the highlands. Most did not benefit at all. In 1975, of economically active families in agriculture, 87 percent in Ayacucho, 82 percent in Apurímac, and 54 percent in Huancavelica were not reform beneficiaries, versus 50 percent in La Libertad and Lambayeque, two north-coast departments.[110] Among southern highlands peasants who were beneficiaries, most were peasant-community members who were not joined to SAIS; as noted above, the average value of the property transferred to a member was less than $50.[111] Whereas in two north-coast departments as of 1975, peasant-community families accounted for only 2 percent of all beneficiaries, they accounted for 42 percent of all beneficiaries in Ayacucho and Apurímac.[112]

Efforts to establish SAIS in the southern highlands were even less successful than elsewhere. The haciendas in these departments were relatively poor; accordingly, the SAIS could not provide significant benefits to peasant communities, and the SAIS collapsed. For example, in the large SAIS Huancavelica, peasant-community members represented about one-sixth of all Huancavelica agrarian reform "beneficiaries"; but the value of the SAIS upon adjudication was only 10 percent that of a well-capitalized SAIS in the central highlands.[113] The peasant communities in the SAIS were angry at the paucity of help from the SAIS, and by the late 1970s peasant-community members began to invade ex-hacienda lands. In 1980, SAIS Huancavelica dissolved.[114]

The prevailing conventional wisdom tends to attribute the problems that emerged in Peru's countryside in the wake of the agrarian reform to the reform policy.[115] As we have just seen, there were problems in the reform and its implementation; however, this interpretation ignores (1) the benefits that accrued to coastal cooperative members who rejected the Shining Path and (2) other agricultural policies that were critically important to peasants' living standards.

What kinds of other policies matter? They are various: policies that try to maintain positive terms of trade for agriculture, government credit for the agricultural sector, public investment in agriculture, and social service programs targeted to the countryside. (By one estimate, 50 percent of poor Latin Americans' incomes are derived from government social services.)[116] Overall, the available data suggest that these policy trends were much more consistently negative in Peru than elsewhere.

Trends in the terms of trade for agricultural products are indicated in the second column of table 4.6.[117] The table shows the change in prices to the producer for key crops in Peru, El Salvador, Ecuador, and the region as a whole. As table 4.6 shows, between 1970 and 1988 real producer prices declined about twice as much in Peru as in El Salvador, and four times as much as in Ecuador.[118]

Table 4.6 also shows that potable-water program targets for the countryside were less vigorous in Peru than in El Salvador. The percentage of the Peruvian rural population that gained access to safe water between roughly 1970 and 1990 was only about 13 percent versus 43 percent in El Salvador. Both nations' records fell below the regional average, however. (The weak public health effort in Peru relative to both El Salvador and the region as a whole is discussed in detail in the next section.)

Data on other government policies for the agricultural sector are limited for El Salvador; a comparison between these policies in Peru and Ecuador, however, shows that policies were much less favorable in Peru. Between 1970 and 1982, the amount of official agricultural credit remained about the same in Peru—in contrast to a 250 percent jump in Ecuador.[119] Similarly, real public investment in agriculture barely

Table 4.6. Trends in Rural Poverty

	Daily Calorie Supply[a] (per person)		Producer Prices[b] (% annual change, 1970–88, in real terms, 7 to 10 crops)	Access to Safe Water[c] (% of rural population)	
	1988	% Change from 25–30 Years before 1988		Most Recent Estimate	% Change from 15–20 Years before 1990
Peru	2,269	−2	−15.4	17	+13
El Salvador	2,415	+29	−5.8	40	+43
Ecuador	2,338	+10	−3.7	31	+287
Regional Average	2,728	+18	−9.3	53	+55

[a]World Bank, *Social Indicators of Development 1990* (Baltimore: Johns Hopkins University Press, 1991), 89, 93, 245, and relevant pages for region. Data indicated in table for 1988 are listed as "most recent estimate" by the World Bank but are indicated as 1988 data in U.S. Agency for International Development, *Latin America and the Caribbean: Selected Economic and Social Data* (Washington, D.C.: U.S. AID, 1992), 78.

[b]Jazairy, Alamgir, and Panuccio (1992, 434–435). Products are rice, wheat, maize, sorghum, groundnuts, coffee, cocoa, tea, cotton, and sugar cane. Data were available for all products for Peru, eight for El Salvador, and seven for Ecuador.

[c]World Bank, *Social Indicators of Development 1990* (Baltimore: Johns Hopkins University Press, 1991), 88, 92, and 244, and relevant pages for region.

increased in Peru between the early 1970s and the mid-1980s, in contrast to large annual increases in Ecuador.[120] Moreover, Peru's agricultural investments were inordinately skewed toward super-high-technology projects benefiting small numbers of families on Peru's coast.[121]

As suggested above, in the context of increasingly severe land scarcity, peasants throughout Latin America have looked more intently to seasonal employment on large enterprises in order to subsist, and accordingly trends in agricultural wages for temporary workers are also very important. On the Peruvian coast, the availability and remuneration of jobs did not appear to change much for agricultural workers during the 1970s; in the highlands, however, these conditions worsened considerably.[122] In Apurímac, the daily agricultural wage was a mere $0.50 in 1982.[123] In El Salvador, data are not available for the key 1970s decade. Between 1978 and the mid-1980s, both job availability and wages in the agricultural sector fell considerably.[124] But, even after these declines, daily agricultural wages in El Salvador—approximately $1.80—were much higher than in Peru.[125]

Accordingly, even in highlands peasant communities that had bene-fited considerably from the Peruvian agrarian reform, peasants were very critical of their plights. Consider, for example, peasants' attitudes in the peasant community Vilca. Vilca had become a member of SAIS Cahuide, one of the most largest and most prosperous of the highlands SAIS.[126] In contrast to most peasant communities that became mem-bers of the SAIS, SAIS Cahuide had made a significant effort to help its peasant communities. However, in an informal survey that my Osores research team carried out in 1980, 84 percent of twenty-five Vilca re-spondents said that the community's progress in recent years had been "bad."[127] Vilca peasants were also asked, "What have been the achieve-ments in your community in recent years?" Despite the optimistic phrase-ology, 92 percent of the respondents answered, "None." My research team asked the same questions in two other sites in 1980, one a coastal cooperative and the other a prosperous peasant community near Huan-cayo. Of fifty-five respondents in these sites, only 7 percent said that progress had been "bad."[128]

Threat to Subsistence?

In Peru, disadvantaged peasants' subsistence was threatened during the late 1970s and 1980s. This does not appear to have been the case in El Sal-vador; unfortunately, although data are available for El Salvador at the national level, they are not available broken down for the rural sector or for specific departments.[129]

Among the most relevant cross-national data that are available are for calorie supply. Calorie supply is calculated from domestic food pro-duction and food imports, minus food exports. The first column of table 4.6 indicates the level of daily calorie supply in Peru and El Salva-dor in 1988, and the trends in supply between about 1960 and 1988. The trend in Peru was negative during this period—an unusual reversal for the region. In Ecuador, the trend was positive; in El Salvador, it was extremely positive—above the regional average. The data in table 4.6 are corroborated by other sources. In the *Statistical Abstract of Latin Amer-ica*, per capita calorie supply in Peru was calculated to have declined from 2,272 calories daily in 1975 to 2,120 in 1980–87 (versus an in-crease in El Salvador from 2,061 to 2,456).[130] Also, a World Bank study in the early 1980s determined that Peru was one of only three Latin

American nations where average food consumption per person was less than 90 percent of national standards.[131]

Even more negative trends are indicated for per capita calorie supply in data reported by Peruvian institutions. Webb and Fernández Baca indicate per capita calorie consumption at only 1,781 calories nationwide in 1985, not only lower than in the 1970s but also lower than in 1947, the earliest date for which a figure is provided (versus the 2,400 calories recommended for Peruvians by international food and health organizations).[132] In another study by a Peruvian research group, daily per capita calorie consumption was estimated to have declined 9.5 percent between 1972 and 1986.[133]

For Peru's poor, the decline in calorie consumption was steeper, and evident earlier. By one estimate, daily per capita consumption among lower-class people throughout the country fell from 1,934 calories in 1972 to 1,486 in 1979.[134] The World Bank reported that, in Peru's rural highlands, per capita calorie consumption dropped from 2,085 calories daily in 1972 to 1,971 in 1980—a 5 percent decline, sharper than the nationwide drop indicated in table 4.6.[135] In the southern highlands, conditions approximated famine; there were reports of consumption of as little as 420 calories a day.[136]

These adverse trends were exacerbated in 1982–83 by bad weather during a severe El Niño. In that year, the southern highlands were devastated by drought. Production of the potato, highland peasants' food staple, plunged by 40 percent to 50 percent, and subsistence was not merely threatened but devastated for many peasants:

> In the southern Andes, severe drought completely destroyed the harvest, forcing peasants to consume surplus seed intended for this year's planting. Starvation is rampant among subsistence farmers; illness, particularly tuberculosis, has spread alarmingly. . . . News reports documented cases of peasants selling their children for $25.[137]

Cross-national data are also available in World Bank sources for malnutrition in children. These data suggest that the rates of malnutrition in children under five were similar in Peru and El Salvador during the 1970s, and that the rate was declining in both countries during the 1980s.[138]

Although data from Salvadoran sources are unfortunately not available by which to corroborate or not corroborate the World Bank data for El Salvador,[139] data from Peruvian sources disconfirm the World

Bank data. Whereas only about 20 percent of children under five were reported malnourished by the World Bank in the mid-1970s and early 1980s, 39 percent of children under six were reported chronically malnourished in 1984 according to Waterlow standards and 45 percent according to Gomez standards by the National Statistical and Information Institute (Instituto Nacional de Estadística y Informatica, INEI), which carried out a national survey of nutrition and health in that year.[140] Of course, in rural areas and especially in poor rural families, the rates were higher. In the same 1984 survey, chronic malnutrition in rural areas was estimated at 57 percent.[141] In another 1984 study, chronic malnutrition was evident in more than 70 percent of the children under six in the homes of subsistence peasants and day agricultural laborers.[142]

What have been my own and other analysts' impressions about hunger during travels in El Salvador and Peru? Briefly, there is much less concern in El Salvador than in Peru.[143] When I was traveling in various departments in El Salvador, including Morazán and Chalatenango, people did not themselves raise the issue of hunger.[144] When I asked the question "Is there hunger in this country?" Salvadorans' answer tended to be, "Only for orphans, or the disabled." Or, on other occasions, "Only if the family has broken down." Of the many times that I posed this question, only once, in the village of Arcatao in Chalatenango, did a peasant respond, "Yes, there are some poor here who can't eat."

By contrast, in Peru, hunger was an intense concern by the early 1980s in the rural highlands and by the late 1980s even in Lima. Journalists were much more likely to report stories about hunger in Peru than in El Salvador; consider, for example, the report in the *Christian Science Monitor* in 1988 that children in a village in the department of Puno were so hungry that they were eating newspaper.[145] Often, without my or my research team's posing a question about hunger, Peruvians expressed rage and despair about it:

> There's no help from the government. On the contrary, everything costs more. Living has just become impossible and every day it's more difficult, especially when you have kids and depend solely on your land.146

> Here, they've always forgotten us. There's no help. Exactly the opposite— the cost of everything has risen too much, and that's not the way to help. They're killing the poor people.[147]

Educated Aspirants to the Middle Class

In virtually all Latin American guerrilla movements, the leaders have been university-educated intellectuals whose origins are middle class or upper middle class, and the Salvadoran and Peruvian cases are no exceptions.[148] Revolutionary movements that have won power in Latin America have also been able to secure considerable political support among professional middle-class groups. In contrast to previous Latin American revolutionary groups, however, at the middle fighting ranks of Shining Path were large numbers of young people—often, from peasant origins —who aspired to enter the middle class and who had gained the education to enter it but then were denied entry.[149] The Shining Path's expansion was due in large part to its appeal not to peasants but to relatively well-educated young people whose professional aspirations had been frustrated. In this section, data additional to that in the first section show this problem to be very severe, much more so than in El Salvador and very probably to a degree unprecedented in Latin America.

After World War II in Latin America, secondary school and university enrollments increased dramatically (see table 4.7). The table shows that secondary school and university enrollments increased especially dramatically in Peru, well above the regional average. Astoundingly, in the early 1990s, the percentage of the relevant age group enrolled in university education in Peru was well above the regional average, and higher by more than 10 percentage points than in much more prosperous Latin American countries, including Chile, Venezuela, and Colombia. The figure was 25 percentage points higher than the number in El Salvador, which was considerably below the regional average.

While the number of university students increased dramatically at the national level in Peru, the growth was even larger in Ayacucho. Between 1960 and 1970, the number of university students nationwide in Peru increased about 3.6 times, versus an explosive 9.7 times in Ayacucho; and between 1960 and 1980 it increased about 8 times nationwide versus a dizzying 20 times in Ayacucho.[150]

During the 1960s and 1970s unemployment was rare among university-educated persons in Latin America, but by the early 1980s the number of university-educated persons was swelling and the number of employment opportunities commensurate with qualifications was not rising

Table 4.7. Trends in Secondary School and University Enrollments

	Secondary School Enrollment (% of age group)			University Enrollment (% of age group)	
	Early 1990s[a]	1975	1965	1993	1970
Peru	70	46	25	40[b]	19
El Salvador	26	9	17	15	4
Ecuador	56	40	17	20[c]	37
Regional Average[d]	50	34	19	15	15

Sources: For early 1990s secondary school enrollment, World Bank, *Social Indicators of Development 1993* (Baltimore: Johns Hopkins University Press, 1993). For 1965 and 1975 data, World Bank, *Social Indicators of Development 1988.* University enrollments in the World Bank, *World Development Report,* 1996 edition (table 7, pp. 200–201), and 1994 edition (table 28, pp. 216–217). Similar trends for university enrollments are reported in James W. Wilkie, Enrique C. Ochoa, and David Lorey, eds., *Statistical Abstract of Latin America,* vol. 28 (Los Angeles: UCLA Latin American Center Publications, 1990), table 904.

[a]Precise year is not available. The data are indicated as "MRE" (most recent estimate). Given that the publication date is 1993, the data are presumably in the range of 1989 to 1992.

[b]Figure in italics in *World Development Report,* and accordingly one or two years distant from 1993.
[c]Figure for 1991.

[d]Regional averages for secondary school enrollment calculated by my research team from the data in the relevant sources (twenty-two nations for MREs and twenty for 1965 and 1975). Regional averages for university enrollments calculated by the World Bank and included in the relevant publications.

accordingly.[151] In the early 1980s, the increase in unemployment among people with a high level of education was about double that for the rest of the unemployed.[152]

In Peru, where the number of educated young people was especially large, the problem of unemployment was especially severe. While presumably most secondary and all university graduates aspired to white-collar employment, the availability of such positions did not increase commensurately. As percentages of total employment for the economically active population, private-sector white-collar employment remained at about 13 percent during the 1980s, and public-sector white-collar employment at about 10 percent.[153] Between 1986 and 1990, the percentage of the economically active population in managerial and administrative positions declined from 4 percent to 3 percent, and the percentage in professional and technical positions from 14 percent to 13 percent; the percentage of employers sank from 2 percent in 1961 to 1 percent in 1988.[154] As of the mid-1980s, about 9 percent of secondary and university graduates were unemployed in Lima.[155] Between 1986 and 1990, the percentage of university-educated family heads whose households were classified as poor increased from 9 percent to 25 percent.[156]

In El Salvador, opportunities for professional employment did not increase dramatically, but the number of well-educated aspirants to these positions was not as large. Although figures on employment in the public sector in El Salvador during the 1980s are imprecise, estimates range from a 10 percent increase to a 20 percent increase.[157] In part because of the significantly larger presence of international agencies in El Salvador during the 1980s, opportunities for highly skilled professionals increased beyond the supply.[158] In my own experience contracting survey researchers in El Salvador and Peru, the cost of the research was roughly five times greater in El Salvador than in Peru—presumably reflecting the much smaller supply of university graduates who could do this kind of work in El Salvador.

In Peru, not only were many well-educated persons' aspirations for professional employment dashed, but also remuneration plummeted. Table 4.8 shows that, whereas in 1980 the average monthly wage in the public sector was approximately $230, by 1985 the wage had fallen to $97 and by 1990 to $39. By contrast, in El Salvador, during the period of the most intense guerrilla challenge in the early 1980s, the average monthly wage in the central government actually increased. As table 4.8 indicates, average monthly wages in the Salvadoran public sector were higher than in Peru at the start of the decade, rose considerably by 1985, and then eroded—but remained at much higher levels than in Peru by the same year.

As chapter 6 describes, teachers were key members of the middle and upper ranks of the Shining Path. Although data on teachers' wages are available only in country-specific documents, it is clear that teachers' wages in Peru plunged during the 1980s, and that they were much lower than in El Salvador. At their nadir after the 1990 "Fujishock," in 1991, average salaries for teachers in Peruvian public schools fell to as low as $40 monthly.[159] Even university professors were earning only about $70 a month at this time.[160] For about three years prior to the nadir and for a few months after it, schoolteachers' average salary was about $90 monthly.[161] Not surprisingly, at such wage levels many schoolteachers

Table 4.8. Wages in the Public Sector, 1980–90, Peru and El Salvador
(average monthly wages in dollars)

	1980	1985	1988	1990
Peru	232	97	111	39
El Salvador	282	324	227	N.A.[a]

Sources: For Peru, Cuánto (1991, 31). Calculation by Cuánto. For El Salvador, my calculation from data in Antonio Orellana, "Desarrollo de los movimientos gremiales en el sector público" (San Salvador, September 1986), and Instituto Nacional de Pensiones de los Empleados Públicos, "Memoria de labores del 1 de enero al 31 Diciembre de 1988" (San Salvador, October 1989, table 3), using exchange-rate data from *International Financial Statistics Yearbook* (Washington, D.C.: International Monetary Fund, 1992), 333. Unfortunately, it is impossible to determine variations in the calculation of what constitutes "average" wages.

[a]Interviews in early 1991 with Antonio Orellana suggested that salaries had increased, especially because of U.S. support for government salaries. He indicated that well-qualified individuals were entering government posts at $250 to $350 a month. Referring to a slightly earlier period, however, Gregory (1991) suggests a decline in salaries, especially at the higher ranks.

could not provide their own children with three meals a day.[162] Teachers' salaries during 1988–91 were less than a third of their 1979–82 levels.[163] In El Salvador in 1990, average salaries for teachers were about $220 monthly—more than double levels in Peru.[164] There is no evidence of sharp increases or decreases in El Salvador.[165]

Wage data are also available for nurses and public health sector personnel in Peru and El Salvador. In Peru in 1990–91, nurses in Huancayo earned about $150 a month prior to the August "Fujishock," and a scant $60 a month after it.[166] By contrast, in early 1990 in El Salvador, nurses earned about $200 a month—more than in Peru prior to the "Fujishock."[167]

This contrasting trend in white-collar salaries in the public sector was also suggested by my own surveys among Ministry of Health employees in Huancayo and officials in five different ministries in El Salvador (see appendix I). In both the Peruvian and Salvadoran surveys, respondents were asked about their "working conditions." Salaries were the first example of a "working condition" mentioned by the interviewer; on-the-job relations were the second condition. In Peru, not a single respondent answered that working conditions were "better now"; an overwhelming majority (86 percent) said that working conditions were worse.[168] By contrast, in El Salvador a majority (52 percent) said that working conditions were the same; a slightly larger number (28 percent) thought that they had improved than the number (13 percent) that believed they had deteriorated.

Economic Decline and State Capabilities

This section examines the capabilities of the Peruvian and Salvadoran states.[169] Focusing on the public health capabilities of the Peruvian and Salvadoran states relative to Latin American norms, the section shows that health outcomes and the public health effort in Peru were inferior to those in El Salvador and Ecuador, and to the regional average. Although these data bolster the argument in the second section of the chapter about lower living standards among Peruvians than Salvadorans, the primary concern here is to explore the reasons for the inferior performance of Peru's state.

Was the primary reason cronyism and corruption in Peru's bureaucracies, as the Shining Path implied?[170] The data in this section are incomplete in numerous respects; in addition, they are based on bureaucrats' and citizens' perceptions of corruption, not on actual observation of corruption. However, it is clear from the data that both bureaucrats and citizens perceived corruption to be a significant problem within the Peruvian state. Also, it appears that Peruvian bureaucrats believed that the problem of corruption was more severe in 1990 than it had been a decade or so previously. For the most part, the Peruvian respondents were comparing corruption during the final months of the García administration with corruption at the end of the Morales Bermúdez military government or the beginning of the Belaúnde government.[171] The evidence of Peruvians' concern about corruption in the data in this section jibe with scholarly analysts' assessments of increasing political patronage by the APRA party and increasing local-level corruption by its partisans.[172]

Overall, however, the data do not suggest that corruption was the most important cause for the inferior performance of Peru's state. It is especially important to note that corruption was perceived to be at least as serious a problem in Ecuador, and was also perceived to be an increasingly serious problem there; yet Ecuador's public health performance was superior to Peru's. Although the data presented in this section are not definitive, they suggest that Peru stands out from El Salvador and Ecuador much less with respect to corruption and much more with respect to resource availability. In other words, the variable that most severely provoked the deterioration of Peru's public health effort was not corruption but scarce resources. Citizens may have been angrier at corruption in Peru than in Ecuador, but that was probably because in the context of Peru's extremely scarce resources, the implications of corruption for citizens' survival were more serious. It was primarily because of the changed implications of corruption in a context of subsistence threats and mortality threats that the Shining Path was able to channel citizens' anger about the problem so effectively.

My focus is on state capabilities in the public health sector for various reasons. First, of course, not all sectors could be analyzed and health is not a politicized issue. In contrast to a policy such as agrarian reform, for example, groups at all points of the political spectrum agree that improving public health is positive; accordingly, the political ideology of incumbent administrations should not be a factor affecting public health performance. Second, considerable data are available—data collected both by my research teams in the two countries and by international agencies.[173] The health statistics reported by the World Bank and other international institutions appear solid relative to statistics in many other areas (military expenditure, for example); however, these institutions do acknowledge flaws.[174]

Trends in Health Outcomes and in Public Health Efforts

Table 4.9 indicates trends in the bottom line for health capabilities: infant mortality and life expectancy rates.[175] The table indicates that, while outcomes in Peru, El Salvador, and Ecuador were all below regional averages, outcomes in Peru were the worst. In Peru, infant mortality rates were the highest and life expectancy was the lowest. With respect to infant mortality rates, the change in Peru between the early 1960s and 1991 was especially scant relative to Ecuador and El Salvador.

Why have the trends in infant mortality and life expectancy been positive in recent decades? Reasons are various: mothers' better educations, better transportation to medical services, and a larger number of doctors.[176] Very important also, however, are public health programs.

Table 4.9. Trends in Health Outcomes

	Infant Mortality Rates (per 1,000 live births)			Life Expectancy (years at birth)		
	1991	% Change from 1980	% Change from 25–30 Years before 1991	1992	% Change from 1980	% Change from 25–30 Years before 1992
Peru	80	−22	−38	64	10	25
El Salvador	56	−33	−53	66	16	22
Ecuador	59	−23	−47	66	6	18
Regional Average[a]	50	−27	−48	68	6	19

Sources: Data for infant mortality in 1991 and life expectancy in 1992 and percentage changes from 1980 in U.S. Agency for International Development, *Latin America and the Caribbean: Selected Economic and Social Data* (Washington, D.C.: U.S. AID, 1992), 65 and 68. The data for 1991 and 1992 are similar to "most recent estimates" in World Bank data, which are the source for the percentage change from 25–30 years earlier. For the percentage change in infant mortality rates, see World Bank, *Social Indicators of Development 1990* (Baltimore: Johns Hopkins University Press, 1991), 88, 92, and 244; for percentage change in life expectancy, see World Bank, *Social Indicators of Development 1993* (Baltimore: Johns Hopkins University Press, 1993), 88, 92, and 244.

[a]Calculated from relevant pages in the sources above for the specific nations.

During the 1980s, most Latin American states waged aggressive immunization campaigns and introduced oral rehydration therapy for diarrhea in children under five, and these programs were extremely helpful in reducing infant and child mortality.[177]

Table 4.10 compares the public health effort in Peru, El Salvador, Ecuador, and the region as a whole. Unfortunately, these data are not available over time, probably because in earlier years the emphasis had been on the development of infrastructure, such as hospital beds, and shifted toward more population-based services only in the 1980s. Table 4.10 indicates that the public health effort in Peru during the late 1980s and early 1990s was inferior to the effort in El Salvador and Ecuador. Only 17 percent of Peru's rural population enjoyed access to health services, in contrast to 40 percent of El Salvador's and 30 percent of Ecuador's, and a mere 25 percent of diarrhea cases in Peruvian children under five were treated by oral rehydration therapy, in contrast to 45 percent in El Salvador and 70 percent in Ecuador. Peru's immunization effort was relatively good, however—slightly better than Ecuador's.

Table 4.10. The Public Health Effort in Peru, El Salvador, and Ecuador

	Access to Health Services (% of rural population, 1980–87)	Oral Rehydration Therapy (% of diarrhea cases in which used, children under five, approx. 1991)	Immunization (% of age group, average, against measles and DPT, approx. 1991)
Peru	17	25	68
El Salvador	40	45	76
Ecuador	30	70	65
Regional Average	48	50	78

Sources: Access to health services for the rural population from Jazairy, Alamgir, and Panuccion (1992, 394–395); application of oral rehydration therapy and immunization rates from World Bank, *Social Indicators of Development 1993* (Baltimore: Johns Hopkins University Press, 1993), 96–97, 100–101, and 262–263. No year is given, only "most recent estimate" indication; however, figures are marked improvements over figures in the 1990 edition and accordingly are assumed to date from about 1991.

Government Expenditure on Public Health

Why, overall, were trends in health outcomes in Peru inferior to those in El Salvador or Ecuador, and why, overall, was Peru's public health effort inferior? Critics of the Peruvian government—in particular the Shining Path guerrillas—contended that the reason for the weak capabilities of the Peruvian state was corruption. However, this argument was not supported by our survey data; these data suggested that these problems were just as severe in Ecuador as in Peru (see below). Rather, the most empirically verifiable answer lies in national health expenditure.[178]

The data on health expenditure are not ideal. Rarely are data on health expenditure expressed in terms of dollars per capita, the most readily comparable measure (but still sensitive to variations in exchange rate calculation). Usually, data on health expenditure are expressed in terms of percentages of central government expenditure or of gross domestic product (GDP). Accordingly, as in this study we are most interested in actual expenditure levels, recall from table 4.1 that prior to the 1980s per capita GDP was greater in Peru than in Ecuador or El Salvador, but by approximately 1989 was very similar in the three nations.

In Peru during the 1970s and 1980s, health expenditure declined, and by the late 1980s it was much lower than in Ecuador or El Salvador.[179]

From 1970 through 1987, Peruvian public expenditure was in the range of 1 percent of GDP annually—as GDP declined (see table 4.1). After 1987, however, expenditure plummeted, perhaps to as low as 0.1 percent of GDP in 1990.[180] By contrast, in Ecuador, a nation whose GDP per capita was similar to Peru's after the late 1970s, expenditure on health was greater: 1.5 percent or more of GDP during the late 1970s, and about 2 percent, twice Peru's figure, during the early 1980s. In the mid- and late 1980s, expenditure fell in Ecuador but much less drastically than in Peru.

In El Salvador, where improvements in health outcomes were most dramatic, government expenditure on health as a percentage of GDP was also higher than in Peru during this period. From the early 1970s to the mid-1980s, government expenditure on health in El Salvador remained steadily above 1 percent of GDP, dipping below this figure only after 1985.[181] Probably most advantageous to health outcomes in El Salvador was the generous international aid that flowed into the health sector and a concomitantly increased role for the private health sector.[182] In 1990, international aid flows were 14 percent of total health expenditure in El Salvador—about double the figure for Ecuador and more than quadruple the figure for Peru. Health expenditure by the Salvadoran private sector was more than double the figure in the two other nations. Accordingly, total 1990 health expenditure as a percentage of GDP in El Salvador was almost twice the figure in Peru, and almost 50 percent more than the figure in Ecuador.

Of course, health outcomes are affected not only by absolute levels of expenditure but also by the kinds of expenditure. Unfortunately, some of the expenditures that were made during the 1960s and 1970s appear to have been cost-ineffective. In particular, the construction of sophisticated hospitals in capital cities helped primarily better-off urban residents.[183] In both Peru and El Salvador, the regional distribution of doctors and hospital beds was heavily skewed in favor of the capital.[184]

However, other major health infrastructure investments were extremely advantageous. A primary example is sanitation. In Peru in the late 1980s and early 1990s, the government was spending less than one-tenth of the sum that the Pan American Health Organization calculates as necessary to provide clean water and sewage to its population.[185] An estimated 40 percent of Lima's mushrooming population and approximately

75 percent of Peru's rural population did not enjoy access to clean water or sewage; in Ecuador, the percentage of the rural population without clean water or sewage was only about 30 percent, and in El Salvador, 41 percent.[186] The figure for Ecuador is an especially dramatic improvement over earlier decades.[187]

The implications of the varying sanitation efforts were especially apparent in early 1991, when an epidemic of cholera—absent from Latin America since the first decade of the twentieth century—broke out in Peru. Cholera bacteria are passed through human feces; infection occurs primarily when water supplies are contaminated by sewage. While other nations in the region were affected too, 72 percent of the 745,000 cases reported in Latin America in 1991 and 1992 occurred in Peru.[188] Similar poverty-related problems of hygiene and overcrowding appear to be related to the high incidence of tuberculosis in Peru. The annual incidence per 100,000 people of tuberculosis in 1990 was 250 in Peru— more than double the incidence for the region as a whole or for El Salvador, and 50 percent more than for Ecuador.[189] Between 1974 and 1991 in Peru, the annual number of notifications of tuberculosis multiplied two and a half times (while the annual number of notifications declined in El Salvador).[190]

At the same time that infrastructure expenditures are necessary, so are funds for basic health services to the rural poor. The data on the public health effort in Peru, El Salvador, and Ecuador in table 4.10 primarily reflect the nations' relative capacities to extend basic health services to this vulnerable group. Although rigorously comparable data are not available, during the 1980s more resources appeared to be allocated to the extension of basic health service in El Salvador than in Peru.[191]

Competing Explanations for the Variations in Public Health Capabilities

This section assesses explanations for the variations in state capabilities in the health sector in Peru, Ecuador, and El Salvador, based on bureaucrats' and citizens' perceptions of the problems in their nation's state bureaucracies. The data are imperfectly comparable in numerous ways —variations in the kinds of sites, in the number of ministries sampled, and so forth. The assessment of trends over time is also complex as time spans were perceived more discretely in Peru and Ecuador than in El

Table 4.11. Bureaucrats' Assessments of Their Ministries
(percentages)

	Peru (N = 99)	El Salvador (N = 100)
1. **"Achievements" of ministry in recent years**		
None	61	31
Don't know	0	27
2. **Most serious problems of ministry in recent years**[a]		
Lack of resources	78	16
Low salaries	39	19
Political appointments	23	0
"Compadrazgo" appointments	16	2
Corruption	9	1
Poor organization, incompetent personnel	32	31
Other[b]	30	15
Don't know	0	16

Sources: For Peru, informal May–June 1990 Osores survey among bureaucrats in the Ministry of Health in Huancayo; for El Salvador, informal May–June 1991 survey among bureaucrats in five different ministries. See appendix I for details. Item was open-ended.

[a]To this question, Peruvian respondents gave more than one answer, whereas Salvadoran respondents did not; accordingly, percentages add to 100 for El Salvador, but not for Peru.

[b]Most problems in the "other" category were specific to a ministry, such as references to AIDS and cholera by health officials.

Salvador; some of our survey items asked respondents to compare bureaucratic practices "now" (1990 or 1991) to bureaucratic practices ten years previously, but Salvadorans were less clear than their Ecuadorean or Peruvian counterparts about who was in power ten years previously.[192] Given these various methodological problems, one of these datasets would probably not be persuasive; but, together, they suggest that neither the degree of corruption nor trends in the problem were flagrantly worse in Peru than elsewhere.

First, table 4.11 indicates much more demoralization among the Peruvian officials than among the Salvadoran. In response to an open-ended item about the achievements of the Huancayo Ministry of Health in recent years, a whopping 61 percent of the Peruvian bureaucrats replied that there had been no achievements whatsoever. Only 31 percent of the Salvadoran bureaucrats said that there had been no achievements in their ministries, although many of the "don't know" responses among the Salvadoran sample should probably be added to the "no achievements" category. The subsample of Salvadoran officials in the health ministry was more upbeat than the sample as a whole; only 20 percent of these respondents said that there had been "no achievements" and only 5 percent "didn't know." Objectively, even in Peru, the "no achievements" response was unfair; as we have seen, vaccination rates improved markedly in the 1980s, and extensive campaigns were made not only in urban Peru but also in remote areas, including those in the Huancayo jurisdiction.[193]

Especially important for this section, table 4.11 highlights the degree to which Peruvian bureaucrats were concerned about the paucity of funds for their ministry—much more concerned than their Salvadoran counterparts. Answering the question, "What for you have been the most serious problems in the ministry in the last few years?" an overwhelming majority of the Peruvian bureaucrats in the Huancayo Ministry of Health responded, "Lack of resources." While Peruvian officials were worried about "political appointments" (patronage), "compadrazgo appointments" (cronyism), and corruption as well as the paucity of funds, the problems of scant resources were the officials' most common complaint by far, cited by 78 percent of respondents. In El Salvador, by contrast, only 16 percent of officials cited scant resources as their most serious concern.[194] Of the twenty respondents in the Salvadoran Ministry of Health, three officials (15 percent) cited scant resources; the most common worry (25 percent) was about AIDS and cholera. Overall, the Peruvian respondents were much more critical than the Salvadoran ones; they were inclined to name many "serious problems" in the ministry, and none said that he or she did not know about "serious problems" in it.

In the Peruvian officials' views, what kinds of resources were most lacking? The concerns were generally not about the establishment of primary care health centers; the available data suggested that the number of these posts expanded considerably in Peru during the 1980s, as they did in El Salvador. Rather, the primary concerns were the supply of medicines at health centers, maintenance of equipment at centers, and funds for health care workers' visits to centers.[195] Perhaps tellingly, given the intensity of these concerns, Peru's Ministry of Health did not gather data on the number of health care workers' visits to such centers, whereas the Salvadoran ministry did.[196]

Table 4.12. Bureaucrats' Perceptions of Cronyism and Corruption (percentages)

	Peru		El Salvador
	Health ($N = 99$)	Agriculture ($N = 52$)	($N = 100$)
1. **Employment by merit**			
Almost always/usually	7	33	8
At times	42	37	33
Almost never	44	27	57
Don't know/other	6	4	7
2. **Promotion by merit**			
Almost always/usually	3	35	4
At times	29	37	34
Almost never	66	25	60
Don't know/other	2	2	2
3. **Purchase prices reported honestly**			
Almost always/usually	5	38	24
At times	39	37	24
Almost never	48	15	30
Don't know/other	2	10	22
4. **In comparison with ten years earlier, merit/honesty is**[a]			
More merit/honesty now	2	17	20
The same	22	23	36
Less merit/honesty now	51	54	15
Don't know/other	24	6	29

Sources: Osores 1990 survey in the ministries of health and agriculture in Huancayo and Orellana 1991 survey of five ministries in San Salvador. See appendix I for details. See table 4.13 for phrasing of the items.

[a]In the Ministry of Health in Peru, figures are not for "in comparison with ten years earlier, control of purchases is . . . " but for "in comparison with ten years earlier, promotion by merit is . . ." Unfortunately, the question about change during the decade was not formatted correctly for the Ministry of Health in Peru.

The data in table 4.12 report officials' own assessments of cronyism and corruption in their ministries. "Cronyism" is measured by officials' responses to items about the frequency of employment and promotion by merit rather than by personal connections. "Corruption" is measured by officials' responses to items about the honest reporting of the purchase price of inputs (or, in the precise language of the surveys, "strict control of prices"). This item reflects the fact that one of the most common forms of corruption in Latin America is for officials to claim that the purchase price of an input was greater than it really was, so that they can pocket some of the difference between the claimed price and the actual price.

The data in the table do not indicate that Peruvian officials are consistently more suspicious of cronyism and corruption than are their Salvadoran counterparts. Rather, perceptions of corruption varied considerably by item, and also in Peru by ministry. On the one hand, Peruvian officials, especially Ministry of Agriculture officials, were not as likely as Salvadoran officials to suspect that employment and promotion were "almost never" by merit. On the other hand, Peruvian officials, especially Ministry of Health officials, were much more likely than Salvadoran officials to doubt that purchase prices were honestly reported and also much more likely to believe that during the ten years before 1990 or 1991 either cronyism or corruption had become worse.[197] One possible reason that Ministry of Health officials were more critical of cronyism and corruption than were Ministry of Agriculture officials in Peru is that the survey was carried out in the final months of the García administration in the Ministry of Health, but in the first few months of the Fujimori administration in the Ministry of Agriculture.

Table 4.13 reports assessments of corruption among Peruvian, Salvadoran, and Ecuadorean citizens. "Cronyism" and "corruption" were indicated by the same items (employment and promotion not by merit and dishonest reporting of purchase prices) as in the surveys among bureaucrats. The table shows that Limeños were more suspicious of cronyism and corruption than were urban Salvadorans, but similarly suspicious as urban Ecuadoreans.[198] Also, responding to another item in the Datum, Orellana, and CEDATOS surveys that is not included in table 4.13, the Ecuadoreans were more likely than the Peruvians, and much more likely than the Salvadorans, to believe that dishonest reporting of purchase prices was increasing.[199] A large plurality of the Ecuadorean respondents (43 percent) suspected that dishonest reporting of purchase prices was more widespread in 1990 or 1991 relative to ten years earlier, versus 28 percent of the Limeños and 13 percent of the Salvadorans.

Table 4.13. Citizens' Perceptions of Cronyism and Corruption in State Bureaucracies (percentages)

	Lima (N = 400)	El Salvador (urban only, N = 165)	Ecuador (urban only, N = 524)
1. Employment by merit			
Almost always/usually	27	38	15
At times	19	21	25
Almost never	49	22	58
Don't know/other	5	2	3
2. Promotion by merit			
Almost always/usually	15	22	17
At times	26	26	30
Almost never	49	49	50
Don't know/other	10	3	3
3. Purchase prices reported honestly			
Almost always/usually	9	24	16
At times	20	22	26
Almost never	59	40	52
Don't know/other	12	15	6

Sources: Datum, Orellana, and CEDATOS surveys (see appendix I). The essence of survey items, which were phrased slightly differently in each nation, was as follows: "When there are openings for work in the government [promotions and salary increases], are these offered according to the merits of the applicants [employees]?" and "Do you think that when government offices make major purchases [for equipment, vehicles, etc.], there is strict control of prices as required by law?"

An Assessment

During the late 1970s and 1980s, poverty in Peru was not a problem of "misery as usual." Rather, as two economists have described it, economic trends in Peru between 1985 and 1990 constituted "one of the worst economic performances in modern history."[200] Despite agrarian reform in the 1970s, a major subsistence threat emerged for Peru's southern highlands peasants. Also, to a degree that was probably unprecedented in Latin America, educated young people could not find professional employment at conventional middle-class wage levels. The country's economic crisis also took a severe toll on the capabilities of the Peruvian state.

By comparison, in El Salvador, economic problems were significant but not as extreme by regional standards. Prior to the emergence of the

FMLN, in the 1970s, the trends for macroeconomic growth and real minimum wages were positive. The most negative trend during the 1970s was land scarcity; especially—but not exclusively—among peasants who were displaced from their traditional lands, land scarcity was a serious grievance. However, the departments where the FMLN gained its key peasant bases were not experiencing dramatically worse living standards than other Salvadoran departments, or dramatically worse living standards than in previous years; absolute living standards in the Salvadoran countryside during the late 1970s and early 1980s were better than in Peru. Nor were professional opportunities particularly unavailable to educated young people. Finally, in part because of U.S. economic support, the capabilities of the state were not drastically reduced by economic crisis.

5

U.S. POLICY AND LATIN AMERICAN REVOLUTIONS

Scholars of revolution tend to underestimate the importance of the international context to the outcome of a revolutionary effort.[1] The tendency during the 1970s and 1980s to downplay the importance of the U.S. role to the outcome of a revolutionary conflict was in part related to the U.S. failure to prevent a revolutionary victory in Vietnam, despite the massive U.S. involvement in Southeast Asia.

Latin America, however, is not Southeast Asia, and in Vietnam the failure of the United States to achieve its goals despite herculean efforts was anomalous. Traditionally, the United States has perceived Latin America as its "backyard"; during the Cold War, the United States considered the maintenance of its power in the region as especially crucial to the strategic imperatives of the struggle against Soviet-backed communism.[2] Given both this commitment and the many advantages that the United States enjoyed in Latin America relative to other regions of the world—in particular, geographic proximity and regimes that were accustomed to the exercise of U.S. power—it is remarkable that three leftist revolutions in the region won power during this era.

Now that the end of the Cold War facilitates historical perspective, it is especially appropriate that scholars consider the ways in which the U.S. government affected revolutionary outcomes in Latin America. The argument here is that it was not necessarily the "strongest" movement that won.[3] By the criteria established in chapter 2, neither the MNR in Bolivia, nor Fidel Castro's 26th of July Movement in Cuba, nor the Sandinistas in Nicaragua were patently "stronger" than the FMLN. As U.S. Colonel James J. Steele commented: "What we're seeing in El Salvador today are some of the best guerrillas, probably the best guerrillas, we've seen in the hemisphere to date. They are certainly better than anything we saw in Nicaragua or in Cuba."[4]

However, in Cuba, Nicaragua, and El Salvador, and to a lesser degree earlier in Bolivia, the character of the revolutionary movement was very much a variable in a Cold War revolutionary equation. The Cuban and Nicaraguan regimes were dictatorships that had endured in good part because of U.S. support, but, as they became more repressive, had alienated the vast majority of their own citizens. The crisis was essentially a political one, and the U.S. response, appropriately enough, was to demand that the regime open politically. In both cases, the dictator refused. Since the opposition to the regime included important leaders or groups whom the U.S. government believed to be more democratic than Marxist, the U.S. government did not consider rescuing the regime to be in the U.S. interest.

In El Salvador, the key problem again was that an authoritarian regime was alienating diverse national political groups. But the Salvadoran regime did respond—albeit belatedly and niggardly—to U.S. requests for reform. Also, although the opposition to the regime was politically diverse, the FMLN was clearly tied to the East bloc in a way that neither Fidel Castro's movement nor the broad-based Nicaraguan opposition had been.[5] Accordingly, the revolutionary movements in Cuba and Nicaragua were perceived at least in part through the prism of the U.S. concern for democracy, whereas the revolutionary movement in El Salvador was perceived primarily through the prism of the Cold War.

During the Cold War, if the U.S. government determined that a democratic or quasi-democratic Latin American regime was threatened by Marxist revolutionaries, a major rescue effort was a virtual certainty.[6] Accordingly, in El Salvador, when U.S. policymakers made this determination, the guerrillas' prospects became bleak. The introduction to this book cites 1982–84 Salvadoran President Alvaro Magaña and FMLN leaders Joaquín Villalobos and Fermán Cienfuegos, as well as numerous scholars, about the importance of U.S. aid to the prevention of a takeover by the FMLN.[7] Many more quotations from Salvadoran and U.S. political actors and from scholars could be added.[8]

Although the years of greatest military activity by the FMLN and the Shining Path roughly coincided, the U.S. government did not perceive the revolutionary movement in Peru through the prism of the Cold War. This perception was correct: the Shining Path was not a movement against an authoritarian regime, and it received no support from the East bloc. But, in part because the Shining Path did not fit U.S. officials' image of a successful revolutionary movement, the U.S. government tended to underestimate the intensity of the threat posed by the Peruvian guerrillas. Prior to Fujimori's April 1992 *autogolpe,* U.S. attention was inordinately focused on free market reform and the antidrug war. Also, when Bush administration officials did become seriously concerned, their primary overt response appeared to be the conventional Cold War era answer: military aid. This reaction was particularly inappropriate to the Peruvian context for various reasons, and it gathered scant approval either in the U.S. Congress or in Peru.

One rough summary indicator of the differing levels of U.S. engagement in El Salvador and Peru is the amount of U.S. aid to each country. The figures on total U.S. economic and military aid to El Salvador and Peru between 1979 and 1990 are provided in table 5.1. During the last half of the decade, U.S. aid to El Salvador was more than six times the amount of U.S. aid to Peru; in per capita terms, U.S. aid to El Salvador would have been more than twenty-five times the amount of U.S. aid to Peru.[9] Even in current dollars, U.S. aid to Peru was less in 1989 than in 1979, when the Shining Path had not yet entered the Peruvian political arena.

This chapter first documents the U.S. decision not to rescue the Bolivian, Cuban, and Nicaraguan authoritarian regimes when they were challenged by political and revolutionary movements. Then it describes the various components of the intense U.S. effort to rescue the Salvadoran government from the FMLN's challenge: U.S. pressure for democratization, U.S. military aid, and U.S. economic aid. The next section examines U.S. policy toward the Peruvian government as it confronted the Shining Path, assessing U.S. policies with respect to democracy, military aid, and economic aid, as well as antinarcotics efforts. The final section provides my own reflections about the positive and negative elements of actual U.S. policy in the two nations, and what the U.S. government might have done differently toward the achievement of a more rapid and effective political peace in the two countries.

Table 5.1. U.S Aid to El Salvador and Peru, 1979–90
(millions of current dollars)

	1979	1980	1981	1982	1983	1984	1985	1986	1987	1988	1989	1990
El Salvador	11	64	149	264	327	413	570	444	574	396	388	328
Peru	76	57	84	60	98	175	88	59	64	71	68	95

Sources: U.S. Agency for International Development, *U.S. Overseas Loans and Grants, July 1, 1945–September 30, 1991* (Washington, D.C.: U.S. AID, 1990); and U.S. Agency for International Development, *U.S. Overseas Loans and Grants: Series of Yearly Data,* vol. 2, *Latin America and the Caribbean: Obligations and Loan Authorizations, FY 1946–FY 1985* (Washington, D.C.: U.S. AID, n.d.).

Note: Aid includes total economic and military assistance.

Table 5.2. U.S. Aid to Bolivia, Cuba, Nicaragua, El Salvador, and Peru during Critical Years of Revolutionary Challenge (millions of current dollars)

Bolivia, 1951	Cuba, 1958	Nicaragua, 1978	El Salvador		Peru	
			1980	1987[a]	1989	1991[a]
0.5	2.6	14	64	574	68	199

Sources: U.S. Agency for International Development, *U.S. Overseas Loans and Grants, Series of Yearly Data,* vol. 2, *Latin America and the Caribbean: Obligations and Loan Authorizations, FY 1946– FY 1985* (Washington, D.C.: U.S. AID, n.d.); *Loans and Grants and U.S. Agency for International Development, U.S. Overseas,* annual editions. Amount is the total for economic and military aid.

[a]Year of greatest amount of U.S. aid between 1980 and 1992.

The United States and Winning Latin American Revolutions during the Cold War

In most analysts' judgments, there were three cases of winning revolutions in Latin America during the Cold War: Bolivia in 1952, Cuba in 1959, and Nicaragua in 1979. All three of the defeated governments were authoritarian and had refused U.S. requests for political opening; accordingly, they were not rescued by the U.S. government when they were challenged by revolutionary movements that included important prodemocratic groups. Table 5.2 indicates the virtual absence of U.S. economic and military aid to Bolivia, Cuba, and Nicaragua—in contrast to the large sums to El Salvador and some support to Peru—during the most critical years.

In Bolivia, Cuba, and Nicaragua, the U.S. administrations weighed an unsavory authoritarian regime against a political opposition that seemed unlikely to produce a government closely allied with the Soviet Union. In part because of the dictatorial character of the incumbent regimes in Bolivia, Cuba, and Nicaragua, large sectors of each country's political actors and middle classes were opposed to the regime; hoping for democracy in their countries, these Cuban and Nicaraguan oppositions were able to lobby elite and mass opinion in the United States. Of course, revolutionary movements were not able to make prodemocratic cases against incumbent regimes that were not considered authoritarian within the United States.

In the cases of Cuba and Nicaragua, the U.S. administrations (under Eisenhower and Carter, respectively) were very concerned about the political crises in the two countries. As the Cuban and Nicaraguan revolutionary movements approached victory, the Eisenhower and Carter administrations feverishly sought political alternatives—"third forces" —to both the incumbent dictators and the revolutionary organizations. In both cases, however, the options for the U.S. administrations had been narrowed by the history of the U.S. relationship with the incumbent regime. Both Fulgencio Batista and Anastasio Somoza retained support within certain quarters of the U.S. government; also, the dictators, whose success in the past had depended in part on their willingness to serve U.S. interests, were not only incompetent but suddenly stubborn, rejecting U.S. demands that their regimes open.

Bolivia, 1952

Relative to the Cuban or Nicaraguan revolution (not to mention the revolutionary attempts in El Salvador and Peru), the Bolivian revolution was brief and bloodless. Moreover, the revolution dissipated. The MNR that won power in April 1952 included ideologically disparate factions; the leftist faction was gradually marginalized. Moreover, the MNR was ousted by a military coup in 1964. For these reasons, foremost scholars of Bolivia consider the country to have experienced a revolution in 1952, but use such qualifying adjectives as "uncompleted."[10]

The government that was overthrown by the MNR was not as repressive as the regimes in Cuba or Nicaragua; nor was it dynastic. It was a military junta that had been in power less than a year. However, the junta came to power illegitimately, and its objective was political exclusion of the MNR.

Between 1946 and 1951, Bolivia was governed by the Socialist Republican Union Party (Partido de la Unión Republicano Socialista, PURS).[11] The PURS party perceived itself as the reformist wing of the traditional elite organizations, counseling reform in an effort to defuse the increasingly powerful MNR; but in reality the party was a poorly organized, motley group, and it was unable to implement its initiatives. Although precise data are not available, considerable numbers of MNR leaders were persecuted, killed, and driven into exile during this period. As in the Cuban and Nicaraguan cases, however, the repression failed to check the growth of the MNR but did provoke public indignation. In May 1951, elections were held.

There was complete agreement among Bolivian political actors that the MNR won the 1951 elections.[12] The MNR itself claimed that it had won 79 percent of the votes. The government, however, said that the MNR had won only a plurality; according to the Bolivian constitution, if no party won an outright majority, a runoff vote in the Bolivian congress was necessary. In any case, the military and the traditional Bolivian economic and political elites successfully pressured PURS President Urriolagoitia to transfer power to a military junta led by General Hugo Ballivián.

The Ballivián government, lacking any claim to political legitimacy, soon confronted major challenges. Bolivia's long-standing economic problems became more severe: The U.S. government announced a drop in the price that it would pay for tin, Bolivia's key export; in response, the Bolivian government halted tin sales to the United States, leading to shortages of many imports, including food.[13] There was increasing popular opposition to Bolivian dependency on international actors for the purchase of tin and also to the control of the mines by a mere three "Tin Baron" families.

Although the Ballivián junta declared the MNR illegal, and many of its leaders were either exiled or arrested, the party was still able to plot and organize vigorously against the government. Led on the scene in La Paz by Hernán Siles Suazo, the MNR conspired with General Antonio Seleme, the minister of the interior and head of the national military police, to stage a coup. The expectation was that the change would be rapid, without widespread popular or labor participation, and that Seleme would become president in a united MNR-reformist military cabinet.[14]

In the event, the insurrection was indeed brief, but its outcome was not as expected. On 9 April, the first day of the revolt, the MNR and Seleme's militarized police were unable either to provoke a popular uprising or to spark major desertions within the Bolivian military. Described a journalist in La Paz:

> Residents cowered behind tightly shuttered doors and windows. . . . Later appeals to students and workers to join the rebellion went unheeded as most of them shrugged their shoulders and stayed out of the way of bullets. No big public demonstrations resulted.[15]

Believing that the rebellion was going badly, Seleme took asylum in the Chilean embassy—giving up any claim to office in a future government.

On the second day, however, the rebels fared better.[16] They were able to rally labor groups, especially miners, to their cause. Although the firepower of the Bolivian army was vastly superior to that of the insurgents, many army officers did not stand fast; some retreated and some disappeared. Pressured by citizens, considerable numbers of rank-and-file soldiers changed sides or surrendered. In Cochabamba, Bolivia's second largest city, the army fell apart quickly in the face of the rebels' advance. In La Paz, the army performed better; it had abandoned the center of the city on the first day, but was gradually retaking it. Then, armed miners seized the railroad station above the city to the north, capturing a munitions train and positioning themselves to attack the army from behind. Another group of armed miners encircled the city of Oruro to the south, obstructing the arrival of reinforcements to the capital. The Bolivian army was trapped, and its general capitulated.

The insurrection had lasted a mere three days. The death toll was approximately 550 Bolivians.[17] Popular participation was underwhelming. As Malloy concluded, "It involved on all sides only a small part of the actual population of Bolivia. . . . Indian peasants played no role."[18]

Through the course of the fighting, the Eisenhower administration was neutral, playing no role. The primary foreign policy concern of the Eisenhower administration was the ongoing Korean War (1950–53). Neither the Bolivian government nor the MNR appeared to try vigorously to enlist U.S. support, and it seems unlikely that either side would have gained it. In the United States, the Bolivian junta was perceived as repressive, illegitimate, and allied to exploitative elites.[19] As one scholar put it:

> The human rights issue tended to evoke additional sympathy for Bolivia in the United States. In a country mired in feudalism and beset by the exploitation of the majority of its people by either the Big Three mine owners or the landlords, the image of the Tin Barons was definitely not good. . . . There was also the fact that Paz Estenssoro had obtained a plurality in the elections of 1951.[20]

Nonetheless, the MNR was questioned on various grounds: first, for its previous links with the 1943–46 Gualberto Villarroel administration (perceived as authoritarian and anti-Semitic within the United States); second, for its ties to the populist Juan Perón government in Argentina (where many MNR leaders had been in exile); and third, and most importantly, for its ties to communism.[21] The underlying assumption for most U.S. journalists, and probably most North Americans, appeared to be that Bolivia was an unstable country, where democracy was unlikely to take root soon.

The MNR government encountered a skeptical U.S. administration.[22] The United States delayed recognition of the new government for seven weeks after its takeover. Numerous U.S. officials and opinion leaders, including two Latin American editors for *Time* magazine, were persuaded that Juan Lechín, a key MNR leader and the head of the Bolivian Miners' Union, was a Marxist, and that other MNR activists were too. When the MNR government moved quickly to nationalize Bolivia's major tin mines, the former mining magnates hired a U.S. public relations firm to portray the MNR government as communist.

Overall, however, the charges that the MNR was Marxist were invalid and were rejected by the Eisenhower administration. Among the top twenty-odd leaders of the MNR, the overwhelming majority were middle-class and upper-middle-class university-educated professionals.[23] Víctor Paz Estenssoro, the president of the 1952–56 MNR government, was described as "a slightly built, nervous man of 43 who could be easily mistaken for a college professor, which he was before he entered Bolivian politics in 1938."[24] In one scholarly description, Paz Estenssoro was

> undoubtedly a fervent nationalist and not above employing certain Marxist categories. Yet his formidable reputation as an intellectual was based principally on long experience in financial administration, a background that had nurtured a deep awareness of the practical problems of bringing about social change as well as a fundamentally managerial approach to politics. Paz was less an ideologue than an intelligent and pragmatic politician in the populist mold but of firmly conservative sensibilities.[25]

Not only were Paz Estenssoro and most of his colleagues populists rather than Marxists at heart, but also they were clear to U.S. officials about their political beliefs.[26] At Paz Estenssoro's inauguration, he proclaimed, "This is not an anti-capitalist government. . . . We want to assure progress for the majority; we take on this task and assume responsibility for it because Bolivia is extraordinarily rich but it needs capital."[27] The Bolivian ambassador to the United States, Víctor Andrade, worked tirelessly in Washington, D.C., to assure American leaders of his government's friendly intentions.[28]

Gradually, the Eisenhower administration decided not only not to oppose the MNR government, but to support it in various ways. Concluded one scholar a few years after the revolution, "The United States has made possible the success of the Bolivian National Revolution thus far."[29] Commented another analyst, "Thus the fact remains that the initial achievement of the revolution—the MNR staying in power—was largely due to United States support for it plus a number of factors which can be summed up in the one statement that without luck nobody fares well."[30]

Cuba, 1959

The coming to power of Fidel Castro's movement in Cuba in 1959 is invariably classified by scholars as a revolution. Yet, the Cuban revolutionary movement was not as "strong" by the criteria used in this book as the movements in El Salvador or Peru. If the Eisenhower administration had clearly withdrawn support from Fulgencio Batista earlier—in 1957 or even during the first six months of 1958—and had promoted new elections at that time, Fidel Castro's revolutionary movement would probably not have won power. Commented one scholar:

> As Fidel recognized, the United States was the final arbiter of Cuban politics: Regardless of the relative strengths of the contenders, if the United States decided to back a group or coalition as replacement for Batista, Washington was likely to have its way.[31]

Unequivocally, former Sergeant Fulgencio Batista was a dictator. In a 12 January 1959 article, *Time* magazine classified Batista's regime as a dictatorship twice in the first paragraph.[32] Batista's power derived in good part from his long-standing support by the U.S. government. In 1933, after authoritarian Gerardo Machado had been overthrown by a popular, nationalistic movement led by students and sergeants, Batista emerged as the commander of the Cuban army and as a leader who was acceptable to both Cuban reformers and the U.S. government. In 1940, Batista's behind-the-scenes power was legitimized in reasonably honest elections; implementing various social reforms but maintaining a good relationship with the United States during his four-year term, Batista was a popular president.[33]

However, when Batista came to power again, leading a coup against the Auténtico Party's President Carlos Prío on 10 March 1952, his administration was not to be popular. Batista's coup preempted presidential elections that were due in three months—elections that candidate Batista wanted to win but was almost certain to lose, probably to the candidate of Cuba's other main political party, the Ortodoxo Party. However, the U.S. government considered Batista a friend of American business and an ally in the Cold War, and the Eisenhower administration recognized the de facto regime within a mere seventeen days.[34]

Although Batista's coup was opposed by both the Auténticos and at first by the Ortodoxos, many of their leaders were exiled, intimidated, or coopted, and their opposition was ineffective.[35] University students were the most active group in opposition to the coup.[36] Batista's response to the opposition was repression, which in turn provoked more intense protest. From the first days of Batista's coup, Fidel Castro, a former law student and Ortodoxo candidate for a congressional seat in the aborted election, was one of the most vigorous opposition leaders. Castro became more prominent after his spectacular, albeit failed, attack on the Moncada Barracks in 1953, after which his 26th of July Movement (Movimiento 26 de Julio, M-26-7) was named. Although the 26th of July Movement proved to be more effective than the other Cuban opposition groups, by the criteria established in chapter 2 it was not as strong as the FMLN or the Shining Path.

The actual number of guerrilla fighters organized under the banner of Fidel Castro's 26th of July Movement was less than the number organized under revolutionary banners in El Salvador or Peru. Fidel Castro reported that his armed fighters numbered a mere three hundred until the final months of the struggle, when they numbered only eight hundred.[37] By most calculations, the maximum number of militants was three thousand—a figure that included many who had no arms and represented a considerable increase in numbers during the final days of the struggle.[38] The leaders' social origins were predominantly middle class, including numerous students; approximately 75 percent of the fighters were peasants.[39]

There are no precise data on the amount of territory controlled by the 26th of July Movement. As of August 1958, the figure appears to have been less than 5 percent: most of southern Oriente province (but not its main cities).[40] Land insecurity was especially severe in Oriente, and the guerrillas implemented a land reform that provided stable tenure. In the November 1958 Batista-controlled elections, it was in Oriente that the electoral boycott called by the rebels was heeded, with only about 5 percent of Santiago's electorate voting.[41] At this time, Castro's revolutionaries controlled rail and bus transportation in the province. By late December 1958, the figure for territory controlled by the 26th of July Movement increased to possibly 20 percent.[42] The revolutionary movement in the Oriente had expanded, controlling virtually all of the province except the capital, and Ché Guevara and Camilo Cienfuegos (who had left the Sierra Maestra in August) were carrying out attacks and gaining supporters in areas of Camaguey and, especially, Las Villas. In these provinces, they controlled the access to the ports from which Cuba's sugar was shipped.

The number of people killed by the rebels in Cuba was much smaller than the numbers in the Salvadoran or Peruvian conflicts: fewer than four hundred.[43] Government casualties were light primarily because Batista's soldiers did not want to fight; when threatened, they surrendered.[44] Between 1952 and 1 January 1959, the entire death toll was a mere fifteen hundred to two thousand, most of whom were civilians killed by Batista's forces in Cuba's cities.[45]

How much popular support did the 26th of July Movement enjoy? Again, a precise calculation is difficult. On the one hand, by 1958, opposition to Batista was virtually universal on the island.[46] Until the final months, however, Castro was only one of various political leaders trying to defeat Batista, and he was not trusted by many of his Havana-based rivals. There is no evidence that urban popular groups were willing to risk their lives for the 26th of July Movement.[47]

The difficulties of successful collaboration among the Cuban rebel groups and popular fears of showing support for the revolutionaries were most apparent in the failure of the one general strike that was consciously attempted, on 9 April 1958.[48] The primary target was Havana, in the expectation that success in the capital would resonate throughout the island. However, some opponents of the Batista regime did not want to participate with the 26th of July Movement, and participation by the Communist Party was rejected by the 26th of July Movement. Planning for the strike was poor. In contrast to similar efforts not only in El Salvador and Peru but in numerous other Latin American nations experiencing revolutionary challenges, the strike was a fiasco in the capital. Batista's forces claimed more than a hundred lives and Havana's residents demonstrated not support for the rebels but fear of political violence. Considerable property damage occurred only in Santiago de Cuba in the Oriente.[49]

During the course of the two Eisenhower administrations, U.S. policy toward Cuba shifted considerably. During Eisenhower's first term and for several years into his second term, anticommunism was a hallmark of his foreign policy.[50] The Eisenhower administration supported numerous military regimes in Latin America, increased military aid to the region, and even approved covert intervention to oust the elected president of Guatemala. U.S. officials were sympathetic to numerous Latin American dictators, espousing anticommunism but ignoring democratic values—as in the case of Batista.[51] Indeed, in early 1955, Vice President Richard Nixon hugged Batista and compared him with Abraham Lincoln in a toast.[52]

However, the Eisenhower administration's close relationship with Batista began to be questioned by various groups in the United States. In early 1957, *New York Times* journalist Herbert L. Matthews traveled to Cuba to interview Fidel Castro in the Sierra Maestra; his series of articles reported that Castro was not only alive (at a time when the Batista government was claiming that he was dead), but thriving. The journalist pointed to the U.S. government's arms shipments to Batista and the U.S. ambassador's public admiration for the dictator as reasons for increasing anti-Americanism within Cuba.[53] Matthews was a seasoned journalist, and his hard-hitting analysis resonated among informed Americans.[54] The cozy U.S.-Batista relationship was criticized by numerous other journalists.[55] Too, the Democratic Party had won control of the U.S. Congress in 1956 and had increased its strength in 1958, and its leaders faulted the administration's support for dictators and emphasis on military rather than economic assistance.[56]

Pressure against the Eisenhower administration's policy toward Cuba was also exerted by Cubans within the United States. Rebel groups, all anti-Batista but favoring different Cuban opponents to Batista, were organized in numerous U.S. cities. These groups coordinated demonstrations and other activities, demanding in particular the end of arms exports to the Batista government.[57] They cheered the revolutionaries on, flew planeloads of arms from small airports in Florida to Cuba, and collected approximately $25,000 a month for the rebels.[58]

Ultimately, the Eisenhower administration placed an embargo on arms shipments to the Batista regime in March 1958. Administration officials hoped that the embargo would prod Batista to moderate his regime's violence.[59] However, the administration's stated explanation was that Batista had used U.S.-supplied tanks and aircraft to subdue a rebellion in Cienfuegos in September 1957, violating the terms of the 1952 Mutual Defense Assistance Agreement, which restricted Cuba's use of weapons to defense against external aggression.[60] The effect of the embargo was more symbolic and psychological than military; although it was perceived by both Batista and his opposition to signify waning U.S. support for the dictator, Batista's military arsenal remained vastly superior to his opposition's.[61]

Although subsequently there were pressures on the Eisenhower administration to resume military shipments, the administration did not accede to them. Indeed, administration officials were increasingly in agreement with the critics of their Latin American policy. In May 1958, Vice President Richard Nixon toured eight Latin American nations; he was met by angry protesters in seven of the eight, and his motorcade was stoned in Caracas.[62] The obvious anger of Latin Americans at the U.S. government prompted serious debate about U.S. policies toward Latin America both within and beyond the Eisenhower administration. Ultimately, the Eisenhower administration began to agree that U.S. support for military dictatorships was not the route to political stability in Latin America, and it endorsed political democracy as an ideal for the hemisphere.[63]

The development of a new U.S. policy toward Cuba—clearly breaking with Batista and persuading him to retire to his house in Florida—was inhibited by the U.S. ambassador to Cuba, Earl E. T. Smith. During most of 1958, Smith believed that the United States should continue to support the Batista regime, trusting that Batista would uphold his promise of free elections observed by the United Nations.[64] Smith continued to hope that elections would produce a legitimate successor to Batista, even after Batista suspended constitutional guarantees and postponed the elections several months, to 3 November.[65] Only after Batista rigged the elections, and his candidate had easily won the presidency, did Ambassador Smith sour on Batista.[66]

Although by November there was a general consensus among U.S. policymakers that Batista was a serious liability, there was no consensus about the appropriate new course; nor was the urgency of the crisis apparent to President Eisenhower or the dying secretary of state, John Foster Dulles.[67] A Florida businessman, William D. Pawley, met with Eisenhower and secured the president's agreement that Pawley would travel to Cuba to ask Batista to retire to Florida, at which time the U.S. government would send arms to a caretaker regime that would coordinate new elections. However, U.S. State Department officials told Pawley not to inform Batista that Pawley's plan had been authorized by Eisenhower. In early December, Batista rejected Pawley's proposal; whether the dictator would have accepted it if he had known that it had been authorized by Eisenhower is not clear.[68]

Only a few weeks later, Batista's tune changed. The fall of Santa Clara, a town of 150,000 inhabitants in Las Villas province, to Ché Guevara's troops on 30 December convinced Batista that his time was up.[69] Although the rebels at Santa Clara numbered only about three hundred, they were able to derail an armored train; the demoralized officers surrendered and the soldiers fraternized with the rebels.[70] Batista's prime minister met with Ambassador Smith and told him that the dictator would resign in favor of a junta, on the condition that the U.S. support the new government, especially with weapons. However, the proposal was rejected by top U.S. State Department officials, who did not believe that such a successor government would be legitimate.[71] After holding his traditional New Year's Eve party, Batista fled by plane to the Dominican Republic. Fidel Castro learned of Batista's flight at dawn on radio broadcasts; he immediately called for the surrender of the Santiago garrison and for a general strike, and his calls were heeded.[72]

The U.S. government's decisions during November and December 1958—in particular, not to foment a military coup, a possibility that worried Castro—were shaped by U.S. assessments of the character and ideology of the revolutionaries.[73] On the one hand, top U.S. policymakers feared Castro, believing that he was "too radical."[74] On the other hand, they did not perceive him as a communist.[75]

Although the precise character of Castro's beliefs in 1958 will probably never be known (given that Castro said different things to different people), the strong probability is that he was not a Marxist at the time.[76] Also, as we have noted, Fidel Castro was only one among several political leaders in the political struggle against Batista; it was not clear that he would emerge at the apex of power.[77] Overall in Latin America, ten dictatorships were to collapse during 1959–60; it was not clear that the collapse of the Batista dictatorship would be different from the others.[78]

Nicaragua, 1979

The Nicaraguan revolutionary equation was similar to the Cuban, except that the flaws of the dictator and probably also of U.S. policy were more extreme. Perhaps the final year before the Sandinistas' victory was somewhat similar to what the twelve months after New Year's Day 1959 might have been in Cuba, had Batista not resigned.

Like Batista, Anastasio ("Tacho" or "Tachito") Somoza Debayle was a dictator. He was the third ruler in a family dynasty; his father had governed between 1936 and 1956 and his older brother between 1957 and 1963.[79] Whereas Anastasio's older brother had been raised to become president of the country, Anastasio had been raised to run the National Guard; Anastasio was much less politically skilled than his father or his brother. Anastasio came to power in presidential elections in 1967 and again in 1974, but they were not judged free or fair either within or without Nicaragua.[80] Still, until 1975 Anastasio enjoyed strong moral support from the U.S. government, especially from the U.S. ambassador during the Nixon administration, Turner Shelton, as well as increased U.S. economic and military assistance.

By the late 1970s, however, Somoza seemed to be more delusional and more indifferent to the suffering in his country than Batista had been, and he was definitely perceived as extreme in these respects in the U.S. media.[81] Somoza was frequently described by U.S. journalists as a "dictator."[82] Also, Somoza's residence was commonly called a "bunker" in Managua, and this fact was frequently mentioned in the media.[83] Even Somoza's inner circle suspected that "Tachito was cracking up under the pressure of events. His family life was a shambles."[84] President Omar Torrijos of Panama told President Jimmy Carter that the problem in

Nicaragua was "simple. A mentally deranged man with an army of criminals is attacking a defenseless population."[85]

Prior to 1978, the Sandinista National Liberation Front (Frente Sandinista de Liberación Nacional, FSLN) was not a strong revolutionary movement. One estimate is that, in early 1978, there were only between five hundred and one thousand FSLN guerrillas.[86] By most accounts, Nicaraguan peasants were not as politically organized as their Salvadoran counterparts.[87] Unfortunately, no electoral or other data are available that would enable rigorous assessment of FSLN support by department in Nicaragua in the mid- to late 1970s. On the basis of both scholarly accounts and the location of FSLN strongholds in later years, it appears that leftist political attitudes were more common among subsistence peasants in the mountainous coffee-producing north-central departments of Matagalpa, Nueva Segovia, and Estelí, and also in the western departments of Chinandega and León, where cotton estates had expanded in recent decades.[88] However, there were various obstacles to FSLN activity in these areas, and the FSLN did not undertake major attacks in them prior to late 1977.[89] They were certainly not "controlled" by the FSLN.

During 1978, however, the FSLN became much stronger. By October–November 1978, the number of FSLN combatants was about twenty-five hundred—more than double the figure at the start of the year.[90] Its expansion was sparked by changes that other actors initiated and changes that the FSLN itself initiated. First, in January 1978, the leader of Nicaragua's political opposition, the Democratic Union for Liberation (Unión Democrática de Liberación, UDEL), Pedro Joaquín Chamorro was gunned down in Managua, and Nicaraguans blamed Somoza for the crime.[91] In the wake of the assassination, UDEL organized a general strike that successfully shut down much of Managua and more of the country's provincial cities.[92] Then, in August 1978, under commander Edén Pastora, the FSLN captured the Nicaraguan National Congress and held more than two thousand hostages, including large numbers of government officials and Somoza relatives; the FSLN gained the release of Sandinista leader Tomás Borge and fifty-eight other Sandinista prisoners, safe passage to Panama, and $500,000. The daring attack revitalized the movement.[93]

It was to be less than a year between the capture of the National Congress and the resignation of Somoza. Within the context of a nationwide general strike called by the Broad Opposition Front (Frente Amplio de Oposición, FAO), the FSLN carried out its first major offensive in September 1978.[94] The FSLN coordinated attacks against National Guard garrisons in Managua, León, Chinandega, Masaya, and Estelí, and gained control of certain neighborhoods in each city.[95] Somoza ordered that the National Guard retake these areas one at a time; National Guard forces concentrated at the target area, cut off its utilities and transport, and then shelled and bombed it.[96] The suppression succeeded in regaining government control over the cities, but it killed thousands of civilians and alienated thousands more.[97]

At this time, revulsion against Somoza became virtually universal. As in Cuba, however, opposition to the dictator was not synonymous with support for the FSLN. Many of the attacks that were made against the National Guard were spontaneous, autonomous uprisings, not FSLN-coordinated attacks.[98] Also, many of the participants in the FSLN's attacks were young people—*los muchachos*—who were not members of the FSLN.[99] When Nicaraguans commented to journalists about the reasons for their participation in attacks, they said, "We all want Somoza to go."[100] Summarized Anthony Lake: "By 1978 the Sandinistas were trying to capture the leadership of a largely spontaneous uprising against a regime that had alienated a whole society."[101] Accordingly, it is impossible to quantify actual popular support for the FSLN.[102]

Among knowledgeable observers in the Carter administration, as well as among scholars, there is now widespread agreement that, by the time of the FSLN's September 1978 offensive and Somoza's brutal response—if not earlier—the appropriate U.S. policy was the achievement of Somoza's resignation.[103] However, as in the case of the Eisenhower administration and the achievement of Batista's resignation, at the time there was consensus in Washington neither about the urgency of the crisis nor about the appropriateness of a U.S. decision to oust a long-standing U.S. ally. Until June 1979, the Carter administration was advised by the Central Intelligence Agency that Somoza's regime could withstand the FSLN's attacks, and in good part for this reason President Carter was not as concerned about the crisis as he might otherwise have been.[104]

The question of the appropriateness of a U.S. decision to oust a long-standing ally was vexing for the Carter administration. First, a decision to achieve Somoza's resignation was not merely a decision not to support him; given that Somoza wanted to remain in Nicaragua despite the crisis, the achievement of his resignation required U.S. action—at a minimum "pressure" or possibly some kind of "force."[105] Although Assistant Secretary of State for Inter-American Affairs Viron Vaky argued that pressure was necessary, he was unable to persuade most other Carter administration officials of his position.[106] Two reasons were especially salient. First, President Carter and other high-ranking foreign policy officials believed that such "force" would constitute "intervention" in internal Nicaraguan affairs, to which they were opposed in principle.[107] Second, such a policy would have been denounced by Somoza's various allies in the U.S. Congress, in particular John Murphy, the powerful chairman of the Merchant Marine and Fisheries Committee of the U.S. House of Representatives.[108] The passage of the Panama Canal treaties was Carter's foreign policy priority for Latin America, and the legislation had to be drafted and approved by Murphy's committee; the treaties were narrowly ratified only in March 1979.

Accordingly, the Carter administration did not itself pressure Somoza to resign after the crisis of September 1978. Rather, the administration suspended U.S. military aid to Nicaragua, reduced economic aid, and supported mediation between Somoza and the FAO by the Organization of American States (OAS). The mediation effort continued until January 1979, when the final OAS mediators' proposal for a plebiscite was rejected by Somoza. In the wake of the collapsed mediation, the Carter administration seemed at a loss for further options; it formally ended the suspended military aid program and called home more than half of U.S. embassy personnel but was otherwise inactive.[109]

The FSLN's final offensive began in May 1979, and it was very successful. The FSLN attacked National Guard garrisons in almost all major Nicaraguan cities, held at least parts of these cities for days or weeks, and established its own provisional capital in León (Nicaragua's second largest city).[110] The FSLN even threatened Managua for seventeen days in June, before retreating to nearby Masaya.[111] The National Guard sought to retake FSLN-occupied cities with the same brutal tactics that it had used during the 1978 offensive; but, although the human cost was even higher than in 1978, military success was much more limited.[112]

The Carter administration struggled to find an effective response. After intense bureaucratic infighting, U.S. Secretary of State Cyrus Vance proposed to the OAS Consultation of Ministers that Somoza be replaced by a national reconciliation government supported by an OAS peace-keeping force; but the proposal was rejected on 21 June, and an alternative proposal supporting Nicaraguan opposition forces and calling for elections was approved. Also, on 20 June, ABC television news correspondent Bill Stewart was murdered in Managua by the National Guard; film of the execution was broadcast to appalled Americans. In response, a group of U.S. congressmen and senators declared Somoza "the Idi Amin of Latin America."[113] Apparently, the combination of these events sowed panic among most of Somoza's colleagues, hundreds of whom crowded the Managua airport in a rush to leave.[114]

Finally, however, Somoza was ready to yield. Apparently, he made his decision on 19 June, and it was immediately relayed to U.S. officials and then reaffirmed personally to incoming U.S. ambassador Lawrence Pezzullo on 28 June.[115] Rather than set an immediate date for his departure, however, the Carter administration hesitated. Administration officials hoped to compose a successor government that would limit the power of the FSLN and in some way maintain the National Guard. But Somoza was duplicitous in his discussions of these issues with U.S. officials; after his departure from Nicaragua on 17 July, U.S. plans for the transition were not realized.[116]

As administration officials assessed their goals for the Nicaraguan transition, they perceived the FSLN leadership as predominantly Marxist and anathema at the apex of the Nicaraguan government, but they also believed that the FSLN leadership's power in the new government could be limited.[117] In June 1979, a five-member "Provisional Junta of National Reconstruction" had been named that included two prominent non-FSLN political leaders and two openly FSLN or pro-FSLN representatives; ironically, Carter administration officials were hoping not that this junta would in fact rule, but rather that it could be expanded to include more "moderates," or even that the FSLN could be totally excluded.[118] Moreover, the FSLN included three "tendencies," of which the largest was the Terceristas; this group was considered ideologically flexible, and among its many non-Marxist members were Edén Pastora, as well as numerous persons influenced by liberation theology.[119] Accordingly, as the Carter administration considered future scenarios for Nicaragua, the prospect of a government dominated by Marxist FSLN leaders seemed remote.

Of the three winning Latin American revolutionary movements during the Cold War, Nicaragua's FSLN was probably the "strongest." Yet, it is very unlikely that the Sandinistas could have won power if the Somoza government had responded to U.S. requests for political opening and the Carter administration had decided that rescue of the regime was in the U.S. interest. Comments Jorge Castañeda: "The Sandinistas' victory was, like all revolutions, . . . the product of exceptional circumstances converging fortuitously."[120] Elaborates Saul Landau:

> The revolution could not have triumphed without the ambivalence of President Carter. . . . The Sandinistas captured world opinion, an intangible factor that nevertheless wove its way through White House thinking and mass media concepts and images. Somoza had made fundamental errors in judgment. His tactics had alienated even the wealthy.[121]

The U.S. Role in El Salvador

The U.S. government was deeply engaged in the effort to thwart the revolutionary movement in El Salvador, intervening on a massive scale to affect the Salvadoran polity, military, and economy.

The total amount of U.S. aid to El Salvador during the 1980s was approximately $3.6 billion. Historically, U.S. aid to El Salvador had been low: in no year between 1965 and 1979 did U.S. aid surpass $14 million.[122] But in 1985, U.S. aid rocketed to a whopping $570 million (see table 5.3). This amount was an unprecedented expenditure for the United States in Latin America.[123] During the course of the decade, El Salvador was the fifth largest recipient of U.S. aid worldwide.[124]

Not only was U.S. aid to El Salvador prodigious relative to U.S. aid to other Latin American countries, but the impact of the aid was especially great in a country about the size of Massachusetts with a population of about five million. Between 1986 and 1988, the U.S. funded between 20 percent and 43 percent of the Salvadoran government's budget.[125] In 1987, U.S. aid totaled more than the country's exports.[126]

Table 5.3. U.S. Aid to El Salvador, 1979–90 (millions of current dollars)

	1979	1980	1981	1982	1983	1984	1985	1986	1987	1988	1989	1990
Total	11	64	149	264	327	413	570	444	574	396	388	328
Economic	11	58	114	182	246	216	434	323	463	314	307	247
Military	0[a]	6	36	82	81	197	136	122	112	82	81	81
Total as % of All U.S. Aid to Latin America and Caribbean	2	12	22	27	25	26	26	26	30	27	24	15

Sources: U.S. Agency for International Development, *U.S. Overseas Loans and Grants and Assistance from International Organizations, July 1, 1945–September 30, 1991* (Washington, D.C.: U.S. AID, 1992), 35 and 49; and U.S. Agency for International Development, *U.S. Overseas Loans and Grants: Series of Yearly Data,* vol. 2, *Latin America and the Caribbean: Obligations and Loan Authorizations, FY 1946–FY 1985* (Washington, D.C.: U.S. AID, n.d.).

[a]Less than $50,000.

During the decade, the U.S. government spent more than $200,000 per guerrilla.[127]

Of course, U.S. aid to El Salvador was not merely a matter of dollars and cents. U.S. aid to El Salvador was a complex set of allocations—allocations that were both military and economic, that were conditioned in various ways, and that were not necessarily coherent. The allocations were made to affect the behavior of different groups within El Salvador and also to satisfy different political constituencies within the United States. Only after Duarte had been elected president in 1984 were the effects of the U.S. role in El Salvador apparently sufficient to prevent the possibility of an FMLN victory.[128]

During the early years of the Reagan administration, most top U.S. policymakers believed that virtually the sole cause of the Salvadoran conflict was East bloc support for the FMLN, and that the sole appropriate response of the United States was military support for the Salvadoran regime.[129] The U.S. public and the U.S. Congress were wary, however, that El Salvador could become a second Vietnam, and in 1981 the U.S. Congress conditioned U.S. aid to El Salvador upon certification by the administration that there was progress in El Salvador toward a political opening.[130]

Prodded in part by the U.S. Congress, the Catholic Church, and human rights groups, and in part by their own observations, most Reagan administration officials came to believe that political authoritarianism was also an important cause of the conflict, and they too sought democratization in El Salvador.[131] For some U.S. officials, U.S. aid to El Salvador was no longer perceived primarily as support for the Salvadoran regime, but as leverage upon it, enabling the U.S. government to push for a political opening. However, other U.S. officials—especially military and intelligence officials on the ground in El Salvador—continued to believe that the U.S. priority should be a military victory for the Salvadoran regime over the FMLN and continued to doubt the value of democratization to this end.[132]

Accordingly, at different moments, different U.S. officials were maintaining different objectives for U.S. aid in El Salvador. The result was confusion. Some components of U.S. aid to El Salvador may have borne contradictory effects. In particular, although U.S. military aid was considered by some U.S. officials as leverage for democratization (and in fact probably did constitute such leverage), the aid of course also strengthened the military institution in numerous ways. Further, as long as U.S. officials continued to aspire to a military victory for the Salvadoran regime over the FMLN (not merely the prevention of a takeover by the FMLN), it is doubtful that any U.S. threat to suspend military aid to El Salvador could be credible to Salvadoran officers.[133] To the extent that Salvadoran officers did not find U.S. threats credible, the officers presumably perceived U.S. military aid as an indication that the war, not democratization, was the "real" U.S. priority.

U.S. Political Pressure on the Salvadoran Government

The U.S. government was more profoundly immersed in the domestic politics of El Salvador than in the domestic politics of any other Latin American country during the decade. As mentioned above, increasingly U.S. officials believed that democratization in El Salvador was necessary, both to assure U.S. congressional support for economic and military aid and to resolve the key problem sparking the revolutionary movement. Throughout the decade, the U.S. government, prodded by the U.S. Congress and numerous U.S. interest groups, promoted the holding of elections. However, although some U.S. government officials did try to improve human rights performance in El Salvador, in general U.S. standards for the "freedom" and "fairness" of these elections were low, and concern for other components of democracy was scant.[134]

As chapter 3 described, from 1979 until 1982 El Salvador was governed by civilian-military juntas that had not been elected and that were complicit in a pattern of flagrant human rights violations. Such a regime was palatable neither to most members of the U.S. Congress nor to many administration officials. The U.S. ambassador to El Salvador, Deane Hinton, vigorously backed the holding of elections for a constituent assembly in March 1982. U.S. embassy officials emphasized to all Salvadoran political actors that elections were necessary for increased economic and military aid. In the event, although evidence accumulated subsequently that the number of voters in the election was greatly inflated and that the real results of the elections could never be ascertained (see chapter 3), turnout for the elections was perceived as high, bolstering the administration's contention that the guerrillas lacked popular support.

The U.S. government played a determining role in the selection of the provisional president for El Salvador after the 1982 elections (see chapter 3). When it appeared that the Salvadoran rightist parties would ally to choose death squad mastermind Roberto D'Aubuisson as provisional president, U.S. Ambassador-at-Large Vernon Walters, a retired U.S. general with a very high profile in Latin American military circles, traveled to El Salvador. Political party leaders and military leaders were invited to meet with him and were reminded that U.S. aid was contingent upon the emergence of a moderate government. The Salvadoran military commanders were particularly concerned that a president emerge who would not threaten U.S. military aid, and ultimately their preferred candidate, Magaña, became president.

Not surprisingly, such an outcome was not overwhelmingly reassuring to the U.S. Congress. Human rights violations continued, albeit in smaller numbers (see chapter 3). The U.S. Congress granted the Reagan administration less than a third of the military aid that it had requested for El Salvador and conditioned it on the achievement of a verdict in the case of the U.S. churchwomen murdered in El Salvador in December 1980.[135] At the same time, the military strength of the FMLN relative to the Salvadoran army was at its apex, and the guerrillas were expanding into more and more areas of the country (see chapter 2). In this context, the Reagan administration became even more engaged in internal Salvadoran politics, and President Reagan himself may have begun to believe that democratization would be important to the resolution of the Salvadoran conflict.[136]

In the fall of 1983, the U.S. government began to send clearer signals to the Salvadoran leadership about the importance of respect for human rights. Ambassador Thomas Pickering arrived in the country and quickly stepped up pressure for a political opening. George Bush, U.S. vice president and former head of the Central Intelligence Agency, visited El Salvador on 11 December 1983 to reinforce the U.S. embassy's criticisms of the death squads. At an official dinner presided over by President Magaña, Bush condemned the death squads:

> Your cause is being undermined by the murderous violence of reactionary minorities. . . . These cowardly death squad terrorists are just as repugnant to me, to President Reagan, to the U.S. Congress, and to the American people as the terrorists of the left. . . . If these death squad murders continue, you will lose the support of the American people.[137]

Apparently, in at least one meeting with top Salvadoran military and civilian leaders, Bush presented a list of death squad members whose withdrawal the U.S. government wanted.[138] The pressure exerted by Bush, and continued after his departure by Pickering, was effective; death squad killings began to decline in November and dropped again in December.[139]

The improvement in the Salvadoran military's human rights record was conditioned on the dramatic increase in U.S. aid for El Salvador described below.[140] As mentioned in chapter 3, a Salvadoran defense minister said, "We know that improving our image is worth millions of dollars of aid for the country."[141] Echoed the chief of staff of the armed forces:

> We knew that public opinion in the United States and the view of many senators and congressmen opposed to military aid for El Salvador were largely due to our bad image because of the squads. Knowing that the aid was absolutely vital for us, we concluded that we had to take a strong decision to get rid of them.[142]

Presidential elections were scheduled for March 1984. Aware that the outcome of the 1982 Constituent Assembly election had been problematic, the Reagan administration sought to assure that Roberto D'Aubuisson, the presidential candidate for ARENA, would not win. U.S. officials in El Salvador were deeply involved in the mechanics of the electoral process; for example, when the Salvadoran computer that was to print out voter lists failed, a U.S. computer was used for that purpose.[143] U.S. officials actively supported Duarte's candidacy. The Central Intelligence Agency channeled approximately $1–$3 million in covert assistance to the Christian Democratic Party for its campaign—an amount that, in per capita terms, would have been $50–$100 million in a U.S. election.[144] Also, U.S. embassy officials overtly lobbied for Duarte, emphasizing as in 1982 that a D'Aubuisson presidency would doom U.S. aid to El Salvador.[145] Ultimately, despite numerous problems (see chapter 3), the 1984 election was perceived as successful by the U.S. government. Not only was it assessed as fair by various delegations, in particular a delegation of members of the U.S. Congress that included U.S. Majority Leader James Wright, but the runoff was won by Duarte.[146]

The election of a civilian president with democratic credentials was the key to fully opening the chest of U.S. aid for El Salvador. Duarte personally traveled to Washington, convincing Democrats in the U.S. Congress that he sought political reforms and peace for El Salvador.[147] Beginning in May 1984, the U.S. Congress dramatically increased U.S. allocations for El Salvador (see table 5.3), and removed most of the conditionalities that had previously been attached to military aid.

Intense U.S. engagement in Salvadoran politics continued during the Duarte administration: "In very few other countries in the world in those years did a U.S. Embassy have the kind of access and influence that the U.S. Embassy in El Salvador had."[148] Both U.S. ambassadors to El Salvador during Duarte's administration (Pickering and Edwin Corr) were top advisers to the Salvadoran president. U.S. embassy officials counseled Duarte and his cabinet not only on relations with Washington and on relationships with other political groups in El Salvador but also on internal Christian Democratic Party politics. At the same time, U.S. officials advanced the policy alternatives favored by the United States, alternatives that may ultimately have been contradictory: democratization but a military victory over the FMLN; social reform programs but free market economics. In part due to these contradictory objectives, the Duarte government gradually lost popular support (see chapter 3).

As the Christian Democratic Party's support eroded, ARENA won the midterm elections of 1988 and became the favorite to win the 1989 presidential elections. Although Alfredo Cristiani, a businessman who had been educated at Georgetown University and had not been tied to the death squads, had replaced D'Aubuisson as ARENA's presidential candidate, U.S. officials were concerned about the implications of the party's victory.[149] Moreover, political violence was again increasing. In early 1989, at the request of the U.S. embassy in El Salvador, Vice President Dan Quayle visited the country and, speaking with Salvadoran leaders, criticized a recent army massacre of ten peasants in the village of San Sebastián.[150]

ARENA's victory in March 1989 followed, of course, the January 1989 inauguration of George Bush as U.S. president. In the context of changes in the Soviet Union, as well as Bush's own foreign policy proclivities, U.S. policy toward El Salvador shifted; the U.S. government began to express interest in a negotiated settlement to the conflict. The Bush administration's interest intensified in November 1989, when the FMLN's offensive convinced most U.S. officials that the war could not be won militarily and—probably most importantly—the Atlacatl Battalion's murder of six Jesuit priests and two coworkers at the Central American University indicated that U.S. efforts to secure the Salvadoran military's respect for human rights had failed.[151] In October 1990, the U.S. Congress voted to halve military aid to El Salvador, and also to end all aid if the Salvadoran government did not negotiate seriously; this decision increased the pressure on Bush and Cristiani administration officials to pursue negotiations.[152]

In short, U.S. pressure on the Salvadoran regime to hold elections and improve human rights performance was considerable. But this pressure was compromised in numerous ways. First, as is discussed below, it was undercut by large amounts of military aid. Also, given the size of the military-aid program, many analysts feared that the transition toward a political opening was merely a result of expediency on the part of the Salvadoran political right, and that the opening would not survive the diminution of the U.S. role in the country.[153] There were also doubts that U.S. intervention to affect electoral outcomes, as occurred in both 1982 and 1984, constituted a positive lesson in democratic behavior.

Moreover, U.S. promotion of democracy in El Salvador was limited primarily to the holding of elections and limiting human rights violations. Only a tiny fraction of U.S. aid was allocated for the strengthening of democratic institutions. According to official U.S. AID/El Salvador statistics, between 1986 and 1989 only 1 percent of all U.S. aid—about $4 million annually—was spent for this purpose.[154] Most of the expenditure was for the American Institute for Free Labor Development (AIFLD), which trained and organized farmworkers under its banner.[155] Judicial reform, which under the circumstances might have been expected to be a priority, was not funded at all until 1989, when it received a bare $1.5 million.[156]

U.S. Military Aid to the Salvadoran Government

The amount of U.S. military aid to El Salvador during the 1980s was much more than the United States had ever allocated to any other country in Latin America. Between 1980 and 1989, according to official U.S. statistics, U.S. military aid to El Salvador was in the range of $1 billion (see table 5.3).[157] In 1984, the year of the highest level of U.S. military aid to El Salvador, the U.S. provided $197 million, more than half the amount of U.S. military aid to the entire Latin American region.[158] Military aid declined somewhat during the last half of the decade, but it was still $81 million in 1990, 35 percent of U.S. military aid to the entire region.[159] Approximately 32 percent of the aid was allocated to equipment and maintenance, 18 percent to ammunition, 10 percent to aircraft, 10 percent to fuel, 10 percent to training, 8 percent to construction projects, 8 percent to medical supplies, and 6 percent to rations.[160]

U.S. aid greatly strengthened the combat capability of the Salvadoran military. Commented one U.S. analyst: "Massive U.S. military aid after 1984 blunted the rebels' growing offensive capability."[161] A U.S. journalist wrote: "Strengthened by U.S. training and weapons, El Salvador's army may be turning the corner in its 4-year-old war against the Marxist-led guerrillas."[162] Added four U.S. lieutenant colonels:

> We would not want to underestimate the magnitude of the American achievement . . . from 1980 through 1984. The transformation of ESAF [El Salvadoran Armed Forces] during that period from a "militia of 11,000 that had no mission" into a much larger and incomparably more capable force that turned back the FMLN stands as a significant feat of arms. . . . Clearly . . . , the Salvadorans could never have succeeded without American arms, advice, and training.[163]

The size of the Salvadoran armed forces more than quadrupled, growing from approximately ten thousand in 1979 to forty thousand by 1984 and to fifty-six thousand by 1987.[164] Whereas in 1980 the ratio of government forces to guerrillas was a mere 1.5 to 1, by the late 1980s the ratio approached 8 to 1.[165] Also, Salvadoran officers became combat-ready:

> The first time I went there [to El Salvador], most of the Salvadoran top military leaders looked like Sergeant Snorkel in the comic strips, they couldn't fit through a door of a helicopter, and their idea of warfare was an 8 to 5 type of convenient schedule and they called it off for the evening and went home. Now they are lean and mean.[166]

The equipment of the Salvadoran armed forces improved dramatically. Whereas in 1980, the Salvadoran soldier carried a worn, obsolete rifle, by 1984 he was well outfitted, brandishing a new M16.[167] Ammunition was scant at the beginning of the war, but plentiful later.[168] Radios numbered a mere 250 in 1980, but about 2,500 by 1987.[169] At the beginning of the decade, the Salvadoran armed forces had about 20 aircraft; by late 1984, it had approximately 46, and a few years later roughly 135.[170] The increase in the number of helicopters meant that, whereas at the beginning of the war only about 20 soldiers could be transported in helicopters, by 1987 some 500 could be.[171] As mentioned in chapter 2, the combat helicopters that the Salvadoran armed forces gained in 1984 facilitated attacks against the large formations that the FMLN was deploying at the time, compelling the FMLN to change its strategy in the war.[172] The maintenance of the Salvadoran armed forces' new equipment was facilitated by the U.S.-financed expansion of a central logistics depot at military headquarters in San Salvador.[173]

U.S. military advisers were also stationed in El Salvador to improve the Salvadoran military's combat effectiveness. By an informal agreement between the U.S. Congress and the Reagan administration, the number of military advisers was limited to 55, but their actual number was higher, approximately 105 to 125.[174] These advisers were backed by about 1,200 more U.S. military personnel stationed in Honduras.[175] U.S. lieutenant colonels worked with the Salvadoran army chiefs of staff on the strategy for the war.[176] Most U.S. advisers, however, were assigned to actual Salvadoran military units; although officially barred from actual combat, many participated.[177] Their role is discussed by U.S. Major Kevin Higgins:

> Stay in the shadows, devote yourself completely to the cause, make sure they get credit for everything you do, don't openly offer advice, but when they come up with an idea that's right-on, support it with everything you've got. If they don't come up with "that" idea on their own, drop some hints. If they come up with an idea you don't care for[,] if you can't turn it into something worthwhile let it die. "Their" ideas will be carried out much more enthusiastically than anything attached to the "stigma" of being your idea. Giving just that little bit of ground allows you to get yourself in a position where you have the entire zone moving in the direction you want, without anyone knowing except yourself.[178]

While the U.S. government was able to strengthen the military capabilities of the Salvadoran armed forces, its efforts to change the political structure and attitudes of the Salvadoran armed forces were less successful.[179] U.S. analysts who closely observed the Salvadoran military were frustrated by its resistance to the development of professional norms and standards:

> [The Salvadoran military] continues to suffer from many of the ills that have plagued it since the war began: a disengaged officer corps, a "garrison

mentality," forced service conscripts with little will to fight, excessive reliance on firepower and helicopters for resupply rather than on ground troops to hold territory. . . . The *tanda* system . . . also hampers the armed forces' warfighting effectiveness since it thereby tolerates unprofessional, brutal, and criminal behavior. The corruption endemic to the Salvadoran armed forces has proved to be resistant to U.S. reform efforts and equally damaging to military capabilities.[180]

Four U.S. lieutenant colonels, at least one of whom had served as a U.S. military adviser to the Salvadoran commanders, were also skeptical about the development of professional norms among the Salvadoran officers.[181] The four lieutenant colonels criticized in particular the continuation of the *tanda* system; the gap between the officer elite and peasant conscripts, without provisions for noncommissioned officers; and the reliance on firepower, without sufficient implementation of small-unit tactics or civil defense programs.[182]

Perhaps most important, although human rights violations by the Salvadoran military declined during the 1980s and regular elections were held, many analysts believed that these changes were perceived by Salvadoran military officers not as inherently positive but merely as necessary to receive U.S. aid (see chapter 3). On the ground in local areas in El Salvador, Salvadoran soldiers were still widely perceived as abusive; in the Orellana research team's survey, for example, a substantial majority of the respondents (58 percent) said that civil defense programs were not helpful, and almost half of these respondents (44 percent) explicitly criticized the soldiers as repressive or arrogant.[183] For most U.S. policymakers, the November 1989 murders at the University of Central America by the U.S.-trained Atlacatl Battalion, especially in the context of the subsequent cover-up, showed that, overall, the Salvadoran military was not convinced that respect for human rights and democratization were important to win popular support and remove the root causes of the insurgency (see chapter 3).

U.S. Economic Aid to El Salvador

Although U.S. military aid to the Salvadoran government was the most controversial part of the U.S. aid package, in absolute quantities U.S. economic aid far surpassed military aid (see table 5.3). As U.S. AID proclaimed, "Wherever one turns in El Salvador, one sees U.S. economic aid at work."[184] This section describes U.S. economic aid and its beneficiaries.

There were various kinds of U.S. economic aid to El Salvador during the 1980s. The largest component was the Economic Support Fund (ESF), sometimes referred to as "economic stabilization." Although ESF funds amounted to a mere $9 million in 1980, between 1984 and 1989 they amounted to approximately $210 million annually, roughly 60 percent of all economic aid.[185] Most ESF funds (approximately 75 to 80 percent) were allocated to offset the deficit in the Salvadoran balance of payments, relieving the government of debt-servicing pressures and enabling the purchase of imports.[186]

Another 20 to 25 percent of ESF funds—about $40 to $50 million annually during the mid- to late 1980s—was allocated to development projects.[187] Over the course of the decade, the largest share of these funds went to restore war-damaged infrastructure. The second largest share was to the Salvadoran private sector for the development of non-traditional exports and the improvement of productivity. Between 1985 and 1988, large sums were also spent for earthquake recovery efforts. Smaller percentages—under 10 percent—were allocated for the agrarian reform program, education, and health, and a mere 4 percent or so for democratization.

The second largest component of U.S. economic aid to El Salvador was classified as "development assistance." Originally, in 1980, development assistance was a larger program than ESF, and its emphasis was the agrarian reform program, in particular the provision of credit to reform beneficiaries and financing for the purchase of lands.[188] The sums for development assistance did not increase anywhere near as dramatically as ESF, however; between 1984 and 1990, development assistance approximated $70 million annually, representing about 20 percent of all U.S. economic assistance to El Salvador.[189] By the late 1980s, projects became more diverse: between 1985 and 1988, 40 percent of the assistance was allocated for agriculture, 21 percent for health, 14 percent for education, and 5 percent for population.[190]

A third component of U.S. assistance for El Salvador was food aid, provided under P.L. (Public Law) 480, the Food for Peace Program.[191] U.S. expenditure for P.L. 480 was steady between 1983 and 1990, in the range of $50 million annually.[192] Although, overall, Salvadorans were helped by the P.L. 480 program, some farmers were hurt to a degree, as prices for some of their food products were lower.[193] Roughly 85 percent of the expenditure was under Title I of the P.L. 480 program, which is for long-term, low-interest loans that facilitate the purchase of U.S. food products.[194] Approximately 15 percent of the expenditure was under Title II of the program, which is for outright food donations, targeted to needy individuals.[195]

Overall, who were ultimately the major beneficiaries of U.S. economic aid in El Salvador? The question is difficult to answer precisely. As indicated above, approximately half of all U.S. economic aid was balance-of-payments support that facilitated imports by Salvadoran businessmen—in other words, assistance to the Salvadoran upper-middle and upper classes. Maximizing the advantages of these programs in various ways, businessmen gained significantly.[196] Further, during the mid- and late 1980s, as the Reagan and Bush administrations placed more emphasis on free market reforms, it appears that private businessmen were able to claim a growing share of the benefits of U.S. aid.[197] Agrarian reform programs were cut back, whereas more U.S. aid was allocated to "agribusiness development."[198] Also, social service expenditures were increasingly channeled through probusiness groups, in particular the Salvadoran Foundation for Social and Economic Development (Fundación Salvadoreña de Desarrollo Social y Económico, FUSADES), raising questions about the percentage of these assistance funds that actually reached target groups.[199]

One key question was also the extent to which the Salvadoran military officers gained from U.S. assistance that was denominated as "economic" rather than "military." Apparently, given the key political roles that military commanders enjoyed during the 1980s, many positioned themselves to take advantage of ESF and other government resources.[200]

Also, in the allocation and implementation of many projects, security force personnel were involved—indeed, many of the projects were referred to within El Salvador as "civic action" by the military.[201] Although much of the development aid for local areas in El Salvador was channeled through the National Commission for the Restoration of Areas (Comisión Nacional de Restauración de Areas, CONARA), which was dependent on the Ministry of Planning, for the most part in practice local military officers controlled the distribution of funds and projects.[202]

Overall, citizens were favorable toward these programs; in the Orellana research team's survey, 13 percent reported that civic action programs had been implemented in their community, and the overwhelming majority of these respondents (84 percent) said that the programs had eroded support for the FMLN.[203] Still, however, in their decisionmaking about aid projects, many officers benefited their personal allies, and more than a few benefited themselves.[204]

This problem was acknowledged by U.S. AID officials in El Salvador, and beginning in 1987 an effort was made to channel U.S. assistance directly to elected civilian officials, in particular mayors, through the Municipalities in Action program.[205] In this program, projects were expected to be proposed by the citizens of the municipality in a *cabildo abierto* (open community meeting). Approximately $30 million was to be channeled through the program annually in 1989 and 1990, and Chalatenango and Morazán were priority target areas. However, many analysts remained skeptical that military commanders would withdraw from this key decisionmaking arena.[206] In the Orellana research team's survey, respondents were at best lukewarm about the program: 68 percent were not familiar with it; another 24 percent knew about it, but said that it had not been implemented in their community; of the 8 percent who said that it had been implemented in their community, only about one-third (18 out of the 621 respondents) were enthusiastic.[207] In other words, 18 out of 621 respondents said that the program had helped "a lot."[208]

Although much of the U.S. economic aid to El Salvador benefited civilian or military elites, it is also clear that some of the aid benefited the poor.[209] As of 1988, U.S. AID/El Salvador reported expenditure during the previous decade of $35 million for essential medicines, pharmaceutical supplies, and medical equipment; $51 million for the construction and rehabilitation of almost a thousand rural classrooms, benefiting seventy-seven thousand students, as well as classroom equipment and teacher training in many more schools; and $50 million for the building or rebuilding of homes, businesses, classrooms, clinics, and other places devastated in the 1986 earthquake.[210] A program to help displaced persons was funded at more than $70 million over the decade; it dispensed daily food rations to about 200,000 people, provided 14,000 temporary jobs a month, and enabled 400,000 visits by medical personnel.[211] Efforts were also made to assure that programs reached remote areas. For example, in 1988, some 102 projects—primarily the construction of roads and bridges, the development of potable water systems, the improvement of school classrooms, and the introduction of electricity—were initiated in the department of Chalatenango versus 96 in San Salvador.[212]

Another important source of foreign economic support for El Salvador was remittances from Salvadorans abroad, primarily in the United States. By 1985, approximately $100 million was remitted annually by Salvadoran families abroad; by 1989, the figure had reached $200 million annually.[213] In other words, by 1989 the amount of remittances was as much as half of all U.S. aid (see table 5.1).

Overall, the primary goal of U.S. economic aid to El Salvador was to assure that, amid the toll of the war on the Salvadoran economy, economic plummet not occur—an economic plummet that it was assumed would have devastating consequences for popular support for the Salvadoran government.[214] For the most part, the U.S. objective was achieved; although U.S. economic aid did not bring prosperity to El Salvador, economic decline would have been much steeper, perhaps as steep as in Peru during 1980–92.[215] Further, during the course of the 1980s, support for the FMLN eroded sharply among middle-class Salvadorans, and the guerrillas' key social base became the peasantry— a trend that occurred for various reasons, but one that probably would not have happened in the context of an economic plummet of Peruvian dimensions.

It is also important to point out that, especially during the Duarte administration, ESF aid was conditioned on the adoption of free market policies—policies that contradicted the traditional populist economic programs of the Christian Democratic Party.[216] The U.S. embassy encouraged devaluation, a reduction in public spending, an increase in interest rates, privatization of state-owned enterprises, trade liberalization, and new investment and export promotion laws. These policies were resisted by President Duarte, who feared a political backlash, and the negotiations between the U.S. and Salvadoran governments were frequently tense. Salvadorans' discontent over the austerity and salary declines of this period was indeed a key factor in the election of the ARENA government in 1989.[217]

The U.S. Role in Peru

Whereas the U.S. role in thwarting a revolutionary victory by the FMLN was major, the overt U.S. role in thwarting a revolutionary victory by the Shining Path was not.[218] As indicated in the introduction to this chapter, for example, in per capita terms during the late 1980s U.S. aid to Peru was less than 4 percent of U.S. aid to El Salvador. In contrast to U.S. aid to El Salvador, U.S. aid to Peru did not increase during the 1980s as the revolutionary challenge became more intense. Indeed, in real terms, aid to Peru averaged $46 million during Peru's previous democratic interlude between 1962 and 1968, but only $26 million between 1980 and 1990.[219] In real terms, U.S. aid to Peru peaked in 1962, a year of a troubled election and a Marxist guerrilla challenge in the country.[220] Table 5.4 provides further specific information about the amount and kinds of U.S. aid to Peru between 1981 and 1992.

There were numerous reasons for the relative lack of U.S. engagement in Peru. First, and most important in my view and accordingly mentioned previously, the Sendero challenge was not a conventional Cold War challenge. Even prior to the collapse of the East bloc, as a Maoist group that vilified the Soviet Union and China, Sendero's advance had minimal implications for the Cold War. Also, although neither Bolivia's MNR nor Cuba's 26th of July Movement defeated the incumbent governments in predominantly military confrontations, the image that many U.S. analysts held of a "strong" guerrilla movement was one that carried out more significant military attacks than Sendero did—movements such as the FMLN and the Viet Cong. Whereas the tendency among U.S. political leaders and officials during the Cold War was to exaggerate the threat posed by most guerrilla movements, between 1980 and 1992 U.S. government officials consistently underestimated the challenge that the Shining Path presented to the Peruvian state.[221]

Second, the fact that Sendero was not a conventional Cold War challenge also meant that "tried and true" U.S. responses were inappropriate. A new and different response was necessary, but the elaboration of such a response was difficult. The problem was suggested in a *Newsweek* article: "U.S. counterinsurgency manuals don't contain much proven advice about how to piece a broken country back together."[222]

Table 5.4. U.S. Aid to Peru, 1981–92
(millions of current dollars)

	1981	1982	1983	1984	1985	1986	1987	1988	1989	1990	1991	1992
Total	84	59	98	175	88	59	64	71	68	95	199	123
Economic[a]	77	52	91	162	77	55	55	63	54	83	155	111
Military	4	5	5	11	9	1	0	0	3	2	25	0.1
Narcotics	3	2	2	3	2	4	8	8	11	10	19	13
Total as % of All U.S. Aid to Latin America and Caribbean	12	6	7	11	4	3	3	5	4	4	14	8

Note: Some figures do not add to the correct sum because of rounding.

Sources: U.S. Agency for International Development, *U.S. Overseas Loans and Grants and Assistance from International Organizations, July 1, 1945–September 30, 1989* (Washington, D.C.: U.S. AID), as well as 1993 edition; and U.S. Agency for International Development, *U.S. Overseas Loans and Grants: Series of Yearly Data,* vol. 2, *Latin America and the Caribbean: Obligations and Loan Authorizations, FY 1946–FY 1985* (Washington, D.C.: U.S. AID, n.d.).

[a]Excludes narcotics assistance, indicated separately on this table.

There were other reasons that the U.S. government tended toward inaction in Peru. Most obviously, as an Andean nation, Peru was geographically more distant than El Salvador or the other Central American nations and, accordingly, problems in Peru did not necessarily spark U.S. strategic interests as much as problems in the Caribbean Basin. Also, since the early 1960s at least, U.S.-Peruvian relations had been tense; in general, U.S. officials perceived successive Peruvian governments as too far to the left—perceptions that the García government in particular did not change. U.S. diplomats' access to top-level Peruvian policymakers was relatively poor. At the same time, there was not as strong a U.S. constituency prodding the U.S. government on its policies toward Peru as had prodded the U.S. government on its policies in Central America.[223]

However, the United States did vigorously pursue policy goals for Peru in the 1980s and early 1990s. It is argued below that the predominant U.S. concerns were the antidrug war and the need for free market reforms. To the extent that the Bush administration sought to support Peru, its overt emphasis was military aid for the antidrug war—aid that was inappropriate to the kind of challenge represented by Sendero and ultimately not a significant factor in its decimation (see chapter 3).

It does appear, however, that the Central Intelligence Agency provided covert support to the GEIN, the select unit within DINCOTE that captured Guzmán, and to DINCOTE as well.[224] Although the CIA probably began to provide small amounts of support to Peruvian intelligence units as early as 1986, and although greater CIA support for these units was urged by Assistant Secretary of State Bernard W. Aronson in early 1990, apparently major support was forthcoming only in early 1991, when the long-standing disagreements between the United States and Peru on free market economic policies and antidrug policies had been resolved (see below).[225] CIA personnel provided the GEIN with sophisticated surveillance equipment and instruction in its use—and, according to some sources, a virtual blank check.[226]

The United States and Democratization in Peru

As noted above, the Reagan and Bush administrations emphasized democratization as a primary U.S. goal in Latin America but defined democracy almost exclusively as elections. In Peru prior to the April 1992 *autogolpe,* democracy by this definition had been achieved—and indeed, as indicated in chapter 3, Peruvian elections were very free and fair relative to the Salvadoran—so support for democratic institutions was not high on the U.S. agenda.[227]

In some periods the U.S. government exerted pressure on behalf of democratic processes in Peru, but these were periods when the prospects for regular elections were threatened. During Alan García's final beleaguered years, the U.S. embassy warned Peruvian officers against a coup.[228] Also, after Fujimori's *autogolpe*, the Bush administration worked to prod the Fujimori regime back into the constitutional fold.[229] U.S. pressure against Fujimori's *autogolpe* included not only suspending economic and military aid that had been programmed for 1991 (but had not yet been disbursed) and reducing aid for 1992, but also working with other nations to withhold all international credits.[230]

As discussed in chapters 3 and 6, however, between 1980 and April 1992 the institutions that compose democratic government were not working well, and the pattern of human rights violations by the Peruvian military raised serious issues. But, to an even greater degree than in El Salvador, the Reagan and Bush administrations did not appear to entertain the question about the enhancement of Peru's democratic institutions —especially democratic institutions whose effectiveness was important to attenuating support for Sendero, such as the judiciary. For example, despite recommendations by the U.S. Congress and U.S. interest groups—beginning by at least 1985—that the U.S. government support Administration of Justice programs in Peru, Peru's judiciary began to receive U.S. support only in 1989, and the total budget for the three-year program was a mere $3.4 million.[231]

U.S. Antinarcotics Policy

During most of the Bush administration, the antinarcotics issue dominated U.S.-Peruvian relations. The "war against drugs" was a centerpiece of President Bush's foreign policy in Latin America; drug summits were organized twice: in Cartagena, Colombia, in February 1990, and in San Antonio, Texas, in February 1992. As the producer of more than half the cocaine that was transported into the United States, Peru was a priority theater in the war. Said Luigi Einaudi, U.S. ambassador to the OAS, for example: "Drugs are the number one problem."[232] Commented Anthony C. E. Quainton, U.S. ambassador to Peru between 1989 and

1992: "Drugs were the principal item in the bilateral agenda."[233] In 1988, the biggest antidrug base in the Americas opened at Santa Lucía in the Upper Huallaga Valley; approximately twenty-five agents of the U.S. Drug Enforcement Administration plus about eight U.S.-supplied helicopters and 450 Peruvians were located at the base.[234] Table 5.4 indicates that increasing (albeit not massive) amounts of U.S. funds were allocated to antinarcotics efforts in Peru between the early 1980s and 1991.

The key debate during most of the period was a U.S. proposal for a $35.9 million military aid package for Peru, stated to be for antinarcotics objectives. Under the U.S. proposal, the United States was to station twenty to fifty U.S. Army Special Forces instructors in Peru to train Peruvian military units; equip the roughly fifty-five hundred Peruvians who would be trained by the U.S. instructors; and enhance Peru's military arsenal by refurbishing twenty ground-attack planes and supplying river patrol boats.[235] It was also expected that the United States would support alternative development programs in coca-producing areas, but precise amounts were not specified.

The proposed military aid package—and the "war against drugs" in general—was extremely controversial. There were many doubts that the "war" could be won in the Andean nations, as well as fears that it would undermine the region's weak civilian institutions and exacerbate the serious pattern of human rights abuse.[236] Also, in the specific case of Peru, analysts worried that the "war against drugs" was not the most important battle for Peru at the time, and that the antinarcotics effort hurt the struggle against Sendero.[237] One U.S. analyst, for example, compared the U.S. request that Peru wage an earnest war against drugs to "asking a country that's fighting the Civil War and going through the Great Depression to take on Prohibition as well."[238] There was also a contradictory worry: that the stated antinarcotics objective of U.S. aid was not the actual objective, and that the actual objective was counterinsurgency, an effort in which the United States should not be involved, given U.S. human rights law or other factors.[239]

The primary concern expressed by Peruvian leaders across the political spectrum was that U.S. antinarcotics aid exaggerated the military dimension of the effort and slighted the economic component.[240] They feared that repressive enforcement measures, if not combined with the promotion of alternative development and crop substitution programs, would only lose Peruvian peasants' hearts and minds to the Shining Path. Said Hector Vargas Haya, an Aprista congressman, for example: "What we need in this country are greenbacks, not Green Berets."[241] Primarily as a result of these concerns, the Bush administration's $35 million military aid proposal was rejected by President García in April 1990 and then by President Fujimori in September 1990.

Finally, however, in May 1991, President Fujimori accepted the package. The shift in Fujimori's position reflected intense U.S. pressure; although U.S. officials denied that U.S. support for Peru in the international financial community was contingent upon Peru's signing the military aid agreement, the Peruvian government repeatedly indicated that it believed this was the case, and Peruvian journalists routinely interpreted the negotiations in this fashion.[242] A second factor was that, in the course of U.S.-Peruvian negotiations between September 1990 and May 1991, the Bush administration compromised.[243] In particular, the Bush administration promised greater economic aid, especially for crop substitution. Also, the administration modified some of its conceptualization; for example, peasants producing coca were not labeled criminals.

But tensions continued. The U.S. military aid proposal was under consideration in the U.S. Congress for several months. Finally, in September 1991, the U.S. Congress reduced the amount of military aid from $35 million to $25 million (see table 5.4); the $10 million that had been earmarked for the Peruvian army—the service most often cited for abuses by human rights groups—was withheld, and the remaining funds were conditioned on various improvements in the Peruvian security forces' human rights performance.[244]

Gradually, the May 1991 agreement unraveled. Both the Fujimori and the Bush administrations had high expectations for the May 1991 agreement, expectations that were dashed.[245] Although the agreement did not specify precise figures for U.S. economic support for antinarcotics efforts, Fujimori assumed a massive allocation. In the event, although U.S. AID reported $19 million for antinarcotics economic programs in 1991, Peruvian experts calculated smaller numbers.[246] For their part, U.S. officials expected improved antidrug performance on the part of Peruvian officials, but the pattern of events suggested that official complicity with drug traffickers remained a serious problem.[247] Accordingly, the U.S. government delayed its disbursements of aid; the delays angered the Peruvians. In February 1992, at the drug summit in Texas that President Bush hoped would showcase his administration's antinarcotics achievements, his policies were sharply criticized by Fujimori.[248] Finally, in April 1992, further U.S. military aid for antinarcotics activities was stopped by Fujimori's *autogolpe*.

U.S. Military Aid to Peru

During the Cold War, support for the military was a key conventional U.S. response to a guerrilla threat in a Third World nation. Reagan and Bush administration officials sought to respond to the guerrilla challenge in Peru with increased military aid, but their proposals were for the most part opposed by both the U.S. Congress and the Peruvian government.[249] Table 5.4 indicates that, with the exception of the year 1991, U.S. aid to the Peruvian military was slight.[250]

There were various reasons for the opposition within the United States to military aid for Peru. First, and especially important during the early and mid-1980s, was the belief among Republican U.S. congressmen in particular that the Peruvian military should not be supported because of its friendly relationship with the Soviet military.[251] The Peruvian military had begun to buy arms from the Soviet Union during the late 1960s and purchased significant quantities until the late 1980s.[252] Republican congressmen also were especially angered by Peruvian military attacks on U.S. aircraft that suggested disrespect for the United States and possibly also complicity with drug traffickers.[253]

Second, and increasingly important by the later 1980s, was the belief that the Peruvian military was engaged in a persistent pattern of gross violations of internationally recognized human rights, and that accordingly any aid to the Peruvian military violated U.S. law. Democratic U.S. Congressmen in particular feared that U.S. aid would signal U.S. condonation of the human rights violations by the Peruvian military; soldiers might become even more indiscriminate in their behavior, provoking more popular support for the guerrillas, and also more arrogant, weakening democratic institutions.[254] From this perspective, the use of military aid as leverage toward greater respect for human rights was problematical at best.[255]

Among Peruvian leaders and citizens, the primary concern was that military aid would not actually help the counterinsurgency effort.

Peruvian leaders and citizens believed that the guerrilla problem was economic and political to a greater degree than it was military; but they perceived the aid proposed by the United States as primarily military and accordingly inappropriate for Peru.[256] Peruvians worried too that a U.S. military role would provoke a nationalistic reaction in Peru and that U.S. military advisers would not understand the Peruvian context.[257] When citizens in a 1990 Lima sample were asked about ways to improve Peruvian military performance, only 3 percent of the respondents called for more international military aid.[258] Even among Peruvian security force personnel, a majority in the Osores research team's sample rejected participation by foreign military advisers.[259] Gradually, however, as noted in chapter 3, a certain desperation developed among many Peruvian military officers, and U.S. military aid was welcomed in numerous quarters.

U.S. Economic Aid to Peru

U.S. economic aid was the kind of U.S. support that Peruvian political leaders and citizens wanted.[260] Table 5.4 shows that, indeed, economic aid was by far the largest component of U.S. aid to Peru during the 1980s. However, table 5.4 also indicates that, relative to U.S. aid to the region as a whole, economic assistance to Peru was low for most of the decade. U.S. economic aid increased only after President Fujimori restored Peru to the good graces of the international financial community.

During the 1980s, approximately half of U.S. economic aid to Peru was allocated for "development assistance" and approximately half went toward food aid.[261] In contrast to El Salvador, ESF funds (primarily for balance-of-payments support) allocated to Peru were scant, primarily because neither the Belaúnde nor the García government was implementing the economic stabilization programs upon which ESF support was conditioned. As in the case of El Salvador, development projects were diverse, and food aid was provided under both Titles I and II of the P.L. 480 Food for Peace program (increasingly under Title II). An exception to this pattern was the year 1984 (see table 5.4), when the U.S. government was trying to entice the Belaúnde government back toward orthodox financial policies and to bolster the center right in Peru for the 1985 presidential election. In that year, "development assistance" for Peru jumped, designated apparently for "land and water management" and for "housing investment guaranties."

Although food aid was thus an important component of U.S. aid to Peru, the amount of aid was small relative to the need. The population of Peru was approximately four times larger than that of El Salvador and hunger was a much more severe problem; yet during the 1980s the amounts allocated through the U.S. Food for Peace program were smaller in Peru than in El Salvador.[262] The intensity of the need for food aid in Peru is suggested by the dramatic increase in food aid in the early 1990s; in 1989 approximately $32 million in P.L. 480 funds were allocated for Peru, but in 1993 the figure was $110 million.[263] Whereas U.S. food aid was reaching less than 5 percent of Peru's population in 1989, it was reaching an estimated 15 percent by 1993.[264]

Why did U.S. economic aid not increase during the mid- to late 1980s as the Sendero threat intensified? Upon his inauguration, García indicated his desire to assume a leadership position for the Third World against "imperialism"; he blamed the Third World's debt crisis in large part upon the United States; and he said that Peru would not pay more than 10 percent of its export earnings toward the service of its debt.[265] The debt issue was an extremely salient one for the U.S. government during most of García's term; for U.S. officials who wanted the U.S. position on the debt to prevail, García's stance was anathema.[266] As one U.S. embassy official put it, "The Treasury Department hates Peru because of its stand on the debt."[267] Although toward the end of García's term it appeared that he might be willing to accommodate the international financial community and shift at least slightly toward free market policies, ultimately major structural adjustment did not occur.

Economic aid increased substantially only in 1991 (see table 5.4), when the Fujimori government reached an accord with the international financial community. As noted above, the United States had planned an even larger increase in aid for Peru in 1991, to $238 million, but some of the funds had not been disbursed during the course of the 1991 fiscal year and were suspended after the *autogolpe.* U.S. aid included the dramatic jumps in food and military aid mentioned above, as well as approximately $60 million in ESF funds.[268]

An Assessment

Are there policies that the United States could have adopted for El Salvador and Peru that might have reduced the human tolls in the two countries and might have brought about more rapidly, and perhaps more permanently, the relative political peace that both nations now enjoy?[269] Could peace negotiations have begun sooner in El Salvador, and could the possibilities for a permanent peace in Peru have been enhanced?

In El Salvador, the U.S. response was massive and comprehensive, combining economic and military aid as well as political pressures. In my view, the most important component of U.S. policy was the pressure toward democratization. In chapters 3 and 6 in this book, it is argued that the gradual political opening in El Salvador was critical to the erosion of middle-class support for the FMLN and to the enticement of first FDR and then FMLN leaders back into the electoral political arena. The pressure exerted by the United States was similar to the human rights pressure that it had previously placed upon the Batista and Somoza governments, without a positive response.

However, U.S. pressure for democratization was compromised in various ways. First, as chapter 3 in particular showed, U.S. standards for bestowing the democratic label on El Salvador were very low. Although numerous factors were important to the FMLN's commitment to a negotiated solution after November 1989, it seems very possible that the maintenance of higher democratic standards—in particular, elections that were perceived by most citizens as "free and fair"—might have tempted the FMLN back into the electoral arena much earlier.[270]

Also, the goal of a political opening in El Salvador was undermined by U.S. military aid. On the one hand, the FMLN's challenge to the Salvadoran government was, to a much greater degree than Sendero's in Peru, a military challenge that required a military response if the incumbent regime were not to succumb; however, as discussed in various chapters in this book, military repression was the primary factor triggering the FMLN's revolt. Given the ideological commitment in some sectors of the U.S. government to a military solution to the conflict, the signal given by U.S. military aid was, for the most part, toleration of the abuses that had originally sparked the conflict. It is interesting to note that Salvadoran citizens themselves were skeptical of the impact of U.S. military aid. For example, even when answering a question about the improvement of military performance, most Salvadorans cited respect for human rights and political dialogue.[271] Indeed, a considerable percentage of the Salvadoran sample—33 percent—said that, overall, the arms sent by the United States to El Salvador had not been helpful to the country, because there had been abuses and/or damages to the civilian population as a result.[272]

There has been a tendency to underestimate the importance of U.S. economic aid to the trajectory of the Salvadoran conflict. Although poverty was not the key factor prompting Salvadoran university students to join the FMLN, poverty would probably have increased much more dramatically during the 1980s if U.S. economic aid had not been so plentiful. Although the political opening in El Salvador did gain middle-class acceptance of the Salvadoran regime, this acceptance might not have been forthcoming if El Salvador had suffered an economic debacle of Peruvian proportions.

In the Peruvian case, it must be acknowledged that the identification of an effective response to the Shining Path was complex and difficult. As has been indicated, the Sendero challenge was a new kind of challenge, requiring a new kind of response. However, it remains the case that the U.S. response was flawed.

First, it is striking that, as U.S. government officials elaborated policy toward Peru, their focus seemed to be virtually exclusively on the implementation of free market reforms and on antidrug policy. The reason may have been underestimation of the Sendero threat, or the belief that only when economic or antidrug policies were changed could counterinsurgency be effective. The result, however, was that the U.S. government appeared virtually oblivious to the concerns of Peru. On numerous occasions in the late 1980s and early 1990s, U.S. diplomats could have engaged in discussion about policies against the Sendero challenge, but did not.[273] For example, when Ambassador Alexander F. Watson was interviewed at length in Peru's leading news weekly in 1989, he did not mention the Sendero threat as a problem for which solutions should be debated.[274] At a Lima symposium attended by scores of Peruvian leaders and scholars in 1990, the U.S. ambassador to the Organization of American States, Luigi Einaudi, was speaking on the OAS and the "war against drugs" when guerrilla bombs went off outside the building; Ambassador Einaudi did not stray from his topic.[275]

To the extent that the Bush administration did try to respond to the Sendero threat, its overt policy was traditional: military aid. In part because military aid for counterinsurgency objectives was restricted by the Brooke-Alexander Amendment, and in part because of human rights and other concerns, the Bush administration usually stated the objective of the military aid to be support for antinarcotics efforts. In a virtually unprecedented response by a Latin American country, the aid was refused by two successive Peruvian governments. Ultimately, the inappropriateness of U.S. military aid as a response to the Sendero challenge was shown by its dénouement (see chapter 3).

The most effective support against the Sendero threat provided by the Bush administration was covert: the CIA's financial and logistical support for the GEIN and DINCOTE. Although this support may have been critical, it was also problematic in various respects. First, it is unfortunate that the aid did not begin earlier—apparently, it became major only after early 1991, when the Fujimori government was acceding to U.S. policy preferences with respect to economic stabilization and antinarcotics efforts. Also, because the U.S. role was covert, the real history of the capture of Guzmán, and accordingly also of the decimation of Sendero, is being withheld from Peruvians. When a true history is not available, valid lessons cannot be inferred from it. Fujimori has been able to appropriate for partisan purposes the capture of Guzmán as his administration's success, when the truth is more complex.

As I discuss in greater length in the concluding chapter, my view is that, although the root causes of the Shining Path challenge in Peru were complex and primary responsibility remains with the Peruvian government, various kinds of U.S. efforts directed at the origins of the challenge were appropriate. As indicated in chapter 3, most Peruvians opted for U.S. economic support. In the context of U.S. objectives for economic policy in Latin America at the time, it is understandable that U.S. officials rejected large-scale economic support for the García government. It is also clear that, if Sendero gained social bases in an area of Peru, it became extremely dangerous to carry out development projects in that area or to deliver food aid. However, more could have been done through Peru's network of nongovernmental organizations in areas not yet controlled by the guerrillas for the satisfaction of basic food needs. The jump in U.S. food aid to Peru should have occurred in the 1980s, not after 1991—after the Fujimori government had adopted free market policies but also for the most part after the capture of Guzmán.

Also, it is not clear, in the context of the serious flaws in democratic governance in Peru under both Presidents García and Fujimori, that large-scale U.S. support for democratic institutions in Peru would have enhanced the capabilities of the state and, in turn, its legitimacy. But there was at least a possibility that U.S. support for the reform of critical democratic institutions, such as the judiciary, would have been advantageous. Perhaps most important, as the conclusion discusses, the U.S. government might have encouraged debate about counterinsurgency within a democratic context.

6

WHY DID THE REVOLUTIONARY MOVEMENTS EMERGE AND EXPAND?

*T*he previous chapters of this book present objective information about each of the key variables in revolutionary equations—revolutionary organization, political regime, economic conditions, and the international context. By contrast, the first two sections of this chapter provide the revolutionaries' subjective explanations for their decisions to take up arms. The first section focuses on the guerrilla leaders, and the second on the rank and file. Information on the militants' political, socioeconomic, ethnic, and personal backgrounds—which are, of course, the contexts within which the militants make their decisions—is also included where available. With respect to Peru, particular attention is given to Guzmán, not only because he was the Shining Path's chief but also because his leadership was cited by many followers as a key factor in their decision to join the organization.

The revolutionaries' subjective explanations for their decisions were given in their own writings or in interviews with me, with my research team, with other scholars, or with journalists. Their interpretations are a crucial complement to the objective information about revolutionary organization, political regime, economic conditions, and U.S. policy in previous chapters.

It is the fit between the implications of the interviews with the revolutionaries in these two sections and the implications of the objective data in previous chapters that informs my own effort at a comprehensive, scholarly analysis in the final section of the chapter. In this final section, I weave the various kinds of information presented in earlier chapters together with other scholars' arguments to assess the significance of each variable in the revolutionary equation in the two nations, as well as the interplay among the variables. In other words, my answer to the key question of this book—Why did the guerrilla movements in El Salvador and Peru emerge and expand?—is provided in a much richer and more scholarly context than in the introductory chapter.

The Top Guerrilla Leaders: Their Backgrounds and Their Explanations

As in almost all Latin American revolutionary experiences, in both El Salvador and Peru the university was the key place where the guerrilla leadership formed. Accordingly, the socioeconomic backgrounds of most of the original leaders were middle class or upper middle class, and teachers were an important constituency.

However, the universities at which the movements emerged were very different. In El Salvador, the university was in the country's capital, whereas in Peru it was in the remote southern highlands department of Ayacucho. The National University of El Salvador was in many respects an actor in the Salvadoran political arena. From the very start, the leaders of the Salvadoran guerrilla groups were engaged in national political debates and were aware of international political events; in such a context, it was difficult for one revolutionary figure to claim exclusive knowledge of the road to revolution. In Peru, however, Ayacucho was a small, remote, provincial town, where awareness of national and international events was limited. In such a place, a pedestrian but well-read professor such as Guzmán could appear to be the sole genius who knew the correct revolutionary road. Also, in Ayacucho, the close and prolonged contact with Guzmán that was critical in the establishment of Sendero's inner circle was facilitated.

As chapter 3 indicated, a nondemocratic regime and severe political exclusion characterized El Salvador during the 1970s and much of the 1980s, and repression of political activism was widespread. Almost all FMLN leaders emphasize the vices of the Salvadoran political regime in their explanations of their own radicalism; many of the original leaders were themselves victims of electoral fraud and repression. By contrast, none of the Shining Path leaders had tried to participate in electoral politics prior to their commitment to the revolutionary movement; nor had any of the leaders personally experienced or witnessed political repression. Specific national political events are not salient for the Shining Path leaders.

From the data in chapter 4, it is evident that economic conditions deteriorated much more severely in Peru during the 1970s and 1980s than in El Salvador. Although the Sendero leaders did not personally experience deprivation, they lived in one of Peru's most impoverished departments, where they directly observed the declining living standards of the southern highlands peasants and the increasing threat to the peasants' subsistence. Unfortunately, ex post facto interviews are not available for the Shining Path leaders—as they are for many of the FMLN leaders—but it is evident from the leaders' writings discussed in chapter 2 that their uppermost concern is economic misery. When they discuss the Peruvian state, the focus is rarely upon repression, but rather upon corruption—a corruption among elites that deprives the poor of the basic right to live. By contrast, at the time the top FMLN leaders became revolutionaries, none of them was living in the poorer departments of El Salvador, and few appeared to be in close observation of particular economic problems in the country.

The FMLN

The birthplace of the revolutionary movements that were to compose the FMLN was the National University of El Salvador. The middle-class and upper-middle-class students there were aware of the international political upheavals of the late 1960s and early 1970s—ranging from the students' uprising in France in May 1968 to the Tupamaros' rebellion in Uruguay and the emergence of liberation theology in the Catholic Church—and they became engaged in the debates of these heady times.[1] Among the five commanders of the organizations that formed the FMLN in 1980, only one had not studied at this university.[2] Many of the second-in-commands had also studied at the university. The exceptions to this pattern were generally leaders from the FPL.

The Salvadoran Communist Party was active at the university beginning in the early 1960s. During the mid-1960s, the political left was sufficiently strong at the university to achieve the election of Fabio Castillo, then a member of the Communist Party and later a founder of the PRTC, as rector.[3] Castillo promoted numerous leftists to high positions within the university, and he encouraged leftist activities among the students. In the 1972 presidential election, many university students campaigned vigorously for the leftist alliance. Enraged by the electoral fraud, the students protested massively, and the government closed the university —exacerbating the students' anger and causing many to despair of an electoral road to political reform.[4]

The background and experiences of Shafik Handal, head of the PCS from 1970 to the present, were archetypal. Of middle-class origin, Handal became a university student, then a radical activist, and also a political prisoner.[5] Born in 1930, Handal was the Caucasian son of Palestinian Christian immigrant parents; his father was a prosperous storekeeper in the provincial city of Usulután. When Handal was only thirteen years old, he was shocked by the bloody, but ultimately successful, civilian and military movement that overthrew the dictatorship of Hernández Martínez. In 1950, as a law student at the National University, he joined a major—and successful—effort for democratic reform of the Salvadoran university structure. However, he also witnessed the forced expulsion of students from a university building by the National Guard, in violation of the constitutional principles of the university:

> This was very instructive for me. It was a first realization that let me know who ruled in the country. Civil society and civil power were superseded by military and police power.[6]

Later that year, Handal joined the Communist Party. In 1992 interviews about his life, Handal did not express any particular interest in the ideology or practice of the Communist Party; rather, he noted, "the PCS was the only revolutionary organization that there was in the country."[7] In February 1951, in his first nonclandestine action for the party, Handal and other militants put a pro-PCS manifesto on walls in the capital; immediately thereafter Handal was persecuted by the police. "It was my baptism as a militant . . . and also my baptism as a target of repression," he said.[8] In 1952, Handal went into exile in Chile.

Returning to El Salvador in 1956, Handal's activism and his repression continued.[9] In 1959, he became a member of the Central Committee of the PCS; in 1973, he succeeded Cayetano Carpio as secretary general of the party. The primary emphasis during most of this period was on electoral politics. A 1960 effort to form a legal party was rejected. But, as a member of a coalition of parties, the PCS participated in three presidential and five legislative and municipal elections between 1966 and 1977. Reported Handal: "We won the presidential elections of 1971 [*sic*] and 1977, but we lost the ballot-counting."[10] However, in particular between 1960 and 1964 and 1970 and 1973, groups within the PCS encouraged military organization and armed struggle; indeed, in 1961 Handal headed a military commission within a PCS school. In subsequent years, Handal focused primarily upon the coordination of strikes and demonstrations. During the 1960s and 1970s, Handal was arrested seven times and beaten, but not tortured.

The other three commanders who became radicals during their studies at the National University of El Salvador were more than a decade younger than Handal; deciding much more quickly to pursue a violent road to revolution, they did not experience direct frustration with electoral politics as Handal did. But, to the extent that their statements about their decisions are available, the electoral frauds and the government repression of the 1970s were extremely salient in their revolutionary development.

The ERP's Joaquín Villalobos was born in 1951 to a large, Caucasian, middle-class family; his father owned a printing shop.[11] Villalobos studied at a traditional Catholic high school. He became radical only after beginning his study of economics at the National University in San Salvador; he participated in a students' strike and then a teachers' strike, and his political views were transformed. In his own discussion of his radicalization, Villalobos emphasized that his commitment was a product of the events of the era rather than of an intellectual analysis: "I hadn't read a page of Marxism."[12] Villalobos said that the crucible for the war was the frustration of Salvadorans' expectations that the Christian Democratic Party would win the elections of 1972, their subsequent activism, and the concomitant repression of both members of the Catholic Church and students at the National University.[13] In 1988, Villalobos continued to believe that the Salvadoran political system excluded the left: "Democracy is a fraud because the left can't participate, we would be shot."[14] After the 1989 offensive, he offered the following explanation for the origins of the conflict:

> The good people of Morazán started to organize, many of them in Christian communities. They began to organize against economic injustice, the repression of the National Guard, and the frauds of the PCN. We adopted armed struggle not because we liked violence, but because we had to fight for the structural changes that would establish new rules for participation.[15]

Information about the commanders of the smaller groups, the RN and the PRTC, is scantier.[16] The RN's Eduardo Sancho Castañeda (alias "Fermán Cienfuegos") was born in 1947 to a wealthy, Caucasian family and educated at a Jesuit high school. At the National University of El Salvador, he was politically active by the late 1960s. He was one of the founders of the ERP and subsequently of the RN. He became the head of the RN after the death of its original commander, Ernesto Jovel Funes, in a plane crash in 1980.[17]

The PRTC's head, Francisco Jovel (alias "Roberto Roca"), became a political activist while at the National University in the early 1970s.[18] Caucasian, he was born in the late 1940s in Usulután to middle-class parents. In 1971, he helped to organize a student strike at the university, and later that year became the vice president of the country's national student organization, the General Association of Salvadoran University Students.

The exception to this pattern of National University recruitment for the FMLN commanders was the FPL's Salvador Cayetano Carpio ("Marcial").[19] Born in 1919 or 1920, he was the oldest FMLN commander. Carpio had been very young when his father, a shoemaker of limited means, died. Carpio was sent to study at a religious seminary; however, he did not complete high school. He began manual labor when he was only fourteen years old. First he picked coffee, and then he worked as a baker. When he was in his early twenties, he became a leader of a bakers' union, and in 1944 he participated in various workers' strikes. In 1945, he joined the PCS and led several strikes; he was arrested in 1946, went into exile in 1947, and was arrested again after his return to El Salvador.

Between 1955 and 1957, Carpio traveled to the Soviet Union for Marxist studies, as well as to China. He was elected secretary general of the PCS in 1964 but eventually became critical of the PCS's political position. After he advocated the adoption of armed struggle by the party in 1970 but lost the argument, he left the PCS to found the FPL:

> After a long process of ideological struggle within the traditional organizations [political parties] it became evident that they ... denied the possibility and necessity of the Salvadorean people undertaking the process of revolutionary armed struggle. ... By the end of 1969 it was very clear that El Salvador, its people, needed an overall strategy in which all methods of struggle could be used and combined in dialectical fashion.[20]

Overall, Carpio was the most doctrinaire of the FMLN commanders. He liked to be referred to as the Ho Chi Minh of Central America. By the time he committed suicide in 1983, he had become a bitter man who used Marxist ideology to justify his own ambition. At least according to his former FPL colleagues, he constantly referred to his working-class origins, claiming that this background gave him the authority to be the number-one commander of the Salvadoran guerrillas: "He had personified the vanguard as himself."[21] However, although Carpio's mind-set was more classically Marxist than the other commanders', his best-known book was about his experience of torture and imprisonment in El Salvador: *Secuestro y capucha en un país del "mundo libre"* (Kidnapping and Hooding in a Nation of the "Free World").

Many of the FMLN seconds-in-command also became political radicals while attending the National University. Indeed, all three original seconds-in-command for which information is available—all women—studied at the university.

Ana Guadalupe Martínez Menéndez was the ERP's second-in-command.[22] She was born in 1953 to a middle-class family; her father was a Salvadoran police chief. Studying at the National University in 1969, she joined a strike protesting discrimination against low-income students. In the 1972 elections, she supported the opposition coalition. She reported that, for her as for so many other guerrillas, this fraudulent election was a turning point, convincing her that "'elections didn't work. So we sought another way to change the politics of the country."[23] In 1973, she abandoned her studies of medicine and became a member of the ERP. In 1976, she was arrested; for seven months, she lived in a tiny cell where she was raped, beaten, and tortured. Like many FMLN leaders, when Martínez wrote, her experience of political repression was her topic; the book was entitled *Cárceles clandestinas de El Salvador* (The Clandestine Prisons of El Salvador).

The PRTC's number two was María Concepción Valladares (better known by her alias "Nidia Díaz").[24] Caucasian, she was born in approximately 1953. The family was essentially middle-class, but home life was unstable and unhappy. Her father hailed from an upper-class landowning family and had studied in the United States, but he had failed professionally. Her mother worked as a secretary during the day and sewed at night for extra money. Díaz was a scholarship student at a private Catholic high school. She was attracted to the political left when she entered the National University in 1970. As a leader among the psychology students in particular, she coordinated strikes and occupied buildings. As early as 1972, she was learning about weapons, and became a "guerrilla militant." At the same time, however, she operated several flower shops and retained aspirations to become a professional psychologist.[25]

In her book, Díaz explains why she became a guerrilla. Her statements are clear and direct, employing universal concepts rather than theoretical or sectarian jargon:

> We felt obliged to take up arms. I love peace, and life; but an unjust war was imposed upon us. . . . [I did not want to take up arms but] there was no alternative. . . . The causes of the struggle are still here, continue to persist: misery, hunger, exploitation, disrespect for human rights.[26]

The background of the FPL's original second-in-command was no exception to this pattern.[27] Indeed, Melida Anaya Montes (alias "Ana María Gómez") was both a student and a teacher at the National University. She rose to prominence as a founding leader of the teachers' union National Association of Salvadoran Educators (Asociación Nacional de Educadores Salvadoreños, ANDES). She suffered government reprisals as early as 1967; after leading an ANDES strike demanding social benefits for teachers, she was sent from San Salvador to the interior of the country by the government. But ANDES demonstrated against the reprisal; allying with other unions, the teachers seized the center of San Salvador and occupied the Ministry of Education. From this experience, "Ana María" wrote her book *La primera gran batalla de ANDES* (The First Great Battle of ANDES).

At some point during the 1960s, "Ana María" became a member of the PCS. In the early 1970s, she left the PCS to join the FPL under Carpio's leadership. During the 1970s, she played a pivotal role in the organization of the BPR, in particular in the establishment of the link between the FPL and the BPR. As a result of her activities as a leader of the BPR, she was arrested in 1977.[28] As mentioned in chapter 2, by the early 1980s she had become much more favorably disposed than FPL commander Carpio toward unification among the FPL and the other guerrilla organizations, and she was murdered by Carpio's order.

A larger number of FPL leaders than of the other groups' leaders hailed from the popular strata. "Leonel González" (Salvador Sánchez Céren), who in 1983 succeeded Carpio as FPL commander, was from a lower-middle-class family living in Quezaltepeque in La Libertad, about forty-five minutes from San Salvador; like his predecessor, he had not been a student at the National University.[29] His father was a carpenter and his mother sold meals in the town's market. Both parents were devout Catholics who sympathized strongly with the plight of poorer persons in the town; his mother gave food to those who could not afford it. After completing primary school in his hometown, "González" studied at a teachers' school in San Salvador that was located near the National University. There he participated in the 1959–60 student protests that led to the overthrow of the Lemus government. After graduating from the teachers' school, he taught for the next thirteen years. Unusually among the top FMLN leaders, "González" reports long-term personal observation of rural poverty: "For seven of the thirteen years that I was a schoolteacher, I was in the rural sector, and this was an experience that sensitized me to the problems and the role of the people of the countryside."[30]

After three years as a teacher, in the early to mid-1960s, "González" became a militant member of the teachers' union ANDES and was active in the teachers' strikes of the 1970s.[31] As a result, he too suffered government reprisals. Although "González" was the leader of the largest organization within the FMLN for many years, his persona is virtually never mentioned by militants as a reason for their decision to become a guerrilla (see next section). Speaking in Washington, D.C., in September 1996, he appeared intelligent but stolid.[32]

Facundo Guardado was one of the highest-ranking FMLN leaders of peasant extraction.[33] A mestizo, he was born in approximately 1955 in the village of Arcatao in Chalatenango, to a peasant father and a mother who had been a schoolteacher in San Salvador. His father, a fervent Catholic, became active in the Christian Democratic Party. Guardado worked from a young age in the fields, and as a teenager he did seasonal work on coffee estates. He hoped to carry out secondary studies in the department capital after he completed the sixth and last grade in his village, but to his dismay his family did not have the necessary money. His first interest in leftist politics was sparked during the 1968 teachers' strike in Arcatao, and gradually he became a militant. He describes his recruitment into the FPL:

> I arrived at the movement in two ways. First, I was an activist in the Christian Democratic Party from the time that I was a small boy; and then, I had become active in the cooperative movement promoted by the Church. Through this movement I began to affiliate with the peasant organizations. This was the story of the majority of us [in the FPL]. Many of us came from the ranks of the Christian Democratic Party; we had lost all hope by this time that we could find a solution through this party; we were people who had developed our human and social consciousness through the Christian movement.[34]

But Guardado was also familiar with places beyond his rural home; in 1980, he was one of the guerrilla leaders who traveled widely—in his case, to Ethiopia, the Soviet Union, and several Eastern European countries—to obtain support for the revolutionary movement.

As the FMLN coalesced and the war became prolonged, the five commanders together issued documents explaining the reasons for their continuing actions. In the commanders' end-of-the-year report for 1988, the focus is on the interplay among the organizational strength of the FMLN, the U.S. government, and the Salvadoran government, and the commanders' perception that trends were favoring the FMLN. Despite the elections of the 1980s, the Salvadoran government is emphatically described as nondemocratic:

> The workers of the city and the countryside are struggling for their demands and rights, unresolved due to the incapacity of the government and the intransigence of the bosses. The deep economic crisis is borne on the backs of the people. The government response towards the economic and political struggle is repression, which went rapidly from being selective to being massive, combined with the most sophisticated techniques of terror and "psychological war". . . .

The action of the death squads increases, but it does not succeed in stopping the people's anger. . . . The crisis in the inner circles of the dictatorship is evident. . . .

The participation of the FDR in the Democratic Convergence . . . has shown that there does not exist the "democratic" opening propagandized [by the North American Embassy, the government, and the military].[35]

As discussed in chapter 2, the FMLN was allied with the FDR, and the FDR's role was important. Although the FDR's leaders were civilians who at no time took up arms for the FMLN, their backgrounds and explanations are also relevant.

The president of the FDR during most of its existence was Guillermo Ungo.[36] Like most Salvadoran political activists, Ungo studied at the National University of El Salvador, earning both his bachelor's and his law degrees from there; he was also personal secretary to its leftist rector during the early 1960s. From a prosperous family that owned a printing business, he had the opportunity to study at a university in the United States, and he became a prominent lawyer and law school professor. In 1969, he became the head of the social democratic MNR, and in 1972 was the vice presidential candidate on the ticket with Duarte. Whatever disillusionment Ungo felt in the wake of the 1972 electoral fraud and his subsequent exile, he persisted in mainstream politics; after the October 1979 coup, he joined the new civilian-military junta. Finally, however, in December 1979 he despaired of the new government being able to control the military's abuses, and he resigned. Soon thereafter, he began to work with the revolutionary leftist groups. Said Ungo shortly before his death in 1991, "Democratization is the main issue. The Salvadoran army must be democratized and changed."[37]

Perhaps the FDR leader best known in the United States was Rubén Zamora, who became the vice presidential candidate of the CD in 1989 and then the presidential candidate of the FMLN/MNR/Democratic Convergence coalition in 1994.[38] From an upper-middle-class background, Zamora was also a student at the National University of El Salvador, where he graduated as a lawyer. He continued his studies abroad, earning a master's degree in political science at the University of Essex in Great Britain. Returning to El Salvador, he became chair of the Political–Social Science Department at the National University, and he also became active in the Christian Democratic Party. In October 1979,

Zamora became the minister of the presidency (chief of staff) for the new civilian-military junta. Like Ungo, however, he became increasingly angry at the failure of the government to control rightist violence. The death of his brother, attorney general Mario Zamora, at the hands of the death squads in January 1980 was the straw that broke the camel's back. He and other PDC dissidents withdrew to form the Social Christian Popular Movement (Movimiento Popular Social Cristiano, MPSC); in April, the MPSC joined the FDR.

Zamora repeatedly emphasized political exclusion as the primary reason for the rise of the revolutionary movement. In one discussion of the formation of the FDR, he said:

> First, we [the Christian Democrats] took part in elections, but they were fraudulent, and then we were arrested. I was jailed after every election in that period. Then, we tried extra-parliamentary means—strikes and protests. But they were met with repression. Every demonstration ended up in a massacre.[39]

On another occasion, Zamora commented:

> The war dates from 1972 and the denial of the presidential election to Duarte. . . . The 1972 election was the last straw; we saw that change was impossible through elections.[40]

The Shining Path

As we have seen, the vast majority of the FMLN leaders were university-educated and came from the middle class or upper middle class; the entire original Shining Path leadership was also from such a background.[41] But whereas most of the FMLN leaders became radical activists as university students, many of the Sendero leaders were professors. Women were well represented at the top ranks of the Senderista leadership, although they appear inordinately likely to have risen to the top on the basis of their abilities to forge a close relationship with Guzmán.[42]

With only one possible exception, the original inner circle of Senderista leaders developed at the Universidad Nacional de San Cristóbal de Huamanga, the Ayacucho university that had reopened in 1959. Guzmán's leadership and his ideology, and its perceived applicability to the poverty of the Peruvian highlands, drew the other leaders to the movement. In the small, remote university town of Ayacucho, a movement centered on one totally committed professor was able to become hegemonic—an unlikely achievement in a larger city, buffeted by a greater variety of political winds. In other words, the provincial origins of Sendero facilitated the development of the quasi-religious character of the organization.[43]

As discussed in chapter 2, Abimael Guzmán was Sendero's "philosopher-warrior" and iron ruler for twenty-two years. Why did Guzmán himself become such a committed revolutionary?

There are few indications from Guzmán's background that he would become a revolutionary leader. Both in high school and at the university, he was a scholar, not a political activist. The factor that stands out in Guzmán's background (as in many revolutionary leaders') is childhood loss.[44] Born in 1934 in Mollendo, a village on Peru's southern coast, Guzmán was an illegitimate child whose mother died when he was only five years old. Although Guzmán's father was a middle-class import wholesaler, he did not take his son in upon the death of his mother; the father was living with another woman and their legitimate children. Guzmán was cared for by uncles in Arequipa for several years. He may not have lived with his father at all until he was twelve, when father and son were in Lima. Returning to Arequipa the next year to study at a private Jesuit secondary school, Guzmán continued to live with his father. However, the relationship was tense; Guzmán felt that his father preferred his legitimate children to him.

Guzmán became interested in political ideology and Marxism while at the university in Arequipa.[45] An excellent student, Guzmán took courses in law and philosophy and was quickly attracted to Marxism. He became the prize pupil of a rigorous, ascetic Kantian philosophy professor and soon thereafter a disciple of a Stalinist painter. In late 1959 or early 1960, he joined the Peruvian Communist Party. Raised in relative privilege, the Caucasian Guzmán apparently first saw with his own eyes the desperate living conditions of poor Peruvian families when he carried out a census in Arequipa after a devastating earthquake, and he became even more committed. By the time that Guzmán was completing his doctorate at the Arequipa university, his scholarship was deeply affected by his political views. For his dissertation in philosophy, he wrote on "The Kantian Theory of Space," rejecting Kant's view in part on Marxist grounds. Guzmán also wrote a second thesis, for a doctorate in law, which is described as an "emotional, uninhibited apologia for revolution."[46]

In 1962, Guzmán took a job as a junior professor of philosophy in the education department at the newly reopened university in Ayacucho, the Universidad Nacional de San Cristóbal de Huamanga. There, he met Augusta La Torre. Only eighteen years old when she married Guzmán in 1964, Augusta quickly came to share Guzmán's political ideology.[47] She was a beautiful Caucasian woman from an elite, albeit downwardly mobile, landowning family, and had attended the local nuns' school; although her father was a Communist Party leader in Ayacucho, he was apparently not very serious about his Marxism.

To what extent was Guzmán's leadership a factor in his movement's appeal to others? Analysts agree that, at the university in the early 1960s, he was "an excellent, even charismatic teacher, as well as reserved, measured, and correct in his relation with faculty and colleagues."[48] They also agree that he was a fierce political infighter and a doggedly persistent organizer who was especially attractive to, and comfortable with, women.[49] It is also clear that, awed by Guzmán's intellectual passion and political conviction, his supporters revered him.[50] "He had an incredible power to convince," said one Senderista.[51] One nickname for Guzmán was "Shampoo," because he was adept at ideological brainwashing.[52] To Guzmán's followers, he was a master of Marxist ideology; in propaganda posters, Guzmán often wore thick spectacles and carried a book.[53]

But was Guzmán truly the genius that his supporters described—or, hungry for ideals, were his followers creating a god to fill their own needs?[54] After Guzmán's capture, it became clear that his militants had indeed exaggerated his brilliance. Commented one journalist:

> The most startling novelty to emerge . . . is how unimpressive he appears to be, either culturally or intellectually. President Gonzalo's captors confess to being somewhat disappointed. His knowledge of Marx, even, is a trifle thin, although he is hot on Mao, to the point of childish obsession in defending even Mao's most banal works. The main impression he creates is that of a studious provincial intellectual.[55]

Another journalist said that his writings "read like bad Mao."[56] Moreover, his interpretation of post-1968 Peru as similar to prerevolutionary China was blatantly wrong.[57]

Nor was Guzmán extraordinarily personally appealing or effective for most people. Even as a young professor in Ayacucho, Guzmán was not strikingly handsome; as a middle-aged man, he became "barrel-chested, jowly . . . with a firmly buttoned collar and a head round as a billiard ball."[58] He suffered from psoriasis; skin peeled off his arms.[59] Guzmán frequently got drunk; after his capture, he was unable to withstand the rigors of prison life.[60] Even in Ayacucho in the 1960s and 1970s, Shining Path members were perceived as "crazies" and "country bumpkins" by most other leftist parties; between 1973 and 1975, they lost control of the key positions they had enjoyed in the university bureaucracy.[61] Perhaps the most important decision made by Guzmán —to take the teaching job at the university in Ayacucho—had been pure chance.[62]

Although Augusta La Torre's influence with her husband may have given her more informal power than anyone else in the organization, to the extent that there was a formal second-in-command, most analysts deemed him to be Osmán Morote.[63] The relationship between Guzmán and Morote was virtually familial. Morote's family was an old, respected, and wealthy mestizo one in Ayacucho. Morote's father, Efraín, was a Marxist anthropologist who was elected rector of the university in 1962. Osmán became acquainted with Guzmán when he studied under him at the university. By 1964, both Osmán and his sister Kayta were active followers of Guzmán; another brother was to follow suit. Osmán became a professor in anthropology at the university and was at Guzmán's side when Sendero Luminoso was founded in 1970.

Julio César Mezzich was at times in the 1980s thought to be competing with Morote for the number-two position in the organization, but his precise status and relationship to Guzmán remain uncertain. Mezzich was the only one of Sendero's apparent top leaders who was not recruited into the movement in the environs of the Ayacucho university.[64] Born in Lima to an upper-class, Caucasian family of Czech origin, he studied at prestigious private schools in the capital—a Jesuit secondary school and then medicine at the University of Cayetano Heredia. While at the university, he undertook social work in the countryside during his vacations. In the early 1970s, as a leader in the Maoist Revolutionary Vanguard, he successfully organized peasants' campaigns for land.[65] As an upper-class Limeño who "went local"—marrying a woman from an indigenous community and donning indigenous garb—he gained his own political following. He apparently began to collaborate with

Guzmán in approximately 1982. Given Mezzich's high socioeconomic status and his independent political base, it is not clear that Mezzich ever completely gained Guzmán's confidence, or that Mezzich wanted to cast his lot completely with Guzmán.

An important early ideological role in the Shining Path was played by Antonio Díaz Martínez, professor of agronomy at the Ayacucho university.[66] Originally from a town in Cajamarca in Peru's northern highlands, Díaz Martínez's Caucasian family was prosperous and he graduated as an agronomist in 1959 from Peru's most prestigious agricultural university, La Molina in Lima. In the early 1960s, Díaz Martínez worked on various agrarian reform projects; then, he became a professor at the Ayacucho university, and between 1965 and 1969 he traveled extensively in the department with student groups to study rural conditions. In his 1969 book *Ayacucho: Hambre y esperanza* (Ayacucho: Hunger and Hope), Díaz Martínez concludes that external "aid" programs in actuality fail to help the peasantry—that, to the contrary, peasants' self-sufficiency is undermined and they are left to the mercy of the forces of the market. After two years in Peking between 1974 and 1976, Díaz Martínez was a firm Maoist and Sendero adherent.

The leader who was to emerge as number one after the capture of Guzmán was Oscar Alberto Ramírez Durand ("Comrade Feliciano").[67] The son of an army general who worked in intelligence, "Feliciano" was born in Arequipa in 1953 and completed his primary and secondary education at religious schools there. An important political influence during these years was his maternal grandfather, who frequently cared for Feliciano and the other children in his family; he was also grandfather to Teresa Durand, who became the wife of Sendero leader Osmán Morote.[68] In 1970, he began to study economic engineering at the Universidad Nacional de Ingeniería (National Engineering University) in Lima, but in 1972 his relationship with his father broke down over politics, and by 1977 he was no longer registering for classes at the university.[69] In 1980, he attended a Shining Path training school in Ayacucho; in 1985, he was the head of the Shining Path's Committee for the Zone of Ayacucho. "Feliciano" has said nothing about his decision to join Sendero.

By the late 1980s, most of the original Shining Path leaders—with the exceptions of Guzmán himself and "Feliciano"—were no longer present. But like the original inner circle, Guzmán's new inner circle was composed primarily of teachers. Most were also Caucasian.[70] The new inner circle, however, had not been recruited into the movement during its period in Ayacucho. Many became familiar with Guzmán in the mid- to late 1970s, however, when he began political work at La Cantuta, a school for teachers strategically located on the outskirts of Lima, on the highway between the capital and Peru's central highlands. A considerable number of women were among the top Senderista leaders at this time; as of 1992, two of the five Political Bureau members were women, and eight of the nineteen Central Committee members.[71]

Representative members of this new inner circle include Elena Iparaguirre, Laura Zambrano, and Martha Huatay, all of whom were captured in late 1992, when information about their backgrounds became available. Number two in the Sendero organization and Guzmán's lover at the time of his capture was Elena Iparaguirre ("Comrade Miriam"). Born in Ica in 1947 and Caucasian, she had earned a bachelor's degree in sociology or psychology, probably at a university in Lima, and had been a teacher.[72] Another important Sendero leader—a member of the Central Committee and the head of the Lima Metropolitan Committee at the time of her capture—was Laura Zambrano ("Comrade Meche"). Born in the mid-1940s and mestizo, she was from a working-class family in the department of Ancash.[73] She studied at La Cantuta and also became a teacher. Sharing many of these background characteristics was Martha Huatay, who among other positions served as president of a Sendero front association of lawyers.[74] Born in the north-coast city of Trujillo and mestizo, she was a teacher first in eastern upper-jungle departments and then in Lima before becoming a lawyer. A long-time union activist and Communist Party member, Huatay joined the Shining Path in the 1970s or very early 1980s. Unfortunately, no personal statements are available from these women providing their own explanations for their decisions to become Senderistas.

The Rank-and-File Guerrillas: Their Backgrounds and Their Explanations

Both the FMLN and the Shining Path gained widespread support in their respective countries (see chapter 2). The emergence of radical university groups is commonplace; the forging of an alliance between the intellectuals and major sectors of the peasantry or other lower-class groups is rare.[75] Both the FMLN and the Shining Path achieved this alliance; intellectuals composed the inner circle of both groups, and peasants were an important rank-and-file constituency in both.

There were, however, important differences in the make-up of the guerrilla groups in the two countries. First, at the midlevel leadership rank, in both the FMLN and the Shining Path a large number were schoolteachers; in Sendero schoolteachers were especially predominant.[76] By contrast, within the FMLN, and in particular within the FPL, a larger number of peasants achieved midlevel leadership status.

Among the rank-and-file guerrillas, the vast majority in the FMLN would have identified themselves as peasants, whereas in Sendero the largest number would have considered themselves students. However, comparisons between El Salvador and Peru on this score should be made cautiously. Because of greater access to education in Peru relative to El Salvador, the fifteen-year-old Peruvian was likely to still be attending school, whereas the fifteen-year-old Salvadoran was not. Although the social origins of the two fifteen-year-olds might have been identical, the Peruvian would be classified as a "student" and the Salvadoran as a "peasant." Also, more Peruvians than Salvadorans from rural backgrounds were still studying part-time into their twenties; although working, perhaps even full-time, they usually considered themselves "students."[77] In other words, there were many more students with professional aspirations, despite their peasant origins, among whom the guerrilla leadership might recruit in Peru than in El Salvador.[78] Overall, however, it would still appear that by the early 1990s there was greater diversity in the social backgrounds of the rank and file in Sendero than in the FMLN.

The key sites where the FMLN and the Shining Path secured lower-class recruits were different. As chapter 4 showed, the southern highlands departments where peasants and their children became Sendero's first militants were the most impoverished in Peru, and becoming more so. By contrast, in El Salvador the departments where the FMLN gained peasant recruits were disadvantaged, but not demonstrably more so than many other departments, and by many indicators were not becoming poorer. The FMLN chose its sites in part because of their poverty, but probably more importantly because of the potential for political organization there. Their strategic location was also a factor: the location of

Morazán and Chalatenango on the border with Honduras (a country with which El Salvador had gone to war in 1969) facilitated the flow of people and weapons; too, the volcanoes near San Salvador were good hiding places for the guerrillas.

Just as most FMLN leaders emphasized the fraudulent and abusive political regime as the primary reason for their decision to join the revolutionary movement, so did the rank and file. However, given the actual day-to-day circumstances of the peasant members, they were more likely to have been directly influenced by progressive Catholic priests, and they were also more likely to have been directly concerned with the improvement of their economic conditions. References by rank-and-file guerrillas to the FMLN as an organization or to Marxist ideology were very rare. By contrast, Shining Path members emphasized economic misery. For Shining Path militants, Christian influences are nonexistent; the principles that are important to them are Guzmán's own, and they frequently cite the movement itself and its ideology as a reason for joining.

The FMLN

As indicated above, the FMLN's inner circle emerged among student activists at the National University of El Salvador. Among the top five or six leaders of each of the five organizations in the FMLN (with the exception of the FPL), almost all had been university students in San Salvador during the 1970s.[79] Roughly 20 percent of these leaders were women.[80]

The backgrounds of midlevel FMLN leaders are only rarely known. During the 1970s, the five groups' inner circles recruited extensively in San Salvador among various unions. There was little success among workers or middle-class groups, with the exception of the teachers.[81] The teachers' union, ANDES, was militant, and several teachers became midlevel FMLN leaders.[82] In one 1982 ERP attack, "Operation Pedrero," the seven leaders included two students, two peasants, two ex-officials of the army, and one worker.[83]

For midlevel leaders and others of urban origins, the authoritarian political regime was the key factor in their decision to join the revolutionary movement. Summarized one midlevel FPL leader: "The repression was the detonator."[84] Commented another FPL leader:

It is evident that, after the 1977 [fraudulent] election, there was a torrent towards armed struggle, because after that other popular orientations—Christian, Christian Democrat and Social Democrat—which had been putting hope in legal parliamentary and electoral forms—realized, not only their insufficiencies, but also the unviability of this mode of struggle to open the channels of democracy. New social sectors understood that only with a more direct, active, and multifaceted participation of the great popular majorities was it possible to advance a democratic process.[85]

Said Irma Segunda Amaya, a student in Aguilares (north of San Salvador) who joined the FPL in 1976 and subsequently became head of Political and Military Instruction in the guerrilla-controlled zones of Chalatenango: "Working with the Catholic Church, we began to organize against the injustice in the area. But the government's response was repression. We had to make the response that we were being given. We had to defend ourselves. It was the only way to survive, and possibly achieve our goals."[86]

The abuses against Catholic priests were pivotal in the decisions of many midlevel leaders and urban professionals to join the guerrillas. In Francisco Emilio Mena Sandoval's account of why he left the National Guard to become a guerrilla, his first chapter is about his shock when he hears Roberto D'Aubuisson acknowledge the murder of Father Rutilio Grande: "I asked myself, 'What are we doing? To be in the Guard is to collaborate in the murder of priests?'"[87] Listening to both Archbishop Romero and Jesuit friends at the UCA, Mena Sandoval began to agree with them that "democratization was the only way to avoid a social explosion, which was approaching like a cyclone."[88] Mena Sandoval's observations of social injustice and corruption within the military also influenced his decision, however: "The officials treated the soldiers like animals."[89] His image of a professional Salvadoran army was destroyed by his observation of soldiers' corrupt and abusive behavior during the Soccer War with Honduras, and he was very critical of the military during his 1981 press conference about his decision to join the ERP.[90]

For many, the assassination of Archbishop Romero in 1980 was the galvanizing atrocity.[91] Said "Apolonio," an electrical engineer who became a technician for Venceremos radio, for example:

I returned to El Salvador a few days after the assassination of Monsignor Romero. The news hit me between the eyes. I could neither believe nor accept it. I was a pacifist. I worked in YSAX [the archdiocesan radio station] because I was convinced that the Monsignor could find a way out of the country's disastrous crisis. A whole lot of people shared that same hope. When they killed him, that was when I said yes to everything the *compas* [guerrillas] proposed. I said yes to armed struggle. The death of the Monsignor helped clarify my beliefs. Not only in my case. I think the same thing happened to many others.[92]

Of course, the murder of priests also greatly influenced other church people. A Catholic priest from Belgium became a pastoral and ideological adviser for the ERP in the midst of the repression: "On Christmas day three years ago [in 1980], after a bomb exploded in our rectory, I realized I had only one option left if I wanted to stay in El Salvador. I traveled that day to northern Morazán."[93]

As the original leaders of the FMLN moved to the countryside in the early 1980s, peasants became overwhelmingly predominant among the rank-and-file guerrillas. Contacts between the guerrilla organizations and peasants in Chalatenango and Morazán had begun much earlier, however, by approximately 1974.[94] As mentioned in chapter 4, the interest was not due to a perception of Chalatenango or Morazán as particularly disadvantaged departments, but rather primarily due to the perception that political organization was viable in these sites.[95] In the eastern departments, memories of the 1932 massacre were not as immediate as in the western departments, and haciendas were not as robust as in the western departments.[96] The influence of the liberation theology sector of the Catholic Church was also essential.[97] Explained a former FPL member: "In part because of poverty in the eastern departments and in part because of the role of the Catholic Church, political organization grew in these departments, and then in the wake of government repression, the FMLN emerged."[98]

Although in neither Morazán nor Chalatenango were there many large, prosperous cotton or coffee estates, the type of peasant recruited by the guerrillas was slightly different in the two departments. Whereas Villalobos liked the social cohesiveness among the Morazán smallholders, the FPL leaders emphasized recruitment among migrant farmworkers. In the FPL leaders' view, migrant workers were more likely to organize politically because they had less to lose from landowners' reprisals.[99]

By one estimate, about 80 percent of the FMLN's rank and file were peasants in the early 1980s, and the figure had reached 95 percent by the late 1980s.[100] After a two-week visit to Morazán in the early 1980s, *New York Times* journalist Raymond Bonner provided a profile of the peasant revolutionary in the zone: "born and raised in Morazán; two years of school; at least one parent or sibling killed by Government soldiers; living brothers and sisters participating in the revolution."[101] The peasant revolutionaries were also young; Bonner estimated that about 80 percent were eighteen years old or younger, and that very few were older than twenty-five.[102] A priest said to Bonner that "the immense majority" of the guerrillas were Christians.[103] Approximately 25 percent to 30 percent were women.[104]

Among the peasants who joined the FMLN, the fraudulent and abusive political regime is again key to their decision. Explained one commander of peasant origins: "Since 1972, they denied us access to power through election, so we took up the armed struggle, not as an end, but as a means."[105]

For most, an egregious violation of human rights was the direct impetus in their decision to join the guerrilla movement.[106] The ex-peasant commander for Guazapa (a volcanic range just north of San Salvador) was Raúl Hercules.[107] In his twenties when he joined the guerrilla movement, Hercules had led the first act of revolutionary violence in Guazapa: killing an ORDEN member whom Hercules believed had assassinated his father (a leader of the local Federation of Christian Peasants). Hercules emphasized that, despite his religious upbringing, violence had appeared to be the only alternative:

> I was raised on the message of Father Alas and Father Grande. Though others [than the priests] said we would never bring change without guns, we thought it was possible. We demonstrated, we organized, and we said "no" for the first time in our lives. You know what it brought. You've heard the stories. . . . [Father] Alas was kidnapped, drugged, beaten, and left for dead. Father Rutilio was machine gunned. My own father was cut into pieces.[108]

For an older peasant, "Magdaleno," the stimulus was again repression.[109] After attending a meeting of the Federation of Christian Peasants, "Magdaleno" had been detained and tortured by soldiers who wanted him to reveal the names of persons at the meeting. Upon his release, "he knew he was marked and that the next arrest could be his last."[110] Fearing both for his life and for his ability to provide for his children, he went to San Salvador and received an audience with Archbishop Romero to discuss his plight. Believing that the archbishop was not condemning his decision, he became a militant.

A twenty-nine-year-old woman told a journalist that she had joined the ERP because she believed that "[it is] the only way to bring democracy and social change to El Salvador. . . . Others join because they fear if they don't organize, they will be killed by the army."[111]

For "Nico," a twelve-year-old boy of peasant origin who was a messenger and guide with the guerrillas, the atrocity that sparked his decision to join the guerrilla movement was his mother's rape and murder. Reported Charles Clements: "He described the crime graphically, dispassionately, a recital of watching the rape itself and then seeing his mother's brains splattered against the wall. . . . 'The soldiers,' he said, 'were no better than animals.'"[112]

But for many peasants, the decision to become a guerrilla was also strongly influenced by leftist Catholic priests and increasing perceptions of economic injustice. Said one FPL peasant militant in Chalatenango:

> What influenced me most politically was learning to read and write. A Sister in my place began teaching me and later I slowly learned more by myself. . . . A book called the *Cartilla*—for the teaching of the ABC—religious books, the New Testament and others were the first books to teach me a better understanding. Another thing that influenced me was the injustice of the landowners towards the poor and the activities of the repressive organizations. Through studying I came to know the exploitation all around us, by the landowners, the authorities, the church even which charged first one *colón* then five, twenty-five and one hundred *colones* for a wedding, or a christening.[113]

The Shining Path

Whereas during most of the 1980s the FMLN was an alliance between university students and peasants, Sendero Luminoso was a more complex, diverse organization. Although university professors and schoolteachers predominated at the top ranks of the movement, by the early 1990s there were many different kinds of people in the middle and lower ranks. In my research team's interviews with thirty-three Senderistas, five (15 percent) were teachers (one university professor, three secondary school teachers, and one primary school teacher); three

(9 percent) were other professionals (one obstetrician, one architect, one government employee); eight (24 percent) were students; six (18 percent) were peasants; six (18 percent) were workers (some of whose jobs were not stable); two (6 percent) were vendors; and three (9 percent) were unemployed. At times, it was difficult to identify the interviewee's social status, or even urban versus rural residence. For example, one of the unemployed persons in our sample was a twenty-five-year-old man who had served as a soldier in the Peruvian army, had completed his university studies, and had been job-hunting for more than a year when he entered the Shining Path; however, he was of peasant origins and his parents had continued to live in a peasant community.[114] There was not as sharp a distinction between "commanders" and "compañeros" in the Shining Path as in the FMLN; midlevel positions were numerous in the Peruvian organization.[115]

There was a greater range of ages among the Shining Path members than among their youthful FMLN counterparts. In my research team's interviews, ages ranged from twenty-one to fifty-six; the average age was thirty-one. Similarly, in a Sendero annihilation squad captured in Puno in 1993, the average age was twenty-eight.[116] In one study of Shining Path inmates, only 57 percent of the convicted terrorists were twenty-five or younger.[117] However, groups of Senderistas in the Upper Huallaga Valley were younger; the age range was between ten and twenty-five in one group and between sixteen and twenty-one in another.[118]

A somewhat smaller percentage of Senderistas than FMLN members were women.[119] In my research team's interviews, 18 percent were women. Similarly, in a band of fifty Senderistas visited by a journalist in the Upper Huallaga Valley in 1987, 20 percent were women.[120] In the study of convicted terrorists, 16 percent were female.[121] Still, there were more women in the Shining Path than in other Peruvian political parties; among the salient reasons are the large number of female teachers in Peru and the important role of Guzmán's wife Augusta in the movement.[122]

Especially after September 1992 and the publication of many photographs of captured Senderistas, statements about their ethnicity can be made.[123] While at least half of the top Sendero leaders were Caucasian, the vast majority of Senderistas appeared to be darker-skinned "mestizos" (a category that in Peru includes a range of complexions and features); a smaller minority appeared of largely indigenous stock.[124]

As early as the 1970s, teachers and university students were a major target of the Senderista inner circle—not only at the university in Ayacucho, but also at La Cantuta in Lima.[125] Subsequently, wherever Sendero was seeking to expand, it focused first on the local university. In Huancayo, for example, high-ranking Senderistas recruited aggressively at the Universidad del Centro; even in the coca-producing Upper Huallaga Valley, the central recruitment site was the university.[126] Said one analyst, "Sendero used the university completely. Lenin used the workers. Mao used the peasants."[127] By the early 1990s, perhaps thirty thousand teachers —or 15 percent of all Peru's teachers—were Senderistas.[128] As mentioned above, 15 percent of the Senderistas interviewed by my research team were teachers; in a sample of 421 terrorists captured in Lima in approximately 1985, 6 percent were teachers.[129] One nine-member ideology and propaganda "support group" for Sendero included two university professors and two primary school teachers, as well as two students and a self-employed public accountant.[130]

In the thirty-three interviews with Senderistas in the Huancayo area carried out by my research team, and also in others' interviews with militants, the Shining Path members emphasize socioeconomic misery as the key impetus to their decision to join the revolutionary movement.[131] The guerrillas bemoan the hunger, malnutrition, and generally abject conditions of living and dying in Peru, and they also contend that the Peruvian government is responsible for these conditions. In a new usage of the word *hambre* (hunger), the Peruvian state is often described as *hambreador*—making the people hungry. Whereas in El Salvador FMLN members who describe the government as committing "genocide" are usually thinking about political murders, in Peru the revolutionaries who describe the government as "genocidal" are often referring to it in that manner because they believe it is intentionally "killing the people with hunger."[132] Also, Senderistas are much more likely than FMLN members to applaud the effective organization of their movement, the validity of its ideology, and the brilliance of their revolutionary leadership.

In sharp contrast to FMLN interviewees, not one of the Senderistas in the Osores sample mentioned political exclusion or problems of the electoral process as reasons for their joining the movement. Three (9 percent) reported a specific human rights abuse (in all three cases, soldiers' killing one or more of their relatives during a raid into a highlands village) as an impetus to their decision—a considerable percentage but much smaller than would have been the case in a Salvadoran sample.

Among my research team's thirty-three Senderista respondents, the highest-ranking seemed to be Rosa, a forty-two-year-old sociologist who had been taught by Guzmán at the Ayacucho university and who served as a political leader for Junín-Huancavelica in Socorro Popular.[133] Rosa explained her decision to join the Shining Path:

> I entered Sendero Luminoso because I could no longer bear seeing on one side so much hunger and misery, and on the other side wealth and extravagance. The exploitation has to stop. There has been enough injustice and abuses, humiliations and contempt. The discussion has finished. It's the hour for action. I think that no one can look objectively at the situation here without trying to remedy it and fight for change.[134]

Responding to the question about what she liked most about Sendero, Rosa said:

> The clarity and firmness with which they develop the war. Their valor and courage to achieve the installation of the dictatorship of the poor. A communist does not fear death, because the communist's life is surrendered to the party. Our moral character stands up to ten cannons of the genocidal soldiers; we try to be the most correct and perfect social models, without letting go of our fury in combat and our valor in our daily action.[135]

Rosa speaks highly of Guzmán:

> He is the man who awoke the political consciousness of the poor people to use violence. . . . As a philosopher and as a valiant man. . . . he equals Marx, Lenin, and Mao; he taught us to apply the law of contradictions.[136]

Similar comments were made by the twenty-nine-year-old Martina, who had been a secondary school teacher in a village in Huancavelica and who appeared to be the second-highest ranking Senderista in my research team's sample:

> I think that everyone who has sufficient courage to rebel against poverty and misery has an important role in our struggle, which is to change this world of misery and oppression into another where there is happiness, liberty, and food. For this reason we combat the oppressor, the assassin of children and women—Fujimori, the man responsible for the hunger and genocide.[137]

Martina and the other three schoolteachers all expressed adulation for Guzmán. Said, for example, Lucho, a twenty-nine-year-old primary school teacher in a Huancavelica community:

President Gonzalo [Guzmán] is the red sun who will illuminate the path towards the conquest of power and the elimination of this decrepit and rotten state. . . . President Gonzalo has shown that he is an intellectual of the highest level, a philosopher and strategist. He fell for tactical reasons; he will be freed and the reconstruction of the party will be made.[138]

A forty-five-year-old who taught secondary school in the mining town of La Oroya laid perhaps the greatest emphasis on ideology as the movement's key appeal:

The Communist Party of Peru is the political-military apparatus of all the ideology of the proletariat, the basis of Gonzalo thought, which will arrive in power to give to the people the opportunity to make up for all the years of exploitation throughout history. . . . What I like most about Sendero is that the ideology maintains you, and you are not servile, and you don't accept the misery that is inflicted by the governments that come and go, puppets of North American capitalism. We must fight to get out of this crisis and our best weapon is our moral valor. Except for power, everything is illusory.[139]

There were also other well-educated professionals among Sendero's ranks. In a sample of convicted terrorists, 37 percent had studied beyond secondary school and almost 5 percent beyond college—much higher percentages than for those convicted of other crimes.[140] As noted above, the Senderistas interviewed by my research team included not only a university-educated sociologist but also an obstetrician, an architect, and a government employee. Explained the thirty-five-year-old architect who had been active in the Lima area:

I entered Sendero Luminoso because of the need to change our country, which for centuries has been the estate and the property of the rich. The injustices and the abuses committed always against the poor pushed me to enter the ranks of the Communist Party of Peru, the only true director of the popular war, aiming at the conquest of power in order to install the dictatorship of the proletariat.[141]

Numerous lawyers were also supporters of the Shining Path. Retorted one to a U.S. journalist who had spoken up for Peru's human rights organizations, "What about the rights of the thousands of children who die of malnutrition every year in Peru?"[142]

Although professors, teachers, and some other professionals predominated in Sendero's top ranks, numerically the largest group within the organization was students.[143] As mentioned above, 24 percent of the

Senderistas interviewed by my research team were students. In a sample of 421 terrorists captured in Lima in the early and mid-1990s, 35 percent were students.[144] In a 1991 nationwide survey, 25 percent of Peruvians between the ages of fourteen and twenty-four (and accordingly mostly students) justified armed insurrection.[145]

In the interviews by the Osores research team, the student members of Sendero were not as consistent and precise in their discussions of their decision to join the revolutionary movement as were the teachers and other professionals. However, the substance of the students' explanations was not different. Said a combatant of peasant origins who had joined Sendero at twenty-four, when he was a student, working part-time in a bakery:

> I could not tolerate the injustice, the poverty, and the corruption in the state. I had to act in order to change the system. There is no place for those who comply with the exploiters who cause hunger and misery for the people. . . . President Gonzalo is a highly prepared brain; he will always be the light that guides us and the guarantee of triumph.[146]

Commented a student at the Universidad del Centro:

> To liberate the country from oppression, misery, and poverty, there had to be born someone and it's our President Gonzalo, the guide who created the armed struggle to defend our people. He is the great world leader of our era.[147]

Various Senderista students spoke with journalists about their decisions. Wrote one U.S. journalist about her discussion with a Senderista student at San Marcos University in Lima:

> He talked on and on, full of confidence in the perfect logic of everything he said. Could I disagree that in Peru the vast majority live lives that are an affront to human dignity? Or that whether dictators ruled or whether elected demagogues were in power has made little difference to the poor? . . . Everyone here knows someone in that Glass of Milk Program who is stealing the supplies, everyone now understands that María Elena Moyano was an enemy.[148]

The Senderista "Javier" was a twenty-three-year-old Limeño law student who also worked in a stockbroker's office. "Javier" was overheard by another U.S. journalist as he responded to his mother's angry criticism of his guerrilla activities:

> "What kind of kid goes around killing people?" she [Javier's mother] said, standing and waving her arms. . . . "Javier" had heard this before. . . . "The

system kills people with hunger," he said. "Sixty thousand children die before their first birthday each year in Peru. What's going to help them?"[149]

The peasantry was cited with the second highest frequency (35 percent) as the social group among which Sendero had the most influence.[150] Peasant support for Sendero in numerous communities of Peru's southern highlands has been reported by Degregori (1986: 252–253); Gorriti (1990: 34–47); González (1989: 45); Rénique (1994: 240); Berg (1986–87: 186–188); Bonner (1988: 44–45) and Granados (1987: 25). As mentioned above, among the Senderistas interviewed by my research team, six (18 percent) were peasants.[151] After interviews with an eighty-member Sendero zonal committee in the southern highlands, a journalist judged 30 percent of the committee members to have been of indigenous peasant stock.[152]

During the late 1970s and early 1980s, the common recruitment pattern was that a teacher, who had become a Senderista during his years at a university or at a "normal school" for teachers, would sponsor meetings in the square of the community, seeking to recruit students and peasants into the movement.[153] Said "Nicario," for example, who at the time of his recruitment was a student in a peasant community in Ayacucho:

Sendero was active [in the community]. . . . they invited me to a meeting. . . . The leader mainly talked about Mao. . . . The meetings were continuous. . . . They spoke about how there was too much bureaucracy in Peru, many delinquents and thieves, abusers, and that this was the objective of Sendero, to make all this disappear.[154]

Three of the six peasants interviewed by the Osores research team said they had been forced into the movement, but only one of these was critical of Sendero throughout the interview; one said he had gradually become sympathetic, and the third appeared to be trying to conceal his sympathy.

In their own discussions of their involvement in the Shining Path, the peasants interviewed by the Osores research team emphasized economic straits. In contrast to the teachers and students, the peasants rarely included Marxist terms in their explanations for their entry into the movement; none appeared to know Guzmán or have achieved a high rank in the organization, and none expressed awe for Guzmán.[155] A twenty-nine-year-old peasant who had worked his own land in the Junín department explained why he became a Senderista military chief:

I came to understand that the popular war is the only way out of the misery and poverty in which we live today, and that many of our brother peasants don't even have anything to eat.[156]

Said a combatant who had worked on a coffee farm east of Huancayo:

In reality, the movement sought to take from the rich to give to the poor and the needy.[157]

Explained a fifty-six-year-old southern highlands peasant who had been active in the Shining Path for almost ten years:

In the talks and classes at night, they said to us that he [Guzmán] was the president, and the new hope of the poor and the peasants, and that soon the Senderistas would take power. . . . When government authorities were killed, they had committed abuses . . . ; that's how to establish justice, and no one for fear of the *compas* would abuse the humble peasants.[158]

Despite their own Maoist ideology, the militants' appeals in peasant communities were also pragmatic and relevant to the particular locality. In Ayacucho, Junín, and Puno, Sendero promised the recuperation of long-lost land from large capital-intensive farms.[159] In the drug-producing Upper Huallaga Valley, Sendero leaders emphasized their ability to protect peasant coca-growers from the Peruvian and U.S. antidrug forces, as well as their ability to gain better prices for the coca from the traffickers.[160]

In the interviews by the Osores research team, one of the peasant Senderistas emphasized local problems in his explanation for entering the movement:

I belonged to the PCP group of Chongos Alto [a community about two hours from Huancayo], and entered the party in order to work on the problems of the workers of the haciendas of the high mountains. We are struggling for the people and we help the people against the hacienda owners who exploit them miserably. . . . We made incursions into haciendas, as in the case of the hacienda Cusipampa, where there had been many abuses and exploitation of our own people.[161]

The peasant members of Sendero were also more likely than the teacher or student members to express satisfaction at the financial benefits of their affiliation with the organization.[162] Said one:

For the actions that were done, they gave us good money. The haciendas of people with money were assaulted, and radios, money, arms, and lots of food were taken. Also, cars were used to move us around, and we stayed at good hotels, with the others in the group.[163]

Said another peasant:

There was food and money. It depended on the rank you had. But there was support, which was good for our families.[164]

Later, in the cities, committed militants would visit house to house, first getting to know the families and providing material support, and then recruiting them to the cause.[165] Although, as mentioned above, the social and rural/urban status of many Peruvians is difficult to identify precisely, approximately eleven of the Senderistas interviewed by the Osores research team were from the lower strata: six workers, two vendors, and three unemployed.[166] Even among the employed workers, complaints about their economic situation were intense. Said a militant who had worked in a Huancavelica mine:

They made us work ten hours [a day] and the pay was not enough to make ends meet, not even to eat; and the bosses treated us with much disrespect, too.[167]

Seconded a vendor who had become a chief for logistical support for the Shining Path:

I had been a vendor, but with the situation as it is, it's impossible to get ahead. For this reason I entered Sendero Luminoso. I liked it and I stayed. . . . I especially liked the military organization within it. Everything was carefully calculated and you couldn't make a mistake, the directives that they gave us had to be executed precisely, because if not you exposed your *compañeros* and endangered the success of the mission. . . . There was money for food, lodging, and our expenses.[168]

For many of the Senderistas whose explanations for joining the revolutionary movement are reported by journalists, information on their social backgrounds are not available. However, their words are often telling. Consider, for example, the explanation by an arrested thirty-four-year-old mestizo political commander, Isidoro Nunja García. Asked "Why are you a Senderista?" he answers, "I think it's the way to make sure that all Peruvians have everything they need."[169] To the same question, a fifteen-year-old guerrilla in the Upper Huallaga Valley replied "Misery, hunger, exploitation, abuse."[170] Said another jailed Senderista:

"The central problem is not race. It's economics. It's class."[171] Said another Senderista supporter:

> Sendero has been created due to a social problem, due to the abandonment of the state. It emerged in Ayacucho, didn't it? Because Ayacucho was abandoned. People lived only from their potatoes, from what they cultivated.[172]

At a Shining Path party with "Javier," Rosenberg asked one of his friends, "How are things?" Answered the Shining Path member: "Great. A million percent inflation, garbage piling up, no jobs, no water, no electricity. The forces of history are really on our side."[173]

One of the most fervent explanations was by a Shining Path leader, giving a eulogy at a funeral for a fifteen-year-old boy who had been a terrorist suspect and was almost certainly killed by Peruvian soldiers:

> They say we are terrorists because, in this land, he who has the most economic power is he who rules, because he who does not have anything is worth nothing. The law, the political constitution of the state, serves only for those who have money, but for those who do not have money, the justice is not justice, it is a tremendous injustice. The terrorists are those who kill us with hunger every day. The terrorists are those who give us a minimum wage that is not even enough to pay for a grave or the most miserable of food; those are the terrorists.[174]

When the Shining Path guerrillas mention political problems, they usually cite corruption. Said, for example, "Comrade Tania," a former Sendero military captain in the Upper Huallaga Valley:

> She [a Shining Path commander and ideologue] made us see that our country was a disaster due to corruption. The political system was rotten; the judges, prosecutors, and lawyers were compromised by the drug traffickers. Also, many leaders and officials behaved like jackals with the people. . . . In key posts, the APRA government was spreading misery and thievery. The desperation—they said—was APRA policy. I believed a lot in the truth of the words of this Shining Path commander.[175]

Despite the ideological emphasis of the Shining Path leaders, many militants were also vague about what the practical implications of a triumphant Shining Path might be. For example, a Senderista in a Lima jail is nonplussed by a U.S. journalist's questions:

> [Gloria is asked] how marriage will be different under the revolution. Will there be day care, abortion? Gloria says she has heard something about day care in Soviet communes. But her contract with the party is not one of

specifics, but glory, sacrifice, the heaven of the New Society. Is there day care in heaven? The question, to her, is ridiculous.[176]

Scholarly Explanations: The Interplay among Politics, Economics, Revolutionary Organization, and International Actors

Integrating various scholars' analyses and information presented previously, this section demonstrates the symbiotic interplay among the variables in the Salvadoran and Peruvian revolutionary equations.[177] Although I identify political exclusion as the sine qua non for the Salvadoran revolutionary equation and economic crisis as the sine qua non for the Peruvian equation, I stress how these variables interacted with the specific revolutionary organization and with the international context to produce revolutionary equations similar to those in figures 1 and 2 in the introduction to this book.[178] The causation in both revolutionary experiences was cumulative and interactive.

El Salvador

In most respects, the Salvadoran experience follows the model of revolution depicted in figure 1. The sine qua non was the authoritarian regime that excluded the political left. Table 6.1 indicates that most Salvadorans perceived the FMLN's paramount objectives as political.[179] Responding to the question, "In general, what is the reason that most people believe the FMLN continues fighting?" about half of the sample said "to win political power." Only 12 percent cited the more economically focused reason, "to achieve justice." In table 6.2, the answers to a question about the origins of the guerrilla movement are reported; about 40 percent of the sample cited either "ambition, struggle for power"—implying the FMLN's desire for political power—or "bad government"—implying various illegitimate actions by the government, including for many respondents political abuses. Table 6.2 indicates that about one-third of the sample attributed the origins of the FMLN's challenge to El Salvador's economic problems, but this figure is only about half the percentage in the Peruvian sample.

Numerous scholarly analysts have emphasized the exclusive, repressive Salvadoran regime as the original catalyst of the country's revolutionary movement.[180] Wickham-Crowley identifies as the "national cause"

Table 6.1. Opinions about Why the Guerrillas Continued to Fight (percentages)

	Peru Junín, 1991 ($N = 130$)	El Salvador Eastern Departments, 1991 ($N = 231$)
To win political power	30	50
To achieve justice	28	12
For ideological reasons	20	10
Whim	5	20
Foreign support	8	4
To change the military	1	3
Other	2	0
Don't know, no answer	6	3

Source: Author's commissioned surveys; see appendix I. Item was not asked in the other surveys. To maximize comparability, alternatives for selection by the respondents were read to him/her. Item read, "In general, what is the reason that most people believe Sendero/the FMLN continues fighting (*luchando*)?"

El Salvador's "old regime" that, like the Nicaraguan, Guatemalan, and Colombian regimes, denied "real political participation to new contenders pounding at the gates of power. . . . these regimes faced 'crises' of participation with which their 'old' institutions were incapable of dealing."[181] In Enrique Baloyra's various studies, his backdrop is the "reactionary despotism" of the Salvadoran regime between 1948 and 1979.[182] Montgomery concludes that the key problem in El Salvador was that the political opposition was "forbade . . . from coming to power."[183] Vilas writes that "the radical intensification of state repression provoked a response from among the popular classes."[184] Seligson argues that extreme political repression may have been a "necessary and sufficient" condition for the rebellion.[185] A journalist's pithy synthesis was "This war began because elections were stolen in El Salvador."[186]

Making their arguments, these scholars point to the events and data on political violence that are presented in chapter 3. Although the Salvadoran authoritarian regime was not traditionally U.S.-backed (a contrast to the Cuban and Nicaraguan revolutionary experiences that are the primary empirical basis for figure 1), the refusal of the regime to tolerate electoral victory by the Christian Democratic Party became increasingly unacceptable to educated, middle-class Salvadorans. Middle-class

Table 6.2. Citizens' Opinions about the Principal Cause of the Guerrilla Movements (percentages)

	Peru				El Salvador	
	Lima, 1990 (N = 400)	Junín, 1990 (N = 200)	Junín, 1991 (N = 130)	Nationwide, 1987[a]	San Salvador, 1991 (N = 175)	Eastern Departments, 1991 (N = 231)
1. Economic crisis, social injustice, and poverty	61	71	55	35	35	30
2. Ambition, struggle for power	7	0	12	25	34	31
3. Bad government	20	8	22	13	9	11
4. Communism	3	0	2	6	3	7
5. Will of God	0	0	0	0	7	9
6. Other	6	11	8	7	3	3
7. Don't know, no answer	3	10	1	11	11	10

Source: Author's commissioned surveys; see appendix I. Exception is data for El Salvador in 1987. In all surveys, item read, "What do you think is the principal reason for the existence of the guerrillas in Peru/El Salvador?"

[a]Martín Baró (1989, 75). Sample size is not given.

frustrations crystallized with the electoral frauds of 1972 and 1977. As we have seen in previous sections of this chapter, when middle-class university students protested these frauds, their protests were repressed, and they decided that revolutionary action was their only option.

There is considerable controversy among scholars about the importance of economic variables to the expansion of the FMLN.[187] As I indicated in chapter 4, and as was reinforced by FMLN militants' statements given in this chapter, in my view economic problems did not detonate the Salvadoran rebellion. Despite ever-more-severe rural inequality and landlessness, overall trends in poverty were not drastically negative during the 1970s or 1980s. Social injustice was one reason why university students and church people began to organize among Salvadoran peasants in the 1970s, and land inequality and land scarcity were reasons why peasants were receptive to their calls. But these problems were—in the terms used by various scholars of revolution—constants or preconditions; there was not the drastic change in overall living standards, in either absolute or relative terms, that would have provoked the kind of violent rage that occurred among Peruvian peasants. Rather, as the FMLN militants emphasize in their statements, the drastic change for Salvadoran peasants was the severity of the government's repression of their originally nonviolent organizational efforts. In other words, there were economic grievances among the Salvadoran peasantry, and if there had not been, neither peasants, nor university students, nor church people would have sought agrarian reform; but, in the absence of state repression, they would not have taken up arms.

This interpretation is shared by various scholars of revolution, including in particular John Booth and Charles Brockett, and also by scholars of the Salvadoran peasantry.[188] For example, discussing the economic straits of Salvadoran peasants in numerous departments and the emergence of Marxist and Christian organizations that sought social and economic reform, Douglas Kincaid concludes that "the radicalization of the movement as a mass phenomenon appears much more the consequence of the repression unleashed against it at a time when it sought much more limited objectives."[189] A similar comment is made by Wood: "Repressive [action] appears to have fueled participation in some areas."[190] Seligson concurs, citing the story of a ten-year-old boy who was traveling with his mother on a bus when the bus was stopped by soldiers who shot his mother dead and poured acid on her face; the boy subsequently joined the FMLN.[191]

Also, as chapter 4 indicates, there was no drastic decline in overall living standards in El Salvador during the 1970s provoking the outrage among middle-class groups, or aspirants to the middle class, that erupted in Peru. In sharp contrast to their Peruvian counterparts, most of the FMLN leaders believed that, if they were allowed to compete freely in fair elections, they would win, and then they would be able to implement socioeconomic reform. In other words, for them, electoral reform was the top priority.[192]

Although during the 1980s scholars of the Salvadoran revolutionary experience focused primarily upon political and/or economic conditions as the detonators of the Salvadoran revolutionary challenge, there was some attention to the role of the FMLN as a revolutionary organization. At first, analysts tended to compare the FMLN with Nicaragua's FSLN —unfavorably, suggesting that the FMLN's shortcomings were one of the reasons why it had not won power as the FSLN had.[193] These analysts pointed to the organization's flaws that were highlighted in chapter 2: the acrimony among the fractious groups that formed the FMLN, which might have cost it victory during 1979–81. Two key FMLN leaders, Salvador Cayetano Carpio and Joaquín Villalobos, were both considered to bear at least some responsibility in the assassinations of other FMLN leaders. The FMLN was also considered more dogmatically Marxist than the FSLN, and more arbitrary in its targets. Of course, the relative lack of scholarly attention to the FMLN as a factor in the revolutionary equation during the 1980s was not shared by Reagan administration officials; in their view, it was the large quantity of East bloc weapons delivered to the FMLN in the early 1980s that created the crisis.[194]

More recently, Byrne has refocused attention on the FMLN as a revolutionary organization that was successful by many criteria.[195] While, as Huntington has pointed out, "the rarity of revolution is in large part due to the difficulties of parallel action by intelligentsia and peasants,"[196] in the late 1970s and early 1980s Salvadoran university students and the peasants of Chalatenango, Morazán, and some other smaller areas forged a strong alliance. To a significant degree, after the death of Salvador Cayetano Carpio, the FMLN overcame its original fractiousness and effectively formulated its revolutionary strategy. At the same time, it retained a flexibility and an openness to dialogue and negotiation that stood it in good stead in the early 1990s.

As chapter 5 indicates, scholars of revolution have underestimated the importance of U.S. policy to revolutionary outcomes.[197] Chapter 5, however, shows the significance of U.S. policy as a variable in El Salvador's revolutionary equation. In 1981, in contrast to the Eisenhower administration's assessment of the revolutionary challenge in Cuba and the Carter administration's assessment of the revolutionary challenge in Nicaragua, the Reagan administration appeared to hope to bolster the Salvadoran regime even if it failed to reform. In this decision, however, the Reagan administration confronted some of the same obstacles that the Eisenhower and Carter administrations would have encountered if they had sought to rescue the Batista or Somoza regimes. Not only most American citizens but also many administration officials could not countenance American support for a government that was killing many citizens whose primary appeal was for democracy in their country. To support such a government was antithetical both to American values and to Americans' understanding of why revolutions occurred. As egregious human rights violations continued in El Salvador in the early 1980s, pressure against the Reagan administration's decision continued, spearheaded by the Catholic Church and human rights groups; as a result, the amount and kind of resources that the Reagan administration committed to the Salvadoran military were limited.

Ultimately, however, as chapter 5 discussed and as virtually all scholars agree, there was a crucial interplay between U.S. policy, political opening in El Salvador, and undermining of popular support for the FMLN.[198] In the phraseology of figure 1 in the introduction, the U.S. government pressured the Salvadoran government to "reform"; the Salvadoran government agreed to this bitter pill, given that it was sweetened by large amounts of U.S. economic and military aid. The outcome was the "rescue" of the regime, albeit a somewhat politically opened regime.

Scholars have less frequently pointed to the prodigious level of U.S. economic aid to El Salvador between 1983 and 1990 as a factor in the erosion of Salvadoran support for the FMLN. In my view, U.S. economic aid was critical to the avoidance of the kind of economic plunge in El Salvador that occurred in Peru—a plunge that might have sparked many more Salvadorans to maintain their original support for the FMLN (see chapter 5).

Peru

Analysts of the Shining Path concur that political exclusion was not a factor in Peru's revolutionary equation. As Palmer writes:

> Sendero did not grow out of a national context of systemic and official repression or a systematic thwarting of opportunities for access to national politics. . . . Democracy should have been a major bulwark against the advance of Shining Path in Peru.[199]

Rather, the revolutionary spark in Peru was economic crisis. Just as socioeconomic misery was emphasized by the Senderistas themselves as the key impetus in their decision to join the movement, economic crisis was overwhelmingly cited by Peruvian citizens as the principal cause of the guerrilla movement. Table 6.2 shows the dramatic difference between Peruvians' and Salvadorans' assessment of the primary reason for the emergence of revolutionary movements in the two countries. Strong majorities of the Peruvian respondents in both Lima and highlands Junín attribute the rise of Sendero to economic crisis, social injustice, or poverty, whereas 35 percent or less of the Salvadoran respondents attribute the rise of the FMLN to such factors. The second most favored explanation in Peru was "bad government," endorsed by a relatively scant 20 percent or so of the respondents.[200] Table 3.11, "Citizens' Opinions about the Way to Achieve Peace," also underscores the emphasis on economic solutions to political violence in Peru, versus the emphasis upon dialogue and political space for the guerrillas in El Salvador. Peruvians' emphasis upon economic factors as the principal cause of Sendero's rise was indicated in other surveys as well. For example, in a June 1991 survey in Lima carried out by Apoyo, those who consider subversion "justifiable" were asked why; of the 76 respondents, 33 percent said "poverty or misery"; 20 percent "social injustice"; 18 percent "abuse" or "exploitation"; 14 percent "economic crisis"; 12 percent "corruption or immorality"; 2 percent "governmental failure"; and 1 percent centralization.[201]

Chapter 4 describes the subsistence threat among Peru's peasants that occurred during the late 1970s and 1980s and the particularly negative trends in the provinces of core early support for Sendero. The chapter includes peasants' statements about their rage and despair at their poverty. This point is also made by anthropologists Starn (1991) and Mitchell (1991), who examined economic and social trends in the Ayacucho community of Quinua from the 1940s through the 1980s. Emphasizing severe population pressure and ever-more-frequent migration in search of work, both Andeanists perceive a "grinding poverty that led so many peasants into angry action" and "explosive pain and discontent in the highlands."[202]

Chapter 4 also describes both the devastation of living standards for Peru's middle class and the blocked opportunities for middle-class aspirants. It focuses in particular on the increasing number of university students and graduates, which implied an increasing number of young people with professional aspirations—at a time when professional jobs and salaries, especially teachers' salaries, were declining. Scholars concur that these economic conditions led to frustration and even rage among many relatively well-educated Peruvians, especially among provincial mestizos who were the first in their families to gain an education and then were unable to meet their own or their families' expectations.[203] Explains sociologist Rodrigo Montoya:

> In provincial universities such as those in Ayacucho or Puno, it is difficult . . . to distinguish a student from a Quechua peasant. Not only are the indigenous physical traits the same, but also the dominance of quechua and the difficulties with Spanish. An economist graduated from the Ayacucho university in these conditions cannot get a job at the Central Reserve Bank and is not resigned to being a low-ranking teacher in a remote village where nobody wants to go. But there is no other way to survive but to go there. In his family and social milieu—where so many hopes were placed in education as the route to social mobility—this exile is interpreted as failure, a very painful failure.[204]

Echo sociologists Gianotten, de Wit, and de Wit:

> Most of the students in the department of education [at the university in Ayacucho] had to go back to their communities after ending their studies. Children of peasants, who had worked themselves upwards with many financial difficulties, and become teachers, had to go back to the poverty from which they came. They went back to villages where there was no drinking-water, no electricity. . . . [Their students] had not even enough money to buy a pencil. . . . The deep frustration of blocked aspirations and a future perspective without any hope of improvement led to a growing militancy.[205]

As Peru's economic crisis grew worse at the end of the 1980s and the early 1990s, it afflicted a much larger number of Peruvians. Even in Lima, there was hunger. It was under these circumstances that Sendero was able to expand even in the capital city. Reported Strong: "The armed revolution thrived on the starvation of the poor, whose numbers multiplied in Lima."[206] One Shining Path member of a Lima shanty town explained his adherence to the movement:

> Here, we get water once a week, and our children are dehydrated in the summer. . . . But in San Isidro and Miraflores [two upper-class neighborhoods] they have water all the time, and they use it to water their flowers.[207]

In chapter 4, the toll taken upon public expenditure by Peru's economic crisis is also indicated, in particular the reduction in resources available for public health and the relatively poor public health outcomes. Similarly, in the third section of chapter 3, the scant resources available for the Peruvian military and the low salaries of security force personnel are described.

However, although the economic crisis was a necessary factor in the expansion of Sendero among Peruvians, it was far from sufficient. Anger made citizens available for violent protest; they sought perpetrators for their increasingly abject poverty, and found violence acceptable if it promised to punish likely perpetrators and facilitate their own survival. But, in other nations or in Peru at different moments, citizens' outrage has not been channeled into a revolutionary movement. Between 1980 and 1992, however, many citizens' hopes and fears were caught up by an organization that was exceptionally adept at identifying local grievances and persuading the aggrieved that Sendero's actions could help end abuses. In short, both economic crisis and revolutionary organization were necessary to the revolutionary equation.

Most foremost theorists of the Shining Path adamantly reject Skocpol's belittlement of the importance of the guerrilla organization in the making of the revolutionary challenge.[208] These analysts—in particular David Scott Palmer, Carlos Iván Degregori, and Gustavo Gorriti—do not deny that Peru was besieged by economic crisis in the 1980s and early 1990s; but, especially because all three scholars were familiar with Senderista leaders in the movement's early years, they were more interested in the revolutionary organization than in its national economic context.[209] Of the three, Gorriti is most emphatic about the vital significance of the Senderista organization for the revolutionary equation: "In the history of guerrilla insurrections, there are few, indeed if any, in which the factor of political will, supported by exhaustive planning, has been so preponderant."[210]

In my own view, as I discuss in chapter 2 and in the first section of this chapter, the merits of Sendero's leadership were somewhat exaggerated, and many of Sendero's "assets"—its authoritarian leadership, rigid Maoist creed, and willingness to use violence—were double-edged swords. But I concur that, in different ways and at different times, Sendero's strategy and tactics were new and effective—much more so, for example, than the relatively conventional strategy and tactics of the rival MRTA revolutionary group. In particular, the quasi-religious, fundamentalist element in Sendero that is stressed by both Degregori and Gorriti indicates that in some respects Sendero is similar to the revolutionary religious movements that appear likely to be predominant among revolutionary movements in the twenty-first century.[211] Ironically perhaps, the openness of Peru's post-1980 democracy led to an emphasis on electoral politics by the country's traditional Marxist parties; to a certain extent these parties abandoned Peru's revolutionary political space to fundamentalist organizations such as Sendero, which of course repudiated elections and prioritized the armed struggle.

As Degregori emphasizes, the strategic genius of Sendero's founders was to target a particular sector: teachers and, through them, students and young people in general.[212] Peruvians' aspirations for education were unusually high, Degregori notes; at school, students were seeking not only "practical tools" but also "truth."[213] Sendero proposed a "simplified and accessible version of a theory that defined itself as the only 'scientific truth,' and was legitimized through references to the Marxist classics."[214] Guzmán was "the caudillo-teacher."[215] Degregori explains:

> "Sendero Luminoso" emerges around 1970 as a product of the previous meeting between a provincial university elite with a youthful, also provincial social base, that had suffered a painful process of uprooting and desperately needed an orderly and absolute explanation of the world as a means of salvation. The provincial university elite . . . does not break ideologically with the classist, authoritarian, and anti-democratic structure of traditional Peru and embraces Marxism-Leninism seeking above all in it order, as much in its explanation of the world as in its project for the new society. . . . [Its] discourse finds an echo principally among young people from rural Andean

areas who were suffering profound changes, . . . who demand security, seek order. . . . They are sectors now without a place in traditional rural society, but who can't find a place either in "modern" Peru asphyxiated by the crisis and the unemployment.[216]

Another anthropologist who studied at the university in Ayacucho also notes the comfort that Sendero's rigid ideology provided to frustrated graduates:

Education is very important [as the explanation for the subversive phenomenon]. It creates new expectations and leads to people unhappy with their status. It awakens a level of political consciousness. A frustrated person is easily captured by [Sendero's] ideology, which permits him to struggle against a system that offers him nothing and also allows him to sacrifice his life for a cause that they consider just.[217]

In Sendero's effort to gain peasant support, the movement tended to succeed in its initial overtures, but then, over time, to lose some of its appeal. Interestingly, the Senderista militants did not at first try to impose their rigid Maoism upon poorly educated peasants. Rather, the militants first appeared to peasants as pragmatists who wanted to meet with them and learn about their problems. In particular, the Senderistas carefully gathered intelligence about the wrongdoers in a community, soon threatened them to change their ways, and punished them if they did not. Often, Sendero assassinated key "public enemies": a hacendado in one village, a corrupt official in a second, a merchant who charged usurious loans in another, or even cattle thieves.[218] Peasants sought revenge against "the rich."[219] In one of the most detailed descriptions of the emergence of peasant support for Sendero, for the period 1981–82 and 1985 in the community of Pacucha in the southern highlands department of Apurímac, Ronald H. Berg explains:

During this time (the 1970s and 1980s), the economy became increasingly polarized and social tension mounted. An entrepreneurial class emerged to fill the commercial vacuum left by departure of the hacendados, and the position of this class was strengthened by its access to bank loans for commercial agriculture. At the same time, the position of the majority of the peasants deteriorated: the real value of wages declined, and the possibility of temporary urban employment for displaced rural-urban migrants declined as well. Sendero moved into this situation, not by organizing people around abstract issues . . . , but by attacking the objects of popular resentment, i.e., the rich peasants and the cooperatives.[220]

In various departments, Sendero was effective in channeling peasants' anger that they had not gained land from the military government's agrarian reform. For the central highlands department of Junín, historian Nelson Manrique describes both frustrated peasant-community members and a Sendero organization that, sensitive to the local SAIS as the target of their frustration, violently destroys the SAIS and then distributes the SAIS's livestock to the peasants.[221] Sendero used a very similar strategy in the southern highlands department of Puno, where conflicts between peasant-community members and SAIS were also intense, but was less successful.[222]

In the late 1980s, when Sendero was expanding in Lima and other previously better-off areas, it again initially sought support by violently punishing persons whom local residents perceived as the cause of their problems. Journalist Michael Smith describes Sendero's inroads into a Lima shanty town: "When Sendero is sizing up a new field of operation or community, it asks a simple question: 'Who is the most hated figure in the community?' The winner of this reverse popularity contest turns up dead a few days or weeks later."[223]

Sendero attracted supporters in other ways as well. To a much greater degree than the FMLN, Sendero sought to provide material benefits to its supporters. In the wake of attacks, Sendero would often be able to transfer money, livestock, or other goods for distribution among community members. Also, as noted in chapter 2 (see note 166) and in the previous section of this chapter, by the late 1980s Sendero was paying salaries to its militants. Both the amounts and the numbers of persons receiving funds appear to have been very large by Latin American standards. The common salary range—$250 to $500 per month—was about three to eight times the salaries of most of Peru's teachers (see chapter 4). In the thirty-three interviews with Senderistas by the Osores research team, 57 percent said that they received salaries, and another 36 percent that they received food, housing, or money for expenses. Only one respondent said he did not receive any goods at all. One thirty-five-year-old former architect said that salaries in the jungle areas were as high as $1,000 a month.[224]

Sendero combined the use of force, material benefits, and symbols to create a sense among many Peruvians that it was a better, and more powerful, alternative than the Peruvian state.[225] This combination is suggested by anthropologist Jaime Urrutia, a professor at the university in Ayacucho at the time:

> Yes, I think that Sendero is growing. . . . They call strikes more easily now; . . . [in November or December 1988] during the course of a strike, Sendero intercepted cars that were going from Ayacucho to Pisco—there, in the highlands, twenty or thirty vehicles, including a university bus. . . . They deflated the tires of all the vehicles that were carrying provisions and took all the food. . . . [The Senderistas] transmit pragmatism. . . . They are transmitting the fact that they have the necessary force, the fact that they can distribute food, the fact that they can convoke the population or some sectors of the population.[226]

One of Sendero's greatest strategic achievements was that, for many Peruvians by 1991 and 1992, their march to power appeared inexorable.[227] Sendero's attacks became a constant drumbeat in the headlines of local newspapers; for example, between 22 April 1989 and 12 May 1989 the headlines of the Huancayo daily *Correo* included "Confrontation Leaves 70 Dead"; "Masked Subversives Sow Terror, Inferno in the Valley"; "They Assassinate Aprista Legislator"; "Huancayo with Military Patrols, Region Paralyzed"; and "More than 15 Attacks during Black-Out."

However, over the longer term, Sendero lost support in some highland peasant communities.[228] As chapter 2 discussed, many of Sendero's "strengths" were also "weaknesses." As Sendero attacked more and more local figures, the bloodshed alienated previous supporters.[229] After Sendero had made inroads into a community, it sought to instill its ideology more deeply, and many citizens resisted.[230] In particular, considering peasant markets a mode of capitalism, Sendero tried to close them, and peasants were upset.

As suggested in figure 2 in the introduction to this book, Sendero's expansion both exacerbated traditional weaknesses in the Peruvian state and provoked new problems—in other words, as Sendero expanded, it further delegitimated a state that had never enjoyed broad or deep support.[231] Accordingly, as Skocpol argues, the weakness of the state was a reason for the expansion of the revolutionary movement; however, contradicting her argument, the weakness of the state in Peru was not independent of the country's economic crisis, nor of the attacks by the guerrilla movement itself. It is also interesting to note that, whereas

Skocpol perceives international military pressure as a key independent variable provoking the political crisis of the state, in the case of Peru the country's crisis appears to have prompted its traditional rival, Ecuador, toward the view that aggressive military action was timely.[232]

Sendero provoked further delegitimation of the Peruvian state in various ways. First, it must be kept in mind that Peru's state officials and its political party leaders had never established strong networks beyond Peru's coast; in the words of one analyst, "Peru's political parties are like flowers in a vase. . . . They look pretty, but they are cut off from their roots."[233] Highlands residents often commented that Peru's political leaders had "abandoned" them. But, if traditionally Peru's political elites were rarely present for highlands residents, their absence was further aggravated by Sendero's violence.[234] As indicated in chapter 2, in contrast to most Latin American revolutionary groups whose primary targets were security force personnel, civilian officials were common victims of Sendero. By one count, Sendero murdered 502 political authorities between 1980 and 1992.[235] In 1989 alone, during the run-up to municipal elections in November, more than eighty mayors were assassinated, including the mayors of Puno, Ayacucho, and Huancayo; not surprisingly, another four-hundred-odd candidates resigned in fear.[236]

Sendero's definition of "civilian official" was extremely broad, including not only elected leaders but development professionals, health care workers, schoolteachers—anyone who was employed by the state. For example, at a time when the García government was trying to implement development projects in the southern highlands, the Shining Path killed twenty-seven agronomists and other development professionals in Ayacucho alone.[237] Not surprisingly, by the late 1980s many schools and clinics were controlled by Sendero, and development professionals would not travel into rural highlands areas.[238]

Again in contrast to conventional Latin American guerrilla groups, Sendero also assassinated members of civil society, especially social and political activists. Although precise numbers for long periods are not available, it appears that between January and May 1989 Sendero killed more than fifty union leaders nationwide,[239] and that between 1991 and 1992 Sendero killed forty-four leaders of grassroots organizations.[240] Many of these victims were members of the United Left (Izquierda Unida), the coalition of Marxist parties that was generally considered

Peru's second strongest electoral force during the 1980s, but—in good part due to Sendero's complex and violent challenge—was relatively weak by the early 1990s.[241]

As chapter 3 discussed, despite considerable civilian authority over the military in Peru between 1980 and 1992, the Peruvian security forces' response to the guerrilla challenge was sorry on all counts: not only was the insurgency not checked, but thousands of innocent civilians were killed and abused (see tables 3.5 and 3.6). In many areas where the security forces were present, citizens' perceptions were that, whereas Sendero killed selectively, the Peruvian army killed blindly.[242] In June 1985 in one Apurímac community, for example, "the security forces beat people indiscriminately, including old people and children. They threatened to massacre the entire population (as occurred in other villages) and in one incident they beat and robbed store owners, beat a man with rifle butts in the village plaza, and raped two women."[243] Not surprisingly, these human rights violations spurred some victims' relatives to join Sendero, and in general they undermined the government's legitimacy and its claim to be democratic. In a Datum survey in March 1993, 74 percent of respondents believed that human rights were not respected in Peru, and almost half—46 percent—said that the government or the security forces were those not respecting human rights.[244]

Together, the perceived failures of successive democratically elected governments to resolve the economic crisis and to defuse the guerrilla challenge gradually eroded Peruvians' perceptions that the country was "democratic." As noted in chapter 3, only 38 percent of respondents in our 1990 sample considered Peru "a lot" or "a good deal" democratic. In a 1993 survey, only 16 percent of Peruvian respondents felt "trust" in the nation's political parties; only 30 percent trusted in the judiciary; and only 40 percent trusted in the congress.[245] To a certain extent, it is surprising that these percentages were not lower, given the increasing attention in the early 1990s to what was apparently egregious corruption at the highest levels of the García administration.[246] Many Peruvians shared the condemnation of Peru's political system made by a member of the Superior Court of Junín, who attributed Sendero's rise directly to the failed political system:

> The traditional political parties are only interested in developing campaigns so that their elites can get to power, even though they have to make campaign

promises that they can't fulfill. In Peru, the political parties have institutionalized political lies, political betrayals, political corruption, which are all protected in the circles of elite power. . . . Every day people's civil rights and
human rights are less protected; there are so many forms of repression by the
state against the popular groups. . . . This "democracy" is deformed, it's a
democracy of party elites who are corrupt and decrepit.[247]

The fusion of economic, organizational, and political variables in
Peru's revolutionary equation is particularly exemplified by Sendero's
exacerbation of the country's economic crisis, which in turn reduced
the capacity of the state and delegitimized it. Analysts affiliated with the
Bernales Commission in the Peruvian Senate estimated the total cost of
guerrilla violence in Peru between 1980 and 1991 at almost $15 billion
(more than half of Peru's GDP during most of those years).[248] Approximately one-third of these costs were "direct": damages to infrastructure
(electricity towers, roads, bridges, buildings, and so forth); about one-
sixth of the costs were for additional expenses for private and public
security; and slightly more than half were "opportunity costs" (lost
tourism, lost production, lost marketing, lost investment, lost hours
worked, and the like).[249] However, higher estimates—in the range of
$20 billion—have also been made by economists.[250] The day-to-day
impact is suggested by journalist James Brooke:

> Because of attacks on power pylons by the Maoist Shining Path guerrillas
> and a shortage of water in Andean hydroelectric dams, most of Lima . . .
> lacks electricity for eight hours each day. Because power is needed to pump
> water to rooftop tanks, apartment dwellers generally have running water for
> only a few hours a day. Most traffic lights do not function. . . . [A doctor said
> that] on two occasions recently his hospital lost electrical power while he was
> performing brain surgery.[251]

As indicated in chapter 5, for a variety of reasons the U.S. government did not try to ameliorate the Peruvian economic crisis as it did the
Salvadoran one. Despite the country's straits, even U.S. support for food
assistance programs in the early 1990s was scant relative to its support
for these programs in El Salvador or in Peru by the mid-1990s, and
overall the quantity of food available for Peru's hungry was insufficient.

By the early 1990s, the variables identified in figure 2 were interacting
as Sendero penetrated Lima's shanty towns. As indicated in chapter 2,
Sendero's expansion in these neighborhoods surprised virtually all

scholarly analysts, who had not anticipated that Sendero could achieve support in areas where grassroots organizations and political parties were active. Sendero even advanced markedly in Villa El Salvador, a "self-built" community that for many years had been a bastion of the United Left.[252] It was in Villa El Salvador that María Elena Moyano—the shanty town's deputy mayor, the founder of its Glass of Milk program, and an active proponent of soup kitchens—was assassinated in February 1992. For many analysts, almost as dismaying as her brutal assassination was the fact that, neither in the last days of her life as she was repeatedly threatened by Sendero nor in her death, did she appear to enjoy widespread support.[253]

How could such a tragedy have happened? The cumulative causes came together in Sendero's capacity to play on the theme of corruption—a chord that, as we have noted, resonated for the guerrillas in peasant communities, but was perhaps even more effective for them in the early 1990s in shanty towns.[254] As chapter 4 discussed in the section on public health, there is no evidence that corruption was actually worse in Peru than in Ecuador or many other Latin American nations; however, poor Peruvians experienced corruption as worse both because Sendero stressed the issue so adroitly and because, in the context of scarce to nonexistent resources, corruption was less often "petty" and more often a life-or-death issue. For example, when public hospital administrators absconded with medicines so that they could sell them, or soup kitchen managers stole food to sell it, the sick or the hungry were more likely to die—and, for many Peruvians, these deaths in turn justified Sendero's killings.[255] Cried a woman who was demonstrating in Lima in the early 1990s on behalf of the Glass of Milk and soup kitchen programs: "*We are fighting for our lives.* The international organizations donate food, but the bureaucracies don't give us anything [emphasis added]."[256]

For the salient case of Villa El Salvador, the interplay of these variables is especially thoughtfully described by Burt (1994).[257] She highlights a "pathology of poverty."[258] After Fujimori's implementation of the "economic shock" in 1990, many of Lima's poor were at "the brink of starvation."[259] The number of families who sought to survive by eating at soup kitchens quadrupled; but the food at the soup kitchens was insufficient.[260] Sendero explained the paucity as the corruption of Villa

El Salvador's mayor, his deputies, and the managers of food assistance programs (such as María Elena Moyano). In fact, there was no evidence of this corruption, but Sendero's rumor became reality for many. The leftist political parties that were supposed to be governing the community were quarreling, and leaders did not stand up for each other. Sendero was both creating an accessible culprit and then, by punishing this culprit, satisfying the popular demand for justice. As Cecilia Blondet synthesizes:

> Poverty and hunger have provoked overall violent relations [in Villa El Salvador]. The conflict between leaders and the social base is sharpened as jealousies become more intense. [In controversies over food-assistance programs], women will acquiesce to an accusation that a leader is a thief. And, some women leaders are corrupt.[261]

7

CONCLUSION
U.S. POLICY AND PATHS TOWARD
POLITICAL PEACE IN LATIN AMERICA

At the threshold of the twenty-first century, revolutionary movements are not an anachronism. Revolutionary conflict of the kind that emerged during the Cold War is over; revolutionary conflict is not. Against the new revolutionary challenges in the post–Cold War era, what kinds of effective policies could be fashioned by the United States and other international actors?

During the Cold War, there was a particular interplay among the variables making up the revolutionary equation in Latin America (see figure 1 in the introduction). As mainstream scholars recognized, the catalyst was political exclusion by an authoritarian regime. University students and other middle-class groups who had been politically repressed by the authoritarian regime allied with aggrieved peasants in order to make a revolution. As these scholars recognized also, critical to the outcome of the conflict was not a militarily "strong" revolutionary organization but a broad-based opposition that appeared at least as prodemocratic as pro-Marxist. As mainstream scholars underestimated, however, this broad-based opposition was critical to a revolutionary equation that included U.S. policy: specifically, a decision by the U.S. government not to rescue a dictator who refused to open his regime (as in the cases of Batista and Somoza). By contrast, in El Salvador, when the authoritarian regime did open somewhat, the opposition to the regime became less broad-based, and the United States decided that rescue was viable.

In 1989, the Cold War ended. Still, the Shining Path in Peru expanded dramatically; new movements, first the EZLN and then the EPR, emerged in Mexico, and old movements reignited in Colombia. But both the political and economic variables in the post–Cold War revolutionary equations are different than during the Cold War, and the nature of the revolutionary organizations is different (see figure 2 in the introduction).

It has been my argument in this book that there is not yet sufficient recognition that post–Cold War revolutionary movements are not mere throwbacks to the Cold War, but rather attest to serious new problems in the post–Cold War era, and that it is in the overall U.S. interest of regional peace and stability to seek to mitigate these problems. We address first new political problems, then new economic problems, and finally the question of revolutionary organization and U.S. and international responses after the emergence of a revolutionary movement.

First, political change has been dramatic in Latin America during the 1980s and 1990s. The U.S. government no longer perceives communism as the most severe threat in the region, against which the U.S. government might decide to support an authoritarian regime. Rather, the United States is engaged in the promotion of democracy in the region. Whereas in the judgment of country specialists on Latin America only Costa Rica qualified as democratic throughout the Cold War and only Venezuela from 1958 until the end of the era, elected regimes have emerged in every nation of the hemisphere except Cuba.[1]

However, as was clear in the Salvadoran case in chapter 3 and was also evident in the 1988 Mexican election, the U.S. government (as well as some journalists and scholars) has pronounced a nation "democratic" even when the election was not considered "free and fair" by the nation's citizens. Much more international effort is necessary to establish clear criteria for free and fair elections.[2] But, with or without clear criteria, international election-monitoring efforts are critical in polarized nations, where citizens' fears of political repression and fraud are usually intense. The Salvadoran experience suggests that parallel "quick counts"—estimates of the results by independent analysts immediately after the closing of the polls, such as the United Nations carried out for the first time in El Salvador in the 1994 elections—are particularly important to the discouragement of fraud and the establishment of public confidence in the electoral outcome.[3]

Also, whereas U.S. government officials and others at times portray the holding of an election that is praised as free and fair as the end of a democratic fairy tale, it is only a beginning. The Peruvian experience described in this book is a vivid example. Despite the freedom and fairness of its elections between 1980 and 1991, most Peruvians did not perceive their country to be truly democratic. Moreover, Peru is not the only Latin American nation where citizens' democratic expectations have not been fulfilled. In the words of several of the foremost scholars of Latin American politics, many Latin American democracies appear to be "low-intensity" democracies or "delegative democracies": the formal constitutional and electoral structures are more or less correct, but they are hollow shells.[4] Elections may enable the "circulation of elites," but not the "displacement of elites"—and the latter may be what citizens want.[5] In the new system, political "inputs" to the government are permitted, but satisfactory "outputs" are not forthcoming.[6] During the 1980s and 1990s, the legitimation and consolidation of democracy have proven elusive.[7]

Although the responsibility for democratic legitimation, of course, lies first and foremost with the Latin American governments themselves, U.S. support can be helpful, through both multilateral and bilateral channels. The Clinton administration has been more sensitive to the need for U.S. support for deepening democracy in Latin America than its predecessors, but funds remain scant.[8] Between fiscal year 1991 and fiscal year 1996, U.S. support for the "Democracy Program" in Latin America and the Caribbean has averaged a scant $98 million annually; the peak year was 1993, at $128 million, and the nadir was 1996, at $74.5 million.[9] When we consider that this total is to be distributed across almost thirty Latin American and Caribbean countries, encompassing not only support for electoral processes but also the redefinition of military roles and the enhancement of civilian political institutions—including in particular the judiciary, the legislature, political parties, unions, and the media—the sum appears small indeed.[10]

Given that the despotic regimes of the Cold War era have ended in Latin America, and that the region's nations are undertaking a difficult transition toward free market economics, economic problems are a likely catalyst of post–Cold War revolutionary movements.[11] Interestingly, for example, whereas when the FMLN and other revolutionary movements sparked during the Cold War used the word "genocide," they were referring to political repression, when Shining Path militants used the word "genocide," they were referring to malnutrition and starvation.

In chapters 4 and 6, we saw that, whatever the long-term results of this economic transition may be, the short-term effects were devastating in Peru. And it is not only in Peru that this transition has been painful. Although the region's inward-looking import-substitution industrialization policies proved untenable by the 1980s, per capita economic growth rates during the 1960s and 1970s averaged about 3 percent annually— much higher than in the 1980s or 1990s (see table 4.1). Per capita growth rates were negative during the 1980s (see table 4.1); between 1991 and 1996, per capita growth was estimated at a scant 1.1 percent.[12] Real wages have not rebounded to their 1980 levels.[13] In many countries, especially as government payrolls have shrunk, formerly middle-class and would-be middle-class sectors have been especially hard hit. Commented an Argentine novelist in 1995: "I always ask a taxi driver what he used to do. They are former engineers, businessmen, teachers, almost anything. And you say this is not explosive?"[14]

Also, it has not been only in Peru that abject poverty has intensified.[15] The World Bank reported that, whereas about 115 million people were living in poverty in Latin America in 1980, the number in 1995 had risen to approximately 160 million; further, whereas the percentage of the population living in poverty declined from roughly 60 percent in 1950 to about 35 percent in 1980, in 1995 the percentage had not declined from the 1980 figure.[16] In the pastoral letter issued after the episcopal conference of Latin American bishops in Mexico in 1995, the priests repudiated the "many signs of death which appear everywhere: extreme poverty, growing unemployment, uncontainable violence and so many forms of corruption and impunity which submerge millions of families in anguish and pain."[17] A journalist describes the poor in Argentina:

> In the bleak and bitter outskirts of Buenos Aires, thousands of people stand in line every morning, eyes glazed by hunger, clamoring for government handouts. The residents of most lower-class neighborhoods have had to fend for themselves. . . . [Two brothers, both working second jobs,] have helped organize a soup kitchen for their hunger-crazed neighbors, lining up donations of food from local companies. The project fed 300 people a day.[18]

Another journalist describes the plight of Mexican children who spend their days on Mexican city streets, washing windshields, selling candy, performing acrobatic tricks, and the like in exchange for drivers' small change:

"People yell at me from their cars that I shouldn't be working, that I should be in school [says an eight-year-old]. . . . But I have no money for school. Working here, at least I can make money for food." Ninety percent of the city's street children are sick on any given day, according to children's rights monitors. The youngsters experience high rates of respiratory ailments because they spend their entire day in the most polluted sections of the city. They suffer diarrhea and other illnesses from poor diet and hygiene.[19]

What might be done by the international community to ease the transition to free market economics in Latin America? Of course, the recommendations are numerous and diverse, and they cannot be fully addressed here. The proposals include more progressive taxation, microenterprise development, enhanced education, improved infrastructure, property titling projects in both the rural and the urban sectors, as well as recommendations (primarily by leftists) for an alternative economic model that maintains a role for the state in the economy—for example, in the provision of subsidies to particularly competitive industries.[20] But what does the Peruvian case, and to a lesser degree the Mexican, suggest to be important efforts that the international community might undertake, or further emphasize?

First, international food aid programs might be increased, not cut.[21] Although it is true that a person given a fish may eat for a day but a person taught how to fish may eat for a lifetime, short-term emergency food aid programs can be helpful. U.S. "Food for Peace" allocations have been an important component of U.S. foreign aid, and should continue to be—especially the "Title II" food that is distributed through nongovernmental organizations.[22] We noted in chapter 5 the much smaller U.S. commitment to food aid in Peru than in El Salvador during the 1980s and early 1990s, and this difference is presumably one of the reasons for the greater hunger in Peru than in El Salvador during this period. We also observed in chapter 6 that the paucity of food became a tense political issue even in Lima, as hungry people accused local authorities and NGO leaders of stealing the food—when most analysts believed that the problem was not corruption but actual food shortages. Although in Peru in the early 1990s food aid was necessary even in Lima, usually the greatest attention should be given to the distribution of food to remote, disadvantaged parts of the country.[23]

Second, the international financial community might further prioritize poverty alleviation. In recent years, most of the economic development funds for Latin America are loans from the Inter-American Development Bank (IDB) and the World Bank (IBRD). Since approximately 1993, the IDB has put much more emphasis upon loans to "the social sector"—primarily basic sanitation, urban development, public health, education, environmental programs, and microenterprise; some 35 percent to 40 percent of all IDB funds have been allocated to the social sector.[24] The IDB also developed a pilot project for Guatemala, called "Community Development for Peace," in which local Guatemalan communities are defining their own priorities for the IDB's funds. These initiatives are welcome and important, but still much more could be done, especially by the World Bank and especially in the area of nutritional education.[25]

Third, given that the Peruvian and Mexican experiences suggest that post–Cold War revolutionary movements are most likely to emerge in destitute regions, special attention might be given to economic development programs for such regions. Although the Peruvian southern highlands and Mexico's Chiapas are perhaps extreme cases of this problem, regional disparities abound in Brazil, Central America, and the Andean nations. Some Latin American governments are likely to resist a focus on development in remote regions; after all, the regional disparities are in part the result of elites' long-standing disregard for the plight of indigenous peoples in their countries, and in part the result of elites' recognition that greater total numbers of supporters and voters reside in capital cities. Currently, however, even at the IDB, virtually no attention is given to the allocation of funds by region; upon discussion with Latin American officials, the long-term significance of equitable regional distribution of funds might be highlighted.[26]

Of course, economic adversity is not a sufficient condition of a revolutionary movement. Rather, economic crisis and the outrage that it provokes among citizens is a challenge that today's Latin American democratic governments must try to meet.[27] This challenge may be addressed somewhat effectively by the government—or totally ineffectively. In the case of Peru, both the Belaúnde government and, after 1987, the García government failed to persuade citizens that their leaders were dedicated to ameliorating Peru's economic straits (see chapter 4). In the case of the García government especially, the widespread popular perception by the late 1980s was not that key government officials were trying hard to overcome the economic crisis, but that they were trying to maximize their personal wealth. Of course, the popular perception of pervasive government corruption was delegitimating in the extreme.

As discussed in chapters 4 and 6, there is no evidence that official corruption was worse in Peru than in other Latin American countries. But, such a statement damns with faint praise; in recent years, the presidents in both Brazil and Venezuela have actually fallen because of allegations of corruption. Moreover, the data in tables 4.12 and 4.13 indicate that, among bureaucrats as well as citizens in Peru, El Salvador, and Ecuador, alarmingly large percentages of respondents perceive rampant cronyism and corruption in government ministries. The prevailing perceptions were that merit was unimportant to employment and promotion, and also that embezzlement was common. What can be done by the international community to combat both corruption and the misperception of corruption?

Again, in part because of Latin American leaders' concerns and in part because of the Clinton administration's concerns, corruption became more salient on the multilateral agenda after 1993. At the Summit of the Americas in December 1994, the "Plan of Action" included an initiative to fight corruption through the development of reforms to make government operations more transparent and accountable; to strengthen internal mechanisms for government oversight, monitoring, and enforcement; and to establish conflict-of-interest standards for public officials and penalties for illicit enrichment.[28] Subsequently, the Organization of American States led the effort to formulate a document, "The Inter-American Convention against Corruption," that would require transnational cooperation against bribery and illicit enrichment. However, the ratification of this document by the signatories has been very slow, and the U.S. government has been one of the laggards.[29] More effort is required if this initiative is to advance.

Also, the mechanisms for official transparency and oversight recommended at the Summit of the Americas might be further discussed and implemented within the Latin American nations. As chapter 4 indicated, much more can be done to establish civil service examinations and similar professional procedures for job appointments and promotion, and

also for honesty in the purchase of supplies and other financial deal-
ings.[30] Further, Latin American leaders might debate the question of the
number of political versus civil service ministerial appointments that
would be made by each administration.

Even together, economic debacle and a state that appears unable to
address the debacle are insufficient variables in a revolutionary equation. Also necessary is a revolutionary organization that does find a way
to process citizens' adversity and their perceptions of its perpetrators.[31]

The revolutionary organization that effectively channels citizens' rage
at their frustrated professional aspirations or their increased poverty
and at the failings of their "democratic" regime is not the same as the
successful revolutionary organization of the Cold War era. In contrast
to most Cold War revolutionary organizations, successful post–Cold
War revolutionary organizations are unlikely to call for "democracy."
Rather, like the Shining Path in Peru (as well as many Islamic fundamentalist groups in the Middle East and Africa), these movements are
likely to reject elections—criticizing their procedural flaws as well as
their failures to produce effective governments—and rather base their
claims to legitimacy on quasi-religious and ideological grounds. The
Shining Path sought to present itself as a group of virtually "born-
again" Peruvians: honest, dedicated, and effective, fighting against a
hopelessly corrupt state. In the Shining Path's interpretation of political
violence and in its formulation of the "quota" (the expectation that
Senderistas would sacrifice their lives in the revolutionary struggle), the
movement was engaging its militants' faith, not their reason.

Whereas successful revolutionary movements during the Cold War
fought their country's regime not only on the ground at home but also
in the U.S. political arena, in the post–Cold War era revolutionary
movements are unlikely to spark the reactions in the United States that
they did previously. Unlike the FMLN and most previous Latin American
revolutionary movements, Sendero did not try to be palatable to particular sets of U.S. political actors; for example, it regularly denounced
U.S.-based human rights groups. Nor was the expansion of a Maoist
movement in Peru the priority for U.S. government officials that the
expansion of a pro-Soviet movement would have been during the Cold
War. In contrast to the Cold War context, in Peru in the 1980s and early
1990s a "strong" revolutionary organization was not in good part an

organization that effectively managed its international context; rather, it was an organization that could convince Peruvian citizens that it had the capacity to win.

As emphasized in chapter 3, the Belaúnde and García governments were delegitimated not only by the perceived ineffectiveness of their economic policies, but also by the perceived ineffectiveness of their counterinsurgency policies. Once the insurgency had erupted, could the international community have helped, or helped more?

First, it must be repeated that, whereas during the Cold War U.S. officials' tendency was to exaggerate the intensity of Marxist threats in Latin American nations, the prevailing current tendency has been to underestimate their significance. Although neither Peru's Shining Path nor Mexico's EZLN won power, both movements' impacts were very great and very costly in different ways. It is important that the U.S. government, international financial institutions, and Latin American governments advance policy priorities—such as free market and antidrug policies—only after considering the effects of these policies on a possible or actual insurgency. Unfortunately, for example, the Bush administration, in its emphasis upon military action in Peru's coca-producing areas as an antidrug initiative, did not appear to analyze in sufficient depth the likely impact of this policy on Peru's counterinsurgency effort. The same appears to be true of the Clinton administration's prioritizing of antidrug efforts in Colombia in the late 1990s.[32]

As U.S. officials acknowledge the possibility of continuing revolutionary challenges in the post–Cold War era, they may begin to discuss the nature of effective responses. Through this discussion, previous U.S. responses can be placed within their Cold War framework, and the new factors in revolutionary equations discerned. In this process, the unfortunate albeit natural tendency to "prepare to fight the last war," as the adage goes, may be overcome.

During the Cold War, U.S. officials often attributed the expansion of a Marxist guerrilla movement to military support from the Soviet Union or Cuba, and—unless the threatened regime was a dictatorship that refused to reform and that the U.S. public would not countenance—bolstered it with various kinds of resources, saliently including military aid. Even during the Cold War, many critics of U.S. policy argued that the U.S. emphasis on military aid was inappropriate given that in most cases—such as the Salvadoran—military repression was itself a cause of the crisis and that U.S. military aid tended to strengthen the military institution and its resistance to the establishment of the democratic norms sought by many of the supporters of the revolutionary movement.

In the post–Cold War era, when no military support for Latin American guerrilla movements from Cuba or Russia is available, U.S. military aid is likely to be even less appropriate. We noted that, in the Peruvian case, when the Bush administration offered military aid as a response to the Shining Path challenge, not even Peruvian military officers enthusiastically endorsed such aid. Peruvian citizens did not perceive Sendero Luminoso as a military problem that had a military solution, and their perception was correct.

But if the U.S. government is not to respond to a guerrilla challenge with a package of military and economic aid, what might be done? Most generally, it is in the U.S. interest that U.S. public awareness of the continuing economic and political problems in many Latin American countries be increased. For example, U.S. political leaders might highlight more often data about the low levels of U.S. expenditure on foreign aid—low relative to Americans' assumptions about this expenditure and also low relative to that by other developed nations in per capita terms. And U.S. leaders might frequently remind citizens of the saying that "an ounce of prevention is worth a pound of cure."

When a "cure" must be found, however, it is necessary that the recommendations made by U.S. and international political leaders be assessed within the context of the specific Latin American country at the specific moment. To a greater degree than in the Cold War era, revolutionary movements in the future will be different from one another, and the paths toward peace will be different. For policy priorities and policy alternatives appropriate to the particular country at the particular moment, it is important that U.S. officials listen closely to the reflections of Latin American citizens and leaders. Context will be crucial.

An apparent example of sensitivity to the Peruvian context is U.S. support for the elite police unit that captured Sendero's leader, Guzmán. As the "philosopher-king" of Sendero and a "sun god," Guzmán's leadership was singularly important to the organization. Accordingly, when Guzmán was captured, the implications were much more serious for Sendero than would have been the case for most Latin American revolutionary organizations. Capture has been important in some cases—for example, the capture of Ché Guevara—but in most cases there were several important leaders and persons who could become viable successors. Not only was Sendero's strategic capacity disabled, but also its mystique was shattered. Although the fundamentalist character of Sendero may be likely in future revolutionary movements, the extraordinary importance of the revolutionary leader seems less likely, and so the lesson from the Peruvian experience is not "try to capture the leader."

In the Peruvian case, however, it seems unfortunate that U.S. support for the capture did not begin earlier and was not yet more intense. As chapter 3 indicated, more than two years elapsed between the identification of the first important Senderista safe house in June 1990 under García and the capture of Guzmán, and more than eighteen months between the identification of a second important safe house in January 1991 under Fujimori and his capture. A more expeditious capture was possible; apparently, the GEIN was tracking the militant who ultimately was to point them toward Guzmán by November 1990 and had observed preparations for Guzmán's birthday on 3 December in the second safe house, but opted to delay breaking into the house.[33] It also seems unfortunate, for numerous reasons, that the likely U.S. role was covert.

With the exception of the capture of Guzmán, however, new strategies toward the decimation of Sendero and the MRTA evolved slowly, under both the García and Fujimori governments, and without U.S. encouragement (see chapters 3 and 5). If greater effort had been made by the United States or other international actors earlier, some of the problems in Peru's counterinsurgency policy that facilitated Fujimori's *autogolpe* might have been overcome, and the *autogolpe* averted. And, of course, thousands of lives might have been saved.

In Peru, one important example of such a path toward peace was judicial reform appropriate to the Sendero threat. As noted in chapter 3, the García government was fully aware that in the late 1980s only 5 to 10 percent of terrorist suspects were being convicted; the García government knew that standards for conviction were too high, and also that many judges were intimidated or bribed by the guerrillas. President García sought changes that were likely to have improved the judicial process; but there was little echo for his initiatives. It would have been in the U.S. interest that debate about these initiatives be sparked.

But, such debate did not occur, and García's initiatives were ultimately not implemented. Then, after the *autogolpe* in 1992 and President Fujimori's radical overhaul of the judicial process, more than 95 percent of terrorist suspects were convicted.[34] Among the estimated five thousand persons jailed for crimes of terrorism or treason since 1992, Peru's National Coordinator of Human Rights has identified 1,504 as probably innocent.[35] Clearly, whereas under García Peru's judiciary was failing because it did not convict the guilty, under Fujimori it was failing because it did not free the innocent. Between the two extremes, a consensus about fair rules in a context of a post–Cold War counterinsurgency movement still has not been forged. Was a system of "faceless judges" really necessary, as President Fujimori contends?[36] If so, what could have been done to assure the rigor, independence, and impartiality of these judges' verdicts? Was it necessary to make mere membership in a violent guerrilla group a crime? If so, what safeguards should have been taken to maintain freedoms of expression and assembly?

Although the most valuable role that the U.S. and other international actors might have played was probably the stimulation of informed discussion, funds would also have been helpful. But, as mentioned in chapter 5, administration of justice programs in Peru began to receive U.S. support only in 1989, and the annual allocation was only about $1 million.[37] In recent years, U.S. AID has been allocating approximately half its "Democracy Program" funds for the administration of justice and, accordingly, support for these efforts in Peru has now increased somewhat.[38] Although the increase is a positive step, the funds would have been more timely at an earlier date.

Another important strategy was enhanced protection of civilians who were targeted by Sendero. To a greater degree than virtually any other Latin American revolutionary movement, the Shining Path sought to eliminate civilians whom it decided were standing in its way and whom it could charge, justifiably or not, with corruption. Government efforts at social and economic development in the southern highlands during the García government failed in part because of the intensity of attacks against government officials in these areas by the guerrillas. Grassroots activists, such as María Elena Moyano, who sought to represent an alternative to both the state and Sendero instead came to represent the absence of an alternative when they were murdered, usually by Sendero. The state itself became absent when few political leaders dared to compete for political office in many areas of the country. Many international organizations did not want a presence even in Lima, much less in Sendero-dominated areas.

What could be done to reduce the danger faced by civilians in contexts such as the Peruvian? As discussed in chapter 3, in the countryside a key initiative proved to be the *rondas:* armed peasant self-defense patrols. Although the Peruvian *rondas* were not without their flaws—and the relationship between the peasant *ronderos* and the military sponsors of the *rondas* has not always been clear—in most analysts' judgments they were on balance very helpful. Probably in part because *rondas* had not worked well in El Salvador or in Peru during the Belaúnde government, *rondas* were not suggested by U.S. officials or other international actors in Peru but emerged first from debates within the García government. The *rondas* might have been vigorously implemented earlier if international actors had prompted more analysis in the mid- and late 1980s about the differences between the Salvadoran and Peruvian revolutionary experiences—in particular, the facts that the Peruvian military's human rights violations were to a greater degree than the Salvadoran's a result rather than a cause of the Shining Path, that in Peru's northern highlands community patrols had already proven successful, and that there was greater chance for success in the late 1980s than in the early 1980s given stronger tendencies among peasants to reject Sendero's increasingly violent tactics.

Could a *rondas* initiative be successfully applied to an urban setting? Only with modifications; virtually by definition, "outsiders" cannot be readily identified in an urban setting, and the police are likely to be the appropriate security force, rather than the military. However, the underlying principle of the *rondas* is that the community can be trusted to oppose advocates of violence and can collaborate toward that end—a principle that can indeed be applied in urban contexts. Whereas each individual in a community cannot bear arms, construct a home security system, and/or hire an armed guard, community leaders as a group may undertake some of these steps at some times or places. In general, as in community policing initiatives in U.S. cities and elsewhere, the community and the police would work together to develop responses appropriate to the particular context. Especially after the grisly murder of María Elena Moyano highlighted Sendero's savage character to North Americans and Europeans, special pleas for international funds for these kinds of initiatives might have succeeded.[39]

None of the above is meant to imply that the development of an effective judicial reform program and appropriate community policing efforts is simple. On the contrary, much effort and some trial and error was necessary before it was appropriate to introduce the *rondas* in Peru; with respect to judicial reform, there is still no consensus about what effective and fair procedures would be within Peru's context.

Indeed, perhaps ironically, during the post–Cold War era revolutionary challenges may be more difficult to confront than during the Cold War. During the Cold War, when dictatorships prevailed in most of Latin America and were the key catalysts to revolutionary movements, opening the regime politically was a relatively straightforward response to the challenge. "Political opening" meant elections—something the United States and other international actors could readily promote, and that was achieved in the Salvadoran case. Now, however, when most countries in the region are already politically inclusive, the simple call for political opening is insufficient. At a time when free market transitions have dashed middle-class expectations and exacerbated poverty in many countries, and also when ample resources may be available to possibly fundamentalist revolutionary organizations, the determination of an appropriate response to the challenge may be extremely complex. At century's end, "democracy"—defined as elections—is not enough to doom revolution.

APPENDIX I
SURVEY RESEARCH IN PERU, EL SALVADOR, AND ECUADOR

*I*n Peru, I had already collaborated in previous years with the public opinion agency Datum. Directed by Manuel Torrado, Datum is one of Peru's best-known and most respected public opinion firms. Datum's polling results are regularly reported in Peru's news dailies and news weeklies, and its pre-electoral forecasts for most elections have been accurate.[1]

In Peru, I also worked with Rodolfo Osores Ocampo, a sociologist trained at the Universidad del Centro in Huancayo who had also earned a postgraduate degree in demography at the Catholic University in Lima. I was fortunate to collaborate with Osores from 1973 until his death in 1997; his expertise on issues of research methodology and his capacity to establish rapport with respondents were excellent. Osores's residence in the central-highlands city of Huancayo was a major boon to this research, enabling a variety of kinds of surveys in one of the areas most directly threatened by Sendero. Over the years, he established a team of university-educated relatives and friends whom he trained in interview techniques and upon whom he could call for distinct types of interviews. This team was socially and politically diverse, including his wife and colleagues at the Ministry of Health in Huancayo, where Osores himself worked for more than a decade; his nephew and one of his friends at the Universidad del Centro, a university where Sendero was very active in the late 1980s and early 1990s; and a second nephew studying at the Catholic University in Lima and residing there with Osores's uncle, a military officer.

In El Salvador, my principal research colleague was Victor Antonio (Toño) Orellana. Director of the Salvadoran Institute of Education and Technical Assistance for Cooperatives (Instituto Salvadoreño de Educación y Asesoría Cooperativa, ISEAC), Orellana had vast research experience. Highly recommended by Roberto Codas Friedmann, the head of the Regional Program for Research on El Salvador (Programa Regional de Investigación sobre El Salvador, PREIS), Orellana had been responsible for education and training at the Konrad Adenauer Foundation in El Salvador and had also been a professor at the public opinion institute of the Universidad Centroamericana José Simeón Cañas (UCA), the Catholic university in El Salvador. At the UCA, Orellana had worked closely with Ignacio Martín-Baró, one of the six priests killed in November 1989 and El Salvador's foremost public opinion scholar until his tragic death.[2] Overall, the UCA is the most respected research institution in El Salvador.[3] Orellana worked closely in our research effort with José Francisco González, a university graduate who was also highly trained in survey research.

In Ecuador, I collaborated with the public opinion agency Centro de Estudios y Datos (CEDATOS). Highly recommended by Dr. Catherine Conaghan, a Canadian-based scholar specializing in Ecuador, CEDATOS is a prestigious firm whose polling results are reported regularly in the Ecuadorean media.[4] Established in 1974, CEDATOS is associated with similar agencies throughout Latin America and beyond, and its Ecuadorean and international public and private clients number more than one hundred. I worked with the director of CEDATOS, Dr. Polibio Córdova, who holds a Ph.D. in economics from the University of Michigan at Ann Arbor, and has also received specialized training in sampling and statistics.

Collaborating with Datum and Osores in Peru, with Orellana in El Salvador, and with CEDATOS in Ecuador, I applied sample surveys in the three countries.[5] Datum carried out a sample survey in Huancayo in May 1990 and in Lima in November 1990. Primarily because the Huancayo survey was performed prior to beginning my research in El Salvador, I revised the questionnaire for reapplication in Huancayo in June–July 1991, so that the items in the survey and the profile of the respondents would be more similar to the ones in the Salvadoran questionnaire. The June–July 1991 Huancayo survey was performed by

Osores's team. Orellana's nationwide Salvadoran survey was carried out in April–May 1991. CEDATOS applied its survey in Quito and Guayaquil in December 1991.

Sampling techniques were similar in the three nations. All the surveys were based on in-person interviews by university students with previous interviewing experience and were carried out after the preparation of maps of sites. In neither Peru nor El Salvador did we conduct interviews in areas considered to be under guerrilla control.

Although sample characteristics and sampling techniques were similar, they were not identical. In Peru and Ecuador, public opinion agencies conventionally restrict their sampling to each country's key cities—Lima in Peru and Guayaquil and Quito in Ecuador. In these two relatively large countries, where Andean geography impedes transportation by land, nationwide samples are considered prohibitively expensive. By contrast, in much smaller El Salvador, where almost any part of the country can be reached by land within a day, nationwide surveys are the rule. Researchers seem to prefer to apply surveys in different parts of the country, perhaps in part so that they do not raise officials' eyebrows. In any case, my own cost limitations prohibited my changing national survey customs, which would have required new sampling maps and so forth.

Sampling strategies were also somewhat different in the three nations. In El Salvador and Peru, the sampling strategy was called "random route": (1) using a map, a set of potential "starting points" for interviewers was established that were representative of the site; (2) a specific route from the starting point (first street on the right, next left, and so on) was randomly decided; and (3) sites for interviewing were set at fixed intervals (for instance, every second workplace, every third house, every fourth store).[6] In Ecuador, however, sampling was based on maps of residences, and the respondents were residents of the particular housing units. While technically the Ecuadorean technique would be considered superior, in El Salvador and Peru researchers perceive biases to at-home interviews. First, respondents interviewed in their homes appear more fearful of retaliation if their views are critical of the government. Second, given high levels of physical insecurity at night, interviews are usually carried out in the daytime, and the daytime at-home population is biased toward housewives and against the working poor (see note 1 to this appendix). For these reasons, the number of at-home interviews in the Salvadoran sample was minimal, and in Peru, Datum was increasingly shifting away from at-home interviews.[7]

Of course, whatever the sampling technique, survey research in countries such as Peru and El Salvador is problematic in numerous respects. Especially in El Salvador, citizens' fear of retaliation for antigovernment answers was intense, and was a major factor in the very high levels of "don't know/no answer" responses in Salvadoran samples (often at 25 percent of total responses).[8] Also, in all three countries, due primarily to low educational levels, some respondents are confused by words and concepts in the surveys, and may in fact not have coherent opinions about the complex political issues in the surveys.

As the survey results of any one scholarly team may be doubted by skeptical analysts, whenever possible I compare my results with those of other institutions. In Peru, where the news media regularly report public opinion polls, there are numerous public opinion agencies, and there are considerable data with which I can compare the results of my research teams. Among these public opinion agencies, Apoyo is especially prestigious. In Ecuador, there are also several respected agencies, in particular the Institute of Social Studies and Public Opinion (Instituto de Estudios Sociales y de la Opinión Pública).

In contrast, in El Salvador the most prestigious public opinion research has been done not by a commercial agency but at a university, specifically at the UCA. In part because of the more problematic nature of survey research in El Salvador and the greater possibility for skepticism about my survey results, I worded as many items as possible in my Salvadoran survey to correspond to items previously asked by UCA teams. Except for the UCA's work, public opinion polling in El Salvador has been scant; not only is this research especially difficult in El Salvador, but also the Salvadoran media have appeared uninterested in polls. The U.S. government often worked with a Costa Rican agency for its polling—a dubious practice for obvious reasons. The only Salvadoran-based firm with whose work I became familiar was Publicidad Rumbo, whose director Ricardo Gonzales generously shared some public opinion results with me.

The research teams also carried out relatively informal surveys among sets of citizens whose views on particular issues would be of special interest. To examine perceptions of the professionalism and effectiveness of state organizations in Peru and El Salvador, we interviewed officials employed in state agencies. During May and June 1990 in Peru, Rodolfo Osores Ocampo's team interviewed ninety-nine employees of the Ministry of Health in Huancayo (including primarily low-level administrators, doctors, nurses, laboratory technicians, and secretaries). In October 1990, Osores's team surveyed fifty-two employees of the Ministry of Agriculture in Huancayo, posing questions about the ministry's professionalism and effectiveness as well as other questions about the agrarian reform in the area. (This survey was also administered to eighteen Agrarian Bank employees and thirteen independent farmers in the area.) In May and June 1991 in El Salvador, Víctor Antonio Orellana's team interviewed one hundred government employees—twenty each in the Ministries of Health, Planning, Education, Agriculture, and Interior. The respondents in these surveys were not selected randomly, but by their willingness to participate in the survey (often due to their acquaintance with the particular interviewer).

Given the importance of the agrarian reform issue in both Peru and El Salvador, I was also interested in comparative information about peasant beneficiaries' perceptions of the reforms. For Peru, Osores and I had been gathering information about these perceptions on a regular basis—in formal surveys in three different cooperatives during 1973–74 and informal follow-up questionnaires in these sites subsequently.[9] In El Salvador, the Orellana team posed similar questions to more than one hundred peasant beneficiaries in eight different cooperatives in three different departments. The cooperatives were selected by Orellana to be as representative as possible of ongoing Salvadoran cooperatives in the 1980s, while at the same time accessible to Orellana's research team through friendship networks in the sites. Orellana was familiar with the universe of Salvadoran cooperatives through his work at ISEAC.

I was also fortunate that, in Peru, the Osores team was able to carry out sets of informal interviews with key groups. Although the number of respondents in these interviews was small, and the samples were not random, I believe that, given the Peruvian context at the time, they were the best that could be done. In the relatively informal context, considerable rapport was achieved in most of the interviews.

To my knowledge, the most systematic interviews that have ever been carried out with Shining Path members were the thirty-three that the

Osores team carried out in Huancayo and its vicinities in April and May 1993. The focus of the questionnaire was on the reasons why the respondent had joined the Shining Path, and what he or she liked and disliked about the movement. Twenty-three of the interviews were carried out by a former Shining Path member ["Pedro Paredes"] who, in the wake of the capture of Guzmán, was trying to extricate himself from the organization. "Pedro Paredes" did not have a permanent job and welcomed the payment for the interviews; he trusted Osores because they were neighbors in the residential area by the Huancayo university, and because Osores had come to know one of his relatives at the Ministry of Health in Huancayo. "Paredes" and Osores conducted some of the interviews together. Raised in the mining town of Cobriza in the department of Huancavelica, "Pedro" was the son of a miner and a street vendor. He completed secondary school, but lacked the funds to study at a university. He joined Sendero when he returned to Cobriza to look for a job in approximately 1988; he was a combatant who participated in numerous attacks and also became a political leader with responsibilities not only in Cobriza but also in Pampas and Huancayo. He became disillusioned after the capture of Guzmán; although he was arrested at least once on charges of terrorism, he was never convicted.

The final ten interviews with Shining Path members were conducted in the Huancayo prison, in the cell block for those arrested on charges of terrorism. These interviews were carried out jointly by Osores and Samuel Sosa (a friend of Osores's nephew), who had recently completed legal studies at the Universidad del Centro and was specializing in terrorist law; Sosa had contacts at the Huancayo jail and brought soap, food, and so forth to gain collaboration from the suspected and convicted Shining Path militants.

Earlier, in June 1990, the Osores team carried out interviews with security force personnel, asking questions about their perceptions of the threat posed by Sendero and alternative strategies for the improvement of the counterinsurgency effort. Sixty interviews were conducted: twelve in the army, six in the navy, and the remainder in an antiterrorist branch of the police. Our respondents' median rank was sergeant but ranged up to the rank of captain and down to private. Almost all had served in at least one "emergency zone"—most in Huancayo but a considerable number in Ayacucho and a variety of other highland areas. About

80 percent were interviewed in Huancayo, 10 percent in Lima, and 10 percent elsewhere. Respondents were not selected randomly, but by their willingness to participate in the survey, which was almost always because of their friendship with the interviewer. At the outset, I had hoped to carry out a similar set of interviews with security force personnel in El Salvador, but I was not able to identify a researcher who could carry out such a delicate research task.

APPENDIX II
DATA ON POLITICAL VIOLENCE IN PERU AND EL SALVADOR

*I*n both Peru and El Salvador, institutions emerged that became the most respected source for political violence data in the particular country: the "Bernales Commission" in Peru and Tutela Legala in El Salvador.[1]

From May 1988 until April 1992 in Peru, the Bernales Commission was a commission of the Peruvian Senate led by Enrique Bernales, a senator for Izquierda Unida from 1985 until 1990 and for Izquierda Socialista from 1990 until 1992—and one of Peru's most rigorous social scientists. Known first as the Special Commission on Pacification of the Senate (Comisión Especial sobre Pacificación del Senado), and then as the Special Commission for the Investigation and Study of Violence and Alternatives for Peace (Comisión Especial de Investigación y Estudio de la Violencia y Alternativas por la Paz), the Bernales Commission's sources included press accounts, direct testimony, and information from human rights organizations and research institutes, as well as official data from the defense and interior ministries and the intelligence services. For the most part, the Bernales Commission was the only political violence institution in Peru that enjoyed access to official data. After the April 1992 *autogolpe*, Enrique Bernales continued his compilation of data on political violence in his capacity as head of the institute publishing the periodical *PerúPaz*. (See also the discussion in Palmer [1995, 306–308].)

However, the Bernales Commission's data were similar to those presented by other institutions in Peru.[2] Indeed, members of these institutions often shared data with one another and collaborated in other ways. With the exception of figures on "terrorist attacks" (indicators for "attacks" were different for different organizations), the figures reported by the gamut of organizations rarely varied by more than 10 percent, and these variations were not patterned to suggest a political bias of one sort or another. Among the other institutions whose data are sometimes cited in this book are the research institute DESCO, whose work was based upon press accounts; human rights groups such as the National Human Rights Coordinating Committee (Coordinadora Nacional de Derechos Humanos) and APRODEH, based to a greater degree on direct testimony; and the U.S.-based RAND Corporation, whose data are presented by Gordon McCormick (1990 and 1992).

In El Salvador, the most respected source for data on political violence was Tutela Legal, the human rights office of the Roman Catholic Archdiocese of San Salvador. Founded in May 1982, Tutela Legal compiled its data by direct investigation of incidences of political violence, including use of personal testimony. Before 1982, the primary source for political violence data was Socorro Jurídico, also affiliated with the Roman Catholic Church. Other human rights organizations reported on political violence in El Salvador, such as the Human Rights Commission of El Salvador (Comisión de Derechos Humanos de El Salvador), but their efforts were not as rigorous or consistent as Tutela Legal's.

In both Peru and El Salvador, analysts of political violence encountered numerous problems. Most obviously, in both countries it was impossible for a researcher to monitor attacks and battles directly. Analysts' primary recourse for these figures was official data. However, most independent analysts feared that a considerable number of the casualties who were reported as guerrillas in the official data were in fact civilians. Especially in Peru, where confrontations often occurred in remote areas and where the numbers of "subversives" killed appeared very high relative to other tallies, human rights monitors believed that the military at times swept into villages in emergency zones, rounded up and killed young men, and counted them all as "subversives."

Also, in both countries but to a greater degree in Peru, analysts believed that the data underestimated the intensity of political violence. Because of the remoteness of many rural areas in Peru, monitors could not investigate incidents of violence and witnesses or relatives could not report them. The security forces also impeded monitors' investigations:

the monitors would not be allowed access to the particular area, witnesses would be threatened, and various cover-up tactics would be used. For these reasons, Peruvian human rights groups fear that actual human rights violations may be as much as double the reported numbers.[3] In El Salvador, access to most of the countryside is much easier than in Peru, and underestimation of the amount of political violence was not widely cited as a key problem.[4]

In El Salvador, by contrast, the primary controversy about political violence data during the 1980s was about the attribution of responsibility for political killings.[5] The U.S. Department of State charged that Tutela Legal overestimated the number of human rights violations by rightist death squads and underestimated the number by the FMLN. However, now that in the more peaceful context of 1992 and 1993, the Truth Commission of the United Nations has determined that 85 percent of the violations were committed by agents of the security forces versus only 15 percent by the FMLN, it is clear that the attributions made by Tutela Legal were relatively accurate.[6] For its part, the U.S. Department of State's data were based exclusively on a review of accounts in the Salvadoran press—an inappropriate methodology in a nation where the print media were overwhelmingly biased towards the political right—and the attributions made by the U.S. Department of State were inaccurate.[7]

NOTES

Introduction

1. This of course was the argument first made by Francis Fukuyama in 1989. See Jensen (1990); and Fukuyama (1992). See chapter 1 for a definition of democracy.

2. Most scholars interpret "social revolution" as Marxist revolution by violent means. See chapter 1 for a definition of revolution.

3. Huntington (1968, 275–276).

4. Goodwin and Skocpol (1989, 495).

5. This is a description of Ché Guevara's view by Wickham-Crowley (1989, 514).

6. Regimes surviving less than a year, such as Alexander Kerensky's in Russia in 1917, are not "established." In Eastern European nations after World War II, initial elections were held under the cloud of Soviet influence; the Soviets did not, however, act as guerrillas.

7. The degree to which these elected governments were truly democratic is problematic (see chapter 7). Considerable numbers of violent attacks were carried out by the guerrillas in the four countries, but by the criteria developed for the establishment of the "strength" of a revolutionary movement in chapter 2—numbers of militants and victims, amount of territory controlled, and popular support—these movements did not rival the Salvadoran or Peruvian. Only in Colombia was any territory controlled by the revolutionaries.

8. In 1962 and 1963, the United States provided $72 million and $60 million respectively to Venezuela, including more than $10 million of military aid each year. President Kennedy visited Venezuela in late 1961 and President Betancourt traveled to Washington, D.C., in February 1963; their relationship was warm (Alexander, 1982, 552–558). Between 1961 and 1971, almost one thousand Uruguayan police were trained under U.S. auspices (Porzecanski, 1973, 53), and in 1973 Uruguay received $22 million, including $9.2 million in military assistance. Between 1971 and 1976, Argentina received about $22 million annually, almost exclusively in military assistance. U.S. economic and military aid to Colombia amounted to more than $100 million in current dollars every year between 1963

and 1973, with the exception of 1965. To compare these amounts to the figures for aid to El Salvador and Peru as of 1985, multiply the 1967 values by roughly 3.3, as indicated by data in the U.S. Department of Commerce, *Statistical Abstract of the United States 1994: The National Data Book* (Washington, D.C., 1994), 488.

9. On the origins of the Venezuelan guerrillas and their actions, see especially Gott (1972, 121–220); and Alexander (1982, 484–495). For estimates of the number of guerrillas, see Wickham-Crowley (1992, 27); and Radu and Tismaneanu (1990, 361). On the government's reforms and the economy (including the brief economic downturn in 1959–60), see Alexander (1982, 502–524). On the weakening of the guerrillas in the face of Venezuelan electoral processes and popular support for the government, see especially Ellner (1980, 1988, 32–63); Hernández (1983, 161–165); and Edelman (1987).

10. Weinstein (1988, 41). See also Lopez-Alves (1989); and Wright (1991, 102–108). Estimate on number of Tupamaros from Radu and Tismaneanu (1990, 348).

11. Gillespie (1982); Andersen (1993); and Wright (1991, 11–116). For estimates of the number of guerrillas, see Gillespie (1982, 178); and Falcoff (1988, 21).

12. Figures as high as fifteen thousand have been estimated. See Americas Watch (1986, 3). Pearce (1990, 281) suggests twelve thousand, as does James Brooke in "Colombia's Rebels Grow Rich from Banditry," *New York Times*, 2 July 1995, 1. For maps designating areas of important guerrilla strength, see Gott (1972, 233); and Pearce (1990, 282).

13. For cautions against the application of the democratic label to Colombia, especially during the National Front period (1958–74), see Bagley (1990); Pearce (1990, 207–208); and Chernick and Jiménez (1990, 1–12). There were, however, serious democratic shortcomings in the other regimes as well. See chapter 1 for a definition of democracy.

14. Wickham-Crowley (1992, 210, 293–296). See also Americas Watch (1986, 3); Collier and Collier (1991, 586); Pearce (1990, 174); Pizarro (1990); Zamosc (1990, 61–62); Jimeno and Volk (1983, 25); Heinz (1989, 257); and *Washington Post*, 4 January 1992, A18.

15. For a description of the guerrilla groups, see Pearce (1990, 281–284); and Wright (1991, 94–95).

16. *New York Times*, 2 July 1995, 1; and 19 January 1992, 6.

17. This is the conventional tally of Latin American revolutions. See, for example, Middlebrook (1994, 1–2); and Blasier (1967). Some analysts, such as Dix (1984), exclude the Bolivian case, not considering the revolution to have been successfully consolidated.

18. Scholars emphasizing global communist forces in their analysis of revolution in Latin America include Radu and Tismaneanu (1990); Ratliff (1976); and Fauriol (1985).

19. Dunkerley (1988, 483–491); Barry (1992, 65–71); and Jonas (1991, 139–142).

Business Latin America, 27 July 1992, 249. For further similar comments from Peruvian and North American analysts, see Radu and Tismaneanu (1990, 339); *Miami Herald,* 14 December 1991, 1, 6A; and *Washington Post,* 28 July 1992, A19.

42. Radu and Tismaneanu (1990, 339).

43. *Philadelphia Inquirer,* 19 December 1991, E1.

44. *Miami Herald,* 14 December 1991, 1A.

45. *Washington Post,* 31 August 1992, A1.

46. Aronson's testimony was entitled "Peru's Shining Path Insurgency: Status and U.S. Counterinsurgency Aid Policy Options," and was delivered on 12 March 1992 before the Subcommittee on Western Hemisphere Affairs, House of Representatives.

47. Jeremy J. Stone, president of the Federation of American Scientists, in an op-ed in the *Washington Post,* 28 July 1992.

48. Inter-American Dialogue, "A Multilateral Dialogue with Peru: Report on Inter-American Dialogue Meeting in Lima" (report issued by Inter-American Dialogue, Washington, D.C., June 1994), 3.

49. Social scientists tend to use the term "correlation" more frequently than "cause"; while it can be shown, as in this book, that independent and dependent variables changed at the same time, it is difficult to prove definitively a link between the changes. In social science terms, "correlation" is proven, but not "causality." There is also the problem of thresholds of change; how much change signifies "real" change? See chapter 1 for further discussions.

50. As figures 1 and 2 indicate, there is a trajectory of, as well as an interplay among, the variables composing a revolutionary challenge. As Wickham-Crowley (1992, 302–326) suggests, a successful revolutionary movement first gains supporters, then gains strength, and then finally comes to power. The reasons for the emergence, expansion, and outcome of the revolutionary challenge may be different.

51. For a more nuanced and thorough discussion of the issues of the "strength" of a revolutionary movement, including the "strength" of the Guatemalan movement, see chapter 5. My argument is about the conditions necessary for revolutionary victory, not revolutionary defeat (as in Guatemala).

52. See also the various quotations and discussion in chapters 4 and 6. I heard the phrase "inhuman salaries" many times in Peru during the years 1987–92. The second comment was made by a peasant in the highlands community Varya in the early 1980s.

53. In the early 1990s, as the possibility of a Shining Path takeover loomed greater, U.S. concern increased, but at the same time U.S. perplexity was heightened by President Fujimori's *autogolpe.* See chapter 5.

54. Of course, as in the case of El Salvador, it is a question not only of U.S. support but also of whether or not a threatened Latin American regime responds sufficiently to U.S. concerns (in the judgment of U.S. officials). With respect to

Peru, the U.S. sought free market reforms from the García government and, after the April 1992 *autogolpe,* democratization from the Fujimori government; many U.S. officials were not satisfied with the Peruvian government's responses. But, as chapter 5 indicates, at no time was the Peruvian government offered the level of incentives to reform that the Salvadoran was.

55. On the status of the Colombian guerrillas, see James Brooke, "Colombia's Rebels Grow Rich from Banditry," *New York Times,* 2 July 1995, 1; Ken Dermota, "Terror Grows in Colombian Region," *Boston Sunday Globe,* 10 September 1995, 9. On the Guatemalan guerrillas, see the series of articles by Robert Collier in the *San Francisco Chronicle,* 27 February 1995, A1–A7; and 28 February 1995, A1–A6.

56. An excellent summary of the origins of the EZLN rebellion is Fox (1994). On the relative poverty of Chiapas, see Collier (1994, 15–16); Russell (1995, 17–19); and Autonomedia (1994, 25–30). On concerns for indigenous peoples' autonomy by the EZLN, see Russell (1995, 38–40); and Autonomedia (1994, 17). On NAFTA as an EZLN concern, see Fox (1994, 13–14); and Russell (1995, 16). The EZLN's demands are also indicated in a volume of documents by their own militants (Autonomedia, 1994). On the specific point of elections as an insufficient answer to the Zapatistas' demands, see *Latin America Weekly Report,* 14 September 1995, 413; and *Latin America Regional Report,* 2 November 1995, 5. Also, on political exclusion and authoritarian practices by the Mexican regime as a factor, see Collier (1994, 125, 139–144); Russell (1995, 8–9, 11–12); and Physicians for Human Rights and Human Rights/Americas Watch (1994, 13).

57. The EPR initiated political violence only in June 1996, and accordingly scholarly accounts are scant. See, however, *Latin America Regional Report,* 18 July 1996, 2–3; 26 September 1996, 4–5; and 19 December 1996, 584.

1. Analytical Framework

1. See, for example, the statements by Goldstone (1991, 19) and Munck (1994, 372).

2. Review essays include Goldstone (1980, 440–445) and Moshiri (1991, 26–29). Critiques include Dix (1983); Knight (1990); Goldstone (1991, 19–21); Colburn (1994, 12–13); and Selbin (1993, 10–11).

3. This is the theme sentence of Skocpol's final paragraph to the book. See Skocpol (1979, 293).

4. Ibid., 29.

5. Ibid., 111.

6. Ibid., 47–111; see, especially, the summary on pp. 110–111.

7. Ibid., 117.

8. Ibid., 115, 156.

9. Ibid., 115.

20. U.S. Department of State, "The Military of El Salvador in its Moment of Crisis," telegram no. 07097 from U.S. Embassy, San Salvador, to Secretary of State, Washington, D.C., 11 December 1979, 1–2, in *The Making of U.S. Policy: El Salvador 1977–1984,* National Security Archive, document no. 00314. Also noted in Byrne (1996, 56).

21. Karl (1992, 149).

22. Sheehan (1989, 148).

23. *Economist,* 25 March 1989, 43.

24. In an interview for the video "Fire in the Mind," no. 9, in the *Americas* series, an Annenberg/CPB project broadcast by WGBH/Boston in 1993.

25. Similar scholarly assessments to those quoted just below are made by Wickham-Crowley (1989, 528); Byrne (1994, 166–167); Walter and Williams (1997, 3); and Dix (1984, 4). A similar assessment is also made by an official in the U.S. Department of State at the time. See Carothers (1991, 31).

26. Jung (1984, 82).

27. Midlarsky and Roberts (1985, 192).

28. Villalobos (1986, 8).

29. Fermán Cienfuegos, cited in Manwaring and Prisk (1988, 33).

30. Magaña, cited in ibid., 238.

31. Not all Peruvian analysts were pessimists. Among the Senderólogos, Raúl Gonzales was the optimist in the debates in the Peruvian media.

32. *Newsweek,* 19 August 1991, 29.

33. Enrique Obando, in an interview with *Peru Report* 7, no. 4 (May 1993): 2.

34. *New York Times,* 11 November 1991, A1.

35. *U.S. News and World Report,* 2 March 1992, 50. For a similar statement by Gorriti, see *La República,* 13 May 1990, 23. In an op-ed for *New York Times,* 24 August 1992, Gorriti similarly concludes his piece noting that the "defeat" of the Peruvian government is "a horrifying but distinct possibility." In *New York Times,* 28 September 1992, 48, Gorriti describes the Shining Path as "close to victory."

36. Carlos Iván Degregori, in his opening words for the talk "The Future of Peru's Shining Path," at the George Washington University Seminar on Andean Culture and Politics, 18 November 1993.

37. Luis Pásara, "Razones para no volver," *Caretas,* 7 December 1995, 33.

38. *Caretas,* 14 October 1991, 12. Poll was by IMASEN.

39. *New York Times,* 1 August 1992, 1.

40. *La República,* 24 October 1992, 16. The quotation is from Strong's interview with a Peruvian journalist.

41. McCormick (1990, 5). McCormick forecast that "If present trends continue, we're looking at a Sendero Luminoso takeover in the next 5 to 10 years" to

10. Ibid., 155.

11. See, especially, ibid., 155–157, where Skocpol presents a table summarizing her argument.

12. Ibid., 14–15.

13. Ibid., 16–33. Although Skocpol departs from Tilly in her emphasis on the state, in other respects Skocpol follows scholarly paths broken by Tilly a few years earlier. Tilly (1973) adamantly criticizes theorists who perceive social, psychological, and economic variables as important to revolution, and argues that political variables are primary. Advancing historical analysis as an appropriate methodology for the understanding of revolution, Tilly (1978) seeks to specify contending power groups' interests, degrees of organization, amounts of resources, and opportunities and threats from the government and other groups.

14. Goodwin and Skocpol (1989, 495–497).

15. Ibid., 496–497.

16. Ibid., 498. The term "neopatrimonial" was first coined by Eisenstadt (1978, 271) to describe regimes or "centers" that increasingly came to monopolize power and political resources, "allowing little independent access to broader groups . . . with only minimal attempts . . . to create social institutions." The concept "sultanistic" originated in Linz (1975), a comprehensive analysis of subtypes of authoritarian regimes.

17. Goodwin and Skocpol (1989, 498–499).

18. Ibid., 490.

19. Dix (1984, 432–438).

20. Wickham-Crowley (1992, 92–130).

21. Blasier (1967, 33).

22. Ibid., 33–34.

23. Ibid., 51.

24. Ibid., 39.

25. Huntington (1968, 275).

26. Ibid., 289.

27. Ibid., 297–303.

28. Ibid., 308.

29. Of course, Skocpol's 1979 study is about social revolutions that occurred prior to the Cold War. Skocpol emphasizes defeats in war as the primary kind of international pressure. However, she did not examine whether or not the external defeat that was an important factor in state breakdown in her three cases also appeared to be relevant in other cases. Goldstone (1986, 16) contends that the relationship between defeat in war and revolution was "virtually nil" during the seventeenth and eighteenth centuries.

30. Goodwin and Skocpol (1989, 498–499); and Wickham-Crowley (1992, 316–325).

31. Wickham-Crowley (1992, 52–54, 184–206).

32. Timothy Wickham-Crowley emphasized this point in a lecture at George Washington University, 19 February 1992.

33. Dix (1984, 438–442); Wickham-Crowley (1989, 528–530); and Midlarsky and Roberts (1985, 191–192).

34. Both Walton (1984, 13) and Booth (1991, 33–34) use the concept of "national revolt." It is defined as "protracted, intermittently violent, nonlocal struggles [with extensive] mobilization of classes and status groups that become recognized claimants of rival sovereignty and engage the state."

35. To my knowledge, this point is made first by Goldstone (1980, 450–451).

36. Davidheiser (1992, 464).

37. Colburn (1994, 42).

38. Gurr (1970, 334–335).

39. Ibid., 24.

40. Ibid., 130–133.

41. Ibid., 46–50.

42. Tutino (1986, 371).

43. Seligson (1996, 135).

44. Muller and Seligson (1987), among other articles.

45. Wickham-Crowley (1989, 528); Dix (1984, 441); and Midlarsky and Roberts (1985, 192).

46. Skocpol (1979, 15–18).

47. Desai and Eckstein (1990, 454–459).

48. Selbin (1993, 139).

49. Wickham-Crowley (1992, 130–153, 324–325).

50. Darhi (1988); and Farhi (1990, 83–101).

51. Walton (1984, 13).

52. Collier and Collier (1991, 12–15).

53. Collier and Collier (1991, 14) point out that "the claim that two countries are similar or different with regard to a particular attribute does not, and is not intended to, assign them the overall status of being similar or different cases."

54. For a thoughtful elaboration of this distinction, emphasizing the possibility of "process tracing" within individual cases, see George and McKeown (1985, 23–24, 54).

55. See Skocpol and Somers (1980, 184–185); and Wickham-Crowley (1992, 14–15) for a discussion of what they both call the "method of difference" in "macro-causal analysis." Various revolutionary movements began in Ecuador

(including the Sol Rojo that hoped to emulate Sendero Luminoso), but did not expand.

56. In 1988, Bolivian GNP per capita was estimated at $570, versus $1,120 for Ecuador and $1,300 for Peru; the percentage of GDP in manufacturing was 17 percent in Bolivia, versus 21 percent in Ecuador and 24 percent in Peru; adult illiteracy was estimated at 26 percent in Bolivia, 18 percent in Ecuador, and 15 percent in Peru. See World Bank (1990, 178–182).

57. The data from both these institutions are the data most frequently cited by scholarly analysts. Both are primary data sources for Americas Watch. For its annual reports on human rights in the late 1980s and early 1990s, the U.S. Department of State relied on the figures of the Bernales Commission as well as the National Human Rights Coordinating Committee (Coordinadora Nacional de Derechos Humanos). The work of the Bernales Commission is discussed in Americas Watch (1992, 13); the work of Tutela Legal is discussed in Congressional Research Service (1989, 77–91).

58. Huntington (1968, 264).

59. Skocpol (1979, 4).

60. Mostafa Rejai, quoted in ibid., 55.

61. Valuable discussions of this question from a current perspective are found in Rueschemeyer, Stephens, and Stephens (1992, 9–11); and Stephens (1990, 160).

62. Dahl (1971, 2–10).

63. See, for example, Jacobs and Shapiro (1994); and Conaghan (1994, 7).

64. See, for example, O'Donnell (1993); Diamond, Linz, and Lipset (1989, xvi); Di Palma (1990, 126); Przeworksi (1991, 10); Inkeles (1991); Weiner (1987, 4); Carothers (1991, 7–8); Mainwaring (1992, 297–298); and Peeler (1985, 5).

65. Huntington (1991, 7).

66. One of the few recent works that begins an examination of these questions is Inkeles (1991).

67. Karl (1990, 2); emphasis added. See also Diamond, Linz, and Lipset (1989, xvi); and Reuschemeyer, Stephens, and Stephens (1992, 43), among many others.

68. Pion-Berlin (1992); and Fitch (1995). These scholars' indicators are discussed in chapter 3.

69. See Carothers (1991, 243–248).

2. Two Revolutionary Organizations

1. Among the analyses of the MRTA, see especially McCormick (1993) and Degregori (1997). For the views of MRTA leader Víctor Polay Campos, see his interview with Tomás Borge in *Caretas*, 9 December 1991, 40–43.

2. The percentages are the author's calculation from data in Comisión Especial de Estudio e Investigación sobre Terrorismo y Otras Manifestaciones de la Violencia (1990).

3. On the FMLN, see especially Baloyra (1982, 64–74; 1990); Barry (1990, 59–61); Byrne (1996); Dunkerley (1983; 1988); Montgomery (1982, 119–157; 1995, 101–126); Leiken (1984); López Vigil (1994, 23); Pearce (1986, 124–139); Prisk (1991); and Zaid (1982). Among valuable newspaper articles, see *New York Times*, 11 July 1982, 3.

4. Quoted from a 1982 Cayetano Carpio statement by Pearce (1986, 125). For background information about Carpio and the other major leaders mentioned in this section, see chapter 6.

5. *New York Times*, 27 February 1981, 8.

6. Harnecker (1993) is the definitive sympathetic work on the FPL. See also Pearce (1986, 124–130).

7. Possibly, the FPL itself sought to establish the BPR.

8. On the number of members, see Dunkerley (1988, 372); and *New York Times*, 27 May 1979, 3.

9. See, especially, Pearce (1986, 130–134); Dunkerley (1988, 370); and Byrne (1996, 34).

10. Miguel Castellanos in Prisk (1991, 37). As, having moved to the right, Castellanos criticizes the revolutionary groups, there is no apparent reason to doubt the sincerity of his perception.

11. Joaquín Villalobos, "Peace and Reconciliation in El Salvador: Lessons Learned" (speech presented at conference, U.S. Army War College, Carlisle, Pa., 8 September 1994). (Translation by author.)

12. Fenton Communications (1984, 13); and López Vigil (1994, 42).

13. See discussion below and in chapter 6.

14. Apparently, many of these were members whose original affiliation had been to the Christian Democratic Party. See Dunkerley (1983, 139).

15. Montgomery (1995, 105).

16. Dunkerley (1983, 129).

17. Pearce (1986, 131–134) is especially valuable on the ideological differences among the groups.

18. Ibid.

19. Harnecker (1993, 328); and Manwaring and Prisk (1988, 76–77).

20. On the FDR, see Dunkerley (1988, 396–398); and Barry (1990, 62).

21. See, for example, FDR criticisms of a 1985 FMLN attack in *New York Times*, 30 June 1985, 3; and 24 August 1985, 2. Differences about the correct policy for Salvadoran elections were heated during the 1989 presidential contest, which

the FMLN boycotted despite participation by the Democratic Convergence (which included many FDR members).

22. On Carpio's personality, ambition, and conflict with other revolutionary leaders, see Bonasso and Gómez Leyva (1992, 71–75); Harnecker (1993, 333–334); Prisk (1991, 49–50); and Moroni Bracamonte and Spencer (1995, 15–16).

23. See, especially, Byrne (1996, 80–81); Moroni Bracamonte and Spencer (1995, 17–21); Leiken (1983, 117); Prisk (1991, 29–32); and Castañeda (1994, 355–356).

24. With respect to the FPL's attitude, see Prisk (1991, 29–32); on the RN, see Moroni Bracamonte and Spencer (1995, 19), citing an FPL source.

25. Montgomery (1995, 113).

26. Estimates on the number of marchers are from *New York Times*, 27 January 1980, sec. 4, 3, and Dunkerley (1988, 146).

27. U.S. embassy assessment, reported in Byrne (1995, chap. 3, 4). In an interview on 27 October 1995 in Washington, D.C., however, Byrne indicated that he believes the U.S. estimate was somewhat high.

28. Handal in Bonasso and Gómez Leyva (1992, 35).

29. Villalobos (1986, 8). During his speech at the U.S. Army War College in Carlisle, Pennsylvania, on 8 September 1994, Villalobos also said: "1980 was the moment for popular insurrection, but the FMLN wasn't even formed yet. Actions were only civilian protest, and there was no good revolutionary effort."

30. Gerson Martínez, cited by Byrne (1996, 67).

31. The discussion by Byrne (1996, 66–68) is especially thoughtful. See also Pearce (1986, 193–194).

32. On the increase in unity after Carpio's death, see Clements (1984, 124); Leiken (1984, 123); Baloyra (1990, 496); and *New York Times*, 25 September 1983, 4. On the events themselves, see Harnecker (1993, 334–335); Radu and Tismaneanu (1990, 197); and Prisk (1991, 48–52).

33. LeMoyne (1989, 113); Leiken (1984, 115, 120); and Prisk (1991, 37, 51–56).

34. López Vigil (1994, 107), speaking of Villalobos as "Atilio." López Vigil was on the Radio Venceremos staff.

35. Clements (1984, 124). Raúl Hercules was a midlevel FMLN commander.

36. Unidentified guerrilla leader cited in *New York Times*, 11 July 1982, 3. For criticisms of *caciquismo* among the commanders, see Colonel Orlando Zepeda in Manwaring and Prisk (1988, 371); and Miguel Castellanos in Prisk (1991, 28). My own assessment is based in part on interviews with Salvador Cortes, FMLN representative in Washington, 6 June 1995; and Hugh Byrne, 15 June 1995, Washington, D.C.

37. San Salvador Radio Senorial, 25 April 1980, printed in *Foreign Broadcast Information Service: Central America*, 29 April 1980, P3. For an emphasis on political vices on other occasions during the early 1980s, see also a communiqué by striking workers, 22 February 1980, in *Foreign Broadcast Information Service: Central America,* 22 February 1980, P4; and ERP demands indicated in *Foreign Broadcast Information Service: Central America,* 14 January 1980, P8.

38. ERP, on San Salvador Radio Cadena Sonora, printed in *Foreign Broadcast Information Service: Central America,* 20 May 1980, P8.

39. A report live from San Salvador on San José Radio Noticias del Continente, reported in *Foreign Broadcast Information Service: Central America,* 15 December 1980, P6–P7. The communiqué was signed by all five FMLN commanders of that period. It is referred to again in *Le Monde,* 9 January 1981, 7. See *Foreign Broadcast Information Service,* 12 January 1981, P13.

40. Interviews with Carpio in Mexico City and in Havana, reported in *Foreign Broadcast Information Service: Central America,* 18 January 1980, P4; and *Foreign Broadcast Information Service: Central America,* 2 January 1981, P5.

41. Villalobos (1983, 52). See also similar statements by the RN's "Fermán Cienfuegos," cited in Barry (1990, 63).

42. "Roberto Roca," *New York Times,* 18 March 1982, A16.

43. Villalobos (1983, 52).

44. See my discussion in chapter 6.

45. Villalobos (1992, front matter).

46. See, for example, Villalobos (1983, 1986, 1989, and 1992) and Harnecker (1989). In author's discussion with Hugh Byrne, 20 August 1995, in Washington, D.C., Byrne mentioned Villalobos's advocacy of Marxism in meetings with other leftists.

47. The article in question is "A Democratic Revolution for El Salvador," in the spring 1989 issue of *Foreign Policy.* For a discussion of the extent to which the article represented Villalobos's actual views at the time, see Massing (1989, 56).

48. *New York Times,* 26 January 1982, A4.

49. *New York Times,* 28 January 1982, A12.

50. For discussions of FPL ideology, see Dunkerley (1988, 370).

51. For such references by FPL leaders, see Harnecker (1993, 64–66, 200). For the use of Marxist terms by FPL peasants in Chalatenango, see Pearce (1986, 157).

52. "Salvador," in Harnecker (1993, 352). For similar comments, see also Harnecker (1993, 12, 112).

53. "Facundo," in Harnecker (1993, 157).

54. Apparently, six foreign businessmen were kidnapped by the RN in 1979 alone. See *New York Times,* 22 May 1979, 3.

55. Author's calculation from the annual reports of Tutela Legal.

56. My calculation from the data in Comisión Especial de Estudio e Investigación sobre Terrorismo y Otras Manifestaciones de la Violencia (1990, 45); and Comisión Especial de Investigación y Estudio sobre la Violencia y Alternativas de Pacificación (1991, 59).

57. For example, during 1989, mayors and numerous government officials were targeted; the FMLN's claims that they were military targets had no basis in international law.

58. Shenk (1988, 42) recounts Villalobos's affability at a New Year's Eve party on 31 December 1987 in Morazán.

59. See, in particular, the descriptions of FMLN grassroots organization in Guazapa by Clements (1984, 124, 155–160). He recounts an incident where a leader is asked to share power with two other commanders after he had covered up the execution of a health worker who had reportedly been a traitor to the FMLN.

60. Pearce (1986, 241–252); Berryman (1994, 76); Metzi (1988); and Alvarez (1988, 86–91).

61. Warren Hoge, "In a Rebel Stronghold in El Salvador," *New York Times,* 22 February 1982, A8.

62. *New York Times,* 22 February 1982, A8; and 26 January 1982, A1, A4; Montgomery (1995, 118–122); Pearce (1986, 252–288); ex-guerrilla María Chichilco interviewed in *New York Times,* 1 May 1995, A15; and my own observation in Morazán, April 1991.

63. Unfortunately, to date most of the accounts of the relationships between the FMLN and the Cuban and Nicaraguan governments have been by defectors or by the U.S. State and Defense Departments during the Reagan administration; it is not clear what flaws or biases may accordingly exist in these accounts. See, for example, Prisk (1991), based on interviews with top FPL leader Miguel Castellanos, who decided to collaborate with the Salvadoran government after his arrest in 1985. Roger Miranda, the source for most of the information in Miranda and Ratliff (1993), left Nicaragua in the late 1980s after serving as chief of the Sandinista Defense Ministry Secretariat and top aide to Defense Minister Humberto Ortega from 1982 to 1987.

64. Smyth (1989, 164), for 1988–89; and Manwaring and Prisk (1988, 474–475), for the early 1980s.

65. U.S. Department of State (1981, 7); and Castellanos in Prisk (1991, 37). However, the assertion by Castellanos in Prisk (1991, 25), that "the Cubans became the managers, and Nicaragua the warehouse and bridge," is an exaggeration.

66. On Cuban and Sandinista influence, see Miguel Castellanos in Prisk (1991, 54, 82); and Miranda and Ratliff (1993, 144–148). On resentment among the FMLN, see Clements (1984, 160).

67. Smyth (1992, 10). The article is based upon FMLN sources.

68. Miranda and Ratliff (1993, 138–140); Hager (1995); and Castañeda (1994, 97–98).

69. Castellanos in Prisk (1991, 63–64).

70. Ibid., 36–38. He does not specify the origins of the remaining 10 percent.

71. Congressional Research Service (1989, 105).

72. Montgomery (1995, 117–118).

73. Ibid.

74. Menzel (1994, 49).

75. Miranda and Ratliff (1993, 143–144); and Miguel Castellanos in Manwaring and Prisk (1988, 474–475). The decline is also mentioned by Smyth (1992, 10) in an article based on FMLN sources. Daniel Ortega admitted that arms shipments to the FMLN continued when he was at a Central America summit in 1987. See Dillon (1988–89, 156); and Robinson (1991, 88).

76. A letter from the FMLN to the Sandinista leadership requesting greater assistance is cited in U.S. Departments of Defense and State (1986, 52–53).

77. Miranda and Ratliff (1993, 147); and Dillon (1988–89, 156).

78. The appearance of surface-to-air missiles in El Salvador generated a great deal of controversy. See *Washington Post,* 26 October 1990, A29; 3 January 1991, A28; and 26 June 1991, A29.

79. *New York Times,* 16 February 1981, 1.

80. Smyth (1989, 164).

81. *New York Times,* 16 February 1981, 1.

82. On the West German donation, see Montgomery (1995, 117); the "Medical Aid for El Salvador" sum is from one of this group's own publications. See also Prisk (1991, 98).

83. Hugh Byrne, interview by author, Washington, D.C., 27 October 1995 (Byrne's statements reflected his interviews with FMLN leaders in El Salvador in mid–1995); and Salvador Cortes, conversation with author, Washington, D.C., 15 May 1997. On communications equipment, see Clements (1984, 125).

84. See Jackson (1989a, 1989b, and 1989c); Quinn (1989); and Rosenau (1994). On Pol Pot's role in the Khmer Rouge, see Jackson (1989c, 242).

85. On Pol Pot's visit, see Quinn (1989, 221–222). On Guzmán in China in 1975, see Lázaro (1990, 246).

86. On the Khmer Rouge, see Quinn (1989, 219–223); and Jackson (1989b, 38–39, 48, 62, 74).

87. Quinn (1989, 217); Jackson (1989a, 7); and Jackson (1989b, 51, 72).

88. Quinn (1989, 232)

89. Ibid., 237–238.

90. Ibid., 217, 232–233.

91. The definitive work on Guzmán's leadership is Gorriti (1990a).

92. *New York Times,* 18 October 1992, 19.

93. *El Diario* (the Shining Path's newspaper), no. 627 (March 1993): 6, 9. Reprinted in English in *Foreign Broadcast Information Service: Latin America,* 19 April 1993, 40–41.

94. Degregori (1990a, 1990/1991); Gorriti (1990c, 18–19); Poole and Rénique (1992, 30–34); and Palmer (1995, 251–252).

95. The Shining Path's most readily available publications include Comité Central Partido Comunista del Perú (1982, 1985); and Arce Borja and Talavera Sánchez (1988). For informed commentaries on Guzmán's ideology, see Degregori (1990a, 174–212); Gorriti (1990a, 129–143); Harding (1988); Mauceri (1991a); and Wheat (1990). On Maoism, see Schram (1969); Terrill (1980); and Wheat (1990, 42–45).

96. Lázaro (1990, 246) is the only available source that provides precise dates. See also Gorriti (1990c, 18).

97. Lázaro (1990); Harding (1988, 70); and Strong (1992, 16).

98. Wheat (1990, 42–45); and Harding (1988, 71).

99. Partido Comunista del Perú (1985, 2).

100. Partido Comunista del Perú (1982, 2–4); and Arce Borja and Talavera Sánchez (1988, 29–32).

101. Partido Comunista del Perú (1982, 27); and Arce Borja and Talavera Sánchez (1988, 9). On Maoist strategy, see Schram (1969, 290–292).

102. Degregori (1990b, 6–7).

103. Arce Borja and Talavera Sánchez (1988, 23–35).

104. *Sí,* 23–30 April 1990, 24–26; *Caretas,* 11 February 1991, 33; *La República,* 19 September 1992, 12. See also *Foreign Broadcast Information Service: Latin America,* 5 October 1992, 37–39.

105. *La República,* 14 September 1992, 12–13; *New York Times,* 14 September 1992, A8; *New York Times,* 20 November 1992, A3.

106. *La República,* 27 September 1992, 3; *La República,* 23 September 1992, 5; and interview with Shining Path commander "Tomás," in *Sí,* 5 October 1992, 32–33.

107. See, for example, Arce Borja and Talavera Sánchez (1988); and a Luis Arce Borja interview in *Expreso,* 10 November 1991, A13. For scholarly discussion, see Instituto de Defensa Legal (1992, 40–43); and Palmer (1994).

108. See numerous statements by Enrique Obando in *Newsweek,* 19 August 1991, 29, as well as McCormick (1992, viii); and *Newsweek,* 3 August 1992, 40. For a general discussion, see Palmer (1994, 3; 1995, 265–267).

109. *Los Angeles Times,* 4 December 1988, part 5, 1. Even midlevel Shining Path militants scorned Moscow, Havana, and Managua. See *Newsweek,* 24 April 1989, 45.

110. Partido Comunista del Perú (1982, 10).

111. Ibid.; and Anderson (1987, 28).

112. Gorriti (1990b, 19); and Anderson (1987, 29).

113. See, for example, *Washington Post,* 6 July 1989, A20. In this 1989 attack, thirty-three Soviet seamen were injured.

114. Partido Comunista del Perú (1985, 7–8).

115. Arce Borja and Talavera Sánchez (1988, 33).

116. See, especially, Starn (1995, 414–415).

117. Mitchell (1991, 197); Berg (1986–7, 187–188); Manrique (1989, 162–169); Flores Galindo (1987, 33); Montoya (1992); Brown and Férnandez (1991, 202–216); Taylor (1983, 20); and Strong (1992, 61).

118. Degregori (1990a, 205) reports that in no document does Sendero even mention ethnic problems in Peru; the country appears to be as ethnically homogeneous as Japan. When it gained control of a community, Sendero often prohibited religious festivals and pressured for the resignation of community authorities. See Gianotten, de Wit, and de Wit (1985, 194–195).

119. Terrill (1980, 151); and Schram (1969, 290–291).

120. Mauceri (1991a, 220–221).

121. Arce Borja and Talavera Sánchez (1988, 10–13). See also virtually any other Shining Path publication.

122. Partido Comunista del Perú (1982, 2).

123. Partido Comunista del Perú (1987, 10).

124. *Caretas,* 20 September 1982, 64.

125. My calculation from statistics in DESCO (1989, 43); Comisión Especial de Investigación y Estudio sobre Terrorismo y Otra Manifestaciones de la Violencia (1990, 45); Comisión Especial de Estudio e Investigación sobre la Violencia y Alternativas de Pacificación (1991, 59); and *PerúPaz* 2, no. 7 (January 1993): 12. Although the data appear to be from different sources, Senator Enrique Bernales was the chief compiler in all cases. From the figures in these sources, I count 2,073 security force victims of Sendero and 12,481 total victims between 1980 and 1992.

126. Ibid., except for the number of ecclesiastics and foreign development workers. Only in some of the sources are the victims specifically attributed to Sendero Luminoso, but a comparison of the tables in the various sources indicates that Sendero was responsible for the overwhelming majority of the victims classified as civilians. Victims killed by security force personnel were almost invariably classified as "presumed subversives." Some sources give higher figures. See, for example, the statistic of 575 municipal authorities murdered in *Latin America Weekly Report,* 23 July 1992, 4. Figure for ecclesiastics from Rosenau and Flanagan (1992, 83); figure for foreign development workers from *Washington Post,* 18 August 1991, A30. Figure includes the three Japanese engineers killed on the north coast in 1991.

127. Guillermoprieto (1993, 70); and Daniels (1990, 10).

128. Interviews with various analysts from Huancayo. See also Daniels (1990, 2).

129. Leger (1989, 3).

130. César Rodriguez Rabanal, cited by Leger (1989, 3).

131. Michael Smith, interview by author, Washington, D.C., 3 May 1989.

132. See chapter 6 for detailed discussion.

133. The head of the Tingo Maria Settlers' Association, in an interview published in *Los Angeles Times,* 5 March 1989, 1.

134. "Trend Report," *Peru Report* 8, no. 4 (May 1994): 2. Consider too the statements by "Comrade Tania" in *Expreso,* 12 May 1992, A11; and by Nicario in Degregori and Ricci (1990, 201).

135. Gonzales (1987, 35); and Rénique (1994, 240). A similar assassination of a former mayor sparked the expulsion of Sendero from Huancasancos, a village in the southern highlands, in 1983. See Bonner (1988, 44–45).

136. A medical worker in Huancasancos in Peru's southern highlands, cited by Bonner (1988, 41). See also Isbell (1992, 77).

137. Juan Pablo Rosas Mesías in *Expreso,* 15 December 1989, 10.

138. *La República,* 27 September 1992, 5; and Arce Borja and Talavera Sánchez (1988, 7). See also Gorriti (1990a, 349–357); and McCormick (1992, 11–15).

139. Quechua (1994, 170–180); Palmer (1995, 267–270); Tarazona-Sevillano (1990, 55–78).

140. See the photographs of the Senderista inmates at Canto Grande prison, dressed as Red Guards, in *Caretas,* 30 July 1991, 1, 34–39. These Senderista practices can also be viewed on several videotapes. See the "Fire in the Mind" segment of the *Americas* series (WGBH/Boston, 1993). See also Malcomson (1987); Bonner (1988); and *New York Times,* 10 July 1991, A4.

141. Bonner (1988, 42).

142. Kirk (1992, 18).

143. Kirk (1991, 18).

144. Alonso Cueto in *Wall Street Journal,* 9 October 1992, A15. See also the comments by Carlos Iván Degregori in Leger (1989, 3).

145. *La República,* 19 September 1992, 12; *Expreso,* 16 September 1992, A10; Strong (1992, xiv–xv); and Kirk (1992, 18).

146. Gorriti (1992, 162–164).

147. Kirk (1991, 554); and Tarazona-Sevillano (1990, 70–71).

148. Tarazona-Sevillano (1990, 70–71); Vivanco (1992, 2); *Expreso,* 20 September 1992, 3; *Sí,* 21 April 1991, 27; and *Foreign Broadcast Information Service: Latin America,* 1 October 1992, 23.

149. *El Comercio,* 16 September 1992, A12; *Expreso,* 17 September 1992, A13; *La República,* 23 September 1992, 13; and 25 October 1992, 4–5.

150. *La República,* 27 September 1992, 5; and *Foreign Broadcast Information Service: Latin America,* 1 October 1992, 23.

151. *Caretas,* 25 February 1991, 33–34; and "Political Report," *Peru Report* 6, no. 11 (December 1992): 2.

152. Quechua (1994, 129 and 242). See also *La República,* 27 September 1992, 5; *Caretas,* 4 March 1991, 32–33; and *Expreso,* 21 September 1992, A5.

153. For versions of this chart, see *Expreso,* 21 September 1992, 17; *La República,* 27 September 1992, 5; and Tarazona-Sevillano (1990, 55–78).

154. For a list of the names of the Central Committee members as of approximately 1989, see Quechua (1994, 242).

155. See the sources in note 152.

156. My research team did not specify precisely whom we meant by "Sendero leaders," so the respondents' report is subjective. On the interviews, see appendix I.

157. *El Comercio,* 9 October 1992, A13. See also Guillermoprieto (1993, 71), as well as Palmer (1995, 268), who suggests greater local autonomy.

158. *Caretas,* 25 February 1991, 33.

159. *Economist,* 19 September 1992, 53.

160. *Caretas,* 30 May 1988, 30. The statement is from a captured Senderista commander interviewed by *Caretas.* Also cited by Tarazona-Sevillano (1990, 58). See also the discussion in *El Comercio,* 9 October 1992, A13.

161. This paragraph is based upon Tarazona-Sevillano (1990, 62–70); and *La República,* 22 September 1992, 16–17. See also *Foreign Broadcast Information Service: Latin America,* 2 October 1992.

162. Consider, for example, the vast array identified in *La República,* 22 September 1992, 16–17. Also reported in *Foreign Broadcast Information Service: Latin America,* 2 October 1992, 37–43.

163. McCormick (1990, 22) estimates $20 to $30 million; another estimate by a U.S. analyst, Stephen G. Trujillo, was $15 to $100 million (*New York Times,* 8 April 1992, A25). Gonzales Manrique (1989, 217) estimates $20 million to $100 million. An estimate of $30 million is found in *Economist,* 19 September 1992, 53; and $40 million in *U.S. News and World Report,* 28 September 1992, 49. The $550 million figure was the estimate of a Peruvian admiral, based on his knowledge of airstrip fees in the Upper Huallaga Valley, in his testimony to the Peruvian congress. See *Latin America Weekly Report,* 24 January 1991, 1. Senderistas admitted the link between the guerrilla organization and drug traffickers. See the interviews with militants in *Caretas,* 7 September 1987, 36; and *Caretas,* 30 May 1988, 32.

164. *La República,* 17 September 1992, 13–15.

165. *La República,* 4 October 1992, 3.

166. The amount of $500 per month is cited in *New York Times,* 26 June 1991, A8; the range of $250 to $500 was suggested in the interviews I conducted in Lima. See also *Expreso,* 15 December 1989, 20, for an interview with an ex-Senderista, in which he says "I lacked nothing." Chapter 6 discusses comments by the thirty-three Senderistas interviewed by Osores on this issue.

167. *Expreso,* 29 July 1990, 8; *La República,* 27 May 1992, 22; *Newsweek,* 24 April 1989, 45; and *Caretas,* 30 May 1988, 32. Weapons were also seized from the police and military, especially before 1986.

168. *Expreso,* 19 September 1992, A12.

169. *Economist,* 25 March 1989, 43; Washington Office on Latin America (1990, 2). García (1989, B280) suggests only sixty-five hundred by early 1987.

170. The 10,000 figure is offered by Colonel James Steele in Manwaring and Prisk (1988, 146, 362); and by Wickham-Crowley (1992, 211). Barry (1990, 60) suggests a peak figure of 12,000; García (1989, B280) indicates 11,000 in 1984; the U.S. Department of State (1984, 7) suggests a range of 9,000 to 11,000 for 1984 (up from a mere 2,000 in 1979–80). Lower estimates, in the 6,000 range, are given by Leiken (1984, 118); and Radu and Tismaneanu (1990, 207).

171. LeMoyne (1989, 114).

172. Bailetti (1990, 23); McCormick (1990, 3); Palmer (1995, 270); *Washington Post,* 27 November 1991, A22; *Washington Post,* 31 August 1992, A14; *Newsweek,* 19 August 1991, 29; and *El Diario de la Nación,* 21 May 1992, 1.

173. Palmer (1995, 270); Enrique Bernales cited in the *Latin America Weekly Report,* 15 August 1991, 10; and Carlos Tapia in *Christian Science Monitor,* 31 July 1992, 4.

174. Estimates varied from approximately five thousand to twenty thousand. See *New York Times,* 16 August 1992, editorial page.

175. Said police chiefs to journalists from the *Peru Report* in early 1992: "Sendero strength is growing so fast, including among the middle class, that mentioning our estimate of the number of militants would just frighten the public." "Political Report," *Peru Report* 6, no. 2 (March 1992): 3.

176. Tapia (1997, 112). The figures excluded the Upper Huallaga Valley, for which Guzmán did not have data.

177. Ibid., 111–112.

178. "Trend Report," *Peru Report* 8, no. 4 (May 1994): 1.

179. "Special Report," *Peru Report* 7, no. 9 (October 1993): 2.

180. *New York Times,* 8 April 1992, A25. Emphasis added.

181. *Le Monde,* 21 August 1991, 7.

182. Ansión, Del Castillo, Piqueras, and Zegarra (1992). See also *New York Times,* 30 August 1992, 8. Michael Smith, an analyst of Sendero in Lima's shanty towns, estimated that Senderistas held one hundred positions just in the secondary schools located on the central highway outside of Lima. See *Foreign Broadcast Information Service,* 9 January 1991, 37.

183. "Politics 1," *Peru Report* 2, no. 5 (May 1988): sec. 7, 1.

184. Of course, a considerable number of the "assumed terrorists" were actually civilians, and many political prisoners were innocent. Data on death toll for assumed terrorists from *PerúPaz* 2, no. 7 (January 1993): 13; data on number of political prisoners and "repentants" from *Latin America Weekly Report,* 9 June 1994, 244.

185. *Proceso* 11, no. 457 (December 1990): 18.

186. COPREFA (Public Affairs Office of the Salvadoran Military), "Recopilación de datos de la fracasada ofensiva del FMLN" (San Salvador, 1990, mimeographed).

187. See also Benítez Manaut (1989, 342); CINAS (1988, 10–11); and Berryman (1990, B244–B255).

188. See the discussion of this issue in Martín-Baró (1987, 89).

189. About half the total respondents did not answer; the question seemed to incite indignation for some, who dismissed out of hand the concept that the FMLN could have any actual support, and fear for others. On the surveys, see appendix I.

190. *New York Times,* 19 March 1982, A12.

191. Martín-Baró (1987, 113–116); Martín-Baró (1989, 153–156); and Instituto Universitario de Opinión Pública (1991, 3).

192. LeMoyne (1989, 114); and Leonel Gómez in an interview with the author in San Salvador, 19 August 1990. LeMoyne was a journalist for the *New York Times* covering El Salvador during the late 1980s; Gómez was an agrarian reform activist who returned to El Salvador in approximately 1990.

193. This paragraph draws primarily upon the interviews with Miguel Castellanos in Prisk (1991, 71–82); Miles and Ostertag (1991, 220); and Menzel (1994, 56–60).

194. Dunkerley (1988, 146); and Byrne (1996, 62).

195. During this period the FMLN claimed one million sympathizers and one hundred thousand militia members. See Leiken (1984, 118). A million sympathizers would be about half the adult population. See also Berryman (1994, 71).

196. See the reports on Salvadoran citizens' attitudes in *Washington Post,* 26 November 1990, 1; and "Editorial: Recrudecimiento de la violencia en El Salvador," *Estudios Centroamericanos* 480 (October 1988): 874–876.

197. Miguel Castellanos in Prisk (1991, 71).

198. Martín-Baró (1987, 89–96).

199. Ibid., 68–69; and Martín-Baró (1989, 65). See also "Editorial: Recrudecimiento de la violencia," 874–876. Menzel (1994, 80, 87) reports that, in a poll of forty-nine families in San Salvador by *New York Times* journalist James LeMoyne, after the November 1989 offensive, "all blamed the FMLN guerrillas for causing their suffering."

200. Carmen Rosa Balbi, "A Disturbing Opinion Poll," *QueHacer* 72 (July–August 1991): 40–45. The article was published in full in *Foreign Broadcast Information Service: Latin America,* 18 October 1991, 33–38.

201. Ibid.

202. *QueHacer* 72 (July–August 1991): 41.

203. Ibid.

204. Ibid.

205. *F.A.S. Public Interest Report* 45, no. 4 (July–August 1992): 9.

206. *Caretas,* 14 October 1991, 13. This position was construed as support for Sendero in the version in *Latin America Weekly Report,* 24 October 1991, 12.

207. *Caretas,* 1 October 1992, 14–15.

208. Berg (1986–87, 186); Starn (1991); Mitchell (1991, 196); Isbell (1992, 61–64); and Bonner (1988, 44–45). See chapter 6 for discussion of the reasons for peasant support in these areas. Approximately three hundred thousand people turned out for the funeral of Sendero leader Edith Lagos in Ayacucho in 1982 (Bonilla [1994, 24]). See also González (1982, 47).

209. *Andean Report* 10 (March 1984): 47.

210. Strong (1992, 109).

211. *Expreso,* 5 February 1993, A10. Also published in *Foreign Broadcast Information Service: Latin America,* 19 February 1993, 41.

212. "Political Report," *Peru Report* 6, no. 1 (February 1992): 3.

213. Manrique (1989, 158–162).

214. Unfortunately, no analysis can be made of pro-Sendero voting, because in Peru ballots are destroyed at the electoral tables after they are tallied.

215. Webb and Fernández Baca (1991, 1021). There was greater effort to provide security for the presidential elections than for the municipal, and Sendero also seemed to target municipal elections more aggressively. Still, in the 1990 presidential elections the rates of absenteeism and invalid balloting in Ayacucho, Huánuco, and Junín were almost twice the nationwide average. See Webb and Fernández Baca (1991, 1028–1030).

216. Tuesta Soldevilla (1987, 189–193, 207–212).

217. *New York Times,* 15 January 1990, A11; 11 November 1991, A6; and 10 December 1991, A9.

218. Just in the central highlands during the first four months of 1991, two hundred teachers resigned. See *La República,* 12 May 1991, 8–9. See also *Foreign Broadcast Information Service,* 12 May 1991, 35.

219. *Washington Post,* 21 April 1992, 1. García (1989, B280).

220. Estimates for the late 1980s and early 1990s by García (1989, B280); and by Antonio Orellana and David Holiday, Americas Watch representative in El Salvador, both interviewed in El Salvador in June 1991. In a government survey in 1991–92, 15 percent of El Salvador's municipalities were not surveyed as a result of security concerns. For the estimates for the early 1980s, see García (1985, 529); Shenk (1981, 13); LeMoyne (1989, 106); and Sharpe (1988, B276). Excellent maps of the FMLN's zones are provided in Shenk (1981, 13); Pearce (1986, viii); and Benítez Manaut (1989, 266–267). The most detailed description of the geography of the FMLN's control is Alvarez (1988, 85).

221. A list of the municipalities where the mayor was currently in exile was kindly provided to me by Dr. Barbara Stephenson, Second Secretary in the Political Section of the U.S. embassy, in June 1991. The list included forty-three municipal-

ities, or 16 percent of the 262 in El Salvador: eighteen in Morazán, sixteen in Chalatenango, six in San Miguel, six in La Unión, four in Usulután, two in Cabañas, and one in Cuscatlán. The list was reviewed by Antonio Orellana and David Holiday and considered accurate. Elections were not able to be held in about 20 percent of El Salvador's municipalities in 1984, but only in 6 to 8 percent in 1988 and 1989. See Baloyra (1985, 236); and García (1985, 529) for the 1984 elections, and Browning (1989, 11) for the 1988 and 1989 elections. During a period in 1989, however, the FMLN explicitly targeted mayors for assassination, and as many as one-third of Salvadoran municipalities were without resident mayors. See *Economist*, 14 January 1989, 41; and *Economist*, 25 March 1989, 37.

222. The most vivid descriptions of the FMLN's role and the people's response are Pearce (1986, 193–286); and Metzi (1988), both with respect to Chalatenango. With respect to Morazán, see López Vigil (1994, 225). I have visited towns in both departments. Pre-1994 electoral data do not indicate much difference in leftist partisanship between Chalatenango or Morazán and the nation as a whole, however, probably because the FMLN was not participating during these years. In the polarized context, residents of these departments who did vote were likely to be on the political right. In these departments, electoral turnout was relatively high, a pattern for which there is scant explanation. See chapter 3 for a discussion of irregularities in pre-1994 Salvadoran elections.

223. In the 1989 municipal elections, authorities were not renewed in 28 percent of Peru's electoral districts. See Rospigliosi (1992, 32–35); reprinted in English in *Foreign Broadcast Information Service: Latin America*, 12 May 1992, 36–40. In 1990, one-quarter of Peru's municipalities were officially without mayors, either because they had never been elected, because they had been assassinated, or because they had resigned. See *Sí*, no. 228, 30 June–6 July 1991, 26; and *La República*, 28 November 1990, 13–15. Forty of Peru's 183 provinces and 339 of its 1,772 districts were without authorities.

224. Figure from Gustavo Gorriti, *New York Times*, 24 August 1992, A15. See also Palmer (1995, 298). The annual reports of IDL include excellent maps that show the expansion of Sendero action. See Instituto de Defensa Legal (1990, 15); and Instituto de Defensa Legal (1991, 11).

225. Gustavo Gorriti, *New York Times*, 13 January 1991, A5; and Strong (1992, front matter). Gordon McCormick estimated 25 to 40 percent in his testimony to the Subcommittee on Western Hemisphere Affairs, U.S. House of Representatives, 11 March 1992, 5. Gabriela Tarazona-Sevillano estimated 33 percent. See *New York Times*, 22 March 1992, 2.

226. For a description of Sendero's hegemony in Huancayo, see *New York Times*, 12 June 1989, sec. 1, 1. In a 1989 Datum poll in Lima, 68 percent of respondents believed that "the subversion" was the most powerful group in Ayacucho, and 61 percent that it was the most powerful group in the central highlands; most respon-

dents believed that the drug traffickers were the most powerful group in the Upper Huallaga Valley. Poll results were by courtesy of Datum.

227. For descriptions of Sendero's control, see *New York Times,* 27 July 1992, A5; and *Washington Post,* 16 February 1992, A51.

228. Rospigliosi (1992, 38). Data on the total number of districts in each department from Webb and Fernández Baca (1990, 26). Similar percentages are reported in *La República,* 28 November 1990, 13.

229. Eyzaguirre (1992, 178). For similar percentages for Huancayo and Jauja, see "Political Report," *Peru Report* 6, no. 1 (February 1992): 1. The highest estimate— 90 percent in Junín—is by Strong (1992, 193).

230. *Sí,* no. 123, 3–10 July 1989, 30.

231. Strong (1992, 193).

232. An outstanding discussion of FMLN strategy from 1980 through 1991 is Byrne (1996). See also Moroni Bracamonte and Spencer (1995); Miles and Ostertag (1991); and Smyth (1989).

233. Colonel James Steele, interviewed in Manwaring and Prisk (1988, 145).

234. The FDR, the PCS, and the PRTC were apparently at the forefront of discussions about the prospects for a negotiated settlement, even as of 1982. See *New York Times,* 28 February 1982, A6; 11 July 1982, 3; and 27 October 1982, A8.

235. See statements by Villalobos and González in Byrne (1996, 73–88). See also the comments by Miguel Castellanos in Prisk (1991, 40–41).

236. Sharpe (1988, B276); and Manwaring and Prisk (1988, 145).

237. *New York Times,* 5 September 1983, A1; and 6 September 1983, A3.

238. Moroni Bracamonte and Spencer (1995, 21).

239. Massing (1989, 56–57); Gibb and Smyth (1990, 7–11); and LeoGrande (1990, 336).

240. See the arguments in internal FMLN documents, including "Balance anual de la Comandancia General del FMLN al pueblo y la nación" (special edition by *Venceremos,* January 1989, mimeographed); "La guerra revolucionaria del pueblo" (FMLN Publications, 1987, mimeographed); and "Guía de trabajo para activistas de masas" (FMLN, January 1988, mimeographed). See also LeMoyne (1989, 112); Miles and Ostertag (1991, 228); Massing (1989, 56–57); and Gibb and Smyth (1990, 7–11). For some FMLN leaders, the guerrillas' approach had two tracks: either goal was acceptable, and the tactics for reaching each goal were the same in the short run. See Berryman (1994, 92). It is also possible that some commanders themselves were uncertain and that some statements were made for public relations purposes.

241. Shenk (1988, 42). Villalobos's view may or may not have evolved toward negotiations as the final objective by 1989. See LeoGrande (1990, 336); and Massing (1989, 56) for conflicting views.

242. Americas Watch (1989); and Washington Office on Latin America (1990). On the military dimension in other Latin American revolutions, see chapter 5.

243. Salvador Cortes, FMLN representative in Washington, D.C., interview by author, 6 June 1995. See also Handal's statement in Bonasso and Gómez Leyva (1992, 46).

244. Americas Watch (1989, 1).

245. Byrne (1996, 158–164) provides an excellent analysis of popular political attitudes at the time.

246. A point made especially well by Bolívar Ocampo (1993); and by Michael Smith in various interviews with the author, 1990–92.

247. Inca (1994, 57).

248. An excellent overview, including the views of pessimists and optimists at a series of roundtables on the advance of Sendero, appears in *Expreso*, 2 March 1991, 6–7; and 3 March 1991, 6–7. The expansion is well documented in annual statistics on guerrilla attacks by department, and on provinces declared in a "state of emergency." Also, the provinces declared in a "state of emergency" are mapped in Instituto de Defensa Legal (1990, 15; 1992, 15); and listed in *PerúPaz* 1, no. 6 (December 1992), 9.

249. González (1982); Degregori (1990a); Harding (1986); Berg (1986–87); and Gianotten, de Wit, and de Wit (1985).

250. González (1987a); Gonzales Manrique (1989); Instituto de Defensa Legal (1990, 57–74). See also *Caretas*, no. 976, 12 October 1987, 47–50; and "Las guerras de San Martín," *Ideéle* 4, no. 41 (September 1992): 8–13. As coca-growing extended eastward into the Ucayali department, it too was gradually affected. See Instituto de Defensa Legal (1992, 247–248).

251. An excellent analysis is Manrique (1989, 149–167). See also Instituto de Defensa Legal (1990, 79–94). In 1990, Sendero gained virtual total control of an eastern coca-crowing jungle sector of Junín, an area of some eighteen thousand square kilometers on the Ene River inhabited by the native Asháninka Indians. See Gorriti (1990b); and Instituto de Defensa Legal (1991, 166–167).

252. On the advance of Sendero in the late 1980s and early 1990s, see Rénique (1993, 14); *Expreso*, 5 June 1991, 4; and "La batalla per Puno," *Ideéle* 4, no. 39 (July 1992): 13–22. On the earlier political resistance to Sendero in Puno, see Rénique (1990); González (1986); and Gonzales Manrique (1987).

253. *Expreso*, 15 January 1991, 8; and 1 October 1991, 10; *Sur* 12, no. 120 (April 1989): 10–11; and Instituto de Defensa Legal (1992, 249–250).

254. *QueHacer* 73 (September–October 1991): 30–34.

255. *La República*, 1 September 1991, 4.

256. *Caretas*, 20 April 1992; and Smith (1992).

257. Kirk (1991, 556); Montoya and Reina (1992, 48–55); and Constable (1992, 2).

258. *Caretas,* 23 March 1992, 40–43.

259. The term "iron wall" was expressed by Montoya and Reina (1992, 34–55). "A giant pincer" was another description. See *La República,* 1 September 1991, 2. For further discussions and maps, see *Caretas,* 16 March 1992, 34–35; *Caretas,* 23 March 1992, 40–43; and *Caretas,* 20 April 1992. See also Smith (1992); and *Washington Post,* 16 February 1992, A51.

260. Instituto de Defensa Legal (1992, 39–72).

261. *Washington Post,* 9 February 1992, A19; *Washington Post,* 12 February 1992, A26; and *U.S. News and World Report,* 24 February 1992, 52.

262. Among the many accounts, see *Resumen Semanal* 15, nos. 658–659 (14 February–5 March 1992): 7–9; and *Andean Newsletter* 64 (9 March 1992): 4–5.

263. *New York Times,* 18 May 1992, A8.

264. *El Comercio,* 24 May 1992, A16; and *Washington Post,* 24 May 1992, A42.

265. *Andean Newsletter* 67 (June 1992): 6.

266. *Ideéle* 4, no. 40 (August 1992): 3; Gepp (1992, 10); *Latin America Weekly Report,* 30 July 1992, 1; and *New York Times,* 18 July 1992, 2.

267. *New York Times,* 23 July 1992, sec. 1, A11. An estimated one thousand apartment buildings lost windows during this period. See *New York Times,* 1 August 1992, sec. 1, 1.

268. On the "armed strike," see *Ideéle* 4, no. 40 (August 1992): 3–5; *Resumen Semanal* 15, no. 680 (24 July–4 August 1992): 2–3; and *New York Times,* 26 July 1992, sec. 1, 14, sec. 4, 2.

269. *New York Times,* 26 July 1992, sec. 1, 14.

270. Strong (1992, 266). Previous attacks had been primarily of the terrorist variety; the organization also used mortars.

271. Instituto de Defensa Legal (1990, 64); *Caretas,* no. 1051, 3 April 1989, 10–15, 84–85; *La República,* 9 April 1989, 10; *Resumen Semanal* 12, no. 511 (24–30 March 1989): 1; and *New York Times,* 8 April 1992, A25.

272. Instituto de Defensa Legal, *Informe mensual* 3, no. 21 (January 1991): 13–16; Strong (1992, 196–197); and *La República,* 6 January 1991, 10.

273. *Washington Post,* 16 February 1992, A51.

274. Bailetti Mackee (1992, 70).

275. Tapia (1992, 72).

276. Between 1988 and 1990, applications from Peruvians seeking visas to go to the United States as tourists nearly doubled; the refusal rate by the U.S. consulate (reflecting consular officers' judgments that the applicants wanted not to tour the United States but to stay there) also doubled, according to *New York Times,* 8 August 1990, A7. See also *New York Times,* 1 August 1992, sec. 1, 1.

277. *Washington Post,* 31 August 1992, A1. See also *Newsweek,* 3 August 1992, 40.

278. "Political and Economic Trend Report," *Peru Report* 6, no. 7 (July 1992): 3. This issue is discussed further in chapter 3.

279. *New York Times,* 24 August 1992, A15.

280. Obando (1993, 51) (translation by author). See also his statement in *Boston Sunday Globe,* 11 October 1992, 4.

281. "Enemy Colleagues" is the title of an article by a Mexican analyst: Zaid (1982).

282. Colonel James J. Steele, in 1986 interview in Manwaring and Prisk (1988, 363).

283. An excellent article that makes many of the points in this paragraph is Obando (1993).

284. *La República,* 19 September 1992, 12; Gustavo Gorriti, interview in *Expreso,* 17 February 1991, 5–7; and *Resumen Semanal* 14, no. 606 (1–7 February 1991): 6.

285. Gustavo Gorriti, interview by author, Washington, D.C., 14 September 1992. Gorriti contrasted the recklessness of Guzmán to the precautions taken by Haya de la Torre during the period when he was hunted by the Peruvian security forces. See also "Political Report," *Peru Report* 6, no. 8 (September 1992): 2. Guzmán had four bodyguards, but they did not have their weapons in their hands when the antiterrorist police entered.

286. This point is emphasized in *New York Times,* 14 September 1992, 1, A8; and in most other accounts of the capture, including, for example, Palmer (1995, 303).

287. Gustavo Gorriti, interview in *Expreso,* 17 February 1991, 5–7.

288. Of course, the analyses and photographs in the Peruvian press were legion. See, for example, *Sí,* 15–20 September 1992; *La República,* 20 September 1992; and the weekly news magazine *Domingo.*

289. *La República,* 19 September 1992, 12; and *Caretas,* 11 February 1993, 33.

290. Obando (1993, 50).

291. This was also Simon Strong's view. See *La República,* 24 October 1992, 17.

3. Political Trends

1. See chapter 1 for a discussion of the definition of democracy. Recall that conventional U.S.-based social science primarily applies the criteria of fair elections at regular intervals and open, nonviolent public contest at all times. Within the Latin American context, many scholars add the criterion of civilian control over the military.

2. As will become evident, "the left" was defined to include most political opponents of the regime, including Christian Democrats and religious and other leaders of popular organizations in El Salvador in the 1970s and early 1980s. The terms "military elites," "civilian elites," "oligarchy," "landowners," and the like will be used somewhat loosely in this chapter. The exact composition of "elites" and analytical issues about their formation of an "oligarchy" are important but beyond the scope of this chapter.

3. See chapter 2 for a chronology of the FMLN's growth.

4. For scholars' views on this point, see chapter 6.

5. Most scholars and journalists who are not country specialists assess democracy as a dichotomous variable—either a regime is democratic, or it is not—and tend to classify a regime as democratic if it holds an election, however unfree or unfair, or whatever the military's behind-the-scenes power. "Democracies" may be "threatened," "troubled," "low-intensity," or "delegative," but they are still "democracies." See Huntington (1991, 11–12); Diamond (1992, 26–27); Weiner (1987); Remmer (1991); Hughes and Mijeski (1984); O'Donnell (1993); and Lowenthal (1992–93). Consider, for example, the case of Colombia. Political violence is rampant—for example, during the mid-1980s, approximately five hundred members of the Marxist Patriotic Union, including a presidential candidate, were killed. In part for this reason, specialists on Colombia qualify the democratic label for the country if they use it at all. See, for example, Hartlyn (1989, 293); and Bagley (1990, 148). However, the country is routinely characterized as democratic in the comparative politics literature. See, for example, Huntington (1991, 15); Weiner (1987, 6); Karl (1990, 9–10); Diamond (1992, 31); Herman (1988); Stallings and Kaufman (1989, 205); Kline (1990); and Peeler (1985). One exception to this pattern is the annual survey *Freedom in the World.* Freedom House offers two seven-point scales: one for "political rights" (primarily rights to participate in the electoral process) and one for "civil liberties" (freedom to develop views, and individuals' autonomy from the state or other coercive groups). Freedom House itself does not try to assess actual conditions in the countries, but relies on the evaluation of a team of experts' scores for a checklist of items. Although Freedom House's methodology is relatively sophisticated, there are not standard thresholds that distinguish one nation's rating from another's. For example, for 1992–93 civil liberties were ranked at "3" in both Ecuador and El Salvador, but the respective explanations of the rankings were quite different. See Freedom House (1993, 77–85 and 210–218).

6. On the stamp of approval from the U.S. government, see U.S. Department of State (1984, 12); and U.S. Department of State (1987, 1–2). For positive scholarly assessments, see Huntington (1991, 15).

7. Werlich (1978, 59).

8. On the War of the Pacific, see Stern (1987, 213–326); Bonilla (1980, 177–225); Morner (1985, 53–157); Werlich (1978, 106–118); and Pike (1967, 139–150).

9. Comments Gilbert (1977, 35), for example: "A sense of national shame and anger over these events lingers to this day."

10. See, especially, Bonilla (1980, 177–225).

11. Werlich (1978, 167–174) suggests that Leguía signed the treaty with Colombia as a U.S.-imposed condition for U.S. mediation in a more positive way of the conflict between Peru and Chile.

12. See, especially, García (1982, 2–5).

13. This paragraph draws upon Williams (1994); García (1982); and Montgomery (1982, 40–43).

14. García (1983, 2–3).

15. Ibid., 13.

16. Thorp and Bertram (1978, 40).

17. Bourricaud, Bresani, Favre, and Piel (1969); Gonzales (1991); and Gilbert (1977, 77–79).

18. Estimates of population by region during the nineteenth century are not precise. However, the 1876 census indicates that about four times as many people lived in the highlands department of Puno or Cuzco than in Lambayeque, the coastal department that became home to much of Peru's sugar industry. See Larson and Bergman (1969, 299). Of course, the Incan Empire was based primarily in the highlands, and its seat was in the Andean department of Cuzco.

19. Morner (1985, 136–137); and Gilbert (1977, 34–42).

20. Gonzales (1991, 528–529), among many scholars.

21. The question of how hacendados expanded their holdings in the highlands deserves more systematic research. See, however, Smith and Cano H. (1978, 166–167); Pike (1967, 222); Handelman (1975, 33); Werlich (1978, 141, 161); and Morner (1985, 186).

22. On the central highlands, see Manrique (1987, 235–261); on the Cuzco area, see Glave (1986).

23. Caravedo Molinari (1978, 23–25); and Morner (1985, 182).

24. In fact, official policy after 1920 was the protection of the peasant community. According to a new constitution drawn up under Augusto Leguía, the peasant community was recognized as a legal corporation and its land was declared inalienable. See Werlich (1978, 160–162).

25. Thorp and Bertram (1978, 40, 208).

26. On the events of the early 1930s and the initiation of the feud between the military and APRA, see Werlich (1978, 187–201), among other excellent studies.

27. On the convergence of anti-APRA interests between the oligarchy and the military, see Villanueva (1962); North (1966, 48–51); and Astiz (1969, 135–139).

28. Villanueva (1962); and Einaudi and Stepan (1971, 42–44) indicate that, in 1963, of the 630 men who belonged to the boards of directors and top management of the eighty-six largest business enterprises in Peru, only four were military men; less than 1 percent of the exclusive "Club Nacional" were military officers. The analysis of right-wing Peruvian political thinking by Bourricaud (1970, 186–194) is especially incisive.

29. See, especially, Villanueva (1962); Werlich (1978, 167); and North (1966).

30. Werlich (1978, 222–225).

31. This point is well documented. See Villanueva (1973); and Einaudi and Stepan (1971). Astiz and García (1972) qualify some of the data in the work of Einaudi and Stepan, but confirm its overall argument.

32. Astiz and García (1972, 672).

33. Ibid., 674.

34. Villanueva (1973); Einaudi and Stepan (1971); and Astiz and García (1972) provide comprehensive discussions of this point.

35. Villanueva (1973); Astiz and García (1972, 677); Einaudi and Stepan (1972, 18–20); and Malloy (1973).

36. Einaudi and Stepan (1971, 66–67).

37. Jaquette (1971, 122–123); and Pinelo (1973, 115–119).

38. Astiz and García (1972, 680); Astiz (1969, 143–144) contrasts the class backgrounds of Peruvian, Argentine, and Brazilian officers. Most analysts concur, although evidence tends to be impressionistic; it is rare in Latin America that region of birth has as strong implications about socioeconomic class as in Peru.

39. Einaudi and Stepan (1971, 56).

40. The literature on the origins and trajectory of the Velasco government is voluminous. Among the excellent studies are Lowenthal (1975); and Pease García (1977).

41. From the "Manifesto of the Revolutionary Government of the Armed Forces, October 2, 1968," reprinted in Del Pilar Tello (1983, 284–285).

42. For specific data on the increase in leftist organization under Velasco, see especially Latin America Bureau (1985, 13); and Parodi (1988, 90).

43. Latin America Bureau (1985, 67).

44. The figure is the sum of the tallies of the four competing leftist parties, calculated from Webb and Fernández Baca (1991, 1028–1030). On the political context of the 1978 Constituent Assembly elections and the elections themselves, see Latin American Bureau (1985, 70–76); and Pease García (1979, 255–322).

45. Montgomery (1982, 52).

46. Stanley (1990, 11). On the military-elite alliance, see also Montgomery (1982, 53); Dunkerley (1988, 351–352); and Baloyra (1982, 14–52).

47. See, for example, Montgomery (1982, 71) on the 1954 and 1955 elections.

48. Especially valuable on this point are Montgomery (1982, 55–96); and García (1983).

49. Scholars disagree about the extent to which El Salvador's 1970s governments represented variations on the earlier model, and about whether or not the model had actually broken down prior to the coup against Romero. See, for example, Baloyra (1982); and Stanley (1990, 14).

50. Webre (1979, 181). Also cited in Montgomery (1982, 55–96); and García (1983).

51. Baloyra (1982, 54); and Dunkerley (1988, 367).

52. Baloyra (1982, 49, 64).

53. See, especially, Dunkerley (1988, 357); and Baloyra (1982, 45–47).

54. Dunkerley (1988, 360–361).

55. Ibid., 361.

56. Ibid.; and Armstrong and Shenk (1982, 63).

57. Dunkerley (1988, 361–362).

58. Vilas (1995, 82).

59. Armstrong and Shenk (1982, 64).

60. Dunkerley (1988, 374).

61. Ibid., 374; and Montgomery (1995, 71–72).

62. Dunkerley (1988, 375); Montgomery (1995, 72); and Armstrong and Shenk (1982, 87–89).

63. Dunkerley (1988, 375).

64. Ibid.; and Armstrong and Shenk (1982, 88).

65. On the Romero administration, see Baloyra (1982, 64–74); Stanley (1991, 15); Dunkerley (l988, 376–381); Armstrong and Shenk (1982, 89–115); and García (1983, 7–8).

66. Dunkerley (1988, 378).

67. Benítez Manaut (1989, 243).

68. Ibid.

69. This group included Carlos Eugenio Vides Casanova, Nicolás Carranza, Jaime Abdul Gutiérrez, and Juan Rafael Bustillo. See Stanley (1991, 15).

70. An especially incisive analysis is Keogh (1984).

71. Montgomery (1982, 10–15).

72. Ibid., 15–17; and Armstrong and Shenk (1982, 116–118).

73. Two prime examples of Majano's ineffectiveness were, first, in January 1980, when a majority of the Salvadoran officers corps demanded the resignations of García and Carranza, and Majano apparently did nothing, and later, in May 1980, when Majano achieved the arrest of Major Roberto D'Aubuisson for coup plotting but could not exert sufficient pressure to indict him. See Baloyra (1982, 106–11); and Montgomery (1982, 160, 177).

74. The validity of these perceptions is not entirely clear. See Keogh (1984, 169). The officers' perception may have been a result of dissent within the U.S. embassy. Apparently, two U.S. military officials maintained close ties with the hardliners, but were eventually ordered out of El Salvador by Ambassador Robert White. See Stanley (1991, 18, 23–24); and Armstrong and Shenk (1982, 126–127).

75. Stanley (1991, 19).

76. This analysis is heavily indebted to Stanley (1991).

77. Stanley (1991, 26) reports that military officers were paid handsome sums. One rumored amount was a $20,000 retainer plus $10,000 per month, with an expectation that the hired officer assassinate one person a month. Also, four reformist officers were killed, and attempts made on the lives of three others, presumably by the hard-line faction. See Stanley (1991, 27).

78. Americas Watch and American Civil Liberties Union (1982a, 37); Simon and Stephens (1982, 61); and Berryman (1994, 75). Similar figures are provided in Vilas (1995, 85). Pearce (1986, 196) indicates thirteen thousand victims for 1980.

79. Of course, there is no exact figure. This figure was established by the United Nations Commission on the Truth for El Salvador (1993, 43). An 80 percent estimate was made by Baloyra (1982, 137), in part on the basis of data from the Socorro Jurídico. A 70 percent figure was suggested by the U.S. Senate (1982, 4). The lower estimates are from the U.S. Department of State and the higher figures from Socorro Jurídico, which was then affiliated with the Roman Catholic Archdiocese of San Salvador. For a thoughtful discussion of this data, see Congressional Research Service (1989, 78–83).

80. Armstrong and Shenk (1982, 135); Stanley (1996, 186 and 205–207).

81. U.S. Senate (1982, 8) states the violence against Christian Democratic political activists.

82. On the FDR, see chapter 2.

83. See, in particular, note 5 to this chapter. My conclusion about the complexity of evaluating elections is based in part on my own experiences as a member of election observation delegations sponsored by the Center for Democracy in El Salvador in 1991 and by the U.S. Citizens Elections Observer Mission (USCEOM) in El Salvador in 1994, as well as on research in Peru during the 1980 election, about a month after the 1985 election, and during the first round of the 1990 election.

84. My concerns jibe with those of Freedom House for "political rights." Between 1982 and 1989, Freedom House scored Peru's "political rights" at 2; El Salvador's "political rights" were ranked at 4 in 1982 and 1983, and at 3 for the years 1984–95 (with the exception of the year 1985 when they were ranked at 2). The fact that Freedom House did not raise El Salvador's "political rights" rank up from 3 after the 1994 elections suggests that its earlier 3 rank may have been generous. See the annual editions of *Freedom in the World,* edited by Raymond D. Gastil and published by Greenwood Press (Westport, Conn.), for the years 1982–88; the same *Freedom in the World,* edited by R. Bruce McColm, for 1990–92; its publication *Freedom at Issue* 112 (January–February 1990) for 1989; and its publication *Freedom Review* for 1993–95.

85. A January 1991 UCA survey, reported in *Proceso,* no. 462, 13 February 1991, 15.

86. Survey by Datum, and results generously provided to the author by Datum's director, Manuel Torrado.

87. Martín-Baró (1989, 65). Survey was nationwide, by the UCA. The distribution of public opinion on electoral fraud in El Salvador had not changed much from 1984, when Baloyra (1985, 237) reported that 63 percent in a predominantly urban UCA survey were "not sure that the election would be clean." About the conduct of the 1994 elections, however, Salvadorans were more positive; see IUDOP (1994, 14).

88. Survey by the firm Opinión Iberoamericana. The exact wording of the item and precise date of the survey are not clear. "Trust" was "confianza." Survey results reported in *La República*, 14 July 1993, 15–17. Carrión (1994) reports extensively on this survey. Although Peruvians were relatively enthusiastic about electoral processes, they were as critical of most other political institutions as Salvadorans and Ecuadoreans were. Across the thirteen Latin American and Iberian nations, more than half the respondents expressed trust in presidential elections in six countries.

89. See the sources in the table.

90. Eriberto Arroyo Mío, Pablo Li Ormeño, and Saúl Cantoral, respectively.

91. My estimate is based upon data in Instituto de Defensa Legal (1990, 91–94); and Americas Watch (1990, 22–23, 49–50).

92. On the Comando Rodrigo Franco, see Piqueras (1990); Crabtree (1992, 205–206); and Obando (forthcoming, 38). At the time, many Peruvian analysts believed that the mastermind of the death squad was Agustín Mantilla, García's close friend and vice minister and then minister of the interior (responsible for the Peruvian police), but this interpretation has come into doubt in recent years. In an interview in Lima on 24 July 1996, Enrique Bernales reported that the current— but similarly unproven—interpretation by many analysts is that the Comando Rodrigo Franco was a component of the Servicio de Inteligencia Nacional and the precursor of the group within the Peruvian security forces that was to carry out some of the most salient atrocities under the Fujimori government. Yet other analysts believe that the Comando Rodrigo Franco was composed of military personnel acting according to the orders of regional commanders or on their own.

93. Americas Watch (1984a, 9–10).

94. Recollect that the figures in the table for El Salvador represent only deaths confirmed by Americas Watch or the American Civil Liberties Union. Tutela Legal did not issue annual reports that note confirmed deaths of politically salient civilians (as various Peruvian human rights groups did).

95. Carothers (1991, 34).

96. Americas Watch (1990, 69–93); and Menzel (1994, 65–66).

97. See also the figures on civilian deaths estimated by Socorro Jurídico for 1979–81 at the end of the first section of this chapter.

98. Enrique Bernales estimated a ratio of one civilian death to two guerrilla deaths. Interview by author, Lima, Peru, 23 July 1996. On Bernales's credentials, see appendix II.

99. In the interview in Lima on 23 July 1996 (see previous note), Bernales confirmed that the figure for "presumed subversives" was precisely the number for guerrilla and civilian deaths in military clashes.

100. As the sources in table 3.5 suggest, during 1989 and 1990 the figures for assassinations were reported by the Bernales Commission, but not by the Coordinadora Nacional de Derechos Humanos; the Coordinadora's data were the data used by the U.S. Department of State, and accordingly the annual human rights report provides data for assassinations beginning only in 1991.

101. Bernales, interview. Bernales has worked closely with Diego García-Sayan, who is very familiar with data collection in El Salvador, and accordingly Bernales was able to provide comparative insights for the Peruvian and Salvadoran data.

102. My own observation of the 1980 elections and of the first round of the 1990 elections, as well as many interviews in Peru in June 1985 shortly after the 1985 presidential elections. Americas Watch (1990), for example, attributes no incidents of election-related violence to the Peruvian security forces.

103. This assessment is based heavily on my own conversations with Salvadorans in various towns in San Miguel, La Unión, and Usulután as an elections observer with USCEOM for the April 1991 midterm elections.

104. Washington Office on Latin America (1991, 13–15); and Center for International Policy (1991, 4).

105. Ibid.

106. *New York Times,* 11 February 1991, A3; and 15 February 1991, A10.

107. Gibb (1992, 18–19). Part of the problem may have been relatively weak support for the Democratic Convergence, but the much stronger representation of the FMLN in the 1994 election suggests that fear was also critical.

108. Ibid., 18.

109. The National Republican Institute for International Affairs (1991, 25) reports more voting-table officials for the CD in 1991 than in 1989, but my observation suggested the total number was still small. I estimate less than 30 percent.

110. Leonel Gómez, quoted in Bonner (1984, 301). Information on ballot-numbering and transparent urns from Washington Office on Latin America (1991, 7–10); and National Republican Institute for International Affairs (1991, 16–20).

111. "Transparent" is the word commonly used in Latin America to indicate "clean," "above-board" electoral processes.

112. In recent major elections, turnout as a percentage of total eligible population was above 70 percent in Australia, South Africa, Denmark, Germany, Britain, and Israel; it was below 70 percent but above 60 percent in Canada and Japan; and below 60 percent in the United States, Russia, Mexico, and India. See *Time,* 23 May 1994, 18.

113. For Peru, see Richard Webb and Graciela Fernández Baca, *Perú en números* (Lima: Cuánto, 1996), 397–399; for El Salvador, see Baloyra (1993, 25).

114. Because the absence of fraud is a "nonevent," there is little documentation of this point. I was in Lima, interviewing political elites and attending campaign rallies during the 1980 and 1990 presidential elections, and was there a few weeks after the first (and ultimately final) round of the 1985 election. I have interviewed Fernando Tuesta Soldevilla, Peru's top elections scholar, many times. See also *Resumen Semanal* 3, no. 71 (17–23 May 1980); 8, no. 312 (13–18 April 1985); 13, no. 564 (6–11 April 1990); and 13, no. 574 (15–21 June 1990), reporting major parties' perspectives on the elections.

115. Exceptions were the 1980 presidential race, when polling techniques were less sophisticated and Popular Action won by a larger margin than anticipated, and the first round of the 1990 contest, when Fujimori's rapid rise eclipsed polls that were legally prohibited to be published after about two weeks prior to the election. Also, most Peruvian polls are based in Lima, and forecasts for municipal contests in other areas were scant.

116. *Resumen Semanal* 3, no. 69 (3–9 May 1980).

117. *Resumen Semanal* 8, no. 312 (13–18 April 1985); 8, no. 313 (19–25 April 1985); 8, no. 314 (26 April–2 May 1985); and 8, no. 315 (3–9 May 1985).

118. *Resumen Semanal* 13, no. 564 (6–11 April 1990); and 13, no. 574 (15–21 June 1990).

119. *Resumen Semanal* 3, no. 98 (22–28 November 1980); and 6, no. 241 (4–11 November l983).

120. García's APRA distributed small gifts to potential voters, inaugurated as many public works as possible, grandiosely endorsed Del Castillo from the presidential balcony the last night of the campaign, and published political advertisements after the legal end to the campaign. See *Caretas*, 11 November 1986, 16–17; and *Resumen Semanal* 9, no. 393 (14–20 November 1986).

121. *Caretas*, 17 November 1986, 12–14; *Resumen Semanal,* all issues between 9, no. 393 (14–20 November 1986) and nos. 398–399 (19–31 December 1986).

122. *Resumen Semanal* 12, no. 545 (10–16 November 1989): 2.

123. Ibid., 1–2.

124. Rospiglios (1992, 38); Palmer (1995, 266); *Resumen Semanal* 12, no. 542 (20–26 October 1989); no. 543 (27 October–2 November 1989); and no. 544 (3–9 November). See also chapters 2 and 6 for data on the number of authorities and candidates killed by Shining Path.

125. *Caretas*, no. 1084, 20 November 1989, 25; and *Resumen Semanal* 12, no. 545 (10–16 November 1989): 3.

126. *Caretas*, 6 April 1992, 32–35.

127. Arriaza Meléndez (1989, 42). Similar criticisms were made by Acevedo (1991a, 30); García (1985, 534–535); *New York Times,* 24 March 1984, 4, citing a member of the Central Elections Council (Jaime Trabanino Llobell); and *New York Times,* 25 March 1984, 12. Also, Salvador Manzano (head of the Electoral Registry), interview by author, 24 January 1991, in San Salvador. Another common tactic was the use of dead persons' cards.

128. The company was ANTEL. See U.S. Senate (1982, 8); and Bonner (1984, 304–306).

129. García (1985, 533).

130. See Bonner (1984, 303–306); and Schulz (1984, 234–236) for description of the UCA's analysis and criticism of it.

131. United Nations (1990, 7).

132. *New York Times,* 1 April 1984, sec. 4, 1. See also *New York Times,* 24 March 1984, A4; and 26 March 1984, A8.

133. *New York Times,* 26 March 1984, A8.

134. Manzano, interview; and interviews in various localities about the electoral process during the 1991 legislative and municipal elections.

135. Gibb (1992, 19–20); Center for International Policy (1991, 4–5); *New York Times,* 13 March 1991, A5; and *Economist,* 16 March 1991, 39; and 23 March 1991, 48.

136. García (1985, 534–535); Baloyra (1985, 236–237); Acevedo (1991a, 30); and *New York Times,* 26 March 1984, A8.

137. Browning (1988, 33); *New York Times,* 14 March 1991, editorial page; *Economist,* 23 March 1991, 48; and Center for International Policy (1991, 5).

138. Browning (1988, 13) explicitly discusses these possibilities.

139. Gibb (1992, 20).

140. *Economist,* 20 March 1991.

141. *Economist,* 16 March 1991, 39; and 23 March 1991, 48.

142. The three members were elected by the Legislative Assembly from sets of names provided by the three parties. See the 1983 Constitution of El Salvador, Chapter 7, Article 208. For the 1991 election, an Electoral Oversight Board, composed of representatives of all legally registered parties, was given access to meetings of the Central Elections Council and to the Electoral Register. In agreements negotiated in April 1991, representatives on the CCE were granted to four parties (enabling the inclusion of the Democratic Convergence for the 1994 election).

143. Until 1989, these officials were also representatives of the three parties with the most votes in the preceding election. In 1989, provisions were made to allow representatives from smaller parties and/or new parties under certain conditions. In 1991, for the first time, all competing parties were allowed to be included in these bodies. See the relevant articles of the electoral codes for each year.

144. Salvador Manzano, interview by author in San Salvador, 7 June 1991. See also the analysis in United Nations (1990, 19–20).

145. United Nations (1990, 19). Argentina, Brazil, and Costa Rica employ nonpartisan procedures similar to Peru's.

146. See chapters 1, 2, and 3 of Decree Law 14250. Article 11 identifies numerous categories of politically linked individuals who are ineligible. The decree law is printed in Ramírez (1989).

147. Few scholars have rigorously grappled with the conceptualization of civilian authority over the military or sought to assess actual degrees of authority on a specific range of issues. Exceptions include Fitch (1989); and Pion-Berlin (1992).

148. For a comprehensive discussion of the Peruvian military's view of its political options, see McClintock (1989c). The theme is the military's attitude that a coup would be "suicidal" (in the word of General Sinesio Jarama in a 1987 interview), primarily because of the likely massive opposition to it. See also Marcella (1990, 64). Given the intense discontent of the Peruvian military during the García administration, however, coups were plotted during his final eighteen months (although by this time new presidential elections were looming). See Obando (1994, 112); and *New York Times,* 15 January 1989, 9.

149. The firm Apoyo carries out the survey and publishes the results in *Debate,* usually in July. See each issue for this period. Fujimori's national security adviser Vladimiro Montesinos, a cashiered army captain, is not classified as a military officer.

150. See, especially, Walter and Williams (1997, chap. 6).

151. In 1985, former military president Francisco Morales Bermúdez was a contestant. See Webb and Fernández Baca (1991, 1029).

152. Polling agencies regularly asked citizens whether their preferred political regime was "democratic" (elected), "socialist" (by revolution), or "military" (by coup). Preferences for democracy in Lima soared almost to 90 percent during the apex of García's popularity during 1985–86, and rarely declined below 70 percent during the decade. See McClintock (1992, table 6). The major shift during the decade was roughly 10 percentage points away from socialism and toward military rule. Popular support for democracy was also widespread in El Salvador, at 90 percent in the Orellana 1991 survey.

153. As of 1990, about 5 percent of El Salvador's 43,250 troops were in the navy, and 5 percent in the air force; by contrast, approximately 20 percent of Peru's 125,000 troops were in the navy, and 12 percent in the air force. See Copley (1991, 297, 781–782).

154. This scholarly consensus is based upon evidence from arms-purchase patterns and institutional support or rejection of Velasco. The explanations for the distinct politics of the services were the greater travel to remote, disadvantaged areas by the army and its relatively inclusive recruitment pattern. See Del Pilar Tello (1983, 2:30, 180); and Pease García (1977, 110–121).

155. Palmer (1993, 282–287) reports that, as of 1992, there were about eight thousand officers in the Peruvian army, two thousand in the Peruvian navy, and at least one thousand in the air force.

156. Copley (1991, 296–297).

157. Among the many sources, see García (1992); *Washington Post,* 9 November 1988, A17; and *Boston Globe,* 25 February 1987, 1, 9.

158. Peltz (1990, 31).

159. Valuable studies include Blachman and Sharpe (1988–89); Miles and Ostertag (1989, 16–20); and Barry (1990, 16–25).

160. Data on military expenditure are controversial and often vary dramatically by source. Data on foreign military assistance, which would have greatly increased expenditure in El Salvador, are not included. In both nations, the military budget is secret; data published by the governments often underestimate total military expenditure. See Velarde and Rodríguez (1989, 80–82); and *Andean Report,* October 1983, 182. The figures from London's International Institute for Strategic Studies best approximate scholarly estimates of the trends in military expenditure in Peru during this period. See, in particular, Scheetz (1992, 183), who meticulously documents dramatic increases in 1977–78 and 1982, and a decline to 1975 expenditure levels in 1985–87; as well as Obando (1990, 60–66); and Marcella (1990, 64). Its *Military Balance* also reports credible figures for years that are missing in other sources. By contrast, the World Bank figures appear to better fit qualitative estimates of trends in military expenditure in El Salvador.

161. This trend is especially apparent for El Salvador in the World Bank data. Given the missing World Bank data for 1984–87 for Peru, the decline in expenditure during the first years of the García administration is evident only from the International Institute for Strategic Studies data.

162. Obando (1994, 108).

163. In general, the Belaúnde administration favored large-scale public investments, and numerous commentators—from Peruvians on the street to Inter-American Development Bank officials—attributed the bias to the desire for pork-barrel possibilities. See, for example, the discussion in *Andean Report,* December 1980, 221–223.

164. Because other sources do not indicate as sharp a drop in expenditure as the International Institute for International and Strategic Studies, see also the comments by Marcella (1990, 64) about García's halving the budget. Marcella is the director of Third World Studies at the U.S. Army War College, and should have access to the best estimates of military expenditure.

165. Palmer (1992b, 165). By another estimate, only 10 percent of Peru's troops were pitted against the guerrillas. See *Latin America Regional Report,* 28 July 1988, 5. See also McCormick (1990, 35). It should also be noted, however, that the per capita number of military personnel was larger in Peru than in almost all other Latin American nations, with the important exception of Chile. See *New York Times,* 26 January 1992, 4E.

166. Rudolph (1992, 119); and cost estimates in *Latin America Weekly Report,* 14 October 1983, 1.

167. McCormick (1990, 42).

168. Obando (1994, 123). For a similar figure for a rear admiral, see *New York Times*, 15 January 1989, 6. Mauceri (1991, 19) reports $120 per month for an army general.

169. Obando (1994, 122).

170. There is scholarly consensus that overall budgetary concerns were the primary reason that there was not a dramatic increase in expenditure under Fujimori. See Palmer (1992, 166); and Obando (1994, 116). Some opponents of the Fujimori government suggest that an additional reason may have been Fujimori's desire to increase his capacity for co-optation.

171. Figure for Peru in *Sí*, 19 March 1991, 13; average for neighboring nations in *Sí*, 19 March 1991, 13–14; a similar version of the same data is reported in Degregori (1994, 97). Similarly low figures for various ranks were reported in *New York Times*, 14 January 1991, A2; *Latin America Weekly Report*, 20 June 1991, 10; and *New York Times*, 25 July 1991, 11.

172. *Sí*, 19 March 1991, 14; figure for El Salvador from interviews at COPREFA (Comité de Prensa de la Fuerza Armada, or Armed Forces' Press Office), 21 August 1990, and Carlos Rivas, head of the army school in El Salvador, 22 August 1990, in San Salvador. They agreed that the salary for the just-recruited officer was 540 colones per month (about $70 at the time), and that after a year's service the salary was 680 colones per month (about $85 at the time). A similar base figure in colones, but higher in dollars at the exchange rate of the time, is reported by Millman (1989, 95).

173. Obando (1994, 124); *Latin America Weekly Report*, 20 August 1992, 10; *El Suplemento de Expreso*, 3 March 1991, 10; and *Washington Post*, 21 April 1992, A16.

174. The primary alternative answer was that salaries should not be raised because the state had no money. For more information on the survey, see appendix I.

175. *Newsweek*, 19 August 1991, 31; and Palmer (1992, 166). With respect to the naval officers' requests, "Political and Economic Trend Report," *Peru Report* 6, no. 7 (July 1992): 3.

176. *Sí*, 23 March 1992, 31; *Debate* 14, no. 67 (December 1991–February 1992): 3.

177. Mauceri (1991, 19); and Palmer (1992, 166).

178. *Newsweek*, 3 August 1992, 46.

179. *Newsweek*, 19 August 1991, 31; *Foreign Broadcast Information Service: Latin America*, 30 April 1991, 2; and *La República*, 17 March 1991, 22–23.

180. *Foreign Broadcast Information Service: Latin America*, 21 June 1991, 29.

181. *Sí*, 23 March 1992, 31.

182. In the first years of the war, high rates of military casualties did prompt many desertions. See CINAS (1988, 34–35). In later years, however, no problems of this variety were mentioned in the scholarly literature or in interviews with Colonel

Mauricio Vargas, 24 January 1991, in San Salvador; Major Jeffrey U. Cole (U.S. Navy attaché), 13 August 1990, in San Salvador; and Philip Cochola (political officer, U.S. embassy in San Salvador), 16 August 1990.

183. Estimate by William Stanley, 26 June 1997, in correspondence with the author, based on his interviews in El Salvador during this period. The most trenchant critic of Salvadoran officers' comfortable lifestyles is Millman (1989).

184. The "most powerful" military position varied somewhat according to the particular interaction between the president and the military. Military leaders who were ranked among the ten most powerful Peruvians between 1981 and 1991 included the minister of defense, the head of the joint command of the armed forces, and the commander of the army.

185. Article 281 of the 1979 constitution. See also Krujit (1991, 100).

186. Interview with General (r) Edgardo Mercado Jarrín, on 11 July 1997, in Washington, D.C., among other sources.

187. Information on the prior professional experience of the officers is available in García Belaúnde (1988, 66–69, 87–89, 208–209, and 257–258).

188. *Debate* 15 (August 1982): 32; and the annual issues of *Debate* between 1981 and 1991 reporting on power in Peru.

189. Interview with General Mercado Jarrín, on 11 July 1997.

190. *Peru Report*, April 1987, sec. 7.

191. In 1986, the head of the joint command was named as sixth most powerful; in 1987, another head of the joint command was eleventh most powerful; in 1988, the minister of defense was tenth most powerful; and in 1989 the army commander was eleventh most powerful. See the relevant annual issues of *Debate*.

192. The establishment of the defense ministry was one of the most politically controversial presidential decisions of 1987. In a futile effort to reverse the president's decision, an angry air force commander buzzed the presidential palace. However, García did scale back his plans for the institution. See Rubio (1990, 113–115).

193. Obando (forthcoming, 34–35); and Crabtree (1992, 111–112).

194. Montesinos was an extremely controversial figure whose power in the Fujimori government and in the military institution was divisive. Montesinos had been expelled from the army on the grounds of dishonesty and disobedience, and had even been tried on charges of treason (for allegedly delivering classified material to a foreign nation), but was not convicted. Subsequently, as a lawyer, he defended persons accused of drug trafficking. For further discussion, see Obando (forthcoming, 45–46). In the first few years of Fujimori's government, Montesinos played an important role but did not have a formal title; he was referred to simply as "an adviser," or as a "shadowy adviser," or as "Fujimori's Rasputin." After the *autogolpe*, he was named chief of the Advisory Committee of the National Intelligence Service (SIN) and was usually politely called Fujimori's "national security adviser," although the title remained de facto.

195. Mauceri (1995, 20). For example, even in 1991, Fujimori achieved the retirement of the politically hostile navy commander.

196. Obando (1994, 114); interview with retired General Luis Cisneros in *Debate* (November 1992–January 1993): 13. These changes were facilitated by Legislative Decree no. 752 in November 1991.

197. Enrique Obando, interview in *Peru Report* 7, no. 4 (May 1993): 4. Thirty-five years of active service was unprecedentedly long.

198. *Debate,* annual poll issues.

199. Ibid. In 1994, de Bari Hermoza became general commander of the armed forces.

200. Walter and Williams (1996, chap. 6, 221–223).

201. Ibid., 228–229.

202. Leonel Gómez, cited in *New York Times,* 5 May 1991, 9.

203. Walter and Williams (1996, chap. 6, 235); and Barry (1990, 50–52). D'Aubuisson himself was a member of the *tandona.* The class also counted among its members Sigifredo Ochoa, the officer whose rebellion had sparked the withdrawal of García as defense minister in 1983, opening the way to Vides Casanova's appointment.

204. Walter and Williams (1996, chap. 6, 236–238, 254, table 6.2).

205. Ibid., 237.

206. Diskin and Sharpe (1986, 74–75); and Duarte (1986, 204–205).

207. Karl (1992, 158); Gibb and Smyth (1990, 16); *U.S. News and World Report,* 5 February 1990, 50; and *Washington Post,* 3 January 1990, A25; and 19 November 1990, A25.

208. Wilde (1992, 10), for example, also reports that a U.S. Information Agency poll in Peru in the summer of 1991 found that the preferred forms of U.S. assistance were economic assistance and technical assistance; the nature of the "technical" assistance was not specified.

209. This is an important topic, but tangential to this book. Unfortunately, in my view, to the extent that there is a spectrum at which aggressive counterinsurgency and toleration of human rights abuses is at one pole and passive counterinsurgency and respect for human rights is at another, Fujimori went way too far toward the first pole.

210. For assessments of Belaúnde's strategy, see Degregori and Rivera (1993); Mauceri (1996, 136–138); and Obando (1994, 108–110).

211. "Ineffective control of corruption, delinquency, and terrorism" was judged the "worst defect" of the Belaúnde government by an elite Lima sample. See *Debate* 7, no. 32 (May 1985): 24–28.

212. Obando (forthcoming, 31); Kruijt (1991, 102); and Gorriti (1990a).

213. Some analysts describe Belaúnde as uninterested in the problem and/or as abdicating his authority to military officials; but, although Belaúnde's key concern was not counterinsurgency, he did have views on the topic. Beyond the sources cited above, see Neier (1984, 148).

214. In Article 231 of the Peruvian constitution, the executive was authorized to make such a decision without approval by the legislature.

215. Berg (1986–87, 184).

216. Degregori and Rivera (1993, 8–10); Rubio (1990, 117); Pease García (1984, 67); Mauceri (1989, 44–46); and Obando (forthcoming, 32–33). On the support for Huamán among his colleagues, see *Resumen Semanal* 7, no. 280 (24–30 August 1984); and *Resumen Semanal* 7, no. 281 (31 August–6 September 1984). Apparently, top military commanders were persuaded to dismiss Huamán less because of their disagreement with his views than because of his politicization of the issue.

217. Mauceri (1989, 49).

218. Webb and Fernández Baca (1991, 436). García dubbed the southern highlands areas where aid would be targeted as "The Andean Trapezoid."

219. Central Reserve Bank, "Ayuda Memoria," (Lima, 1986, mimeographed); and *Peru Report* 1, no. 4 (April 1987), sec. 7.

220. Banco Central de Reserva, "Programa de apoyo al ingreso temporal (PAIT)" (Lima, 1987).

221. Mauceri (1989, 55–56); Crabtree (1992, 55); and author's interview with Carlos Bendezu (director of CORFA, the Ayacucho development agency), 22 November 1987, in Ayacucho.

222. See *Peru Report,* April 1987, sec. 7; Mauceri (1989, 54–56); and Crabtree (1992, 110).

223. See Rénique (1994, 236–242) on Puno; and Manrique (1989) on Junín.

224. Air Force General Cesar Enrico Praelli, General Sinesio Jarama Davila, and General Wilfredo Mori Orzo, respectively.

225. Charges were brought against General Clemente Noel, who had commanded the Ayacucho emergency zone during the 1983 massacre of journalists in Uchuraccay; civil guardsmen in Cuzco charged with torture; and police believed responsible for a 1983 massacre in the village of Soccos near Ayacucho (of whom eleven were convicted).

226. Rubio (1990, 118); Obando (forthcoming, 37); Degregori and Rivera (1993, 12); and author's interviews at the military headquarters in Ayacucho, November 1987.

227. Degregori and Rivera (1993, 12–13).

228. While the military's view was "to the left" on the socioeconomic component of counterinsurgency, it was "to the right" on human rights. See Rubio (1990, 117); McCormick (1990, 44); General Sinesio Jarama in *Debate* 11, no. 55 (March–May 1989): 8–10; General Guillermo Monzón (head of the joint command and

commander of the army) in *Caretas,* 10 February 1986, 26; and Diego García-Sayan, author's interview, 21 October 1987, in Lima.

229. The clearest description of the events in English is Americas Watch (1986, 99–112). Americas Watch (1988, 61–65) discusses in detail the Senate Commission's report; and Americas Watch (1990, 35–37) updates the legal outcomes. See also Bonner (1988, 57–58); Crabtree (1992, 110–111); Obando (forthcoming, 36–37); and Rubio (1990, 118).

230. *New York Times,* 15 January 1989, 6.

231. *Andean Report,* June 1988, 14–142; and *Washington Office on Latin America Update* 8, no. 4 (July–August 1988): 5.

232. Crabtree (1992, 204).

233. See tables 3.5 and 3.6. In the comparison of the Belaúnde and the García years, however, it should be noted that the military was operating in a much larger swath of Peruvian territory in the late 1980s than in the early years of the decade. Also, military assassinations of civilians occurred during the early 1980s, but in the remote southern highlands, and they were grossly underreported.

234. Daniels (1990, 11) wrote: "I have seen soldiers enter a village in convoy to steal all its chickens."

235. For example, Palmer (1990, 8) reports that the percentage of provinces under military control (under "emergency" laws) increased from 7 percent in 1984 to 31 percent in July 1989. See also chapter 2.

236. See, for example, Degregori (1994, 93); and Basombrío (1996, 205). On many of the points below, further elaboration is provided in McClintock (1997).

237. In the November 1990 sample survey by Datum in Lima, only 5 percent of the respondents cited "improving intelligence" as an important way to improve counterinsurgency performance. In the Osores team's interviews with sixty middle-ranking members of the security police, technical police, and army, mostly in Huancayo, in June–July 1990, less than 7 percent of the sample cited "improving intelligence" as important. Among both the civilian and military samples, better arms, equipment, and training were the priorities, cited by at least 30 percent of the civilian Lima sample and 42 percent of the military sample. See appendix I for more information about the surveys.

238. José Bailetti (director of INIDEN), interview by author, Lima, 14 August 14, 1991; and Alejandro Deustua (research analyst at CEPEI), interview by author, Lima, 4 August 1991. See also Marks (1996, 68); and *La República,* 20 September 1992, 6–7.

239. On the formation of the GEIN and its strategy, see Reina (1995); Gorriti (1996); and Jiménez Baca (1996). My account is also based on interviews in Lima with Enrique Bernales, 23 July 1996; Fernando Rospigliosi, 23 July 1996; Carlos Chipoco, 27 July 1996; Agustín Mantilla, 16 June 1997; Carlos Tapia, 20 June 1997; and other off-the-record interviews.

240. See chapter 5 for a thorough discussion of this point.

241. *Caretas,* no. 1112, 12 June 1990, 34–38; *Latin America Weekly Report,* 21 June 1990, 2; *Resumen Semanal* 13, no. 572 (1–7 June 1990): 1–2; and interviews by author in Lima with Marcial Rubio, 9 November 1990; and José Bailetti, 12 November 1990.

242. See the sources cited in note 239.

243. Reina (1995, 49).

244. For example, in the Osores research team's survey of security force personnel in mid-1990, only 37 percent of the respondents favored the establishment of armed *rondas;* 52 percent were opposed.

245. See the interview with General Howard Rodríguez (former military commander in the Ayacucho emergency zone) in *La República,* 11 June 1989, 10–11, in which he expressed a view that he repeated to me in an interview in Lima, 12 November 1990. See also *U.S. News and World Report,* 18 September 1989, 49; and *Latin America Weekly Report,* 8 August 1991, 3; and comments by General Sinesio Jarama in *Foreign Broadcast Information Service: Latin America,* 14 May 1991, 43. The point was also made by Bruno Revese in a talk at Georgetown University, on 30 January 1990.

246. *Ideéle* 27 (July 1991): 8; *La República,* 20 April 1991, 10; and *Americas Watch* 6, no. 6 (August 1992): 23–24.

247. See, for example, *Ideéle* 28 (August 1991): 15–16; and *La República,* 8 March 1992, 18–22.

248. Mauceri (1996, 144).

249. Among many sources, see Clutterbuck (1995); and *New York Times,* 8 October 1992, A3.

250. *Andean Newsletter,* no. 51, 11 February 1991, 5; *Newsweek,* 26 December 1988, 37; and *New York Times,* 31 August 1988, 8.

251. Pablo Rojas, head of the Commission on Human Rights, in *Washington Post,* 12 August 1991, A12.

252. See statements by García in *New York Times,* 16 November 1986, E3; and 21 August 1988, 9.

253. See Americas Watch (1990, 29–37); and McClintock (1997).

254. Interviews in Lima with Lourdes Flores, 22 July 1996; Rolando Ames, 23 July 1996; and Fernando Rospigliosi, 23 July 1996. Also, with respect to the military, *Peru Report* 1, no. 10 (October 1987): 3C-1; and, with respect to the judges, Henry Pease García, speaking at George Washington University, Washington D.C., 17 March 1992; and Luis Pásara, in *Caretas,* 7 October 1991, 33.

255. *PerúPaz* 2, no. 10 (April 1993): 7.

256. The leader throughout 1990–92 was Benedicto Jiménez Baca, an officer with many years of experience in DINCOTE.

257. Reina (1995, 49–50); and Clutterbuck (1995, 84).

258. On these events discussed in the paragraph below, see Reina (1995); Clutterbuck (1995); and Gorriti (1996), among other sources.

259. Bolívar Ocampo (1994, 426). On the U.S. support, see chapter 5.

260. Degregori (1994, 89); Bolívar Ocampo (1994, 424); and Basombrío (1996, 206). This collaborative relationship between the military and the peasants was noted especially in the southern highlands areas that were studied by Degregori et al. (1996). In other areas, in particular Junín, my interviews in July 1996 indicated that military compulsion had been common.

261. Degregori (1994, 89).

262. On the judicial reform, see Comisión de Juristas Internacionales (1994), among other sources.

263. There were more captures in the eighteen months between June 1992 and December 1993 than during the entire twelve years 1980–91, and almost double the number of suspects were convicted. See *El Peruano,* 17 March 1994, A3.

264. *Washington Post,* 5 January 1997, A20.

265. Youngers (1995, 9).

266. Answering the question, "How do you think that the military can improve its performance?" 38 percent of the Salvadoran sample cited one of these two alternatives, whereas a mere 8 percent cited strictly military alternatives, such as more arms or better training. (Thirty-one percent did not respond, 16 percent gave a different kind of answer altogether, and 6 percent cited the vague "fighting steadfastly.") Survey by Orellana research team in 1991 ($N = 621$).

267. *Americas Watch* (February 1994), 4. A decline in the combined total of death squad killings and disappearances from an average of 152 in July and August 1983 to forty-six in December 1983 is reported.

268. Arnson (1993, 143); Douglas Farah, "Salvadoran Death Squads Threaten Resurgence," *Washington Post,* 28 August 1988, A1; and Walter and Williams (1996, chap. 6, 231–232).

269. Walter and Williams (1996, chap. 6, 232).

270. Vides Casanova, cited in Diskin and Sharpe (1986, 75), in turn citing *New York Times,* 1 July 1984, sec. 1, 8. A similar statement made by Vides Casanova is cited in Karl (1988, 186).

271. Preston (1985, 30).

272. Schwarz (1991); and Karl (1992, 156–157) are especially explicit on this point.

273. "Summary" section at the top of a Directorate of Intelligence memorandum of 20 January 1984, entitled "El Salvador: Dealing with Death Squads," printed in *New York Times,* 17 December 1993, A39.

274. Congressional Research Service (1989, 91–98); Popkin (1991); and Americas Watch (1991b). Walker and Williams (1996, chap. 6, 222) argue that, prior to

his inauguration, Duarte promised defense minister Vides Casanova that he would not prosecute military officers for past human rights abuses as one component of his pact with the Salvadoran military.

275. Walker and Williams (1996, chap. 6, 211, 226–228).

276. Byrne (1996, 130–132, 161–163); Walker and Williams (1996, chap. 6, 240); and Carothers (1991, 32).

277. Millman (1989); and U.S. Congress, *Bankrolling Failure: A Report to the Arms Control and Foreign Policy Caucus,* Washington, D.C., November 1987, 5–9.

278. Note that, despite the military aid, there were numerous rightist coup plots during this period. See Lane (1990, 27); an excellent general analysis is Sharpe (1988). My interpretation of Duarte's reasoning is indebted to thoughts by Leonel Gómez, in an interview in Washington, D.C., 2 July 1996.

279. *New York Times,* 4 April 1985, sec. 1, 15; Duarte (1986, 238–239).

280. *New York Times,* 16 November 1985, sec. 1, 16.

281. Preston (1985, 35) comments: "[While] an independent-minded, populist reformist when he was robbed of the presidency in 1972 . . . now . . . he seems a different, far more conservative man."

282. Farah, "Salvadoran Death Squads," A1, A29. Another factor was the November 1989 offensive itself.

283. Preparations for an offensive had begun in 1987, but it appears that many FMLN leaders would not have gone ahead with the plan if their plan for the postponement of the 1989 elections by six months and various changes in the electoral process had been accepted, or if they had thought that the government was serious in talks with FMLN representatives that had begun in September. See Montgomery (1995, 213–217); and Byrne (1996, 152).

284. Byrne (1996, 174–175).

285. Montgomery (1995, 216).

286. Byrne (1996, 177); Montgomery (1995, 214); and Vickers (1992, 36–37).

287. Interviews with Roberto Codas of Preis in San Salvador, August 1991; Karl (1992, 152); Baloyra (1992, 74–75); *Economist,* 11 August 1990; and *New York Times,* 3 October 1990, A9.

288. Walter and Williams (1996, chap. 6, 241–242); Byrne (1996, 179–180); Schwarz (1991, 31–35); *New York Times,* 17 November 1991, A1; *New York Times,* 30 September 1991, A1; *Economist,* 5 October 1991, 45; and *Washington Post,* 30 September 1991, A1. See also the report of the United Nations Truth Commission. In an interview in Washington, D.C., on 2 July 1996, Leonel Gómez, an expert on the Salvadoran military who investigated the case, reported that Bustillo had been the chief instigator of the crime and that Ponce had acceded to Bustillo's view. Apparently, Cristiani himself had been told that some action of this type was likely, but could not prevent it.

289. Walter and Williams (1996, chap. 6, 242); and Vickers (1992, 40).

290. The paucity of references to Cristiani in scholars' discussions of the peace process is striking. See, for example, Vickers (1992); and Montgomery (1995, 220–228). President Cristiani apparently had to be persuaded to fly to New York on 28 December in order to achieve the final agreement before the end of the term of Secretary General Javier Pérez de Cuéllar. For a more positive assessment of Cristiani, see Byrne (1996, 190).

291. Vickers (1992); and Byrne (1996, 169–191). Just as the Salvadoran military faced declining U.S. support, the FMLN faced the loss of Soviet and Sandinista support. However, the FMLN did continue military attacks in 1990 and to a lesser degree in 1991; indeed, in November 1990, the FMLN used surface-to-air missiles against an air force plane for the first time.

292. *Economist,* 16 October 1993, 48.

293. *Mucho* or *bastante* was the Spanish for "a lot" or "a good deal." For details on the Datum survey, see appendix I.

294. Orellana survey. For details, see appendix I. The figure for the Ecuadorean sample was 32 percent.

4. Economic Trends

1. A similar argument is made by Seligson (1996, 151–155).

2. For a comprehensive analysis of economic declines and recoveries during the 1970s and 1980s, see Paredes and Sachs (1991).

3. Inter-American Development Bank (1984a, 415); and Inter-American Development Bank (1992, 285).

4. De Soto (1986).

5. See the discussions in Sheahan (1993, 155–157); and Hamann and Paredes (1991, 59–60). Estimates range from about 20 percent of Peru's GDP to almost 40 percent.

6. This is the customary practice in economic analyses of Peru as other Latin American nations. For examples, see Paredes and Sachs (1991); Sheahan (1993); and Gonzales de Olarte (1996).

7. The data in the first three columns of the table are World Bank data for absolute levels of GNP, expressed in current dollar values; the data in the second three columns are Inter-American Development Bank figures for rates of growth in GDP per capita. Clearly, the data do not jibe well. The reasons are various. GNP figures include transfer payments and are not the same as GDP figures. Also very important are variations in officials' per capita product calculations and difficulties in exchange-rate calculation.

8. Paredes and Sachs (1991, 73).

9. Inter-American Development Bank (1992, 286).

10. For the 1970s, see Bulmer-Thomas (1983, 272). Bulmer-Thomas provides a thoughtful analysis for the reasons for GDP growth from the 1920s through the late 1970s in El Salvador.

11. The data are from Funes (1992, 44). A similar interpretation of the 1980 plummet is made by Vilas (1995, 84).

12. Boyer (1991, 11); and Funes (1992, 44).

13. See, for example, ECLAC (Economic Commission for Latin America and the Caribbean) (1993, 44). The key problem is that, in nations without safety nets for the unemployed, the unemployed cannot subsist and accordingly make work for themselves in the "informal sector." Few can afford to be "unemployed."

14. However, calculations of "inadequate employment" are often actually made only on the basis of persons receiving extremely low wages.

15. Some other estimates of underemployment are slightly lower, but—at above 85 percent—still excruciatingly high. See, for example, U.S. Embassy, Lima (1993); and *Latin America Weekly Report,* 8 August 1991, 2.

16. The real minimum wage is the wage received by most manual workers in Latin American countries—approximately one-third of the economically active population in Peru. See Cuánto (1991, 30).

17. The source given in the table, Funes (1992), provides comprehensive data for every year and is based on official data. The data in Booth and Walker (1993, 179) imply a very slight fall in Salvadoran wages during the 1970s, but their figures are derived from 1973 as a base year, a historical high in El Salvador; also, their source is Wilkie and Haber (1981), a U.S.-based statistical abstract, and the source in turn for its data are not clear.

18. Inter-American Development Bank (1990, 28).

19. This is especially true in many Latin American nations during the 1970s and early 1980s, when inflation was high and exchange rates frequently distorted.

20. *Perú Económico* 13, no. 8 (August 1990), 43–44. The article was also published in *Foreign Broadcast Information Service,* 4 January 1991, 14. The figures jibe with the author's own interviews with citizens in El Salvador and Peru.

21. Calculated from Webb and Fernández Baca (1992, 524).

22. Author's estimate from data in *EIU Country Report* no. 3, 1991, 24, and Wood (1996, 27).

23. Cuánto (1991, 30–31). See also Carol Graham, "Peru's Blighted Path," *Christian Science Monitor,* 30 April 1991, 19.

24. Webb and Fernández Baca (1992, 524 and 1951).

25. *Washington Post,* 9 February 1992, A18.

26. "Radiografiá del Hambre," *Savia,* no. 1 (6 July 1989), 4

27. The study, by a Peruvian research team, is reported in Crabtree (1992, 146, 147).

28. *Washington Post,* 27 November 1991, 22A; *New York Times,* 15 December 1991, 21. A Lima street vendor's comment, "Sometimes you eat and sometimes you don't," was reported in *New York Times,* 7 July 1991, 8.

29. Consider, for example, that income distribution at the national level (not exclusively rural) was more skewed in Peru than in El Salvador; Mahler (1989, 81) reports that the Gini index for income distribution in Peru in 1972 was .536 versus .384 in El Salvador in 1976–77. The statistic for El Salvador was the lowest for the seven nations in the study. As will be evident below, data for rural areas in El Salvador are available, but are broken down by department much less frequently than would be helpful for this study. Also, as Zuvekas (1993, 26–27) discusses, household surveys in El Salvador were flawed in various respects; as a consequence, analysis over time using these surveys was not possible.

30. Martínez and Tealdo (1982, 39).

31. Ibid.

32. Ibid., 15–16.

33. Brockett (1990, 73).

34. Taylor and Hudson (1972, 267).

35. Barry (1987, 9); Brockett (1990, 73–74); and DeWalt (1985, 50).

36. The figure is a ballpark estimate based on data in McClintock (1981, 61, appendix 3). It includes the roughly 10 percent of farm families who were workers or sharecroppers on haciendas, plus the 15 to 20 percent of families who were temporary workers for one or more haciendas. It does not include the roughly 35 percent of Peruvian farm families who were members of "peasant communities," where land was held by the community as a whole. Some of the "landless families" were headed by sons of peasant community members who might expect to become full members in the future. The statistics on total farm families in Peru varied widely.

37. Brockett (1990, 149); Lehoucq and Sims (1982, 2); Ruben (1991, 15); and Simon and Stephens (1982, 2). However, as Seligson (1995) emphasizes, the "landless" include workers and sharecroppers on haciendas, some of whom probably preferred wage labor to private parcels. In contrast to Peru, by the 1970s in El Salvador there were very few traditional indigenous communities. Seligson (1995, 46) believes that the jump in landlessness between 1971 and 1975 reflects a change in the estimation technique of the United Nations (the source for most of these data).

38. Seligson (1995, 45–48).

39. Ibid., 60.

40. From Martínez and Tealdo (1982, 16); and Lehoucq and Sims (1982, 2).

41. McClintock (1981, 77–83).

42. Browning (1975, 405–437), in particular his map of "agricultural regions" on p. 406.

43. Kincaid (1993, 139–140).

44. Mason (1986, 500–501); Pearce (1986, 28–29); and Simon and Stephens (1982, 2).

45. Wickham-Crowley (1992, 243–244). See also Seligson (1996, 151); and Paige (1996, 132), who discuss Wickham-Crowley's data.

46. Pearce (1986, 45–49); Browning (1975, 406–417); and Simon and Stephens (1982, vi).

47. Williams (1986, 172–173) for the 1961–71 period.

48. Paige (1996).

49. Joaquín Villalobos, interview by author, Washington, D.C., 11 September 1994. For further discussion of this issue, see chapter 6.

50. Alberto Enríquez, interview by author, Washington, D.C., 9 December 1994.

51. Caballero (1981, 208).

52. North (1985, 49). Calculation into dollars for Peru by Caballero, for El Salvador by author.

53. Data for Peru from Figueroa (1983, 68); for El Salvador from Diskin (1989, 432). Calculations into dollars in the original text. Diskin writes that the Salvadoran incomes were "below" about $225.

54. Figure is calculated as 18 percent in Peru by McClintock (1984, 61), drawing upon Webb (1977, 39); Caballero (1981, 207–208); and World Bank (1981, 155); and as 15 percent in El Salvador by Morales Velado (1989, 88); and North (1985, 48).

55. McClintock (1984, 61); and *Andean Report*, October 1985, 168–169.

56. In El Salvador, by the mid-1970s, official socioeconomic data were no longer broken down by department. Rather, data were broken down by "region" (west, central, paracentral, and east). Unfortunately, relatively poor and relatively prosperous departments were subsumed under this new geographic demarcation; for example, Chalatenango and San Salvador were both subsumed under the demarcation of "central region." Accordingly, the new demarcation was useless for this study. Also, analysts are less likely to analyze regional variation in El Salvador simply because it is a small country.

57. Zschock (1988, 50–51).

58. CONADE (1982, 8, 27, 21); and Zschock (1988, 50, 51, 117).

59. McClintock (1984, 60); and McClintock (1989a, 66–67).

60. McClintock (1984, 60).

61. Webb (1977, 119–129).

62. CELADE (1988, 18).

63. Ministerio de Educación and Ministerio de Salud Pública (1989, 41).

64. Fiedler (1986, appendix E).

65. Grupo Asesor Económico y Social (1990, 112).

66. CONADE (1982, 8, 21, and 27).

67. Ibid.

68. Data for Ecuador from Luzuriaga and Zuvekas (1983, 48); data for Peru from Webb (1977, 119–129).

69. The value of property transferred per beneficiary in the "agrarian zone" of Ayacucho was a mere 3 percent of the value of property transferred per beneficiary in the Lima zone. See McClintock (1984, 66) for a comprehensive discussion.

70. McClintock (1981, 48–63); and Deere (1990, 236–246). "Reserves" (sectors of the estates that usually included the best land) were not allowed for former owners, and compensation was minimal.

71. Wise (1986, 25–31); Diskin (1989, 441); and Pelupessy (1991, 44). On expropriated estates, "reserves" were allowed, and compensation was considerable.

72. In the final years of the reform, the government seemed to be augmenting the figures. Contrast the data in Martínez and Tealdo (1982, 20) with Matos Mar and Mejía (1980, 68); and McClintock (1981, 60).

73. Figure includes all members of Agrarian Production Cooperatives (CAPs) and the approximately 20 percent of Agrarian Social Interest Society (SAIS) constituents who were former hacienda workers. Peasant community members of the SAIS benefited much less. See McClintock (1981, 48–63); Caballero and Alvarez (1980, 63); and Matos Mar and Mejía (1980, 64–70).

74. McClintock (1984, 64), based on data from Peru's Ministry of Agriculture.

75. McClintock (1982, 142). These three cooperatives were representative of the universe of Peruvian cooperatives at the time of my initial field work in 1974. Subsequently, however, as agrarian reform officials were adjudicating land of lower quality in disadvantaged highlands regions, my three cooperatives became more prosperous than average. See McClintock (1981, 89–92).

76. McClintock (1981, 288–296).

77. U.S. AID bases its figures on those collected by ISTA (Instituto Salvadoreño para la Transformación Agricola). However, the Salvadoran Ministry of Agriculture and its subagencies report lower numbers; see Ruben (1991, 36); Ministerio de Agricultura y Ganadería (1989, 236); and FINATA (1990, 8). The figures are especially high in the U.S. AID data for "Phase 1" beneficiaries. It appears that U.S. AID may include "beneficiaries" who have abandoned the cooperatives in its statistics.

78. "Phase 1" encompasses decrees 154 and 842 of March 1980. "Phase 3" encompasses decree 207 of April 1980. "Phase 2," which was targeted primarily at the adjudication of the country's prime coffee estates, was not implemented. Data on numbers of beneficiaries and percentages of agricultural families are based on U.S. AID data for June 1991, which are higher than data from Salvadoran sources, especially for Phase 1 beneficiaries. See note 77.

79. Gore, McReynolds, and Johnston (1987, 95). For this survey, contracted by U.S. AID in El Salvador, respondents from a 1978 nonmetropolitan household

survey were interviewed again. Collaborating with U.S.-based scholars and numerous officials in Salvadoran ministries, the chief investigators for this survey were meticulous. The bias toward optimism that tended to mark U.S. government publications on El Salvador was not apparent. Unfortunately, however, the sixty-nine beneficiaries are not distinguished by phase.

80. Ibid., 53, 96.

81. Survey by Antonio Orellana. One hundred fourteen members of eight sites of agrarian reform beneficiaries, about half of whom were beneficiaries under Phase 1 and half under Phase 3, were interviewed in three departments in May 1991. Most were affiliated with the Unión Comunal Salvadoreña (UCS), which received considerable support from the U.S.-based American Institute for Free Labor Development (AIFLD). Also, in contrast to the Gore, McReynolds, and Johnston survey, in which individual household members were interviewed at their residences, Orellana was seeking permission for the interviews from the directors of the cooperatives, and members may have felt that their answers should be diplomatic.

82. Gore, McReynolds, and Johnston (1987, 95); Wise (1986, 22); and Orellana survey (1991). Ministerio de Agricultura y Ganadería (1989, 184–216) indicates that these improvements were in fact realized in the Phase 1 cooperatives.

83. Whereas incomes for landless rural families averaged about $315 in El Salvador in 1975 (North, 1985, 48), in 1989 family incomes for Phase 1 beneficiaries averaged about $880. See Diskin (1989, 432); and FINATA (1990, table 15). Although these figures are nominal data in current dollars, they yet suggest a significant improvement. Incomes for Phase 1 beneficiaries in 1989 were slightly higher than for Phase 3 beneficiaries.

84. Gore, McReynolds, and Johnston (1987, 95); and 1991 Orellana survey (see chapter 3, note 266).

85. Strasma (1989, 422, 427); and Wise (1986, 62). The increase was from $371 in 1982 to $732 in 1984, in current dollars.

86. For Peru, my comments are based primarily on my original field research and numerous follow-up visits to three cooperatives (two coastal CAPs and one highlands SAIS) spanning fifteen years. See, especially, McClintock (1981, 219–258). For an excellent analysis of a set of reform enterprises in a disadvantaged highlands department, see Deere (1990, 246–254). For El Salvador, my comments are derived primarily from secondary sources, including Gore, McReynolds, and Johnston (1987, 95); Diskin (1989); Reinhardt (1989); Barraclough and Scott (1987); Wise (1986); Ruben (1991); Pelupessy (1991); Strasma (1989, 425); Mason (1986); Mason (1990, 19); and Ministerio de Agricultura y Ganadería (1989, 147–184). In October 1990, I also visited the Phase 1 cooperative, Escuintla, a former cotton estate in the department of La Paz.

87. The most salient fears on these issues were expressed for Peru by Quijano (1975); and Cotler (1975). Although the debt owed by the cooperatives was originally large in Peru, it was not indexed for inflation, and its real amount decreased

markedly in the late 1970s; finally, in 1979 the outstanding debt was canceled. See McClintock (1981, 62). On these concerns with respect to El Salvador, see Diskin (1989, 444–445); and Barraclough and Scott (1987, 73–74). On the amelioration of the debt burden under the Duarte government, see Pelupessy (1991, 51).

88. Mason (1986, 507); and DeYoung (1982, A1, A16).

89. Dickey (1993, A2). He suggests that the death squads were responsible for most of the violence, but that the FMLN was also responsible for some. See also Strasma (1989, 414); and FINATA (1989, 3). The FMLN forcibly compelled some cooperatives which had grown cotton for export to diversify away from cotton. See Strasma (1989, 415).

90. Diskin (1989, 441–446).

91. Pelupessy (1991, 45).

92. Barraclough and Scott (1987, 74).

93. Prosterman, Riedinger, and Temple (1981, 66); Mason (1986, 508); and FINATA (1990, table 1).

94. Diskin (1989, 435); and Dickey (1983, A2) reported that only forty of three hundred peasants theoretically eligible for Phase 3 benefits in the municipality of San Francisco Chinameca applied for land. Twenty-seven of these forty were murdered—nineteen by death squads and eight by the FMLN. Some of the eligible peasants not claiming Phase 3 land refrained because the owner was their relative—often their parent (Strasma, 1989, 423).

95. Wise (1986, 20). Slightly different figures for different years are provided in Dickey (1983, A2); and FINATA (1989, 8).

96. McClintock (1981, 369–370).

97. Wise (1986, 61–63). In 1982, 41 percent of Phase 3 families were earning less than $200 per year, and the average for Phase 3 families was $371. See Wise (1986, 61–63). Diskin (1989, 432) identifies the "rural poor" as those living on an income below $225 in 1977. A slightly higher income figure is suggested by North (1985, 49).

98. Data on the impact of the reform by department were very difficult to gather in El Salvador. Even when taking into account the small size of the country and the regional rather than departmental breakdowns, I concluded that the regional variation was a fact that official analysts were downplaying.

99. U.S. Department of State (1984b, 6). The pattern indicated in the U.S. Department of State data is also suggested in the data on numbers of Phase 3 beneficiaries by department as of January 1989 given to me by FINATA.

100. Precise figures are not available. See the map of Salvadoran departments. Most figures are reported by region, not department.

101. Ibid.

102. Ministerio de Agricultura y Ganadería (1989, table 1).

103. Matos Mar and Mejía (1980, 20).

104. Deere (1990, 246–254).

105. Caballero and Alvarez (1980, 63).

106. Majos Mar and Mejía (1980, 20).

107. Caballero and Alvarez (1980, 63); and McClintock (1984, 66).

108. The terms of this joint structure varied considerably. See McClintock (1981, 35–37). In my category of "agrarian cooperative members" above, I include the ex-hacienda workers in SAIS but not the peasant community members. The figure for ex-hacienda workers in SAIS is an estimate based on my own knowledge of various Peruvian SAIS. See McClintock (1981, 92).

109. For SAIS and Peasant Group beneficiaries as percentages of all beneficiaries, see Matos Mar and Mejía (1980, 20).

110. McClintock (1989a, 74). Calculation is based on families benefited by department in Ministry of Agriculture (1975, table 4); and 1972 economically active population in agriculture by department in Marletta and Bardales (n.d., 216–222). I have used the figure of 1.5 economically active persons in agriculture per agricultural family. The 50 percent figure is an average for the two north-coast departments.

111. Ministry of Agriculture (1975, table 4). Calculation of the exact number of peasant-community members is impossible because they are joined with ex-hacienda workers in the SAIS in the Ministry of Agriculture's data.

112. Ministry of Agriculture (1975, table 4).

113. Ibid.; Vela (1980); and Padrón Castillo and Pease García (1974, 47).

114. Vela (1980).

115. See, for example, Seligmann (1995).

116. Osvaldo Hurtado, "Los pobres: Otra vez en la escena," *Opinión*, 6 May 1993, 1.

117. Of course, especially as governments implement free market policies, the prices for agricultural products are a result of market forces rather than government policies. During the 1970s and 1980s, however, Latin American governments did intervene in various ways to affect producer prices in agriculture, and their actions were widely perceived to be important to these prices by peasants.

118. The terms of trade for the basic grains that are most important for disadvantaged peasants were adverse between 1978 and the mid-1980s in El Salvador, but improved considerably after 1990. See Ruben (1991, 26); and Zuvekas (1993, 14).

119. McClintock (1987, 103). The data available for El Salvador suggest that the amount of agricultural credit remained the same between 1980 and 1984, but declined markedly after the mid-1980s. See Wise (1986, 43); and Ruben (1991, 26).

120. McClintock (1987, 105).

121. Ibid., 104–108.

122. Deere (1990, 255–260); and Mitchell (1991).

123. Berg (1986–87, 182).

124. Ruben (1991, 22, 60).

125. Menzel (1994, 33, 49); and Rosenberg (1991b, 246). Both report the wage in dollar terms.

126. Vilca was one of the sites of my long-standing research in rural Peru. In much of my previous work, I used pseudonyms in an effort to protect the identities of specific leaders. I referred to SAIS Cahuide as SAIS Huanca, and Vilca as Varya. Now, however, time has passed and it is necessary to compare my scholarly results with other studies of the SAIS.

127. This was a nonrandom application, primarily to men, of a brief questionnaire. For further information on Vilca and on the nature of these surveys, see McClintock (1981, 102–105).

128. For information on these nonrandom surveys, see ibid.

129. For example, data are missing for El Salvador's rural sector in Jazairy, Alamgir, and Panuccio (1992, 386). Although the absence of data by department or by rural sector is in part a function of El Salvador's relatively small size, it probably also reflects a relative lack of concern about the issue in El Salvador.

130. Wilkie and Contreras (1992, 170–172).

131. Haiti and Bolivia were the other two countries. The results of the study are reported by U.S. AID (1984, 3), but publication information about the World Bank study is not provided.

132. Webb and Fernández Baca (1991, 241); and Mitchell (1991, 128).

133. *Savia*, no. 1 (6 July 1989), 5.

134. Fernández Baca (1982, 89–90).

135. World Bank (1981, 140).

136. González (1982, 43), for unspecified southern highlands zone as of approximately 1980.

137. Data on decline in potato production in McClintock (1984, 69); the quotation is from *Andean Focus* (November–December 1983), 1. The map provided by Torres Guevara (1997, 14) shows the close correlation between the zones of drought during El Niño and the southern highlands areas where Sendero was expanding at the time.

138. World Bank (1995, 104 and 270).

139. Attempts were made to secure Salvadoran data, but without success. The relative lack of data about malnutrition in El Salvador may reflect the relative paucity of malnutrition there, and the concomitant paucity of conern about it.

140. The exact World Bank figure is 15 percent in 1970–75 and 13 percent in 1980–85; see World Bank (1995, 270). The Peruvian-source data are reported in Webb and Fernández Baca (1992, 313–314).

141. *Savia*, no. 1 (6 July 1989), 4.

142. Mitchell (1991, 128).

143. Concurring with this analysis are, among others, Gabriel Marcella (in a conversation in Carlisle, Pa., 8 September 1994). Recall also the comments by Alberto Enríquez above, and see the discussion of scholars' interpretations and the interviews with militants in chapter 6.

144. Interviews, as a member of a delegation of the Commission on United States–Central American Relations, with peasants in the villages of San Francisco Gotera and Delicias de Concepción in Morazán, 19 January 1983; conversations, as a member of the Center for Democracy's International Election Observation Mission, in Morazán communities on 10 March 1991. Also, as a member of the election-monitoring delegation of the U.S. Citizens Elections Observer Mission (USCEOM), I posed this question on 20 March 1994, in the town of Aguilares, which is in the department of San Salvador but near the border with Chalatenango, and in the town of Arcatao in Chalatenango.

145. Kathryn Leger, "Peruvians Struggle to Get by as Economy Deteriorates," *Christian Science Monitor,* 1 November 1988, 9. Although the Shining Path did not advance in Puno in the early 1980s, and there were major setbacks to its advance in the department in the later 1980s due to what was perceived by many citizens as unfair attacks, it did indeed gain many supporters in the department; see note 252 in chapter 2.

146. Peasant in Canchapalca, a peasant community in SAIS Huanca, to my research team, 1981.

147. Peasant in CAP María Laura (referred to as Marla in my previous work), on the north coast near Virú, 1983.

148. Wickham-Crowley (1992, 23–28, 213–215); and chapter 6.

149. See chapter 6. The possibility of similar economic concerns as stimuli to political alienation is discussed for several European cases by Davies (1962).

150. Degregori (1990, 253). All Ayacucho university students were at the National University at San Cristóbal de Huamonga, where Sendero originated (see chapter 6).

151. Inter-American Development Bank (1987a, 130).

152. Ibid.

153. Crabtree (1992, 9).

154. Webb and Fernández Baca (1992, 492); and Crabtree (1992, 9).

155. Webb and Fernández Baca (1990, 211). For reasons discussed in the first section of this chapter, unemployment data are not good indicators of poverty in most Latin American countries.

156. Cuánto (1991, 79).

157. Gregory (1991, 7).

158. Ibid., 19, 28.

159. *New York Times,* 26 June 1991, A8.

160. *Wall Street Journal,* 31 December 1990, 1.

161. Ansión, Del Castillo, Piqueras, and Zegarra (1992, 44); and Burgos (1991, 42). Kirk (1992, 21) reports that a kindergarten teacher's salary was $55 a month in approximately 1990. Strong (1992, 259) reports $85 in June 1991. Calculations into dollars are especially difficult for the late 1980s and early 1990s because of extremely high inflation.

162. *New York Times,* 8 December 1991, E3.

163. Ansión et al. (1992, 44).

164. Gregory (1991, 23). I am assuming that teachers have thirteen or more years of schooling. Exchange-rate calculations from data in *International Financial Statistics Yearbook.*

165. Another interesting comparison is the minimum teachers' salary of $172 in Chile in the early 1990s. See *Latin America Weekly Report,* 16 September 1993, 425. Helen Atkinson-Barnes, a Ph.D. candidate at the University of Michigan who lived in Quito for several months in 1992, reported that teachers' salaries in Ecuador were at about $100 in the early 1990s.

166. Data collected by Rodolfo Osores from documents in the Huancayo Ministry of Health, in *Intis* and *Nuevo Soles.* Exchange-rate calculations made through data published in *El dólar día a día,* of Cuánto. Rosenberg (1991b, 11) reports a scant $45 monthly salary for nurses.

167. Gregory (1991, 30)

168. The time frame in Peru was the period during which the respondent had been working at the ministry; in Peru the average was about twelve years. In El Salvador the year of comparison was roughly 1983, "before Duarte became president."

169. The definition of the state in this book follows Skocpol (1985, 7), who in turn is following Weber: "compulsory associations claiming control over territories and the people within them. Administrative, legal, extractive, and coercive organizations are the core of any state." In other words, the key components of "the state" are bureaucratic agencies. For a similar emphasis, see Geddes (1990). A review of the various definitions of the concept is provided by Rosenau (1988).

170. This question has been salient among analysts of state capabilities. See, for example, Geddes (1990); and Anderson (1987).

171. The surveys were carried out in the Huancayo Ministry of Health in June, July, and August 1990 and in the Huancayo Ministry of Agriculture in September and October 1990. President García was succeeded by President Fujimori on 28 July 1990.

172. See, for example, Crabtree (1992, 162); and Graham (1992, 198–199).

173. Both the head of my Peruvian research team, Rodolfo Osores, and his wife were employed at the Huancayo Ministry of Health. Both Osores in Peru and Orellana in El Salvador were able to collect survey data on relatively sensitive issues from health bureaucrats (see appendix I).

174. World Bank (1993, 195–206) discusses in depth the procedures used in data collection and the various flaws. In particular, in poor nations where significant percentages of the population reside in remote rural areas, comprehensive data can rarely be collected. In Peru, El Salvador, and Ecuador more than 10 percent of deaths are not registered, for example. The problem has become more severe since 1990. See World Bank (1993, 197, 200). The Salvadoran Ministry of Health estimated that 20 percent of infant deaths were not reported in 1989. See *Anuario salud pública en cifras* no. 20 (1989): 4. Carlos Indacochea, an official at UNICEF in Peru with a Ph.D. in demography from Cornell University, estimated on 31 January 1993 that 33 percent of infant deaths in Peru were not reported.

175. Infant mortality rates are reported in the table rather than children-under-five mortality rates or maternal mortality because these data are missing for the earlier decades in the *Social Indicators of Development* series published by the World Bank.

176. World Bank (1993, 43); and Sollis (1992, 337). The increase in the number of doctors was especially dramatic in El Salvador; by the 1980s, however, the number of doctors per capita in Peru and Ecuador was still about double the number in El Salvador. See World Bank, *Social Indicators of Development, 1993* (Baltimore: Johns Hopkins University Press, 1993), 97, 101, 263. By contrast, the provision of hospital beds was not an important factor.

177. World Bank (1993, 52–86).

178. Data from the Economic Commission for Latin America and the Caribbean, the Inter-American Development Bank, and the World Bank are not consistent. The data for health expenditure in World Bank (1993) are higher than in the other sources. The higher figures are probably the result of including food aid under the health rubric, an inclusion usually not made by the governments. See World Bank (1993, 197). The data of ECLAC (1993, 53) and the data of the Inter-American Development Bank (1988, 75–76) are both from official government sources and jibe relatively closely.

179. All figures in this paragraph from ECLAC (1993, 53); and Inter-American Development Bank (1988, 75).

180. ECLAC (1993, 53). The World Bank (1993) does not, however, suggest such a drastic decline in expenditure in Peru in 1990.

181. ECLAC (1993, 53).

182. All subsequent figures in this paragraph from World Bank, *World Development Report, 1993*, 210.

183. Ibid., 52–71; article by Lawrence K. Altman, *New York Times,* 7 July 1993, A8.

184. In El Salvador in 1978, 70 percent of the doctors lived in San Salvador (IDHUCA, 1991, 666); in 1985, 46 percent of all hospital beds were in San Salvador. See Inter-American Development Bank (1987b, annex 8). In Peru, 67 percent of

doctors were located in Lima in 1985 and 55 percent of all beds were in Lima/Callao at that date (Zschock, 1985, 115, 146). In Ecuador, 27 percent of hospital beds were in Pichincha (the department where Quito is located) and 33 percent in Guayas. See CONADE (1982, 121).

185. *New York Times,* 21 April 1991, A7.

186. The figure for Lima is for 1990–91. See ibid. The figures for the rural populations are for 1985–87. See Jazairy, Alamgir, and Panuccio (1992, 394–395). Figures are averages for percentages of the population with access to safe water and access to sanitation.

187. Ecuador's "most recent estimate" figure for percentage of the rural population with access to safe water was a 287 percent improvement over the figure for fifteen to twenty years previously, in comparison to a 43 percent improvement in El Salvador and a scant 13 percent improvement in Peru. See World Bank, *Social Indicators of Development, 1990,* 88, 92, 244.

188. World Health Organization, "Cholera in the Americas," data sheet kindly provided to me. See also *New York Times,* 8 March 1992, E4.

189. World Bank (1993, 206), 206.

190. Data courtesy of Pan American Health Organization, "Annual Notifications of Tuberculosis 1974 to 1991, American Region."

191. For El Salvador, IDHUCA (1991, 664) calculates that 40 percent of the public health budget was allocated to support urban hospitals, while 60 percent was allocated to smaller health centers providing primary health care to the urban and rural poor. By contrast, in Peru the figures were 75 percent for urban hospitals versus 25 percent for primary health care centers, according to Zschock (1988, 4). As these different sources probably used different methodologies, the cross-national comparison should be considered only suggestive.

192. The year of the survey was 1990 in Peru, and 1991 in El Salvador and Ecuador. There was a clear perception in both Ecuador and Peru that the nation's regime had changed from military to civilian at the turn of the decade. In El Salvador, by contrast, regime labels and chronologies were murkier for most citizens. In El Salvador, my research team often found respondents thinking in terms of changes between the Duarte and Cristiani administrations, rather than changes between the precarious military juntas of the early 1980s and the Cristiani administration.

193. Data on vaccination campaigns in the Huancayo jurisdiction in 1990 were collected by Rodolfo Osores.

194. Percentages are imperfectly comparable because Peruvian respondents cited more than one "serious problem," whereas Salvadoran respondents cited only one. However, the plural word "problems" was used in the Salvadoran survey.

195. My own review of the questionnaires from the Huancayo Ministry of Health.

196. My own review of the annual reports of the Peruvian and Salvadoran Ministries of Health.

197. As table 4.13 indicates, the question about honest reporting of purchase prices was unfortunately asked only in the Ministry of Agriculture in Peru.

198. One important variable that affects these results is education. In all three nations, better-educated respondents are more likely to be critical of cronyism and corruption, and our Peruvian and Ecuadorean samples are better educated than our Salvadoran (due primarily to the better educational levels in Peru and Ecuador than in El Salvador).

199. The cynicism about the Ecuadorean regime of the early 1990s in the CEDATOS sample is indicated by other Ecuadorean survey research firms as well. See, for example, the survey by Instituto de Estudios Sociales y de la Opinión Pública reported in Isaacs (1991, 228).

200. Glewwe and Hall (1994, 715).

5. U.S. Policy and Latin American Revolutions

1. See chapter 1. For example, Wickham-Crowley (1992, 12) acknowledges that his study excludes "the international level of analysis." Note also that my emphasis is on the importance of international actors to the outcome of a revolutionary challenge, not its emergence or its expansion.

2. For excellent overviews, see Blasier (1985); and Molineu (1990). Nations in Central America and the Caribbean, such as El Salvador, have traditionally been the focus of especially intense U.S. concern. However, the levels of aid to Colombia cited in the introduction to this book, as well as U.S. policy toward Bolivia after the 1952 revolution and toward Chile between 1964 and 1973, when the United States was rejecting even democratically elected Marxist leadership for the country, highlight the geographical extension of the U.S. "backyard."

3. This is an argument that among the conditions necessary for a victory by a revolutionary movement in Latin America during the Cold War was a U.S. decision not to rescue the beleaguered regime. It is not an argument that among the conditions necessary for a defeat of a revolutionary movement during the Cold War was a U.S. decision to rescue the regime. Although, as I suggest in the introduction, U.S. support was a factor in the defeat of numerous Latin American insurgencies during the Cold War, the United States played virtually no role in the defeat of the Guatemalan National Revolutionary Unity (Unidad Revolucionaria Nacional Guatemalteca, URNG) in Guatemala in 1981–82. The Guatemalan insurgency was large and its attacks intense; but, poorly equipped or prepared militarily, it was defeated—and defeated quickly, within about a year—amid a savage military onslaught. If the defeat had not been so rapid and decisive, both the United States and East bloc actors would have likely played a more important role in its trajec-

tory. On the revolutionary challenge and its defeat, see Wickham-Crowley (1992, 289–291); Dunkerley (1988, 483–491); and Barry (1992, 65–71).

4. Colonel James J. Steele, in Manwaring and Prisk (1988, 363). Wickham-Crowley (1989, 512) estimates that the number of Salvadoran guerrillas was about double the number of Nicaraguan guerrillas. See also Castañeda (1994, 98); and Dix (1984, 440).

5. See chapter 2 for a discussion of East bloc support for the FMLN. For the perception of Democratic Senator James Exon of an FMLN victory as a "Communist guerrilla takeover," see *New York Times*, 4 February 1982, 1. A comprehensive analysis of this topic is beyond the scope of this book.

6. On U.S. support for threatened democratic or quasi-democratic regimes during the Cold War, see the introduction.

7. See note 11 in the introduction.

8. Most focus on the increased power of the Salvadoran military. See, for example, Peltz (1990, 44); Migdail (1983, 20–22); Colonel René Ponce in Manwaring and Prisk (1988, 61–62); and Bacevich et al. (1988, 36–37).

9. Calculation is for the years 1985–89; the population of El Salvador during this period was approximately five million, and that of Peru approximately twenty million. See figures in the annual volume *Economic and Social Progress in Latin America*, issued by the Inter-American Development Bank. Longer-term trends and components of U.S. aid are specified in subsequent sections of this chapter.

10. Malloy (1970).

11. This paragraph is based primarily on ibid., 126–150. On repression under the PURS government, see ibid., 127, 134, 135; and Alexander (1958, 43).

12. On the elections and their aftermath, see Malloy (1970, 151–154); Mitchell (1977, 31–32); and Alexander (1958, 39–43).

13. Mitchell (1977, 32); and Malloy (1970, 154–155).

14. Malloy (1970, 156–157); Alexander (1958, 44); Selbin (1993, 39); and *Time*, 21 April 1952, 38.

15. *New York Times*, 10 April 1952, 3.

16. This paragraph draws upon Mitchell (1977, 32–33); Malloy (1970, 157); and Dunkerley (1984, 38–40).

17. Mitchell (1977, 33). See also the estimates of four hundred in *Time*, 28 April 1952, 39; and approximately five hundred by Dunkerley (1984, 39).

18. Malloy (1970, 164).

19. *Newsweek*, 28 May 1951, 46–47; and 28 May 1951, 36; *Time*, 28 May 1951, 43–44; *New York Times*, 15 May 1951, 18; 17 May 1951, 1, 15; 18 May 1951, 15; 19 May 1951, 6; 20 May 1951, 30; 16 April 1952, 8, L8; and 20 April 1952, 22; and *Time*, 21 April 1952, 38; and 28 April 1952, 39.

20. Zondag (1982, 29).

21. See periodicals cited in note 19, as well as Blasier (1985, 129–130); and Zondag (1982, 254–270).

22. A cogent account is Blasier (1985, 129–131). See also Andrade (1976, 126–156).

23. Mitchell (1977, 18, 27). Among the thirty MNR leaders whose education is indicated by Mitchell, only three (one of whom was Lechín) lacked a university education. See also Zondag (1952, 30).

24. *New York Times,* 15 May 1951, 18.

25. Dunkerley (1984, 42).

26. Malloy (1970, 217).

27. *El Diario,* 17 April 1952, quoted in Dunkerley (1984, 42).

28. Andrade (1976, 126–186).

29. Alexander (1958, 255).

30. Zondag (1982, 29–30). For similar assessments of the U.S. stance, see Malloy (1970, 217–218); and Dunkerley (1984, 58).

31. Wright (1991, 11).

32. *Time,* 12 January 1959, 32.

33. Benjamin (1990, 92–104); and Domínguez (1978, 54–109).

34. Bonsal (1971, 11). One indication of Batista's pro-U.S. position was his immediate breaking of relations with the Soviet Union.

35. Thomas (1977, 4–10); Matthews (1975, 13); and Wright (1991, 7–8).

36. Franqui (1980, 45); Bonsal (1971, 11); and Thomas (1977, 7–16).

37. Blackburn (1963, 80); Matthews (1975, 122); and Thomas (1971, 191).

38. Thomas (1977, 260); Blackburn (1963, 76); Geyer (1993, 198); Matthews (1975, 122); and Dix (1983, 283). A higher estimate (seven thousand by December 1958) is given by Paterson (1994, 200), but neither Fidel Castro nor Ché Guevara claimed such numbers.

39. Wickham-Crowley (1992, 327–328); Thomas (1977, 261); Blackburn (1963, 76–77); and *Time,* 12 January 1959, 32.

40. On territorial control in Oriente, but only there, see Thomas (1977, 261); Domínguez (1978, 435–437); Paterson (1994, 141, 176, 243); Franqui (1980, 461); Geyer (1993, 192–193); and Szulc (1986, 455). The Sierra Maestra mountains are in the Oriente province.

41. Paterson (1994, 195); and Smith (1990, 155). See also Bonsal (1971, 22); the boycott was apparently somewhat successful in Camaguey as well.

42. My calculation from descriptions and maps that designate areas of rebel control as of December 1958. See *Time,* 1 December 1958, 34; and *Newsweek,* 5 January 1959, 38. Estimates do vary; Montaner (1981, 11) suggested 10 percent. On the expansion by the various rebel groups, see Matthews (1975, 112); and Thomas (1977, 238).

43. Thomas (1977, 262); and *Time*, 26 January 1959, 47.

44. Blackburn (1963, 75); Smith (1990, 168); Thomas (1977, 242, 248, 256–259); and Geyer (1993, 193–194).

45. Thomas (1977, 262); and Montaner (1981, 10, 18–19). These are careful estimates to which both authors devote considerable discussion.

46. Pérez-Stable (1993, 62); Wickham-Crowley (1992, 158); and *Time*, 1 December 1958, 34.

47. See discussion below of the general strike and the summary statement in *Time*, 1 December 1958, 34.

48. Paterson (1994, 141–145); and Thomas (1977, 206–222).

49. Smith (1987, 18); and Paterson (1994, 144).

50. For overviews of the Eisenhower administration's policies in Latin America, see Rabe (1988); and Benjamin (1990, 136–140).

51. Benjamin (1990, 119–126); Rabe (1988, 119–120); and Bonsal (1971, 11–17).

52. Rabe (1988, 87).

53. Paterson (1994, 78).

54. Ibid., 79–80; and Bonsal (1971, 20).

55. Paterson (1994, 84–85, 117–118, 176).

56. Ibid., 135–136; Rabe (1988, 106); and Benjamin (1990, 138).

57. Paterson (1994, 87).

58. *Time*, 26 January 1959, 47.

59. Paterson (1994, 125).

60. Benjamin (1990, 152); and Domínguez (1978, 64).

61. Benjamin (1990, 152); Paterson (1994, 135, 199, 247); Thomas (1977, 203); and *New York Times*, 28 March 1958, 9. Batista harped about the arms embargo, but scholars are virtually unanimous that the regime's problem was not the quantity of arms available to it but its misuse of its weapons.

62. Rabe (1988, 100); and Smith (1987, 46–47).

63. Rabe (1988, 105, 174).

64. Paterson (1994, 126–128); and Smith (1990).

65. Paterson (1994, 133).

66. Ibid., 196; Bonsal (1971, 22); and Smith (1990, 155).

67. Paterson (1994, 219, 247).

68. On the Pawley initiative, see Paterson (1994, 208–210).

69. Franqui (1980, 476); and Szulc (1986, 456–458).

70. Thomas (1977, 242).

71. Paterson (1994, 222).

72. Szulc (1986, 458).

73. On Castro's concern, see Paterson (1994, 200–201).

74. Ibid., 219; and Benjamin (1990, 155).

75. Benjamin (1990, 155); and Rabe (1988, 122).

76. Thomas (1977, 272–274); Rabe (1988, 118); Geyer (1993, 187–194); and Welch (1985,10). This was also the conclusion of an exhaustive assessment by the U.S. Bureau of Intelligence and Research in December 1958. See Smith (1987, 15); and Benjamin (1990, 155–156).

77. The post-Batista president of Cuba was to be not Castro but Manuel Urrutia, a career jurist from Santiago who was in exile; former President Prío had also provided considerable financial support for the 26th of July Movement and was expecting a role in the next government, as were numerous other middle-class financial supporters of the revolutionaries. See *Time*, 12 January 1959, 33; and Benjamin (1990, 155–156).

78. Figure from Paterson (1994, 249).

79. There were brief periods in which hand-picked successors governed.

80. At this time, Latin American elections were not monitored and no rigorous evaluations were attempted. But there was journalistic and scholarly consensus that "what the Somozas would never entertain was the idea that they should permit the opposition, however moderate, to come to power." See Christian (1985, 25). Just a few weeks before the 1967 election, more than two hundred persons at an opposition rally were killed by the National Guard. See Pezzullo and Pezzullo (1993, 256). On the censorship, repression, and co-optation that Anastasio's father used against potential opposition forces, see Walter (1993, 226–230).

81. See the suggestion of madness in *Time*, 25 June 1979, 31.

82. The label "dictator" was used in the title of some stories. See, for example, *Time*, 11 September 1978, 26; and 30 July 1979, 34. The term was used in the text of articles in *Time* in the following issues: 4 September 1978, 24; 25 September 1978, 30; 23 April 1979, 38; 25 June 1979, 38; 2 July 1979, 36; 16 July 1979, 29; and 13 August 1979, 22. It was also used in the text of articles in *Newsweek* in the following issues: 25 September 1978, 48; 2 October 1978, 65; and 20 July 1979, 45.

83. As *Newsweek* (25 September 1978, 48) reports: "the dictator [was] inside his fortified bunker in Managua, circling within the thick walls that separated him from the realities of this tortured nation." I have counted five references to his bunker in stories in *Time* during 1978–79, three in *Newsweek*, and two in the *New York Times*.

84. Crawley (1979, 155–156). In the mid-1970s, Somoza's drinking became more excessive. He appeared in public with his mistress, and his American-born wife prepared to leave Nicaragua. One of his daughters had fled to London after the National Guard tortured and exiled her boyfriend, a Sandinista. In July 1977, Somoza suffered a second heart attack; he was in Miami recovering for almost two months and feared a third, fatal heart attack.

85. Torrijos as quoted by Pastor (1987, 89); and Pezzullo and Pezzullo (1993, 51).

86. Booth (1985, 145, 150).

87. See, for example, Dunkerley (1988, 250); and Dunkerley (1983, 143).

88. See Booth (1985, 116–121), Gould (1990); Wright (1991, 185); and Wickham-Crowley (1992, 232). Following Booth (1985, 150), Wickham-Crowley (1992, 232) also identifies departments to the east and northeast (Jinotega and Zelaya) as Sandinista "fronts"; however, empirical evidence is lacking. These were scantily populated areas, and they were not areas of especially intense Sandinista attacks in 1978–79.

89. Dunkerley (1988, 240).

90. Ibid., 248; Booth (1985, 168); Chavarría (1982, 34); and *Time,* 2 July 1979, 37.

91. Pedro Joaquín Chamorro had broken with the Conservative Party over its collaboration with the Somoza family. UDEL had been formed in 1974 and included Christian Democrats, trade unionists, and some Socialists. See Pezzullo and Pezzullo (1993, 259). Chamorro was also the editor of the leading opposition daily, *La Prensa.*

92. On the general strike, see Pezzullo and Pezzullo (1993, 262).

93. See especially Booth (1985, 144–146, 163–165).

94. Led by Alfonso Robelo, the FAO included UDEL, the Socialist Party, and the MDN (Nicaraguan Democratic Movement), made up of about two hundred businessmen, professionals, and commercial farmers. See Everingham (1996, 142–144); and Pezzullo and Pezzullo (1993, 263–265).

95. Pezzullo and Pezzullo (1993, 265); Booth (1985, 165); and Everingham (1996, 153). Rebels had gained control of Matagalpa a week or so before the coordinated offensive.

96. Booth (1985, 166); and *Time,* 2 October 1978, 39–40.

97. Estimates of the number of deaths range from 1,500 to 5,000. See Booth (1985, 166); Charvarría (1982, 33); and Pezzullo and Pezzullo (1993, 266).

98. Chavarría (1982, 35); Booth (1985, 165); and Pezzullo and Pezzullo (1993, 263, 265).

99. *Time,* 25 September 1978, 30; 2 July 1979, 38; *Newsweek,* 11 September 1978, 44; 18 June 1979, 43; and 23 October 1978, 69.

100. *Time,* 11 September 1978, 26. For similar comments, see *Time,* 25 September 1978, 30; *Newsweek,* 11 September 1978, 44; *Newsweek,* 2 October 1978, 66.; *New York Times,* 11 June 1979, A9.

101. Lake (1989, 270).

102. By July 1979 the number of militants was usually estimated at about five thousand, but again it is impossible to know how many of these members were really pro-FSLN, rather than merely anti-Somoza. For the estimate of five thousand, see Wickham-Crowley (1989, 512); Booth (1985, 176); Chavarría (1982, 36);

and *Time,* 30 July 1979, 34. The U.S. government's estimate was lower: two thousand in May 1979. See Pezzullo and Pezzullo (1993, 71). Wright (1991, 185) suggests two thousand armed members plus some three thousand "irregular militia."

103. Smith (1994, 250); Pezzullo and Pezzullo (1993, 244–245); and Lake (1989, 274–275). Presumably the resignation would have been followed by elections.

104. Pastor (1987, 132, 137); and Lake (1989, 212–213, 278).

105. Pastor (1987, 79); and Smith (1994, 250). There was division among the U.S. actors about what U.S. "force" might have to be. Potentially, "force" was President Carter's summons of Somoza to the White House and request that he resign (Pezzullo and Pezzullo, 1993, 53), but at times in the past its meaning had been extended to include assassination.

106. Pastor (1987, 79); Pezzullo and Pezzullo (1993, 244); and Lake (1989, 43).

107. Pastor (1987, 79); and Lake (1989, 275).

108. Pastor (1987, 97–98); Lake (1989, 277); Christian (1985, 87–88); and Morley (1994, 176).

109. Christian (1985, 88); and Smith (1994, 250).

110. Besides León, the controlled cities included Estelí (actually captured in April before the onset of the offensive, then retaken and recaptured several times); Masaya (in June); Matagalpa, Nicaragua's third largest city (in July); among numerous other smaller cities. See, especially, Chavarría (1982, 35). Given that, for obvious reasons, reporters could not investigate the rival groups' claims to control of different areas, it is impossible to know exactly how much of Nicaraguan territory was controlled by the FSLN. In any case, there were continued clashes between the FSLN and the National Guard in numerous areas. See the maps in *Time,* 16 July 1979, 28; and *Newsweek,* 2 July 1979, 40; as well as Pezzullo and Pezzullo (1993, 270–274); and Christian (1985, 94).

111. Chavarría (1982, 35).

112. *Time,* 25 June 1979, 28–29.

113. Pezzullo and Pezzullo (1993, 55).

114. Booth (1985, 177).

115. Christian (1985, 102); Pezzullo and Pezzullo (1993, 245); and Booth (1985, 178).

116. Pezzullo and Pezzullo (1993, 246–247); Christian (1985, 102–118); and Morley (1994, 192–217).

117. Especially in the final weeks of the revolutionary challenge, Carter administration officials perceived significant Cuban support for the FSLN. See, for example, *Newsweek,* 9 July 1979, 39.

118. Pezzullo and Pezzullo (1993, 271–273); Pastor (1987, 151–152); Lake (1989, 237–243); and Dunkerley (1988, 257).

119. On the FSLN, see Booth (1985, 144); and Wright (1991, 181–182).

120. Castañeda (1993, 107). Castañeda notes the importance of "political and international factors" to the Sandinistas' victory.

121. Landau (1993, 33). For similar statements, see Smith (1995, 252).

122. For figures on aid between 1946 and 1979, see U.S. Agency for International Development, *U.S. Overseas Loans and Grants, Series of Yearly Data*, vol. 2, *Latin America and the Caribbean, FY 1946–FY 1985* (Washington, D.C.: U.S. Agency for International Development), n.p.

123. Compare figures for total economic and military aid to Latin American countries in U.S. Agency for International Development, *U.S. Overseas Loans and Grants: Latin America and the Caribbean, FY 1946–FY 1985* and subsequent annual editions of this publication. The expenditure was unprecedented both in terms of current dollars, and in terms of real dollars per capita. Since 1946, one country received more aid in real terms over a five- and ten-year period than El Salvador— Brazil during the 1960s. Per capita, however, the aid to El Salvador dwarfed the aid to Brazil.

124. The rank order for the top fourteen recipients of U.S. aid during the period 1980–90 was Israel, Egypt, Turkey, Pakistan, and then El Salvador, followed by Greece, the Philippines, India, Honduras, Bangladesh, Portugal, Costa Rica, Morocco, and Guatemala. See the annual editions of U.S. Agency for International Development, *U.S. Overseas Loans and Grants*.

125. Congressional Research Service (1989, 55–56). As this report discusses, there were various ways by which to calculate the percentage of the Salvadoran government's budget funded by the United States. Some analysts' estimates were much larger. A report to the Arms Control and Foreign Policy Caucus of the U.S. Congress estimated that, for the first time in history, in fiscal year 1987 U.S. assistance to El Salvador surpassed the contribution of the government to its own budget. See Senator Mark O. Hatfield, Representative Jim Leach, and Representative George Miller, *Bankrolling Failure: United States Policy in El Salvador and the Urgent Need for Reform* (Report of Arms Control and Foreign Policy Caucus of the U.S. Congress, November 1987), 1–2.

126. Compare aid figure in table 5.3 to figure for exports in Inter-American Development Bank (1988, 408).

127. This calculation is based on a figure of 15,000 guerrillas. This figure assumes deaths and turnover within the FMLN, whose numbers are discussed in chapter 2.

128. There has been a scholarly consensus about the correlation between these two events. For a succinct statement, see Carothers (1991, 31).

129. Arnson (1993, 55–74); and Carothers (1991, 16–18, 23–24).

130. Arnson (1993, 69–71) and, on popular attitudes, p. 92.

131. Ibid., 128–130, 136–143); and Carothers (1991, 18–29).

132. Carothers (1991, 26, 34); Stanley (1990, 16–17); and *New York Times*, 14 December 1993, A1. Although the overall tone of the report by the four U.S. lieu-

tenant colonels is reformist, they make critical comments about the value of democracy in a counterinsurgency effort. See Bacevich et al. (1988, 43–44). In my own interviews in El Salvador in 1990–91 with U.S. officers, they frequently expressed skepticism about democratic norms.

133. This point is made by Carothers (1991, 34); and Schwarz (1991, 82–83), among others.

134. Sober analyses include Arnson (1993, 95–105); and Carothers (1991, 25–30). These are key sources for the subsequent paragraphs in this section.

135. Arnson (1993, 139–141).

136. Ibid., 128; and Carothers (1991, 32). The evidence is contradictory, however; a statement by President Reagan criticizing the concept of death squads is cited in Americas Watch (1984a, 6).

137. U.S. Department of State, Bureau of Public Affairs, *Current Policy*, no. 533, 11 December 1983, 1–2. Cited in Arnson (1993, 143).

138. Arnson (1993, 143).

139. Americas Watch (1984a, 4); and Americas Watch (1984b, 2–3).

140. This point is especially well made by Schwarz (1991).

141. General Eugenio Vides Casanova, cited in Diskin and Sharpe (1986, 75), citing in turn *New York Times*, 1 July 1984, 8. See also the 1985 "Day of the Soldier" speech by Vides Casanova, cited by Karl (1988, 186).

142. General Blandón, cited by Preston (1985, 30).

143. Carothers (1991, 30).

144. Ibid., 30, 268.

145. Ibid., 30; Byrne (1996, 93–94); and Arnson (1993, 151–158).

146. The importance of Wright's assessment is emphasized by Arnson (1993, 159–160).

147. Ibid., 162–163.

148. Carothers (1991, 32). Note that Carothers was in the Reagan administration at the time. This paragraph draws upon Carothers (1991, 32–36); and Byrne (1996, 110–125).

149. This paragraph draws upon Arnson (1993, 242–243).

150. Byrne (1996, 174–175).

151. See chapter 2 for further discussion of the murders. Byrne (1996, 179–181) emphasizes in particular U.S. ambassador William Walker's frustration at the Salvadoran command's refusal to investigate the murders; Arnson (1993, 247–252) points out that some U.S. officials made errors suggesting that perhaps they too hoped to cover for the Salvadoran government and armed forces.

152. Byrne (1996, 179–182); Arnson (1993, 252–264); and Carothers (1991, 38).

153. On this point, see, for example, Schwarz (1991, 36–37).

154. U.S. AID Mission to El Salvador, "U.S. Assistance to El Salvador, 1979–1991" (data sheets provided to the author in San Salvador, courtesy of U.S. AID). Figures vary only slightly from those in U.S. AID reports from Washington, D.C.

155. Ibid.

156. Ibid.

157. Including some types of officially "economic" aid, and assuming certain other covert transfers, skeptical analysts believe that the actual amount of military aid was considerably higher. See, for example, Goodfellow (1984) and Landau (1993, 101).

158. U.S. Agency for International Development, *U.S. Overseas Loans and Grants: Latin America and the Caribbean, FY 1946–FY 1985,* n.p.

159. U.S. Agency for International Development, *U.S. Overseas Loans and Grants and Assistance from International Organizations, July 1, 1945–September 30, 1991* (Washington, D.C.: U.S. Agency for International Development, 1992), 35 and 49.

160. U.S. Government Accounting Office (1990, 11). Percentages do not add to one hundred because of rounding.

161. Peltz (1990, 4).

162. Carl Migdail, "El Salvador—Is Tide Turning Reagan's Way?" *U.S. News and World Report,* 22 August 1983, 20–22.

163. Bacevich et al. (1988, 36–37). Quotes in the original without a reference.

164. Ibid. Figures include security forces.

165. Ibid., 28. Calculation can also be made from the figures just given and the data in table 2.1. A conventional recommendation to governments is that the ratio be ten to one.

166. Enrique Baloyra in Subcommittee on Western Hemisphere Affairs of the Committee on Foreign Affairs, U.S. House of Representatives (1988, 100).

167. Bacevich et al. (1988, 29).

168. Ibid. On scant ammunition in the early 1980s, see the interview with President Magaña in Manwaring and Prisk (1988, 100).

169. General Vides Casanova, in Manwaring and Prisk (1988, 284).

170. Bacevich et al. (1988, 32); and Montgomery (1989, 51).

171. Casanova, in Manwaring and Prisk (1988, 284).

172. Former U.S. ambassador to El Salvador Robert White indicated in an interview on 10 April 1996, in Washington, D.C., that some of the U.S. aircraft were equipped with infrared cameras that could detect body heat and take photographs, which could be processed immediately in the United States and then relayed back to El Salvador.

173. Bacevich et al. (1988, 29).

174. *Washington Post,* 4 January 1991, A12.

175. Ibid.

176. Doyle and Duklis (1989, 45); Bacevich et al. (1988, v); and Montgomery (1989, 37).

177. In 1993, U.S. soldiers in the group "Veterans for Special Operations" argued that they should be eligible for combat medals for their service in El Salvador. See *Newsweek*, 5 April 1993, 4. A scholar who indicates the involvement of U.S. soldiers in combat is Montgomery (1989, 37–40). In the television program *60 Minutes* it was reported that CNN had photographed American soldiers in combat in El Salvador—possibly as many as five thousand in the course of the war.

178. Doyle and Duklis (1989, 44–45). Major Kevin M. Higgins was with the 5th Brigade in San Vicente from October 1983 to August 1984 and was a chief in the Third Military Zone in El Salvador from September 1986 to March 1988. His comments were in response to a questionnaire by Doyle and Duklis.

179. Sober accounts that cannot be attributed to a leftist or Democratic Party bias include Bacevich et al. (1988), by four U.S. lieutenant colonels; Schwarz (1991), a study that was sponsored by the Office of the Secretary of Defense, based primarily on interviews with U.S. military and civilian officials, and published by the RAND Corporation; and Carothers (1991, 34–35), a study by an analyst in the U.S. Department of State during the Reagan administration.

180. Schwarz (1991, vi, 18). For detailed criticism of corruption within the Salvadoran military, see Millman (1989).

181. Bacevich et al. (1988, vii). For the professional backgrounds of the lieutenant colonels, see Bacevich et al. (1988, 52).

182. Ibid., 24–43.

183. That 139 of 621 respondents would openly criticize soldiers to an interviewer in the context of El Salvador in 1991 is remarkable. It should be assumed that many of the respondents whose criticisms were vaguer felt the same way. For information on the 1991 survey by the Orellana research team, see appendix I.

184. U.S. AID/El Salvador (1988, 5).

185. The U.S. AID data in U.S. AID's annual reports categorize the components of economic aid primarily only as "AID and Predecessor" or "Food for Peace." My calculation here is from "Total Assistance to Central America 1980–90" (data sheet from the Central America Office at the Latin America and Caribbean Bureau of the U.S. Department of State, as of 28 February 1991). See also U.S. AID/El Salvador (1988, 7–8). On the ESF program in El Salvador, see Congressional Research Service (1989, 32–36); and U.S. AID/El Salvador (1988, 7–9).

186. The percentage calculation is a rough one by the author, from a graph that does not provide precise figures, in Congressional Research Service (1989, 34). ESF dollars were provided to the Central Bank of El Salvador, which in turn sold dollars at a reduced "official" rate to the Salvadoran private sector for the purchase of imports. When the difference between the price of the dollar on the open market

and the "official" rate was calculated for 1983 by Goodfellow (1984, 2), the subsidy provided to Salvadoran importers was 59 percent.

187. Again, calculations are approximate because they are based upon a graph that does not include precise numbers. See Congressional Research Service (1989, 34). On the allocation of the ESF development aid, see Congressional Research Service (1989, 39).

188. U.S. AID, "Congressional Presentation Fiscal Year 1990," Annex III, Latin America and the Caribbean, "Country: El Salvador."

189. Congressional Research Service (1989, 37); and "Total Assistance to Central America 1980–1990."

190. Congressional Research Service (1989, 38).

191. A straightforward discussion of the P.L. 480 program in El Salvador is Congressional Research Service (1989, 32–33).

192. "Total Assistance to Central America 1980–1990"—see note 185 above.

193. The competition with domestic farmers that is implicit in the P.L. 480 program is one reason for the controversy about it in some countries.

194. "Total Assistance to Central America 1980–1990." The food imported through Title 1 is distributed for sale at prevailing prices through regular commercial channels. The beneficiaries of the program include the purchasers of the food imports; without the program, the supply of food would be less, and prices higher. The government is also a beneficiary; without the program, the Central Bank would have to use more of its foreign exchange to finance food imports.

195. Ibid.

196. One of the most rigorous analyses is Goodfellow (1984, 2). Goodfellow discusses the problems of corruption and capital flight in particular.

197. Barry (1990, 143–144); and Siegel and Hackel (1987, 126–128).

198. See data for FY 1988 and FY 1989 in U.S. AID Mission to El Salvador, "U.S. Assistance to El Salvador 1979–1991" (data sheets provided to the author in San Salvador, courtesy of U.S. AID).

199. Barry (1990, 146–147); and Siegel and Hackel (1987, 127–128).

200. Among my interviewees in San Salvador during 1990–91, there was a strong consensus on this point. See also Doyle and Duklis (1989, 456–457).

201. U.S. AID/El Salvador (1988, 5).

202. Roberto Codas, PREIS, interview by author, San Salvador, 21 August 1990; and author's interviews of U.S. AID officials in San Salvador, 15–16 August 1990.

203. 1991 survey by Orellana research team. For information about the survey, see appendix I.

204. Author's interviews of U.S. AID officials in San Salvador, 15–16 August 1990; Millman (1989); and Barry (1990, 144–145).

205. Information about the program in this paragraph is based on U.S. AID/El Salvador (1988, 11); and author's interviews with U.S. AID officials in San Salvador, 15–16 August 1990.

206. Codas, interview.

207. 1991 Orellana survey.

208. Ibid.

209. U.S. AID/El Salvador (1988) does not specify whether these projects were financed through ESF or through U.S. AID development assistance.

210. U.S. AID/El Salvador (1988, 12–13, 23, 25).

211. Ibid., 9.

212. "Información de proyectos ejecutados: Plan de acción 1988, al 15/07/90" (courtesy of U.S. AID officials in San Salvador, 15 August 1990).

213. Stahler-Sholk (1994, 31).

214. U.S. AID/El Salvador (1988, 7) provides one of the many examples.

215. Chapter 4 contrasts national economic trends in El Salvador and Peru. For an analysis of the implications of U.S. aid for the Salvadoran economy, see Barry (1990, 143–144).

216. On this conditioning and its upshot, see Congressional Research Service (1989, 36–37); U.S. AID/El Salvador (1988, 7); Byrne (1996, 129–130); and Barry (1990, 146–147).

217. On wage and employment trends during the 1980s, see chapter 4.

218. This section draws upon interviews between 1981 and 1997 with U.S. officials, including U.S. Deputy Chief of Mission John Youle, 14 July 1986; U.S. ambassadors David Jordan, 30 July 1987 (in Washington, D.C.); Alexander Watson, 6 December 1987 and 6 July 1989; U.S. Assistant Secretary of State Bernard W. Aronson, 30 May 1997; and other interviews with notable U.S. embassy officials, including Dan Clare, 11 July 1983; Charles Loveridge, 7 July 1989 and 7 April 1990; Gene Bigler, 17 August 1991; and Steve McFarland, 20 August 1993. However, many U.S. government documents on this issue remain classified; only when these documents have become accessible can a definitive analysis be made.

219. Real values calculated with 1967 = $1, on the basis of consumer price index data in the U.S. Department of Commerce, *Statistical Abstract of the United States* (Washington, D.C., 1994), 488. Figures for aid in current dollars from U.S. Agency for International Development, *U.S. Overseas Loans and Grants: Series of Yearly Data, Obligations and Loan Authorizations FY 1946–FY 1985*; and U.S. Agency for International Development, *U.S. Overseas Loans and Grants*, annual editions.

220. In current dollars, U.S. aid to Peru in 1962 was $80.5 million. Between 1968 and 1977, when Peru was governed by a reformist military regime, U.S. aid to Peru was low, in the range of $25 million a year; U.S. aid increased when the democratic transition began. See U.S. Agency for International Development, *U.S. Overseas Loans and Grants: Latin America and the Caribbean, 1946–1985*.

221. At the same time, it is only fair to point out that virtually everyone (including scholars such as myself) underestimated Sendero, and also only fair to point out that, especially by 1990, U.S. concern was mounting. For example, Assistant Secretary of State Bernard Aronson himself testified to the U.S. Congress about the Sendero threat in March 1992. However, from my interviews with U.S. officials during 1982–92, I can cite numerous underestimations of the Sendero threat. For example, U.S. officials said that insurgents would not attack the Santa Lucía antidrug base, but they did. See Joseph B. Treaster, "Cocaine Prices Rise, and Police Efforts May Be Responsible," *New York Times,* 14 July 1990, A10; James Brooke, *New York Times,* 18 March 1990, A60; James Brooke, *New York Times,* 12 April 1990, A1, A12.

222. "Into the Crossfire," *Newsweek,* 19 August 1991, 32.

223. Although U.S.-based human rights groups were active and effectively made their voices heard, religious and other groups advocating a concern for Peru's poor were less active.

224. For information about the GEIN and the capture, see chapter 3. On CIA support for the GEIN, see Simpson (1995, 641); Reyna (1995, 50); Sally Bowen, "Political Indicators," *Peru Report* 5, no. 2 (1991), 44; and "Political Interview," in *Peru Report* 6, no. 8 (1992), 3. CIA support for the GEIN was also indicated in an interview with Agustín Mantilla (interior minister at the time of the GEIN's formation), in Lima, 16 June 1997, as well as numerous off-the-record interviews with knowledgeable Peruvian and U.S. analysts. CIA support for DINCOTE in general was indicated by Jeremy Bigwood, a U.S. journalist and photographer who was detained by DINCOTE for a week in 1993, in an interview in Washington, D.C., 3 November 1996. Documents have been sought through Freedom of Information Act requests, but relevant ones have not yet been forthcoming.

225. Interview with Agustín Mantilla, in Lima, 16 June 1997, and off-the-record interviews with U.S. officials.

226. Ibid. The kind of CIA role is also suggested by Gorriti (1996, 130) when he writes of "*a man* who was a photographic and electronic wizard who designed for the group all kinds of equipment and accessories to film, photograph, and tape suspects. He taught the GEIN agents to intervene public telephones using microphones and developed a suitcase especially for a video camera that permitted the operation of the equipment without the necessity of opening the suitcase [emphasis added]."

227. Interviews with U.S. officials as indicated in note 218. U.S. ambassador Alexander F. Watson, in an interview in *Caretas,* 3 July 1989, 20, discusses Peru's democracy as a set of values and institutions shared with the United States and Europe. Ambassador Watson was relieved that he was able to maintain as positive a relationship with Peru as he did, given the animosity that began between President García and Reagan administration officials soon after García's inauguration. In interviews with Peruvian leaders, including Minister of Foreign Relations Alan

Wagner, 25 July 1986, little discussion with U.S. officials about the strengthening of Peru's democratic institutions was reported.

228. See, for example, *New York Times,* 15 January 1989, 6.

229. McClintock (1993, 115–116); and Palmer (1996).

230. *New York Times,* 18 May 1992, A8. Bruce Williamson, the desk officer for Peru at the U.S. Department of State at the time, reported to me in a memorandum of 21 April 1993 that the U.S. had planned to spend $237.8 million in Peru in fiscal year 1991, and that as a result of the *autogolpe* only about 80 percent was disbursed (see table 5.4). The reduction in aid between 1991 and 1992 is evident in table 5.4.

231. For sample recommendations, see the U.S. House of Representatives Foreign Affairs Committee, "FY 1986–1987 Foreign Assistance Recommendations," Title VII—Latin America and the Caribbean, Section 707 Assistance for Peru, item c, dated March 18, 1985; and "Memorandum re Peru Certification," from Holly Burkhalter, Americas Watch, to Representative Bonker, 6 February 1985. On the amounts in the 1989–91 program, see *New York Times,* 15 April 1992, A12. Also, interview with U.S. State Department desk officer for Peru, Bruce Williamson, 20 April 1993. An additional $500,000 from another program was allocated for the training of judges and police officers, but the allocation between the two kinds of professions is not available to me.

232. U.S. ambassador Luigi Einaudi, in an address to a symposium at CEPEI, 6 November 1990. A similar scholarly assessment is made by Palmer (1992, 72).

233. U.S. ambassador Anthony C. E. Quainton, addressing the conference "Peruvian Counternarcotics Efforts: A Contextual View," at the Meridian International Center, 11 January 1993, in Washington, D.C.

234. Joseph B. Treaster, "On Front Line of Drug War, U.S.-Built Base Lags in Peru," *New York Times,* 31 October 1989, A1, A10.

235. James Brooke, "U.S. Will Arm Peru to Fight Leftists in New Drug Push," *New York Times,* 23 April 1990, 1, 18; Eugene Robinson, "Anti-Drug Effort Turns to Military," *Washington Post,* 25 April 1990, A31; and an interview with U.S. ambassador to Peru Anthony C. E. Quainton, "Las condiciones de la Ayuda," *Caretas,* 30 April 1990, 16–17, 32.

236. For analytical overviews including various perspectives, see García-Sayan (1989); and Smith (1992). Cogent critical statements include the Washington Office on Latin America (1991b); and Congressman Peter H. Kostmayer, "Opening Statement: The Andean Initiative (Part II)," Subcommittee on Western Hemisphere Affairs, U.S. Congress, June 20, 1990.

237. In McClintock (1988, 130–139), I argue that antinarcotics efforts in the Upper Huallaga Valley provoked the social tensions that the Shining Path in turn exploited. My argument drew upon Gonzales Manrique (1987a, 59–72); González (1988, 40–47); and *Peru Report* 2, no. 11 (November 1988): 7-1 through 7-8. Other

scholars and I have also argued, pointing in particular to the effective campaign by General Alberto Arciniega in the area, that counterinsurgency was most effective when antinarcotics efforts were restricted. See McClintock (1990); Massing (1990, 88–92); and Instituto de Defensa Legal (1990, 61–70).

238. Quoted in Peter Andreas, "Peru's Addiction to Coca Dollars," *Nation,* April 16, 1990, 515.

239. Juan E. Mendez, "U.S. Joins Peru's Dirty War," *New York Times,* 7 May 1990, 16. This interpretation is supported by the fact that until as late as 1992 the Brooke-Alexander Amendment severely restricted conventional military assistance to nations that were in arrears on their official debt to the U.S. government, but not military aid for counternarcotics purposes. Especially during the García administration, Peruvians worried about this question as well. See the interview with Ambassador Alexander F. Watson, *Caretas,* 3 July 1989, 18.

240. See "Interior Minister: U.S. Drug Aid 'Ridiculous,'" *Foreign Broadcast Information Service,* 11 September 1989, 47; James Brooke, "Peru's Leader Proposes a Market to Fight Coca," *New York Times,* 28 October 1990, A12; Jack Anderson and Dale Van Atta, "America's Phony Drug War," *Washington Post,* 18 November 1990, C7; and Eugene Robinson, "U.S. Efforts Against Coca Run into New Peruvian Drug Policy," *Washington Post,* 4 November 1990, A29. See also Congressman Peter H. Kostmayer, "Opening Statement on the Andean Initiative (Part 11)," Subcommittee on Western Hemisphere Affairs, 20 June 1990, 6; and Diego García-Sayan, "Prepared Statement before the Subcommittee on Western Hemisphere Affairs," 6 June 1990; and Palmer (1992, 72).

241. *Christian Science Monitor,* 3 May 1990, 3.

242. *Washington Post,* 2 March 1991, A8; *Latin America Weekly Report,* 14 March 1991, 7; *Washington Office on Latin America Andean Initiative Legislative Update,* July 1991, 5; *Caretas,* 1 April 1991, 36–37; *Caretas,* 29 April 1991, 16–17; *Andean Report,* April 1991, 53; and *Resumen Semanal,* 3–9 May 1991, 3.

243. Palmer (1992, 72–74); and sources in note 242.

244. *Washington Post,* 17 September 1991, A25; and 24 November 1991, A 28; and *New York Times,* 6 October 1991, 8.

245. Quainton (address presented to the conference "Peruvian Counternarcotics Efforts: A Contextual View")—see note 233 above.

246. In February 1992, Fujimori said that the amount was $9.8 million. See *Foreign Broadcast Information Service,* 27 February 1992, 24. A $10-million figure was also given to me by the U.S. Department of State desk officer for Peru, in a U.S. Department of State paper, "Economic Support for Peru," March 1992. From the data in a memorandum of 21 April 1993 by Bruce Williamson, U.S. desk officer for Peru at the U.S. Department of State during this period, it appears that the antinarcotics funds classified by AID as "economic" actually included a significant component for law enforcement programs. Soberón (1992, 3) reported that at most

$2 million would be allocated for alternative development programs in the coca-growing areas.

247. *New York Times,* 11 November 1991, international edition; and *New York Times,* 28 March 1992, 4.

248. *Washington Post,* 27 February 1992, A4; and 3 March 1992, A13.

249. On Reagan administration proposals for military aid, see *New York Times,* 30 January 1985, A4; on the Bush administration's, see discussion in the previous section on antinarcotics efforts in this chapter.

250. During much of this period, the Brooke-Alexander Amendment prohibited military aid to countries that were in arrears on their official debt service to the U.S. government. As mentioned in note 239, it is possible that one factor in the Bush administration's emphasis upon antinarcotics as the purpose of U.S. military aid to Peru was to circumvent Brooke-Alexander.

251. Dan Clare (U.S. embassy official), interview by author in Lima, 11 July 1983, in particular. At the conference "Soviet Activities in Latin America," U.S. Department of State, 7 May 1987, U.S. ambassador David Jordan said that one of his instructions as ambassador had been to break the tie between the Soviet and Peruvian militaries, and that he had tried hard, with some success. Reagan administration officials periodically sought military aid for Peru on the grounds that it would provide an alternative for the Peruvian military, but obviously this argument did not prevail. See "The U.S. Position on Peru," *Inter-American Economic Affairs* 39, no. 2 (autumn 1985): 86–88 (transcript of hearings in the U.S. House of Representatives). Peruvian military officers usually said that the motives behind their arms relationship with the Soviet Union were exclusively pragmatic.

252. See annual editions of U.S. Arms Control and Disarmament Agency, *World Military Expenditures and Arms Transfers* (Washington, D.C.: Government Printing Office). McClintock (1989b, 375–376) discusses the original dispute between the U.S. and Peruvian governments that prompted the Peruvian military to seek arms from the Soviet Union.

253. For example, in April 1990, Peruvian army troops fired on two U.S. government helicopters chasing a suspected drug plane; also, in April 1992, the Peruvian armed forces shot at a U.S. C-130 Hercules plane, killing one U.S. soldier and wounding two others, and even presented the U.S. government with a bill (subsequently withdrawn) for $20,000 to cover the costs of its operation. The Peruvians' argument was that the plane was off course and had not responded to the armed forces' warning call. See *Newsweek,* 2 April 1990, 5; and Youngers (1995a, 6).

254. See, for example, Washington Office on Latin America (1991b, 108–129); and Youngers (1992). These fears were well founded. In the sample of 130 respondents in the Huancayo area in June 1991 by the Osores research team (a relatively well-educated sample), 60 percent said that the army had performed badly in the counterinsurgency effort, and repression and abuse were by far the most common criticisms. See further discussion in chapters 3 and 6.

255. A cogent statement is Youngers (1992). The Salvadoran experience was believed to have this lesson for the U.S. government.

256. *Christian Science Monitor*, 3 May 1990, 3. See also Carla Anne Robbins, "Cocaine, Communism, and Crisis in Peru," *U.S. News and World Report*, 18 September 1989, 46. Among the numerous Peruvian leaders making this point in interviews with the author in Lima were General (r) Edgardo Mercado Jarrín, 18 July 1986; General (r) Sinesio Jarama Davila (director of the CAEM), 27 July 1987; General Luis Alcantara (vice minister of Interior), 11 November 1990; and General Howard Rodríguez (commander of several highlands emergency zones), 12 November 1990. Peruvian leaders repeated that the strategy for the resolution of Peru's guerrilla problem should be *"integral"* ("integral," "whole"). For the views of Peruvian citizens, see table 6.2.

257. These were the primary concerns expressed among the sixty security force personnel interviewed by the Osores research team, and these concerns are also mentioned in the articles cited in this section about García's and Fujimori's skepticism toward U.S. military aid. Said General (r) Sinesio Jarama, director of Peru's CAEM at the time, in an interview on 27 July 1987: "The United States doesn't understand the nature of the Communist threat in Latin America or Peru."

258. 1990 Datum survey in Lima ($N = 400$), commissioned by the author. See appendix I. In a mid-1990 poll, 84 percent of Peruvians rejected direct U.S. military intervention in Peru. See *Debate* 12, no. 61 (August–October 1990): 40. Wilde (1992, 10) reports that in a U.S. Information Agency poll in the summer of 1991, 12 percent of the sample responded favorably to U.S. military aid and 5 percent favorably to the presence of U.S. military trainers.

259. Survey of sixty security force personnel, mostly in Huancayo, June–July 1990, by Osores research team. For more information on the survey, see appendix I.

260. See table 3.11.

261. "Peru: AID Assistance FY 81–84" (document courtesy of U.S. AID official Jerome Hulehan, 15 March 1983); "U.S. Aid to Bolivia, Colombia, and Peru" (document prepared by Larry Nowels, Foreign Affairs and National Defense Division, Congressional Research Service, for the years 1984–89); and "United States Assistance to Peru," for FY 1986 through FY 1992, document no. 9792 from ARA/AND (Office of Andean Affairs, Bureau of Inter-American Affairs), revised January 1992.

262. The Food for Peace program and its various components are discussed in the section on U.S. economic aid to El Salvador. The allocations between 1980 and 1989 averaged about $50 million annually to El Salvador, versus roughly $43 million to Peru. See U.S. Agency for International Development, *U.S. Overseas Loans and Grants*, annual editions.

263. Ibid.

264. U.S. Department of State, "Economic Support for Peru" (1991 memorandum, Washington, D.C.), 3.

265. President Alan García's inaugural address to the Peruvian Congress, 28 July 1985, reprinted in full by *Andean Report* (August 1985). The U.S. was referred to as "the richest and most imperialist country on earth" (p. 16).

266. Overviews of Peru's international financial relations during the García period include Crabtree (1992); and Larrain and Sachs (1991).

267. Interview with Russ Graham, Economics Officer in USIS, 19 August 1987, in Lima. Ambassador Alexander Watson believed that his efforts had been important just to maintain economic aid at levels not very different from the early 1980s.

268. Memorandum from Bruce Williamson, U.S. desk officer for Peru, U.S. Department of State, 21 April 1993, Washington, D.C.

269. See chapter 7 for my views about the appropriate U.S. role for the enhancement of political peace in Latin America in the post–Cold War era generally.

270. This is not to deny that, until the November 1989 offensive did not prompt a popular insurrection, a major segment of the FMLN continued to hope for a military victory. Among other scholars, Byrne (1996) is very clear on this point. It is also clear that, after 1989, external factors such as the defeat of the Sandinistas at the polls and the collapse of the Soviet Union were important in the inclination of the FMLN toward negotiations. At the same time, however, to the extent that political exclusion was the key impetus to the formation of the revolutionary movement—as is argued in chapters 3 and 6—the significant limitations of the political opening and the significant flaws in the Salvadoran electoral process could not but have been factors maintaining the FMLN's desire for a military victory.

271. See note 266 in chapter 3. A similar argument is made by Evans (forthcoming).

272. 1991 survey by Orellana research team ($N = 621$). Item read: "In a particular moment of the armed conflict, the government of El Salvador received new arms that arrived from the United States for the military. In your opinion, what was the role of these arms in the war? How do you think they were used?" Besides the 33 percent that said the arms had not been helpful, 53 percent said that they had been helpful; 10 percent did not know, and 4 percent gave a different response of some kind. Given the context of continuing war and intimidation in El Salvador at the time, it is probable that a higher percentage were actually critical of the U.S. arms. See appendix I for more information about the survey.

273. Of course, there were exceptions. Various U.S. embassy personnel resented the extent to which the drug issue dominated the bilateral agenda.

274. *Caretas,* 3 July 1989.

275. Symposium organized by CEPEI (Peruvian Center for International Studies), 6 November 1990.

6. Why Did the Revolutionary Movements Emerge and Expand?

1. Harnecker (1993, 43–45, 71, 94, 155). Hugh Byrne made the point with me in an interview in Washington, D.C., 19 July 1995.

2. See chapter 2 for a discussion of these organizations. The five commanders as of 1980 were Joaquín Villalobos of the ERP; Shafik Handal of the PCS; Eduardo Sancho Castañeda (alias "Fermán Cienfuegos") of the RN; Francisco Jovel (alias "Roberto Roca") of the PRTC; and the FPL's Salvador Cayetano Carpio (the one who had not studied at the National University).

3. Commission on U.S.-Central American Relations (1982); and Pearce (1985, 123).

4. Harnecker (1993, 43–45).

5. Bonasso and Gómez Leyva (1992, 7–32); *New York Times,* 27 February 1981, 8; and Radu and Tismaneanu (1990, 188–189).

6. Handal's words in January 1992 interviews, quoted in Bonasso and Gómez Leyva (1992, 18).

7. Ibid., 20.

8. Ibid.

9. The material in this paragraph is based on ibid., 20–30.

10. Ibid., 29. Handal said that he expected fraud, but believed that it was necessary to demonstrate to the Salvadoran people the unviability of the electoral route to power.

11. For information about the background of Villalobos, see Dunkerley (1988, 370–371); Shenk (1988, 42); and Radu and Tismaneanu (1990, 208). The paragraph is also based on the address by Villalobos at the conference "Peace and Reconciliation in El Salvador" (U.S. Army War College, Carlisle, Pa., 8 September 1994); and my interview with Villalobos, 11 September 1994, in Washington, D.C.

12. Villalobos, Army War College address.

13. Ibid.

14. Joaquín Villalobos, interview for the PBS television series *Frontline,* 14 June 1988.

15. Joaquín Villalobos, interview for "Fire in the Mind," program no. 9 of the video series *The Americas* (produced by WGBH/Boston in 1993; Annenberg/CPB collection), filmed in 1992.

16. For information about Sancho Castañeda, see Commission on U.S.-Central American Relations (1982); and Radu and Tismaneanu (1990, 223).

17. Information about Jovel Funes is scanty. Wickham-Crowley (1992, 337) reports that he was a lawyer. Radu and Tismaneanu (1990, 222) say that he was extremely hostile to Villalobos.

18. *New York Times,* 18 March 1982, A16. Photograph is included. Commission on U.S.-Central American Relations (1982); and Fenton Communications (1984, 14–15).

19. For information about the background of Cayetano Carpio, see Harnecker (1993, 47–49); Wickham-Crowley (1992, 337); and Radu and Tismaneanu (1990, 195–197).

20. Quoted from a mimeographed document in Montgomery (1995, 103).

21. Harnecker (1993, 328).

22. Fenton Communications (1984, 4–7); Commission on U.S.-Central American Relations (1982); and Radu and Tismaneanu (1990, 209).

23. Quoted in Fenton Communications (1994, 4), apparently from their interview with her.

24. Díaz (1988). On her family background and early life, see pp. 76–77; on her radicalization at the university, see pp. 53–54, 140, 211.

25. Ibid., 211–214.

26. Ibid., 20, 63, 213.

27. Harnecker (1993, 38–39); and Commission on U.S.-Central American Relations (1982). Conflicting information about her background is offered by Wickham-Crowley (1992, 337); Radu and Tismaneanu (1990, 197); and others.

28. Commission on U.S.-Central American Relations (1982).

29. "Leonel González," interview by Salvador Cortes (FPL leader and Ph.D. candidate at American University), San Salvador, July 1995. The tape of the interview was kindly shared with the author. All information in this paragraph is based on this interview.

30. Ibid.

31. Harnecker (1993, 41); Radu and Tismaneanu (1990, 197); Prisk (1991, 59); and *New York Times,* 25 September 1983, 4.

32. Lecture at the Washington Peace Center, Washington, D.C., 12 September 1996. Also, Hugh Byrne, interview by author, Washington, D.C., 16 June 1995.

33. Facundo Guardado, interview by author, Washington, D.C., 10 August 1995; Hugh Byrne, interview by author, Washington, D.C., 19 July 1995; Wickham-Crowley (1992, 337); and Commission on U.S.-Central American Relations (1982).

34. Harnecker (1993, 153–154).

35. Comandancia General del FMLN, "Balance anual de la Comandancia General del FMLN al pueblo y la nación," *Edición especial venceremos* (Chalatenango), January 1989, 4.

36. Fenton Communications (1984, 1–3); Commission on U.S.-Central American Relations (1982); and Dunkerley (1983, 140–143).

37. Guillermo Ungo, at a breakfast discussion of the Inter-American Dialogue, 30 January 1990, in Washington, D.C. Ungo (1984, 219–230) makes a similar emphasis upon political exclusion.

38. For information about Zamora, see Fenton Communications (1984, 8–10); and Dunkerley (1983, 140–143).

39. Rubén Zamora, interview for "Fire in the Mind," *Americas* video series.

40. Zamora, at a talk for the Washington Office on Latin America, 16 June 1994, in Washington, D.C.; and in an interview for the El Salvador segment of the four-part Public Broadcasting System video series *Crisis in Central America* (produced by WGBH-TV Boston in 1985, distributed by Blackwell Corp). In actuality, the Christian Democrats did participate in elections again in 1977.

41. There are no precise criteria for the calculation of "middle class" or "upper middle class" in Latin America.

42. As of 1992, of the five Political Bureau members, two were women; about eight of the nineteen Central Committee members were women. See data following in this section, and Kirk (1992, 16). For an interesting discussion of the role of women leaders in Sendero, see *New York Times,* 22 September 1992, A4.

43. Among scholars of Sendero, Degregori (1986, 1990a, 1990b, 1990–91) and Palmer (1986; 1995, 253–263) place the greatest emphasis on the importance of Sendero's origins in Ayacucho.

44. The most comprehensive discussion of Guzmán's background is by Strong (1992, 3–31). See also Palmer (1995, 259–261); Guillermoprieto (1993, 67); and *La República,* 13 September 1992, 4–5. Unfortunately, to date Guzmán himself has not offered reflections on his decisions. His only statements are the ideological ones described in chapter 2.

45. Gorriti (1990b, 16–17); and Strong (1992, 5–10).

46. Strong (1992, 9).

47. A view of La Torre as more politically fervent than Guzmán himself is presented by Guillermoprieto (1993, 68); Gorriti (1990b, 18); and Strong (1992, 3–4), but she is portrayed as a naive follower of her husband by Kirk (1997, 90).

48. Palmer (1995, 259). Palmer was an academic colleague of Guzmán's at the university in 1962 and 1963.

49. Kirk (1992, 19).

50. Gorriti (1990b); and Strong (1992, 3–31), among others.

51. "Trend Report," *Peru Report* 8, no. 4 (May 1994): 2. See also Strong (1992, 4).

52. Gorriti (1990b, 15); and Guillermoprieto (1993, 68).

53. Gorriti (1990b, 17–19); Guillermoprieto (1993, 68); Strong (1992, 14); and Daniels (1990, 11).

54. On the phenomenon of the "ideal-hungry" follower in revolutionary movements, see Post (1986).

55. "Political Report," *Peru Report* 6, no. 11 (December 1992): 1. See also Guillermoprieto (1993, 68); and the discussion in *New York Times,* 14 September 1992, A8.

56. Guillermoprieto (1993, 72).

57. Kirk (1991, 552); McClintock (1992b, 231–233); and Harding (1986, 186–187).

58. A 1962 photograph is included in Palmer (1994, 299). See also the 1970 police photograph of Guzmán, widely reprinted in Peruvian publications, such as *La República,* 23 March 1991, 15. On the middle-aged Guzmán, see Kirk (1992, 17).

59. Kirk (1991, 552); and "Political Report," *Peru Report* (December 1992): 1.

60. "Political Report," *Peru Report* (December 1992): 1; and Guillermoprieto (1993, 68).

61. Poole and Renique (1992, 39); Harding (1986, 186); Guillermoprieto (1993, 68); and Palmer (1986, 128).

62. "Political Report," *Peru Report* (December 1992): 1.

63. For Morote's background, I am indebted to comments on an earlier draft of this manuscript by David Scott Palmer. See also Gorriti (1990b, 18); Harding (1986, 189); Tarazona-Sevillano (1990, 70); Kirk (1991, 554); and Palmer (1989, 8).

64. For Mezzich's background, see Harding (1986, 188); Tarazona-Sevillano (1990, 71); *Sí,* 21 April 1991, 26–27; and *Expreso,* 20 September 1992, A3. I am also indebted to David Scott Palmer for various pieces of information.

65. In his comments on a first draft of this chapter, David Scott Palmer indicated that the area of Mezzich's activities was Huaraz, where Mezzich's family may have owned a farm.

66. For background on Antonio Díaz Martinez, see Harding (1986, 183); Harding (1988); and Kirk (1991, 554).

67. For Ramírez Durand's background, see *Caretas,* 4 March 1991 and 8 April 1991, 20; *Expreso,* 7 July 1992, A11; *La República,*16 September 1992, 8; *Foreign Broadcast Information Service: Latin America,* 1 October 1992, 23; and *El Comercio,* 6 August 1995, A12–A15.

68. *Expreso,* 28 June 1994, A5; and *El Comercio,* 6 August 1995, A13.

69. Ibid.

70. See photographs of Shining Path leaders in *Caretas,* 4 March 1991, 32–33; *Caretas,* 22 October 1992, 26–31; and *La República,* 16 September 1992, 8.

71. See chapter 2 for their identities. Some of these women, however, rose to leadership positions at least in part due to a close personal relationship with Guzmán. See *New York Times,* 22 September 1992, A4.

72. For background on Iparaguirre, see *La República,* 16 September 1992, 8; and *Expreso,* 23 September 1992, A11.

73. *La República,* 16 September 1992, 12.

74. *Caretas,* 22 October 1992, 26–30, 77–78.

75. As indicated in chapter 1, this point was originally highlighted by Huntington (1968, 288–290).

76. Scholars concur on this point. See Gianotten, de Wit, and de Wit (1985, 190); Palmer (1986, 138); Smith, Michael L. (1992, 141); Degregori (1986, 251; 1991, 26; 1992, 43); Poole and Rénique (1992, 38–41); Guillermoprieto (1993, 68); and Rénique (1994, 233).

77. See, for example, interview no. 32 by the Osores research team (see appendix I for more information about these interviews).

78. Among the eight "students" interviewed by the Osores research team, for example, four specified their origins, and two of these were of peasant origins.

79. Analysis by Hugh Byrne after numerous interviews in El Salvador in mid-July 1995 with former FMLN leaders, made in an interview with the author in Washington, D.C., 19 July 1995. See also the backgrounds of the five top ERP commanders in Mena Sandoval (n.d., 311).

80. Montgomery (1995, 123); and Byrne, interview.

81. Harnecker (1993, 145–146).

82. See Harnecker (1993, 38–40, 145–146); and Baloyra (1990, 490).

83. Mena Sandoval (n.d., 309).

84. Alberto Enriquez (former member of FPL), interview by author, Washington, D.C., 9 December 1994.

85. "Valentín" (Gerson Martínez) in Harnecker (1993, 190).

86. Irma Segunda Amaya, in an interview on 10 March 1995 in Washington, D.C. She believed that her experience was typical, and I agree; see also, for example, the story of "Arlena" reported by Clements (1984, 82).

87. Mena Sandoval (n.d., 12).

88. Ibid., 13, 172. Precise words are attributed to Father Ellacuría.

89. Ibid., 23.

90. Ibid., 76–77, 209–210, 241.

91. Pearce (1986, 193).

92. López Vigil (1994, 9).

93. Father Rogelio Poncel, cited in *Christian Science Monitor,* 5 January 1984, 1–2.

94. Montgomery (1995, 120).

95. See, especially, the statement by Joaquín Villalobos quoted in chapter 4.

96. This point was made clearly by Irma Seguna Amaya during an interview by author, Washington, D.C., 10 March 1995.

97. Dunkerley (1988, 418) observes that "progressive Catholicism had a stronger political impact in the north-central zone than anywhere else in the country," and cites Morazán in particular. See also Barry (1990, 62); and López Vigil (1994, 42). On their importance in Chalatenango, see Pearce (1986, 178). Although

the strategic advantage of strongholds near the border with Honduras was a factor, it was not mentioned by FMLN leaders.

98. Alberto Enriquez, interview by author, Washington, D.C., 9 December 1994. Author's loose translation.

99. Harnecker (1993, 160). Also, Segunda Amaya, interview.

100. Estimate by FPL leader Facundo Guardado in an interview in El Salvador with Hugh Byrne, reported to the author by Byrne on 19 July 1995, in Washington, D.C. See also Mena Sandoval (n.d., 340); *New York Times,* 15 March 1981, 4; and *New York Times,* 26 January 1982, A1.

101. *New York Times,* 26 January 1982, A4.

102. Ibid., 28 January 1982, A12.

103. Ibid., 26 January 1982, A4.

104. Harnecker (1993, 269); Shenk (1988, 42); and Montgomery (1995, 123).

105. Cited by Adler and Long (1992, 26).

106. Caesar Sereseres, professor of political science at the University of California at Irvine, carried out interviews with about thirty FMLN members at different ranks from the five groups within the coalition. He reported that a "very high percentage" said they joined because of abuses to their relatives and/or to priests. Interview by author, Carlisle, Pa., 8 September 1994.

107. Clements (1984, 122). Hercules is talking directly to Clements. Montgomery (1995, 101) reports that the commander's real name was Fidel Recinos.

108. Clements (1984, 122–123).

109. Ibid., 169–171.

110. Ibid., 170.

111. *New York Times,* 26 January 1982, A4. Raymond Bonner is the journalist reporting the interview.

112. Clements (1984, 28).

113. Pearce (1986, 155). Other similar accounts are offered in this book.

114. Interview no. 9, Osores research team.

115. With respect to El Salvador, see Clements (1984, 124). With respect to Peru, a wide variety of ranks and sections were reported by the thirty-three respondents interviewed by my research team. See appendix I for information about the survey.

116. *Foreign Broadcast Information Service: Latin America,* 18 March 1993, 59.

117. Chávez de Paz (1989, 26). Forty-one percent of those convicted for any type of crime were twenty-five or younger.

118. *Los Angeles Times,* 4 December 1988, 1; and *Newsweek,* 24 April 1989, 45.

119. Kirk (1992, 16). Sendero claimed that 40 percent of its members were women, but this claim was not borne out in the various samples.

120. *Caretas,* 7 September 1987, 34. See also *Newsweek,* 24 April 1989, 45, which reports that "most of the rebels were males."

121. Chávez de Paz (1989, 27).

122. An interesting discussion is provided in *New York Times,* 22 September 1992, A4.

123. For full discussions of ethnicity in Peru and ethnicity as a factor in the expansion of the Shining Path, see McClintock (1993).

124. Sendero's ethnic composition would thus be similar to that in the country as a whole. Comments about skin color are very rare in Peruvian publications. For photographs of captured Shining Path members, see *Caretas,* 20 September 1982, 20–24; *Caretas,* 7 September 1987, 34–35; *Caretas,* 9 March 1992, 36; *La República,* 4 April 1993, 17; and *Correo* (a Huancayo newspaper), 18 June 1993, 6.

125. Although the teachers' university in Lima is usually referred to as La Cantuta, its formal name is the Enrique Guzmán Valle National University. For a discussion of Sendero's hegemony there, see *Expreso,* 15 October 1991, 8–9.

126. For the Huancayo area, my own observation; for the Upper Huallaga Valley, see *Ideéle* 4, no. 41 (September 1992): 10. The rector of the state university in the department of Huánuco was a Senderista. See *Latin America Weekly Report,* 10 November 1994, 508.

127. Manuel Jesús Granados, cited by Bonner (1988, 35). An excellent comprehensive analysis is Ansión, Del Castillo, Piqueras, and Isaura Zegarra (1992).

128. This estimate was made in late 1990 by Gloria Helfer, a member of one of Peru's leftist parties, and minister of education at the time in the Fujimori government. The estimate was frequently cited. See INIDEN (1991, 43). See also the statement by Enrique Obando in *La República,* 25 April 1993, 9. In teachers' union elections in a poor Lima neighborhood in the early 1990s, about 15 percent (236) of the teachers cast ballots for a Shining Path slate. See *New York Times,* 30 August 1992, 8. In an election at the education faculty of the prestigious University of San Marcos in Lima, the figure was 10 percent. See *Wall Street Journal,* 31 December 1990, 1A, 4.

129. *El Comercio,* 4 April 1985, 3.

130. *Foreign Broadcast Information Service: Latin America,* 26 March 1993, 34. See also *La República,* 14 April 1993, 12–16. A considerable number of this group had either studied or taught at La Cantuta in Lima.

131. For information about the interviews by my research team, see appendix I. Overall, the interviews conducted with Senderistas by journalists in Peru were probably not as solid as the ones conducted with FMLN members in El Salvador. Many of the interviews of the Shining Path members were carried out in jail, and they were sometimes supervised by the guerrilla respondent's superior. Usually, the degree of confidence established between respondent and interviewer was less than in the Salvadoran case. On the other hand, there may have been a greater tendency

among the FMLN members to try to advance a particular vision of the organization; many journalists were at least slightly sympathetic to the FMLN, but few were to the Shining Path. A thoughtful discussion of some of these issues is provided in Kirk (1992).

132. See, for example, the interview with Isidoro Nunja García in *Caretas,* 30 May 1988, 32. A segment of the interview is also published in Poole and Renique (1992, 67). *Hambreador* was used many times by respondents in my research team's interviews.

133. The leadership status of Rosa and the next Senderista to be discussed, Martina, was inferred from their comments in response to a question by the Osores research team about familiarity with Sendero's top leaders.

134. Interview no. 19, Osores research team.

135. Ibid. The variation in pronouns is Rosa's own.

136. Ibid.

137. Interview no. 10, Osores research team. Again, rank was indicated primarily by comments about her familiarity with Sendero's inner circle.

138. Interview no. 33, Osores research team. See also interviews no. 4, 10, and 31.

139. Interview no. 4, Osores research team.

140. Chávez de Paz (1989, 41). Although the study was of inmates in Lima jails only, approximately 90 percent of all those convicted on charges of terrorism were transferred to Lima. See Chávez de Paz (1989, 17). Dietz (1992) also found that illegal protesters (who included both Senderistas and citizens of other leftist political persuasions) were more likely to have had some university training than legal protesters.

141. Interview no. 18, Osores research team.

142. Shining Path human rights lawyer cited by Guillermoprieto (1993, 74).

143. In a May 1990 survey by Datum, students were the social group among whom 46 percent of respondents believed that Sendero had the most influence. Survey results courtesy of Manuel Torrado, director of Datum. Keep in mind, however, the caveats about comparisons to El Salvador with respect to "students" and "peasants" at the beginning of this section.

144. *El Comercio,* 4 April 1985, 3.

145. Survey was by the agency CEDRO, reported in *Sendero File* 5 (November 1992): 2. The survey is also cited by Julio Cotler in "Political Trend Report," *Peru Report* 5, no. 10 (November 1991): 3.

146. Interview no. 32, Osores research team.

147. Interview no. 6, Osores research team.

148. "Julián," cited by Guillermoprieto (1993, 74).

149. Rosenberg (1991, 148).

150. National-level survey by Datum, 10–12 May 1990. Survey results courtesy of Manuel Torrado, director of Datum.

151. Includes two former workers on what they describe as haciendas and four peasants who described themselves as working their own plots, without indicating whether or not they were members of peasant communities.

152. Casas (1991, 30).

153. This model is described by Bonner (1988, 42–44); Rénique (1994, 233); and Gianotten, de Wit, and de Wit (1985, 190–191).

154. "Nicario," cited in Degregori and Ricci (1990, 193–195).

155. Interview nos. 3, 7, 21, 26, 28, and 29, Osores research team. Only the peasant in interview no. 26 used some of the terms that were common among the teacher and student interviews, but said "We were told that he was the guide and philosopher" rather than "he is the guide and philosopher," etc.

156. Interview no. 26, Osores research team.

157. Interview no. 28, Osores research team.

158. Interview no. 21, Osores research team.

159. For Puno, Rénique (1994, 235); for Huancayo, Manrique (1989).

160. Strong (1992, 109); Gonzales (1992); and "Political Report," *Peru Report* (March 1992): 1.

161. Interview no. 7, Osores research team.

162. Five of the six peasant respondents said that they received food and money as a result of their activities for Sendero. Only the peasant who had been recruited by force and had not been persuaded by the militants' appeals reported that he did not receive economic support.

163. Interview no. 28, Osores research team.

164. Interview no. 26, Osores research team.

165. Cecilia Blondet and Maruja Barrig, at the George Washington University Andean Seminar, 22 November 1991.

166. The workers include an assistant with car transport, an electrician, a mechanic, a cook, a miner, and a man who said he did any odd job available.

167. Interview no. 20, Osores research team.

168. Interview no. 24, Osores research team.

169. *Caretas,* 30 May 1988, 30. A segment of the interview is also published in Poole and Renique (1992, 67).

170. Mark R. Day, *Los Angeles Times,* 4 December 1988.

171. *New York Times,* 2 June 1992, A4.

172. "Tito," cited by Degregori, Blondet, and Lynch (1987, 244).

173. Rosenberg (1991a, 186).

174. Félix Cóndor, in Raucana, a Shining Path stronghold near Lima, cited in Strong (1992, 263).

175. *Expreso,* 12 May 1992, A11.

176. Kirk (1992, 20).

177. I am indebted to Hugh Byrne for his apt use of the word "symbiotic" in a conversation in December 1995.

178. Both Degregori (1986, 230); and Mayer (1994, 143) suggest that some scholarly analysts of the Peruvian revolutionary challenge perceive economic crisis as a sufficient factor. To my knowledge, none has, and in any case, I certainly do not.

179. The table reports results for war-torn departments in El Salvador in order to be comparable with the Junín sample in Peru. However, as was usually the case in the Salvadoran survey, results varied little by geographic region. The percentage that responded "to win political power" was 47 percent in San Salvador. Respondents in the capital cited "whim" less frequently (only 13 percent), and international support more frequently (8 percent) than their counterparts in conflictive departments.

180. For statements similar to those cited in this paragraph, see LeoGrande (1990, 144); Dunkerley (1988, 375); and Carothers (1991, 14).

181. Wickham-Crowley (1992, 228–229).

182. Baloyra (1982); Baloyra (1985); and Baloyra (1993, 4).

183. Montgomery (1995, 269). The comment is in the last paragraph of her book.

184. Vilas (1995, 82).

185. Seligson (1996, 155).

186. James LeMoyne, ABC News *Nightline,* 30 January 1992, transcript no. 2789, 5.

187. A debate on this issue appeared in *Latin American Research Review* 31, no. 2. Diskin (1996, 111–126); and Paige (1996, 127–139) argue that rural social tensions were a major cause of the Salvadoran revolt; Seligson (1996, 140–158) contends that they were not. Arguments advancing rural poverty as a key impetus to the rebellion have also been made by North (1985); Acevedo (1996); and Pearce (1986).

188. Booth (1991); and Brockett (1991).

189. Kincaid (1993, 140).

190. Wood (1996, 16). See also Dunkerley (1988, 365–366).

191. Seligson (1996, 153–154).

192. See, for example, Castañeda (1994, 103). Such an interpretation is also supported by the emphasis in the peace accords on political rather than economic reform. As Wood and Segovia (1995, 2087) point out, "The core of the peace agreement . . . was the agenda of extensive reforms of the coercive apparatus of the state."

193. See, for example, Leiken (1984); and Wickham-Crowley (1989, 518–519). Bracamonte and Spencer (1995) are also primarily critical.

194. For a brief summary of what was, of course, an intense debate at the time, see Carothers (1991, 16–20). In recent years, scholars such as Castañeda (1994, 98) have acknowledged that the FMLN received considerable quantities of East bloc weapons, but point out that thousands of guerrilla fighters must be willing and able to use them if a rebellion is to occur.

195. Byrne (1995); and Byrne (1996).

196. Huntington (1968, 301).

197. Although some scholars acknowledge the importance of U.S. policy, they did not analyze it in any detail. See, for example, Wickham-Crowley (1989, 528); Montgomery (1995, 22); and Baloyra (1982, 184).

198. Scholars making this point include Baloyra (1982, 174–175); Baloyra (1993); Wickham-Crowley (1992, 211, 285); Carothers (1991, 30–34); and Arnson (1993, 71–74).

199. Palmer (1995, 253, 302). See also Huntington (1991, 15); Werlich (1987); McClintock (1989b); Graham (1993); Ferrero (1993); and Cameron and Mauceri (1997).

200. The data suggest a likely increase in the percentage of respondents attributing Sendero's rise to "bad government" between 1990 and 1991 in Junín. The difference in the two samples' responses might also reflect the higher educational level of the 1991 Junín sample.

201. *QueHacer,* no. 72 (July–August 1991): 41.

202. Starn (1991, 79). See also Mitchell (1991, 196–197).

203. Huntington (1968, 289) was the first to emphasize that "typically the first middle-class elements to appear on the social scene are intellectuals with traditional roots but modern values. . . . The first elements of the middle class to appear are the most revolutionary."

204. Montoya (1992, 91).

205. Gianotten, de Wit, and de Wit (1985, 190–191). This same point is also made by Guillermoprieto (1993, 68); Harding (1986, 189); Ansión, del Castillo, Piqueras, and Zegarra (1992, 90–91); and Enrique Obando, in an interview with *La República,* 25 April 1993, 9.

206. Strong (1992, 189). A similar point is made, for the country as a whole, by Brown and Fernández (1991, 203).

207. A Villa El Salvador mechanic cited in *New York Times,* 15 April 1992, A12.

208. The three scholars described here as "foremost" are those who have both explicitly sought a theoretical understanding of Sendero's challenge and published extensively on it. On the "foremost" position of Degregori and Gorriti, see Starn (1992). Beyond works mentioned below, see Poole and Rénique (1992) for a detailed but primarily historical approach; Strong (1992) for the cogent account of a British journalist; and articles by the Peruvian sociologist Raúl González (1982, 1986, 1987, 1988, and 1990).

209. For example, Palmer (1995, 253) writes that "Shining Path in a real sense made the revolution in Peru," but also comments that "Sendero took full advantage of the opportunities presented it" (p. 302), acknowledging that these opportunities were important. In general, Palmer (1986); and Palmer (1995) emphasize the remarkable fit between Sendero's Ayacucho-born character and the political space available to the movement. Degregori's key works (1986 and 1990a) acknowledge problems of poverty but emphasize his interest in social and political dynamics. Gorriti (1992b, 94) comments that Sendero was "feeding on despair," but suggests despair to have been obvious, unnecessary to analyze in much detail.

210. Gorriti (1990a, 172). See also Gorriti (1990c, 17, 21); and Gorriti (1992) for a similar assessment. Gorriti covered the Shining Path for Peru's leading weekly magazine *Caretas* during the early 1980s. See also Gorriti (1990b, 1990c, and 1992).

211. Writes Palmer (1995, 270–275) about this interpretation of Sendero: "The Sendero ideology provides a recognizable alternative value system in a group-solidarity setting that, when combined with actions, enhances one's self-worth. . . . [The Senderista] changes personal behavior and feels much better about himself or herself."

212. Degregori (1986, 261; 1989b, 28; and 1991, 26).

213. Degregori (1990–91, 15).

214. Ibid., 16; and Degregori, "The Future of Peru's Shining Path" (speech at Andean Seminar, sponsored by George Washington University and Washington Office on Latin America, Washington, D.C., 18 November 1993).

215. Degregori (1990–91, 16).

216. Degregori (1986, 260). These sentences constitute the bulk of Degregori's "Conclusions" to this work.

217. Manuél Jesús Granados, interviewed in *La República*, 29 December 1987, 16.

218. Isbell (1992, 65–68); Berg (1986–87, 186); and Harding (1986, 190). The point was also made by Cecilia Blondet, in a talk at the Andean Seminar, George Washington University, 22 November 1991; and in an interview with William Loker, on the basis of his year-long research in the Pucallpa area, in Washington, D.C., 3 May 1989.

219. See especially Berg (1986–87, 186).

220. Berg (1986–87, 191–192).

221. Manrique (1989, 160).

222. Rénique (1993); and Rénique (1994). Emphasis upon peasants' pragmatism and their focus upon local problems is also made by Smith (1989, 233–235).

223. Smith, Michael L. (1992, 25). See also González (1988).

224. Senderista interview no. 18, Osores research team.

225. Peasants, of course, are sensitive to changes in power balances. See Starn (1995, 405). Among some peasant groups, in particular the Asháninkas in the Peruvian Amazon, millenarian attitudes were exploited by Sendero.

226. Urrutia, in an interview with González (1989, 42–46). Urrutia was also director of the Instituto de Estudios Rurales José María Arguedas in Ayacucho from the mid–1980s until 1988; also, in 1986, he was elected lieutenant governor of Ayacucho on the Izquierda Unida ticket.

227. This point has been made by Smith, Michael L. (1992, 29); and David Scott Palmer, in "Political Interview," *Peru Report* 7, no. 7 (August 1993): 1.

228. The degree to which Sendero lost support is controversial, and for obvious reasons precise figures are not available. The two poles of the debate were González (1990), who argued that Sendero was emphasizing the cities because it had lost most of its support in the countryside, and Strong, who believed that Sendero was emphasizing the cities for strategic reasons but "had most of the rest of the country at its disposal" in 1992. See "Political Interview," *Peru Report* 6, no. 9 (October 1992): 2.

229. See chapter 2.

230. Harding (1986, 191); and Isbell (1992, 73).

231. This point has also been made by Palmer (1995, 301–303); and especially Mauceri (1991, 3, 28).

232. Full discussion of Peru-Ecuador relations is beyond the scope of this book. However, many analysts believe that, when the Ecuadorean government began to establish military outposts in disputed territory, it saw itself as taking advantage of the Peruvian government's preoccupation with its internal conflict. See, for example, Palmer (1996, 15).

233. *New York Times,* 20 September 1992, sec. 4, 5.

234. Mauceri (1991, 10). Of course, the mere "presence" of the state is not necessarily positive. As we have seen, some civilian authorities were corrupt, and some security force personnel abusive. Prior to 1968, the primary "representative" of the state in highlands Peru was the hacendado. As Mauceri (1996, 124–125) points out, Sendero's advance in the southern highlands was facilitated by the fact that, after hacendados departed in the wake of the agrarian reform, no other pro-status-quo authorities established a presence.

235. 1980–92 figure is cited in chapter 2, page 68.

236. Mauceri (1991, 10); *Economist,* 18 November 1989, 46; and *New York Times,* 26 October 1989, A6.

237. *Sí,* 16 March 1987, 82.

238. Carlos Tapia, in a roundtable discussion of the internal war, sponsored by the *Expreso* newspaper, in *Expreso,* 4 March 1991, 6. Tapia, an analyst at CEPRODEP (Center for the Promotion and Development of the Population), had been a professor at the Ayacucho university and also a representative in Peru's legislature from 1985 to 1990. A similar analysis is made by Henri Favre, in an interview with Mariella Balbi, *La República,* 17 December 1989, 14. See also Mauceri (1991, 11).

239. Poole and Rénique (1992, 94).

240. *PerúPaz* 2, no. 7 (January 1993): 12.

241. Sendero's attacks were targeted especially against the PUM (the furthest-left group within the Izquierda Unida and thus an ideological rival to Sendero) in particular. For an outstanding analysis of these trends in Puno, see Rénique (1993).

242. William Loker, interview by author, based on more than a year's research in Pucallpa, 1986–87, in Washington, D.C., 3 May 1989; and Bruno Revese, S.J., researcher at Centro de Investigación y Promoción del Campesino (CIPCA), talk at Georgetown University, Washington, D.C., 30 January 1990.

243. Berg (1986–87, 184).

244. *PerúPaz* 2, no. 10 (April 1993): 7.

245. These data were the Peruvian results for a cross-national survey; in Peru, the survey research was carried out by the Apoyo agency. The word for trust was *confianza*. Interestingly, however, the percentage of people who trusted their political institutions in Peru was higher than in Bolivia or Ecuador, and—on some items—in Colombia as well. See *La República*, 14 July 1993, 16–17.

246. After García left the presidency and his party no longer controlled the legislature, investigations of "illicit enrichment" were intense. Most Peruvians believe that García was guilty as charged. However, there has not been a satisfactory trial, and there also is little doubt that Fujimori's desire to discredit a leader whom he perceived as a challenger in the 1995 elections was also a factor. The media's focus upon high-level corruption was not surprising, but it also unfortunately played into Sendero's advance.

247. Loose translation from an off-the-record interview with the judge by Rodolfo Osores, 8 July 1991. The statement employs terms used by both Sendero and President Fujimori and suggests how common these criticisms had become at all points on the political spectrum.

248. My addition of data in Webb and Fernández Baca (1990, 259); and Carbajal Pérez and Uiarte Otoya (1993, 103). Both these publications report data collected by the Bernales Commission.

249. Ibid.

250. Alvarez and Cervantes (1996, 155). A $20 billion figure for 1980–92 is also reported in *La República*, 7 October 1992, 15.

251. James Brooke, *New York Times*, 1 August 1992, 1.

252. As of April 1992, approximately one-third of Villa El Salvador's neighborhood block groups had links with Sendero Luminoso, according to *New York Times*, 15 April 1992, A12. See also Montoya and Reyna (1992); and Burt (1994).

253. Burt (1994, 7–8).

254. For the emphasis upon corruption by the Sendero leadership, see especially one report by a repentant Senderista in *Expreso,* 12 May 1992, A11: "[Our teacher] made us see that our country was a disaster because of corruption."

255. This was the case not only among the very poor. Through the years, numerous middle-class or upper-middle-class Peruvians have said to me, sometimes with sheer satisfaction and sometimes with dismay at their satisfaction, the following words, more or less: "Yes, I was happy when Sendero killed him. He was guilty of so many crimes. He had hurt so many." Carol Graham heard the same comments; see her "Sendero's Law in Peru's Shantytowns," *Wall Street Journal,* 7 June 1991, A13.

256. "Fire in the Mind," segment of *The Americas* video series on PBS.

257. Sendero's effective use of the corruption theme in Lima's shanty towns has also been highlighted by Poole and Rénique (1992, 92–94).

258. Writes Burt (1994, 14): "In a context of scarce resources, institutional breakdown, and weak or inexistent mechanisms of conflict resolution, certain patterns of behavior seem to arise that fundamentally challenge the social movements literature's portrayal of grassroots movements as inherently democratic and participatory. In such a context, internal conflicts in grassroots organizations arise over multiple issues, and mistrust, envy, favoritism, manipulation, and petty corruption become common currency." Earlier in her paper, she notes "in a context of extreme poverty that feeds mistrust, rumors of corruption often become reality and, like a self-fulfilling prophecy, corrupt leaders are sanctioned by Sendero, and many times the sanction is perceived as deserved." See Burt (1994, 11).

259. *Washington Post,* 27 November 1991, A22.

260. Ibid.

261. Cecilia Blondet, speaking at the Andean Seminar, George Washington University, Washington, D.C., 22 November 1991.

7. Conclusion

1. See chapters 1 and 3 for discussions of democracy, and chapter 6 for a discussion of U.S. promotion of democracy in Latin America. Although many scholars include Colombia as democratic after 1959, I do not. See chapter 3. Gurr (1991, 664–665) counts thirty-eight states worldwide with institutionalized democratic systems in 1986, half of which had been continuously democratic since 1945.

2. See the discussion in chapter 3.

3. A similar point is made by Castañeda (1994, 379).

4. Lowenthal (1992–93); Rothstein (1992); Naím (1993); Naím (1995); O'Donnell (1994); Conaghan and Espinal (1990); and Diamond (1996).

5. Claude Ake speaking at the conference "Elections and Conflict Resolution in Africa," cited in *PeaceWatch* 1, no. 5 (August 1995): 6.

6. A conceptualization of "inputs" versus "outputs" was suggested in comments on a first draft of this study by David Scott Palmer, 10 August 1995.

7. See, especially, Diamond (1996) for a recent, comprehensive, and thoughtful analysis. Among the numerous recent scholarly works on democracy that I have reviewed, I have not found a single definition of "legitimacy." In Max Weber's original explication of the term (Weber, 1968, 24–38), he associates legitimacy with validity, which is achieved by tradition, by faith, by rationality, and/or by law. Until recently, the scholarly tendency was to dismiss legitimacy as at best secondary; for example, Di Palma (1990, 149) argues that "legitimacy . . . is both rare and unneeded."

8. During the 1980s, there were few if any U.S. programs that were specifically classified as democracy promotion. Diamond (1992, 46) estimates that U.S. AID spent about $200 million worldwide on democracy promotion at that time, and U.S. AID and USIA together about $400 million. Carothers (1994, 124) reports that AID spent about $400 million on democracy promotion worldwide in FY 1994, a substantial increase. As of AID's 1995 annual report, a separate classification for "democratic initiatives" programs was not being made; the classifications were only economic, military, antinarcotics, and food aid programs.

9. Data generously provided by Margaret J. Sarles, Team Leader, Democracy and Human Rights, Bureau for Latin America and the Caribbean, U.S. Agency for International Development, Washington, D.C. Additionally, in FY 1997, the Organization of American States was to spend $4 million on its Unit for the Promotion of Democracy, and "Good Governance" has been a new theme at the IDB and the World Bank as well. See Shifter and Neill (1996, 4).

10. The $100 million-odd total averages out to about $6 million for each of the seventeen noninsular countries conventionally identified as "Latin American" (rather than Caribbean).

11. For example, in a recent survey on "most important problems," exacerbated poverty and inequality were most frequently reported. See *Latin America Regional Report*, 14 November 1996, 4–5.

12. ECLAC (1996, 14). Figure for GDP per capita.

13. Ibid., 8–9. Among the nine Latin American nations for which data were available, only in Chile and Bolivia were real wages in 1995 above their 1980 and 1990 levels. See ibid., 15, and compare with the data in table 4.3 for real wages in the region between 1980 and 1989.

14. *New York Times*, 7 September 1995, A8.

15. Castañeda (1994); Green (1995); Naim (1993); and Broad and Cavanagh (1995–96), among other scholars.

16. Data from the World Bank, reported in *Economist*, 30 November 1996, 19. See also *Washington Post*, 29 December 1996, A27.

17. From the Celam document "América Latina, levántate y echa a andar," quoted in *Latin America Weekly Report* 95, no. 18 (18 May 1995): 205.

18. *Time*, 6 November 1989, 64.

19. *Washington Post*, 10 December 1996, A1, A23.

20. Among the many sources, see, for example, Nancy Birdsall, "Social and Economic Development" (remarks for the Secretary's Open Forum, U.S. Department of State, Washington, D.C., 3 March 1997); and Castañeda (1994, 426–476).

21. Although U.S. "Food for Peace" (P.L. 480) resources have not declined as much in real terms between 1990 and 1996 as other U.S. AID programs, they have declined slightly—at a time when the total numbers of Latin American poor have increased. See "Total Program Funds for LAC," a graph elaborated by the Democracy and Human Rights Office at the U.S. Agency for International Development, Bureau for Latin America and the Caribbean, December 1996.

22. See, for example, Garst (1992); and comments on this chapter by Dr. Jindra Cekan, food security adviser, Catholic Relief Services, 30 January 1997, in Baltimore, Maryland.

23. Garst (1992); and recommendations in comments on this chapter by Dr. Jindra Cekan, 30 January 1997. This question has apparently come under discussion at U.S. AID but has not yet been resolved, as reported in a telephone interview with Stan Specht, desk officer for Peru at the U.S. Department of State, 13 May 1996.

24. Interviews with Eric Olson, associate at the Washington Office on Latin America, Washington, D.C., 9 May 1996 and 2 January 1997; and with John Ruthrauff, executive director, Center for Democratic Education, Washington, D.C., 30 December 3 1996. See also the IDB's annual reports.

25. Ibid. Precise IDB strategies for the classification of a loan as for "the social sector" are often unclear. Also, of course, the design of "social sector" projects is not necessarily uncontroversial; further, a social sector project is not necessarily a "poverty alleviation" project. See also *Washington Post*, 15 May 1995, A18.

26. The point was indicated by Ronald Scheman, U.S. executive director of the Inter-American Development Bank, at a presentation to the Atlantic Council, Washington, D.C., 7 May 1996, and the recommendation was made by interviewees cited in note 24.

27. Foremost Latin Americanists agree that economic crisis is the most intense challenge to democratic legitimacy in Latin America today. See Lowenthal (1992–93); Naím (1995); O'Donnell (1994); and Diamond (1996).

28. Elliott (1996, 3).

29. Ibid., 4–6.

30. On the importance of these reforms, see also Geddes (1990).

31. The term "political processing of adversity" is used by Diamond (1996, 77), who cites Juan Linz and Alfred Stepan as its originators.

32. Said the Clinton administration's top antidrug official, Barry R. McCaffrey, in a telephone interview with journalist Dougals Farah about U.S. policy in Colombia, for example: "We are adamant in our view that the counter-drug agenda is dominant." Cited in *Washington Post*, 4 October 1997, A16.

33. Reyna (1995); and Gorriti (1996).

34. Youngers (1995b, 9) reports a conviction rate of 97 percent in military tribunals.

35. *Washington Post*, 5 January 1997, A20.

36. Secret "faceless" civilian tribunals try those accused of terrorism, and secret "faceless" military tribunals try those accused of treason.

37. See note 231 in chapter 5.

38. Interview with Margaret J. Sarles, Team Leader, Democracy and Human Rights, Bureau for Latin America and the Caribbean, U.S. Agency for International Development, Washington, D.C., 31 December 1996.

39. An important example of U.S. civilians' standing by threatened civilians in order to reduce the possibility of attacks was the Witness for Peace effort in Nicaragua, where U.S. citizens lived with Nicaraguan peasants to prompt international criticism of attacks upon Nicaraguan civilians by the U.S.-backed contras. See Ed Griffin-Nolan, *Witness for Peace* (Louisville, Ky.: Westminster/John Knox Press, 1991).

Appendix I

1. A comparative study of Peruvian polling agencies by the Universidad del Pacífico in 1989 identifies Datum as the most respected agency in Peru. See Universidad del Pacífico, "Estudio sobre compañías de investigación" (mimeographed). On Datum and other agencies' electoral forecasts, see *Caretas*, 14 February 1983, 31; 29 March 1985, 5–14; 1 September 1986, 30; 30 October 1989, 11; and compare with actual electoral tallies in Cuánto (1991, 1020–1032). However, especially when there has been a more marked tendency for lower-income groups to support candidates of the political left, Datum and other agencies have underestimated the tally for the leftist candidates. See, especially, the forecasts for the Lima mayoralty race in November 1983 in *Caretas*, 7 November 1983, 20–21.

2. Víctor Antonio Orellana collaborated with Ignacio Martín-Baró on the article "La necesidad de votar: Actitudes del pueblo salvadoreño ante el proceso electoral de 1984," *Estudios Centroamericanos* 39 (April–May 1984): 253–264. Martín-Baró is the author of two books on Salvadoran public opinion. See Martín-Baró (1987); and Martín-Baró (1989). Martín-Baró's death was a serious loss for public opinion research in El Salvador for a period; when I was in El Salvador in August–October 1990 considering alternative opportunities for research collaboration, the UCA's research team was not yet reestablished. Most recently, Orellana was

the head of the research project "América Central: Descentralización y fortalec-imiento municipal," coordinated by FLACSO—Program El Salvador and financed by the Ford Foundation.

3. Although the public opinion institute at the UCA is perceived in some quarters as politically left, it estimated the size of the political shift away from the Christian Democrats and toward the ARENA better than other institutions. See, for example, Martín-Baró (1989, 153); and IUDOP (1991, 2).

4. Jocelyn Nieva, my research assistant at the United States Institute of Peace, reviewed the Ecuadorean news dailies available in Washington, D.C., for the month of June 1991 and found CEDATOS to be the only public opinion agency whose results were reported during that period. Its survey about the reform of labor laws was reported in *Hoy*, 19 June 1991, A1.

5. Datum, Orellana, and CEDATOS used somewhat different classifications for age and social class; accordingly, exact comparisons across the three samples cannot be made for these demographic indicators. However, using the classifications made by the organizations themselves, the samples appear roughly similar, except with respect to the rural group in the Salvadoran sample. Datum's November 1990 Lima sample included 400 respondents, of whom 50 percent were male and 50 percent were female; 49 percent were between 18 and 34 years of age and 51 percent were 35 or over; 17 percent were upper class or upper middle class, 20 percent were middle class or upper lower class, and 63 percent were lower class. Orellana's April–May 1991 nationwide Salvadoran sample included 400 respondents, of whom 54 percent were male and 46 percent female; 53 percent were under 30 years of age and 47 percent were aged 30 or older; 21 percent were middle or upper class, 38 percent were from the popular class, and 41 percent were rural. The December 1991 CEDATOS survey included 524 respondents, of whom 50 percent were in Quito and 50 percent were in Guayaquil; 48 percent were male and 52 percent were female; 34 percent were between 18 and 25 years of age, 35 percent were between 26 and 40, and 31 percent were over 40; 19 percent were upper class, 41 percent were middle class, and 39 percent were lower class.

The two Huancayo samples varied somewhat. The May 1990 Datum Huancayo sample included 200 respondents, of whom 81 percent were urban and 19 percent rural; 49 percent were male and 51 percent were female; 55 percent were between 18 and 35 years of age, and 45 percent were 35 years or older; and 35 percent were upper or middle class and 65 percent lower class. The June–July 1991 Osores Huancaya sample included 130 respondents, of whom 68 percent were urban and 32 percent rural; 65 percent were male and 35 percent were female; 50 percent were between 18 and 34 years, 46 percent were 35 and over, and 4 percent did not indicate their age; 16 percent had primary education or less; 30 percent secondary or some secondary or technical education; and 54 percent had university or some university education.

6. On the "random route" procedure, see Gerald Hainville and Roger Jowell, *Survey Research Practice* (London: Heinemann, 1978), 87–88.

7. Manuel Torrado, "Post-Test Electoral" (mimeographed paper distributed by Datum), 2. A major advantage of at-home interviewing is that it facilitates spot checks of interviews by the supervisors of the research. This could not be done in El Salvador. In El Salvador, the supervisor of the research directly accompanied small interview teams in the field.

8. William Bollinger, "Public Opinion and Democracy in El Salvador and Nicaragua" (paper presented at the Latin American Studies Association meeting, Los Angeles, September 1992).

9. For information about the formal surveys and the research sites, see McClintock (1983, 85–105). The subsequent informal surveys were carried out in the same sites; the survey items depended upon my specific interests at the time; respondents usually numbered in the range of 25 to 35 per site, with total numbers of respondents about 50 to 70.

Appendix II

1. The data from both these institutions are the data most frequently cited by scholarly analysts. See, for example, Schwarz (1991) for El Salvador and Chipoco; Schwarz (1992) for Peru. Both are the primary data source for Americas Watch. For its annual reports on human rights in the late 1980s and early 1990s, the U.S. Department of State has relied on the figures of the Bernales Commission as well as the National Human Rights Coordinating Committee. The work of the Bernales Commission is discussed in Americas Watch (1992, 13); the work of Tutela Legal is discussed in Congressional Research Service (1989, 77–91). Tutela Legal is described as "the main human rights investigative agency in El Salvador . . . [that is] well respected internationally" in U.S. Department of State, *Country Reports on Human Rights Practices for 1990* (Washington, D.C.: Government Printing Office, 1990), 619. Bernales is identified as the "person who has most meticulously tracked the course of Peruvian political violence over the past decade" in "Political Report," *Peru Report* 7, no. 4 (May 1993): 3.

2. Direct comparisons are made in DESCO (1989, 1:23–47). During the later 1980s and early 1990s, collaboration among the various reporting groups increased, and the 10 percent variation figure that I present below is based on my own review of the data of these various institutions.

3. Interviews at CEAPAZ, 15 November 1990; and with Pablo Rojas, the director of the human rights group COMISEDH and executive committee member of the National Human Rights Coordinating Committee of Peru, 16 September 1992. On some of the tactics used by the military to prevent investigation, see Bonner (1988, 56). For example, when it became clear that the bodies in mass graves might be discovered, the security forces began to burn the bodies instead.

4. See, for example, Congressional Research Service (1989, 78–91). However, the tallies of deaths made by Tutela Legal and other groups suggest a total death toll

in El Salvador during the 1980s of about forty thousand; the fact that journalists routinely use figures in the range of seventy thousand suggests a consensus that total deaths were considerably higher than reported deaths.

5. For a careful review of this issue, see Congressional Research Service (1989, 78–91).

6. For brief discussions of the work of the Truth Commission, see *New York Times,* 21 March 1993, 1, 10; and *Washington Post,* 21 March 1993, 1, A36. In its report summarizing tallies of violations from 1982 through 1990, Tutela Legal estimated that about 95 percent of the violations were the responsibility of security force agents and 5 percent the responsibility of the FMLN. However, these tallies reflect very high numbers of deaths during the early 1980s and Tutela Legal's assigning responsibility for the vast majority of these deaths to security force agents. In the mid- and late 1980s, Tutela Legal reported the FMLN to be responsible for more than 20 percent of violations.

7. Congressional Research Service (1989, 84–85). The U.S. State Department claimed that the guerrillas were responsible for more than 65 percent of violations, and security force agents 10 percent or less.

BIBLIOGRAPHY

Acevedo, Carlos. 1991a. "El Salvador's New Clothes: The Electoral Process (1982–1989)." In *A Decade of War*, edited by Anjali Sundaram and George Gelber. New York: Monthly Review.

———. 1991b. "El significado político de las elecciones del 10 de marzo." *Estudios Centroamericanos* 509 (March): 151–168.

———. 1996. "The Historical Background to the Conflict." In *Economic Policy for Building Peace: The Lessons of El Salvador*, edited by James K. Boyce, 19–30. Boulder, Colo.: Lynne Rienner.

Adler, Daniel, and Thomas Long. 1992. "El Salvador: Tales of the Struggle." *NACLA Report on the Americas* 26, no. 3 (December): 25–31.

Alexander, Robert J. 1958. *The Bolivian National Revolution*. New Brunswick, N.J.: Rutgers University Press.

———. 1982. *Rómulo Betancourt and the Transformation of Venezuela*. New Brunswick, N.J.: Transaction.

Alvarez, Elena, and Francisco Joel Cervantes. 1996. "The Economic Consequences of the 'Peruvian Disease.'" In *The Peruvian Economy and Structural Adjustment: Past, Present, and Future*, edited by Efrain Gonzales de Olarte, 147–176. Coral Gables, Fla.: University of Miami, North-South Center.

Alvarez, Francisco A. 1988. "Transition before the Transition: The Case of El Salvador." *Latin American Perspectives* 15, no. 1 (winter): 78–92.

Americas Watch *(on countries other than El Salvador or Peru)*

1985. "Guatemala Revised: How the Reagan Administration Finds 'Improvements' in Human Rights in Guatemala." New York: Americas Watch (September).

1986. "The Central-Americanization of Colombia? Human Rights and the Peace Process." New York: Americas Watch (January).

Americas Watch *(on El Salvador)*

1984a. *Protection of the Weak and Unarmed: The Dispute over Counting Human Rights Violations in El Salvador*. New York: Human Rights Watch (February).

1984b. *Free Fire: A Report on Human Rights in El Salvador.* New York: Americas Watch (August).

1985a. *Draining the Sea: Sixth Supplement to the Report on Human Rights in El Salvador.* New York: Americas Watch (March).

1985b. *The Continuing Terror: Seventh Supplement to the Report on Human Rights in El Salvador.* New York: Americas Watch (September).

1986. *Settling into Routine: Human Rights Abuses in Duarte's Second Year: Eighth Supplement to the Report on Human Rights in El Salvador.* New York: Americas Watch.

1987. *The Civilian Toll: Ninth Supplement to the Report on Human Rights in El Salvador.* New York: Americas Watch.

1988a. *Labor Rights in El Salvador.* New York: Americas Watch.

1988b. *Nightmare Revisited 1987–88: Tenth Supplement to the Report on Human Rights in El Salvador.* New York: Americas Watch (September).

1988c. *Human Rights in El Salvador on the Eve of Elections 1988.* New York: Americas Watch (March).

1989. *Carnage Again: Preliminary Report on Violations of War by Both Sides in the November 1989 Offensive in El Salvador (November 24).* New York: Americas Watch.

1989. *Update on El Salvador: The Human Rights Crisis Continues in the Wake of the FMLN Offensive (December 16).* New York: Americas Watch.

1990. *A Year of Reckoning: El Salvador a Decade after the Assassination of Archbishop Romero.* New York: Americas Watch.

1991a. *El Salvador and Human Rights: The Challenge of Reform.* New York: Americas Watch.

1991b. *El Salvador's Decade of Terror.* New Haven, Conn.: Yale University Press; Americas Watch.

Americas Watch *(on Peru)*

1984. *Abdicating Democratic Authority: Human Rights in Peru.* New York: Americas Watch.

1986. *Human Rights in Peru after President García's First Year.* New York: Americas Watch.

1987. *A Certain Passivity: Failing to Curb Human Rights Abuses in Peru.* New York: Americas Watch.

1988. *Tolerating Abuses: Violations of Human Rights in Peru.* New York: Americas Watch.

1990. *In Desperate Straits: Human Rights in Peru after a Decade of Democracy and Insurgency.* New York: Americas Watch.

1991. *Into the Quagmire: Human Rights and U.S. Policy in Peru.* New York: Americas Watch.

1992. *Peru under Fire: Human Rights since the Return of Democracy.* New Haven, Conn.: Yale University Press.

Americas Watch and American Civil Liberties Union. 1982a. *Report on Human Rights in El Salvador.* New York: Vintage.

———. 1982b. *July 20, 1982. Supplement to the Report on Human Rights in El Salvador.* Washington, D.C.: Center for National Security Studies.

———. 1983a. *January 20, 1983. Second Supplement to the Report on Human Rights in El Salvador.* Washington, D.C.: Center for National Security Studies.

———. 1983b. *July 19, 1983. Third Supplement to the Report on Human Rights in El Salvador.* Washington, D.C.: Center for National Security Studies.

———. 1984. *As Bad as Ever: A Report on Human Rights in El Salvador. January 31, Fourth Supplement.* Washington, D.C.: Center for National Security Studies.

Amnesty International. 1989. *Caught between Two Fires: Peru Briefing.* New York: Amnesty International.

———. 1992. *Peru: Human Rights during the Government of Alberto Fujimori.* Washington, D.C.: Amnesty International.

Andersen, Martin Edwin. 1993. *Dossier Secreto: Argentina's Desaparecidos and the Myth of the "Dirty War."* Boulder, Colo.: Westview.

Anderson, Ken, and Jean-Marie Simon. 1987. "Permanent Counterinsurgency in Guatemala." *Telos* 73 (fall): 9–46.

Anderson, Lisa. 1987. "The State in the Middle East and North Africa." *Comparative Politics* 20, no. 1 (October): 1–18.

Andrade, Víctor. 1976. *My Missions for Revolutionary Bolivia, 1944–1962.* Pittsburgh: University of Pittsburgh Press.

Andreas, Peter, and Coletta Youngers. 1989. "'Busting' the Andean Cocaine Industry: America's Counterproductive War on Drugs." *World Policy Journal* 6, no. 3 (summer): 529–562.

Ansión, Juan et al. 1992. *La escuela en tiempos de guerra.* Lima: Centro de Estudios y Acción para la Paz.

Arce Borja, Luis, and Janet Talavera Sánchez. 1988. "La entrevista del siglo: El presidente Gonzalo rompe el silencio." *El Diario,* 24 July, 2–73.

Armstrong, Robert, and Janet Shenk. 1982. *El Salvador: The Face of Revolution.* Boston: South End.

Arnson, Cynthia J. 1983. "The Salvadoran Military and Regime Transformation." In *Political Change in Central America: Internal and External Dimensions,* edited by Wolf Grabendorff et al., 97–113. Boulder, Colo.: Westview.

———. 1989. *Cross-Roads: Congress, the Reagan Administration, and Central America.* New York: Pantheon.

———. 1993. *Crossroads: Congress, the President, and Central America, 1976–1993.* University Park: Pennsylvania State University Press.

Arriaza Meléndez, Jorge. 1989. *Historia de los procesos electorales en El Salvador.* San Salvador: Instituto Salvadoreño de Estudios Políticos.

Asociación Peruana de Estudios e Investigaciones para la Paz. 1985. *Siete ensayos sobre la violencia en el Perú.* Lima: Fundación Friedrich Ebert.

Astiz, Carlos A. 1969. *Pressure Groups and Power Elites in Peruvian Politics.* Ithaca: Cornell University Press.

Astiz, Carlos A., and José Z. García. 1972. "The Peruvian Military: Achievement, Orientation, Training, and Political Tendencies." *Western Political Quarterly* 25, no. 4: 667–685.

Autonomedia. 1994. *Zapatistas! Documents of the New Mexican Revolution (December 31, 1993–June 12, 1994).* Brooklyn, N.Y.: Autonomedia.

Bacevich, Andrew J., et al. 1988. *American Military Policy in Small Wars: The Case of El Salvador.* Washington, D.C.: Corporate.

Bagley, Bruce. 1989. *The State and the Peasantry in Contemporary Colombia.* Allegheny College: Allegheny College Press, Monograph Series on Contemporary Latin American and Caribbean Affairs, no. 6.

———. 1990. "Understanding Colombian Democracy." *Journal of Interamerican Studies and World Affairs* 32, no. 2 (summer): 143–155.

Bailetti Mackee, José. 1990. "La violencia subversiva en el Perú a setiembre de 1990." Lima: Instituto de Investigación de la Defensa Nacional. October. Mimeographed.

———. 1992. "La violencia subversiva en el Peru a junio de 1992." Lima: Instituto de Investigación de la Defensa Nacional. Mimeographed.

Balbi, Carmen Rosa, and Juan Carlos Callirgos. 1992. "Sendero y la mujer." *QueHacer* 79 (September–October): 50–53.

Baloyra, Enrique. 1982. *El Salvador in Transition.* Chapel Hill: University of North Carolina Press.

———. 1985. "Dilemmas of Political Transition in El Salvador." *Journal of International Affairs* 38, no. 2 (winter): 220–242.

———. 1990. "El Salvador." In *Latin American Politics and Development,* edited by Howard J. Wiarda and Harvey F. Kline, 483– 497. Boulder, Colo.: Westview.

———. 1992 "Salvaging El Salvador." *Journal of Democracy* 3, no. 2 (April): 70–81.

———. 1993. "The Salvadoran Elections of 1982–1991." *Studies in Comparative International Development* 28, no. 3 (fall): 3–30.

Barraclough, Solon L., and Michael F. Scott. 1987. *The Rich Have Already Eaten: Roots of Catastrophe in Central America.* Washington, D.C.: Institute for Policy Studies.

Barry, Tom. 1987. *Roots of Rebellion: Land and Hunger in Central America.* Boston: South End.

———. 1990. *El Salvador: A Country Guide.* Albuquerque, N. Mex.: Inter-Hemispheric Education Resource Center.

———. 1992. *Inside Guatemala.* Albuquerque, N. Mex.: Inter-Hemispheric Education Resource Center.

Basombrío, Carlos. 1996. *La paz: Valor y precio. Una visión comparativa para América Latina.* Lima: Instituto de Defensa Legal.

Bénitez Manaut, Raúl. 1989. *La teoría militar y la guerra civil en El Salvador.* San Salvador: UCA.

Benjamin, Jules R. 1990. *The United States and the Origins of the Cuban Revolution: An Empire of Liberty in an Age of National Liberation.* Princeton, N.J.: Princeton University Press.

Berg, Ronald H. 1986–87. "Sendero Luminoso and the Peasantry of Andahuaylas." *Journal of Inter-American Studies* 28, no. 4 (winter): 165–196.

Berryman, Phillip. 1990. "El Salvador." In *Latin America and Caribbean Contemporary Record.* Vol. 7, *1987–1988,* edited by James M. Malloy and Eduardo A. Gamarra, B241–B258. New York: Holmes and Meier.

———. 1994. *Stubborn Hope: Religion, Politics, and Revolution in Central America.* New York: New Press; Orbis.

Biondi, Juan, and Eduardo Zapata. 1989. *El discurso de Sendero Luminoso: Contratexto educativa.* Lima: Consejo Nacional de Ciencia y Technología.

Blachman, Morris J., and Kenneth E. Sharpe. 1988–89. "Things Fall Apart in El Salvador." *World Policy Journal* 6 (winter): 107–139.

Black, George. 1983. "Garrison Guatemala." *NACLA Report on the Americas* 17, no. 1 (January–February): 2–35.

Blackburn, Robin. 1963. "Prologue to the Cuban Revolution." *New Left Review* 21 (October): 52–91.

Blank, Stephen et al. 1990. *Responding to Low-Intensity Conflict Challenges.* Maxwell Air Force Base, Ala.: Air University Press.

Blasier, Cole. 1967. "Social Revolution: Origins in Mexico, Bolivia, and Cuba." *Latin American Research Review* 2, no. 3 (summer 1967): 28–64.

———. 1985. *The Hovering Giant: U.S. Responses to Revolutionary Change in Latin America 1910–1985.* Pittsburgh: University of Pittsburgh Press.

Bolívar Ocampo, Alberto. 1993. "La geopolítica y los orígenes de la subversión en el Perú." *Defensa Nacional* 12, no. 13 (October): 57–66.

———. 1994. "Intelligence and Subversion in Peru." *Low Intensity Conflict and Law Enforcement* 3, no. 3 (winter): 410–429.

Bonasso, Miguel, and Ciro Gómez Leyva. 1992. *Cuatro minutos para las doce: Conversaciones con el Comandante Schafik Handal.* Puebla, Mexico: Magno Graf Publishers.

Bonilla, Heraclio. 1980. *Un siglo a la deriva: Ensayos sobre el Perú, Bolivia y la guerra.* Lima: Instituto de Estudios Peruanos.

———. 1994. "Introducción: La metamorfosis de la violencia en el umbral del siglo xxi." In *Perú en el fin del milenio,* edited by Heraclio Bonilla. Xoco, Mexico: Consejo Nacional para la Cultura y les Artes.

Bonner, Raymond. 1984. *Weakness and Deceit: U.S. Policy and El Salvador.* New York: Times Books.

———. 1988. "Peru's War." *New Yorker,* 4 January, 31–58.

Bonsal, Philip W. 1971. *Cuba, Castro, and the United States.* Pittsburgh: University of Pittsburgh Press.

Booth, John A. 1985. *The End and the Beginning: The Nicaraguan Revolution.* Boulder, Colo.: Westview.

———. 1991. "Socioeconomic and Political Roots of National Revolts in Central America." *Latin American Research Review* 26, no. 1: 33–73.

Booth, John A., and Thomas W. Walker. 1993. *Understanding Central America.* 2d ed. Boulder, Colo.: Westview.

Bourricaud, Francois. 1970. *Power and Society in Contemporary Peru.* New York: Praeger.

Bourricaud, Francois et al. 1969. *La oligarquía en el Perú.* Lima: Instituto de Estudios Peruanos.

Boyer, Christopher. 1991. "Keeping the People in: An Examination of Non-Revolution in Honduras." *LASA Forum* 22, no. 2 (summer 1991): 1, 5–11, 20.

Bracamonte, José Angel Moroni, and David Spencer. 1995. *Strategy and Tactics of the Salvadoran FMLN Guerrillas.* Westport, Conn.: Praeger.

Brady, Martha. 1988. "USAID: El Salvador." San Salvador: United States Agency for International Development.

Broad, Robin, and John Cavanagh. 1995–96. "Don't Neglect the Impoverished South." *Foreign Policy* 101 (winter): 18–36.

Brockett, Charles D. 1990. *Land, Power, and Poverty: Agrarian Transformation and Political Conflict in Central America.* Winchester, Mass.: Unwin Hyman.

———. 1991. "The Structure of Political Opportunities and Peasant Mobilization in Central America." *Comparative Politics* 23, no. 3 (April): 253–274.

Brown, Michael F., and Eduardo Fernández. 1991. *War of Shadows: The Struggle for Utopia in the Peruvian Amazon.* Berkeley: University of California Press.

Browning, David. 1975. *El Salvador: La tierra y el hombre.* San Salvador: Ministerio de Educación.

———. 1988. *Report on the Conduct and Context of the National and Municipal Elections in El Salvador on 20 March 1988.* London: Her Majesty's Stationery Office.

———. 1989. *Report on the Conduct and Context of the Presidential Elections on 19 March 1989.* London: Her Majesty's Stationery Office.

Bulmer-Thomas, V. 1983. "Economic Development Over the Long Run—Central America Since 1920." *Journal of Latin American Studies* 15, no. 2 (November): 269–294.

Burgos, Hernando. 1991. "Adiós a las aulas: Del ajuste económico al "Shock" educativo." *QueHacer* 73 (September–October): 37-50.

Burt, Jo-Marie. 1994. "Poverty, Violence, and Grassroots Organizing in Urban Peru." Paper presented at the Latin American Studies Association meeting, Atlanta, 10–13 March.

Byrne, Hugh. 1996. *El Salvador's Civil War: A Study of Revolution.* Boulder, Colo.: Lynne Rienner.

Caballero, José María. 1981. *Economía agraria de la sierra peruana antes de la reforma agraria de 1969.* Lima: Instituto de Estudios Peruanos.

Caballero, José María, and Elena Alvarez. 1980. *Aspectos cuántitativos de la reforma agraria (1969–1979).* Lima: Instituto de Estudios Peruanos.

Cameron, Maxwell A., and Philip Mauceri. 1997. *The Peruvian Labyrinth: The Polity, Society, and Economy.* University Park: Pennsylvania State University Press.

Caravedo Molinari, Baltazar. 1978. *Desarrollo desigual y lucha política en el Perú, 1948–1956.* Lima: Instituto de Estudios Peruanos.

Carbajal Pérez, Jaime, and Percy Uriarte Otoya. 1993. *Economía y violencia: Los costos ocasionados por el terrorismo: Un marco teórico y un modelo de estimación.* Lima: Instituto Constitución y Sociedad.

Carothers, Thomas. 1991. *In the Name of Democracy: U.S. Policy toward Latin America in the Reagan Years.* Berkeley: University of California Press.

———. 1994. "The NED at 10." *Foreign Policy* 95 (summer): 123–139.

Carrión, Julio F. 1994. "The 'Support Gap' for Democracy in Peru: Mass Public Attitudes towards Fujimori's Self-Coup." Paper presented at the Latin American Studies Association meeting, Atlanta, 10–13 March 1994.

Casas, Luis. 1991. "En un cuartel Senderista." *Sí* 223 (26 May–1 June): 24–31.

Castañeda, Jorge G. 1994. *Utopia Unarmed: The Latin American Left after the Cold War.* New York: Vintage.

Castro Morán, Mariano. 1987. *Función política del ejército salvadoreño en el presente siglo.* 2d ed. San Salvador: UCA.

CELADE (Centro Latinoamericano de la Demografía).1988. *La mortalidad en la niñez en Centro América, Panama, y Belize.* San José, Costa Rica: CELADE.

Center for International Policy. 1991. *El Salvador: The Military Obstacle.* Washington, D.C.: Center for International Policy.

Chavarría, Ricardo. 1982. "The Nicaraguan Insurrection." In *Nicaragua in Revolution,* edited by Thomas W. Walker, 25–40. New York: Praeger.

Chávez de Paz, Dennis. 1989. *Juventud y terrorismo: Características sociales de los condenados por terrorismo y otros delitos.* Lima: Instituto de Estudios Peruanos.

Chernick, Marc W. and Michael F. Jiménez. 1990. "Popular Liberalism and Radical Democracy: The Development of the Colombian Left, 1974–1990." Paper presented at the research conference "Violence and Democracy in Colombia and Peru," Columbia University, New York, 30 November–1 December 1990.

Chipoco, Carlos. 1992. *En defensa de la vida.* Lima: Centro de Estudios para la Paz.

Christian, Shirley. 1985. *Nicaragua: Revolution in the Family.* New York: Random House.

CINAS (Centro de Investigación y Acción Social). 1988. *El Salvador: Guerra, política y paz (1977–1988).* San Salvador: CINAS; CRIES (Coordinadora Regional de Investigaciones, Económicas y Sociales).

Cleaves, Peter S. 1992. "Comments at LASA Panel, Los Angeles, California, September 24, 1992." Unpublished notes.

Clements, Charles. 1984. *Witness to War: An American Doctor in El Salvador.* New York: Bantam.

Clutterbuck, Richard. 1995. "Peru: Cocaine, Terrorism and Corruption." *International Relations* 12, no. 5 (August): 77–92.

Colburn, Forrest D. 1994. *The Vogue of Revolution in Poor Countries.* Princeton, N.J.: Princeton University Press.

Collier, George A. 1994. *Basta! Land and the Zapatista Rebellion in Chiapas.* Oakland, Calif.: Institute for Food and Development Policy.

Collier, Ruth Berins, and David Collier. 1991. *Shaping the Political Arena.* Princeton, N.J.: Princeton University Press.

Comisión de Juristas Internacionales. 1994. *Informe sobre la administración de justicia en el Perú.* Lima: Instituto de Defensa Legal.

Comisión Especial de Estudio e Investigación sobre Terrorismo y Otras Manifestaciones de la Violencia. 1990. *La violencia en el Perú.* Lima: Senado de la República.

Comisión Especial de Investigación y Estudio sobre la Violencia y Alternativas de Pacificación. 1991. *10 años de violencia en el Perú.* Lima: Senado de la República.

———. 1992. *Violencia y pacificación en 1991.* Lima: Senado de la República. Manuscript.

Comisión Especial del Senado de la República sobre las Causas de la Violencia y Alternativas de Pacificación en el Perú. 1992. *La violencia en el Perú, 1991.* Lima: Senado de la República.

Comité Central Partido Comunista del Perú. 1982. "¡Des arrollemos la guerra de guerrillas!" Mimeographed.

———. 1985. "No votar. Sino, i generalizar la guerra de guerrillas para conquistar el poder para el pueblo." Lima: Ediciones Bandera Roja.

Commission on U.S.-Central American Relations. 1982. "Biographies of FMLN and FDR Leaders." Information sheet distributed to 1982 delegation to El Salvador, Washington, D.C. Photocopy.

CONADE (Consejo Nacional de Desarrollo). 1982. *Indicadores socio-económicos.* Quito, Ecuador: Planificación Global.

———. 1993. *Agenda para el desarrollo.* Quito, Ecuador: CONADE.

Conaghan, Catherine M. 1994. "Democracy That Matters: The Search for Authenticity, Legitimacy, and Civic Competence in the Andes." Paper presented to the Academic Workshop and Public Policy Forum on Democracy in the Americas: Approaching the year 2000. Helen Kellogg Institute for International Studies, University of Notre Dame, Ind., 29–30 April.

Conaghan, Catherine M., and Rosario Espinal. 1990. "Unlikely Transitions to Uncertain Regimes? Democracy without Compromise in the Dominican Republic and Ecuador." *Journal of Latin American Studies* 22, no. 3 (October): 553–574.

Congressional Research Service. 1989. *El Salvador, 1979–1989: A Briefing Book on U.S. Aid and the Situation in El Salvador.* Washington, D.C.: Library of Congress, Congressional Research Service, Foreign Affairs and National Defense Division.

Constable, Pamela. 1992. "A Salvadoran Struggle That Won't End." *Boston Globe,* 12 March 1992.

Copley, Gregory R., ed. 1991. *Defense and Foreign Affairs Handbook.* International Media Corporation: Alexandria, Va.

Córdova, Ricardo M. 1988. "Periodización del proceso de crisis (1979–1988)." In *El Salvador: Guerra, política, y paz (1979–1988),* edited by CINAS and CRIES, 83–98. San Salvador: CINAS and CRIES.

Cotler, Julio. 1975. "The New Mode of Political Domination in Peru." In *The Peruvian Experiment,* edited by Abraham F. Lowenthal, 44-78. Princeton, N.J.: Princeton University Press.

Crabtree, John. 1992. *Peru under García: An Opportunity Lost.* Pittsburgh: University of Pittsburgh Press.

Crawley, Eduardo. 1979. *Dictators Never Die: A Portrait of Nicaragua and the Somoza Dynasty.* New York: St. Martin's.

Cuánto. 1991. *Ajuste y economía familiar 1985–1990.* Lima: Cuánto.

Dahl, Robert A. 1971. *Polyarchy: Participation and Opposition.* New Haven, Conn.: Yale University Press.

Daniels, Anthony. 1990. "Dirty War in Peru." *Spectator,* 28 July, 9–11.

Davidheiser, Evelyn B. 1992. "Strong States, Weak States: The Role of the State in Revolution." *Comparative Politics* 24, no. 4 (July): 463–476.

Davies, James C. 1962. "Toward a Theory of Revolution." *American Sociological Review* 27, no. 1 (February): 5–19.

Deere, Carmen Diana. 1990. *Household and Class Relations: Peasants and Landlords in Northern Peru*. Berkeley: University of California Press.

Degregori, Carlos Iván. 1986. "Sendero Luminoso: Los hondos y mortales desencuentros." In *Movimientos sociales y crisis: El caso peruano*, edited by Eduardo Ballón. Lima: DESCO.

————. 1989a. *Que difícil es ser Dios: Ideología y violencia política en Sendero Luminoso*. Lima: El Zorro de Abajo Ediciones.

————. 1989b. "En los origenes de Sendero Luminoso." *QueHacer* 59 (June–July): 24–28.

————. 1990a. *Ayacucho 1969–1979: El nacimiento de Sendero Luminoso: Del movimiento por la gratuidad de la enseñanza al inicio de la lucha armada*. Lima: Instituto de Estudios Peruanos.

————. 1990b. "Violencia política y respuestas desde la sociedad y desde el estado: El caso Peruano." Conference Paper no. 48, presented at the research conference "Violence and Democracy in Colombia and Peru," Columbia University, New York, 30 November–1 December.

————. 1990–91. "A Dwarf Star." *NACLA Report on the Americas* 24, no. 4 (December–January): 10–19.

————. 1991. "Al filo de la navaja." *QueHacer* 73 (September–October): 26–29.

————. 1992. "The Origins and Logic of Shining Path." In *Shining Path of Peru*, edited by David Scott Palmer, 51–63. New York: St. Martin's.

————. 1994. "Shining Path and Counterinsurgency Strategy since the Arrest of Abimael Guzmán." In *Peru in Crisis: Dictatorship or Democracy?* edited by Joseph S. Tulchin and Gary Bland, 81–100. Boulder, Colo.: Westview.

————. 1997. "El capítulo que falta." *QueHacer* 105 (January–February): 46–53.

Degregori, Carlos Iván, and José López Ricci. 1990. "Los hijos de la guerra: Jovenes Andinos y criollos frente a la violencia política." In *Tiempos de ira y amor*, edited by DESCO (Centro de Estudios y Promoción del Desarrollo), 183–220. Lima: DESCO.

Degregori, Carlos Iván, and Carlos Rivera. 1993. *Peru 1980–1993: Fuerzas armadas, subversión y democracia*. Lima: Instituto de Estudios Peruanos.

Degregori, Carlos Iván; Cecilia Blondet; and Nicolás Lynch. 1987. *Conquistadores de un nuevo mundo: De invasores a ciudadanos en San Martín de Porres*. Lima: Instituto de Estudios Peruanos.

Degregori, Carlos Iván, et al. 1996. *Las rondas campesinas y la derrota de Sendero Luminosa*. Lima: Instituto de Estudios Peruanos.

Desai, Raj, and Harry Eckstein. 1990. "Insurgency: The Transformation of Peasant Rebellion." *World Politics* 42, no. 4 (July): 441–465.

DESCO (Centro de Estudios y Promoción del Desarrollo). 1989. *Violencia política en el Peru, 1980–1988*. 2 vols. Lima: DESCO.

De Soto, Hernando. 1986. *El otro Sendero: La revolución informal*. Lima: Instituto Libertad y Democracia.

DeWalt, Billie R. 1985. "The Agrarian Bases of Conflict in Central America." In *The Central American Crisis: Sources of Conflict and the Failure of U.S. Policy,* edited by Kenneth M. Coleman and George C. Herring, 43–54. Wilmington, Del.: Scholarly Resources.

DeYoung, Karen. 1982. "Salvadoran Land Reform Imperiled, Report Says." *Washington Post,* 25 January, A1, A16.

Del Pilar Tello, María. 1983. *Golpe o revolución? Hablan los militares del 68*. Lima: Impressión Servicios de Artes Gráficas S.A. (SAGASA).

Diamond, Larry. 1992. "Promoting Democracy." *Foreign Policy* 87 (summer): 25–46.

———. 1996. "Democracy in Latin America: Degrees, Illusions, and Directions for Consolidation." In *Beyond Sovereignty: Collectively Defending Democracy in the Americas,* edited by Tom Farer, 52–106. Baltimore: Johns Hopkins University Press.

Diamond, Larry; Juan Linz; and Seymour Martin Lipset, eds. 1989. *Democracy in Developing Countries: Latin America*. Boulder, Colo.: Lynne Rienner.

Díaz, Nidia. 1988. *Nunca estuve sola*. San Salvador: UCA.

Díaz Martínez, Antonio. 1969. *Ayacucho: Hambre y esperanza*. Ayacucho, Peru: Waman Puma.

Dickey, Christopher. 1993. "Dream of Agrarian Reform Seems to Be Dying in El Salvador." *Washington Post,* 3 October, A2.

Dietz, Henry. 1992. "Who Protests? Social and Psychological Correlates of Rebellious Political Action." Paper presented at the Latin American Studies Association meeting, Los Angeles, September.

Dillon, Sam. 1988–89. "Dateline El Salvador: Crisis Renewed." *Foreign Policy* 73: 153–170.

Di Palma, Giuseppe. 1990. *To Craft Democracies: An Essay on Democratic Transitions*. Berkeley: University of California Press.

Diskin, Martin. 1989. "El Salvador: Reform Prevents Change." In *Searching for Agrarian Reform in Latin America,* edited by William C. Thiesenhusen, 429–450. Boston: Unwin Hyman.

———. 1996. "Distilled Conclusions: The Disappearance of the Agrarian Question in El Salvador." *Latin American Research Review* 31, no. 2: 111–126.

Diskin, Martin, and Kenneth E. Sharpe. 1986. "El Salvador." In *Confronting Revolution,* edited by Morris J. Blachman, William M. LeoGrande, and Kenneth Sharpe, 50–87. New York: Pantheon.

Dix, Robert H. 1983. "The Varieties of Revolution." *Comparative Politics* 15 (April): 281–294.

———. 1984. "Why Revolutions Succeed and Fail." *Polity* 16, no. 3 (spring): 423–446.

Domínguez, Jorge I. 1978. *Cuba: Order and Revolution.* Cambridge, Mass.: Harvard University Press, Belknap Press.

Doyle, Kate, and Peter Duklis, Jr. 1989. "The Long Twilight Struggle: Low-Intensity Warfare and the Salvadorean Military." *Journal of International Affairs* 43, no. 2: 431.

Duarte, José Napoleon. 1986. *Duarte: My Story.* New York: Putnam's.

Dunkerley, James. 1983. "Class Structure and Socialist Strategy in El Salvador." In *Crisis in the Caribbean,* edited by Firzroy Ambursley and Robin Cohen, 125–147. New York: Monthly Review.

———. 1984. *Rebellion in the Veins: Political Struggle in Bolivia, 1952–82.* London: Verso.

———. 1988. *Power in the Isthmus.* New York: Verso.

Durand, Francisco. 1992. "The New Right and Political Change in Peru." In *The Right and Democracy in Latin America,* edited by Douglas A. Chalmers, Mario do Carmo Campello de Souza, and Atilio A. Boron, 238–255. New York: Praeger.

ECLAC (Economic Commission for Latin America and the Caribbean). 1993. *Statistical Yearbook for Latin America and the Caribbean.* 1992 ed. Santiago: United Nations.

———. 1996. *Economic Panorama of Latin America 1996.* Santiago: United Nations.

Edelman, Marc. 1987. "Venezuela's Petkoff: From Guerrilla to Congressman." *NACLA Report on the Americas* (May–June): 9–12.

Einaudi, Luigi R., and Alfred C. Stepan. 1971. *Latin American Institutional Development: Changing Military Perspectives in Peru and Brazil.* Santa Monica: RAND.

Eisenstadt, S. N. 1978. *Revolution and the Transformation of Societies.* New York: Free Press.

Elliott, Kimberly Ann. 1996. "Implementing the Summit of the Americas: Combating Corruption." Working Paper Series. Coral Gables, Fla.: University of Miami, North-South Center.

Ellner, Steve. 1980. "Political Party Dynamics and the Outbreak of Guerrilla Warfare in Venezuela." *Inter-American Economic Affairs* 34, no. 2 (autumn): 3–25.

———. 1988. *Venezuela's Movimiento al Socialismo: From Guerrilla Defeat to Innovative Politics.* Durham, N.C.: Duke University Press.

Evans, Ernest. 1997. "El Salvador's Lessons for Future U.S. Intervention." *World Affairs Quarterly* 160, no. 1 (summer): 43–48.

Evans, Peter B.; Dietrich Rueschemeyer; and Theda Skocpol. 1985. *Bringing the State Back In.* New York: Cambridge University Press.

Everingham, Mark. 1996. *Revolution and the Multiclass Coalition in Nicaragua.* Pittsburgh: University of Pittsburgh Press.

Eyzaguirre, Graciela. 1992. "Los escenarios de guerra en la región Cáceres." *Allpanchis* 23, no. 39 (first semester): 155–184.

Falcoff, Mark. 1984. "Small Countries, Large Issues: Studies in U.S.–Latin American Asymmetries." Washington, D.C.: American Enterprise Institute for Public Research.

———. 1988. "Between Two Fires: Terrorism and Counter-Terrorism in Argentina, 1970–1983." Paper presented at the School of Advanced International Studies, Johns Hopkins University, Washington, D.C., 10 May.

Farah, Douglas. 1992. "Salvadorans Greet 'Authentic Peace,' at Celebration, Quayle Conceals $46 Million in War Debts." *Washington Post,* 16 December, 1.

———. 1993. "Look at Us Now—We Are Worse Off Than Ever." *Washington Post,* 1 June, final edition, 1.

Farhi, Farideh. 1988. "State Disintegration and Urban-Based Revolutionary Crisis: A Comparative Analysis of Iran and Nicaragua." *Comparative Political Studies* 21, no. 2 (July): 231–256.

———. 1989. "Military Professionalism, National Security, and Democracy: Lessons from the Latin American Experience." Paper presented at the Latin American Studies Association meeting, Miami, Fla., December.

———. 1990. *States and Urban-Based Revolutions: Iran and Nicaragua.* Urbana and Chicago: University of Illinois Press.

Fauriol, Georges. 1985. *Latin American Insurgencies.* Washington, D.C.: Georgetown University, Center for Strategic and International Studies.

Fenton Communications. 1984. "Biographical Sketches of FDR and FMLN Leaders." Unpublished materials of the El Salvador Education Project, New York.

Fernández Baca, Jorge. 1982. "La producción de alimentos en el Peru." *Quehacer,* no. 17 (June): 89–90.

Ferrero, Eduardo. 1993. "Peru's Presidential Coup." *Journal of Democracy* 4, no.1 (January): 28–40.

Fiedler, John. 1986. *An Economic Analysis of Segments of the Public Health Sector of El Salvador.* PN-ABG-589. Institute for Resource Development/Macrosystems, Inc. USAID Mission to El Salvador (sponsor). Washington, D.C.: U.S. Agency for International Development.

Figueroa, Adolfo. 1983. *La economía campesina de la sierra del Perú.* Lima: Pontificia Universidad Católica del Perú.

FINATA (Financiera Nacional de Tierras Agrícolas). 1989. "Incidencia del accionar de terrorismo del FMLN en el proceso de la reforma agraria." San Salvador: FINATA, December. Mimeographed.

———. 1990. "Analisis comparativo de las fases 1 y 3 de la reforma agraria." San Salvador: FINATA. Mimeographed.

Fitch, J. Samuel. 1989. "Military Professionalism, National Security, and Democracy: Lessons from the Latin American Experience." Paper presented at the Latin American Studies Association meeting, Miami, Fla., December.

————. 1995. "Military Role Beliefs in Latin American Democracies: Context, Ideology, and Doctrine in Argentina and Ecuador." Paper presented at the Latin American Studies Association meeting, Washington, D.C., September.

FitzGerald, E. V. K. 1979. *The Political Economy of Peru 1956–78.* New York: Cambridge University Press.

Flores Galindo, Alberto. 1987. *Buscando un Inca: Identidad y utopia en los Andes.* Lima: Instituto de Apoyo Agrario.

Foran, John. 1992. "The Causes of Latin American Social Revolutions: Searching for Patterns in Mexico, Cuba, and Nicaragua." Paper presented at the Latin American Studies Association meeting, Los Angeles, Calif.

Fox, Jonathan. 1994. "The Challenge of Democracy: Rebellion as Catalyst." *Awe:kon: A Journal of Indigenous Issues* 11, no. 2 (summer): 13–20.

Franqui, Carlos. 1980. *Diary of the Cuban Revolution.* New York: Viking Press.

Freedom House. 1993. *Freedom in the World: The Annual Survey of Political Rights and Civil Liberties, 1992–1993.* New York: Freedom House.

Fukuyama, Francis. 1992. *The End of History and the Last Man.* New York: Free Press.

Funes, Carlos Mauricio. 1992. "El Salvador: Déficit fiscal y gestión macroeconómica, 1970/89." *Cuadernos de Investigación* 3, no. 11 (January).

García, José Z. 1982. "Origins of Repression and Moderation in the Militaries of El Salvador and Honduras." Department of Government, New Mexico State University, Las Cruces, May. Photocopy.

————. 1983. "Political Conflict within the Salvadorean Armed Forces." Department of Government, New Mexico State University, Las Cruces, October. Photocopy.

————. 1985. "El Salvador." In *Latin America and the Caribbean Contemporary Record.* Vol. 3, *1983–84,* edited by Jack Hopkins, 517–543. New York: Holmes and Meier.

————. 1989. "El Salvador." In *Latin America and Caribbean Contemporary Record.* Vol. 6, *1986–1987,* edited by Abraham F. Lowenthal, B279–B299. New York: Holmes and Meier.

————. 1992. "The Tanda System and Institutional Autonomy of the Military." In *Is There a Transition to Democracy in El Salvador?* edited by Joseph S. Tulchin and Gary Bland. Boulder, Colo.: Lynne Rienner.

García Belaúnde, Víctor Andrés. 1988. *Los ministros de Belaúnde.* Lima: Editorial Minerva.

García Sayan, Diego, ed. 1989. *Coca, cocaína y narcotráfico: Laberinto en los Andes.* Lima: Comisión Andina de Juristas.

Garst, Rachel. 1992. "La ayuda alimentaria al Istmo Centroamericano." *Temas de Seguridad Alimentaria,* no. 13 (June).

Geddes, Barbara. 1990. "Building 'State' Autonomy in Brazil, 1930–1964." *Comparative Politics* 22, no. 2 (January): 217–236.

George, Alexander L. 1979. "Case Studies and Theory Development: The Method of Structured, Focused Comparison." In *Diplomacy: New Approaches in History, Theory, and Policy,* edited by Paul Gordon Lauren. New York: Free Press.

George, Alexander L., and Timothy J. McKeown. 1985. "Case Studies and Theories of Organizational Decision Making." *Advances in Information Processing in Organizations* 2: 21–58.

Gepp, Charles. 1992. "Peru Awaits Reforms and an End to Terror." *Insight,* 16 August, 10–29.

Geyer, Georgie Anne. 1993. *Guerrilla Prince: The Untold Story of Fidel Castro.* Kansas City, Mo.: Andrews and McMeel.

Gianotten, Vera; Tom de Wit; and Hans de Wit. 1985. "The Impact of Sendero Luminoso on Regional and National Politics in Peru." In *The State and the New Social Movements in Latin America,* edited by David Slater. Amsterdam: CEDLA.

Gibb, Tom. 1992. "Elections and the Road to Peace." In *Is There a Transition to Democracy in El Salvador?* edited by Joseph S. Tulchin, with Gary Bland, 17–24. Boulder, Colo.: Lynne Rienner.

Gibb, Tom, and Frank Smyth. 1990. *El Salvador: Is Peace Possible?* Washington, D.C.: Washington Office on Latin America (April).

Gilbert, Dennis. 1977. *The Oligarchy and the Old Regime in Peru.* Cornell University, Latin American Studies Program Dissertation Series, no. 69.

Gillespie, Richard. 1982. *The Soldiers of Perón: Argentina's Montoneros.* Oxford: Clarendon.

Gitlitz, John. 1984. "Sendero Luminoso in Cajamarca, Peru." Paper presented to the New England Council of Latin American Studies meeting, October.

Glave, Luis Miguel. 1986. "Agricultura y capitalismo en la sierra sur del Perú." In *Estados y naciones en los Andes,* edited by J. P. Dler and Y. Saint-Geours, 213–244. Lima: Instituto de Estudios Peruanos.

Glewwe, Paul, and Gillette Hall. 1994. "Poverty, Inequality, and Living Standards during Unorthodox Adjustment: The Case of Peru, 1985–1990." *Economic Development and Cultural Change* 42, no. 4 (July): 689–717.

Goldfrank, Walter L. 1979. "Theories of Revolution and Revolution without Theory: The Case of Mexico." *Theory and Society* 7: 135–165.

Goldstone, Jack A. 1980. "Theories of Revolution: The Third Generation." *World Politics* 32, no. 3 (April): 425–453.

———. 1991. *Revolution and Rebellion in the Early Modern World.* Berkeley: University of California Press.

Goldstone, Jack A., ed. 1986. *Revolutions: Theoretical, Comparative, and Historical Studies.* New York: Harcourt, Brace, Jovanovich.

Goldstone, Jack A.; Ted Robert Gurr; and Farrokh Moshiri. 1991. *Revolutions of the Late Twentieth Century.* Boulder, Colo.: Westview.

Goldstone, James. 1990. "Down the Salvadoran Drain." *New York Times,* 28 September.

Gonzales, José E. 1992. "Guerrillas and Coca in the Upper Huallaga Valley." In *Shining Path of Peru,* edited by David Scott Palmer, 123–144. New York: St. Martin's.

Gonzales, Michael J. 1991. "Planters and Politics in Peru, 1895–1919." *Journal of Latin American Studies* 23, no. 3 (October): 515–541.

Gonzales Manrique, José. 1987. "Se despunta Sendero?" *Debate* 9, no. 47 (November): 33–39.

———. 1989. "Peru: Sendero Luminoso en el Valle de la Coca." In *Coca, cocaína, y narcotráfico: Laberinto en los Andes,* edited by Diego García-Sayan, 207–220. Lima: Comisíon Andina de Juristas.

González, Raúl. 1982. "Ayacucho: Por los caminos de Sendero." *QueHacer* 19 (September–October 1982): 36–78.

———. 1986. "Puno: El corredor senderista." *QueHacer* 30 (February–March): 49–58.

———. 1987a. "Coca y subversión en el Huallaga." *QueHacer* 48 (September–October): 59–72.

———. 1987b. "Sendero vs. MRTA." *QueHacer* 46 (April–May): 47–53.

———. 1988. "El retorno de lo reprimido: El Huallaga, un año despues." *QueHacer* 54 (August–September): 40–47.

———. 1989. "Ayacucho: Un rincón para vivir? Una entrevista con Jaime Urrutia." *QueHacer* 57 (February–March): 42–57.

———. 1990. "Sendero: Duro desgaste y crisis estratégica." *QueHacer* 64 (May–June): 8–16.

Gonzales de Olarte, Efraín, ed. 1996. *The Peruvian Economy and Structural Adjustment: Past, Present, and Future.* Coral Gables, Fla.: University of Miami, North-South Center.

Goodfellow, William. 1984. *U.S. Economic Aid to El Salvador: Where Is the Money Going?* Washington, D.C.: Center for International Policy.

Goodwin, Jeff, and Theda Skocpol. 1989. "Explaining Revolutions in the Contemporary Third World." *Politics and Society* 17, no. 4 (December): 489–509.

Gore, Peter H.; Samuel A. McReynolds; and Thomas M. Johnston. 1987. *The 1987 Resurvey of the 1978 El Salvador Non-Metropolitan Household Survey.* Washington, D.C.: National Cooperative Business Association.

Gorriti, Gustavo. 1990a. *Sendero: Historia de la guerra milenaria en el Perú.* Vol. 1. Lima: Apoyo.

———. 1990b. "Terror in the Andes." *New York Times Magazine,* 3 December, 40–70.

———. 1990c. "The War of the Philosopher-King." *New Republic,* 18 June, 15–22.

———. 1992a. "Shining Path's Stalin and Trotsky." In *Shining Path of Peru,* edited by David Scott Palmer, 149–170. New York: St. Martin's.

———. 1992b. "Peru's Prophet of Terror." *Reader's Digest* (September): 93–99.

————. 1996. "El día que cayó Sendero Luminoso." *Selecciones del Reader's Digest* (December): 117–142.

Gott, Richard. 1972. *Guerrilla Movements in Latin America*. Garden City, N.Y.: Anchor Books.

Gould, Jeffrey L. 1990. *To Lead as Equals: Rural Protest and Political Consciousness in Chandega, Nicaragua, 1912–1979*. Chapel Hill: University of North Carolina.

Gouldner, Alvin W. 1979. *The Future of Intellectuals and the Rise of the New Class*. New York: Seabury Press.

Government Documents. 1984. *Inter-American Economic Affairs* 38, no. 2 (autumn).

Graham, Carol. 1992. *Peru's APRA: Parties, Politics, and the Elusive Quest for Democracy*. Boulder, Colo.: Lynne Rienner.

————. 1993. "Government and Politics." In *Peru: A Country Study*, edited by Rex A. Hudson, 205–258. Washington, D.C.: Library of Congress.

Granados, Manuel Jesús. 1987. "Ideología del PCP Sendero Luminoso." *Socialismo y Participación* 37 (March): 17–31.

Green, Duncan. 1995. *Silent Revolution: The Rise of Market Economics in Latin America*. New York: Monthly Review.

Gregory, Peter. 1991. "Project for Increasing the Efficiency of the Public Sector." Report prepared for U.S. AID El Salvador, 26 September.

Grupo Asesor Económico y Social, Ministerio de Planificacíon. 1990. *Evolución económica y social*. Informe trimesteral no. 3 (January–September).

Gruson, Lindsey. 1990. "Salvador Arms Aid: Will Congress's Tactic Work?" *New York Times*, 21 October, 8.

Guidos Véjar, Rafael. 1988. *El ascenso del militarismo en El Salvador*. 4th ed. San Salvador: UCA.

Guillermoprieto, Alma. 1993. "Down the Shining Path." *New Yorker*, 8 February, 64–75.

Gurr, Ted Robert. 1970. *Basic Courses in Comparative Politics*. Beverly Hills, Calif.: Sage Publications.

————. 1991. "America as Model for the World? A Skeptical View." *PS: Political Science and Politics* 24, no. 4 (December 1991): 664–667.

Hadar, Arnon. 1991. *The United States and El Salvador: Political and Military Involvement*. Berkeley, Calif.: U.S. El Salvador Research and Information Center.

Hager, Robert P. 1995. "Soviet Bloc Involvement in the Salvadoran Civil War: The U.S. State Department's 1981 'White Paper' Reconsidered." *Communist and Post-Communist Studies* 28, no. 4: 437–470.

Hamann, A. Javier, and Carlos E. Paredes. 1991. "The Peruvian Economy: Characteristics and Trends." In *Peru's Path to Recovery: A Plan for Economic Stabilization and Growth*, edited by Carlos E. Paredes and Jeffrey D. Sachs, 41–70. Washington, D.C.: Brookings Institution.

Handelman, Howard. 1975. *Struggle in the Andes: Peasant Political Mobilization in Peru.* Austin: University of Texas Press.

Harding, Colin J. 1986. "The Rise of Sendero Luminoso." In *Region and Class in Modern Peru,* edited by Rory Miller, 179–207. Institute of Latin American Studies Monograph Series, no. 14. Liverpool: University of Liverpool.

———. 1988. "Antonio Díaz Martínez and the Ideology of Sendero Luminoso." *Bulletin of Latin American Research* 7, no. 1: 65–73.

Harnecker, Marta. 1989. *Propuesta del FMLN un desafío a la estrategia contrainsurgente: Entrevista a Joaquín Villalobos.* El Salvador: Editorial Sistema Venceremos.

———. 1993. *Con la mirada en alto: Historia de las fuerzas populares de liberación Farabundo Martí.* San Salvador: UCA Editores.

Hartlyn, Jonathan. 1989. "Colombia: The Politics of Violence and Accommodation." In *Democracy in Developing Countries: Latin America,* edited by Larry Diamond, Juan J. Linz, and Seymour Martin Lipset, 291–334. Boulder, Colo.: Lynne Rienner.

Heinz, Wolfgang S. 1989. "Guerrillas, Political Violence, and the Peace Process in Colombia." *Latin American Research Review* 24, no. 3: 249–258.

Herman, Donald L. 1988. *Democracy in Latin America: Colombia and Venezuela.* New York: Praeger.

Herman, Edward S., and Frank Brodhead. 1984. *Demonstration Elections: U.S.-Staged Elections in the Dominican Republic, Vietnam, and El Salvador.* Boston: South End.

Hernández, Ramón. 1983. *Teodoro Petkoff: Viaje al fondo de sí mismo.* Caracas: Editorial Fuentes.

Hoagland, Jim. 1993. "Ramsey Clark: Wrong Again." *Washington Post,* 23 March, OP/ED.

Huber Stephens, Evelyne. 1989. "Capitalist Development and Democracy in South America." *Politics and Society* 17, no. 3: 281–352.

Hughes, Steven W., and Kenneth J. Mijeski. 1984. *Politics and Public Policy in Latin America.* Boulder, Colo.: Westview.

Huntington, Samuel P. 1968. *Political Order in Changing Societies.* New Haven, Conn.: Yale University Press.

———. 1984. "Will More Countries Become Democratic?" *Political Science Quarterly* 99, no. 2: 193–218.

———. 1991. *The Third Wave: Democratization in the Late Twentieth Century.* Norman: University of Oklahoma Press.

Inca, Géronimo. 1994. *El ABC de "Sendero Luminoso" y del "MRTA."* Lima: Grupo Editorial Géronimo Inca.

IDHUCA (Instituto de Derechos Humanos de la UCA). 1991. "La salud en tiempos de guerra." *Estudios Centroamericanos* 513–514 (July–August): 653–673.

INIDEN (Instituto de Investigación de la Defensa Nacional). 1991. *Educación para la pacificación.* Lima: La Imprenta del Ejército.

Inkeles, Alex, ed. 1991. *On Measuring Democracy: Its Consequences and Concomitants.* New Brunswick, N.J.: Transaction.

Instituto de Defensa Legal (IDL). 1990. *Perú 1989: En la espiral de violencia.* Lima: IDL.

———. 1991. *Perú 1990: La oportunidad perdida.* Lima: IDL.

———. 1992. *Peru hoy: En el oscuro Sendero de la guerra.* Lima: IDL.

Instituto Democracia y Socialismo (IDS). 1990. *Perú 1990: Encrucijada.* Lima: IDS.

Instituto Universitario de Opinión Publica (IUDOP). 1994. "Encuesta de evaluación post-electoral y expectativas hacia el nuevo gobierno." San Salvador: UCA.

Inter-American Development Bank. 1984a. *Economic and Social Progress in Latin America: 1984 Report.* Washington, D.C.: Inter-American Development Bank.

———. 1987b. "Proyecto de mejoramiento de servicios de salud." Office of Evaluation of Operations, Washington D.C., June. Mimeographed.

———. 1987. *Economic and Social Progress in Latin America: 1987 Report.* Washington, D.C.: Inter-American Development Bank.

———. 1988. *Economic and Social Progress in Latin America: 1988 Report.* Washington, D.C.: Inter-American Development Bank.

———. 1989. *Economic and Social Progress in Latin America: 1989 Report.* Washington, D.C.: Inter-American Development Bank.

———. 1990. *Economic and Social Progress in Latin America: 1990 Report.* Washington, D.C.: Inter-American Development Bank.

———. 1992. *Economic and Social Progress in Latin America: 1992 Report.* Baltimore, Md.: Johns Hopkins University Press.

International Monetary Fund. 1992. *International Financial Statistics Yearbook.* Washington, D.C.: International Monetary Fund.

Isaacs, Anita. 1991. "Problems of Democratic Consolidation in Ecuador." *Bulletin of Latin American Research* 10, no. 2: 221–238.

Isbell, Billie Jean. 1992. "Shining Path and Peasant Responses in Rural Ayacucho." In *Shining Path of Peru,* edited by David Scott Palmer, 59–82. New York: St. Martin's.

IUDOP (Instituto Universitario de Opinión Pública). 1991. "Los Salvadoreños ante las elecciones de deputados y alcaldes municipales del 10 de marzo de 1991." San Salvador: IUDOP. Mimeographed.

Jacobs, Lawrence R., and Robert Y. Shapiro. 1994. "Studying Substantive Democracy." *PS: Political Science and Politics* 27, no.1 (March): 9–16.

Jackson, Karl D. 1989a. "The Ideology of Total Revolution." In *Cambodia 1975–1978: Rendezvous with Death,* edited by Karl D. Jackson, 37–78. Princeton, N.J.: Princeton University Press

———. 1989b. "Intellectual Origins of the Khmer Rouge." In *Cambodia 1975–1978: Rendezvous with Death,* edited by Karl D. Jackson, 241–250. Princeton, N.J.: Princeton University Press

Jackson, Karl D., ed. 1989. *Cambodia 1975–1978: Rendezvous with Death.* Princeton, N.J.: Princeton University Press.

Jaquette, Jane S. 1971. *The Politics of Development in Peru.* Ithaca, N.Y.: Cornell University Latin American Studies Program Dissertation Series.

Jazairy, Idriss; Mohuiddin Alamgir; and Theresa Panuccio. 1992. *The State of World Rural Poverty.* New York: University Press; International Fund for Agricultural Development.

Jensen, Kenneth M., ed. 1990. *A Look at "The End of History?"* Washington, D.C.: United States Institute of Peace.

Jiménez Baca, Benedicto. 1996. "Así fue la captura del siglo." *La República,* September 12–14.

Jimeno, Ramon, and Steven Volk. 1983. "Colombia: Whose Country Is This, Anyway?" *NACLA Report on the Americas* 17, no. 3 (May–June): 2–35.

Jonas, Susanne. 1991. *The Battle for Guatemala: Rebels, Death Squads, and U.S. Power.* Boulder, Colo.: Westview.

Jung, Harald. 1984. "The Civil War in El Salvador." In *Political Change in Central America: Internal and External Dimensions,* edited by Wolf Grabendorff, Heinrich-W. Krumwiede, and Jorg Todt, 82–96. Denver, Colo.: Westview.

Kamen, Al. 1990. "U.S. Encourages Soviets to Aid Salvadoran Talks." *Washington Post,* 18 October, 34.

Karl, Terry Lynn. 1988. "Exporting Democracy: The Unanticipated Effects of U.S. Electoral Policy in El Salvador." In *Crisis in Central America,* edited by Nora Hamilton et al., 173–191. Boulder, Colo.: Westview.

———. 1990. "Dilemmas of Democratization in Latin America." *Comparative Politics* 23, no. 1 (October): 1–22.

———. 1992. "El Salvador's Negotiated Revolution." *Foreign Affairs* 71, no. 2 (spring): 147–164.

Keogh, Dermot. 1984. "The Myth of the Liberal Coup: The United States and the 15 October 1979 Coup in El Salvador." *Journal of International Studies* 13, no. 2 (summer): 153–183.

Kincaid, A. Douglas. 1993. "Peasants into Rebels: Community and Class in Rural El Salvador." In *Constructing Culture and Power in Latin America,* edited by Daniel H. Levine, 119–154. Ann Arbor: University of Michigan Press.

Kirk, Robin. 1991. "Shining Path is Gaining in Peru." *Nation,* 21 April, 552–556.

———. 1992. "The Deadly Women of the Shining Path." *Image* (Sunday magazine of the *San Francisco Chronicle*), 22 March, 14–21.

———. 1997. *The Monkey's Paw: New Chronicles from Peru.* Amherst: University of Massachusetts Press.

Klare, Michael T. and Peter Kornbluh, eds. 1987. *Low-Intensity Warfare: Counterinsurgency, Proinsurgency, and Antiterrorism in the Eighties.* New York: Pantheon.

Kline, Harvey F. 1990. "Colombia: The Struggle between Traditional 'Stability' and New Visions." In *Latin American Politics and Development,* edited by Howard J. Wiarda and Harvey F. Kline, 231–257. Boulder, Colo.: Westview.

Knight, Alan. 1990. "Social Revolution: A Latin American Perspective." *Bulletin of Latin American Research* 9, no. 2: 175–202.

Kober, Stanley. 1991. "Revolutions Gone Bad." *Foreign Policy* 91 (summer): 63–84.

Krauthammer, Charles. 1993. "Stiffing the Neocons—Again: Who Really Believes in Human Rights?" *Washington Post,* 15 January, 23.

Kruijt, Dirk. 1991. *Entre Sendero y los militares.* Barcelona: Editorial Robles.

Lake, Anthony. 1989. *Somoza Falling.* Amherst: University of Massachusetts Press.

Landau, Saul. 1993. *The Guerrilla Wars of Central America: Nicaragua, El Salvador and Guatemala.* New York: St. Martin's.

Lane, Charles. 1990. "The Pilot Shark of El Salvador." *New Republic,* 24 September, 27–31.

Larraín, Felipe, and Jeffrey D. Sachs. 1991. "International Financial Relations." In *Peru's Path to Recovery: A Plan for Economic Stabilization and Growth,* edited by Carlos E. Paredes and Jeffrey D. Sachs, 228–252. Washington, D.C.: Brookings Institution.

Larson, Magli S., and Arlene G. Bergman. 1969. *Social Stratification in Peru.* Berkeley: Institute of International Studies, University of California.

Latin America Bureau. 1985. *Peru: Paths to Poverty.* Nottingham, England: Russell.

Lawyers' Committee for Human Rights. 1990. *Critique: Review of the Department of State's Country Reports on Human Rights Practices for 1989.* New York: Lawyers' Committee for Human Rights.

Lázaro, Juan. 1990. "Women and Political Violence in Contemporary Peru." *Dialectical Anthropology* 15: 233–247.

Leger, Kathryn. 1989. "Peru's Leftist Rebels Gain Ground." *Christian Science Monitor,* 2 May, 3.

Lehoucq, Edward F., and Harold Sims. 1982. "Reform with Repression: The Land Reform in El Salvador." Philadelphia: Institute for the Study of Human Issues.

Leiken, Robert S. 1984. "The Salvadoran Left." In *Central America: Anatomy of Conflict,* edited by Robert S. Leiken, 111–130. New York: Pergamon.

LeMoyne, James. 1989. "El Salvador's Forgotten War." *Foreign Affairs* 68, no. 3 (summer): 105–125.

———. 1992. "Out of the Jungle." *New York Times Magazine,* 8 February, 24–29, 56, 58.

LeoGrande, William M. 1990a. "After the Battle of San Salvador." *World Policy Journal* 7, no. 2 (spring): 331–356.

———. 1990b. "Central America." In *Revolution and Political Change in the Third World,* edited by Barry M. Schutz and Robert O. Slater, 142–160. Boulder, Colo.: Lynne Rienner.

Linz, Juan J. 1975. "Totalitarian and Authoritarian Regimes." In *Macropolitical Theory.* Vol. 3 of *Handbook of Political Science,* edited by Fred I. Greenstein and Nelson W. Polsby. Reading, Mass.: Addison-Wesley.

López, Roberto. 1986. "The Nationalization of Foreign Trade in El Salvador: The Myths and Realities of Coffee." Latin American and Caribbean Center, Florida International University, Occasional Papers Series, no. 16. March.

López-Alves, Fernando. 1989. "Political Crises, Strategic Choices, and Terrorism: The Rise and Fall of the Uruguayan Tupamaros." *Terrorism and Political Violence* 1, no. 2 (April): 202–241.

López Vigil, José Ignacio. 1994. *Rebel Radio: The Story of El Salvador's Radio Venceremos.* Willimantic, Conn.: Curbstone Press.

Lowenthal, Abraham F. 1992–93. "Latin America: Ready for Partnership?" *Foreign Affairs* 72, no. 1: 74–92.

Lowenthal, Abraham F., ed. 1975. *The Peruvian Experiment.* Princeton, N.J.: Princeton University Press.

Luzuriaga C., Carlos, and Clarence Zuvekas, Jr. 1983. *Income Distribution and Poverty in Rural Ecuador, 1950–1979.* Tempe: Arizona State University, Center for Latin American Studies.

Mahler, Vincent A. 1989. "Income Distribution within Nations: Problems of Cross-National Comparison." *Comparative Political Studies* 22, no. 1 (April): 3–29.

Mainwaring, Scott. 1992. "Transitions to Democracy and Democratic Consolidation." In *Issues in Democratic Consolidation: The New South American Democracies in Comparative Perspective,* edited by Scott Mainwaring, Guillermo O'Donnell, and Samuel Valenzuela, 297–298. Notre Dame, Ind: University of Notre Dame Press.

Malcolmson, Scott L. 1987. "On the Shining Path." *Village Voice,* 5 May, 24–31.

Maletta, Héctor, and Alejandro Bardales. N.d. *Perú: Las provincias en Cifras 1876–1981.* Lima: Ediciones Amidep; Universidad del Pacífico.

Malloy, James M. 1970. *Bolivia: The Uncompleted Revolution.* Pittsburgh: University of Pittsburgh Press.

———. 1973. "Dissecting the Peruvian Military." *Journal of Interamerican Studies and World Affairs* 15 (August): 375–382.

———. Forthcoming. "Markets and Democracy in Latin America: Some Reflections on the New Economic Policy of Bolivia." In *Annali of the Fondszione,* edited by Torouato S. Di Tella. Milan: Feltrinelli.

Manrique, Nelson. 1987. *Mercado interno y región: La sierra central 1820–1930.* Lima: DESCO.

———. 1989. "La década de la violencia." *Márgenes* 3, nos. 5–6 (December): 137–182.

———. 1990–91. "Time of Fear." *NACLA Report on the Americas* 24, no. 4 (December–January): 28–37.

Manwaring, Max G., and Court Prisk, eds. 1988. *El Salvador at War: An Oral History.* Washington, D.C.: National Defense University Press.

Marcella, Gabriel. 1990. "The Latin American Military, Low Intensity Conflict, and Democracy." *Journal of Interamerican Studies and World Affairs* 32, no. 1 (spring): 45–81.

Marks, Tom. 1996. "Shining Path to Oblivion?" *Soldier of Fortune* 21, no. 7 (July): 54–69.

Martín-Baró, Ignacio. 1987. *Así piensan los salvadoreños urbanos (1986–1987)*. San Salvador: UCA Editores.

———. 1989. *La opinión pública Salvadoreña (1987–1988)*. San Salvador: UCA.

Martínez, Daniel, and Armando Tealdo. 1982. *El agro peruano 1970–1980: Análisis y perspectivas*. Lima: CEDEP.

Martínez, Julia Evelin et al. 1990–1991. "La erradicación de la pobreza en El Salvador: Elementos para un enfoque alternativo." *Política Ecónomica* 1, no. 4 (December): 1–37.

Mason, T. David. 1986. "Land Reform and the Breakdown of Clientelist Politics in El Salvador." *Comparative Political Studies* 18, no. 4 (January): 487–516.

———. 1990. "Land Reform, Repression, and Revolution: A Comparison of El Salvador and Peru." Paper presented at the annual conference of the American Political Science Association, San Francisco, 30 August–2 September.

Massing, Michael. 1989. "Sad New El Salvador." *New York Review of Books*, 18 May, 53–60.

———. 1990. "In the Cocaine War, the Jungle Is Winning." *New York Times Magazine*, 4 March, 88–92.

Matos Mar, José, and José Manuel Mejía. 1980. *Reforma agraria: Logros y contradicciones 1969–1979*. Lima: Instituto de Estudios Peruanos.

Matthews, Herbert L. 1975. *Revolution in Cuba*. New York: Scribner's.

Mauceri, Philip. 1989. *Militares: Insurgencia y democratización en el Perú, 1980–1988*. Lima: Instituto de Estudios Peruanos.

———. 1991a. "State under Siege: The Limits of State Power in Peru, 1973–1990." Ph.D. diss., Department of Political Science, Columbia University.

———. 1991b. "The Impact of Violence on a Weak State: Peru, 1980–1990." Paper presented at the Latin American Studies Association meeting, Washington D.C., April.

———. 1995. "State Reform, Coalitions, and the Neoliberal *Autogolpe* in Peru." *Latin American Research Review* 30, no. 1: 7–37.

———. 1996. *State under Siege: Development and Policy Making in Peru*. Boulder, Colo.: Westview.

Mayer, Enrique. 1991. "Peru in Deep Trouble: Mario Vargas Llosa's 'Inquest in the Andes' Reexamined." *Cultural Anthropology* 6, no. 4 (November): 466–504.

———. 1994. "Patterns of Violence in the Andes." *Latin American Research Review* 29, no. 2: 141–170.

McCarthy, Colman. 1993. "Achievement Unmasked in El Salvador." *Washington Post,* 6 April, final edition, 22.

McClintock, Cynthia. 1981. *Peasant Cooperatives and Political Change in Peru.* Princeton, N.J.: Princeton University Press.

———. 1982. "Post-Revolutionary Agrarian Politics in Peru." In *Post-Revolutionary Peru: The Politics of Transformation,* edited by Stephen M. Gorman, 135–156. Boulder, Colo.: Westview.

———. 1983. "Velasco, Officers, and Citizens: The Politics of Stealth." In *The Peruvian Experiment Reconsidered,* edited by Cynthia McClintock and Abraham F. Lowenthal, 275–308. Princeton, N.J.: Princeton University Press.

———. 1984. "Why Peasants Rebel: The Case of Peru's Sendero Luminoso." *World Politics* 37, no. 1 (October): 48–84.

———. 1987. "Agricultural Policy and Food Security in Peru and Ecuador." In *Agrarian Reform in Reverse: The Food Crisis in the Third World,* edited by Birol A. Yesilada, Charles D. Brockett, and Bruce Drury, 73–129. Boulder, Colo.: Westview.

———. 1988. "The War on Drugs: The Peruvian Case." *Journal of Interamerican Studies and World Affairs* 30, nos. 2, 3 (summer–fall): 127–142.

———. 1989a. "Peru's Sendero Luminoso Rebellion: Origins and Trajectory." In *Power and Popular Protest,* edited by Susan Eckstein, 61–101. Berkeley: University of California Press.

———. 1989b. "Peru: Precarious Regimes, Authoritarian and Democratic." In *Democracy in Developing Countries.* Vol. 4, *Latin America,* edited by Larry Diamond, Juan J. Linz, and Seymour Martin Lipset, 335–386. Boulder, Colo.: Lynne Rienner.

———. 1989c. "The Prospects for Democratic Consolidation in a 'Least Likely' Case: Peru." *Comparative Politics* 21, no. 2 (January):127–148.

———. 1990. "Washington's Anti-Narcotics Policy: Exacerbating Peru's Crisis?" *The Peru Report* 4, no. 10 (November): section 7.

———. 1992a. "Democracy and Civil Society in the Context of Economic Decline: Peru, 1980–1992." Paper presented at the conference "Economy, Society, and Democracy," Hoover Institution, Washington, D.C.

———. 1992b. "Theories of Revolution and the Case of Peru." In *Shining Path of Peru,* edited by David Scott Palmer, 225–247. New York: St. Martin's.

———. 1993. "Ethnic Conflict in the Andes: Ethnicity as a Factor in the Expansion of the Shining Path." Paper presented at the American Anthropological Association conference, Washington, D.C., 17–21 November.

———. 1997. "The Decimation of Peru's Sendero Luminoso." Paper presented at the conference "Comparative Peace Progress in Latin America," Woodrow Wilson Center, Washington, D.C., 13–14 March.

McCormick, Gordon H. 1990. *The Shining Path and the Future of Peru.* Santa Monica, Calif.: RAND; National Defense Research Institute.

———. 1992. *From the Sierra to the Cities: The Urban Campaign of the Shining Path.* Santa Monica, Calif.: RAND.

———. 1993. *Sharp Dressed Men: Peru's Túpac Amaru Revolutionary Movement.* Santa Monica, Calif.: RAND; National Defense Research Institute.

Mena Sandoval, Francisco Emilio. N.d. *Del ejército nacional al ejército guerrillero.* San Salvador: Ediciones Arcoiris.

Menzel, Sewall H. 1994. *Bullets vs. Ballots: Political Violence and Revolutionary War in El Salvador, 1979–1991.* Coral Gables, Fla.: University of Miami, North-South Center.

Metzi, Francisco. 1988. "The People's Remedy: Health Care in El Salvador's War of Liberation." *Monthly Review* 40, no. 3 (July–August): 5–123. (Translation from the book in Spanish, published in San Salvador by UCA.)

Middlebrook, Kevin J. 1994. *The Paradox of Revolution: Labor, the State, and Authoritarianism in Mexico.* Baltimore: Johns Hopkins University Press.

Midlarsky, Manus I., and Kenneth Roberts. 1985. "Class, State, and Revolution in Central America: Nicaragua and El Salvador Compared." *Journal of Conflict Resolution* 29, no. 2 (June): 163–193.

Migdail, Carl. 1983. "El Salvador—Is Tide Turning Reagan's Way?" *U.S. News and World Report,* 22 August, 20–22.

Miles, Sara, and Bob Ostertag. 1989. "D'Aubuisson's New Arena." *NACLA Report on the Americas* 23, no. 2 (July 1989): 14–38.

———. 1991. "The FMLN: New Thinking." *A Decade of War: El Salvador Confronts the Future,* edited by Anjali Sundaram and George Gelber, 216–246. New York: Monthly Review.

Millman, Joel. 1989. "El Salvador's Army: A Force unto Itself." *New York Times Magazine,* 10 December, 46–47.

Ministerio de Agricultura y Ganadería. 1989. *VIII Evaluación del proceso de reforma agraria.* San Salvador: Oficina Sectorial de Planificación Agropecuaria, September.

Ministerio de Educación y Ministerio de Salud Pública y Asistencia Social. 1989. "Primer censo nacional de talla en escolares de primer grado de educación básica de El Salvador—1988." San Salvador, October. Mimeographed.

Ministry of Agriculture [Peru]. "Reforma agraria en Cifras." Working Document no. 11, Statistical Unit, November.

Miranda, Roger, and William Ratliff. 1993. *The Civil War in Nicaragua: Inside the Sandinistas.* New Brunswick, N.J.: Transaction.

Mitchell, Christopher. 1977. *The Legacy of Populism in Bolivia: From the MNR to Military Rule.* New York: Praeger.

Mitchell, William P. 1991. *Peasants on the Edge: Crop, Cult, and Crisis in the Andes.* Austin: University of Texas Press.

Molineu, Harold. 1990. *U.S. Policy toward Latin America.* Boulder, Colo.: Westview.

Montaner, Carlos Alberto. 1981. *Secret Report on the Cuban Revolution.* Translated by Eduardo Zayas-Bazán. New Brunswick, N.J.: Transaction.

Montes, Segundo. 1989. "Las elecciones presidenciales del 19 de marzo de 1989." *Estudios Centroamericanos* 485 (March): 199–209.

Montgomery, Tommie Sue. 1982. *Revolution in El Salvador: Origins and Evolution.* Boulder, Colo.: Westview.

———. 1989. "Fighting Guerrillas: The United States and Low-Intensity Conflict in El Salvador." Paper presented at the meeting of the Latin American Studies Association, Miami, Fla., December.

———. 1995. *Revolution in El Salvador: From Civil Strife to Civil Peace.* 2d ed. Boulder, Colo.: Westview.

Montoya, David, and Carlos Reyna. 1992. "Sendero: Informe de Lima." *QueHacer* 76 (March–April): 34–55.

Montoya, Rodrigo. 1992. *Al borde del naufragio: Democracia, violencia, y problema etnico en el Perú.* Lima: SUR.

Morales Velado, Oscar. 1989. "La estructura productiva agraria, antes y después de la Reforma Agraria." *Presencia* 1, no. 4 (January–March): 75–105.

Morley, Morris H. 1994. *Washington, Somoza, and the Sandinistas.* New York: Cambridge University Press.

Moroni Bracamonte, José Angel, and David E. Spencer. 1995. *Strategy and Tactics of the Salvadoran FMLN Guerrillas: Last Battle of the Cold War, Blueprint for Future Conflicts.* Westport, Conn.: Praeger.

Morner, Magnus. 1985. *The Andean Past: Land, Societies, and Conflicts.* New York: Columbia University Press.

Moshiri, Farrokh. "Revolutionary Conflict Theory in an Evolutionary Perspective." In *Revolutions of the Late Twentieth Century*, edited by Jack A. Goldstone, Ted Robert Gurr, and Farrokh Moshiri, 4–36. Boulder, Colo.: Westview.

Muller, Edward N., and Mitchell A. Seligson. 1987. "Inequality and Insurgency." *American Political Science Review* 81, no. 2 (June): 425–452.

Munck, Gerardo. 1994. "Democratic Transitions in Comparative Perspective." *Comparative Politics* 26, no. 3: 355–375.

Naím, Moises. 1993. "Latin America: Post-Adjustment Blues." *Foreign Policy* 92 (fall): 133–150.

———. 1995. "The Morning After." *Foreign Affairs* 25 (July): 45–61.

National Republican Institute for International Affairs. 1991. *The 1991 Elections in El Salvador.* Washington, D.C.: National Republican Institute.

Neier, Aryeh. 1984. "Peru's Dirty War." *Nation,* 11 February, 148–149.

North, Lisa. 1966. *Civil-Military Relations in Argentina, Chile, and Peru.* Berkeley: Institute of International Studies, University of California.

———. 1985. *Bitter Grounds: Roots of Revolt in El Salvador.* 2d ed. Westport, Conn.: Lawrence Hill.

Obando, Enrique. 1990. *Adquisición de armamentos y dependencia en América del Sur.* Lima: CEPEI (Centro Peruano de Estudios Internacionales).

———. 1992. "Después de la caída de Abimael Guzmán: Situación de la subversión." *Debate* 15, no. 70 (September–October): 19–22.

———. 1993. "La subversión: Situación interna y consecuencias internacionales." *Analísis Internacional* 1 (January–March): 45–62.

———. 1994. "The Power of Peru's Armed Forces." In *Peru in Crisis: Dictatorship or Democracy?* edited by Joseph S. Tulchin and Gary Bland. Boulder, Colo.: Lynne Rienner.

———. Forthcoming. "Peru: Subversion, Drug-Trafficking, and Civil-Military Relations." In *Civil-Military Relations towards the Year 2000,* edited by Louis Goodman, Johanna Mendelson, and Juan Rial. Lexington, Mass.: D.C. Heath.

O'Donnell, Guillermo. 1993. "On the State, Democratization and Some Conceptual Problems: A Latin American View with Glances at Some Postcommunist Countries." *World Development* 21, no. 8: 1355–1369.

———. 1994. "Delegative Democracy." *Journal of Democracy* 5, no. 1 (January): 55–69.

O'Donnell, Guillermo; Philippe C. Schmitter; and Laurence Whitehead, eds. 1986. *Transitions from Authoritarian Rule.* Baltimore: Johns Hopkins University Press.

Padrón Castillo, Mario, and Henry Pease García. 1974. *Planificación rural, reforma agraria, y organización campesina.* Lima: DESCO.

Paige, Jeffery M. 1975. *Agrarian Revolution: Social Movements and Export Agriculture in the Underdeveloped World.* New York: Free Press.

———. 1983. "Social Theory and Peasant Revolution in Vietnam and Guatemala." *Theory and Society* 12, no. 6 (November): 699–737.

———. 1991. "Coffee and Power in El Salvador." Paper presented at the annual meeting of the Latin American Studies Association, Washington, D.C., April.

———. 1996. "Land Reform and Agrarian Revolution in El Salvador: Comment on Seligson and Diskin." *Latin American Research Review* 31, no. 2: 127–139.

Palmer, David Scott. 1973. *"Revolution from Above": Military Government and Popular Participation in Peru, 1968–1972.* Cornell University, Latin American Studies Dissertation Program, no. 47.

———. 1986. "Rebellion in Rural Peru: The Origins and Evolution of Sendero Luminoso." *Comparative Politics* 18, no. 2 (January): 127–146.

———. 1989. "La amenaza para Sendero es la izquierda." *La República,* 24 October, 7–8.

———. 1990. "Peru's Persistent Problems." *Current History* 89, no. 543 (January): 5–8, 31.

———. 1992a. "Peru, the Drug Business, and Shining Path: Between Scylla and Charybdis?" *Journal of Interamerican Studies and World Affairs* 34, no. 3 (fall): 65–81.

———. 1992b. "The Shining Path in Peru: Insurgency and the Drug Problem." In *Low-Intensity Conflict: Old Threats in a New World*, edited by Edwin G. Corr and Stephen Sloan, 151–172. Boulder, Colo.: Westview.

———. 1993. "National Security." In *Peru: A Country Study*, edited by Rex A. Hudson, 259–318. Washington, D.C.: Library of Congress, Federal Research Division.

———. 1995. "The Revolutionary Terrorism of Peru's Shining Path." In *Terrorism in Context*, edited by Martha Crenshaw, 249–308. University Park: Pennsylvania State University Press.

———. 1996a. "Collectively Defending Democracy in the Western Hemisphere: The Case of Peru." In *Beyond Sovereignty*, edited by Tom Farer, 257–276. Baltimore: Johns Hopkins University Press.

———. 1996b. "Missed Opportunities and Misplaced Nationalism: Continuing Challenges in Multilateral Peacekeeping Efforts in the Peru-Ecuador Border Conflict." Paper presented at the conference "Multilateral Approaches to Peacekeeping and Democratization in the Hemisphere," University of Miami, North-South Center, Coral Gables, Fla., 11–13 April.

Palmer, David Scott, ed. 1992. *Shining Path of Peru*. New York: St. Martin's.

———. 1994. *Shining Path of Peru*. 2d ed. New York: St. Martin's Press.

Paredes, Carlos E., and Jeffrey D. Sachs, eds. 1991. *Peru's Path to Recovery: A Plan for Economic Stabilization and Growth*. Washington, D.C.: Brookings Institution.

Parodi, Jorge. 1988. "Los sindicatos en la democracia vacía." In *Democracia, sociedad y gobierno en el Perú*, edited by Luis Pásara and Jorge Parodi. Lima: CEDYS (Centro de Estudios de Democracia y Sociedad).

Partido Comunista del Perú. 1982. *Desarollemos la guerra de guerrillas*. [Lima]: Ediciones Bandera Roja.

———. 1986. *Desarrollar le guerra popular sirviendo a la revolución mundial*. [Lima]: Ediciones Bandera Roja.

———. 1987. *Gloria al día de la heroicidad!* Lima: Ediciones Bandera Roja.

Pastor, Robert A. 1987. *Condemned to Repetition: The United States and Nicaragua*. Princeton, N.J.: Princeton University Press.

Paterson, Thomas G. 1994. *Contesting Castro: The United States and the Triumph of the Cuban Revolution*. New York: Oxford University Press.

Pearce, Jenny. 1990. *Colombia: Inside the Labyrinth*. London: Latin American Bureau.

———. 1986. *Promised Land: Peasant Rebellion in Chalatenango, El Salvador*. London: Latin America Bureau.

Pease García, Henry. 1977. *El ocaso del poder oligárquico*. Lima: DESCO.

———. 1979. *Los caminos del poder*. Lima: DESCO.

———. 1984. "Avances y retrocesos de la democratización en Perú." In *Transición a la democracia*, edited by Augusto Varas, 53–68. Santiago, Chile: Asociación Chilena de Investigaciones para la Paz (ACHIP).

Peeler, John A. 1985. *Latin American Democracies: Colombia, Costa Rica, Venezuela*. Chapel Hill: University of North Carolina Press.

Peltz, Maxwell S. 1990. "El Salvador 1990: An Issues Brief." Washington, D.C.: Commission on U.S.-Latin American Relations.

Pelupessy, Wim. 1991. "Agrarian Reform in El Salvador." In *A Decade of War*, edited by Anjali Sundaram and George Gelber, 38–57. New York: Monthly Review.

PERA (Proyecto de Evaluación de la Reforma Agraria). 1990. "Beneficiarios del proceso de reforma agraria." Ministerio de Agricultura y Ganadería, San Salvador. Mimeographed.

Peterson, Robert L. 1985. "Guatemala." In *Latin America and Caribbean Contemporary Record*. Vol. 3, *1983–1984*, edited by Jack W. Hopkins, 545–560. New York: Holmes and Meier.

———. 1991. *Democracy and the Market: Political and Economic Reforms in Eastern Europe and Latin America*. Cambridge: Cambridge University Press.

Pezzullo, Lawrence, and Ralph Pezzulo. 1993. *At the Fall of Somoza*. Pittsburgh: University of Pittsburgh Press.

Physicians for Human Rights, and Human Rights/Americas Watch. 1994. *Waiting for Justice in Chiapas*. Boston and San Francisco: Physicians for Human Rights.

Pinelo, Adalberto J. 1973. *The Multinational Corporation as a Force in Latin American Politics: A Case Study of the International Petroleum Company in Peru*. New York: Praeger.

Pike, Frederick B. 1967. *The Modern History of Peru*. New York: Praeger.

Pion-Berlin, David. 1992. "Military Autonomy and Emerging Democracies in South America." *Comparative Politics* 25, no. 2 (October): 83–102.

Piqueras, Manuel. ed. 1990. *Una lucha cívica contra la impunidad*. Lima: Comisión Investigadora de Grupos Paramilitares.

Pizarro, Eduardo. 1990. "Insurgencia crónica, movimiento guerrillero y proceso de paz en Colombia." Paper presented at the research conference "Violence and Democracy in Colombia and Peru," Columbia University, New York, 30 November–1 December.

Poole, Deborah, and Gerardo Rénique. 1992. *Peru: Time of Fear*. London: Latin America Bureau.

Popkin, Margaret. 1991. "Human Rights in the Duarte Years." In *A Decade of War: El Salvador Confronts the Future*, edited by Anjali Sundaram and George Gelber, 58–84. New York: Monthly Review.

Popkin, Samuel L. 1979. *The Rational Peasant: The Political Economy of Rural Society in Vietnam.* Berkeley: University of California Press.

Porpora, Douglas. 1990. *How Holocausts Happen: The United States in Central America.* Philadelphia: Temple University Press.

Porzecanski, Arturo C. 1973. *Uruguay's Tupamaros: The Urban Guerrilla.* New York: Praeger.

Post, Jerrold M. 1986. "Narcissism and the Charismatic Leader-Follower Relationship." *Political Psychology* 7, no. 4: 675–687.

Preston, Julia. 1985. "What Duarte Won." *New York Review of Books,* 15 August, 30–35.

Prisk, Courtney E., ed. 1991. *The Comandante Speaks: Memoirs of an El Salvadoran Guerrilla Leader.* Boulder, Colo.: Westview.

Prosterman, Roy L.; Jeffrey M. Riedinger; and Mary N. Temple. 1981. "Land Reform and the El Salvador Crisis." *International Security* 6, no. 1 (summer): 53–74.

Przeworski, Adam. 1991. *Democracy and the Market: Political and Economic Reforms in Eastern Europe and Latin America.* New York: Cambridge University Press.

Quechua, Victor Manuel. 1994. *Perú . . . 13 años de oprobio.* 2d ed. Lima: Tetis Graf.

Quijano Obregón, Aníbal. 1975. "La 'segunda fase' de la 'Revolución Peruana' y la lucha de clases." *Sociedad y Política,* 2 (November): 4–19.

Quinn, Kenneth M. 1989. "Explaining the Terror." In *Cambodia 1975–1978: Rendezvous with Death,* edited by Karl D. Jackson, 215–240. Princeton, N.J.: Princeton University Press.

Rabe, Stephen G. 1988. *Eisenhower and Latin America: The Foreign Policy of Anticommunism.* Chapel Hill: University of North Carolina Press.

Radu, Michael, and Vladimir Tismaneanu. 1990. *Latin American Revolutionaries.* Washington, D.C.: Pergamon-Brassey's.

Ramírez, Ramón. 1989. *Legislación electoral y partidos políticos.* Lima: Instituto de Estudios Peruanos.

Ratliff, William E. 1976. *Castroism and Communism in Latin America, 1959–1976.* Washington, D.C.: American Enterprise Institute for Public Policy Research.

Reid, Michael. 1985. *Peru: Paths to Poverty.* London: Latin America Bureau.

Reinhardt, Nola. 1889. "Contrast and Consequence in the Agrarian Reforms of El Salvador and Nicaragua." In *Searching for Agrarian Reform in Latin America,* edited by William C. Thiesenhusen, 451–482. Boston: Unwin Hyman.

Remmer, Karen L. 1991. "The Political Impact of Economic Crisis in Latin America." *American Political Science Review* 85, no. 3 (September): 777–800.

Rénique, José Luis. 1990. "La batalla por Puno: Violencia política en la sierra del Perú." Paper presented at the research conference "Violence and Democracy in Colombia and Peru," Columbia University, New York, 30 November–1 December.

———. 1993. "Apogeo y crisis de la 'Tercera Vía': Campesinismo, guerra popular, y contrainsurgencia en Puno." Paper presented at the international seminar "La violencia política en el Perú," Lima, 12–14 July.

———. 1994. "Political Violence, the State, and the Peasant Struggle for Land (Puno)." In *Unruly Order: Violence, Power, and Cultural Identity in the Southern Highlands Provinces of Peru*, edited by Deborah Poole, 223–246. Boulder, Colo.: Westview.

Reyna, Carlos. 1995. "Cómo fue realmente la captura de Abimael Guzmán." *Debate* 17, no. 82 (July–August): 46–50.

Robinson, Linda. 1991. *Intervention or Neglect: The United States and Central America Beyond the 1980s.* New York: Council on Foreign Relations.

Rosenau, James N. 1988. "The State in an Era of Cascading Politics: Wavering Concept, Widening Competence, Withering Colossus, or Weathering Change?" *Comparative Political Studies* 21, no. 1 (April): 13–44.

Rosenau, William. 1994. "Is the Shining Path the 'New Khmer Rouge'?" *Studies in Conflict and Terrorism* 17: 305–322.

Rosenau, William, and Linda Head Flanagan. 1992. "Blood of the Condor." *Policy Review* 59 (winter): 82–85.

Rosenberg, Tina. 1991a. *Children of Cain: Violence and the Violent in Latin America.* New York: William Morrow.

———. 1991b. "Time of Cholera." *New Republic,* 29 July, 10–12.

Rospigliosi, Fernando. 1992. "Shining Path's Impact on Elections Assessed." *Foreign Broadcast Information Service: Latin America,* 12 May, 36–40. Originally published in *Caretas,* 6 April 1992, 32–35.

Rothstein, Robert L. 1992. "Weak Democracy and the Prospect for Peace and Prosperity in the Third World." In *Resolving Third World Conflict: Challenges for a New Era,* edited by Sheryl J. Brown and Kimber M. Schraub, 15–50. Washington, D.C.: United States Institute of Peace Press.

Roush, James L.; James O. Bleidner; and J. Demetrio Martinez. 1994. "Evaluation of the Peace and National Recovery Project: El Salvador." Arlington, Va.: Development Associates, Inc.

Ruben, Raúl. 1991. "El problema agrario en El Salvador: Notas sobre una economía agraria polarizada." *Cuadernos de Investigación* 2, no. 7 (April).

Rubio, Marcial. 1990. "The Perception of the Subversive Threat in Peru." In *The Military and Democracy,* edited by Louis W. Goodman, Johanna S. R. Mendelson, and Jual Rial, 107–122. Lexington, Mass.: Lexington.

Rudolph, James D. 1992. *Peru: The Evolution of a Crisis.* Stanford, Calif.: Hoover Institution Press.

Rueschemeyer, Dietrich; Evelyne Huber Stephens; and John D. Stephens. 1992. *Capitalist Development and Democracy.* Chicago: University of Chicago Press.

Russell, Philip L. 1995. *The Chiapas Rebellion*. Austin, Tex.: Mexico Resource Center.

Sanders, Sol. 1983. "The Heat on Reagan to Negotiate with El Salvador's Guerrillas." *Business Week*, 21 February, 54.

Scheetz, Thomas. 1992. "The Evolution of Public Sector Expenditures: Changing Political Priorities in Argentina, Chile, Paraguay and Peru." *Journal of Peace Research* 29, no. 2: 175–190.

Schram, Stuart R. 1969. *The Political Thoughts of Mao Tse Tung*. New York: Praeger.

Schulz, Donald E. 1984. "El Salvador: Revolution and Counterrevolution in the Living Museum." In *Revolution and Counterrevolution in Central America and the Caribbean*, edited by Donald E. Schulz and Douglas H. Graham, 189–268. Boulder, Colo.: Westview.

Schutz, Barry, and Robert O. Slater. 1990. *Revolution and Political Change in the Third World*. Boulder, Colo.: Lynne Rienner.

Schwarz, Benjamin C. 1991. *American Counterinsurgency Doctrine and El Salvador: The Frustrations of Reform and the Illusions of Nation-Building*. Santa Monica, Calif.: RAND.

Scott, James C. 1976. *The Moral Economy of the Peasant: Rebellion and Subsistence in Southeast Asia*. New Haven, Conn.: Yale University Press.

Sederberg, Peter C. 1994. *Fires Within: Political Violence and Revolutionary Change*. New York: HarperCollins.

Selbin, Eric. 1993. *Modern Latin American Revolutions*. Boulder, Colo.: Westview.

Seligmann, Linda J. 1995. *Between Reform and Revolution: Political Struggle in the Peruvian Andes, 1969–1991*. Berkeley: University of California Press.

Seligson, Mitchell A. 1987. "Democratization in Latin America: The Current Cycle." In *Authoritarians and Democrats: Regime Transition in Latin America*, edited by James M. Malloy and Mitchell A. Seligson, 3–12. Pittsburgh: University of Pittsburgh Press.

———. 1995. "Thirty Years of Transformation in the Agrarian Structure of El Salvador, 1961–1991." *Latin American Research Review* 30, no. 3: 43–74.

———. 1996. "Agrarian Inequality and the Theory of Peasant Rebellion." *Latin American Research Review* 31, no. 2: 140–158.

Sharpe, Kenneth E. 1988. "El Salvador." In *Latin America and Caribbean Contemporary Record*. Vol. 5, *1985–1986*, edited by Abraham F. Lowenthal, B275–B298. New York: Holmes and Meier.

Sheahan, John. 1993. "The Economy." In *Peru: A Country Study*, edited by Rex A. Hudson, 137–204. Washington, D.C.: Library of Congress.

Sheehan, Michael. 1989. "Comparative Counterinsurgency Strategies: Guatemala and El Salvador." *Conflict* 9, no. 2: 127–154.

Shenk, Janet. 1981. "El Salvador." *NACLA Report on the Americas* 15, no. 3 (May–June): 2–20.

———. 1988. "Can the Guerrillas Win?" *Mother Jones,* April, 35–44.

Shifter, Michael, and Sean Neill. 1996. "Implementing the Summit of the Americas: Guaranteeing Democracy and Human Rights." Working Paper Series. Coral Gables, Fla.: University of Miami, North-South Center.

Shugart, Matthew Soberg. 1989. "Patterns of Revolution." *Theory and Society* 18: 249–271.

Siegel, Daniel, and Joy Hackel. 1987. "El Salvador: Counterinsurgency Revisited." In *Low-Intensity Warfare: Counterinsurgency, Proinsurgency, and Antiterrorism in the Eighties,* edited by Michael T. Klare and Peter Kornbluh, 112–135. New York: Pantheon.

Simon, Laurence R., and James C. Stephens. 1982. *El Salvador Land Reform 1980–1981: Impact Audit.* 2d ed. Boston: Oxfam.

Simpson, Christopher. 1995. *National Security Directives of the Reagan and Bush Administrations: The Declassified History of U.S. Political and Military Policy, 1981–1991.* Boulder, Colo.: Westview.

Skocpol, Theda. 1979. *States and Social Revolutions.* New York: Cambridge University Press.

———. 1982. "Rentier State and Shi'a Islam in the Iranian Revolution." *Theory and Society* 11, no. 2 (May): 265–283.

———. 1985. "Bringing the State Back In: Strategies of Analysis in Current Research." In *Bringing the State Back In,* edited by Peter B. Evans, Dietrich Reuschemeyer, and Theda Skocpol, 3–43. New York: Cambridge University Press.

Skocpol, Theda, and Margaret Somers. 1980. "The Uses of Comparative History in Macrosocial Inquiry." *Comparative Studies in Society and History* 22, no. 2 (April): 174–197.

Smith, Earl E. T. 1990. *The Fourth Floor: An Account of the Castro Communist Revolution.* Washington, D.C.: Selous Foundation.

Smith, Gavin. 1989. *Livelihood and Resistance: Peasants and the Politics of Land in Peru.* Berkeley: University of California Press.

Smith, Gavin A., and Pedro Cano H. 1978. "Some Factors Contributing to Peasant Land Occupations in Peru: The Example of Huasicancha, 1963–1968." In *Peasant Cooperation and Capitalist Expansion in Central Peru,* edited by Norman Long and Bryan R. Roberts, 163–190. Austin: University of Texas Press.

Smith, Michael L. 1992. "Shining Path's Urban Strategy: Ate Vitarte." In *Shining Path of Peru,* edited by David Scott Palmer, 127–148. New York: St. Martin's.

Smith, Peter H., ed. 1992. *Drug Policy in the Americas.* Boulder, Colo.: Westview.

Smith, Tony. 1994. *America's Mission: The United States and the Worldwide Struggle for Democracy in the Twentieth Century.* Princeton: Princeton University Press.

Smith, Wayne S. 1987. *The Closest of Enemies: A Personal and Diplomatic History of the Castro Years.* New York: W. W. Norton.

Smyth, Frank. 1989. "Negotiations or Total War." *Nation,* 7–14 August, 164–170.

———. 1992. "Salvadoran Rebels Anticipated Soviet Fall, Shifted Tack." *Christian Science Monitor,* 6 May, 10.

Snyder, Richard. 1992. "Explaining Transitions from Neopatrimonial Dictatorships." *Comparative Politics* 24, no. 4 (July): 379–399.

Soberón, Ricardo. 1992. *The War on Cocaine in Peru: From Cartagena to San Antonio.* Washington Office on Latin America Briefing Series, Issues in International Drug Policy, no. 6. Washington, D.C.: Washington Office on Latin America, 7 August.

Sollis, Peter. 1992. "La disminución de la pobreza en El Salvador: Una evaluación del programa social del gobierno de Cristiani." *Estudios Centroamericanos* 522 (April): 333–354.

Stahler-Sholk, Richard. 1994. "El Salvador's Negotiated Transition: From Low-Intensity Conflict to Low-Intensity Democracy." *Journal of Interamerican Studies and World Affairs* 31, no. 4 (winter): 1–59.

Stallings, Barbara, and Robert Kaufman. 1989. *Debt and Democracy in Latin America.* Boulder, Colo.: Westview.

Stanley, William. 1990. "Partners in Crime: Intra-Elite Conflict and the Dynamics of State Terrorism in El Salvador." Paper presented at the Annual Meeting of the American Political Science Association, San Francisco, August 30–September 2.

———. 1991. "The Elite Politics of State Terrorism in El Salvador." Paper presented at the Latin American Studies Association meeting, Washington, D.C., April.

———. 1996. *The Protection Racket State: Elite Politics, Military Extortion, and Civil War in El Salvador.* Philadelphia: Temple University Press.

Starn, Orin. 1991. "Missing the Revolution: Anthropologists and the War in Peru." *Cultural Anthropology* 6, no. 1 (February): 63–91.

———. 1992. "New Literature on Peru's Sendero Luminoso." *Latin American Research Review* 27, no. 2: 212–226.

———. 1995. "Maoism in the Andes: The Communist Party of Peru-Shining Path and the Refusal of History." *Journal of Latin American Studies* 27, no. 2 (May): 399–422.

Starn, Orin; Carlos Iván Degregori; and Robin Kirk, eds. 1995. *The Peru Reader.* Durham, N.C.: Duke University Press.

Stephens, Evelyne Huber. 1990. "Democracy in Latin America: Recent Developments in Comparative Historical Perspective." *Latin American Research Review* 25, no. 2: 157–176.

Stern, Steve J., ed. 1987. *Resistance, Rebellion, and Consciousness in the Andean Peasant World.* Madison: University of Wisconsin Press.

Strasma, John. 1989. "Unfinished Business: Consolidating Land Reform in El Salvador." In *Searching for Agrarian Reform in Latin America,* edited by William C. Thiesenhusen, 408–428. Boston: Unwin Hyman.

Strong, Simon. 1992. *Shining Path: Terror and Revolution in Peru.* New York: Times Books.

Szulc, Tad. 1986. *Fidel: A Critical Portrait.* New York: William Morrow.

Tapia, Carlos. 1992. "La captura de Abimael y la derrota de Sendero." *Ideéle* 45–46 (December): 72–74.

———. 1995. *Autodefensa armada del campesinado.* Lima: CEDEP.

———. 1997. *Las fuerzas armadas y Sendero Luminoso.* Lima: Instituto de Estudios Peruanos.

Tarazona-Sevillano, Gabriela, with John B. Reuter. 1990. *Sendero Luminoso and the Threat of Narcoterrorism.* New York: Praeger; Washington, D.C.: Center for Strategic and International Studies.

Taylor, Charles L., and Michael C. Hudson. 1972. *World Handbook of Political and Social Indicators.* 2d ed. New Haven, Conn.: Yale University Press.

Taylor, Lewis. 1983. "Maoism in the Andes: Sendero Luminoso and the Contemporary Guerrilla Movement in Peru." Working Paper no. 2. Liverpool: University of Liverpool, Centre for Latin American Studies.

Tello, María del Pilar, ed. 1983. *Golpe o revolución? Hablan los militares del '68.* Lima: Sagsa.

Tenneriello, Bonnie. 1991a. *Proposed Legislation on El Salvador and Recent Related Developments in El Salvador.* Washington, D.C.: Washington Office on Latin America, 5 July.

———. 1991b. *Update on El Salvador Negotiations and Human Rights Developments since August 1991.* Washington, D.C.: Washington Office on Latin America, 18 October.

Terrill, Ross. 1980. *Mao.* New York: Harper and Row.

Thomas, Hugh. 1977. *The Cuban Revolution.* New York: Harper and Row.

Thorp, Rosemary, and Geoffrey Bertram. 1978. *Peru 1890–1977: Growth and Policy in an Open Economy.* New York: Columbia University Press.

Tilly, Charles. 1973. "Does Modernization Breed Revolution?" *Comparative Politics* 5, no. 3 (April): 425–447.

———. 1978. *From Mobilization to Revolution.* Reading, Mass.: Addison-Wesley.

Torres Guevara, Juan. 1997. "El Niño": Un fenómeno satanizado. *Andenes,* no. 98 (June/July): 14–15.

Trimberger, Ellen Kay. 1978. *Revolution from Above: Military Bureaucrats and Development in Japan, Turkey, Egypt, and Peru.* New Brunswick, N.J.: Transaction.

Tuesta Soldevilla, Fernando. 1987. *Perú político en cifras.* Lima: Fundación Friedrich Ebert.

———. 1989. "Cartilla de Información Electoral." Lima. mimeographed.

Tutino, John. 1986. *From Insurrection to Revolution in Mexico: Social Bases of Agrarian Violence, 1750–1940.* Princeton, N.J.: Princeton University Press.

Ungo, Guillermo M. 1984. "The People's Struggle." In *Crisis and Opportunity: U.S. Policy in Central America and the Caribbean,* edited by Mark Falcoff and Robert Royal, 217–230. Washington, D.C.: Ethics and Public Policy Center.

United Nations Commission on the Truth for El Salvador. 1993. *From Madness to Hope: The 12-Year War in El Salvador.* New York: United Nations.

United Nations Technical Mission of the Secretary General. 1990. "Análisis del sistema electoral y de registración de El Salvador." San Salvador, June.

U.S. AID (U.S. Agency for International Development). 1984. *Country Development Strategy Statement FY 1986: Peru.* Washington, D.C.: U.S. AID.

U.S. AID/El Salvador (U.S. Agency for International Development, Mission in El Salvador). 1988. "Partners in Economic Growth and Democratic Development." San Salvador: U.S. AID/El Salvador.

U.S. Department of State. Annual. *Country Reports on Human Rights Practices.* Washington, D.C.: Government Printing Office.

———. 1981. *Cuba's Renewed Support for Violence in Latin America.* Washington, D.C.: Bureau of Public Affairs. Special Report no. 90, December.

———. 1984a. "Democracy in Latin America and the Caribbean." Washington, D.C. Bureau of Public Affairs. Current Policy no. 605, August.

———. 1984b. "El Salvador: Revolution or Reform?" Washington, D.C., Bureau of Public Affairs. Current Policy no. 546, February.

———. 1985. *Revolution Beyond Our Borders: Sandinista Intervention in Central America.* Washington, D.C.: Bureau of Public Affairs.

———. 1987. *Democracy in Latin America and the Caribbean: The Promise and the Challenge.* Washington, D.C.: Bureau of Public Affairs. Special Report no. 158, March.

U.S. Departments of Defense and State. 1986. *The Challenge to Democracy in Central America.* Washington, D.C.: Government Printing Office.

U.S. Embassy, Lima. 1993. "How the Poor in Peru Cope." Cable from U.S. Embassy in Lima. Courtesy of U.S. Department of State.

U.S. Government Accounting Office. 1989. *Limited Use of U.S. Firms in Military Aid Construction.* Washington, D.C.: Government Accounting Office.

———. 1990. *El Salvador: Accounting for U.S. Military and Economic Aid.* Washington, D.C.: Government Accounting Office.

———. 1990. *Foreign Aid: Efforts to Improve the Judiciary System in El Salvador.* Washington, D.C.: Government Accounting Office.

U.S. House of Representatives, Committee on Foreign Affairs, Subcommittee on Western Hemisphere Affairs. 1988. *The Status of Democratic Transitions in Central America.* Washington, D.C.: Government Printing Office.

U.S. Institute of Peace. 1990. *A Look at "The End of History?"* Dialogues from Public Workshop no. 3. Washington, D.C.: United States Institute of Peace.

U.S. Senate, Committees on Foreign Relations and Appropriations. 1982. *El Salvador: The United States in the Midst of a Maelstrom*. Washington, D.C.: Government Printing Office.

USCEOM (U.S. Citizens Elections Observer Mission). 1994. *Free and Fair? The Conduct of El Salvador's 1994 Elections*. June. Washington, D.C.: SHARE Foundation.

Vela, Jaime. 1980. "Hasta la mujer me van a pedir: La disolución de la SAIS Huancavelica." *QueHacer* 4 (April): 60–71.

Velarde, Julio, and Martha Rodríguez. 1989. *Impacto macroeconomico de los gastos militares en el Perú*. Lima: Centro de Investigación de la Universidad del Pacífico y APEP.

Vickers, George. 1992. "The Political Reality after Eleven Years of War." In *Is There a Transition to Democracy in El Salvador?* edited by Joseph S. Tulchin and Gary Bland, 25–58. Boulder, Colo.: Lynne Rienner.

Vickers, George, and Jack Spence. 1994. "Elections: The Right Consolidates Power." *NACLA Report on the Americas* 38, no. 1 (July–August): 6–11.

Vilas, Carlos M. 1995. *Between Earthquakes and Volcanoes*. New York: Monthly Review.

Villalobos, Joaquín. 1983. *Por qué lucha el FMLN?* Morazán, El Salvador: Ediciones Sistema Radio Venceremos.

———. 1986. *El estado actual de la guerra y sus perspectivas*. Madrid: Textos Breves.

———. 1989. *Una revolución democrática para El Salvador*. El Salvador: Ediciones Sistema Venceremos.

———. 1992. *Una revolución en la izquierda para una revolución democrática*. San Salvador: Arcoiris.

Villanueva, Victor. 1962. *El militarismo en el Perú*. Lima: Empresa Gráfica T. Scheuch.

———. 1972. *El CAEM y la revolución de la fuerza armada*. Lima: Instituto de Estudios Peruanos.

———. 1973. *Ejercito peruano: Del caudillaje anárquico al militarismo reformista*. Lima: Mejía Baca.

Vivanco, Miguel. 1992. "Golpe moral al terrorismo en el Perú." *El Diario de la Nación*, 17 September, 1–3.

Waller, Michael J. 1991. *The Third Current of Revolution: Inside the North American Front of El Salvador's Guerrilla War*. Lanham, Md.: University Press of America.

Walter, Knut. 1993. *The Regime of Anastasio Somoza, 1936–1956*. Chapel Hill: University of North Carolina Press.

Walter, Knut, and Philip J. Williams. 1997. *Militarization and Demilitarization in El Salvador's Transition to Democracy*. Pittsburgh: University of Pittsburgh Press.

Walton, John. 1984. *Reluctant Rebels: Comparative Studies in Revolution and Underdevelopment.* New York: Columbia University Press.

Washington Office on Latin America. 1990. *El Salvador: Is Peace Possible?* Washington, D.C.: Washington Office on Latin America.

————.1991a. *A Step toward Peace? The March 1991 Elections in El Salvador.* Washington, D.C.: Washington Office on Latin America.

————. 1991b. *Clear and Present Dangers: The U.S. Military and the War on Drugs in the Andes.* Washington, D.C.: Washington Office on Latin America.

Webb, Richard. 1977. *Government Policy and the Distribution of Income in Peru, 1963–1973.* Cambridge, Mass.: Harvard University Press.

Webb, Richard, and Graciela Fernández Baca. 1990. *Perú en numeros 1990.* Lima: Cuánto.

————. 1991. *Perú en Numeros 1991.* Lima: Cuánto.

————. 1992. *Perú en Numeros 1992.* Lima: Cuánto.

Weber, Max. 1968. *Economy and Society.* New York: Bedminister.

Webre, Stephen. 1979. *José Napoleon Duarte and the Christian Democratic Party in Salvadoran Politics, 1960–1972.* Baton Rouge: Louisiana State University Press.

Weiner, Myron. 1987. "Empirical Democratic Theory." In *Competitive Elections in Developing Countries,* edited by Myron Weiner and Ergun Ozbuden, 1–34. Durham, N.C.: Duke University Press.

Weinstein, Martin. 1988. *Uruguay: Democracy at the Crossroads.* Boulder, Colo.: Westview.

Welch, Richard E. Jr. 1985. *Response to Revolution: The United States and the Cuban Revolution, 1959–1961.* Chapel Hill: University of North Carolina Press.

Werlich, David P. 1978. *Peru: A Short History.* Carbondale: Southern Illinois University Press.

————. 1987. "Debt, Democracy and Terrorism in Peru." *Current History* 86, no. 516 (January): 29–32, 36–37.

Wheat, Andrew. 1990. "Shining Path's 'Fourth Sword' Ideology." *Journal of Political and Military Sociology* 18, no. 1 (summer): 41–55.

White, Robert. 1991. Letter to author. May.

Wiarda, Howard, ed. 1984. *Rift and Revolution: The Central American Imbroglio.* Washington, D.C.: American Enterprise Institute for Public Policy Research.

Wickham-Crowley, Timothy P. 1989. "Understanding Failed Revolution in El Salvador: A Comparative Analysis of Regime Types and Social Structures." *Politics and Society* 17, no. 4 (December): 511–537.

————. 1992. *Guerrillas and Revolution in Latin America.* Princeton, N.J.: Princeton University Press.

Wiener, Raúl A. 1990. *Guerra e ideología: Debate entre el PUM y Sendero.* Lima: Amauta.

Wilde, Alexander. 1992. Testimony before the House Subcommittee on Western Hemisphere Affairs. 11 March 1992. H381–69.1, "Threat of the Shining Path to Democracy in Peru."

Wilkie, James W., and Steven Haber, eds. 1981. *Statistical Abstract of Latin America* 21. Los Angeles: University of California at Los Angeles, Latin American Center.

Wilkie, James W., and Carlos Alberto Contreras, eds. 1992. *Statistical Abstract of Latin America*, vol. 29. Los Angeles: University of California at Los Angeles, Latin American Center.

Williams, Robert G. 1994. *States and Social Evolution: Coffee and the Rise of National Governments in Central America*. Chapel Hill: University of North Carolina Press.

———. 1986. *Export Agriculture and the Crisis in Central America*. Chapel Hill: University of North Carolina Press.

Wise, Michael L. 1986. "Agrarian Reform in El Salvador: Process and Progress." San Salvador: U.S. AID/El Salvador. September. Mimeographed.

Wood, Elisabeth J. 1996a. "Redrawing the Boundaries: The Transformation of Property Rights and Political Culture in Usulután, El Salvador." Paper presented at the State-Society Relations Workshop, University of Washington, Seattle, 17 April.

———. 1996b. "Economic Structure, Agrarian Elites, and Democracy: The Anomalous Case of El Salvador." Revision of a paper presented at the Latin American Studies Association meeting, Washington, D.C., September.

Wood, Elisabeth, and Alexander Segovia. 1995. "Macroeconomic Policy and the Salvadoran Peace Accords." *World Development* 23, no. 12: 2079–2099.

World Bank. 1979. *Ecuador: Development Problems and Prospects*. Washington, D.C.: World Bank.

———. 1981. *Peru: Major Development Policy Issues and Recommendations*. Washington, D.C.: World Bank.

———. 1990. *World Development Report 1990: Poverty*. New York: Oxford University Press.

———. 1993. *World Development Report 1993: Investing in Health*. New York: Oxford University Press.

———. 1995. *Social Indicators of Development 1995*. Baltimore, Md.: Johns Hopkins University Press.

Wright, Thomas C. 1991. *Latin America in the Era of the Cuban Revolution*. New York: Praeger.

Youngers, Coletta. 1992. *Peru under Scrutiny: Human Rights and U.S. Drug Policy*. Washington Office on Latin America Briefing Series, Issues in International Drug Policy, no 5. Washington, D.C.: Washington Office on Latin America, January.

———. 1995a. *Fueling Failure: U.S. Drug Control Efforts in the Andes*. Washington Office on Latin America Briefing Series, Issues in International Drug Policy. Washington, D.C.: Washington Office on Latin America, April.

———. 1995b. "Administration of Justice Programs in Andean Countries: Do They Make Any Difference?" Paper presented at the Latin American Studies Association meeting, Washington, D.C., September.

Zaid, Gabriel. 1982. "Enemy Colleagues." *Dissent* (winter): 13–39.

Zamosc, Leon. 1990. "The Political Crisis and the Prospects for Rural Democracy in Colombia." *Journal of Development Studies* 26, no. 4 (July): 44–78.

Zondag, Cornelius H. 1982. "Bolivia's 1952 Revolution: Initial Impact and U.S. Involvement." In *Modern-Day Bolivia: Legacy of the Revolution and Prospects for the Future*, edited by Jerry R. Ladman, 27–40. Tempe: Arizona State University, Center for Latin American Studies.

Zschock, Dieter K. 1988. *Health Care in Peru: Resources and Policy.* Boulder, Colo.: Westview.

Zuvekas, Jr., Clarence. 1993. *Economic Crisis and Recovery in El Salvador, 1978–1992.* Washington, D.C.: Bureau for Latin America and the Caribbean, Agency for International Development, June.

INDEX

Page references in italic type indicate tables, and page references in bold type indicate figures. Most foreign organizations are listed under their English-language name; cross-references are provided for acronyms and Spanish-language names. In most cases, the name of each foreign organization is followed by the name of the country (in parentheses) in which it is located.

Cynthia McClintock is professor of political science and international affairs at George Washington University. A leading authority on democracy and revolution in Latin America, she earned her Ph.D. from the Massachusetts Institute of Technology, has conducted extensive field research in Central and South America since the early 1970s, and has acted as an elections monitor in both El Salvador and Peru. She has analyzed current political events for a variety of research institutes, for numerous television and radio networks, and for the U.S. State Department and Congress. A former consultant to Inter-American Dialogue and former president of the Inter-American Council, she served in 1994–95 as president of the Latin American Studies Association, an international scholarly association of more than four thousand members. McClintock has contributed numerous articles to edited volumes and to scholarly journals such as *World Politics* and *Comparative Politics;* her books include *Peasant Cooperatives and Political Change in Peru* (1981) and *The Peruvian Experiment Reconsidered* (coeditor; published in English in 1983 and in Spanish in 1985). McClintock received a Fulbright Award in 1987 and was a peace fellow at the United States Institute of Peace in 1990–91.

Jennings Randolph Program for International Peace

This book is a fine example of the work produced by senior fellows in the Jennings Randolph fellowship program of the United States Institute of Peace. As part of the statute establishing the Institute, Congress envisioned a program that would appoint "scholars and leaders of peace from the United States and abroad to pursue scholarly inquiry and other appropriate forms of communication on international peace and conflict resolution." The program was named after Senator Jennings Randolph of West Virginia, whose efforts over four decades helped to establish the Institute.

Since 1987, the Jennings Randolph Program has played a key role in the Institute's effort to build a national center of research, dialogue, and education on critical problems of conflict and peace. More than a hundred senior fellows from some thirty nations have carried out projects on the sources and nature of violent international conflict and the ways such conflict can be peacefully managed or resolved. Fellows come from a wide variety of academic and other professional backgrounds. They conduct research at the Institute and participate in the Institute's outreach activities to policymakers, the academic community, and the American public.

Each year approximately fifteen senior fellows are in residence at the Institute. Fellowship recipients are selected by the Institute's board of directors in a competitive process. For further information on the program, or to receive an application form, please contact the program staff at (202) 457-1700.

Joseph Klaits
Director

REVOLUTIONARY MOVEMENTS IN LATIN AMERICA

This book is set in Minion; the display type is Universe. Hasten Design Studio designed the book's cover, and Joan Engelhardt and Day Dosch designed the interior. Pages were made up by Helene Y. Redmond. Tables and graphics were prepared by Ken Allen. Wesley Palmer edited the notes and bibliography; Lise Markl copyedited the text. The index was prepared by Susan Nedrow. The text was proofread by Catherine Cambron. The book's editor was Nigel Quinney.